ETERNAL GARDEN

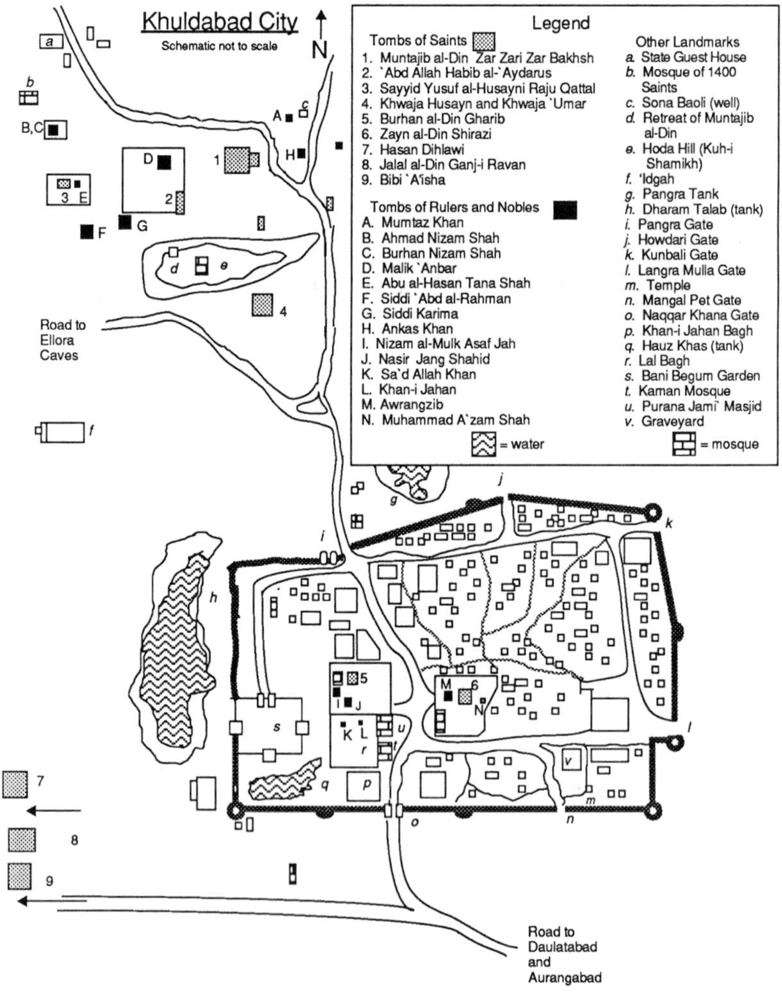

Map 1. Khuldabad City

ETERNAL GARDEN

Mysticism, History, and Politics at a South Asian Sufi Center

Carl W. Ernst

Foreword by Annemarie Schimmel

STATE UNIVERSITY OF NEW YORK PRESS

SUNY Series in Muslim Spirituality in South Asia
Annemarie Schimmel, editor

Published by
State University of New York Press, Albany

Printed in the United States of America

For information, address State University of New York Press, State University Plaza, Albany, N.Y., 12246

Production by Dana Foote
Marketing by Bernadette LaManna

Library of Congress Cataloging in Publication Data

Ernst, Carl W., 1950-
Eternal garden : mysticism, history, and politics at a South Asian Sufi center / Carl W. Ernst.
p. cm.—(SUNY series in Muslim spirituality in South Asia)
Includes bibliographical references and index.
ISBN 0–7914–0883–3 (alk. paper).—ISBN 0–7914–0884–1 (alk. paper) : pbk.)
1. Chishtīyah—India—Khuldabad—History. 2. Khuldabad (India)—Religious life and customs. 3. Sufism—India—History. I. Title. II. Series.
BP189.7.C49E76 1992
297′.65—dc20 90-28514
CIP

10 9 8 7 6 5 4 3 2 1

For Sophie and Teresa

روضهٔ خلدبرین خلوتِ درویشان است

حافظ

CONTENTS

PART III
The Khuldabad Sufis in History

PART IV
Conclusions

PART V
Appendixes

ILLUSTRATIONS

TABLES

MAPS

FIGURES

Table 1. Initiatic Genealogy of the Khuldabad Chishtīs

1. Muḥammad the Prophet (d. 10/632)
2. ʿAlī ibn Abī Ṭālib (d. 40/661)
3. Ḥasan al-Baṣrī (d. 110/728)
4. ʿAbd al-Wāḥid ibn Zayd
5. Fużayl ibn ʿIyāż (d. 187/802)
6. Ibrāhīm ibn Adham (d. 163/779)
7. Ḥużayqa al-Marʿashī
8. Hubayra al-Baṣrī
9. ʿAlū Dīnawarī
10. Abū Isḥāq Chishtī
11. Abū Aḥmad Chishtī (d. 355/966)
12. Muḥammad Chishtī (d. 411/1020)
13. Yūsuf Chishtī (d. 459/1067)
14. Mawdūd Chishtī (d. 520/1126)
15. al-Sharīf al-Zandanī
16. ʿUsmān Hārwanī (d. 607/1211)
17. Muʿīn al-Dīn Chishtī (d. 633/1236)
18. Quṭb al-Dīn Bakhtiyār Kākī (d. 633/1235)
19. Farīd al-Dīn Ganj-i Shakkar (d. 664/1265)
20. Niẓām al-Dīn Awliyā' (d. 725/1325)
21. Burhān al-Dīn Gharīb (d. 738/1337)
22. Zayn al-Dīn Shīrāzī (d. 771/1369)

Table 2. Dynasties of Indo-Muslim Rulers

(Dates given are dates of accession except at the end of a dynasty)

Khaljīs (Delhi)	
Jalāl al-Dīn Fīrūz	689/1290
Rukn al-Dīn Ibrāhīm	695/1296
ʿAlā' al-Dīn Muḥammad	695/1296
Malik Nā'ib/Malik Kāfūr	715/1316
Quṭb al-Dīn Mubārak Shāh	716/1316
Nāṣir al-Dīn (Khusraw Khān)	720/1320
Tughluqs (Delhi)	
Ghiyās al-Dīn	720/1320
Muḥammad ibn Tughluq	725/1325
Fīrūz Shāh	752/1351
Ghiyās al-Dīn II	790/1388
Abū Bakr	791/1389
Muḥammad Shāh	792/1390
Nāṣir al-Dīn Maḥmūd II	795/1393
Dawlat Khān Lodī	816/1413–817/1414

(*continued*)

Table 2. (*Continued*)

(Dates given are dates of accession except at the end of a dynasty)

Bahmanīs (Deccan)	
ʿAlāʾ al-Dīn Ḥasan Bahman Shāh	748/1347
Muḥammad ibn Ḥasan	759/1358
ʿAlāʾ al-Dīn Mujāhid	776/1375
Dāʾūd	780/1378
Muḥammad II	780/1378
Ghiyās al-Dīn	799/1397
Shams al-Dīn	799/1397
Aḥmad I Walī	825/1422
ʿAlāʾ al-Dīn Aḥmad II	839/1436
ʿAlāʾ al-Dīn Hūmayūn	862/1458
Niẓām	865/1461
Shams al-Dīn Muḥammad III	867/1463
Shihāb al-Dīn Maḥmūd	887/1482
Aḥmad III	924/1518
ʿAlāʾ al-Dīn	927/1521
Walī Allāh	928/1522
Kalīm Allāh	931/1525–934/1527
Fārūqīs (Khandesh)	
Malik Rājā Fārūqī	772/1370
Nāṣir Khān	801/1399
ʿĀdil Khān I	841/1437
Mīrān Mubārak Khān I	844/1441
ʿAynā or ʿĀdil Khān II	861/1457
Dāʾūd Khān	909/1503
Ghaznī Khān	916/1510
ʿĀlam Khān	916/1510
ʿĀdil Khān III	916/1510
Mīrān Muḥammad I	926/1520
Aḥmad Shāh	943/1537
Mubārak Shāh II	943/1537
Mīrān Muḥammad II	974/1566
Ḥasan Shāh	984/1576
Rājā ʿAlī Khān or ʿĀdil Shāh IV	985/1577
Bahādur Shāh	1005/1597–1009/1601
Mughuls (Hindustan)	
Bābur	932/1526
Hūmayūn	937/1530
Akbar	963/1556
Jahāngīr	1014/1605
Shāhjahān	1037/1628

(*continued*)

Table 2. (*Continued*)

(Dates given are dates of accession except at the end of a dynasty)

Awrangzīb	1068/1658
Bahādur Shāh	1119/1707
(etc.)	
Niẓāms (Hyderabad)	
Niẓām al-Mulk Āṣaf Jāh	1137/1724
Muḥammad Nāṣir Jang	1161/1748
Muẓaffar Jang	1164/1750
Āṣaf al-Dawla Ṣalābat Jang	1165/1752
Niẓām ʿAlī	1175/1762
Akbar ʿAlī Khān Sikandar Jāh	1803
Nāṣir al-Dawla Farkhanda ʿAlī Khān	1829
Afżal al-Dawla	1857
Maḥbūb ʿAlī Khān	1869
ʿUsmān ʿAlī Khān	1911–1948

FOREWORD

Khuldabad . . . the name conjures up a sunny day in early November, one of those days when everything seems to be in perfect order. We had reached the small town in the morning and were walking around in the vast cemetery with its impressive mausoleums and modest tombs. The huge trees were slowly shedding their golden leaves as though they were preparing to become real dervishes, opening their arms in prayer. Our Indian friend, Dr. Zia Shakeb, led us through the softly undulating area until we reached the cave on top of Kūh-i Shāmikh, where Muntajibuddīn Zarzarī used to meditate in the early fourteenth century.

For a few moments we rested near the small mosque on the very top of the hill. The landscape showed steep slopes and some sharp edges, and extended to a hill range. One could well understand that the elite of Delhi's population who were sent here in 1327 felt unhappy in this area, which was so different from the wide plains of the Ganges-Jumna doab. But the air was strong and healthy, so it seemed to us, and we walked to pay our respects to one of those who had left Delhi to settle here, and who had died soon after his arrival: perhaps from longing for his lost home, for the mausoleum of his beloved master Niẓāmuddīn Auliyā in Delhi. It was Ḥasan Sijzī Dihlawī, the first to compile *malfūẓāt*, the sayings of his master, to preserve his words for future generations. At the same time he was, like his friend Amīr Khusrau, a poet who expressed his love in sweet and tender words, less sophisticated than Amīr Khusrau, but moving. Their music seemed to permeate the peaceful morning. And Ḥasan Dihlawī's model of compiling *malfūẓāt* had triggered off a whole literature, which, to this day, tells of the feats, the daily life, and the miracles of Sufi saints and which, properly sifted, constitutes an important source for Indo-Muslim history.

We turned to another tomb, modest like his, which is the depository of the earthly remnants of a man whose importance for the history of Muslim India comes to light only slowly—a man who was not only an excellent historian of his beloved Deccan, and especially of Khuldabad, but also a poet who can easily compete with, and perhaps surpass, most Indo-Persian writers of the eighteenth century: Ghulām ʿAlī Āzād Bilgrāmī. We had visited his library in

Aurangabad the day before; now we stood near his simple tomb, filled with admiration for a scholar who, in his *Khizāna-i ʿāmira*, produced one of the finest anthologies (*tadhkiras*) of Persian poets, but whose most fascinating work is the *Subḥat al-marjān*, an attempt to prove that India is truly the ideal country for Muslims. Did not Adam come from paradise straight to Sri Lanka, part of the subcontinent, and did not the Prophet himself talk about the Indians? Were not numberless great scholars and poets during the history of Islam connected with, or native of, the subcontinent?

Āzād Bilgrāmī tried to prove these points, but perhaps the most valuable part of his book, and a moving expression of his twofold allegiance to Islam and to Indian soil, is his attempt to compare literary and rhetorical forms of Arabic and Sanskrit. We recited our *Fātiḥa* for this unusual scholar and walked from tomb to tomb, with Dr. Shakeb recapitulating for us the whole history of the Deccan, which could be studied by simply wandering through the vast cemetery of Khuldabad. We entered the precincts of Burhānuddīn Gharīb's shrine, and Mr. Saleem kindly welcomed us, telling with pride of Carl Ernst's visit to the shrine a few years back. We modestly asked whether there would be some *qawwālī*, and after we had paid our respects to the various members of the saint's family and his friends, especially to the ladies (or rather, their tombs!), we set out for a visit to the other shrines in Khuldabad while the *qawwālī* would be arranged. There was the shrine of Zainuddīn Dāūd Daulatābādī, where the emperor Aurangzēb as well as his son Aʿẓam are buried. The simple tomb of Aurangzēb filled us with awe: there was nothing of the glorious architecture for which his father Shāh Jahān, and his grandfather Jahāngīr, were famed; nothing reminiscent of the artful red and white arabesques of Akbar's tomb in Sikandra, or of the simple grandeur of Humāyūn's mausoleum in Delhi. Aurangzēb, who spent the last thirty years of his long life in the Deccan, lies under the blue sky in a simple marble enclosure, similar to that of his ancestor, the founder of the Mughal dynasty, Bābur, who left the wealth of Hindustan behind him to find his last resting in an open enclosure in Kabul. Who would not remember in such a place Ātish's Urdu prayer:

> O God, give long life to the dark blue sky—
> It is the tent above poor people's tombs!

And looking at the tombs both of famous rulers, founders of dynasties like Āṣaf Jāh I, and of dervishes, "the kings without belt and crown," which were stretching before our eyes, Āzād Bilgrāmī's lines came to mind:

> In the end, glory turns again to poverty;
> The rose's crown turns into a beggar's bowl.

In the early afternoon the *qawwāl*s had arrived, and we were transported into the world of mystical delight, carried back through the centuries to the days when the music-loving Burhānuddīn Gharīb lived here and expressed his love of God in mystical dance. It was an hour outside time and space, and, after looking at some manuscripts, we left the place full of gratitude, carrying with us the orange-colored headgear of the Chishtī order, which the friends in the *dargāh* in Khuldabad had bestowed upon us. We drove back to the threatening fortress of Daulatabad. We returned to Aurangabad where we watched, in a late hour, how a weaver produced the famous double-sided silk fabric for which the city was famous. It was still produced according to centuries-old techniques, with a very young boy selecting the thin threads for the patterns with nimble fingers in the dim light of a weak electric bulb. Had anything changed from the days of Burhānuddīn Gharīb?

To be sure, much had changed, and while we enjoyed a day in a truly blessed place and were fortunate enough to be transported back through layer and layer of profane and religious history, the historian's eye could not be content with this merely impressionistic picture of a place saturated with valuable memories.

Carl Ernst returned to Khuldabad to study the documents that he had seen, in part, during his first stay, and that Mr. Saleem and the members of the *dargāh* put at his disposal. Thus, he was able to place the history of Khuldabad into a larger framework, similarly to what Richard Eaton had done a dozen years earlier, although not always agreeing with him on the interpretation of Deccani Sufism. The question of the reliability of the *malfūẓāt* literature had to be tackled, and the much-discussed topic of conversion at the hand of Sufis taken up again. Likewise, the generally accepted view that the Chishtīs had no relations with the government and shunned any official contacts, had to be investigated afresh. The testimony of the documents studied by Carl Ernst show some very interesting features of all these important problems.

There are still many questions to be asked, and many documents from other shrines to be studied—whosoever has seen the scrolls with the *shajara*s, the lineages of the great Sufis in Gulbarga and other places in the Deccan—scrolls that extend over thirty feet and more—knows the immense task before the student of Deccani history. It is important that Carl Ernst has opened a door into this historical field, and I am sure that the book will trigger off a number of further studies in the history of Sufism in southern India. The reader will find much new information, and new light on traditional points in Carl Ernst's study. That his book is written not from the viewpoint of a detached historian who investigates his material without empathy for the human aspects of the documents he is using, but shows the author's warm feelings and his personal interest in Khuldabad and those who have lived and are still living there, seems to me particularly helpful. Without this love and respect for Burhānuddīn Gharīb and his tradition the book would not have been written, for as St. Augustine held, *res tantum cognoscitur quantum* *diligitur*—"one can understand something only to the extent that one loves it."

We hope that the book will attract many students of history and show the enormous wealth of the Sufi tradition in southern India, and the numerous possibilities that still lie before the researcher and the admirer of the Indian Sufi tradition.

Annemarie Schimmel

PREFACE AND ACKNOWLEDGMENTS

In March 1666, the French traveler Jean de Thevenot took a one-day excursion from the city of Aurangabad in western India, and paused briefly in the town of Rawza on his way to visit the Ellora caves. Having passed by the impressive Daulatabad fort to reach Rawza that morning, he visited the imposing tombs, but he was unable to learn anything about them, being ignorant of the language of the old men who welcomed him:

> When I arrived there, I discovered a spacious Plain of well cultivated Land, with a great many Villages, and Bourgs amidst Gardens, plenty of Fruit-trees and Woods: We Travelled at least for the space of an hour over Plow'd Land, where I saw very fair Tombs several stories high, and covered with domes built of large grayish Stones, and about Half an hour after seven, having passed by a great *Tanquie*, I alighted near a large Court paved with the same Stones. I went in, but was obliged to put off my Shoes; at first I found a little *Mosque*, where I saw the Bismillah of the *Mahometans* writ over the Door; the signification of the Inscription is, *In the Name of God*. There was no light into the *Mosque*, but what entered by that Door; but there were many Lamps burning in it, and several old Men that were there, invited me to come in, which I did. I saw nothing rare in it, but two Tombs covered with Carpet: And I was extreamly troubled for want of an Interpreter, for else I had known a great many particulars, that I could not be informed of.[1]

Nearly seventy-five years later, in March 1740, the poet and scholar Āzād Bilgrāmī returned to India after a prolonged residence in the holy cities of Arabia. He had a very different encounter with Rawza, now also called Khuldabad. Āzād was so charmed by the place that he at once resolved to write a book about the saints buried there, a book that might have answered many of Thevenot's questions:

> In a time of travel and journeying, the divine attraction drew me to the kingdom of the Deccan. Traversing certain stations of the journey

> of life in this kingdom, and obtaining the happiness of visiting the resting saints of sacred Rawza (*rawża-i muqaddasa*, the sacred garden), I began to investigate the lives and sayings of those saints. Since the lives and sayings of those saints can be seen scattered in the books of the ancients, an inspiration appeared in my devoted heart from the hidden world, that I should collect in brief a sample of their sublime states and events and their sacred words and sayings, and that I should assemble a book called *Garden of the Saints* (*Rawżat al-awliyā'*).[2]

Especially during the summer rainy season, when the brown hills are suddenly clothed in green, and the cool rains refresh the heart, Āzād felt that this valley was close to paradise, as he and others have recorded in Persian and Urdu verse. Āzād himself would be buried in Khuldabad in 1786, in a small enclosure next to the tomb of the poet Amīr Ḥasan Dihlawī, who had come to this valley with the rest of the Sufis four and a half centuries earlier. The religious importance of Khuldabad continued to be such that, in the 1880s, the Nizam's gazetteer called the town "the Kerbella of Dekhan Mussulmans," remarking that "these numerous tombs have, as it were, consecrated the place, and caused it to be regarded by Mahomedans as a place of great sanctity."[3]

The modern visitor is no more exempt from the charms of the place than was Āzād. When I first visited Khuldabad in 1975, I too was enchanted, and was possessed by a great curiosity about the figures buried in the stately whitewashed tombs. What sort of people were Muntajib al-Dīn "Zar Zarī Zar Bakhsh" ("the giver of gold"), and his brother Burhān al-Dīn Gharīb? Local tradition relates that they led a procession of fourteen hundred Sufi saints from Delhi in the fourteenth century, and this figure is believable when one sees how many carefully tended white tombs dot the hills and valleys around Khuldabad (see Table 3 and Map 1 for a partial list of the tombs of Khuldabad). Among their company most were adherents of the Chishtī order of Sufis, which remains the most popular Sufi brotherhood in south Asia. A few saints are thought to have come even earlier, when the Deccan was ruled by the Hindu Yadava kings—so one is told when visiting Mu'min ʿĀrif's tomb, colorfully painted yellow and green, on the Daulatabad road. A similar tale is heard at the rural shrine of Jalāl al-Dīn Ganj-i Ravān ("flowing treasure"), which overlooks a scene of stunning pastoral beauty, next to the pond called the Fairies' Tank.

Striking too are the numerous royal tombs, mostly dark and gloomy in their disrepair. Although many are unidentified, among their number are found kings and nobles from many of the dynasties that have ruled the Deccan. The most famous of them include Aḥmad Niẓām Shāh (d. 1508), first king of Ahmednagar, his son Burhān Niẓām Shāḥ (d. 1553), and the redoubtable general of Ahmednagar, Malik ʿAnbar (d. 1629); Abū al-Ḥasan Tānā Shāh (d. 1699), the last Quṭbshāhī king of Golconda; and Awrangzīb (d. 1707), the great Mughul emperor, who is buried in a simple tomb within the precincts of Zayn al-Dīn Shīrāzī, the chief disciple of Burhān al-Dīn Gharīb. What, indeed, drew them all to be buried here?

Some years later, when doing research on Sufism in India, I came across the work of Āzād, and realized that it was indeed possible to entertain the notion of a historical study of Khuldabad; in this way I could advance beyond the puzzlement of Thevenot. Āzād's work alone would not suffice, however; it was limited by the constraints of later hagiography, which has its own purposes as a genre. He and other medieval writers had mentioned older texts ("the books of the ancients"), which were written down by the disciples of the first Sufis who came to Khuldabad in 1329. The immediate task was to find out how many of these texts survived.

In 1981 I visited Khuldabad again, and through the generosity of the attendants of the shrines, I was allowed to photograph a remarkable series of Persian documents preserved there. These were indeed "the books of the ancients" mentioned by Āzād: four Persian *malfūẓāt* texts recording the oral discourses of the fourteenth-century Sufi saints, plus a record of the financial operation of the shrines during the fifteenth century. The shrine's library also contained a unique manuscript of a Persian hagiography from the Mughul period and an unusually complete series of revenue documents recording the shrines' land endowments over several centuries, beginning with Akbar and ending with the Nizams of Hyderabad. There were also several rare lithographed Urdu hagiographies. Now it was possible to begin the lengthy task of analysis, but this was complicated by the diversity of the sources, which were written from widely varying points of view; this diversity was especially problematic once the political histories of the medieval period were included. The picture that gradually emerged from the Khuldabad documents was in some ways strikingly different from the standard view of early Sufi history that developed in northern India, and they richly filled in major gaps in our knowledge about a period that is otherwise poorly attested.

Without considering the Khuldabad documents, a full appreciation of the development of Sufi literature in India is not possible. The discourses of Burhān al-Dīn and Zayn al-Dīn, and the writings of their disciples, constitute a formidable resource for the religious and social history of early Indian Islam. Why had these materials been neglected up to now? Although favored by the Mughuls and the Nizams, Khuldabad had been bypassed by the British, and the saints of Khuldabad are now hardly known outside the Deccan. The absence of any readily available printed texts on Khuldabad, despite the wealth of materials preserved in the shrines, seemed to correspond to a lack of

Table 3. Principal Saints and Rulers Buried in and near Khuldabad

The main shrines are indicated below first by geographical location, and then in roughly chronological order, with less prominent figures buried in or around the larger complexes listed under the name of the chief saint's tomb. Saints and their disciples are indicated in **bold** while kings and nobles are shown by *italics*. Dates given are death dates, followed by the date of the *ʿurs* festival, if one is currently observed. It is to be noted that many more of the secular tombs around Khuldabad and Daulatabad remain unidentified.

I. Inside Khuldabad
   A. **Burhān al-Dīn Gharīb** (1337; 6 Ṣafar)
      1. The tombs (14th cent.) of many disciples, including the Kāshānī brothers **Rukn al-Dīn** and **Majd al-Dīn.**
      2. *Niẓām al-Mulk Āṣaf Jāh* (1748; 4 Jumādī II), the first Nizam, and his wife *Sayyidat al-Nisāʾ Bēgam.*
      3. *Niẓām al-Dawla Nāṣir Jang* (1750; 17 Muḥarram), the second Nizam, and his wife.
      4. *Hidāyat Muḥyī al-Dīn Khān Muẓaffar Jang* (1751), the third Nizam.
      5. A number of dignitaries are buried just south of the main tomb, including *ʿIważ Khān* (d. 1730–31), *Mutawaṣṣil Khān* the uncle of Muẓaffar Jang, *Jamāl al-Dīn Khān* (d. 1746), *Shāh Karīm al-Dīn, Shāhzāda Janglī,* and *Saʿīd al-Dīn Siwwum* the taʿalluqdār of Aurangabad.
      6. *Banī Bēgam,* a noblewoman of the Mughul period, is buried in a garden southwest of the complex. Her garden and that of *Khān-i Jahān* (northwest of the Naqqār-khāna gate), both now in ruins, formerly were the adornments of the town. The tombs of *Khān-i Jahān* and *Saʿd Allāh Khān* are in the Lal Bagh garden just south of the complex.
   B. **Zayn al-Dīn Shīrāzī** (1369; 25 Rabīʿ I)
      1. **Mawlānā Khwān Bībī** (14th cent.), "adoptive daughter" of Zayn al-Dīn.
      2. The tombs (14th cent.) of many other disciples, such as **Shams al-Dīn Fażl Allāh, Muḥammad Lashkar**, and **Mīr Ḥasan**.
      3. *Awrangzīb* (1707; 22 Dhū al-Qaʿda), Mughul emperor.
      4. *Muhammad ʿAẓīm al-Shaʾn Bahādur* (1707), and his wife *Awrangī Bībī.*
      5. *Sayyid Manṣūr,* Mughul governor of Baglana, and his wife; he built this mosque and other buildings in 1663.

II. Outside Khuldabad
   A. **Jalāl al-Dīn Ganj-i Ravān** (1247 [?]; 26 Dhū al-Qaʿda), several miles west of Khuldabad.
   B. **Muntajib al-Dīn Zar Zarī Zar Bakhsh** (1309; 7 Rabīʿ I), north of Hoda Hill.
      1. Inside the complex
         a. **Bībī Hājira,** mother of Burhān al-Dīn and Muntajib al-Dīn (14th cent.; 11 Shawwāl).

(*continued*)

Table 3. (*Continued*)

- b. **Sōnā Bā'ī,** Hindu princess (14th cent.).
- c. The tombs of some relatives (14th cent.), plus several of Burhān al-Dīn's disciples, such as **Farīd al-Dīn Adīb** (1337; 29 Muḥarram), **Pīr Mubārak Karwān** (1340; 5 Shawwāl), etc.

2. West of the complex
   - a. **Badr al-Dīn Naw-lakha** (14th cent.).
   - b. **ʿAbd Allāh Ḥabīb al-ʿAydarūs** (1631; 5 Ṣafar).
   - c. *Malik ʿAnbar* (1626; 29 Shaʿbān), Abyssinian general of Ahmednagar.
   - d. *Siddī Karīma,* wife of Malik ʿAnbar.
   - e. *Siddī ʿAbd al-Raḥman,* grandson of Malik ʿAnbar.
3. East of the complex
   - a. *Ankas Khān* (14th cent.), a noble of the Tughluq period.
   - b. *Mumtāz Khān.*

C. **Sayyid Yūsuf al-Ḥusaynī Rājū Qattāl** (1330; 5 Shawwāl), north of Hoda Hill.
1. Inside the complex
   - a. **Sayyid Chandan Ṣāḥib**.
   - b. *Abū al-Ḥasan Tānā Shāh* (1699; 13 Rabīʿ I), the last Quṭb Shāhī king of Golconda, who was imprisoned in the Daulatabad fort until his death.
   - c. *Nawwāb Marḥamat Khān,* a Mughul governor of Awrangabad.
   - d. *Dā'ūd Khān* (d. 1715), a Mughul governor of Burhanpur, and his brothers and sisters.
2. North of the complex
   - a. Mosque of the **1400 Saints** (14th cent.), also containing the graves of scholars such as **Ẓahīr al-Dīn B'hakkarī.**
   - b. *Aḥmad Niẓām Shāh* (1508), first king of Ahmednagar.
   - c. *Burhān Niẓām Shāh* (1553), second king of Ahmednagar.

D. **Amīr Ḥasan ʿAlā' Dihlawī Sijzī** (1336; 29 Ṣafar), west of Khuldabad.
1. **Āzād Bilgrāmī** (1786).

E. **Khwāja Ḥusayn** (1349; 27 Sha'bān) and **Khwāja ʿUmar,** uncles of Zayn al-Dīn Shīrāzī, just south of Hoda Hill.

F. **Bībī ʿĀ'isha** (14th cent.; 7 Shaʿbān), daughter of Farīd al-Dīn Ganj-i Shakkar, south of Ḥasan Dihlawī's tomb.

G. **Shāh Khāksār** (17th cent.; 26 Rajab), two miles southwest of Ganj-i Ravān's tomb.

III. Near Daulatabad Fort

A. **Mu'min ʿĀrif** (13th cent. [?]; 20 Ṣafar).

B. **Mardān al-Dīn** (1335; 17 Ṣafar).

C. **Niẓām al-Dīn Pēsh Imām** (1370; 1 Rabī' II), in Kaghzipura.

D. **'Alā' al-Dīn Żiyā'** (14th cent.; 5 Ṣafar).

E. **Bahā' al-Dīn Anṣārī** (1515; 19 Ṣafar).

---

official interest in an area now regarded as provincial. Bringing these materials back into the light makes it possible to compensate for the distortions caused by the adventitious omission of Khuldabad from history.

To balance these new discoveries against the received view of Indian Sufism, I found it necessary to develop an approach that would allow for the historiographical interpretation of each document as a literary text, something that has been done often in other fields but rarely in south Asian history. Thus the main object of this book is to present a method for reading Sufi texts historiographically, rather than to produce an "objective" history of Sufism in this region.[4] The Khuldabad texts were not to be privileged over other well-known texts, but each had to be read, or reread, as an independent and legitimate testimony, to be overlaid upon, compared with, or differentiated from the rest. Since this approach covers the full range of textual sources for south Asian Islam, it necessitates a rethinking of the basic categories of this field. The problems in the study of Islam in south Asian history, discussed in detail in Part I, frequently derive from an inappropriate politicization of texts in a way that reflects contemporary issues. What I would like to do is to restore, as far as possible, the original political context of each document under consideration. The conceptual difficulties that underly much received terminology can best be attacked, in my opinion, by an intensive study of a tightly circumscribed field, a microstudy, in other words. By closely examining the perspectives in all the available textual materials from a single location, and then plotting their trajectories through history, it is possible to reconsider the fundamental ideas that are in common use. This study is also, therefore, a reconsideration of the study of Islam in south Asia.

The plan of the book is to begin with the most general aspects of the study of south Asian Islam, to narrow the focus to the Khuldabad Sufis themselves, and then to expand outward, following the impact of the Sufi establishment in Khuldabad on later society. Part I, "Historiographical Orientation: Sufism and Islam in India," surveys the early Sufi tradition in Islam and analyzes the principal religious and political historiographies that underly the different medieval texts. One of the main concerns of this section is to separate contemporary ideological issues from the quite different political context of the sources. Part II, "Chishtī Sufism at Khuldabad," begins by describing current debates over the role of Sufism in relationship to the expansion of Turkish imperialism in India. The core of this section, however, is an account of the establishment of the Chishtī Sufi tradition in the Deccan and a description of their principal religious practices as revealed in the earliest sources. This is followed by a consideration of the Sufis' relation to the Indian environment, and especially the controversial question of their role regarding conversion to Islam by non-Muslims. Part III, "The Khuldabad Sufis in History," discusses the political involvement of the early Chishtī masters of Khuldabad, and then documents the later role of the Sufi shrines in Indian politics, up to the nineteenth century. This section also deals with the development of a local hagiography of Khuldabad, which integrated the early Chishtī saints into a sacred geography partly derived from local Maharashtran cosmologies.

The result is intended to be, not a definitive account of the "facts" at Khuldabad, but a presentation of the multidimensional impact of the Sufis of Khuldabad as preserved in a variety of testimonies. Thus, as the subtitle indicates, this book is about the interaction of Sufi mysticism, politics, and history in one particular location, Khuldabad, in the hope that this will tell us more about how to understand Islam in south Asia.

Khuldabad poses many other questions that are beyond the scope of this book. Its close proximity to Ellora, the site of splendid rock-cut caves and temples, puts the valley of Sufi saints nearly on top of some of the most ancient Hindu, Buddhist, and Jain monuments in the region. While it is perhaps common for new religious centers to be established at places already sacralized by previous religious traditions, it is striking to contemplate the spectacle of Sufi shrines so close to majestic Buddha statues, Jina figures, and the great Kailash temple to Shiva. Khuldabad as a monumental funerary complex also needs to be compared to other extensive Muslim graveyards, such as Makli Hill in Sind or Gulbarga in the Deccan. The phenomenon of royal tombs in juxtaposition with Sufi shrines calls out for further investigation. Architectural historians will surely be able to shed light on the historical development and ritual uses of these complexes, which remain so far unstudied. The special local rituals performed at the shrines throughout the year present fascinating materials for the fields of ethnomusicology and religious studies. The testimonies of Urdu poets such as Walī and Sirāj contain unexplored literary perspectives on the saints of Khuldabad. South Asia holds many such centers of religious authority, and I am certain that in cities such as Lucknow, Allahabad, Burhanpur, and many others, rich documentary collections in private hands still offer ample opportunities for patient researchers.

This book is intended for several audiences, including scholars of Islam, Indology, history, and comparative religion; the notes contain particular details and sources of interest to them. But I also have in mind a wider public, including many friends from south Asia, who are seriously interested in Sufism and its history. I hope that all these groups may find something of value in this study, and that this book may contribute to the clarification of the issues at stake in the study of south Asian Islam. More than anything else, this is a book about stories. I hope this book may make readers more aware of the many different kinds of story that form the basis for our knowledge of the past.

The epigraph that suggested the title for this book, *Eternal Garden*, is the first line of a poem by the great Persian poet Ḥāfiẓ (d. 1392), "The cloister of the dervishes is an eternal garden" (*rawża-i khuld-i barīn khilvat-i darvīshān-ast*).[5] This verse suggested itself not only because of its aptness as a description of the shrines of Khuldabad, but also due to the verbal similarity: *rawża*, "garden," was the original name of the town, and *khuld-i barīn*, "utter eternity," is reminiscent of the town's later name Khuldabad, "eternally flourishing."[6] A secondary meaning of *rawża* is "mausoleum," above all the tomb of the Prophet Muḥammad in Medina. Since the Prophet and, to a lesser degree, the Sufi saints, are regarded as being admitted to the divine presence, their earthly remains constitute for their followers a focus radiating the influence of heaven. Rawza was, then, a most appropriate name for this town, which was the first major Sufi shrine and center of pilgrimage in the Deccan. The verse of Ḥāfiẓ has an ambiguity as applied to Khuldabad, since it meant symbolically that Sufis keep their seclusion in the highest paradise, the archetypal eternal garden. By using *Eternal Garden* as the title for the book, I have perhaps done violence to the poem, for the subtitle brings this garden down to earth and historicizes it. Yet it is my feeling that Ḥāfiẓ would have enjoyed this ambiguity, and the curious spectacle of kings seeking after death the protection of those who rejected the world of the court. After all, his poem concludes with praise of his patron as one who possesses "the form of the ruler and the morals of the dervishes." One imagines that Ḥāfiẓ would certainly have taken the opportunity to contemplate the atmosphere of these Sufi shrines, had he accepted the invitation of the Bahmanī Sultan to come from Shiraz to the Deccan in the 1380s.

I would like to express here my profound thanks, first of all, to Fariduddin Saleem, President of the Committee Dargahjat-i Hadd-i Kalan, as well as Mohd. Abdul Hai, Nuruddin, and the other *khādim*s of the shrines of Khuldabad. Without their generosity, which permitted me to have access to the Khuldabad manuscript collection, this project would not have been possible. I would like also to thank them for inviting me to Khuldabad as a speaker at the observance of the 700th *ʿurs* festival of Shaykh Muntajib al-Dīn Zar Zarī Zar Bakhsh in 1987. There are many others I would like to thank, for their valuable help over the years, especially Prof. Annemarie Schimmel of Harvard University, who guided me in the study of both classical Sufism and south Asian Islam, and Prof. K. A. Nizami of Aligarh Muslim University, who initiated me into the study of Indo-Muslim history and historiography. I would also like to thank many others who have generously commented on earlier drafts of this study, but who are not to be held responsible for my final judgments; these include Bruce Lawrence of Duke University, Richard Eaton of the University of Arizona, A. Kevin Reinhart of Dartmouth College, Shantanu Phukan of the University of Chicago, L. Carl Brown of Princeton University, Clifford Geertz of The Institute for Advanced Study at Princeton, Beatrice Manz of Tufts University, Peter Jackson of the University of Keele, Paul L. Hanson of California Lutheran College, and Robert Woods of Pomona College. Brannon Wheeler of the University of Chicago provided valuable assistance in compiling the bibliographical material in Appendix A and preparing all the maps, to which Hiba Awad also contributed. Many others helped in significant ways, including Dr. Muhammad Afzal of the International Islamic University, Islamabad; Omar Khalidi of the Aga Khan Program at MIT; Dr. Christopher Shackle of the University of London; and Eruch Jessawala of Ahmednagar, who first introduced me to Khuldabad. I would like to express my special thanks to my wife Judy Ernst, who designed the cover for the book, for her understanding, encouragement, and support.

The research for this book was supported by a Senior Research Fellowship from the American Institute of Indian Studies in 1981, and by a Fulbright Islamic Civilization Research Fellowship in Pakistan in 1986. Portions of this book have been presented previously in other forms: chapter 2 at the conference on Islamization in South Asia, Oxford University, July 1989; parts of chapter 3 at the conference on South Asian Politics and Religion, UC Santa Barbara, April 1989; chapter 4 at the conference on Transmission of Religious Thought in Islam, Princeton University, April 1989, and in *Texts and Contexts: Traditional Hermeneutics in South Asia*, ed. Jeffrey Timm (State University of New York Press, forthcoming in 1991); part of chapter 7 (on *samaʿ*) at the conference on Ameer Khusro's Impact on Literature and Culture, Chicago, June 1987; part of chapter 10 at the conference of the American Academy of Religion, Boston, December 1987; chapter 11 in *Islam and Indian Regions 1000–1750 A.D.*, ed. A. L. Dallapiccola and S. Zingel-Avé Lallemant (Südasien-Institut der Universität Heidelberg, forthcoming in 1991). Figure 10 is reproduced courtesy of the Museum of Fine Arts, Boston (gift of Denman W. Ross). Figure 14 is reproduced by courtesy of the Trustees of the Chester Beatty Library, Dublin.

The transliteration system employed here for Persian and Arabic names and terms is that of the *International Journal of Middle Eastern Studies*. Words of Indic origin are shown with underdot for retroflex consonants, tilde on nasal *n*, and apostrophe before the *h* of aspirated consonants. Despite occasional ambiguities, this system seemed to be the best compromise between accuracy and simplicity. Spellings of place names follow current usage in south Asia, while spelling of Muslim personal names omits Persian *iżāfa*, which is not pronounced in south Asia. Calendrical equivalents were determined with the aid of Prof. John Woods's "Taqwim" computer program, using Julian equivalents for the lunar Muslim *hijrī* era up to October 4, 1582, and the Gregorian thereafter. When taken from original sources, the *hijrī* date is given first, followed by a slash and the Common Era date; centuries, dates taken from secondary sources, and other well-established dates are given only in the Common Era.

PART I

Historiographical Orientation: Sufism and Islam in South Asia

Before beginning to discuss the Sufis of Khuldabad, it is necessary to explore the historical background of the Sufi tradition of Islamic mysticism and the problems of historical interpretation surrounding the Islamic presence in the Indian subcontinent. The Sufis of Khuldabad saw themselves as the carriers of a teaching that went back to the Prophet Muḥammad, and their literature depends greatly on the writings of the early Sufis and Islamic scholars of the Near East and central Asia. Into this "classical" heritage they incorporated the oral traditions and teachings of the Chishtī order, which from its obscure origins in Afghanistan became the most widespread Sufi order in India. The Sufis were also participants in a society organized under the sultanate of Delhi, which was nominally Islamic, and which was the latest example of a Turkish empire of conquest to be carved out of India.

There are many conflicting modern views on the nature of the entrance of Islam into India, but most of these views derive from much later political preoccupations, such as Mughul imperialism, British colonialism, Indian or Pakistani nationalism, and other ideological concerns foreign to the medieval period. Consequently it is necessary to bring out the underlying reasons for these conflicting historiographical approaches so that we may consciously discard these irrelevant modern biases, as far as possible. Bringing out at the same time some of the complex views that medieval Muslims held of India, and the equally complex views that Indians held of Muslims, helps to measure the distance between modern ideologies and the culture of seven centuries ago. The question of the religious orientation of the Delhi sultanate can then be more easily addressed, in terms of its basis in Persian kingship and its overlay of Islamic symbolism. This will help to clarify the sultanate's policies toward non-Muslim institutions, and above all its constant tension over against Sufism. The historiographical picture will be rounded out by a sketch of the development of the Sufi literature of "discourses" (*malfūẓāt*) and a brief analysis of the types and purposes of Indian Sufi hagiography in different historical periods.

1

Sufism

The Sufi Tradition

We can best approach the Sufi tradition from the standpoint of the history of religion by understanding it as the conscious participation in Islamic mysticism as attested by one's formal initiation into a Sufi lineage or involvement as a lay follower. We must rely mostly on literary sources for our knowledge of the religious history, practices, and teachings of Sufism. From early Arabic Sufi sources it is apparent that Sufism as a distinctive way of life did not come into being immediately at the founding of the Islamic community by the Prophet Muḥammad; rather, it slowly emerged as an emphasis on seeking salvation through intensive devotion to the commands of the creator of heaven and earth, and absorption in the word of God revealed in the Qur'ān. Early Sufi authorities acknowledge that the term "Sufi" (derived from *ṣūf*, the wool worn by pre-Islamic prophets and ascetics) was not in general use before the time of Abū Hāshim al-Ṣūfī, though some assert that the term was known to early Muslim religious figures such as Ḥasan al-Baṣrī (d. 728) and Sufyān al-Thawrī (d. 778).[1] Nonetheless, Sufis regard the Prophet Muḥammad as their chief example and inspiration. For that very reason, argued Abū Nasr al-Sarrāj (d. 988), during Muḥammad's lifetime no higher title than "companion [of the Prophet]" could exist. Thus it was quite some time after the death of the Prophet that the need arose for a new term to designate those holy people who acquired the prophetic qualities of asceticism, devotion, trust in God, poverty, and patience.[2] In practice, the term "Sufi" tends to be less used than a variety of other terms that describe the different aspects or vocations of Sufism: "devotee" (*ʿābid*)," "poor" (Ar. *faqīr* or Pers. *darvīsh*), "ascetic" (*zāhid*), "lover" (*ʿāshiq* or *yār*), "gnostic" (*ʿārif*), etc.

In modern times, European orientalists sometimes argued that Sufism was not really Islamic, basing themselves on an abstract definition of Islam that was often derived from the hostile context of European colonialization of Islamic countries. A number of alternative hypotheses were proposed, suggesting that Sufism was "derived from" Neoplatonic, Christian, Buddhist, or Hindu sources. According to this approach, the speculative and mystical qualities of Sufism could be explained away as foreign elements somehow imported into the Islamic faith (some of these theories followed racial stereotypes, portraying mysticism as the Aryan influence that Persians introduced into the static Semitic religion of the Arabs). In this way one could still retain the convenient picture of Islam as a sterile and fanatic religion of legalism.

Two factors have helped to discredit this old orientalist theory. First is the slow realization that scholars were allowing their judgment to be affected by Christian hostility toward Islam (an old quarrel going back to the crusades and perpetuated in secular form since the colonial period). Second is the growth of a more solid understanding of Sufism based on informed and sympathetic reading of the original sources as they are understood within the Islamic tradition.[3]

It is of course true that a tremendous variety of cultures flourished in the cosmopolitan milieux of the Umayyad and ʿAbbasid Caliphates (ca. 632–945), which was also the formative period of the Sufi movement. But the quest for "influences" on Sufism tells us nothing about the *meaning* of religious doctrines and practices in their Islamic context. The appropriation of terms and practices from earlier religious traditions is scarcely a passive transaction, no matter what the context in which it occurs. "Influence" is nothing but a rather physical metaphor suggesting the flowing in of a substance into an empty vessel. This is hardly a satisfactory model for the complicated process by which people of one culture interpret and put to new uses themes and symbols from another culture.[4] Taking for instance the argument that the rosary came from India into the hands of first Muslims and then Christians, it is hard to attribute any Indian "influence" upon those who use it to count Christian or Islamic prayers. This kind of analysis only has meaning in an outsider's perspective shared at most by a few specialists; its significance is limited, since it is essentially irrelevant to those who participate in the tradition. Since both the texts and the living expositors of Sufism universally point to Muḥammad and the Qur'ān as the twin fountainheads of Sufism, it has become clear that the search for external "influences" has nothing to do with what it means to be a Sufi. These were academic games intended to reveal the derivative, and hence inauthentic, nature of any otherwise admirable aspects of Islamic culture.[5]

To give one example of how insiders understand the Sufi tradition, we may summarize the way that Abū Naṣr al-Sarrāj presents Sufism in his tenth-century *Kitāb al-lumaʿ fī al-taṣawwuf* (*Book of glimmerings on Sufism*). The book consists of an introduction, twelve main chapters, and an appendix. The introduction discusses Sufism as a science in the curriculum of Islamic religious sciences. The first chapter deals with the spiritual states (*aḥwāl*) and stages (*maqāmāt*) of Sufism, the second with the interpretation of the Qur'ān, the third with following the example of the Prophet Muḥammad, the fourth returns to the mystical interpretation of the Qur'ān and prophetic sayings, while the fifth chapter discusses the companions of the Prophet. Special Sufi topics only begin with the sixth chapter on Sufi practices (their "manners" [*ādāb*] in religious rituals, social customs, and ethics), followed by the seventh on Sufi writings (including letters, poetry, and prayers), the eighth on listening to recited poetry (*samāʿ*), the ninth on ecstasy (*wajd*), and the tenth on miracles. The eleventh chapter is a lexicon of Sufi terminology, while the twelfth chapter is a commentary on the apparently outrageous ecstatic sayings (*shaṭḥiyyāt*) of the Sufis. These are followed by a final section on erroneous practices and opinions that are to be found among Sufis. Sarrāj wrote this book intending to characterize the genuine basis of Sufism in mystical experience, and to refute both the critics of Sufism and its unqualified exponents; neither of these groups, in his view, had the necessary experience or learning to understand the subject.[6] From the presentation of Sarrāj, which remained an authoritative and influential classic in later centuries, it can be seen that Sufism constitutes itself as a tradition rooted in the Qur'ān and in the Prophet Muḥammad. Sufism includes the study of Islamic religious learning, which then takes on a distinctively mystical quality from the constant interpretation of traditional subjects in terms of the internal experiences of the soul.

Sufism seems to have originated first in Iraq and then became established in northern Iran, especially Khurasan.[7] By the tenth century, Sufism was a well-established movement with a large literature. The handbooks and biographical treatises produced at this time linked Sufism with noted ascetics from the earliest periods of Islam, so that the public presentation of Sufism emphasized that it was a rigorous form of practical discipline and knowledge comparable to the principal Islamic religious sciences. Sufi literature covered many different subjects, to some extent overlapping the main Islamic religious and literary fields, since Sufi masters were frequently authorities in Islamic law, theology, and related subjects.

Primary was the study of the Qur'ān, and Sufi writers have created an enormous literature on the mystical interpretation of the sacred book. The earliest Sufi Qur'ān commentaries took as a nucleus the commentary of the sixth imam of the Shīʿa, Jaʿfar al-Ṣādiq (d. 765). The comments of many masters (Sahl al-Tustarī, Ḥallāj, and others) were preserved and collected, particularly in the voluminous commentaries of Sulamī (d. 1021), Rūzbihān Baqlī (d. 1209), and other Sufi scholars.[8] Biography, too,was a favorite form of literature in Sufism, because of its value as an entertaining way to convey norms of behavior. Sufi biographical works initially followed the model of *ḥadīth* scholarship, which collected the sayings of the Prophet Muḥammad. These biographies initially focused on the Sufis as the transmitters of religious knowledge, but they gradually expanded from being the records of the sayings of the saints to become a voluminous narrative literature filled with stories of the deeds of the saints. Numerous popular biographical works on Sufis are available, from the classical writings of Abū Nuʿaym al-Iṣfahānī (d.1037) in Arabic and Farīd al-Dīn ʿAṭṭār (d. 1220) in Persian, to the many hagiographies in a variety of modern languages.[9].

Some of the earliest prose treatises concerning Sufism were apologetic works designed to show that Sufism was not in conflict with the Islamic religious sciences, but complemented and perfected them. Demonstration of the authenticity of Islamic mysticism had become necessary in the wake of the highly politicized persecution of certain Sufis, particularly Ḥusayn ibn Manṣūr al-Ḥallāj (d. 922).[10] To this class of defensive writing belong the works of Sarrāj, Abū Bakr al-Kalābādhī (d. 990), and Abū al-Qāsim al-Qushayrī (d. 1074), who related Sufism to Ḥanafī jurisprudence and Ashʿarī theology. Similar to the apologetic works were the large comprehensive surveys of the mystical practice of religion by Abū Ṭālib al-Makkī (d. 996) and Abū Ḥāmid al-Ghazālī (d. 1111). These treatises, which were firmly grounded in Islamic learning and piety, served to introduce and popularize the interiorizing approach of the Sufis among the more conservative Islamic religious scholars. Speculative metaphysics also became a special topic among some Sufi writers, notably al-Ḥakīm al-Tirmidhī (d. ca. 932), Shihāb al-Dīn Yaḥyā al-Suhrawardī (d. 1191), and Muḥyī al-Dīn ibn ʿArabī (d. 1240). These gnostics (using the Arabic term *ʿārif* in its etymological sense of "knower") explored the intellectual aspects of mystical experience, and even employed the terminology of Neoplatonic philosophy to clarify the metaphysical implications of Sufi teachings. Again, this was not a case of mechanical influence, but a sophisticated appropriation of metaphysical concepts to mystical experience.

Sufis also communicated their insights through poetry, from the dense Arabic mystical verses of the early Sufis quoted by Sarrāj through the vast inspired epics in Persian by Sanāʾī (d. 1131), ʿAṭṭār (d. 1220), and Rūmī (d. 1273). In letters, too, Sufi authors such as Junayd of Baghdad (d. 910) developed an elliptical style of writing aimed at others who were qualified to understand their inner meaning. The most intense of all the literary expressions of Sufism were the ecstatic utterances (*shaṭḥiyyāt*) that emerged from overwhelming experiences of divine unity and the annihilation of selfhood. Many of these sayings, such as Abū Yazīd's "Glory be to me!" and Ḥallāj's "I am the Truth," still retain much of their original shock value.[11] The special technical terminology developed in all these types of Sufi writings, which was designed both to clarify for the initiates and to exclude the unworthy, even led to the writing of lexicons of mystical terms.[12]

The Sufi approach to Islamic practice is that of interiorization, beginning with the broad path of the religious law (*sharīʿa*), and proceeding via the path (*ṭarīqa*) of the Sufis to the divine reality (*ḥaqīqa*).[13] To put it in other terms, everything has an external (*ẓāhir*) and a corresponding internal (*bāṭin*) aspect. If the religious law and practices of Islam are taken as the external form, then Sufism is its inner meaning. The inner and the outer are inseparable; one cannot approach the divine, internal reality except through the external religious structure.

An example of the interiorized Sufi approach to traditional Islamic religious practices is Sarrāj's account of ritual prayer (*ṣalāt*), from the chapter on "manners." Sarrāj insists that from the beginning a Sufi must know all aspects of prayer as discussed by the religious scholars. This learning is necessary because of the paramount place of ritual prayer in religion, and particularly because it is the locus in which the whole range of internal spiritual experience becomes available. "Ritual prayer is the station of union, nearness, awe, humility, fear, glorification, gravity, witnessing, contemplation, secrets, intimate conversations with God Most High, standing in the presence of God, acceptance by God, and turning away from that which is other than God."[14] While the ordinary believers must consult the religious scholars about the subjects of their various specialities, the elite Sufis, who concentrate exclusively on God, know the subject of ritual prayer better than anyone else. A similar attitude governs the Sufi treatment of the other Islamic religious practices (fasting, pilgrimage, alms, etc.): not only do the Sufis perform the literal requirements of the law, but also they fulfill it more perfectly than others do. As Sarrāj points out with reference to Sufis' pilgrimage to Mecca, "Their custom is hold firmly to the most comprehensive [interpretation] of religious duties, and to seize the most perfect part of the science of religious law; dependence on being excused is the way of the masses, and accepting comfort and rationalization is the condition of the weak."[15] Sufism is therefore unthinkable without the basic Islamic religious practices. This point may be obvious to those who have studied the subject, but since one still meets with the facile assertion that Sufism is not really Islamic, it is worth repeating here: Sufism is the mystical intensification of Islamic religious consciousness.[16]

The articulation of internal experiences in Sufism was broadly divided into the two categories of "states" (*ḥāl*, pl. *aḥwāl*) and "stations" (*maqām*, pl. *maqāmāt*). The states were typically described as temporary conditions of the soul caused by God's spontaneous manifestations in one's consciousness. Junayd of Baghdad (d. 910) defined the state as "an event that descends on hearts and does not last."[17] Rūzbihān Baqlī called it "that which reaches the heart from the hidden lights. . . . It is the whim of [divine] manifestation."[18] While the states could not be induced by human effort, the stations in contrast were described as the results of the soul's striving to attain the qualities of God. Sarrāj gives the meaning of station as "the station of the creature before God, in terms of where one stands from devotions, exertions, meditations, and concentrating on God."[19] Repentance (*tawba*), asceticism (*zuhd*), poverty *(faqr)*, patience *(ṣabr)*, trust in God *(tawakkul)*, and satisfaction *(riḍā')* are some of the principal stations.[20]

The elaboration and refinement of these psychological categories became increasingly refined over time, so that the Sufis developed a complex technical vocabulary to describe a wide variety of states and stages.[21] Sufis practised many forms of religious exercises and meditations, most of which could be best described as prayers linked to the states and stages of Sufi experience. A variety of terms describe the forms of verbal address of God, ranging from the most spontaneous to the literary and the ritualistic. Simple free prayer *(du'ā)*, frequently modeled on the prayers of Muḥammad, was perhaps the most common form of addressing God.[22] There are also long and eloquent invocations *(da'awāt)*, in which the early Sufis expressed their supplications and praise of God, and beautiful "intimate conversations" *(munājāt)* expressing the most delicate shades of meaning.[23] The most distinctive category of Sufi prayer is *dhikr* (pl. *adhkār*), the Qur'ānic term for "recollection" of God.[24] From being a general term for remembering God at all times, *dhikr* gradually came to mean the repetition of the names of God or other formulas, either silently or aloud, as a form of meditation. By the time of al-Ghazālī (d. 1111), there were numerous accepted rules and techniques of *dhikr*, and later Sufis considered *dhikr* to be one of the most important of religious exercises.

In addition to prayer, Sufis also were fond of listening to the recitation of mystical poetry, often with musical accompaniment, in what came to be known as *samā'*, literally "listening."[25] The use of music, and occasionally spontaneous dancing, in Sufi assemblies, was one of the most controversial of Sufi practices. Arguments raged over the question of legitimacy of *samā'* according to Islamic law, and long treatises were written on both sides, debating the somewhat inconclusive *ḥadīth* reports that indicated the Prophet Muḥammad's attitude toward music and poetry.[26] Sufi mystical poetry in both Arabic and Persian tended to incorporate the imagery of love and intoxication, but used it in an allegorical or symbolic sense, so that the beautiful beloved and the glass of wine were symbols of God and divine love. In this way *samā'* was frequently an occasion for experiencing ecstasy *(wajd)* from hearing the recited verses. Nevertheless, Sufi authorities recognized that musical sessions could potentially degenerate into sensual excesses, and they accordingly established strict guidelines, stressing purity of intention as the most important criterion for *samā'*.[27]

The concept of sainthood *(wilāya)* was the culmination of Sufism as a path *(ṭarīqa)* leading toward direct experience of God. The term *walī* (pl. *awliyā'*), usually translated as "saint," is a Qur'ānic term best illustrated in 10:62, "The friends of God *(awliyā' allāh)*—they have no fear, neither do they grieve." Since *walī* has the connotations of friendship and authority or trusteeship, the Islamic concept of sainthood implies the saint's closeness to God and also the saint's role as executor and implementer of divine commands. From the earliest period of Sufism, saints were regarded as the invisible supports of the universe; an invisible hierarchy headed by the *quṭb* or "axis" of the world carries out the will of God in all things. Sainthood is the foundation of Sufism, according to Hujwiri, and the internal basis of sainthood forms one of the most important topics of Sufi literature.[28]

Divine knowledge (*maʿrifa*), revelation (*kashf*), love of God (*ʿishq*), and annihilation in God (*fanāʾ*) are the characteristics of the perfect saint; these internal attainments provide the certainty that lifts the saint above worldly fears. Saints are also endowed with external abilities to perform extraordinary deeds, "miracles," which form the subject of many stories. Insofar as the concept of sainthood verged upon that of prophecy, another controversy emerged. Determining the relationship between the prophet and the saint was a delicate and difficult matter, similar to the problem of defining the relationship between the prophet and the imam in Shiʿi Islam. The vast majority of Sufis agree that sainthood is just the beginning of prophethood, and that the Prophet Muḥammad remains the perfect exemplar to be imitated by the saints.

Sufism in Islamic Society

Although the early social history of Sufism is obscure, from later biographical sources we can get a picture of the slow emergence of a distinct group of pious ascetics. Living to some extent on the margins of society, many early Sufis appear from their names to have been townspeople who made their living at minor trades and crafts: the weaver (Khayr al-Nassāj), the blacksmith (Abū Ḥafṣ al-Ḥaddād), the saddler (Sarrāj), the ragpicker (Saqaṭī), the fuller (Qaṣṣār), the cobbler (Kharrāz), the draper (Bazzāz), the butcher (Qaṣṣāb), are all titles that Sufis bore. Some formerly practised unlawful professions such as usury (Ḥabīb al-ʿAjamī) and highway robbery (Fuḍayl ibn ʿIyāḍ) before their repentance. Several early Sufis, such as Ibrāhīm ibn Adham and Fāṭima, the wife of Aḥmad ibn Khaḍrūya, are said to have renounced positions of royalty to take up religious life. The two great centers of Sufism were Baghdad and the cities of Khurasan (north-western Iran). The early Sufi movement was relatively unstructured, consisting of like-minded people freely associating in loose circles rather than any formal organization as in later times.

Nonetheless, the recognition of the importance of spiritual authority was fundamental to Sufism, and over time this led to the articulation of the master-disciple relationship. Sufis counted several among the Prophet Muḥammad's associates as their spiritual forebears, especially those who had ascetic tendencies, such as Abū Dharr, or were renowned for their religious knowledge, such as ʿAlī, Ibn ʿAbbās, or Uways al-Qaranī. The first four caliphs are generally mentioned with reverence in early Sufi writings, as are the four founders of the principal Islamic legal schools, and the imams of the Twelver Shīʿa. The growth of the tradition can be seen in the oral transmission of sayings from the most eminent masters, passed on in much the same way as the hadith reports of the Prophet Muḥammad. Association (*ṣuḥba*) with the leading Sufis was the best way to get in touch with their teachings. In this way the basis was established for a chain of transmission of Sufism from master to disciple, going back all the way to the Prophet Muḥammad as in hadith.

The instruction of Sufi masters at this early period was personal and direct, and did not yet have the form of a systematic rule. An example of the general ethical maxims that characterized early Sufi teaching is a list of ten injunctions that Abū al-Ḥusayn al-Nūrī (d. 907) gave to his friends in his testament (*waṣīya*):

> I heard ʿAlī ibn ʿAbd Allāh al-Jaḥḍāmī say, I heard ʿAlī ibn ʿUbayd Allāh al-Khayyāṭ say, I heard Abū Muḥammad al-Murtaʿish say, I heard Abū al-Ḥusayn al-Nūrī say, when he was giving his testament to some of his associates: There are ten things in which you should persevere and exert yourself.
>
> 1. He whom you see claiming to be with God (who is great and mighty) in a state that takes him beyond the limit of the learning of the religious law—do not on any account approach him.
> 2. He whom you see relying on those other than his kinsmen and mixing with them—do not on any account approach him.
> 3. He whom you see sitting in authority, the object of respect—do not on any account approach him, do not receive his assistance, even if he aids you, and do not hope for success from him.
> 4. He whom you see a poor man (*faqīr*) who returns to the world—even if you are dying of hunger, do not on any account approach him, and do not receive his assistance if he aids you, for if he aids you, your heart will be hardened for forty days.
> 5. He whom you see self-sufficient in his own knowledge—beware of his ignorance.
> 6. He whom you see claiming a state for which his internal nature furnishes no guide, and to which the safeguarding of his external nature does not testify—suspect his religion.
> 7. He whom you see satisfied with himself and relying on his own momentary state (*waqt*)—know that he is deceived, and warn him with the strongest warning.
> 8. An aspirant who listens to [secular] poetry and inclines towards luxury—do not expect any good from him.
> 9. A poor man whom you do not see present at a music session (*samāʿ*)—suspect him and know that he obstructs the blessings

of that because of the confusion of his conscience and the scattering of his concentration.

10. He whom you see depending on his friends, brothers, and companions while claiming to possess perfect character—testify to the feebleness of his intellect and the weakness of his religion.[29]

In each case, Nūrī is warning the novices against association with certain types of people: those who think they are above the law, social climbers, people in power, hypocrites, smug ignoramuses, boasters, the self-deluded, the self-indulgent, the unsociable, and the weak in character.

Beginning around the eleventh century, Sufi activity started to become more formalized, centering on communal life in a hospice or retreat (Pers. *khānqāh*, Ar. *zāwiya*), and at this point the need arose for systematic rules to govern the behavior of novices. In contrast to the general advice of Nūrī on the types of people to avoid, the rule of the Iranian master Abū Saʿīd ibn Abī al-Khayr (d. 1047) set up a series of definite rules and practices for Sufi residents at the hospice. Here is Abū Saʿīd's list of ten rules:

1. The disciple should keep his garments clean and be always in a state of ritual purity.
2. One should not sit in a holy place for gossiping.
3. The prayer should be performed in the congregation, particularly by the beginner.
4. Much night prayer is recommended.
5. At dawn, the disciple should pray for forgiveness.
6. Then, in the early morning, he should read the Qur'ān, abstaining from talk till sunrise.
7. Between the two evening prayers, he should be occupied with his recollection (*dhikr*) and the special litany (*wird*) given to him by his master.
8. The Sufi should welcome the poor and needy, and look after them.
9. He should not eat without another person participating—to eat alone is considered unpleasant and unlawful; to offer even the smallest morsel to a brother who may be hungrier than the host is highly appreciated.
10. The disciple should not absent himself without permission.[30]

All the rules in this list presuppose a communal living situation with a regular routine of worship, and the relationship of the individual Sufi aspirant to the community, lay visitors, and the spiritual director. As the Sufi movement became more widely established, the need to define appropriate modes of behavior eventually resulted in handbooks containing hundreds of rules for novices.[31]

The Sufi movement crystalized into a series of "orders" (*silsila*s, lit. "chains"), which formed around a number of charismatic Sufi leaders in the twelfth and thirteenth centuries.[32] The concept of master-disciple relationship was the basis for the *silsila*, which stretched back as a line of transmission all the way to the Prophet Muḥammad. The most widely known orders include the Qādiriyya, named after ʿAbd al-Qādir al-Jīlānī of Baghdad (d. 1166), the Kubrawiyya, after Najm al-Dīn Kubrā of central Asia (d. 1220), the Suhrawardiyya, after the Iranian Abū Najīb al-Suhrawardī (d. 1168), and the Shādhiliyya, after the North African Abū al-Ḥasan al-Shādhilī (d. 1258). Special rituals of initiation developed, frequently involving the use of a patched garment (*khirqa*) of a distinctive blue color, and headgear. The authority of the master as spiritual director of the disciple became all-important.[33] Sufi centers throughout the Islamic world provided hospitality for travelers and disseminated Sufi practices. In the fourteenth century, Ibn Baṭṭūṭa, the great world traveler, visited a Sufi center in Spain filled with dervishes from Iran and Hindustan, and observed that it was conducted exactly along the lines of *khānqāh*s in those distant eastern countries.[34]

The Sufi orders and their material establishments were a part of the larger Islamic society in which they lived, and their fortunes were often tied to the vicissitudes of the political arena. The social manifestation of the Sufi orders was in part a response to the void created by the erosion of the caliphate as a meaningful center of legitimate authority in the Islamic ecumene. After 945, when the Būyid princes, an Iranian Shīʿī dynasty, seized control of the central lands, the caliph was robbed of most of his temporal power and was reduced to figurehead status. The sultanate as a distinct political entity emerged slowly, starting from obscure families of empire-builders (such as the Ghaznavids of Afghanistan) and ending as a widespread monarchical type of organization with close ties to the Islamic religious classes. Jurists reluctantly granted the title *sulṭān allāh*, originally meaning "power of God," to upstart rulers whose only claim to legitimacy was the sword. The political theorist al-Māwardī invented the term "amirate by seizure" to give a semilegal status to governments derived, not from succession to the Prophet of Islam, but from victories gained by adventurous clans of Iranian or Turkish origin. When the Seljuk Turks established their supremacy in the late eleventh century, they sought to strengthen their tenuous legitimacy by extensive patronage of Islamic religious institutions.

It is from this period that the classical institution of the *madrasa*, or Islamic college, derives, under the patronage of the great Seljuk wazīr Niẓām al-Mulk. And it is also during this time that the Seljuk rulers began cultivating eminent Sufi masters to gain both spiritual and political support. It is quite likely that the Seljuk-Sufi alliance was also designed to make political inroads on the Ismāʿīlī Shīʿī movement (the Assassins of Syria and Iran, and the Fatimid rulers of Egypt), by making available on a wide scale the Sunniminded interiorization of Islam. At the same time, Sufi orders began to form links with *futuwwa* men's clubs and craft guilds, and in this way helped to articulate a religious vision for the nonroyal strata of society.

Sufis responded cautiously and even suspiciously to the overtures of the sultans, and their attitude toward royal sponsorship varied considerably. On the one hand, some Sufis sought to influence the sultanate to make it genuinely Islamic in character, but others on the other hand opposed the injustice of the kings and tried to avoid having any contact with rulers whose wealth was illegally extorted from the people. (Of course there were also plenty of greedy dervishes who were happy to live on the largesse of kings, as Saʿdī's *Gulistān* shows so well.) Niẓām al-Mulk founded many *khānqāh*s, and donated large sums to the Sufi orders.[35] Likewise he appointed the famous theologian Abū Ḥāmid al-Ghazālī as a professor in the Niẓāmiyya Madrasa in Baghdad, and even after he left the post to pursue Sufism, Ghazālī returned to teach in a Seljuk madrasa in Tus. Another Seljuk wazir, Abū al-Qāsim Darguzīnī, cultivated the company of the Sufi poet Sanā'ī, who addressed several letters and poems to the wazir.

These early associations between Sufis and sultans later broadened into extensive cooperation. Shaykh Shihāb al-Dīn al-Suhrawardī dedicated his classic Sufi work, the *ʿAwārif al-maʿārif* (*The givens of knowledge*), to the reigning caliph al-Nāṣir, who tried to revive the power of the caliphate with the aid of Sufi and *futuwwa* orders. The Suhrawardī shaykhs in general never accepted the idea of revolt against any king, no matter how unjust.[36] In the thirteenth century, Najm al-Dīn Rāzī addressed his treatise on Sufism, the *Mirṣād al-ʿIbād* (*The path of devotees*), to the Seljuk ruler of Rum, and placed obedience to the king on a par with obedience to God and his prophet, citing the Qur'ānic passage "Obey God, obey the prophet, and those who have authority among you."[37] In Ottoman lands the Mevlevī order in particular, and also the Bektashī to some extent, had close alliances with the ruling power. In medieval Hindustan the Suhrawardī order especially continued the tradition of trying to influence kings for the better. One of their objectives was to intercede with the kings on behalf of the people, and they also were willing to accept positions of employment as Shaykh al-Islām, representing the religious classes in the bureaucracy.[38] During the Mughul period, the Naqshbandī order, which had a strong tradition of association with kings in central Asia, became prominent in political affairs; Shaykh Aḥmad Sirhindī sought to change Mughul religious policies, Shah Walī Allāh invited the Afghan king Aḥmad Shāh to invade India and fight the Marathas, and later Sayyid Aḥmad Shahīd led militant activists against the Sikhs.

Sufi criticism of unjust kingship derives from the strong tradition of pious opposition led by *ḥadīth* scholars and conservative legal circles from a very early date. Sufis were, for instance, to be found among those who attacked the caliph's palace and smashed the jars of unlawful wine that often found their way to the royal table. In ninth-century Baghdad, Abū al-Ḥusayn Nūrī once saw a shipment of suspicious-looking jars being carted into the palace, and at once began smashing them as offences against the law of God (the caliph sent him off in exile for his pains). Similar incidents of Sufis leading attacks on vice are recorded down through the fourteenth and fifteenth centuries in Mamluk Damascus.[39]

Another form of resistance against royal injustice was the Sufis' criticism of the illegal methods used by kings to amass wealth, and their consequent refusal to accept gifts and endowments except under the most stringent conditions. Ghazālī, for example, devotes three chapters of his encyclopedic "Revival of Religious Sciences" to examining the legitimacy of gifts from kings, and emphatically prohibited accepting many kinds of gifts.[40] Although Ghazālī appears to have violated this principle in his own academic career, Sufi tradition maintains that he have vowed toward the end of his life never again to accept any money from kings.[41] In Hindustan, the Chishtī order is best known for its consistent refusal to ask kings for financial support. As one Persian verse states, "How long will you go to the door of prince and sultan? This is nothing but going to the foot of Satan."[42] The tension between accommodation and resistance to royal authority by Sufis will find expression in the conflicting historiographies employed by court historians and hagiographers.

Despite the wide variation in Sufi attitudes toward kings, a fairly consistent pattern of royal patronage of Sufi institutions emerged throughout the Muslim East. Sultans set up charitable trusts (*awqāf*) as endowments for *khānqāh*s or hospices, which, particularly in Egypt, Syria, and Iraq, were likely to be splendid and well-equipped residences with spacious individual quarters. Though rarely themselves of a mystical temperament, kings often specified that their tombs be attached to Sufi tomb shrines and lodges, much like the royal abbeys of Christian Europe. In this way they could borrow sanctity from the tombs of Sufi saints nearby, while benefitting from the blessings of prayers and Qur'ān recitations that were underwritten by royal grants.[43] The technical form taken by these grants was a benefice (*inʿām*) deriving from a land tax collected directly by the recipient without going through the state treasury. This form of revenue assignment (*iqṭāʿ*), originally developed to pay armies in lieu of salary, was standardized by the Būyids and, from the time of the Seljuks, was the most common way of making religious endowments.[44] The Turkish sultans of Delhi as well as the Mughuls regarded the administration of such endowments as a major function of government.[45] Though many of the Indian Sufi centers were modest and self-sustaining (particularly among the Chishtīs), in Syria and Egypt the *khānqāh*s tended to be large establishments, most of which received their suport from amīrs and the king.[46] As early as the eleventh century, the conservative Ḥanbalī scholar Ibn al-Jawzī had noted the luxurious way of life observed in some Sufi establishments, where food, drink, singing, and dancing were of more importance than Islamic scholarship and piety. "They ask every tyrant for the world," he observed, "and do not scruple about the gift of the tax-collector. And most of their hospices are built by tyrants who endow them with ill-gotten wealth." To Ibn al-Jawzī, this seemed a far cry indeed from the seriousness and asceticism of the early Sufi movement.[47]

Just as Sufis had to establish relationships with the kings, so they also played a definite role with the populace. A great Sufi master after death became in some ways more influential than in life. The saint's tomb became the center of rituals of pilgrimage both for Sufi disciples and for the general public, though the aims of the two groups generally differed; the Sufis sought spiritual guidance from the departed saint, while ordinary folk typically asked for help with the problems of everyday life.[48] The Islamic laws of inheritance tended to encourage the creation of a hereditary establishment, since the sons of a saint would usually inherit the property and would be entrusted with the care of the saint's tomb. The descendants of saints would carry some of the charisma of their ancestors, regardless of whether they possessed any spiritual qualifications themselves. So while the intensive training of Sufis continued as before, with the growth of the Sufi orders a great many people became peripherally involved with Sufi shrines as an institutional form. Miracles, healing, and various kinds of assistance in matters both occult and ordinary were the standard features of this approach to Sufism, and from time to time it involved practices of which the stricter jurists disapproved, such as music, prostration, and excessive reverence for saints both living and dead.[49]

Parallel to the main Sufi movement and closely related to it were some manifestations of mysticism that were defiant of social convention. An early branch of Sufism was the path of "self-blamers" (*malāmatiyya*), who humbled their egos by deliberately incurring society's reproaches through objectionable behavior. Such behavior was only intended to outrage, and did not include actually breaking Islamic law.[50] Yet there were others, particularly the free-wheeling *qalandar*s, who resembled dropouts rather than ascetics, and who were known more for irreverence and bizarre behavior than for their observance of religious proprieties.

By the thirteenth century, the Sufi movement was very broad. It built upon the individual contributions of loosely associated ascetics and mystics of early Islam and constructed from them a series of discrete hierarchical organizations extending throughout the Islamic world, undisturbed by political borders. As Marshall Hodgson observed regarding the growth of medieval Sufi orders, "a tradition of intensive interiorization re-exteriorized its results and was finally able to provide an important basis for social order."[51] Sufism functioned as a typical part of Islamic society, and its social extension inevitably had to find some kind of modus vivendi with the ruling power, whether in collaboration or in opposition. This is the background that stood behind the Sufis of medieval India.

2

Historiographies of Islam in India

The Problem of Nationalist Historiography

Those who deny the significance of historiography are most likely to be at the mercy of their own presuppositions. Historiography, or the narrative interpretation of historical data, lies at the core of our knowledge of the past. Isolated "fact" is a myth of nineteenth-century positivism. Modern historians of medieval India, whether British or Indian, have tended to focus on medieval historical chronicles from an exclusively political point of view, treating these works as "sources" and "authorities" from which history may be constructed by the "cut and paste" method.[52] For any appreciation of the religious dimension of medieval India, or any other civilization, it is necessary to go beyond this "factual" approach. The religious element in human life is based upon awareness of the divine-human intersection, which may then be expressed in art, story, social structure, gesture, or ritual. Intentions and contexts are essential parts of religious meaning, just as genres or "kinds" of writing are appropriate divisions in the study of literature.

In considering a civilization such as medieval India, in which religious perceptions played an important role, it is necessary to examine the sources critically, in terms of their professed objectives, interests, and contexts. Chronicles, epics, hagiographies, dramas, inscriptions, and poems may all treat the same subjects and persons, but with widely varying purposes and points of view. Our purpose is not to sift through the sources to establish an "objective" historical account of the Sufis of Khuldabad, but to establish as far as possible the historiographical positions of each source, the main interpretive stances that governed the narrations of history.

For the past century and a half, the writing of Indian history has been dominated by contemporary political concerns, beginning with the British attempt to justify their colonial rule over India. The great monument of the

British study of Indian history is Sir H. M. Elliot's massive collection of extracts from Arabic and Persian sources.[53] While lopsided in its selections and containing frequent mistakes, "Elliot and Dowson" is still a valuable resource.[54] Nonetheless, Elliot presented a peculiarly jaundiced view of India's past. In his view, the medieval historians of India scarcely deserved the name, since they presented:

> Nothing but a mere dry narration of events, conducted with reference to chronological sequence, never grouped philosophically according to their relations. Without speculation on causes or effects; without a reflection or suggestion which is not of the most puerile and contemptible kind; and without any observations calculated to interrupt the monotony of successive conspiracies, revolts, intrigues, murders, and fratricides, so common in Asiatic monarchies, and to which unhappily India forms no exception.[55]

Elliot's lengthy diatribe on the lamentable deficiencies of the Indian historians (whether Muslim or Hindu) culminates, however, in his oft-quoted assessment of the one major benefit that these histories still hold:

> They will make our native subjects more sensible of the immense advantages accruing to them under the mildness and equity of our rule. . . . We should no longer hear bombastic Bábús, enjoying under our Government the highest degree of personal liberty, and many more political privileges than were ever conceded to a conquered nation, rant about patriotism, and the degradation of their present position. If they would dive into any of the volumes mentioned herein, it would take these young Brutuses and Phocions a very short time to learn, that in the days of that dark period for whose return they sigh, even the bare utterance of their ridiculous fantasies would have been attended, not with silence and contempt, but with the severer discipline of molten lead or empalement.[56]

As a result of this line of thinking, Elliot's collection tended to focus on selections that would demonstrate the evils of the medieval Indian period, focusing almost exclusively on political chronicles as the essence of history.[57]

The main distorting presupposition in Indian historical thinking today reads the medieval past in terms of modern religious nationalism. In this view, historical events are implicitly seen as prefiguring the partition of British India into an Islamic Republic of Pakistan and an overwhelmingly Hindu Indian Union.[58] The modern creed of nationalism, born of the French revolution, has effectively converted the world; it requires an effort to realize that the modern concept of ethnic and linguistic nationality did not exist prior to the nineteenth century.[59] In general, though, it is often assumed that the conflict between

Hinduism and Islam (construed as political entities) is one of the eternal verities. Although there are many notable critics of this kind of ideological historiography among south Asian historians, the tendency toward nationalism, especially in popular literature and journalism, is nonetheless widespread enough to require an analytical treatment here. Partisan accounts of medieval battles, in which modern authors blatantly champion their own side against the enemy, are still encountered in south Asian historical writing. To give examples: some Hindu historians decry the "Muslim" invasions (with the stress on religious identity) as the savage onslaught of cruel barbarians and fanatics, whose delight in destroying temples was only exceeded by their love of violence against persons; certain Muslim authors in contrast view the Islamic conquests in India as the liberating force of a democratic and universal faith, which freed the oppressed from the shackles of the Hindu caste system.[60] Modern writers, following to some extent the depictions of medieval epics, have seized upon certain historical figures as heroes and villains of a drama that has finally culminated in modern times. These examples of historiomachy are only slightly exaggerated summaries of positions that are familiar to every student of Indian history.[61]

The terms of the historiomachy are simple. Outstanding historical figures are labelled as heroes by one side, and as villains by the other. To take one example: Maḥmūd of Ghazna's invasions of India, though primarily a series of looting expeditions, have loomed in the modern Hindu consciousness as a national catastrophe. As one prominent Hindu historian has written:

> The most crucial age in Indian history began in A. D. 998, when the Turkish conqueror, Mahmūd, captured Ghazni . . . . No code circumscribed the destructive zeal of the conqueror; no canon restrained the ruthlessness of their hordes. When, therefore, Mahmūd's armies swept over North India it saw torrents of barbarians sweeping across its rich plains, burning, looting, indulging in indiscriminate massacre; raping women, destroying fair cities, burning down magnificent shrines enriched by centuries of faith; enforcing an alien religion at the point of sword.[62]

The undoubtedly destructive effect of Maḥmūd's armies has here taken on an apocalyptic tone, which has become a typical element in the formation of the modern Hindu consciousness; Maḥmūd is now associated in the Indian mind with the destruction of temples and enforced conversion to Islam. Yet attention to sources from Maḥmūd's own time shows that his raids on temples were motivated more by lust for gold, slaves, and jewels than by intolerance of idolatry. Maḥmūd did not even attempt to convert his large contingent of Indian soldiery to Islam, much less the masses of northern India; his Indian campaigns occupy only a small fraction of the court histories that record his exploits.[63] Although Maḥmūd and his court historians did attempt to legitimate his regime and conquests in the name of Islam, it was not because of personal piety or fanaticism. Maḥmūd's only religiously based expedition was to wipe out the Isma'īlī heretics of Multan, but here too, loot was an underlying motive. As C. E. Bosworth has observed, "in some ways, the absence of a motive of burning religious zeal makes his cold-blooded manipulation of religion for pure reasons of state all the less excusable."[64] Still, seeing Maḥmūd's invasions as an Islamic victory over Hinduism has caused much anguished soul-searching over the causes of the Hindu defeat, and the failure of the Hindu kings to unite against the enemy.[65] In Islamicate literature, on the other hand, Maḥmūd of Ghazna became a larger-than-life figure who was idolized by poets and litterateurs for generations.[66] Similarly polarized opinions can be found regarding all the prominent figures of Indo-Muslim history, especially Akbar, Aḥmad Sirhindī, Dārā Shikūh, and Awrangzīb, whose religious views are variously categorized and judged (from a modern perspective) as secular, orthodox, fanatic, or apostate.

Some of the most extreme ideological portrayals of Indian history at the same time are the loudest in claiming to rely on objective "facts" that are ignored by their opponents. The language and rhetoric of positivism is most often invoked (perhaps unconsciously) when ideology is most nakedly displayed. One needs especially to be on guard when a historian, with unintended irony, recommends Ranke's positivist injunction to history, "to show what actually happened"; this is usually a sign that some particularly disingenuous judgments are about to be unleashed.[67]

Modern Indian nationalism began precisely as a reaction against the condescension toward Indian culture exhibited by the colonial regime, but it ended by creating triumphalist historiographies glorifying Islam or Hinduism. Nationalist writers and politicians seized upon the images of the past that were most useful for state formation. This meant drawing upon either the Muslim court histories or the Hindu epic and puranic traditions for images that could be adapted to the exigencies of the modern situation. The practical political goals of nationalist historiography have politicized medieval texts in a manner that is foreign to their original political context.

The picture changes dramatically if we repoliticize the medieval sources in their own terms. What emerges is not a nationalistic and religious concept of identity, but a variety of ethnic ones, based on common Indian and Islamic cosmologies. There are consequently many medieval historiographies of Islam in India, few of which have any direct bearing on modern concepts of religious nationalism. The modern symbols of nationalist ideologies belong to that class of secondary and tertiary symbols that have come to clutter up the realm of public discourse to such an extent that the scholar can sometimes be most useful in helping to clear them away.[68] The sections immediately following are tentative sketches intended to reveal the multiplicity of historiographic approaches underlying the apparently monolithic Islamic and Indian perspectives on Islam in India.

Medieval Islamic Views of India

Arab lore on India certainly goes back to pre-Islamic times, since trade has been carried out on the monsoon winds across the Arabian Sea for many centuries. References to Indian religion are generally scanty in Arabic sources, and must be sifted out from writings of widely differing types.[69] The earliest Arabic literature on India dates from the expeditions that culminated in the Arab conquest of the Indus valley region in 711–712. al-Balādhurī's Arabic chronicle of conquests treated India in the context of the massive expansion of Arab power in the first Islamic century. Other Arabic sources, preserved in Persian translation, expand on the account of the Arab conquest, and describe how the Arab governor Muḥammad ibn Qāsim exempted the local brahmans from the poll tax (*jizya*) on non-Muslims and confirmed the existing nobility in their positions.[70] Probably the most popular variety of writing about India, however, was the literature of the marvelous (Ar. *ʿajāʾib*), which mixed geographical lore with the tall tales of sailors. Legends about the wonders of the East had been popular literary fare in Hellenistic times, in the works of the Greek paradoxographers and the Latin compilation of Pliny.[71] Sandwiched between Sindbadlike adventure stories are occasional references to odd and bizarre religious behavior in India, such as ritual suicide, worship of idols, and the powers of magicians.[72] Scientific writers on world geography, such as the Persian Ibn Khurradādhbih (d. 894) and the Sicilian Arab al-Idrīsī (ca. 1154), included learned accounts of the Indian topography with occasional references to religion; al-Idrīsī was impressed with the remarkable variety of Indian religions, which he (following Ibn Khurradādhbih) numbered at forty-two, though he could not begin to describe them in full.[73] Islamic encyclopedic writings typically touched upon Indian religions by categorizing them as heresies, and the picture of Indian "heresies" that these sources provide is peculiar and far from accurate.[74]

In examining the early Arab accounts of India, an important terminological question must be raised: Why do the Arab authors never employ any term equivalent to "Hinduism"? To begin with, the term "Hindu" originated as the ancient Persian word for "river" (Sanskrit *sindhu*), above all the great river now known (through the Greek pronunciation) as the Indus; the term then became the outsider's geographical name for the region where the river flowed, hence the Greek word "India." In Arabic, *Hind* is the general term for the south Asian subcontinent. *Hindūstān* in Persian refers to the northern plains of India. Only after the Turkish invasions of northern India in the eleventh century did the term *hindū* (with the pseudo-Arabic plural *hunūd* or *ahānid*) emerge, not in Arabic but in modern Persian, initially as an ethnic term, and only later as a religious designation. From Persian, "Hindu" entered modern European languages by the seventeenth century, although the abstract term "Hinduism" does not occur before the nineteenth century.[75] The terms "Hindu" and "Hinduism," then, essentially represent foreigners' concepts of India; they do not correspond to any indigenous Indian concept, either of geography or religion. The lack of any Arabic term for "Hinduism" was, therefore, fairly accurate. The Arabs perceived a number of different religious communities (Arabic *milla* or *madhhab*) in India, with different customs and teachings; some of these were regarded as prophetic and monotheistic, compatible with Islamic beliefs, and others were not. So while we can speak of Arabic views of Indian religions, there was no early Arabic concept of Hinduism, as indeed there was no Indian concept of Hinduism.

The beginnings of the concept of "Hindu" religion are to be sought in the Persian literature of the Ghaznavid period, beginning about 990. The term "Hindu" still had a primarily geographic reference in Ghaznavid times, but the ethnic pride of the Turkish rulers of central Asia helped create an Indian ethnic stereotype in the Persian literature that Sultan Maḥmūd sponsored at his court.[76] For the early classical Persian poets, "Hindu" referred primarily to the black complexion of the Indian, who became the poetic opposite of the light-skinned Turk. "Hindu" as an adjective described anything black, whether the beloved's tresses, a mole on the cheek, or the planet Saturn. The "Hindu" also was associated with slavery (in opposition to the Turkish ruler), and even became mythologized as the demonic resident of hell. In the Persian epic *Shāh nāma* (*The book of kings*), which Maḥmūd commissioned, Alexander the Great could still be portrayed as addressing a letter to the Indian king, beginning with an invocation of the creator, and this salutation: "Best of the Hindus, wise, knowing, and clear minded."[77] But in some of the panegyric poems addressed to Maḥmūd, the sultan is hailed as the conqueror of "infidel India" (*hindūstān-i kāfir*), so that India is identified as the land of the unbelievers.[78] Histories written during the Ghaznavid period also employ the rhetoric of holy war against infidels to describe the raids on India, but this rhetoric was a stock reconstruction by religious scholars to inflate the significance of routine military actions.[79] The traces of religious imperialism that are detectable during the time of Maḥmūd are relatively slight; India does not even become a major object of conquest in epic literature until a hundred years after Maḥmūd, when Rājā Jaypāl of the Panjāb figures as the principal opponent in the *Farāmurz nāma*.[80] Here at any rate is the first clue to the religious concept of the Hindu, as an adjunct to the deeds of a conqueror.

We owe the more precise formulation of the concept of Hindu religion to the superb scientific analysis of Indian civilization by the Ghaznavid scholar al-Bīrūnī (d. 1048).[81] A model of learning and detachment, al-Bīrūnī's Arabic study of India nevertheless stands as the first statement that clearly puts the Hindu in opposition to the Muslim in religious terms. Writing at the same time that Maḥmūd of Ghazna and his successor Masʿūd conducted their raids on northern India, al-Bīrūnī spent years studying Sanskrit with Indian pandits, and mastered the religious, philosophical, scientific, and geographical literatures of India. al-Bīrūnī was sympathetic but critical; he presented Indian doctrines as he found them in the Sanskrit texts, and compared them to the teachings of Greek philosophers and scientists. His book was designed "as a help to those who want to discuss religious questions with them [the Indians], and as a repertory of information to those who want to associate with them."[82] Despite his appreciation of Indian civilization, al-Bīrūnī could not help seeing it in opposition to the Islamic: "The Hindus entirely differ from us in every respect."[83] He described the differences between the two cultures in terms of language, Indian xenophobia, custom (especially exclusionary purity rules), and the bitter legacy of Arab and Turkish invasions. In his final analysis, from a Muslim point of view Hindus were "our religious antagonists."[84] Al-Bīrūnī's concentrated study of the Brahmanical learning of northern India had accustomed him to applying the Islamic concept of religion (*dīn*) to India.[85] He recognized that Indians had a very different religious attitude from Muslims, caring little for doctrinal controversy but zealously guarding their caste purity, but he was probably unaware of the novelty of his synthetic creation of the concept of Hindu religion. With al-Bīrūnī, Hindus become identified for the first time as a distinct religious group, precisely insofar as they are distinct from Muslims.

To trace the development of the concept of Hindu religion would require a lengthy investigation, which no one, to my knowledge, has yet attempted. To the brief summary just presented, which is based on well-known materials, I would add a tentative observation, that the crystalization of the term "Hindu" as a religious designation took place as a result of the Mongol invasions of Islamic countries. To reiterate: the connotations of "Hindu" in early Persian poetry were primarily ethnic; though the religious concept was present to some degree, the Hindu was always opposed to the Turk, not to the Muslim. Al-Bīrūnī's study, which established the theoretical opposition between Hindu and Muslim on religious terms, was a specialized work of scholarship and not widely read. Yet in Persian historical works written in India, especially after the Mongol invasions of the thirteenth century, the opposition of Hindu and Muslim (Persian *musulmān*) becomes proverbial.[86]

What is the reason for the increasing stress on religious identity in post-Mongol India? The answer may be sought in the devastating consequences of the Mongol incursions. From a material and personal point of view, the attack of the Mongols on the great Islamic cities of central Asia was disastrous. But from a religious point of view, the most terrible result was the destruction of the central Islamic institution of the caliphate by an army of pagans. The first great historian of the Delhi sultanate, Qāżī Minhāj-i Sirāj (d. ca. 1270), reflects a widespread consensus of his time when he states that the Mongol invasions are the dreaded apocalyptic sign of the end of time, as foretold by the Prophet Muḥammad.[87] Writing just after Hūlagū Khān's execution of the last ʿAbbāsid caliph in 1258, Minhāj-i Sirāj concludes his history with that terrible event, but his portrayal of the Turkish sultans of Delhi makes it clear that he regards them as the saviors of Islam:[88]

> Notwithstanding that, by the will of the Almighty, and the decrees of Destiny, the turn of sovereignty passed unto the Chingīz Khān, the Accursed, and his descendants, after the kings of Iran and Turan, that the whole of the land of Turan and the East fell under the sway of the Mughals [Mongols], and that the authority of the Muḥammadan religion departed from those regions, which became the seat of paganism, *the kingdom of Hindūstān*, by the grace of Almighty God, and the favour of fortune, under the shadow of the guardianship of the Shamsī race, and the shade of the protection of the Iltutmishī dynasty [i.e., the sultans of Delhi], *became the focus of the people of Islam, and orbit of the possessors of religion.*[89]

In this view, the extermination of the Islamic dynasties of the central and western Asian lands left India as the sole remaining bastion of Islamic civilization, and the Turkish sultan of Delhi became the last defender of the faith against the pagan Mongol threat. In short, India was the last haven for Islam.[90] Under these conditions, with the flood of Muslim refugees fleeing to India from the Mongol massacres, it is scarcely surprising that the attention of Indian Muslims turned to the alarming threat posed by another "pagan" population, within their own domain.[91] Although for Minhāj-i Sirāj, the Mongols remained the infidels par excellence,[92] the aftermath of the Mongol invasions provided the conditions for creating a concept of Hindu religion, conceived of in opposition to Islam.

The formation of an Islamic concept of Hindu India, then, increasingly ascribed a religious identity to the Hindu, but it was a negative identity, formed under the pressure of political circumstances. As Peter Hardy has remarked, "the Hindus are not mentioned, for the most part, except as the passive material on which Muslims impose their will. . . . [The Hindus] are never interesting in themselves, but only as converts, as capitation tax-payers, or as corpses."[93] The most extravagant negative treatment of Hindus occurs in the triumphalist poetic epics of Amīr Khusraw (d. 1325), court poet to seven successive sultans of Delhi. Describing the Khaljī sultan's conquest of the Indian Deccan, Khusraw writes:

> There were many capitals of the *devs* (meaning Hindu gods *or* demons) where Satanism had prospered from the earliest times, and where far from the pale of Islam, the Devil in the course of ages had

> hatched his eggs and made his worship compulsory on the followers of the idols; but now with a sincere motive the Emperor removed these symbols of infidelity . . . to dispel the contamination of false belief from those places through the muezzin's call and the establishment of prayers.[94]

This display of literary skill depicts Hindus only as mythical incarnations of evil, a foil for the implausibly righteous conquests of a disinterested ruler. In the works of Khusraw as in the court histories, "whatever happens is brought under the categories of Muslim thought whether or not religion is an element in the situation."[95] Likewise ʿIṣāmī's epic poem *Futūḥ al-salāṭīn* (*The conquests of the sultans*, 1350) treats Islam in India not as a religion but as the triumph of Muslim kings over hapless Hindus, using Firdawsī's *Shāh nāma* as a literary model.[96] Finally, the court historian Baranī reveals the extremes of prejudice in his work on political theory, *Fatāwā-i jahāndārī* (*The institutes of world empire*, ca. 1357). According to Baranī, religious repression of Hindus has been the cornerstone of Turkish rule in India since the time of Maḥmūd of Ghazna; Baranī even claimed that the Prophet Muḥammad himself commanded that Hindus should be killed and enslaved whenever possible, since they were the worst enemies of Islam.[97] Although this spiteful and anachronistic attitude may be explained as the result of Turkish racism and Baranī's personal resentment against Hindu courtiers, the virulent perception of Hindus as the opponents of Islam was a perceptible element in the climate of opinion in fourteenth-century Delhi. The shrill tone of Baranī's exhortations to militancy against Hindus may also be taken as a sign of the extent to which the sultans felt free to ignore anti-Hindu ranting.[98] In any case, the negative concept of the Hindu as anti-Islamic clearly emanated from the poets and historians who formulated the imperialist ideology of the Delhi sultanate.

Perhaps the fullest dramatic development of the Islamic conquest of "infidel" India is a work that takes the form of a religious martyrology, the *Mir'āt-i Masʿūdī* (*The mirror of Masʿūd*). Written by a Sufi named ʿAbd al-Raḥmān Chishtī (d. 1655), ostensibly on the basis of a work dating from the Ghaznavid period, this book is a romance depicting the valiant life and death of Sālār Masʿūd, "the Prince of the Martyrs."[99] Inspired by a visitation of the spirit of the deceased martyr, ʿAbd al-Raḥmān Chishtī described Sālār Masʿūd's exploits in the service of Sultan Maḥmūd of Ghazna against the heathen foes. The martyr initially escapes poisoning by refusing food from a treacherous Hindu host: "The Prophets . . . never eat food prepared in the house of a Hindu, nor will I," says Sālār Masʿūd.[100] The story portrays Sultan Maḥmūd as a dedicated opponent of idolatry who exults in the destruction of temples; he "laid down the image of Somnát at the threshold of the Mosque of Ghazní, so that the Musulmáns might tread upon the breast of the idol on their way to and from their devotions."[101] The culmination of the story comes when Sālār

Masʿūd determines to destroy a temple of the sun in the town of Bahraich. "Here will I often come, till the crowds of unbelievers, and the darkness of unbelief, be removed from hence. Until this place be cleansed from idolatry, it is impossible for the faith of Islám to spread in the land of India."[102] After titanic struggles with vast Hindu armies, the hero dies tragically, on June 14, 1033. Despite the intrinsically improbable nature of the story, this kind of martyrology has had a wide acceptance. Ironically, the shrine of Sālār Masʿūd is greatly revered among Hindus, who celebrate the anniversary of his martyrdom according to the Hindu calendar with rituals of obviously Hindu origin.[103] As I have discussed elsewhere, martyrology as a literary form became increasingly popular among Indian Muslims from the seventeenth century onward. Sufi writers, including ʿAbd al-Raḥmān Chishtī, expanded the stories of Sufi martyrs in their hagiographies.[104] The association of religious martyrs with sultans was natural in this kind of edifying literature, but it could also play into the political ambitions of rulers who wished to identify their expansionism with holy warfare.

In contrast to the secular literature of poetry and history, the Islamic religious law (*sharīʿa*) had very little to say about Indian religions, and so no Islamic religious concept of the Hindu could be said to exist. The Qur'ān makes frequent reference to Jews and Christians, but not to any adherents of Indian religions. The Arab conquest of Iran had exposed Muslims to the Zoroastrian community, which they generally treated along the same lines as the Christian and Jewish *dhimmīs* (legally protected religious minorities). Yet the Islamic legal texts written in India contain surprisingly few references to Indian religions. Most of the Indian lawbooks are based on works of the Ḥanafī legal scholars of Samarqand and Bukhara written two or three centuries earlier; therefore they incongruously retain judgments covering the subject of Muslim interaction with Zoroastrians, Christians, and Jews, which can scarcely have had any relevance in northern India.[105] A typical judgment forbids Muslims to wear the Zoroastrian headgear (*kulāh-i mughān*), belt (*zunnār*), or Jewish hat (*qalansuwa*).[106] Rarely, Indian Muslim legists made analogies between Zoroastrian or Christian practices to forbid Muslims from participating in Indian religious festivals:

> If on the day of the feast of the Hindus (*ʿīd-i hinduwān*) one is present in approval of them or frolics with them, is happy on that account, and gives them some gift, Abū Ḥafs Kabīr (God's mercy upon him) has maintained that if a man has performed fifty years of worship of God, and, when their New Year (*nawrūz*) comes, sends a gift to the infidels for the glorification of that day, even if it is only an egg, all of his worship of fifty years is in vain.[107]

The example given is a hybrid one, based on the Zoroastrian New Year festival and the Christian use of Easter eggs (which Muslim jurists in Egypt had condemned); its presence in an Indian legal work is simply a sign of the conservative nature of the legal tradition. To the extent that they noticed Hindu religious practices at all, Muslim legal scholars simply classified them in the negative category of *dhimmī* ("non-Muslim") or *kāfir* ("infidel"). Since Islamic law did not distinguish between Christian, Jew, Zoroastrian, and Hindu, we cannot point to any distinctive Islamic concept of Hinduism from a religious point of view.

Despite the negative concept of the Hindu that developed variously in poetic, political, and legal contexts, it must not be forgotten that India occupied a special position in the medieval Islamic cosmos. A number of early *ḥadīth* reports of the Prophet refer to the conquest of India in an apocalyptic tone, equating the warriors who attack India and those who will fight the Antichrist at the end of time.[108] The participants in the first Arab expeditions against India may well have had these traditions in mind. A host of other stories attempt to show that even during the lifetime of the Prophet, south Indian kings influenced by the miracle of the splitting of the moon converted to Islam.[109] Also popular is the legend of the Indian merchant Ratan Sen, who is said to have served Muḥammad at Medina, and being blessed with miraculous longevity, for the next six hundred years continued to relate *ḥadīth* that he had heard personally from the Prophet.[110] Contemporary Urdu writers have collected a multitude of details concerning the relationships between India and Arabia during the early Islamic period. According to one traditional Indian Muslim scholar, "In the eastern Islamic world, India is that fortunate land which, in the very age of the Prophet had, to a great extent, become acquainted and familiar with Islam. Its portion of devotees so built the Islamic realm (*dār al-islām*) that today also in that land Islam and the Muslims are living and established with all their religious and intellectual distinctness and particularity."[111]

The most remarkable legendary accounts in *ḥadīth* reports attributed to the Prophet Muḥammad relate that India (more precisely, Ceylon) was the site of Adam's descent to earth after his expulsion from paradise. On the mountaintop in Sri Lanka called Adam's Peak, pilgrims of different religions still pay homage to the massive footprint variously ascribed to Adam, Shiva, or the Buddha. While modernists may dismiss such reports as legendary, one should not underestimate the power of myth as a major element in the formation of worldview. The first to give notable literary expression to these stories in India was Amīr Khusraw, who refers repeatedly to Adam's descent to India, in his seven poetical arguments demonstrating that India is indeed paradise on earth.[112] Āzād Bilgrāmī, the hagiographer of Khuldabad, has summarized the symbolic significance of Adam's descent to Ceylon in a remarkable Arabic treatise, *Subḥat al-marjān fī āthār Hindūstān* (*The coral rosary of Indian antiquities*), which he completed in 1764. It is a work in four parts, dealing with the references to India in the sayings of the Prophet Muḥammad, biographies of eminent Indian Muslim scholars, rhetoric in Arabic and Sanskrit, and love poetry in the Islamic and Hindu traditions. From the numerous accounts that he culled from many literary sources (e.g., al-Ghazālī, al-Suyūṭī), Āzād concluded that Adam's peak is the second holiest place on earth next to Mecca; India was the site of the first revelation, the first mosque on earth, and the place from which pilgrimage was first performed.[113] Using the Sufi concept of Muḥammad's primordial prophetic nature, Āzād described India as the place where the eternal light of Muḥammad first manifested in Adam, while Arabia is where it found its final expression in the physical form of the Prophet.[114] The black stone of Mecca descended with Adam, the staff of Moses grew from a myrtle that Adam planted on the peak, and all perfumes and craft tools derive from Adam's descent to India.[115] The modern editor of Āzād's work dismisses these traditions as unreliable in terms of *ḥadīth* criticism, due to their weak sources and transmitters; they are, moreover, "semi-historical, based on legends."[116]

While these objections to Āzād's collection of *ḥadīth* are perhaps valid from a strictly textual point of view, they fail to explain the mythical significance of Āzād's portrait of a sacred Islamic land of India. Āzād was perfectly aware of the strictures of *ḥadīth* criticism about unreliable reporters. He had studied *ḥadīth* in Medina with the celebrated Indian scholar Muḥammad Ḥayāt al-Sindī, who trained an entire generation of scholars and sufis in the study of *ḥadīth*.[117] Āzād's purpose in writing his *Coral Rosary* was not, however, to write a standard work of *ḥadīth*; he wanted instead to describe "the land of Hind, which [God] made the realm of vicegerency [*dār al-khilāfa*] and singled out with this distinction."[118] Since it was in India that Adam first exercised the authority that God gave humanity over the earth, it has the unique status of being the first place on earth where human vicegerency (*khilāfa*, also "caliphate") was established. From another innocent statement carefully placed at the beginning of the second (biographical) portion of his book, it appears that Āzād was concerned to show that India was in all ways closely linked to the essence of the Islamic faith. The earliest figure he picked for his lives of Indian Muslim scholars was Rabīʿ ibn Ṣabīḥ al-Saʿdī (d. 776–777), whom he casually describes as "the first one to write [books] in Islam."[119] This statement audaciously places the beginning of Islamic scholarship in India. While not insisting on the factual veracity of these stories, Āzād treated them as appropriate symbolic vehicles for making India central in the Islamic cosmos. In this perspective, India is no longer the hostile frontier of paganism; India plays an essential role in the drama of Islam.

Medieval Indian Views of Islam

What were the attitudes of Indians toward Islam and the Muslims? This apparently simple question is complicated by the apparent absence of any concept of Islamic religion in Indian sources. Brahmanic authorities writing in

Sanskrit, whether discussing Hindu law (*dharmaśastra*) or philosophy, continued to carry out polemics against Buddhists long after they ceased to be an effective force in India, but the Sanskrit tradition has never taken official notice of the existence of Islam.[120] Nor is there any tradition of historical writing in India (except for the Kashmir chronicle), comparable to the dynastic chronicles of the Islamic and European historians, to which one might look for systematic reflections on the Islamic presence in India.[121] The concept of an exclusive confessional religious community was basically unknown in India before Muslims arrived. As W. C. Smith has observed, "Never before, however, had an organized, systematic, and exclusive community carrying (or being carried by) what was in theory an organized, systematic and exclusive idea arrived violently from the outside to reject all alternatives and to erect a great conceptual wall between those who did and those who did not belong."[122] It was long before Indians would entertain the notion of Islam as a separate religion, and longer still before they adopted the even more abstract European concept of "Hinduism." To piece together a comprehensive picture of the Indian perceptions of Islam would require the labors of many specialized Indologists, and would require a survey of many inscriptions and literary texts in a variety of languages; this has not been done, as far as I know.

In the absence of any full study of Indian concepts of Islam, the following brief overview (with special attention to the Deccan region) will suggest some of the main lines along which Indian perceptions of the Islamic presence developed. Like the Islamic concepts of the Hindu, Indian concepts of Islam were forged in the heat of conflict, and reflect the impact of the imperial expansion of the Turkish regime in India. Indians initially conceived of Turks and other invaders in ethnic terms, and later on, when the Turks were domiciled in India, as a separate caste within the Indian social order. Indian resentment at the destruction of temples found dramatic expression in epic poetry, but Indians for long resisted the concept of religious exclusivism that Islam introduced, but which would eventually triumph in the self-consciousness of modern "Hinduism."

Epigraphic sources almost unanimously describe the invaders of northern India in ethnic or geographic terms. Early Sanskrit inscriptions refer to *Tājika*s or Arabs (738), *Valaca* or Baluch (ca. 735), and *Turuṣka*s or Turks (ca. 835); the latter term is sometimes used as a vague place name. The foreigners also come under the ancient terms *Yavana* (815), originally meaning "Greek" (from Ionia), and *Śaka* or Scythian (1316), though they are more frequently referred to as *mleccha* (852), the Sanskrit equivalent of "barbarian."[123] These terms are also found in regional languages in exactly the same style; as an example, a royal inscription in Kannada from the Belgaum district in southern India, dated 1223–24, refers to the king of "Turuṣka" in a list of more than a dozen kings of different regions of India.[124] A Tibetan pilgrim's memoir in

1234–36 likewise referred to the depradations of Turuṣka soldiers in Bihar.[125] Turkish rulers were called by the name Hammīra, from the Arabic title *amīr*, "commander, ruler." Since the royal inscriptions were mainly concerned with recording the exploits of Indian kings, it was natural that they refer primarily to military foes; the theological background of the Turks was of no interest to their Indian opponents on the battlefield.

Sanskrit epic literature dealing with the Turkish invasions makes few references to religion. In the thirteenth century, Vastupala, the minister to the Vaghela ruler of Gujarat, inspired three epic poems in Sanskrit that contain some references to battles with Turkish forces. Another Sanskrit epic, the *Prithvīrājā Vijaya* of Jayānaka (ca. 1178–1200), chronicles the life of the last Hindu king of Delhi, Prithvīrāj.[126] The focus of these works was heroic and military; religion was not an issue, except insofar as the Turks violated the purity of sacred lakes and disrupted the traditional royal patronage of temples and brahmans.[127] For Jayānaka, the Turks were simply demonic, "fiends in the shape of men."[128] A Sanskrit drama sponsored by the son of Vastupala depicted a Turkish invasion being defeated by spies, using standard dramatic plot twists that had been employed for centuries.[129] Literary devices took priority over historical circumstance in this kind of conventional writing.

Particularly in the vernacular Indian languages, epic literature has continued to portray the heroic struggles of Rajput princes against the Turks. The Hindi *Prithvī Rāj Rāsō* attributed to Prithvīrāj's minister Chānd Bardai was successively reworked by different bards, and summarizes generations of reflection on the significance of the king's defeat. "Its anti-Muslim epic-content goes far beyond the tragic situation of a single historical event, and weaves around it an accumulated arena of heroic resistance spreading over several centuries and anachronistically telescoping within the time and space of Ghūrīd invasions the eponymous representatives of later ethnic groups of Muslim invaders."[130] Like the tales of Maḥmūd of Ghazna in Persian literature, the Indian stories of Prithvīrāj became the focus of intensely romantic, not religious, sentiment.[131] In a similar way the fifteenth-century legend of Rājā Hammīr Dev and his fight against Sultan ʿAlāʾ al-Dīn Khaljī (ca. 1300) sets forth the ideals of Rajput chivalry against the ruthless invaders, making an epic story of the unconquered resistance of the Rajputs; battles and exploits that occurred centuries apart are collapsed into a single anachronistic event in the Hammīr legend. Typical themes in the Hammīr cycle are the alliance of the Rajputs and the Mongols against the Delhi sultan and the humiliation of Muslim women.[132]

Perhaps the most remarkable of the Indian epics in Hindi was written by a Muslim: Malik Muḥammad Jāyasī's *Padmāvat*, an allegorical retelling, from a Sufi point of view, of the Hammīr story, using all the elements of Indian religious mythology and literature. Written for a sophisticated audience familiar with Indian imagery, Jāyasī's poem is didactic and mystical rather than epic and heroic. It shows the unsubstantial nature of the victory of ʿAlāʾ al-Dīn (illusion) over the fortress of Chitore (the body), after Padmāvatī (intelligence) and Ratan Sen (the mind) escape on the funeral pyre. At the end of this Hindi poem, the phrase "Chitore became Islam" is simply an allegorical indication of the illusory nature of the world.[133] Yet historical Islam was not a topic for the vernacular Indian epics.

The very few known cases where Indians discussed the religion of Muslims suggest that Hindus regarded Islam as another form of worship of the supreme being, and they described it in terms derived from the Indian theological vocabulary. A Sanskrit inscription on the famous Quṭb Minār in Delhi, dated 1368, records an Indian architect's repair of the tower for Sultan Fīrūz Shāh. The invocation of the deity Viśvakarma, the divine architect of the universe, suggests that the architect was comfortable using a Sanskrit title for the deity of the Muslims. In a recent article, M. C. Joshi has challenged the original translation of the inscription, which was first published by Daya Ram Sahni over sixty years ago. Joshi writes:

> Sahni has translated the fourth and fifth line as "the restoration of the Minār was carried out in the palace or temple of Visvakarman [*sic*]," which cannot be accepted for the reason that no Hindu architect would ever like to call a mosque or its attached Minār as the temple of Visvakarman, the supreme deity of the Hindu Builder-community.[134]

Exactly why an Indian architect should refuse to call the God of Islam Viśvakarma is not clear, except that Joshi seems to regard it as impossible for a "Hindu" to see anything familiar in Islam. He therefore translates the line in question thus: "The work was completed by the grace of Shri Visvakarman," but this translation is problematic.[135]

Yet there is another instance suggesting that Indians did not find it at all strange to regard a mosque as a temple to a familiar deity. A Sanskrit inscription from Kathiawar dated 1264 records the dedication of a mosque by one Nūr al-Dīn Fīrūz, an Iranian sailor and trader from Hormuz. The opening invocation addresses the supreme being by the names Viśvanātha ("lord of the universe"), Śunyarūpa ("one whose form is of the void"), and Viśvarūpa ("having various forms"). The next line records the date as "662 of the Rasūla Mahammada, the preceptor (*bōdhaka*) of the sailors (*nau-jana*) devoted to Viśvanātha."[136] The explicit identification of the Muslim group as sailors who follow the Prophet (*rasūl*) Muḥammad also gives the Sanskrit title "lord of the universe" to the god worshiped in the mosque. The Indians who helped Fīrūz acquire the land from a temple and some shops were not Muslims, but regarded Fīrūz as a "supporter of his faith" (*dharma-bhāndava*).[137] In their view, it was entirely natural to think of a mosque as a place where a recognizable god was worshiped. According to architectural historian R. Nath, there was even a fifteenth-century Sanskrit text written in Gujarat for the guidance of Indian architects employed to build mosques. In it, the god Viśvakarma says of the mosque, "There is no image (as idol-worship is prohibited) and there they worship, through dhyāna (contemplation), the formless, attributeless, all-pervading Supreme God whom they call Rehamāṇa [i.e., Arabic *raḥman*]."[138] It is only the modern politicized view of Hinduism, to which Joshi testifies, that cannot imagine Indians seeing Islam as a form of worship comparable to any other in India.

Even in dangerous political situations where one might suppose that Indians would be wary of the religion of the enemy, they continued to appreciate Islamic faith as compatible with their own. The last Hindu king of Gujarat, Karna Deva Vāghela, though he suffered a devastating attack from Delhi in 1299, managed to survive for another decade until a second campaign from Delhi overcame him. A bilingual Persian-Sanskrit inscription of 1304 records how the Rājā, along with two Mongol officers (who had deserted Delhi for the Hindu king) and another Muslim official, endowed the revenue from a village for the upkeep of a mosque in Cambay.[139] Karna Deva's approval of the endowment to the mosque was simply the usual form of patronage that the kings extended to all types of religious centers, including temples of Shiva, Vishnu, and the goddess. The Rājā was perfectly happy to support the Islamic religion of some of his officials, but he clearly separated that element from the military threat of the Turks in Delhi.

The very terms "Islam" and "Muslim" are scarcely to be found in Indian sources before recent times, and when they do occur, it is within the distinctively Indian context of the caste system. In the Kathiawar mosque endowment mentioned above, the inscription also mentions that among the trustees of the mosque are the sailors, oilmen, limeburners, and "the Muśalamānas among the *patrapatis*." D. C. Sircar identifies the latter group as carriage drivers.[140] From an anthropological point of view, Muśulamāna (the Sanskritized form of the Persian term *musulmān*, from Arabic *muslim*) here probably designates the Muslim subset of a caste of drivers similar to modern *tāngāwālās*; it is not exactly a religious description, but a term for an endogamous kin-group (Sanskrit *jāti*) that follows a particular profession. From an Indian point of view, "Muśalamānas" would be distinguished not primarily by their beliefs or rituals, but by their profession and by the subset of that kin-group within which they married. The three other professional groups mentioned in the inscription (sailors, oilmen, and limeburners) are not described as Muslims; caste was a more prominent indicator of status than religion as it is commonly understood today.

Several centuries later, the Rajput nobility's integration into the Mughul administration led to a comparable recognition of the Muslim elite as a subset of the Rajput caste:

> The traditions generally represent the Rajpūt *jāti* (caste) as being divided into two categories: Muslim (or Turk) and Hindu. This

> category of "Muslim" within the Rajpūt *jāti* did not include all Muslims, but only those who were warriors and who possessed sovereignty and power equal to or greater than the Hindu Rajpūt. The Muslim Emperor in particular held a position of high rank and esteem, and the traditions often equate him with Rām, the pre-eminent Kṣatriya cultural hero of the Hindu Rajpūt.[141]

Equating "Muslim" with a section of the Rajput caste indicates how Indians consistently viewed Muslims in terms of their own social system, without any reference to the distinctive and exclusive aspects of Islamic theology.

The impact of the Islamic presence on the Maharashtran region is of special importance because of the dominant role of Maratha culture in the formation of modern Hindu identity. The Khaljī invasion of the Deccan in 1296 led to the overthrow of the ruling Yādava dynasty in 1313, but reactions in Marathi literature were few. With the exception of the religious writings of the Mahānubhāvas and the Vārkarīs, Marathi literature is said to have entered a "dark age" that lasted over two centuries, due to the end of traditional royal patronage.[142] Religious thinkers such as the Vārkarī poet Nāmadeva (d. 1350) lamented the destruction caused by the Yāvana (Turkish) kings. The Mahānubhāvas, who had been persecuted by the Hindu Rājās of Deogir, saw the Turkish defeat of the Yādavas as a divine punishment. But the first major literary reaction to the Muslims was in the writing of Eknāth (d. 1599), one of the great theologians of Hindu devotion (*bhaktī*) and a supreme master of Marathi. He wrote a series of satirical dialogues in popular idiom as a way of expressing his teachings on the nature of God and the transcendence of caste through the path of devotion. One of these dialogues, the *Hiṇdu-Turk Saṃvād*, reveals the religious arguments that might typically have taken place between Hindus and Muslims in the sixteenth century, while at the same time arguing that both are fundamentally in search of the same divinity:

> The goal is one; the ways of worship are different.
> Listen to the dialogue between these two:
> The Turk calls the Hindu "Kafir!"
> The Hindu answers, "I will be polluted—get away!"
> A quarrel broke out between the two;
> A great controversy began.[143]

Like the earlier antisectarian leaders of the *sant* movement, Kabīr (d. ca. 1448) and Guru Nānak (d. 1539), Eknāth found the exclusivist religious consciousness typified by Islam to be intolerable.[144] In this poetic dialogue, the Turk reproaches the Hindu for crass idolatry, ridiculous scriptures, purity regulations, and caste distinctions. The Hindu replies by making parallels between the stories of the Hindu and Islamic scriptures, and criticizes the worship of Sufi tombs, animal sacrifices, and above all the desire to convert Hindus into *musulmāns* (the term *musulmān* only occurs in the verses mentioning conversion). At the end the two become reconciled, realizing that in God all distinctions disappear. By Eknāth's time, it was generally realized that Islamic exclusiveness had called forth a countermovement of exclusivity on the Hindu side, but sectarian religious identity did not yet comfortably fit with the structure of Indian society.

Another depiction of the tension between Hindu and Islamic identities, once again conceived in terms of caste, occurs in the work of the later Marathi hagiographer Mahīpati (d. 1790). In his lengthy compendium of lives of Maratha saints, Mahīpati described the curious case of Bahīrambhaṭ (or Bahīra Jātaveda, ca. 1400), who had resolved to become totally indifferent to the world. This saint decided to avoid conventional renunciation as a forest-dweller, on the grounds that he would only attract reverential disciples that way. "Still," he thought, "I must plan that my relations with my own caste should suddenly break so that no one should question me." By breaking with his caste, he will incur the greatest amount of dishonor among men; social censure will, however, be the test that purifies him. "Everyone will spit on me. They will offend me with slander. It is fitting that exactly this should come to pass. If things happen in this way, my body will become pure." So Bahīrambhaṭ did the most dreadful thing he could imagine: he went to the *qāżī* and asked to become a Muslim. "Take me into your caste. Know ye, that making a Muslim out of a Hindu is considered to be meritorious (*puṇya*) in your *śastra* (holy book). So don't hesitate. Make me like yourself." The surprised *qāżī* asked what was wrong, and offered to help, but he was unable to comprehend why the high-caste pandit wished to become a Muslim. "I have not become free of desires. (But) yours appears to be a direct way of reaching *Bhagavaṃta* (God)." Bahīrambhaṭ was accordingly "defiled"—that is, circumcised—and officially converted, and his family and friends bitterly criticized him for entering into a low caste. Bahīrambhaṭ then repented his conversion, and begged to be reinstated in his community, and the Brahmans relented and prescribed a penance. Unfortunately Bahīrambhaṭ's circumcision could not be undone, but when Muslims reproached him for apostasy, he pointed out to them that he still had the pierced ears of a Brahman too. He no longer knew what he was, for he no longer belonged to either caste. Wandering in a daze and regarded as insane, Bahīrambhaṭ at last met the saint Nagnath, who knocked Bahīrambhaṭ unconscious, pounded his body into jelly with a pestle, reformed it into an image, and cremated it. Then Nagnath brought the body to life with a glance, and Bahīrambhaṭ was reborn, foreskin restored, in "a divine body with all good qualities, such as Yogis enjoy."[145] In this tale of conversion to Islam and apostasy, there is only the vaguest notion of Islamic religion; becoming a Muslim is primarily seen as an estrangement from one's caste group, with the impressively distinctive rite of circumcision as an apparently irrevocable price of admission. Typical of the *bhakti* position, the story also sees conventional religion, whether Hindu or Islamic, as a detour from the esoteric truth of the self. The ingenious solution to Bahīrambhaṭ's dilemma is an example of the initiatic death rituals of yoga, which replace the normal body with an immortal body of adamant.[146]

Militant religious opposition to Islam began to take form in the late seventeenth century and early eighteenth century, when a resurgent Maratha kingdom under Shivaji challenged Mughul authority. Parallel with the Maratha revival was the militarization of the Sikhs under the pressure of Mughul persecution; such was the influence of the Islamic model of exclusivism that the Sikhs even adopted the Arabic term *shahīd* for their martyrs. But in Maharashtra the elaboration of religious separateness was to be more extensive, founded upon a longer cultural tradition and a larger social base than the Sikhs had in the Punjab. The militant Maratha religious leader Ramdas spoke bitterly of the injustices of Mughul rule:

> Many were those who were taken by the Muslims (*Tamra*) . . . many were the good women who were abducted; many were converted to Islam. . . . Under the Muslim kings Muslim fairs (*ʿurs*) are held everywhere. The holy places (of the Hindus) have been desecrated, the homes of Brahmans are destroyed, the whole Earth has been shaken up, the religion (*dharma*) is lost.[147]

Inspired by the successes of Shivaji, Ramdas envisioned a new heaven on earth, when "the land of the Hindus is now strong. . . . The sinful Awrangzēb is destroyed, the *mlechchas* are destroyed, the holy places that were destroyed are now re-established . . . and there is plenty of everything for the performance of the sacred rites."[148] Shivaji's exploits, especially his assassination of the Mughul soldier Afżal Khān, became the nucleus of a totally new bardic tradition in Marathi that contributed importantly to the formation of a regional identity.[149]

The spirit of the Maratha revival acquired its modern nationalistic form in the late nineteenth century, when Maratha writers began to debate the significance of Muslim institutions and British rule. Probably Bal Gangadhar Tilak (d. 1920) more than anyone else can be credited with the creation of a modern Maratha historiography, in which he denounced the idol-smashing Maḥmūd, the bloodthirsty Tīmūr, and the violent Awrangzīb. These dramatic images would become the stereotypes of Islam in modern Hindu nationalism.[150] The more extreme manifestations of anti-Muslim sentiment are visible in today's popular culture in Maharashtra; examples that come to mind include the Shivaji comic book that portrays Mughul soldiers as Islamic *mullās*, and the eccentric P. N. Oak, whose "Committee to Rewrite Indian History" maintains that there is no Islamic architecture in India, only defaced Hindu buildings.[151]

As Indians were slowly coming to terms with a religious group that defined itself as an exclusive community, the notion of a separate Hindu community must have been encouraged. Wilfred Cantwell Smith has suggested that "the crystallization of religious communities" intensified throughout India from the seventeenth century onward, increasingly formalizing the Hindu and Sikh communities as well as the Islamic.[152] It is not certain when the term "Hindu" first became common as a religious designation in Indian languages, but we have seen some indications of how the term originated in Arabic and Persian, as a negative counterpart, first of Turk, then of Muslim. A roughly similar process seems to have occurred in both Hindu and Islamic contexts (using these terms now lightly, with an awareness of their changing content over time for different Indian audiences). That is, while the Persian term "Hindu" moved from ethnic and geographic reference to religious designation, the various Indian terms for Muslim ethnic groups began, much more slowly, to include a consciousness of religious separateness. The internal reflex of recognizing a separate Islamic community was for Indians to become self-conscious. The even more abstract European concept of religion, with all its condescending colonial and missionary accents, dramatically intensified Indian self-consciousness. As W. C. Smith observed, "When something called 'Hinduism' was attacked, Indians arose to defend it."[153] The modern term for this self-consciousness in India is "communalism." The traumatic partition of India, and the uncertain creation of an Islamic state in Pakistan, created further tensions in the Hindu-Muslim relationship. The current political impasse between India and Pakistan is an ironic testimony to the efficacy, and perhaps the irreversibility, of communal self-consciousness.

3

Religion and Empire in the Delhi Sultanate

Medieval Hindustan in the thirteenth and fourteenth centuries was a society dominated by a power-seeking aristocracy of Turkish origin, who fought to establish their authority in a complex historical and political situation. The symbolism and psychology of world domination formed the underpinning of the Delhi sultanate. The Turkish sultanate of Delhi was based on Persian royal symbolism, qualified by superficial acknowledgment of the Islamic political tradition of the caliphate; its main objectives were defense against the rival Mongol imperium and expansion into the Indian subcontinent. While Turkish ethnicity and Islamic religious identity did have some symbolic prominence in the sultanate, in practice the patronage of the regime clearly included support of non-Muslim religious institutions, incomprehensible as that may seem in nationalist terms. In contrast to other areas such as the Anatolian frontier, where centuries of warfare between Christians and Muslims made religious identity a self-conscious and politically charged factor, medieval India did not regard religion as politically decisive. Pragmatism was dominant over ideology, or rather, nationalistic ideology was simply not yet present. The Sufis could not help but respond to the powerful center of gravity that was the sultanate. The tensions between the sultanate and Sufi institutions led to the production of rival historiographies mirroring the concerns of both groups.

Persian Kingship and the Indo-Muslim State

The quest for world dominion is an old one, which in a compact form coincided with the cosmic symbolism of kingship in many traditional civilizations. The world or cosmos was identified with the inhabited realm. Beyond the borders of the cosmos were the demonic forces of chaos, incarnated in troublesome nomads or rival kingdoms. The Persian empire of Cyrus was perhaps the first explicitly to break out of the protective shell of cosmic symbolism into an empirical world whose receding borders excited an insatiable thirst for conquest. Alexander of Macedon embodied the Persian imperial dream even more successfully than the Persians themselves, and his conquests across Asia became the stuff of enduring romances and legends.[154] Roman Caesars and Persian shahs of later centuries were all followers of this dream of world conquest, which their court ceremonials and symbolism proclaimed in a hundred ways. The sudden establishment of an Arab state by the successors of the Prophet Muḥammad catapulted a tribal people into the command of a vast empire. It is not surprising that the Arab caliph (*khalīfa*) soon began to display all the signs and ceremonies of universal kingship that the conquered shah and the rival Caesar used.[155]

Iranian political theory entered the ʿAbbāsid court through such influential Persian advisers as Ibn al-Muqaffaʿ and the Barmakī family, and the ethical and political maxims of Iran became the staples of the new *adab* courtly literature in Arabic.[156] By the third/ninth century, Iranian court poets, in an endless stream of Persian panegyric odes (*qaṣīdas*), were lauding their patrons as modern rivals of Alexander, Caesar, and Khusraw (Chosroes). The practice of the ancient Iranian kings was also the subject of the famous *Siyāsat nāma* (*Book of government*), which the wazīr Niẓām al-Mulk wrote as a guidebook for the Seljuk sultan Malik Shāh.[157]

In the eastern Islamic lands, new rulers of Turkish ancestry entered in waves of nomadic resettlement, driven by the turmoil of the central Asian steppes in search of better fortune. Their appearance coincided with the renaissance of Persian royal traditions encouraged by Iranian vassals of the caliph. Yet it was a Turk of slave origin, Maḥmūd of Ghazna, who commissioned the complete edition of the Persian royal epic, Firdawsī's *Shāh nāma*.[158] This enormous poem, containing over sixty thousand verses, draws on Iranian legends and heroic cycles to portray the history of kingship from the creation of the first man Gāyumars up to the extinction of the Sāsānian monarchy by the Arab conquest. Kingship in this tradition is of divine origin, symbolized by the king's halo or aura of light called the "royal glory" (*farr-i shāhī*), which is a lesser manifestation of the "divine glory" (*farr-i īzadī*). The *Shāh nāma* became a favorite text for all the royal dynasties in the lands from Anatolia to central Asia and India where Persian was the court language.[159] The magnificent illustrated copies of this work prepared for the Ṣafavī prince Tahmāsp, for the Mongol Īl-khāns, for the Mughuls, and the like, testify to the unfailing popularity of Firdawsī's poem as an expression of royalist sentiments.[160] Kings commissioned a host of imitations of the *Shāh nāma* to immortalize their own exploits, though few of these poems have the sonorous and majestic qualities of their model.[161]

The renaissance of Persian royalism only became politically significant because of the decay of the central Islamic institution of the caliphate. As a world imperial structure, the caliphate had reached its apogee in the third/ninth century, and by 945 had fallen into a position of subservience to an upstart Iranian dynasty, the Būyids. A combination of factors were responsible for this decline, including the increasing independence of provincial governors, agrarian rebellions, sectarian movements, and pretorian coups by Turkish guards. The result was that the caliphs were reduced for the next few centuries to controlling a small area of land around Baghdad. Because of the prestige of the caliphate as an office traced back to authority of the Prophet Muḥammad, princes continued to pay lip service to the caliphs and went through the ritual of asking the caliphs for investiture with positions they had already gained by force of arms. This procedure gave the fiction of legitimacy to rulers whose only claim to authority was the sword. The pretense of caliphal supremacy was upheld until a rival imperial power determined to extinguish it; Hūlagū Khān's Mongol troops sacked Baghdad and killed the last caliph, al-Mustaʿṣim, in 1258. The authority of the caliphate was now virtually meaningless in any practical sense, although the Mamlūk rulers of Egypt kept a branch of the ʿAbbāsid family under a demeaning house arrest in Cairo for several centuries, producing the nominal caliph only for ceremonial occasions. In the absence of a meaningful caliphate, Turkish and Mongol rulers in the eastern Islamic lands increasingly buttressed the authority of their kingship with the royal symbolism of Iran.

The Turkish sultans of Delhi were well aware of the Iranian royal tradition, which their Ghaznavid and Ghūrid predecessors in Afghanistan had employed so strenuously. In Delhi, as in Ghazna and Ghur, *darī* or "court" Persian continued to be the language of administration, acting as a natural medium for the expression of Iranian notions of kingship. A clear restatement of the Persian monarchical tradition was Fakhr-i Mudabbir's *Adab al-ḥarb wa al-shujāʿa* (*Manners of war and bravery*), a partly political but primarily military treatise dedicated to Sultan Iltutmish (d. 633/1236). The Delhi sultans combined the symbolism of divinely ordered kingship with a racialistic bias in favor of the Turks. The light complexioned Turk, already a staple figure of beauty in Persian poetry, was paired off against the dark Indian in an antithetical pairing that became proverbial.[162] Sultan Ghiyās al-Dīn Balban (d. 686/1287), a Turk who was once purchased in the slave market of Baghdad, imaginatively traced his ancestry to the mythical Turanian hero Afrāsyāb from the *Shāh nāma*, and likewise insisted on the use of Persian royal ceremonial in the court. Such was his sense of Turkish superiority that he was infuriated when advisers admitted into his presence a low-born Indian Muslim, whom they recommended to the sultan for no better reason than ability.[163] But Turkish racialism was not fundamental to the institution of the Delhi sultanate, though it continued to be a powerful factor at court. From the time of ʿAlā' al-Dīn Khaljī (d. 717/1316), the sultans recognized that Indianizing their administration was a sound governing policy, and by the time of Sultan Muḥammad ibn Tughluq (d. 752/1351), Indian converts to Islam and Hindus formed a significant proportion of the administrative officials.[164] Regardless of the ethnic composition of the Delhi sultanate, however, it remained an imperial state with a symbolic basis in Persian kingship.

Indian traditions of kingship do not seem to have had any impact on the Turkish sultans of Delhi. The antiquity of the world ruler (*cakravartin*) concept is attested in both the Buddhist Jātaka stories and in the Hindu literature (Kautilya's *Arthaśāstra* and the *dharmaśāstra* tradition), and many an Indian king has claimed this lofty status.[165] The Persians had not been utterly unaware of Indian political traditions, for Indian classics such as the *Hitopadeśa* had been translated into middle Persian at an early date (later Ibn al-Muqaffaʿ would translate this into Arabic as the famous *Kalīla wa Dimna*). But the absence of any concrete world imperial program in India since Harsha (d. 648) left the monarchical principle primarily in the hands of minor dynasties. Battle was certainly the main vocation of the Indian warrior caste, but the practice of seasonal raids on an almost ritual basis did not contribute to the consolidation of a great empire. Modern Indian nationalist historians have frequently bemoaned the "fratricidal" warfare among the Hindu kings, which prevented them from uniting to meet the "Muslim" threat, but this modern communalistic language is a product of twentieth-century ideologies. Nothing could have been further from the minds of these thirteenth-century rulers than Hindu *svarājya* (self-rule) or the Pakistan movement.[166] At any rate, compared to the expansionism of the early Arab caliphate, or central Asian empires such as the Qara Khitai and the Mongols, the Rajputs and other Indian kings offered the Turks no awe-inspiring imperial spectacle, despite their ability on the battlefield. The Turkish sultans constructed their imperial edifice with reference to Irano-Semitic and central Asian traditions, and in their proclamations they generally remained oblivious to the native traditions of India, despite the wholesale absorption of existing local Indian administrations into the Turkish empire.

Granted the presence of the Iranian symbols of monarchy at the Delhi court, what was the psychological significance of this tradition of kingship? Żiyā' al-Dīn Baranī, the historian and disappointed courtier, is one of the main sources for the Delhi sultanate, and both in his historical and in his political writing he has brilliantly portrayed the unbounded ambition that is necessary for the true king seeking world dominion. Baranī had been a courtier in the service of Sultan Muḥammad ibn Tughluq for seventeen years, from 1334 to 1351. He fell from grace at the accession of Sultan Fīrūz Shāh, possibly because of being implicated in the abortive coup of Aḥmad Ayāz. During his last exile from court, he produced the only surviving work (in a unique manuscript) of political theory written during the Delhi sultanate, the *Fatāwā-i jahāndārī* (*Institutes of world dominion*). Baranī presented his views on kingship in the guise of being a record of the principles and laws current during the reign of Maḥmūd of Ghazna (d. 1030), but there was a great distance separating his romanticized portrait of the king from the historical reality. Using historical figures like Maḥmūd was merely a device Baranī used to endow his analysis of kingship with the aura of tradition; he was thus freely able to criticize the shortcomings of the sultans of Delhi by discussing safely distant examples from history and legend. The *Fatāwā-i jahāndārī*, even more so than Baranī's history of the Delhi sultans, the *Tārīkh-i Fīrūz Shāhī*, gives a superb portrait of the tensions and motivations characterizing the world imperial ambition of the Delhi sultanate.[167]

Baranī begins from the Arabic form of the old Persian adage, "religion and kingdom are twins" (*al-dīn wa al-mulk tu'amān*), but the actual relationship between religion and politics is tantalizingly ambiguous. He gives this proverb a mythological embodiment, maintaining that the two sons of Adam, Seth and Gāyumars (*sic*), were assigned prophecy and kingship as their respective provinces.[168] Seth's successors the prophets were to show the way of God's commandments to humanity, while Gāyumars led the kings in ordering and chastising humanity according to justice in order to found world dominion.[169] Baranī in this way incorporates kingship, via the Iranian primeval man Gāyumars, into the divine economy of the Islamic religious tradition. The accommodation of kingship with Islam is, however, full of inconsistencies, so that it appears to be a secular regime's mere lip service to religion.[170] On the level of ethics, Baranī permits the ruler personally to engage in behavior forbidden by Islamic law as long as the ruler's ultimate aim is to support the practice of Islam socially as the state religion.[171] The customs of Persian kingship, he candidly admits, are opposed to the example (*sunnat*) of the Prophet Muḥammad, and the secular laws necessary for empire contradict and supersede the Islamic legal system (*sharī'at*).[172] Politically, Baranī ignores the question of the caliphate as the supreme Islamic institution, maintaining that the sultan is the ultimate authority both in religious and secular terms.[173]

Baranī attempts to resolve the apparent contradictions between kingship and Islam by stating that kingship is the reflection of divinity on earth, and is thus superior to prophecy in this respect. Prophecy is the perfection of religiousness and kingship is the perfection of the world, but they are contradictory perfections. Religiousness is servantship, which is characterized by weakness, poverty, and need, while worldly kingship has the qualities of lordship, such as power, greatness, and bounty. The qualities of kingship are thus more properly divine attributes than those of prophecy.[174] "Kingship (*pādshāhī*) is the vicegerency (*khilāfat*) of God and the representation (*niyābat*) of God."[175] Since the king is "the shadow of God on his earth" (*ẓill allāh fī arḍih*), the Persian court ritual of prostration (*sijda*) to the king is technically permitted, though otherwise prostration is only performed before God.[176] Theoretically, the ideal king is the metaphorical world ruler (*jahāndār-i majāzī*), who imitates the example (*ittibāʿ-i sunnat*) of the real world ruler (*jahāndār-i ḥaqīqī*)—that is, God.[177] Like God, the king possesses the divine attributes of both grace and wrath to reward the good and punish the evil.[178] While both kings and prophets must have the qualities of greatness, intellect, and piety, the kings must avoid any appearance of miserliness and lack of ambition; it is necessary for kings to mingle their good qualities with infidelity and pathology (*kufr wa maraż*), for they must have the magnificence and ambition required to thwart the powers of evil among men.[179] It is not possible to rule successfully with the poverty and thorough moral uprightness of a prophet; it is for this reason that the first four caliphs after Muḥammad all fell martyrs to the swords of assassins. Imperial ambition is not permissible for the prophet. The example (*sunnat*) of the Prophet Muḥammad is fundamentally opposed to the customs (*rusūm*) of Khusraw.[180] Baranī maintains that it is one of the great tribulations of kings, that despite their true piety, they are forced by the requirements of office to commit acts forbidden by Islamic law. For them, drinking wine, the pomp and ritual of court, and the grandeur of military might are mere show, for the true kings, like Alexander (*sic*), are really only concerned about the next world.[181]

The institute of kingship would be inconceivable, according to Baranī, without an insatiable ambition for world conquest.[182] It is a limitless form of egotism, requiring "obtaining supremacy over the world and its inhabitants, conveying to the ears of the world the cry of 'I and no other,' making his court the resort in need of the seventy-two sects, and conceiving his equals as under his power."[183] The key to this ambition is the search for domination over the whole world, for anything less will not suffice to convince his subjects of his seriousness. The desire for world conquest also amounts to religious imperialism, for the true king "desires to bring the inhabited quarter under his command and rule, to illumine the children of Adam with the light of Islam, to bring the seventy-two sects into the monotheistic faith, and to make sure that the example of the Prophet is followed."[184]

It is important to realize that the ambition for world conquest need not be attained literally to be valid; the mere presence of the desire for dominion is the essential thing. Baranī makes use of the ancient symbolism of the "kings of the world" to make this point. He says, as mentioned above, that a king's ambition requires "*conceiving* his equals as under his power" (the emphasis is mine). The "equals" (*ham-sar*) are the other monarchs who pretend to world rule: during the reign of the Persian king Qubād, his equals were the Caesar of Rome, the Khān of China, the ʿAzīz of Egypt, the Pādshāh of Syria, the Tabaʿ of Yemen, the sultan of the Franks, and the Ray [raja] of Qannauj.[185] A nearly identical symbolism is found in the wall paintings of a princely palace of the Umayyad caliphate, Quṣayr ʿAmra, dated to around 710; there, the caliph is pictured on the throne of world rule, with the Caesar, the Khusraw (Kisrā), the Khān, the ʿAzīz, the Negus of Ethiopia, and the last Visigothic king of Spain, all acknowledging his suzerainty with salutations.[186] It seems that the Umayyad pretensions to world conquest remained partially imaginary too, for by no means all these rulers had submitted to Arab dominion. The concept of the great kings of the world was well-known throughout the Islamic world in Baranī's time. Ibn Baṭṭūṭa's motive for his remarkable peregrination from Morocco to China and back was apparently the desire to encompass the world by meeting face to face with "the Seven Mighty Kings."[187] Baranī stresses that in fact any full-scale war between equals should be avoided, because it causes immense destruction that threatens the existence of one or both societies. He undoubtedly had in mind the Mongol conquest, which caused unimaginable devastation from Central Asia to the Mediterranean, and extinguished the ʿAbbāsid caliphate. With this very practical limitation, Baranī allows the desire for world conquest to remain as a prerequisite for kingship.[188]

Another interesting example of Baranī's analysis of royal ambition, from the *Tārīkh-i Fīrūz Shāhī*, is the lengthy conversation that Sultan ʿAlā' al-Dīn Khaljī reportedly had with Baranī's uncle, the wazīr ʿAlā' al-Mulk. Baranī enumerates the string of remarkable successes that the sultan had enjoyed by the third year of his reign (698/1299), with a great victory over the Mongols, countrywide prosperity, and unprecedented wealth in the royal treasury. Finding himself the unopposed master of "two or three climes" of the earth's seven, he grew so intoxicated with his power that he formed an audacious idea, which Baranī disingenuously claims "had never occurred to the mind of any emperor" before. He told his courtiers that he wanted their advice about two plans that he had conceived to deal with his fellow kings (*mulūk-i ḥarīf*). The first was this: the Prophet Muḥammad with his four companions (the first four caliphs), by their strength and courage, had invented (*paydā kard*) the religious law (*sharīʿat*) and religion (*dīn*), and thereby he had earned the name of prophet, which would endure until the resurrection. God had also given ʿAlā' al-Dīn four friends, whom he named, and with their swords he proposed to bring all humanity into his path, so that from this religion and teaching (*mazhab*) their names would likewise endure until the resurrection. At this point, "he called for wine for the assembly and asked the assembly's advice about publicizing (*paydā āwardan*) the religion and teaching, especially with the kings." He then emphasized again his desire that his name should endure after his death, and revealed his second plan: pointing out his great wealth, numerous elephants, and other resources, he said, "I want to entrust Delhi to someone and go myself, like Alexander, after world conquest, and bring the 'inhabited quarter' (*rubʿ-i maskūn*) under my control." Baranī noted that with this very folly in mind, ʿAlā' al-Dīn had already called himself "the Second Alexander," both in his coinage and in the *khuṭba* sermon proclaimed in the congregational mosque. "In his drunkenness he boasted, 'Every clime that I conquer I will entrust to one of the nobles of my kingdom, and I will go after and conquer another clime. Who is there who will stand before me?'" One imagines at this point a pregnant pause, while the courtiers rack their brains for an adequate response to the proposal. They knew that some people laughed at the young king's folly while others feared it.[189]

Baranī's uncle ʿAlā' al-Mulk was a trusted drinking companion of the sultan, and though not present at the assembly, had been informed of the sultan's unusual plans. On being asked his opinion, ʿAlā' al-Mulk gently requested that the ever-present wine be taken away and that their audience be restricted to the two of them and the sultan's four companions. Apologetically he urged the sultan not to discuss religious law, religion, and teaching, for these were the affairs of prophets, not the craft of kings; religion and the religious law are related to heavenly inspiration, and can never be constructed by human opinion and action. Never in all time could kings play the role of prophets, for kings are concerned with world conquest and world dominion, and moreover prophecy has been sealed by the mission of Muḥammad. The sultan should abandon this sort of talk altogether, or else his Muslim subjects would desert him, and so his kingdom would be destroyed. ʿAlā' al-Mulk then explicitly equated the attempt to found a new religion by force with the Mongol conquest, which was ultimately unsuccessful as a world religion. "As many rivers of blood as Chingīz Khān made flow from cities of Muslims, he could not establish the Mongol religion and Mongol laws among the people. Rather, most Mongols became Muslims and accepted the religion of Muḥammad, while no Muslim became a Mongol and accepted the Mongol religion."[190] Fortunately for the courtier, Sultan ʿAlā' al-Dīn accepted his advice and praised ʿAlā' al-Mulk's honesty and loyalty.

With regard to the second proposal, to conquer the world, the courtier was not so negative. "It is the goal of ambitious sultans, and the practice of world conquest is that they want to conquer all the world and bring it under their control." ʿAlā' al-Mulk observed that with the considerable resources at his disposal, the sultan could doubtless make great strides toward world conquest. On principle he could therefore make no objection, but he did caution that leaving his capital to imitate Alexander's conquest of the inhabited world would leave room for rebellion to take place in Delhi in the king's absence. And where could he find a wazir as wise and trustworthy as Aristotle, who kept Alexander's home regions safe and sound for the thirty-two years the conqueror was away? The clime of India was in any case difficult to rely on in the sultan's absence, because of the untrustworthy people found there. To this tactful advice, the sultan replied, "What good are the wealth, elephants, and horses that have come into my hands, if I do not conquer the world and conquer no other climes, but remain satisfied with the mere kingdom of Delhi? How can I obtain the name of 'World Conqueror'?" ʿAlā' al-Mulk ventured to suggest two other projects to replace the ones rejected. The first project would be to put all the clime of Hindustan, east, west, and south, under his command, so that the very word "rebel" will no longer be spoken. The second, and greater, project would be "to close the Multan road to the Mongol catastrophe, and to close the road for the Mongols to enter, by strengthening fortresses in that area with trustworthy officers and repair of forts, digging trenches," and other necessary military preparations. "In order to completely remove the power of the Mongols to injure Hindustan," it is especially important to appoint experienced and trustworthy officers in each of the strategic points of the frontier. These two projects—removing any opposition among the inhabitants of Hindustan, and placing great and famous commanders in the path of the Mongol invasion—will perfectly satisfy the heart of the king, so that he can sit in the center of his kingdom in Delhi, ruling in splendor and performing the tasks of world conquest and world dominion. ʿAlā' al-Mulk concluded by delicately suggesting that the sultan's policy-making would be improved if he refrained from drinking wine, a suggestion that the repentant ruler humbly embraced.[191]

The conversation as reported by Baranī fifty years afterward, need not be supposed a literal transcription of an actual discussion, but it gives a wonderfully clear picture of unlimited ambition colliding with the political realities of the Delhi sultanate. Like the conversations reported by Thucydides, Baranī's accounts are summaries of his analysis of the issues at stake. It is not necessary to reject this account merely on the grounds that it is not strictly in accord with what is known of ʿAla al-Dīn Khaljī's policies; its significance is not as a report but as an analysis.[192] The sultan's first proposal, to found a new world religion by force of arms, appears at first sight the simplistic plan of a blockheaded warrior-king. But ʿAlā' al-Mulk's criticism of the plan, after distinguishing the roles of emperor and prophet in exactly the terms Baranī uses elsewhere, then dwells on the failure of the Mongols to achieve the conversion of the world despite all their savage destruction. From this perspective, Baranī views the Mongol empire as a failed attempt to subjugate the kings of the world by religious imperialism. Baranī blurs the boundary line between state religion and the naked quest for world dominion. The second proposal, to emulate Alexander and conquer the inhabited world, is really just another form of the project to convert the world by force. Both ambitions seek a form of immortality through fame, based on the elimination of all opposition and boundless expansion of the ego. Baranī's added touch of ascribing the king's madness to excessive wine is his way of providing an external touchstone to the imperial psychosis, but he finds only the creation of a new religion horrifying, whereas world conquest is a laudable if generally impractical goal.

The moralistic tone of the conclusion to this conversation, in which ʿAlā' al-Mulk persuades the repentant sultan to give up wine, is historically unconvincing.[193] The courtier's concrete advice to the sultan, to secure his conquest of India and strengthen the frontier against Mongol invasion, is nevertheless an accurate analysis of the two imperatives of the Delhi sultans' policy, and forms the imperialistic rationale of the program of raiding the Deccan that led to the temporary annexation of most of south India.[194]

Non-Muslims and the Sultanate

Questions remain about Baranī's description of the religious basis of the Turkish imperium, in particular regarding the strength of Islamic religious imperialism at the court. Baranī clearly favored a repressive policy of persecuting Hindus, advice that the sultans persistently ignored. Yet by blatant misrepresentation, Baranī gave the impression that religious repression of Hindus was the basis of Turkish rule in India since the time of Maḥmūd of Ghazna. He maintained, for example, that the Khaljī system of direct taxation was a method for humbling Hindu notables, which the sultans adopted as a repressive measure only after rejecting the preferred alternative of massacring Hindus as impractical. He pictured the rationale for the sultans' policy in another fictitious conversation, in which Sultan ʿAlā' al-Dīn Khaljī asked the advice of one Qāżī Mughīs al-Dīn about the status in Islamic law of Hindus in relation to the land tax (*kharāj*). The sultans had in fact followed the ancient precedent of the Arab conquerors of Sind, by treating Hindus on an analogy with Christians and Jews, and giving them protected status (*zimma*) and exemption from military duty on payment of a capitation tax (*jizya*). The qāżī presented Baranī's argument to the king, saying that care should be taken to humiliate the Hindus while collecting the tax, to make the non-Muslim obedient and exalt the pride of the true religion over falsehood.

The anti-Hindu policy, the qāżī claimed, was required, because Hindus are the worst enemies of the Prophet Muḥammad, who himself had clearly stated that they should be killed and looted and enslaved whenever possible (the historical impossibility of this fantastic claim does not seem to bother Baranī). Hindus in reality must either adopt Islam or die, and their property must be all looted, according to a legal ruling that Baranī elsewhere (falsely) attributed to the Shāfiʿī school of Islamic law.[195] He pretended that except for the school of Abū Ḥanīfa, which is unfortunately followed in Hindustan, all the other schools of law agree that the capitation tax and protected status cannot apply to Hindus, so they must choose Islam or death (once again Baranī fabricates, as Hindus are not even mentioned in classical legal texts).

The conversation then continued, describing how the Hindu village headmen lived like nobles and ignored their tax payments, so that the king's authority was flouted. The sultan replied to the learned qāżī that he had much experience in these matters, and it would not be possible to exterminate all the Hindu masses in India. Talk then turned to development of a severe taxation system that would effectively humble these Hindu officials and build up the treasury for conquests abroad.[196] Baranī was clearly disappointed in the failure of the Delhi sultans to follow his enlightened policy. Baranī's hatred of Hindus, whose prosperity he blamed for his own misfortunes, was behind this episode. The virulent anti-Hindu tone of Baranī's rhetoric gave a tone of religious persecution to the sultan's tax policy, although it appears to have been rather a revenue reform designed to eliminate middlemen.[197]

Baranī's stress on Islamic religious imperialism in the Delhi sultanate is undoubtedly overstated. Even his hero Maḥmūd of Ghazna, when offering loot from a desecrated Hindu temple to a Muslim religious scholar, found that the scholar refused it, regarding it as stolen property.[198] To be sure, there was a large influx of Muslim religious scholars into Hindustan from the time of the Mongol invasions, which helped bring about a renaissance in the Islamic sciences, particularly *ḥadīth* and law.[199] It would be natural, too, to assume that these religious scholars would have a much heightened horror of paganism, after the destruction of the great Islamic cities of central Asia and Iran at the hands of the heathen Mongols.[200] Islamic legal literature is conservative, however. As shown above (Part I, chap. 2), few works on Islamic law from the Delhi sultanate took cognizance of the existence of Hindus. Baranī's own disgruntled depiction of the lofty position of Hindu nobles argues against any actual policy of religious repression or imperialism in the early Delhi sultanate.[201] Baranī blamed his own loss of position at court on the lack of a policy favoring Muslims of noble birth over all others, so in the end a political factor lay behind his religious fanaticism.[202] Sultan Fīrūz Shāh, probably after 776/1374–75, was the first sultan of Delhi to undertake enforcement of discriminatory sanctions against non-Muslims as well as persecution of Muslim heretics.[203] But even Fīrūz Shāh's ostentatiously militant orthodoxy, as proclaimed in a lengthy inscription that once filled the octagonal dome of old Delhi's principal mosque, must be measured against the actions of his regime.[204]

The commitment to Islamic symbolism, important as it was to the Delhi sultans, did not in practice preclude support for non-Islamic religious institutions. It was a characteristic policy of most Indo-Muslim rulers to give endowments and exemptions to Brahmans and temples when it suited their political purposes. Large numbers of documents testify to land endowments and tax exemptions conferred by Muslim kings on Brahmans, Jains, Jogis (yogis), Parsis, and on temples to Shiva, Vishnu, and the goddess. Two valuable collections of revenue documents from a Jogi establishment and a Vaiṣnava center in the Punjab show a continuous record of support by all the Mughul emperors from Akbar to Awrangzīb and later.[205] Although some of these documents conferred new land revenues or dealt with problems of shrine administration, others, like Akbar's grant to a Zoroastrian in 1578, were resumptions or expansions of grants from previous rulers.[206] Although few pre-Mughul revenue documents survive, the language of some later documents indicates a continuation of the grants of earlier sultans as well as of the grants of Hindu kings. A Quṭbshāhī document of 1684 confers village revenues for the upkeep of the Malleshwara Swami temple, specifically referring to it as *agrahāram* land, a Sanskrit term denoting land endowment set aside for the support of Brahmans; this grant must have been a continuation of an ancient pre-Islamic foundation.[207] Many more examples could be adduced.[208] What conclusion is the historian to draw from this documentation?

Turkish successor states since the Seljuks had legitimized their authority through their patronage of religious institutions, principally academies for scholars of the Islamic religious sciences and Sufi establishments. Granted the structural similarities between Turkish and Indian kingship, it was not a large step to assimilate Hindu religious establishments into this patronage structure. The Mongols practiced a similar type of patronage of different religions, since, as David Morgan put it, they "believed in taking out as much celestial insurance as possible."[209] The very same terminology covered both types of religious endowment; the Arabic term *a'imma* (plural of *imām*, "religious leader") denoted by extension the grants and exemptions extended to the religious leaders, whether Muslim or Hindu.[210] All were alike expected "to remain occupied with prayer for the permanence of the conquering dynasty," a phrase that, with slight variations, inevitably appears in the grant documents. Although the sultans of Delhi could not be expected to have read the authorities of Hindu law, they may have surmised a connection between the kings of India and the wealthy temples that presented such a tempting spectacle to invaders. But many questions remain. Under what circumstances did it occur to Muslim kings that donations to temples would carry weight with a large group of their Indian subjects? How extensive was the support of non-Muslim shrines in comparison to Islamic institutions? What was the proportion of non-Islamic grants that continued under Turkish rule? We have no way of knowing at present. Documentation from the sultanate period is scarce. War and disaster have reduced the vast archives of the Mughul bureaucracy to a small fraction of their former size, and court histories rarely focused on measures designed to please nonelite groups. Until scholars make a systematic attempt to collect from many private sources the revenue documents concerning royal support of non-Muslim religious institutions, generalizations about the political status of non-Muslims in medieval India will remain speculative.

The problematic kernel in the sultans' support of non-Muslim religious institutions deserves methodological reflection. Why are we surprised by this official support of non-Muslim religions? The standard answer has been in the plausibly argued concept of an Islamic state: despite official toleration of *zimmī* religions, it is the duty of an Islamic sovereign to prevent public display of non-Islamic religions or expansion of their physical or social base. The concept of enforcing disabilities for non-Muslim religions has a history in

Islamic law that can probably be traced back to the Umayyad caliph ʿUmar ibn ʿAbd al-ʿAzīz (d. 101/720). At different times, rulers have invoked a number of disability statutes forbidding non-Muslims to ride horses, requiring special dress, and so forth; Islamic legal scholars disagree about the legitimate extent and application of such disability rules. The relative infrequency with which these rules have been applied in India suggests that political and historical contexts may have a great deal to do with royal policies of harassing particular religious groups.

The problem is not in historical analysis, but in the *idée fixe* inherited from the older orientalism, that Islam is a religion of intolerance, spread by the sword. Under this handy assumption, true Muslim rulers will try to convert all heathens by any means necessary; idol-smashing is their favorite occupation. In this vein, a Western Indologist writes about Muḥammad ibn Tughluq: "Being a pious Muslim, he systematically destroyed every temple and shrine dedicated to Hindu Gods and had all their images smashed. If the great temple of Pandharpur had been spared by the Muslims in 1218 [sc. 1318], it was certainly destroyed by [the time of his reign]."[211] From this point of view, it would be inconceivable that this same sultan's Muslim officials would repair a temple of Shiva and urge the resumption of worship at Kalyan, not far from Pandharpur, after disturbances caused by a rebellion in 1326, yet a Sanskrit inscription informs us that this was the case.[212] Most popular histories of India excoriate the late Mughul emperor Awrangzīb (d. 1707) for his bigotry and intolerance toward Hindus, which resulted in the imposition of the hated *jizya* tax and the destruction of many temples; many feel that Awrangzīb's fanaticism was the cause of the downfall of the Mughul empire. This atemporal and ideological portrait does not explain the historical circumstances that led half the Hindu nobility to support Awrangzīb in the war of succession against the liberal, supposedly pro-Hindu Dārā Shikūh.[213] Nor does it explain the reasons behind Awrangzīb's well-documented support for a variety of Hindu religious institutions.[214] If we wish to understand the actions of either ruler, we must have a more advanced set of categories than "fanatic Muslim ruler" and its opposite, "not really a Muslim ruler."

The Turks ruled in India as a minority, and they typically reinstated conquered Indian kings as tributaries. In remote and mountainous areas the sultan's command might be freely ignored, and sometimes the sultan might have to treat Indian kings as independent rulers. The running of government depended in part on the retention of an existing Indian bureaucracy that collected land revenue and received appropriate perquisites.[215] Some of these Indian rulers and officials continued to act as sources of patronage for traditional religious institutions as before, even while they acknowledged Turkish suzerainty.[216] Although the data on state patronage of religion under the Delhi sultanate is still too fragmentary to justify confident generalizations, a brief comparison with the European Turkish frontier in Anatolia suggests a significant difference between the two cases. The data collected by Vryonis led him to conclude that in Anatolia, "the sultans confiscated the vast majority of Christian lands, revenues, and buildings and bestowed them upon their Muslim secular and religious followers. Consequently, mosques, medresses, tekkes, hospitals, and the like spread across Anatolia, often in the very buildings and on the same lands formerly belonging to the Greek church."[217] The Delhi sultans certainly looted temples and built mosques out of the ruins of destroyed temples, and they doubtless appropriated land revenues from temples that had previously enjoyed the rājās' patronage. But the Turkish rulers in Anatolia seem to have been more intent on religious imperialism than their counterparts in Delhi. The centuries of warfare between Byzantine Christians and Arab and Turkish Muslims contributed to an intense aggression in which religious identity played a major role.[218] Support for Christian institutions does not seem to have been a regular feature of Seljuk or Ottoman policy in Anatolia. India, with its many faiths and diverse kingdoms, did not represent a religiously homogeneous counter-empire for the Turks, as did Byzantium. In other words, there was less historical residuum of religious imperialism in Indian Islam than in the Turkish sphere; Indian Muslim rulers, accordingly, could more freely give patronage to non-Muslim institutions, when it was to their interest to do so.

To what extent was the Delhi sultanate recognizably an Indianized regime? Peter Hardy has pointed out the ambiguous power relations between Muslim and Hindu authorities: "It was as if, provided the Muslim conquerors offered certain tokens publicly that they were not going to introduce a wholly new language and vocabulary of politics, but rather to add new words to the stock of existing words or new layers of meaning to old words, then (while not going out of their way to be sociable) the conquered chiefs would not refuse all conversation."[219] Despite theoretical similarities between the Indian and Turkish-Islamic polities, however, Hardy questions whether, in concrete terms, Indian chiefs were invited to royal installation ceremonies in Delhi, and if so, whether they were impressed. Inscriptional evidence supplies a partial answer to this question, suggesting that, while Indians may not have had access to the Iranian and Islamic symbolism employed by the sultans, they were quite ready to view the sultans as fulfilling the royal imperatives of the Indian tradition. A Sanskrit inscription from a well and pilgrims' hospice from Rohtak in the Punjab, dated 1281, gives a dynastic list of the Turkish rulers of Hariyāna (the area around Delhi), beginning with the conqueror of Delhi, Shihāb al-Dīn Ghūrī, and ending with a eulogy of the reigning sultan Balban (under whose authority, presumably, the well and building were constructed). According to the editor's summary, the text:

> Gives a highly classical account of Balban in a tone which could describe any Hindu king. . . . All the kings of India from Gauḍa

> (Bengal) to Gajjana (Ghaznī), and the Dravidian settlements of Setubandha (Far South) paid respect to Balban; his soldiers daily bathed in the Bay of Bengal and Arabian Sea; he conquered the Gauḍas, Andhras, Keralas, Karṇāṭas, Mahārāṣṭras, Gūrjaras and Lāṭas.[220]

The highly exaggerated tone of the inscription, attributing to Balban conquests that he had only dreamt of, should not obscure the important message of this inscription: Balban's putative conquests of the entire south Asian subcontinent, considered as the realm of ecumenic empire, made him a full-fledged universal emperor in Indian eyes.[221]

The sultans of Delhi made gestures toward Indianization most notably in their coinage. Coinage was one of the prerogatives of the sovereign, and the presentation of authority in coins must be partially construed as a statement of the ruler's concept of authority. It is difficult to make too much of symbolism in coins, however, because their practical use in local circulation also needed to be acceptable to the populace. Therefore it was common among Muslim conquerors to imitate previous types of coinage until consolidation of their authority permitted them to issue new types more to their liking. The early sultans of Delhi continued to use the coins of the Cauhān Rajputs, which featured a horseman on one side and the bull of Shiva on the other with Devanagari inscriptions. Sultans of Bengal also used coins featuring the goddess Lakṣmi.[222] A most curious example of the use of Indian media was a coin issued by Sultan Maḥmūd of Ghazna in 418/1018, containing a Sanskrit translation of the Islamic profession of faith. On one side the coin gives in Arabic the name of the ʿAbbāsid caliph, the Arabic profession of faith, and the name of Maḥmūd, surrounded by a legend with the date and mint town. The obverse dispenses with the caliph, but gives in Sanskrit, *avyaktam ekaṁ Muhamadaḥ avatāraḥ nṛpatiḥ Mahamūdaḥ*, meaning roughly "There is One unlimited, Muḥammad is the *avatār*, the king is Maḥmūd." This is an ingenious translation of "There is no god but God, Muḥammad is the messenger of God" (*lā ilāha illā allāh, Muḥammad rasūl allāh*), with the title of the ruler conspicuously forming a sequence with God and the Prophet. The selection of the term *avatār* to translate the Arabic *rasūl*, "messenger," is striking, since *avatār* is a term reserved in Indian thought for the "descent" of the god Vishnu into earthly form, as for instance Rāmā and Krishna. In the margin is the formula *avyaktīya-nāmni* or "in the name of the unlimited," the mint town, and the date, given as *tājikīyena saṁvatā 418*, "418 in the Arab era."[223] It is hard to do more than wonder at the theological originality of equating the Prophet with the *avatār* of Vishnu, since it is impossible to extrapolate any religious policy from this brief motto. Still, it seems unmistakable that Maḥmūd meant by this coin that his Sanskrit-reading subjects should have some officially sanctioned means of recognizing his authority in terms familiar from their own tradition. While no later coin contains anything as remarkable as this Sanskrit version of the Islamic profession of faith, Sanskrit continued to be used by many Turkish, Afghan, and Mughul rulers of northern India up through the seventeenth century.[224] Sometimes the Sanskrit simply gave the name of the ruler, but most often it gave the hybrid title Śrī Hamīr (based on the Arabic *amīr*). A number of these coins from the sultanate period give the name of the ʿAbbāsid caliph as well. The mixture of Indian and Islamic language and symbolism in the coins of these Muslim rulers suggests that they wished to present their regimes to some extent as fulfilling Indian norms of legitimate government in addition to Islamic ones.

Indians expected Muslim sultans to extend patronage to all religions like any other legitimate Indian sovereign. A seventeenth-century Assamese chronicle gives a mythical account of the origins of the Delhi sultanate that shows the first sultan's deliberate assumption of this royal responsibility. The chronicle, entitled *Badshahi Buranji*, was written by an anonymous author between 1663 and 1685. It is impossible to tell whether the author was a Hindu or a Muslim, since the text shows equal familiarity with the Assamese vocabulary of Vaiṣnava devotionalism and the Persian terminology of the Mughul court.[225] The text relates how the great king Rungaddin was born, thanks to the blessing of a Sufi saint, to Muḥammad Shāh of Nako, who traces his ancestry back to the Indian epic heroes of the Mahābhārata. After conquering the king of Rum (Anatolia), Rungaddin turned to Delhi, where he battled Pithor Raj for the throne of India. Pithor Raja (the same Prithvi Raj made famous in the Rajput bardic tales) died accidentally on his own sword, and his wives were consumed on the funeral pyre in accordance with Rajput tradition. So far the mythical Rungaddin has entered into the heroic cycle on terms familiar to the epic poems. After his victory, Rungaddin consulted with Sarbabhaum-Chandra, "the family priest of the late King Pithor Raja," about the religious policy he is to follow.[226] The priest replied, "O Pādshāh, what shall I say? You are yourself acquainted with all laws and traditions. God has created the nations of the earth in separate groups, each different from the other; and He has not provided uniform customs and religions for all. If the different castes and creeds are protected, God will protect you also, and you will be able to remain at Delhi without any trouble or fear." The king therefore announced, "The laws and traditions which existed before will remain unaltered." Investigating "matters relating to the sacred shrines of Musalmans and Hindus" then becomes his chief business every Thursday.[227] The story of Rungaddin, through its reinterpretation of the fall of Prithvi Raj, cleverly resolves the tensions created by Muslim rule in India. It acts as a foundational myth, and legitimizes the authority of the new emperor, first by his fictitious Indian ancestry, and then by his acceptance of the Brahman priest's advice to take on the religious duties of an Indian sovereign. Here also the sultan has been assimilated to the Indian norm.

The authority of the sultans, too, had its impact on Indian political thinking.[228] The story of the foundation of the Vijāyanagar empire has been often told, how the two Hindu soldiers Bukka and Hārihāra joined the Turks after the defeat of the Hindu kings of the Deccan, becoming Muslims in the process. As the seventeenth-century historian Firishta tells the tale, they seized the opportunity created by the breakup of the Delhi sultanate, apostatized from Islam, and founded the city of Vijāyanagar as the center of a revived Hindu empire. Vasundhara Filliozat's publication of the earliest inscriptions of Vijāyanagar shows that Bukka had adopted the title "sultan" along with the customary titles of Indian kingship. The complete phrase in which the term "sultan" occurs, in inscriptions dated from 1354 to 1369, is a peculiar one (*hiṃdurāyasuratrāṇa*, five times with slight variations). Filliozat has, with some uncertainty, translated the compound in three different ways: "sultan of the Hindu kings" (three times), "protector of the gods for the Hindu kings," and "sultan of the kings of the lunar family" (from Indu, a name of the moon god Soma, claimed as the ancestor of the Vijāyanagar kings).[229] If a founder of Vijāyanagar intended to call himself "sultan of the Hindu kings," it meant that he recognized the Turkish perspective as significant—he adopted with pride not only the title used by the alien conqueror, but also the term that the conqueror had employed for the once subject people. These inscriptions, from rulers who had spent time in the Turkish court, may well be the earliest uses of the term "Hindu" in an Indian source.

The interplay between religion and political authority in medieval India was extraordinarily complex, and Muslims and Hindus recognized this. Muslim rulers saw the importance that temples could have as counters in the game of political supremacy. In a struggle with Afghans and the Quṭbshāhīs over the territory of Orissa, the Mughuls used the temple of Puri in order to secure their own dominance. Although the Afghans had attempted to stake their claim by permitting the rebuilding of the temple in 1591, the Mughul general Mān Singh (himself a devotee of Vishnu) claimed Puri for the Mughuls and personally did pilgrimage there to set up the conditions for the eventual Mughul takeover.

By 1633, it was observed that a Mughul official would help lead the procession of the festival at Puri, since it was a considerable source of revenue through the pilgrim tax. Awrangzīb's policies did not substantially change this situation, since many new temples were built in Puri even while a few were destroyed for symbolic purposes.[230] Turkish raids on temples became part of later political symbolism in temple chronicles. Now temple restoration and reconsecration became an action of political legitimation for the new Hindu dynasties that arose in southern India, as they took control of the remnants of the overextended Tughluq empire. Malik Kāfūr's raids on the temples of Śrirangam and Madura in 1327 were recorded in temple chronicles as a catastrophe. Using epic and heroic imagery, Tamil and Sanskrit sources depict the subsequent reconquest and reconsecration of these temples late in the fourteenth century as a triumph for the new dynasty of Gingee.[231] The Muslim intrusion was now an integral part of the temple's legitimation of the Hindu ruler.

Political and administrative continuities linked the Delhi sultanate to the traditional Indian regimes that preceded it as well as to its successors. These links are much stronger than the conventional distinction of "Islamic" from "Hindu" governments would indicate. In all these regimes, the notion of legitimacy and patronage worked in a similar fashion, whether in ancient Hindu polity, under the sultans and padshahs, or later on under the Marathas and the Sikhs. Muslim rulers favored Islamic religious establishments, and sometimes enforced disabilities on non-Muslims such as pilgrimage taxes, but the political realities of legitimation required some patronage of non-Muslim institutions as well. The religious basis of the state was not by any means as narrowly construed as it is today, in modern religious nationalism. The system established by the sultans was basically, in André Wink's phrase, "the new bureaucratic grid superimposed on the pattern of vested rights by the Muslim conquerors."[232] Although theorists like Baranī (and his modern counterparts) posited an absolute collision between an exclusive Islam and an abstract Hinduism, in practice the Indo-Muslim polity was a much more complex, multilayered society.

Sultanate and Caliphate

In Sunnī theory, the caliphate (*khilāfat*) was the supreme Islamic political authority, constituted as the legitimate succession to the political office of the Prophet Muḥammad. The question of the orientation of the sultanate toward the ʿAbbāsid caliphate also needs to be answered, as an index of the interest of the sultans in having an Islamic foundation for their rule. Given the dominance of Iranism at the Turkish court, and the effective impotence of caliphal recognition, why, then, did seven of the Delhi sultans apparently rule in the name of the caliph? Iltutmish sought recognition from the caliph al-Mustanṣir, who sent the Indian-born *ḥadīth* scholar Ḥasan Ṣaghānī to present his investiture in 626/1229.[233] His next three successors had reigns too brief to consolidate their power, but ʿAlā' al-Dīn Maḥmūd (r. 639/1242 to 644/1246) minted coins in the name of the reigning caliph al-Mustaʿṣim (r. 1242–58). Oddly enough, after the fall of Baghdad in 1258, Balban continued to mint coins and read the Friday public sermon (*khuṭba*) in the deceased caliph's name. In the same way, the independent Muslim sultans of Bengal still minted coins in the name of the last ʿAbbāsid caliph after 1258.[234] The next two sultans of Delhi, who reigned to 689/1290, and the founder of the Khaljī dynasty Jalāl al-Dīn Fīrūz (r. to 695/1296), all issued coins in the name of the deceased al-

Musʿtaṣim.[235] Although ʿAlā' al-Dīn Khaljī was not interested in this form of protective symbolism, Sultan Muḥammad ibn Tughluq had begun correspondence with the caliph as early as 731/1330–31. He became seriously interested in the authority of the "captive" caliph in Cairo during the difficult period beginning about 1339. In coins dated 742, 743, and 744, he used the name of the recently deceased caliph al-Mustakfī Billāh (d. 740/1339–40), with the curious motto, "May God make his Caliphate abide for ever."[236] Sultan Muḥammad ibn Tughluq then applied for and received a formal document from the new caliph al-Ḥākim II in 744/1343, and yearly thereafter.[237] Fīrūz Shāh Tughluq (r. 752/1351–790/1388) also received this caliphal investiture.[238] Were not all these statements of caliphal authority simply attempts to put the sultanate on a religious footing?

The symbol of caliphal recognition had considerable political importance in the Delhi sultanate, but it was not so much an appeal for recognition by pious Muslims as it was a challenge to the Mongol claim to world domination. To be sure, in the case of Sultan Muḥammad ibn Tughluq, it has been convincingly argued that his approach to the nominal ʿAbbāsid caliph was a countermeasure against the resistance of the ʿulamā' to his policies, designed to show him as the faithful upholder of the heir of the Prophet.[239] Fīrūz Shāh too wished to gain this sort of religious respectability, which was thoroughly in consonance with his abolition of non-*sharīʿa* practices at court and his energetic sponsorship of the study of Islamic law. But the earlier Turkish sultans were far more concerned with the threat of the Mongols than with satisfying the religious classes in their own domains, and this political factor continued throughout the Tughluq period. Chingīz Khān himself had reached the Indus in 1221, and the Mongol armies continued to pose a serious threat to northern India for many years. And it was Chingīz Khān's putative descendant Tīmūr (Tamerlane) who finally gave the coup de grace to the tottering Tughluq dynasty when he sacked Delhi in 1398. The Turks for their part were quite familiar with the Mongols' conviction that God had awarded them world sovereignty. The caliphate was the supreme political symbol of the Islamic *sharīʿa*, and was thus the only Islamic legitimating factor that could challenge Mongol world rule. The caliphal investiture of Iltutmish in 1226, and even more so the minting of coins in the name of the dead caliph after 1258, were not merely events controlled by the dead hand of tradition.[240] They were direct affronts to the supremacy of the Mongol khāns, proclaiming that the authority of the Delhi sultanate was guaranteed by the successors of the Prophet.[241]

The historian Minhāj-i Sirāj reported that in 658/1260 Sultan Nāṣir al-Dīn Maḥmūd entertained Chingīz Khān's grandson Hūlāgū at an imperial reception, not long after Hūlāgū's extirpation of the caliphate; in a calculated move, the sultan's golden throne was decorated with "the caliphal seat" (*masnad-i khalīfatī*) to advertise pointedly Delhi's challenge to the Mongols, and

Minhāj-i Sirāj celebrated the occasion with a suitable poem celebrating the Delhi world ruler's triumph over the khān in religious terms: "Congratulations to Islam for this feast of the world's king; from this adornment India became much sweeter than China."[242] As late as 1404, Muslim advisers to Tīmūr's grandson Pīr Muḥammad urged him to stake his claim as emperor by obtaining caliphal recognition from Cairo, and so jettison the Mongol traditions. This alternative had little attraction, however, for the heirs of the khān who had destroyed the last of the ʿAbbāsid caliphs.[243]

With Baranī's description of the world-conquering mentality in mind, it is instructive to return to Sultan Muḥammad ibn Tughluq's investiture from the powerless ʿAbbāsid caliph in Cairo, and examine his court poet's treatment of this event as an imperial triumph. The easy coexistence of the motifs of Persian kingship alongside the Islamic symbolism of the caliphate shows a shrewd appreciation for the public relations value of both sets of images, and a lack of concern for any possible conflict between the two. Here are some salient verses from the ode (*qaṣīda*) that Badr-i Chāch composed to celebrate the caliph's conferral of the title of "emperor" (*pādshāh*) on Muḥammad ibn Tughluq:

> Last night when the [black] clothing of the house of ʿAbbas came from Syria and reached the emperor who chose the orient sky for his parasol [i.e., when night eclipsed the sun, a poetic metaphor for the time of arrival of the caliph's emissary in the Tughluq court],
>
> Saturn said to Jupiter, "When the letter of oath from Khusraw came as a petition before the throne, the caliph did it honor."
>
> When he became aware of its contents, the imam's command was this: "May his commands govern the land assignment (*iqṭāʿ*) of the seven climes,
>
> "Let his throne be from Jamshīd's brow, his carpet from the solar crown, his standard eternal felicity, his title 'Sultan of the days.'"
>
> For the minister of the king's realm [Muḥammad ibn Tughluq], his majesty's [the caliph's] mercy was this: "Let his pens' writ run over land and sea."
>
> For the kitchen of his [the sultan's] glory, the imam of the realm decreed, "Let the cash of this world and the next be his fortieth portion of charity."
>
> The Commander of the Faithful ordered, "Let him be proclaimed to the seven climes every Friday from the pulpit (*minbar*) as Emperor of Islam."
>
> May the quilt of life adorn his breast, the sultan's crown his head, heaven be at his throne's foot, angels in his retainers' ranks.

Know that a Badr-i Chāch is a sweet-spoken slave at this door, if
the Khusraw of the world names him "the pride of time."[244]

This poem shows all the blissful confusion of symbols that characterized the conventions of world empire in the Delhi sultanate. Badr-i Chāch puts the caliph in the position of the religious leader (imam) who is able to confer on the sultan the position of world ruler, cloaked in Islamic religious language. The caliph's utter powerlessness to enforce his position evidently does not deter him from awarding the seven climes to the sultan as a land revenue assignment, according to the traditional princely method of rewarding ministers and subordinates. Nonetheless, despite the Islamic veneer, the underlying meaning of the sultanate is still the ancient Persian concept of world empire. The poet's references to Islamic religious charities, Friday sermons, angels, and the like, are only introduced as parts of poetical conceits exalting the sultan's authority over the world. The cosmic symbolism (sun, planets, heavens, climes), court ritual (parasol, throne, crown, door), and the names of ancient Persian kings (Khusraw, Jamshīd), all blatantly proclaim Sultan Muḥammad ibn Tughluq's attainment of world empire according to the Persian model.

Many more examples of this kind could be produced from the fulsome and bombastic panegyrics of Badr-i Chāch, whose odes, nearly all in praise of the same sultan, fill more than a hundred pages in the lithograph edition.[245] It may be doubted, however, whether sultan Muḥammad ibn Tughluq listened to each and every line of these repetitions of poems in his praise. He was interested only in the main point. Once another court poet, Jamāl al-Dīn, began to recite an ode to the sultan, beginning with this verse: "God, as long as the world lasts, watch over this world-keeper (*jahānbān*): Muḥammad Shāh Tughluq, son of Tughluq, son of the Sultan!" When the poet pronounced this opening line, the sultan stopped him, saying he would not be able to reward the rest of the verses adequately. As it was, he gave the poet a pile of gold as high as his head.[246] The plain assurance of his divine right to eternal world dominion was what the sultan wanted to hear. Badr-i Chāch probably received a fitting reward as well.

The Tughluqs' manipulation of the symbolism of the caliphate was thus part of a long tradition of imperial political policy, and it did not matter much whether one claimed to have the support of the caliph, or whether one claimed to be the caliph himself. For a poet like Amīr Khusraw, the title of caliph had been simply one more epithet to use in praising kings, and he had applied it to Quṭb al-Dīn Mubārak Khaljī and Ghiyās al-Dīn Tughluq without worrying about the ʿAbbāsid pretender.[247] He was simply following the lead of the sultans; Quṭb al-Dīn Mubārak even issued coins proclaiming himself "Vicegerent (*Khalīfa*) of the Lord of Creation."[248]

The idea of caliphal investiture as a source of authority now began to appeal to Deccani rebels as the Delhi empire crumbled. They too made contact with the ʿAbbāsid caliph, and bought their own diplomas of investiture to persuade sultan Muḥammad ibn Tughluq to keep from trying to reconquer them. This appears to have happened in the breakaway kingdom of Maʿbar in the far south, which had been independent since 1335. There, sultan Nāṣir al-Dīn Maḥmūd Damghān Shāh, in a coin of 745/1344–45, claimed to be "helper of the Commander of the Faithful," a phrase that could only mean he sought investiture from the caliph.[249] The panegyrist of the first Bahmanī sultan, ʿIṣāmi, in 751/1350–51, went to the extent of calling his patron the rightful caliph (*khalīfa bar ḥaqq*).[250] At his coronation, the first Bahmanī sultan also adopted the black parasol of the ʿAbbāsid caliphs as part of his court ritual.[251] Later, however, the second Bahmanī sultan, Muḥammad (r. 759/1358–776/1375), sent the queen mother on a state pilgrimage to Mecca, during which she obtained investiture and appropriate symbols from the ʿAbbāsid caliph in Egypt. According to a contemporary source, the explicit purpose of this gesture was to keep future sultans of Delhi from attempting to reconquer the Deccan.[252] The caliph notified Fīrūz Shāh in Delhi that the Deccan had been properly awarded to the Bahmanis, so Fīrūz Shāh, eager to retain his own caliphal investiture, never troubled the Bahmanīs. For all the pious posturing, though, caliphal symbolism was only useful as a support for kingship.

Sultanate Imperialism and Sufism

The Sufi movement had existed in tension with the emerging monarchical structure of the sultanate ever since the Seljuk Turks had come to power as protectors of the caliph in the late eleventh century. Sufis both supported the sultans as the theoretical upholders of Islamic law and questioned them as rulers whose morals and legitimacy might be doubtful in practice. Sultans in turn had made state patronage of Sufis as a cornerstone of policy. In the polity of the sultans of Delhi, Sufis formed a disparate but recognizable political group, alongside others such as the military, the Turkish nobility, and the religious scholars. From time to time alliances occurred between Sufi and sultan, while just as often conflicts arose. Yet the tension between the two never disappeared.

I propose, as a methodological principle, that it is essential to classify correctly literary accounts, especially when they obliterate the tension between Sufis and sultans; proper classification is just as important for individual stories as for entire works. Narratives that show Sufi saints giving limitless praise of the virtue and wisdom of rulers are no different from political panegyric, whether they occur in royal chronicles or hagiographies.[253] They must therefore be examined in terms of the political objectives of the author, which may be quite different from the political context of the Sufis being described. The same question can be raised about Sufi writings dedicated to kings, in what amounts to an interference of royal motives. The tension between saintly and royal hagiographies comes out in the open when conflicting accounts of the same event from different literary genres are set side by side. On the other extreme, hagiographies that show Sufis humbling or destroying impious kings with their miraculous powers may be considered pardonable attempts to achieve just restitution through the imagination. To this category belong the martyrologies that depict, for example, the sack of Delhi by Tīmūr in 1398 as divine punishment for Fīrūz Shāh Tughluq's execution of two would-be Sufis.[254] This type of hagiography is a testimony to saintly power rather than a journalistic report on day-to-day events, so it is a much better guide to popular attitudes toward sainthood than it is to royal policy. In short, identifying genre is the first task in studying Sufi literature.

The problem of tension between Sufis and sultans may be illustrated by Baranī's relationship with Sufism. It is no exaggeration to say that Baranī's ideas were opposed to Sufi views on politics, even among those Sufis who accommodated royalty in their treatises. Writing a "mirror for princes" during the Seljuk period, a Sufi-minded theologian like al-Ghazālī did not attempt to provide an Islamic religious or mystical basis for politics, and contented himself with an exposition of the Persian royal tradition, yet he did uphold ethical standards.[255] Sufi writers of the post-Mongol period had written political treatises that glorified monarchy as equal to or even superior to prophecy. Najm al-Dīn Razī (d. 654/1256) wrote that the just king is the true vice-gerent of God, and manifests the divine attributes of lordship.[256] Likewise Ḥusayn Wāʿiẓ Kāshifī (d. 910/1504–05) in the *Akhlāq-i Muḥsinī* (*Muhsinian ethics*) rated kingship as equal in some respects to prophethood.[257] Although these Sufi and Sufi-influenced writers used concepts of royalty similar to Baranī's, there was a great distance separating their insistence on ethical behavior from Baranī's Machiavellian amoralism. The Sufi shaykh ʿAlī Hamadānī (d. 786/1385), in his *Naṣīḥat al-mulūk* (*Advice for kings*), was strict in demanding that kings follow the example of the Prophet and the first four caliphs; he would not have tolerated Baranī's pragmatic concept of following royal customs that systematically infringed upon Islamic law.[258] Baranī's elevation of kingship above Islamic law and ethics in the name of Islamic imperialism destroyed the independent authority of religion, at the same time making Sufism irrelevant.

Baranī himself was a lay disciple of Niẓām al-Dīn Awliyā'. Chishtī circles in Delhi generously viewed Baranī's last years of poverty in exile from court as his deliberate choice of the dervish life.[259] Baranī's writings, as discussed above, nonetheless show that he had learned little from the Chishtī masters; the royal glory that he admired so much they treated with the healthy respect one gives to a large and unpredictable animal.[260] Baranī's distortion of Sufi teachings on politics and ethics is particularly clear in his account of the meeting between the ʿAbbāsid caliph Hārūn al-Rashīd and the Sufi ascetic Fużayl ibn ʿIyāż. In Baranī's version, the caliph went to see the ascetic to ask how to compensate for the sins he had committed as a ruler. Fużayl was very reassuring, and told Hārūn that God would forgive his sins and even make the kingdom prosper as long as his faith was sound and his intentions pure.[261] The versions of this encounter in classical Sufi literature are quite different. Sufi authorities are agreed that Fużayl gave the caliph such a stiff lecture on the pains he would undoubtedly suffer in hell fire that the caliph finally fainted and had to be carried away.[262] The inconsistency between the two narratives should not merely lead to the conclusion that one is right and the other wrong. Baranī's variance from the standard Sufi story had a contemporary political significance. It was Muḥammad ibn Tughluq's policy to employ Sufis as members of his administration, whether they liked it or not, and Baranī by this anecdote indicated his approval of this policy.[263] He used Maḥmūd of Ghazna (and here Hārūn al-Rashīd) as symbols of ideal royal behavior, and Fużayl ibn ʿIyāż, a member of the Chishtī initiatic lineage, was to represent the proper behavior of the mystics. Observing the degree of tension between Sufis and sultans, and identifying the dominant historiographical genres, are interpretive tactics that are crucial to the understanding of the sources on Indo-Muslim history.

4

The Textual Formation of Oral Teachings in the Early Chishtī Order

The historical formation of Sufism in India is a process that has taken centuries, and its origins are available to us only through a series of later reconstructions. From the time of Hujwīrī (d. 1074), the northwestern cities of India were home to a number of Sufis, though Hujwīrī is one of the few whose writings have come down to us. Later tradition records that in the late twelfth century, when most of the great Sufi orders began to crystalize in different parts of the Islamic world, the Chishtī order first became established in India. Probably the most popular order in the subcontinent, the Chishtiyya originated in the town of Chisht in Afghanistan. Although later authors such as Jāmī (d. 1492) tell stories of the early Sufis of Chisht, the first Chishtīs themselves wrote nothing, nor do contemporary witnesses tell us anything of their lives.[264] Even in the case of Muʿīn al-Dīn Chishtī (d. ca. 1233), whom tradition identifies as the founder of the Indian Chishtiyya, in order to find any connected written account of him we must wait until the fourteenth century, when the Chishtī order suddenly reveals itself in a full-blown literary tradition written in Persian.

The oral teachings of the Chishtīs, as revealed in the "oral discourses" (*malfūẓāt*) literature, took on a canonical textual form that soon became the authoritative and normative genre both for members of the order and for their lay followers. The transition from oral to written form was reflected in diverse literary styles adapted to different audiences. Modern critical debates about the authenticity of some of the Chishtī *malfūẓāt* have put into prominence the question of the Chishtī canon, yet the imposition of Western models of literary criticism needs to be supplemented by attention to the elaboration of internal critical categories that help explain the textual mediation of mystical Islam in India.

From Oral Teaching to Written Text In Sufism

The explosion of Sufi literary activity in India in the thirteenth and fourteenth centuries had a powerful formative effect on Indian Sufism. The widespread Suhrawardī order, which came from Baghdad, boasted outstanding mystical writers in its Indian branch, such as Qāżī Ḥamīd al-Dīn Nāgawrī (d. 1244), who wrote sophisticated meditations on the ninety-nine names of God and on mystical love.[265] While the Chishtīs did not at first express themselves in writing, they eventually produced a broader and more sustained literary tradition than any other Indian Sufi order. Neither Muʿīn al-Dīn Chishtī nor his two main successors, Quṭb al-Dīn Bakhtiyār Kākī (d. 1235) and Farīd al-Dīn "Ganj-i Shakkar" (d. 1265), wrote any books (the spurious discourses attributed to them are discussed below). The first generations of Indian Chishtīs continued to emphasize oral instruction, although masters such as Farīd al-Dīn also taught standard Arabic works on religion and mysticism, such as the *ʿAwārif al-maʿārif* of Shihāb al-Dīn Suhrawardī. Yet in the next generation, the Chishtī master Niẓām al-Din Awliyā' (d. 1325) made such a profound effect on his contemporaries that a new genre of literature, the *malfūẓāt*, emerged to embody his teachings.

In theory, the *malfūẓāt* was as close as one could get in words to the actual presence of the Sufi master. Although the authors of the *malfūẓāt* texts did not actually take dictation at the time when the master was speaking, they typically tried to write out his talks from memory as soon as a daily session ended, and in some cases they had the good fortune to have their work corrected by the master. Nonetheless, in the act of rewriting the master's words, the writer inevitably exercised some kind of selection and interpretation, and so produced a narrative structure depicting the Sufi teaching from a particular point of view. This combination of oral transmission and narrative recasting naturally had precedents in Sufi tradition. By the tenth century, the collecting of Sufi biographical dictionaries, with emphasis on sayings, had become an established category in Arabic religious literature; Sufi hagiography insofar as it stressed sayings was basically an outgrowth of the *ḥadīth* literature, which collected the sayings of the Prophet Muḥammad.[266]

Oral traditions from several outstanding personalities in the early Sufi movement, such as Abū Yazīd and al-Ḥallāj, were collected in Arabic in monograph form; typically these traditions were related as disconnected episodes, often introduced (as in *ḥadīth*) by the chain of transmitters (*isnād*).[267] In Persian the first monographic Sufi biographies concern Abū Saʿīd ibn Abī al-Khayr (d. 1049). His two biographies, written by his descendants some one hundred to one hundred fifty years after his death, narrate a long series of incidents that reveal his actions and sayings as a Sufi teacher.[268] Other works, no longer extant, recorded the sayings of Abū Saʿīd from two hundred different "sessions" (*majālis*), and Abū Saʿīd's contemporary al-Qushayrī is said to have recorded the sessions of his teacher Abū ʿAlī al-Daqqāq.[269] Disciples also preserved the oral discourses of some Iranian Sufis of the thirteenth and fourteenth centuries, such as Jalāl al-Dīn Rūmī (d. 1273).[270] In India, however, the *malfūẓāt* quickly became a dominant literary form for the transmission of Sufi teaching, so that later generations of Indian Sufis found it almost indispensable to commit their discourses into this textual mold.

How accurate is the *malfūẓāt* literature as a written record of oral teaching, and what criteria should be used to analyze it? The early Iranian Sufi biographies illustrate the same problem that occurs in the Indian *malfūẓāt* texts. In the case of the sayings of Abū Saʿīd, the modern Iranian literary critic Bahār believes that, on linguistic grounds alone, these sayings as recorded in his biographies must be considered a fairly accurate record of the actual words of the shaykh:

> The Sufis preserved the words of their saints, as the *ḥadīth* reports have to be preserved, word by word and letter by letter, and they permitted little change or interpolation in them. The credibility of some of the sentences and terms and their chain of transmission and correctness is such that no room remains for doubt or denial. . . . The style of *Asrār al-tawḥīd* in its totality, i.e., from the viewpoint of grammar and syntax, is without the slightest discrepancy equivalent to the style of the Sāmānids.[271]

This general observation on style and language is valuable and doubtless accurate as far as it goes, but it unfortunately does not shed any light on the process of literary composition that gave the text its form. To say that the compilers of hagiographical texts used the method of *ḥadīth* reporting glosses over two separate problems. First, the *ḥadīth* literature has its own historiography and redactions, raising questions concerning the transition from oral to written form and canon formation. Regrettably, most discussions of *ḥadīth* tend toward extremes, as traditionalists assert its absolute authority while modernists and some Western scholars reject it altogether on hypercritical grounds. Second, the interval of three to four generations between Abū Saʿīd's death and the writing of his biographies raises the question of how his sayings were chosen and preserved, and to what end. We may legitimately ask, too, about the political background of the biographies of Abū Saʿīd, since the *Asrār al-tawḥīd* was the first Sufi biography dedicated to a ruling monarch, in this case the Ghurid sultan Muḥammad ibn Sām (d. 1203).[272] The question of reliability, which tends to dominate critical discussions, should yield to the analysis of oral and written styles, canonical function, literary composition, and audience, as the basis for study of *malfūẓāt* texts.

The Foundation of the Chishtī *Malfūẓāt* Literature: Niẓām al-Dīn

The development of the Chishtī *malfūẓāt* literature may be sketched in two stages. First it is necessary to describe the discourses of Niẓām al-Dīn Awliyā' and compare them with those of his two disciples Naṣīr al-Dīn Maḥmūd Chiragh-i Dihlī (d. 1356) and Burhān al-Dīn Gharīb (d. 1337). These texts may be called, for convenience, the "original" *malfūẓāt*. The prominence of the first two of these texts among the many *malfūẓāt* is evident in the fact that they are the only ones to have been published in modern critical editions, and only Niẓām al-Dīn's has been translated into English.[273] The discourses of Burhān al-Dīn and his successor Zayn al-Dīn are preserved in several unedited texts, which up to now have received hardly any attention from scholars. An analysis of these texts, which form the basis for the study of the Sufis of Khuldabad, considerably adds to our understanding of the development of the *malfūẓāt* literature. Next, these "original" texts, all written by literate and courtly disciples, may be juxtaposed with another series of *malfūẓāt* purporting to be dictated by the principal Chishtī shaykhs to their successors, illustrating the main line of initiatic authority in the order. These "retrospective" texts, the authenticity of which has been challenged, stressed the hagiographic mode of personal charisma and authority, while the "original" ones focused on the teaching element consisting of practice and speculation, but all the *malfūẓāt* texts made the person of the Sufi master an essential part of the teaching.

The recording of the oral teachings of Niẓām al-Dīn Awliyā' was evidently the spontaneous decision of his disciple, the poet Amīr Ḥasan Sijzī Dihlawī (1253–1336). Beginning in 1307, until 1322, Ḥasan recorded as much as he could of his teacher's conversations, whenever leisure from his official duties as court poet permitted him leave in Delhi. The resulting book is called *Fawā'id al-fu'ād* (*Morals of the heart*).[274] Ḥasan was a skilled and eloquent poet in Persian; his poetic output includes several hundred lyric poems (*ghazal*s) as well as panegyric odes (*qaṣīda*s) addressed to the sultans of Delhi.[275] Although much of his poetry was of the standard erotic type popular at court, Ḥasan also injected the symbolism of Sufism into his verse. Mīr Khwurd called him "Amīr Ḥasan ʿAlā' Sijzī, whose burning lyrics brought forth the fire of love from the flint of lovers' hearts, whose pleasing verses conveyed solace to the hearts of the eloquent, and whose invigorating subtleties are the sustenance of the discerning."[276]

Fawā'id al-fu'ād is a beautifully written account of the Sufi teaching of Niẓām al-Dīn, and it is certainly one of the most popular Sufi works in India.

It was some time before Ḥasan revealed to Niẓām al-Dīn that he was recording the conversations in the shaykh's circle:

> It is more than a year that I have been connected to my master, and every time that I have had the happiness of kissing your feet, I have heard useful morals (*fawā'id*) from your pearl-bearing speech: sometimes preaching, advice, and encouragement of virtue, and sometimes stories of the shaykhs and their states; on every subject your inspiring words have reached the writer's hearing. I have wanted that to be the model for this helpless one's state, or rather the guide of the path for this wretch. I have written it down to the best of my understanding, inasmuch as your blessed speech has frequently mentioned that one ought to keep before one's eyes the books of the masters and the indications that they have made about the spiritual path. Since no collection can be superior to the refreshing sayings of my master, for this reason I have collected whatever I have heard from your blessed speech. Until this time I have not revealed it, and I [now] await your command.[277]

On hearing this declaration, Niẓām al-Dīn replied that, when he had attended upon his own master Shaykh Farīd al-Dīn, he too had formed the resolve to write down his teacher's sayings; he still vividly recalled the Persian verse with which Farīd al-Dīn had first greeted him:

> The fire of separation from you has burnt up hearts,
> the flood of longing for you has laid souls waste!

Ḥasan, greatly affected, was momentarily overcome by the attempt to express his own feelings. But then Niẓām al-Dīn requested him to show some samples of his notes, which fortunately Ḥasan had brought along. The shaykh complimented Ḥasan on his writing, but was puzzled by several blank spots in the manuscript. Ḥasan explained that those were places where he did not know the rest of the words—that is, his memory was not clear about those points. Niẓām al-Dīn then graciously told him what was missing, so that the account became complete.[278] This tender exchange between master and disciple illustrates Ḥasan's purpose in writing *Fawā'id al-fu'ād*: just as Niẓām al-Dīn had previously urged reading the classical writings of the Sufi shaykhs along with religious ritual and worship,[279] so now Ḥasan wrote his diary as an evocation of his master's presence as well as his teaching.

Several years later, another conversation took place between Ḥasan Sijzī and Niẓām al-Dīn that underlined the role of the *malfūẓāt* as a nearly sacred text that served as a religious standard. When Ḥasan brought out the completed first volume of *Fawā'id al-fu'ād*, Niẓām al-Dīn read it over with approval, saying, "You have written well, you have written like a dervish, and you have also given it a good name." The shaykh "in connection with this state" went on to make lengthy comments about the sayings of the Prophet Muḥammad as recorded by his associates, implicitly suggesting a comparison between Ḥasan's rendering of his own conversations and the collection of the prophetic *ḥadīth* literature. Such was the devotion of Abū Hurayra toward the Prophet, he noted, that Abū Hurayra, despite knowing the Prophet only three years, managed to transmit more *ḥadīth* than all the other companions put together; it was his concentration on the person of the Prophet that enabled Abū Hurayra to remember all those *ḥadīth*. Niẓām al-Dīn said that the Prophet told Abū Hurayra to extend the skirt of his garment whenever the Prophet spoke, slowly gather in the garment when the words were finished, and place his hand upon his breast; this routine would enable him to memorize Muḥammad's words.[280] Niẓām al-Dīn laid particular stress on Abū Hurayra's collection of religious knowledge, but he explicitly extended it to encompass mystical knowledge.[281] As the *ḥadīth* conveys ethical and ritual norms to the Muslim community, so the *malfūẓāt* now establish the principles of mysticism. In both cases the focus upon the personal source of the teaching is an essential part of the disciple's ability to remember the teacher's words, to preserve them for himself and others. In this way the Sufi *malfūẓāt* function as a parallel to the primary canon of Islam, the Qur'ān and *ḥadīth*.

The success of *Fawā'id al-fu'ād* as an exposition of Chishtī Sufism was tremendous. The court historian Baranī, in an oft-quoted passage, has recorded the popularity of *Fawā'id al-fu'ād* as an instance of the great influence that Niẓām al-Dīn exerted over the whole population of Delhi:

> Owing to the influence of the Shaikh, most of the Mussalmans of this country developed interest in mysticism, prayers, and aloofness from the world, and came to have a faith in the Shaikh. The hearts of men having become virtuous by good deeds, the very name of wine, gambling, and other forbidden things never came to anyone's lips. . . . Most of the scholars and learned men, who frequented the Shaikh's company, applied themselves to books on devotion and mysticism. The books *Qut-u'l-Qulub, Ihya-u'l-'Ulum* [etc.] . . . found many purchasers, as also did the *Fawa'id-u'l-Fu'ad* of Amir Hasan owing to the sayings of the Shaikh which it contains.[282]

While Baranī's account of the mystical and religious inclinations of the Muslim populace is perhaps exaggerated, it does testify to the extraordinary respect that Niẓām al-Dīn commanded among the people.

What were the reasons for the popularity of *Fawā'id al-fu'ād*? The book's popularity was doubtless a measure of Ḥasan Dihlawī's success in evoking the presence of Niẓām al-Dīn. The skilled pen of this poet, combined with the close relationship between master and disciple, made *Fawā'id al-fu'ād* an effective presentation of the teaching relationship in the Chishtī order. While

Fawā'id al-fu'ād inspired a host of imitations, few of these survive. Four other disciples of Niẓām al-Dīn compiled his *malfūẓāt*, but only one of these texts, "an inferior work," can still be found in manuscript.[283] In addition, the contents of Niẓām al-Dīn's teachings were in this way made available to a wide public, so that the book in reality became "the guide of the path" for many, as Ḥasan had hoped.

A recent Urdu biography of Ḥasan stresses the significance of *Fawā'id al-fu'ād* for its original audience in terms of explaining Islamic religious duties in detail, clarifying problems of mystical practice, and rejecting and correcting ethically dubious customs and traditions.[284] In modern times, scholars have, in contrast, valued this important *malfūẓāt* text less for its religious contents than for its historical value, as a corrective to the exclusively dynastic focus of the court historians. As K. A. Nizami observed:

> Through these records of conversations we can have a glimpse of the medieval society, in all its fullness, if not in all its perfection—the moods and tensions of the common man, the inner yearnings of his soul, the religious thought at its higher and lower levels, the popular customs and manners and above [all] the problems of the people. There is no other type of literature through which we can feel the pulse of the medieval public.[285]

The *malfūẓāt* texts certainly do throw light on aspects of social history that are ignored in dynastic chronicles, but the main reason for their initial popularity is the success with which they have expounded and evoked the Sufi teaching.

The Elaboration of the *Malfūẓāt* Tradition: Chirāgh-i Dihlī

With Niẓām al-Dīn's successor in Delhi, Naṣīr al-Dīn Maḥmūd "Chirāgh-i Dihlī" ("the lamp of Delhi," d. 1356), the *malfūẓāt* took on an uneven character, derived from the contrast in temperament between the serious legal and ascetic emphasis of the shaykh and the immaturity of the compiler, Ḥamīd Qalandar. When Chirāgh-i Dihlī discussed topics such as fasting, Ḥamīd would confess his own inability to fast, and admitted his preference for composing mediocre Persian verse instead of meditating.[286] Ḥamīd has given an elaborate description of how the collection of *Khayr al-majālis* (*The best of assemblies*) began, in 1354. After taking it upon himself to record five sessions in the circle of Chirāgh-i Dihlī, Ḥamīd brought his compilation and showed it to the master. Much to Ḥamīd's delight, Chirāgh-i Dihlī approved of it, and related a long story about the value of memorizing the words of the saints.

Typical of Chirāgh-i Dihlī's concern with the study of Islamic law, his example was drawn from the life of a legal scholar. The story concerned

Mawlānā Ḥamīd al-Dīn Żarīr ("the blind") of Bukhara, who had memorized the Qur'ān and a text on ritual prayer before becoming a disciple of Mawlānā Shams al-Dīn Gardīzī. Moving from the elementary classes to the advanced ones, Ḥamīd al-Dīn Żarīr would sit before the master with his skirt (*dāman*) extended, and at the conclusion of the lesson would gather up his skirt to his chest, as if he carried in it the literal fruit of the teacher's discourses (precisely recapitulating the technique that Niẓām al-Dīn had described to Ḥasan Dihlawī, which Abū Hurayra had used when memorizing the words of the Prophet Muḥammad). Ḥamīd al-Dīn Żarīr eventually succeeded to his master's place and wrote famous commentaries on works of Islamic law. On hearing this story, Ḥamīd Qalandar took the example to heart: "I extended my skirt before the revered master, who is my teacher and instructor and leader, and asked him for a *Fātiḥa* for the sake of memory. I formed the intention that I would not love anyone who was not a lover and adherent of the master, nor go to such a one's place, nay, as far as possible I would not look upon his face."[287] Ḥamīd enthusiastically equated his own personal devotion to Chirāgh-i Dihlī with the years of scholarly apprenticeship described in the story.

We cannot be so confident, however, regarding the scholarly pretensions of Ḥamīd Qalandar. Ḥamīd has indicated that at times Chirāgh-i Dihlī took pains to correct the manuscript of *Khayr al-majālis*, even in matters of Arabic vocabulary.[288] Other disciples of Chirāgh-i Dihlī reported that when shown sections of Ḥamīd's compilation, the shaykh remarked that they were inaccurate, and threw them away, having no time to correct them.[289] Ḥasan himself reflected that at times he did not understand the shaykh's words, but "if I do not comprehend, let me write down once what I do understand, so that it is a memorial."[290] From the "telegraphic" manner in which Chirāgh-i Dihlī's teachings are summarized in *Khayr al-majālis*, and on the basis of the apparent shortcomings of its compiler, Paul Jackson has admitted to having "very serious reservations" about the accuracy of this text as a record of the teachings of Chirāgh-i Dihlī.[291] The editor of *Khayr al-majālis*, K. A. Nizami, remarked that Ḥamīd Qalandar "had no real and genuine aptitude for mysticism."[292] For his own part, Ḥamīd Qalandar confidently compared his own compilation to *Fawā'id al-fu'ād*, and called *Khayr al-majālis* his auspicious "religious child" that would bring him great reward.[293] Despite these strictures on his accuracy, Ḥamīd Qalandar's compilation is nonetheless an important link in the recording of Chishtī teachings. Some of the stories of Chirāgh-i Dihlī that he records, such as the tale of Moses and the idolater in the thirty-sixth session, demonstrate how Sufis adapted traditional materials to portray contemporary situations; in this case, the idolater addresses his deity in Hindi, making the situation much more vivid for Chirāgh-i Dihlī's listeners.[294]

More importantly from the perspective of this study, Ḥamīd Qalandar's work reflects from the beginning a certain tension with the *malfūẓāt* texts of

Burhān al-Dīn Gharīb as rivals for canonical status. The *malfūẓāt* texts had begun to take on the canonical function of acting as a normative text that serves as vector for religious authority as well as individualist piety.[295] The flattering tone of Ḥamīd Qalandar's first conversations with Chirāgh-i Dihlī suggests that one of his motives was to establish the political supremacy of Chirāgh-i Dihlī within the Chishtī succession. When Ḥamīd Qalandar first came into the assembly of Chirāgh-i Dihlī, it happened to be the day when the latter was celebrating the death-anniversary (*ʿurs*) of his old friend and fellow-disciple Burhān al-Dīn Gharīb; this would have taken place on 11 Ṣafar 755/7 March 1354, seventeen lunar years after the death of Burhān al-Dīn Gharīb. Ḥamīd Qalandar immediately introduced himself to Chirāgh-i Dihlī and informed the shaykh that he had associated with Burhān al-Dīn Gharīb in Deogīr, and that he had in fact recorded the conversations of Burhān al-Dīn Gharīb in a *malfūẓāt* containing twenty sessions.[296] This remark reveals how the genre of *malfūẓāt* had already been established as a model among the Deccan Chishtīs. The very example that Ḥamīd Qalandar then related from memory was Burhān al-Dīn Gharīb's account of how he had sought and received spiritual advice from Chirāgh-i Dihlī when he had lost a hat given to him by Niẓām al-Dīn Awliyā'; Chirāgh-i Dihlī had emerged from a trance, and correctly predicted that Burhān al-Dīn Gharīb would receive even greater gifts from Niẓām al-Dīn.[297] After hearing Ḥamīd Qalandar's story, Chirāgh-i Dihlī confirmed its truth, and was very happy to be reminded of this incident with his old friend after so many years (Ḥamīd would retell this story in more high-flown and dramatic language in the biography of Chirāgh-i Dihlī attached as a supplement to *Khayr al-majālis*, where he specifically called this event a miracle).[298]

Ḥamīd Qalandar further observed that Burhān al-Dīn Gharīb had great faith in Chirāgh-i Dihlī, so Ḥamīd as an admirer of Burhān al-Dīn Gharīb was especially eager to see a man who was even greater. Chirāgh-i Dihlī's response to this flattery was to change the subject.[299] Ḥamīd Qalandar at their next meeting continued in the same vein, though, saying, "Lord! Mawlānā Burhān al-Dīn was a dervish who attained union, but the revered master [Chirāgh-i Dihlī] is an Abū Ḥanīfa in learning, and in asceticism and mastery is the Shaykh Niẓām al-Dīn of the age. God willing, I shall record the master's sessions."[300] Nonetheless, the figure of Burhān al-Dīn Gharīb looms over the composition of *Khayr al-majālis* at the end as well as at the beginning. In the one hundredth and final session, Ḥamīd Qalandar reports that Chirāgh-i Dihlī told a story that Ḥamīd had previously heard from the lips of Burhān al-Dīn Gharīb. That very night he had a dream in which Burhān al-Dīn Gharīb appeared and announced that the book of *Khayr al-majālis* was now complete, handing a luminous copy of the book to Ḥamīd Qalandar.[301]

Curiously, neither Ḥamīd Qalandar himself nor the incident of the hat is even mentioned in any of the genuine *malfūẓāt* of Burhān al-Dīn Gharīb. In fact, one of Burhān al-Dīn Gharīb's disciples pictured his relationship to Chirāgh-i Dihlī in quite the opposite fashion. Majd al-Dīn ʿImād Kāshānī, one of the four Kāshānī brothers, took up the task of recording Burhān al-Dīn Gharīb's miracles and revelations in a work called *Gharā'ib al-karāmāt* (*The rare miracles*).[302] In this account, Majd al-Dīn maintains that at their first meeting, Burhān al-Dīn Gharīb at once perceived the great spiritual potential of the youthful Chirāgh-i Dihlī, and warned him to be heedful and take advantage of the guidance of Niẓām al-Dīn, in this way acting as a preceptor rather than as a suppliant.[303]

Majd al-Dīn also tells a story in which Chirāgh-i Dihlī states that he learned the ability to perceive the states of souls after death from Burhān al-Dīn Gharīb.[304] Ḥamīd Qalandar's remarks betray the competition that must have come into existence between the centers established by various disciples of Niẓām al-Dīn Awliyā'; other followers of Chirāgh-i Dihlī would make deprecatory statements about Burhān al-Dīn Gharīb in later years. Regardless of the historicity of the incident of the hat, the unusual prominence of that story and Ḥamīd Qalandar's obsequious praise of Chirāgh-i Dihlī suggest a deliberate design to elevate the latter to a central position in the Chishtī order, at the expense of Burhān al-Dīn Gharīb. Stressing the primacy of one co-disciple over another was perhaps an inevitable result of the canonical focus on the authority of the Sufi master.

The Elaboration of the *Malfūẓāt* Tradition: Burhān al-Dīn Gharīb

Most existing accounts of the early *malfūẓāt* literature have neglected the largely unpublished texts produced in the circle of Burhān al-Dīn Gharīb (d. 1337), another major disciple of Niẓām al-Dīn, who led the Sufis who participated in the enforced migration of the Muslim elite of Delhi to the Deccan capital of Daulatabad in 1329. Strangely enough, there is no trace of any *malfūẓāt* text recording teachings by Burhān al-Dīn's brother Muntajib al-Dīn, despite the latter's great popularity in the Deccan; Muntajib al-Dīn is known only through legends (below, Part III, chap. 11). As we have seen, Ḥamīd Qalandar's account of his compilation of *Khayr al-majālis* presupposed the existence of a developed *malfūẓāt* tradition among the Deccan Chishtīs. Without appreciating the wide scope of the *malfūẓāt* texts written in the Deccan by Burhān al-Dīn Gharīb's disciples, it is impossible to form a complete understanding of the origin of this genre of Sufi writing among the Chishtīs.

The first and perhaps most important of the *malfūẓāt* texts emanating from the circle of Burhān al-Dīn Gharīb also followed the model of *Fawā'id al-fu'ād*. This was *Nafā'is al-anfās wa laṭā'if al-alfāẓ* (*Choice sayings and elegant words*), compiled by Rukn al-Dīn Dabīr Kāshānī in forty-eight sessions between Muḥarram 732/October 1331 and 4 Ṣafar 738/1 September 1337.[305] Rukn al-Dīn, as his title *dabīr* indicates, was a secretary in the service of Sultan Muḥammad ibn Tughluq's administration at Daulatabad. In his preface, Rukn al-Dīn remarks that in hearing the oral teachings of Burhān al-Dīn Gharīb, he had found that "no wayfarer has seen written in the writings of bygone shaykhs any of those subtleties and cyphers, nor has any seeker of truth read a word of those subjects and rarities."[306] Just as the admired Ḥasan Dihlawī (himself an emigré to Khuldabad) had collected and arranged the discourse of Niẓām al-Dīn Awliyā', now Rukn al-Dīn had determined to do the same with the words of Burhān al-Dīn Gharīb, whom he addresses by the loftiest of epithets. In a style considerably more prolix than that of Ḥasan, Rukn al-Dīn states that the purpose of his book is to see that "speakers with the brides of the meanings of the path by this means attain the throne-place of union with the real beloved, and seekers of the maidens of the subtleties of wayfaring by reading it may gaze on and contemplate the world-adorning beauty of the essential goal of desire."[307] He therefore at the first session he recorded, proposed this project to Burhān al-Dīn Gharīb, who approved wholeheartedly, saying, "For a long time, this idea has been established in my mind," and thanking God that it had been preordained that this book should be written by Rukn al-Dīn. Burhān al-Dīn Gharīb further encouraged Rukn al-Dīn by quoting from the poet Niẓāmī: "Freshen me with the heart of David, and make my psalms cry aloud." In other words, Rukn al-Dīn was to proclaim like David the psalmlike words that would constitute his book.[308] Toward the end of the session, the shaykh turned to Rukn al-Dīn and said, "Amīr Ḥasan, who has written the *Fawā'id*, [acted] in this way: whatever tale the shaykh [Niẓām al-Dīn] told, he turned toward Amīr Ḥasan. He [Ḥasan] wrote down whatever words were spoken." Rukn al-Dīn understood from this that he would have the great fortune to play the same role for Burhān al-Dīn Gharīb as Ḥasan had been performing for Niẓām al-Dīn as recently as ten years previously.[309]

As in the case of Ḥasan Dihlawī, Rukn al-Dīn Kāshānī was intent on accurately communicating the teachings of his master. *Nafā'is al-anfās* contains discussions, questions directed at Burhān al-Dīn Gharīb, stories both personal and legendary, and the explanation and performance of religious duties with an emphasis on Sufi rituals and their interpretation. While a number of famous early Sufis are mentioned, the greatest stress lies on Burhān al-Dīn Gharīb's teacher Niẓām al-Dīn, who is mentioned on every other page; the next most prominent figure in Burhān al-Dīn Gharīb's conversations is "the great shaykh," Farīd al-Dīn Ganj-i Shakkar. *Fawā'id al-fu'ād* clearly exerted a profound influence on Burhān al-Dīn Gharīb as it had on Niẓām al-Dīn's other disciples, and it suggested itself as a model that was eagerly followed in the recording of Burhān al-Dīn Gharīb's own teachings, even in the selection of the diary format and the preservation of its oral character.

Later texts from the circle of Burhān al-Dīn Gharīb took on a much more literary character, and while they retained oral elements, they abandoned the diary *malfūẓāt* structure for other genres. A more systematic approach characterized the *malfūẓāt* compiled by Rukn al-Dīn's brother Ḥammād al-Dīn Kāshānī (d. 761), entitled *Aḥsan al-aqwāl* (*The best of sayings*).[310] This book is divided up into twenty-nine chapters, each called a *qawl* or saying, covering all aspects of Sufi practice, summarized as follows:

1. On the practices (*rawish-hā*) of the masters of the path and the customs (*sunan*) of the lords of reality.
2. On the order of the manners (*ādāb*) of the shaykhs' assemblies.
3. On the firm faith of disciples in the matter of the master and other ascetics.
4. On the manners of the aspirant in the presence of the master.
5. On the manners of initiation (*bayʿat*) and the explanation of people's intentions and the conditions of discipleship.
6. On the virtue of obeying the master.
7. On the explanation of guarding the cloak (*khilʿat*) and other articles received from the master.
8. On disciplining the soul.
9. On the excellence of good actions.
10. On the excellence of good morals.
11. On the manifestation of the greatness and miracles of the saints.
12. On the excellence of fasting.
13. On the excellence of truthfulness.
14. On the influence of the prayers of the saints.
15. On the internal states of love.
16. On the manners of accepting gifts.
17. On avoiding consumption of unlawful things.
18. On the manners of trust in God, patience, and enduring poverty and hunger.
19. On the companions of excellence and contentment.
20. On the excellence of seclusion.
21. On the excellence of harmony and beneficence.
22. On the poor and the rich.
23. On the condemnation of begging.
24. On the excellence of charity.
25. On the excellence of prayers.
26. On the manners of the assembly of audition (*samāʿ*).
27. On the miracles of Burhān al-Dīn Gharīb.
28. On the explanation of the dreams of the companions of Burhān al-Dīn Gharīb.
29. On the words of the master regarding his disciples.

As a handbook, it presents under each heading a series of principles and practices (*rawish*) in the words of Burhān al-Dīn Gharīb, usually followed by a concrete example, drawn from the experience of the Chishtī masters, that will serve as a proof (*burhān*, a play on the name of the shaykh). Some of the sayings preserve distinct characteristics of speech rather than written composition, so the words of Burhān al-Dīn Gharīb have a decidedly spoken flavor.[311] At the beginning of most chapters, Burhān al-Dīn Gharīb is introduced by a distinct set of lofty epithets in accordance with the topic of that chapter. The title of the book is drawn from two passages from the Qur'ān (39.18 and 41.33) that stress both hearing and following good advice. This text, which was begun in the year of Burhān al-Dīn Gharīb's death (738/1337), is fortunately also available in a scholarly Urdu translation.[312]

While the emphasis of *Aḥsan al-aqwāl* is again on Sufi teaching, it imitates Rukn al-Dīn's *Nafā'is al-anfās* as a *malfūẓāt* text and claims a similar authority. The emphasis of *Aḥsan al-aqwāl* is on social, ethical, psychological, and ritual practices (by far the longest chapter is the twenty-fifth, on prayers); only the last three chapters are devoted to the miracles and experiences of Burhān al-Dīn Gharīb and his disciples. The structured format of this work does not reveal as much of the personality of the author as do the works written in diary form, although at the end he reveals that Burhān al-Dīn Gharīb prayed that Ḥammād al-Dīn should become a living saint (the implication is that the prayer of Burhān al-Dīn Gharīb would be answered).[313] It seems that the author may have reedited the book later on, perhaps in the writing of the last three chapters, whose biographical content does not fit well with the very practical subject matter of the first twenty-six chapters; in chapter twenty-seven, Ḥammād al-Dīn quotes from his brother Majd al-Dīn's *Gharā'ib al-karāmāt*, a work that was certainly begun much later than the original edition of *Aḥsan al-aqwāl*.[314] The language of the preface to *Aḥsan al-aqwāl* is closely modelled on the preface to Rukn al-Dīn's *Nafā'is al-anfās*, quoting some phrases nearly verbatim. Ḥammād al-Dīn follows Rukn al-Dīn's language very closely, but with greater rhetorical luxuriance, when he insists that no written source has ever indicated the profound depths of knowledge to be found in the present treatise.[315] Although the topical organization of this work seems on the surface to be a departure from the diary format of *Fawā'id al-fu'ād*, through the concrete examples that it gives for each practice, *Aḥsan al-aqwāl* retains the essential focus on the person of the master as the embodiment of the teaching.

The third *malfūẓāt* text to be written by a member of this remarkable family was Majd al-Dīn Kāshānī's *Gharā'ib al-karāmāt wa ʿajā'ib al-mukāshafāt* (*rare miracles and wondrous unveilings*),[316] a work that falls more nearly into the category of narrative hagiography. Although the date of its composition is not known, the benedictory formulas addressed to Burhān al-Dīn Gharīb indicate that it was begun after the latter's death. Majd al-Dīn in his preface observed that for some time the idea for this book had been on his mind, that he "should make a book of the influential words of the Shaykh al-Islām."[317] His friends urged him to follow the example of his two brothers, whose works have been described above; since they all have been constantly praising and remembering Burhān al-Dīn Gharīb, no gift could provide them more joy and ecstasy than a book chronicling the miracles (*karāmāt*) and unveilings (*mukāshafāt*) of the shaykh.

The preface continues with an extended narration of the severe discipline (*riyāżat*) that enabled Burhān al-Dīn Gharīb to attain the powers and knowledge that occupy the bulk of this book.[318] The focus of this work is much more on the man than on his teachings. The way that Majd al-Dīn was persuaded to write the book suggests that its purpose was primarily devotional. Yet in comparison with the fantastic events described in the spurious *malfūẓāt*, Burhān al-Dīn Gharīb's miracles are modest enough. He himself was quite conscious of the manner in which the popular imagination tended to attribute events such as healing to the prayers of saints, but he disclaimed responsibility for such feats, and regarded miracles as a distraction from the goal.[319] In *Gharā'ib al-karāmāt*, there are no accounts of teleportation or nightly visits to Mecca. Of the fourteen events described as miracles, nearly all concern the saint's foreknowledge of the future,[320] while the nineteen "unveilings" are mostly occasions when he reads the thoughts or unspoken questions of others.[321] In effect, these were teaching miracles, evidences of the saint's transmission of Sufi teaching. The disciples of Burhān al-Dīn Gharīb evidently had a great desire for material of this kind, for Majd al-Dīn later authored a supplementary collection of narratives entitled *Bāqiyat al-karāmāt* (*The rest of the miracles*), which is apparently no longer extant.[322] In any case, this work is primarily aimed at the devotee: "His disciples reached from the level of discipleship to the rank of mastery, and those accepted by him transformed the world; because they saw his blessed face, their sins were forgiven. [Verse:] I also have become his servant / so that the sins of this fool are forgiven. // He is an intercessor with God / so that he may bestow the cloak of acceptance."[323] As in the more narrowly construed hagiographies, this book reveals the shaykh as the one who has the power to read the disciple's heart and intercede with God on the disciple's behalf.

The fourth *malfūẓāt* work oriented toward Burhān al-Dīn Gharīb also came from the pen of Rukn al-Dīn Kāshānī, but its encyclopedic literary scope makes it only in part a record of the sayings of the shaykh. This monumental treatise is entitled *Shamā'il al-atqiyā' wa dalā'il al-anqiyā'* (*Virtues of the devout and proofs of the pure*), the only one of the Khuldabad texts to be published in Persian.[324] *Shamā'il al-atqiyā'* is an enormous collection (455 pages in the rare lithographed edition) of excerpts from Sufi writings and oral traditions, covering a full range of topics related to mystical thought and practice. In his preface, Rukn al-Dīn has presented a list of over two hundred fifty classical authorities on Sufism and religion that he consulted, which are scrupulously cited as sources on every page of the book. This bibliography, including both Arabic and Persian sources, comprises about seventy-five works on the standard Islamic religious sciences (Qur'ānic exegesis, *ḥadīth*, theology, and law), about one hundred twenty-five books on Sufism, and another fifty sources of oral traditions.[325] A number of these titles are evidently no longer extant aside from the quotations in this work. *Shamā'il al-atqiyā'* also includes excerpts from several other lost treatises on Sufism written by the Kāshānī brothers.[326] Rukn al-Dīn's bibliography thus constitutes what Jonathan Z. Smith would call an ordered catalogue of texts rather than a closed canon.[327] Its inclusion of oral sources makes it essentially open-ended. The Chishtī *malfūẓāt*, which straddle the boundary between text and speech, are prominently featured in this catalogue.

Rukn al-Dīn began writing *Shamā'il al-atqiyā'* during the lifetime of Burhān al-Dīn Gharīb, who approved the first few sections and bestowed upon Rukn al-Dīn the title "the spiritual secretary" (*dabīr-i maʿnawī*). The book was not completed, however, until some unspecified time after the shaykh's death.[328] The subjects that Rukn al-Dīn included in *Shamā'il al-atqiyā'* address a select audience of educated Sufis. The two principal sections are, first, a discussion in fifty-two chapters of Islamic rituals and the interior stations (*maqāmāt*) of Sufism. Second is an analysis of mystical states (*aḥwāl*). The third and fourth sections, on theology and anthropology, are miniscule in comparison and function only as appendixes. As is common in Sufi manuals, each chapter begins with quotations from the Qur'ān and *ḥadīth*, followed by excerpts from works of exegesis, Islamic law, theology, and from a multitude of Sufi sources. The popularity of *Shamā'il al-atqiyā'* can be gauged from its translation into Dakhani Urdu in the seventeenth century.[329] The special interest of this text for the development of *malfūẓāt* is due to its incorporation of many of Burhān al-Dīn Gharīb's oral teachings.[330] Rukn al-Dīn did not intend merely to make a compilation based on written sources, but viewed the preceding Sufi tradition as a heritage alongside the oral teaching received from Burhān al-Dīn Gharīb. He formed this resolve:

> In this book should be written and recorded the different sayings and virtues of the devout and the saints, and the kinds of spiritual states and customs of the virtuous and the pure, which have issued from these treatises and writings, [and] from the conceptual wonders and esoteric rarities that have been heard from the jewel-bearing tongue and pearl-scattering discourse of that unveiler of scriptural difficulties and clarifier of intricate proof, that is, my master and patron, my elder and teacher.[331]

Unlike the *malfūẓāt* written in diary form, which strive to recreate the living presence of the master, this scholarly production places the master's oral teaching in the context of a vast historical tradition. The ordered catalogue of texts that forms its bibliography, while not a closed canon, confers canonical authority on the Chishtī *malfūẓāt* texts while still recognizing the importance of oral sources.

The Problem of "Inauthentic" *Malfūẓāt*

It was probably the impact of Niẓām al-Dīn Awliyā' through the teachings of *Fawā'id al-fu'ād* that led to the reconstruction of earlier Chishtī tradition along similar lines, through the fabrication of spurious *malfūẓāt* texts. As Baranī observed, one of the effects of Niẓām al-Dīn's popularity was to arouse people's curiosity about the teachings and practices of the earlier Chishtī masters, such as Farīd al-Dīn and Quṭb al-Dīn.[332] It was in this spirit that the grandson of Shaykh Ḥamīd al-Dīn Suwāli Nāgawrī (d. 1276) compiled the latter's sayings, in a large and rambling *malfūẓāt* composed around 1350.[333] As shown above, the purpose of the *malfūẓāt* was to evoke the personal presence of the Sufi master as well as to record the shaykh's teachings. Niẓām al-Dīn had also attempted to record some of the conversations of his master Farīd al-Dīn to this end, though no trace of this survives. But somehow a series of books, attributed to the earlier Chishtī shaykhs, began to appear. By a kind of principle of plenitude, every great teacher in the Chishtī succession was credited with a book of teachings. Even before the completion of the first part of *Fawā'id al-fu'ād*, a book falsely ascribed to Niẓām al-Dīn was in circulation in Awadh; Niẓām al-Dīn, who firmly denied having written that or any other book, reflected that problems of plagiarism and inauthentic books had also plagued Indian Sufi authors even in the time of ʿAlī Hujwīrī.[334] Perhaps the most telling piece of evidence against the false *malfūẓāt* occurs in the conversations of Naṣīr al-Dīn Maḥmūd "Chirāgh-i Dihlī" (d. 1356), a chief disciple of Niẓām al-Dīn; when a disciple asked about these writings, Naṣīr al-Dīn rejected them as unworthy of the Chishtī masters, none of whom had ever written a book.

In a brilliant article, Mohammad Habib called attention to these spurious *malfūẓāt*, demonstrating their variance from accepted Chishtī teachings, their historical anachronisms, and their lack of authenticity according to the testimony of the Chishtī masters themselves. Habib concentrated on six unauthentic works, listed here according to their ostensible chronological order:

1. *Anīs al-arwāḥ*, the conversations of ʿUsmān Hārwanī allegedly collected by Muʿīn al-Dīn Chishtī;
2. *Dalīl al-ʿārifīn*, the conversations of Muʿīn al-Dīn Chishtī collected by Quṭb al-Dīn Bakhtiyār Kākī;
3. *Fawā'id al-sālikīn*, the conversations of Quṭb al-Dīn Bakhtiyār Kākī collected by Farīd al-Dīn Ganj-i Shakkar;

4. *Asrār al-awliyā'*, the conversations of Farīd al-Dīn Ganj-i Shakkar collected by Badr al-Dīn Isḥāq;
5. *Rāḥat al-qulūb*, the conversations of Farīd al-Dīn Ganj-i Shakkar as collected by Niẓām al-Dīn; and
6. *Afżal al-fawā'id*, and its continuation *Rāḥat al-muḥibbīn*, the conversations of Niẓām al-Dīn as recorded by the poet Amīr Khusraw.[335]

These books lack the personal touch that made *Fawā'id al-fu'ād* such an effective presentation of Niẓām al-Dīn's teaching. The false *malfūẓāt* focus on establishing the authority of the Chishtī masters at all costs—describing, for instance, the Prophet's miraculous recognition of the Chishtī saints during their pilgrimages to Mecca—although reliable Chishtī tradition firmly records that none of these masters ever made the *ḥajj* pilgrimage. While the genuine *malfūẓāt* contain lively conversations, the audiences in the fabricated works are silent witnesses to the monologues of saints. The spurious *malfūẓāt* are characterized by a profusion of exaggerated miracles designed to enhanced the saint's prestige, and by an extreme fascination with chants (*awrād*) and their benefits. Although the unauthentic works are not devoid of merit, they betray their secondary status by plagiarizing at length from *Fawā'id al-fu'ād*. The reconstruction they offer of the early Chishtī order tends toward the simplistic, dwelling on charisma and miraculous power rather than evoking a guiding presence.[336] The stress on presenting the unbroken initiatic line of the early Chishtīs may have been due to anxiety about the dispersal of the Chishtī order after the death of Niẓām al-Dīn in 1325.[337] The primary concern of these texts is to establish the mere fact of spiritual authority rather than to convey the teachings upon which that authority rested. At a loss to explain the popularity of these works, Habib finally suggested that they were forgeries commissioned by booksellers in order to drum up trade.[338]

Despite the criticisms of Habib, it must be acknowledged that traditional Chishtī circles from an early date generally accepted these documents as genuine, and they are still very popular in Urdu translation. The authenticity of these *malfūẓāt* has been defended by a number of traditionally-minded scholars.[339] Today, most followers of the Chishtī order in fact rely primarily on the "inauthentic" *malfūẓāt* for their understanding of the early Chishtī masters; the only exception to this rule is *Fawā'id al-fu'ād*, which has continued to be universally popular up to the present day. The discourses of Chirāgh-i Dihlī and Burhān al-Dīn Gharīb can be found only in a few rare Persian manuscripts preserved in private libraries and Sufi shrines, and on the rare occasion when they have been translated into Urdu, these publications remain extremely hard to get. Nizami, finding only three manuscripts of *Khayr al-majālis*, attributed their rarity to the rigor of Chirāgh-i Dihlī's teachings, since the shaykh insisted on observance of Islamic law, criticized hereditary succession in Sufi lineages, and rejected the "inauthentic" *malfūẓāt*. This strict approach necessarily lacked the popular appeal of the "inauthentic" *malfūẓāt*.[340] At shrines such as the tomb of Farīd al-Dīn Ganj-i Shakkar in Pakistan, the most commonly available text today consists of the Urdu translations of eight *malfūẓāt* texts in a single volume entitled *Hasht bihisht* or *Eight Heavens*. This contains seven "inauthentic" texts plus one original one: *Anīs al-arwāh*, *Dalīl al-ʿārifīn*, *Fawāʾid al-sālikīn*, *Rāḥat al-qulūb*, *Miftāḥ al-ʿāshiqīn* (discourses attributed to Naṣīr al-Dīn Maḥmūd), *Fawāʾid al-fuʾād*, *Rāḥat al-muḥibbin*, and *Asrār al-awliyāʾ*. The eclipse of the early *malfūẓāt* texts by other writings believed to be inauthentic constitutes a problem for critical scholarship. The problem is that Habib's critical approach, while partly framed in terms of traditional standards, draws primarily upon modern Western categories of analysis that are foreign to the material under consideration. His distaste for miracle stories might even be said to reveal a positivistic bias.

The theoretical distinction I have attempted to make between the genuine and spurious *malfūẓāt* is compromised by the appearance of some of the "inauthentic" works in *Shamāʾil al-atqiyāʾ*. In his bibliography, Rukn al-Dīn Kāshānī lists the apocryphal *malfūẓāt* of the early Chishtī shaykhs right along with Ḥasan Dihlawī's *Fawāʾid al-fuʾād* and his own *Nafāʾis al-anfās*.[341] The citations of Chishtī apocrypha in *Shamāʾil al-atqiyāʾ* appear to be the earliest literary reference to the spurious *malfūẓāt*. Only a small number of citations from these works appear in *Shamāʾil al-atqiyāʾ*, however: seven quotations in all, as far as I can determine.[342] The subjects covered in these quotations are for the most part concerned with Sufi practice, although one anecdote refers to the power of the master to discern the thoughts of prospective disciples (a prominent hagiographic theme in *Gharāʾib al-karāmāt*). The distinction between the genuine and false *malfūẓāt* is not absolute; it must be admitted that this distinction is significant primarily from the academic point of view. Both kinds of texts contain extracts from Sufi teaching, and both illustrate the charisma of the Sufi teacher; the difference is primarily in emphasis. Rukn al-Dīn, too, was attempting to represent the breadth of the Sufi tradition in the widest possible way. His concern was not to establish rigid standards of textual authenticity but to summarize the range and depth of Sufi teaching available to the Chishtī masters in his day, and in his experience the literary tradition was closely tied to the oral one. He cites over thirty authorities simply as "the treatise of so-and-so," refers to over fifty oral sources as "the saying of so-and-so," and reserves an extra catchall category for anonymous sayings. In compiling *Shamāʾil al-atqiyāʾ*, Rukn al-Dīn was probably happy to include some references to the spurious Chishtī *malfūẓāt*, insofar as they contributed to his overall presentation of Sufi teaching. The anachronisms and contradictions that they contain would not have presented a problem for him, since he only extracted materials that were relevant to his purpose. Since Rukn al-Dīn felt free to give excerpts from these apocryphal works in his Sufi encyclopedia, we can only conclude that even at this early date the hagiographic interest in the early Chishtī order had already reached a fairly high level; in other words, the "inauthentic" *malfūẓāt* were popular manifestations of religious sentiment among Indian Muslims attached to the Chishtī order.

The last of the *malfūẓāt* texts written in Khuldabad was devoted to recording the teachings of Burhān al-Dīn Gharīb's principal successor, Zayn al-Dīn Shīrāzī (d. 1371). A court official and Chishtī disciple known only as Mīr Ḥasan compiled Zayn al-Dīn Shīrāzī's discourses under the title *Hidāyat al-qulūb wa ʿināyat ʿullām al-ghuyūb* (*Guidance of hearts and aid for knowers of the hidden*) between 745/1344 and 769/1367.[343] Ḥasan obviously used *Fawāʾid al-fuʾād* as a model for his compilation, since he started off imitating its diary format, and he even adopted the same epithet for himself (*banda-i kamīna*, "lowly servant") that Ḥasan Dihlawī had used in *Fawāʾid al-fuʾād.* Ḥasan begins his account with verbal echoes of the epithets used by previous *malfūẓāt* writers to describe their enterprises:

> Having collected from the pearl-bearing and jewel-scattering words of the Shaykh of Islam and of the Muslims, the revered king Zayn al-Ḥaqq wa al-Ḥaqīqa wa al-Dīn Dāʾūd Ḥusayn Shīrāzī (may God sustain the Muslims by prolonging his existence), according to the measure of my weak intelligence and infirm expression, this *Guidance of Hearts and Aid for Knowers of the Hidden* comes forth so that all the people of the heart may collect their scattered thoughts through this comprehensive collection, find salvation from external and internal dissipation, and help the author by praying for his good reward.[344]

Nonetheless, the formal similarity with the earlier *malfūẓāt* texts is not close. *Hidāyat al-qulūb* contains only eight dates in what is a very long manuscript, and in much of the text simply recounts anecdotes without any temporal sequence, so that the diary structure is more apparent than real.[345] References to discussions that took place earlier and materials referred to "above" and "below" reinforce the literary character of the work.[346] Perhaps because he has followed his own initiative in collecting Zayn al-Dīn Shīrāzī's teaching, Ḥasan reveals more of his own personality than do other *malfūẓāt* writers. Mīr Ḥasan's compilation begins with his first meeting with the shaykh, and it indirectly reveals his growing closeness to Zayn al-Dīn Shīrāzī over a period of nearly twenty-five years. Ḥasan frequently asks questions and records his gradual initiation into the inner circle of disciples. In addition, *Hidāyat al-qulūb* has a much stronger narrative character than other *malfūẓāt*. Zayn al-Dīn Shīrāzī's stories are told at length and in leisurely detail, in contrast to the often brief and abbreviated tales recorded from Burhān al-Dīn Gharīb and Niẓām al-Dīn. He repeatedly emphasized how stories can be understood on different levels according to the capacity of the audience.[347] Zayn al-Dīn Shīrāzī's scholarly training in the study of the Qur'ān and its commentaries is displayed frequently, and he also recites a surprisingly large number of verses in an old dialect of Hindi.

Other Sufi orders in India besides the Chishtīs possessed quasicanonical *malfūẓāt* texts. Although the state of research on the literature of these other Sufi orders is not as far advanced as in the case of the Chishtīs, it appears that the Chishtī *malfūẓāt* literature in most cases served as a model for non-Chishtī orders. No contemporary writings record the history of the establishment of the Suhrawardī order in northwestern India in the thirteenth century. The founder of the Suhrawardiyya in Multan, Bahā' al-Dīn Zakariyyā (d. 1262) wrote several works on prayer, retreat, and Sufi practice, but they lack the personal dimension of *malfūẓāt* texts.[348] Later hagiographers who sought to reconstruct the life and teachings of Bahā' al-Dīn Zakariyyā had to resort to the Chishtī *malfūẓāt* or fourteenth-century Suhrawardī sources to find extensive anecdotal material about him.[349] Hagiographers of the Mughul period refer to *malfūẓāt* texts recording the teachings of Bahā' al-Dīn's successors in Multan, but it is generally agreed today that these works have not survived.[350] This judgment appears to have been premature, however, and mistaken in assuming that all *malfūẓāt* texts were written in Persian. A disciple of Bahā' al-Dīn's grandson Rukn al-Dīn Abū al-Fatḥ (d. 1335), one Fażl Allāh al-Mājawī, actually compiled the teachings of the Suhrawardī saints in 1316 in Arabic, under the title *al-Fatāwā al-Ṣūfiyya fī ṭarīq al-Bahā'*iyya (*Sufi decrees on the Bahā'ian path*), which can be found in manuscript in several European and Turkish libraries.[351] Since the first book of *Fawā'id al-fu'ād* had only been completed a couple of years previously, it appears that *al-Fatāwā al-Ṣūfiyya* was exceptional in being composed without reference to *Fawā'id al-fu'ād*; a preliminary examination indicates that the work is organized topically on the model of the classic Suhrawardī handbook of Sufism, 'Umar al-Suhrawardī's *'Awārif al-ma'ārif*, although it still employs the *ḥadīth*-based narrative as found in the Chishtī *malfūẓāt*. In any case, the Suhrawardī materials clearly call for further investigation. The abundant compilations devoted to the teachings and miracles of the later Suhrawardī saint Jalāl al-Dīn Bukhārī "Makhdūm-i Jahāniyān" (d. 1383) provide extensive documentation of popular Muslim religiosity in the fourteenth century.[352] In the Firdawsī order based in Bihar, another impressive series of *malfūẓāt* texts chronicled the teachings of Sharaf al-Dīn Manērī (d. 1381) and his successors, from the late 1340s onward. These compilations are mostly in diary form like *Fawā'id al-fu'ād*, and record Sharaf al-Dīn's conversations with many visitors. Thanks to the researches of Paul Jackson these writings are becoming better known, but much work remains to be done before we shall have a complete understanding of their literary tradition.[353]

If we set aside the problem of authenticity and turn to other axes of comparison, we can nevertheless distinguish between the two classes of texts in terms of the previously mentioned categories of oral or written character, canonicity, and audience. We have referred to the discourses of Niẓām al-Dīn, Chirāgh-i Dihlī, and Burhān al-Dīn Gharīb as the "original" *malfūẓāt* texts for purposes of discussion. These works preserve many unmistakable features of oral style. Here, the Sufi masters in their conversations frequently use the typically oral mnemonic devices of clustering related items into groups of three, four, or five. Questions, exclamations, impromptu quotations of poetry, and occasional dramatic interaction with interlocutors dominate these early texts. What may be called the "retrospective" *malfūẓāt* texts in contrast show them delivering monotonous sermons and narrative pericopes that betray a purely literary hand at work.[354] This increasingly literary quality of *malfūẓāt*, and the loss of oral character, is characteristic of the later proliferation of *malfūẓāt* texts that emerged from subsequent generations of Chishtī masters (in most of these cases there is no question about the authenticity of these works). By the fifteenth century, the oral element in *malfūẓāt* is in many cases entirely eliminated. It should be noted that the recognition of the importance of oral modes of textuality in Islamic culture has only recently begun to appear in scholarly literature.[355] The orality of the *malfūẓāt* texts is also suggestive for the oral aspect of *ḥadīth*, which was so strongly emphasized as being the basis of the *malfūẓāt*. It is noteworthy that the story of Abū Hurayra's mantle and his remarkable memory has recently come under criticism from modernist interpreters in Egypt, who have questioned the vast number of *ḥadīth* reports circulating in his name. These scholars have applied exclusively literary textual standards derived from Western scholarship, so it is not surprising that they are in the process becoming alienated from oral portions of their tradition.[356]

As far as indigenous categories are concerned, while both the original and retrospective texts function canonically, they can be distinguished in terms of their relative emphasis on normative teaching or religious authority. Following the model of *ḥadīth* reports, the original *malfūẓāt* as described above stress the contents of Sufi teaching, particularly with regard to practice. The retrospective works, on the other hand, move largely in the direction of hagiography in emphasizing personal charisma and authority over teaching. Of course, hagiographic elements of authority do appear in the original *malfūẓāt*, and the retrospective works pay attention to practices such as the efficacy of chants, but the main tendencies tend to break along these lines. This distinction is further demonstrated in the authorship of the texts. The compilers of the original *malfūẓāt* were disciples trying to preserve and convey their masters' teachings: Ḥasan Dihlawī was a court poet, the Kāshānī brothers of Khuldabad were all court officials, and Ḥamīd Qalandar was a marginal Sufi hanger-on and poet. The retrospective texts, on the other hand, form an extended literary elaboration of the initiatic genealogy, unambiguously guaranteeing and concretizing the authority of the order. Even miracle stories tend to break down in the same fashion, with the original *malfūẓāt* stressing miracles as part of the teaching and the retrospective texts using them to demonstrate authority.

The original *malfūẓāt*, finally, differ from the retrospective works in terms of their audience. The recorders of the original *malfūẓāt* were addressing elite members of the Turkish nobility and military class that ruled northern India in the thirteenth and fourteenth centuries. These were people who could put themselves in the place of a Ḥasan Dihlawī, imagining themselves to be the disciple of the Sufi shaykh, and using the text as what Ḥasan Dihlawī called "the guide of the path." The audience of the retrospective *malfūẓāt*, on the other hand, was less concerned with Sufi practice and Islamic law, but much more interested in the powers of the saints as intercessors with God. For them, the value of the *malfūẓāt* was relational rather than informational; the *malfūẓāt* functioned scripturally to put them in touch with the heart of the Chishtī lineage, and therefore in close relationship with God's representatives on earth. Because of the pseudonymous character of the retrospective works, it is difficult to identify their "popular" audience with much more precision than this on purely internal grounds. Yet *Fawā'id al-fu'ād*, the foundational text of the genre, was not limited by these restrictions and appealed to both audiences.

The Sufi teaching is essentially a personal mediation of a complex teaching tradition. In its normative aspect, it follows the model of *ḥadīth* by transmitting religious guidelines through a chain of reliable witnesses. Hagiographical writing in its most extreme form disregards the teaching aspect of Sufism and concentrates instead on authority. In the Chishtī Sufi order, the original *malfūẓāt* by their dialogical format used the *ḥadīth* method of oral transmission to embody the teaching process in a written form. The process of textualization of oral teaching led to the formation of a kind of secondary canon of Indian Sufi literature, in which the retrospective elaboration of the discourses of the early Chishtī masters supplemented the original texts, proceeding along purely literary lines. The modern debate about the authenticity of the *malfūẓāt* literature has been conducted in terms of Western critical standards that are sometimes quite removed from the self-understanding of the tradition. Wilfred Cantwell Smith has observed that "we have tended to derive our concept of scripture from the Bible; I am suggesting that we are now in a position where our understanding of the Bible, and of much else across the world, may begin to be derived from a larger concept of scripture."[357] In trying to understand the emergence of the canon of Chishtī *malfūẓāt* texts, or any other non-Western religious texts, it may be tempting to apply the same standard techniques of literary criticism that were developed in biblical studies, in terms of a scriptural model that was basically Protestant. But the limitations of this kind of approach become apparent when the interpreter ends up dismissing as "inauthentic" and "apocryphal" a literature that continues to have a demonstrably canonical function for its community. By observing how this tradition has interpreted its own canonical texts, we can not only enlarge our comprehension of this particular phenomenon, but also we can expand our categories of analysis so that they may more adequately reflect the global scope of the study of religion.

5

The Interpretation of the Sufi Biographical Tradition in India

After the *malfūẓāt* texts, the most important sources for the development of Sufism in India are biographical dictionaries, both purely hagiographic collections and lives of the saints conceived as a supplement to political history. The difference between religious and political biography is by no means as clear as one might suppose. In classical Islamic literature, the lives of Sufi saints are often found in local biographical works devoted the notables of a particular city. Books of lives of the saints frequently have an explicitly political context, signaled by a dedication to a sultan or other powerful political figure, or by reference to disputes over precedence within Sufi orders. Implicit political motives can also be inferred by reference to contemporary events or by comparison with other hagiographic texts ostensibly describing the same period. What follows is a brief outline of some of the most important works on Sufi biography relating to the Chishtīs from the sultanate period and the Mughul era to the present. The increasing overlap of religious and political objectives is one of the fundamental themes of these texts.

By far the most useful and reliable early Chishtī biographical text is *Siyar al-awliyā'* (*Lives of the saints*), written around 1350 by Sayyid Muḥammad ibn Mubārak ʿAlawī Kirmānī, known as Mīr Khwurd (d. 1368). Although Mīr Khwurd had been brought up in a family devoted to Niẓām al-Dīn Awliyā', he had entered government service and worked in the Deccan for some fifteen years; he later referred to this period of secular employment as having been devoid of any association with Sufism. Sometime after the Bahmanī dynasty ended the Delhi sultanate's control over the Deccan in 1348, Mīr Khwurd returned to Delhi and reestablished his contacts with the Chishtī order, eventually experiencing a renewal of his initiation in a dream of Niẓām al-Dīn Awliyā' on the night of April 17, 1357.[358] On Mīr Khwurd's return to the Chishtī order in Delhi, he accepted Naṣīr al-Dīn Maḥmūd Chirāgh-i Dihlī as the legitimate successor to Niẓām al-Dīn Awliyā'. Mīr Khwurd's book is an

extremely valuable source, not least because of his incorporation of documents from Chishtī archives as well as oral traditions from his family. It is the
first attempt at a biographical sketch of the Chishtī order in chronological
order. The focus of the book, not surprisingly, is Niẓām al-Dīn Awliyā'. The
latter portions, which are arranged by topic, contain extensive excerpts from
Fawā'id al-fu'ād. But Mīr Khwurd moves in the direction of hagiography; he
borrows incidents and sayings from the portraits of the early Chishtīs in the
"retrospective" *malfūẓāt*, sometimes changing the names of the main characters.[359] He stresses charisma and miracle, so that in comparison with the best
malfūẓāt works, Mohammad Habib concluded that "his work, though very
informative and quite indispensable, is not an equally safe guide."[360]

The narratives in a hagiography like *Siyar al-awliyā'* are not isolated
facts, but function as part of a presentation designed to highlight Chishtī
teachings through exemplary personalities. A comparison of several highly
circumstantial episodes with earlier and contemporary sources reveals that
some of the stories in *Siyar al-awliyā'* are not descriptions of actual events at
all, but are narrative elaborations of Sufi maxims and popular stories. As an
example, we can take Mīr Khwurd's biography of one of Niẓām al-Dīn
Awliyā's chief disciples, Shaykh Fakhr al-Dīn Zarrādī. This shaykh, we are
told, had once defied Sultan Muḥammad ibn Tughluq's attempt to force him
into government service, but was constrained to join the emigrants to
Daulatabad.[361] Yet he chafed at the enforced move, and hoped to leave for
pilgrimage to Mecca. He expressed this wish to the chief religious official of
the empire, Qāżī Kamāl al-Dīn Ṣadr-i Jahān, an old friend from student days
in Hansi.[362] The qāżī pointed out that he would have difficulty in obtaining the
sultan's permission to leave Daulatabad. Fakhr al-Dīn was dejected by this
advice, and told Mīr Khwurd's father Sayyid Muḥammad Kirmānī that he had
given up the plan. Sayyid Muḥammad rebuked him for accepting the qāżī's
advice and abandoning his heart's desire, and told him, "This is no good;
there is no consultation in love." He urged Fakhr al-Dīn to go ahead on
pilgrimage, but to conceal his plan from Qāżī Kamāl al-Dīn. On the pretext of
attending a wedding, Fakhr al-Dīn left Daulatabad and escaped to Mecca
where he accomplished his pilgrimage. After a sojourn in Baghdad he perished at sea while attempting to return to his beloved Delhi.[363]

The story of Fakhr al-Dīn Zarrādī's pilgrimage is so circumstantial, especially with reference to Mīr Khwurd's father, that we are inclined to treat it as
a reliable report. But nearly the same account, with minor variations, occurs
as a stock teaching story in the Chishtī *malfūẓāt*. Niẓām al-Dīn Awliyā' related
the story in his assembly in Delhi on 2 Dhū al-Qaʿda 720/4 December 1320,
telling how an unnamed person requested permission from the qāżī of Lahore
to go on pilgrimage to Mecca. This differs from Mīr Khwurd's story in that
the qāżī at first gives the man a present and asks him to remain and preach to
the people, but later in exasperation tells him to go to Mecca when the man

keeps asking him for permission to go. The story is told only for the moral that "there is no consultation in love"—the true lover does not ask the advice of others about love.[364]

Burhān al-Dīn Gharīb likewise told a version of this story in Daulatabad on 20 Sha'bān 734/16 April 1334, with the only difference that the qāżī this time is from Hansi, as in Mīr Khwurd's account.[365] Niẓām al-Dīn Awliyā' and Burhān al-Dīn Gharīb were not concerned with the story's historical accuracy or the identity of the characters when using it for teaching purposes. Yet Mīr Khwurd relates it as a historical event. This is most unlikely, however, since Fakhr al-Dīn Zarrādī as a senior disciple of Niẓām al-Dīn would have been quite familiar with the teaching story, and would scarcely have acted the part of the naive would-be pilgrim. Mīr Khwurd was happy to retain the moral of the story (with his habitual addition of a forgettable Persian verse), but his application of this tale to a historical person, buttressed with first-person testimony from his father, is odd. It is tempting to suspect that Fakhr al-Dīn did actually leave the Deccan surreptitiously to go to Mecca, and that Mīr Khwurd has faithfully recorded the resentment that the sultan's manipulative policies aroused among independent religious figures. Yet he could not refrain from introducing a typical Sufi anecdote into the account to give it more rhetorical force.

Another comparable case is the story, encountered by the traveler Ibn Baṭṭūṭa, of the dervish whose disciples ate a baby elephant, whereupon the enraged mother elephant killed them all, sparing only the master after smelling his breath to determine his innocence. Ibn Baṭṭūṭa was told that the story concerned the famous Iranian Sufi Ibn al-Khafīf (d. 983), who never went to India, but the same anecdote occurs, without names, as a teaching story in the *malfūẓāt* of Burhān al-Dīn Gharīb.[366] In terms of the interpretation of a hagiography like *Siyar al-awliyā'*, this kind of example suggests that a great deal of cautious comparison and examination of literary treatment is necessary before the author's strategy as a biographer can be evaluated.

The value of a balanced biographical source like *Siyar al-awliyā'* is all the more apparent when it is compared to unrestrained hagiographies that glorified the authority of Sufi saints to the limit. A good example of this is the late fourteenth-century work entitled *Ḥālāt-i mashāyikh-i Chisht* (*States of the Chishtī shaykhs*), written by Bahā' al-Dīn Maḥmūd "Rāja" Nāgawrī (grandson of the famous Sufi saint Qāżī Ḥamīd al-Dīn Nāgawrī).[367] The text is organized in the form of a chronological chain or *silsila* of the Chishtīs, beginning with the Prophet Muḥammad and concluding after seventeen master-disciple transmissions with the author's own master, 'Imād al-Dīn.[368] Practically every anecdote in the book is a miracle story, mostly related from the oral accounts of 'Imād al-Dīn. The tendency in this kind of extreme hagiography is to stress the fact of holiness rather than its content, as was pointed out earlier. One story in this text brings out this charismatic focus especially well. This is the account of how Muʿīn al-Dīn Chishtī, the founder of the Chishtī order in India, was meditating in the Kaʿba in Mecca, and by divine order was granted the boon that all future disciples of his line would be blessed by God.[369] This promise, which would have been especially appreciated by later Chishtī devotees, tells us nothing about why Muʿīn al-Dīn was so singled out for God's favor, but merely assures us that his authority has divine support until the resurrection. This "blank check," giving unlimited power of mediation to a Sufi saint, is a kind of apotheosis of saintly authority. It will recur not only in Sufi hagiographies but also in political chronicles that legitimize dynasties in the names of Sufi saints.

In dynastic histories, the role of Sufi saints has generally been limited to their influence on politics. This in itself is not surprising, but the extent to which these political portraits have influenced the received image of Sufis has not been sufficiently appreciated. From the viewpoint of the British colonial historians, all of this emphasis on Sufism in the dynastic histories was inexplicable. When Briggs published his translation of Firishta's history in 1829, he omitted the entire concluding section on Sufi saints, on the grounds that it was irrelevant to history.[370] But many of the Mughul-era historians of India felt that inclusion of lives of the saints was a necessary part of their task.[371] The reason for the importance of saints' lives in works of political history is not hard to discover. It is the literary reflex of the quest for legitimacy, dating back to the Seljuk period, which led sultans to regard patronage of Sufism as a vital state policy.

From the viewpoint of historiography, however, ambiguity arises when comparison of Sufi sources with dynastic histories reveals widely differing concepts of the nature of the relationship between Sufis and sultans. The question is further complicated by hagiographies that have been dedicated to rulers or produced in an imperial context; it is always necessary to ask to what extent such a hagiography has been interfered with, as it were, by imperial perspectives. In the same way, Sufi hagiography is a factor in the descriptions of saints refusing to accept land endowments for fear of becoming too closely dependent on the court. Choice of language and narrative structure are necessary ingredients in the complicated and sophisticated process of biographical writing. Whether the Sufi-sultan relationship was portrayed in positive or negative terms, the choice of approach was a choice between historiographies.

The polarity between mystical and royal historiographies should not be taken as absolute and exclusive, but as a symbiotic relationship. In medieval Islamic society, Sufism and the court were never totally separate from one another. For all that the early Chishtīs may have refused land endowments from sultans, they nonetheless relied on gifts (*futūḥ*) from all classes of society, especially the wealthier classes. Many leading Chishtī disciples were members of the court or the administration. Far from being anarchists or even democrats, the Chishtī masters clearly regarded the royal institution, with appropriate Islamic orientation, as the normal form of regulating society. The ambiguity that appears in the gap between the writings of the Sufi *khānqāh* and the court was part of the tension between human nature and the divine order, between the unbounded assertion of imperial authority and the renunciation of human desires, as it was experienced in the Delhi sultanate. The paradoxical symbol of a dervish wearing a crown, and the adoption of courtly ceremonial in Sufi circles, were indications of how close the symbiosis between the two institutions was in practice. Often one and the same author could write both political histories and sacred biographies, or hybrid works uniting the characteristics of both.[372] It is precisely because of this institutional symbiosis that it is necessary to reconsider the classification of literary accounts that annihilate the tension between the two historiographies.[373]

To enumerate and describe the details of the evolution of Sufi biography, and its relation with royal historiography, is beyond the scope of this study, but some general characterizations may be attempted. Although the number of biographical dictionaries of Sufi saints written in Persian is enormous, they have not yet been subjected to scarcely any critical analysis.[374] The principles of selection and arrangement, of inclusion and exclusion, have not been clarified, especially for the larger works. Some criteria are more obvious than others. The monographic biography devoted to a single saint is the simplest category. The next stage of complexity is the anthology (usually indicated by the term *tazkira*, "memoir") of local saints' lives, focused on a single city or town; this is a well-attested genre of Islamic biography, which continues to be produced up to the present day. Yet when we reach the level of organization by Sufi order or lineage, it is necessary to ask a number of questions about the way in which large biographical works have been organized. One place to begin this inquiry is with Sufi genealogies preserved in ritual *shajara* ("tree") documents. Many Sufi shrines preserve such documents, which Sufi initiates would often receive as part of their admission into the order. In written biographies of the pre-Mughul period there is not much of a problem with classification by order, since fewer Sufi orders were active in India and the lines of affiliation remained fairly clear. But by the sixteenth century, a new phenomenon of multiple initiations became common. Shaykh Muḥammad Ghaws Gwāliyārī, for example, claimed initiation in twelve different lineages: one Shaṭṭārī, one Madārī, one Uwaysī, one Qādirī, two Chishtī, two Firdawsī, and four Suhrawardī.[375] Under these circumstances it becomes difficult to unravel the different lines of initiation and decide on a method of organization.

In addition, many hagiographers used the archaic system of sects introduced by Hujwīrī in his *Kashf al-maḥjūb* in the eleventh century. Originally adapted from the works of heresiographers, Hujwīrī's system described twelve sects within Sufism, all but two of which were acceptable. In reality this division was based on psychological tendencies attributed to the "founders" of the different sects, although Hujwīrī admitted that scarcely any of these schools existed in a coherent form in his day.[376] This arrangement, which was composed at least a century before the emergence of the recognized Sufi orders, was poorly adapted to describe the historical development of the orders. Later on a parallel model of fourteen families (*chahārdah khānwāda*) came into play, but the imposition of such a model onto hagiographies containing hundreds of individual notices often creates the impression of haphazard and arbitrary arrangement. Yet the construction of linear history is an interpretative act that has been a constant factor in the articulation of social order from antiquity to the present day.[377]

In a recent paper, Bruce Lawrence has raised important questions about the composition of Sufi biographical works, arising from his comparison of two Mughul-era hagiographies written by members of the Qādirī order: ʿAbd al-Ḥaqq Dihlawī's *Akhbār al-akhyār* and Dārā Shikūh's *Safīnat al-awliyā'*. His research has shown that the two works exhibit widely diverging concepts of the Qādirī order and its linear development.[378] It is clear that extensive comparative analysis of many different hagiographies will be necessary before we can form a coherent picture of the way in which the historical construction of Sufism took shape in India.

Beyond the technical problem of lineages is the more substantive issue of political context. The hagiographies of the Mughul period were composed in an era of imperial expansion, which made possible the concept of a pan-Indian scope in historical writing. Despite the momentary expansion of the Tughluq empire in the early fourteenth century to include the south of India as well as Bengal, the dynasties centered on Delhi remained kingdoms of Hindustan (i.e., northern India, especially the Gangetic plain). But with the expansionist policy initiated by Akbar, the Mughuls asserted their dominion over the entire subcontinent as a world imperial gesture. Hagiographies produced in the post-Akbar period reflect this pan-Indian vision of Sufi sainthood, which might be said to carry with it an implicit acknowledgment of Mughul sovereignty. In Mughul-era hagiographies one also finds frequent mention of the activities of earlier Sufi saints with regard to converting the local populace to Islam. This topic is strangely absent in Sufi writings of the thirteenth and fourteenth centuries, reflecting the very restricted arena in which the early Indian Sufis carried out their activities. The new emphasis on conversion uses much of the rhetoric of imperial expansion, in this way linking the ruling power with both Sufi saints and the expansion of the Islamic basis of society. With many portrayals of Sufis and their relations with sultans, a slippage takes place, so that the tension between Sufi historiography and royal historiography becomes blurred. In some cases it becomes impossible to find anything to differentiate a hagiography from a dynastic history. Thus, in a case discussed later in this study (Part III, chap. 10), the anonymous author of a local hagiography of Burhanpur took up entire passages from the dynastic historian Firishta to complete his biographies of the Chishtī saints of Khuldabad. If anything, this text (*Fatḥ al-awliyā'*) has a much more stridently imperialistic tone than does Firishta. Rather than characterize this text as a hagiography with an imperial dedication, it may be better to call it an imperial manifesto with a hagiographical extension.

The subsequent development of Sufi hagiography after the Mughul period is a subject that still awaits investigation, but it may safely be predicted that questions of new political and social contexts will prove to be just as important as in earlier ages. The topic of conversion to Islam, which authors of the Mughul period used to make a connection between Sufi saints and political power, takes on an altogether different hue in Urdu hagiographies of the nineteenth and twentieth centuries. Clearly under pressure from the Christian missionaries who had free reign in British India, Muslim authors reconceived the role of the Sufi into that of Islamic missionary. One even finds the English word "mission" transliterated into Urdu in some of these accounts. Many tribal and ethnic groups formulated their own relationship with Islam in terms of contact with some great Sufi master of the past. The nineteenth-century British gazetteers are full of oral traditions that relate the spectacular conversion of large groups to Islam following the miraculous deeds of noted Sufi saints. In more recent times, literature produced in postpartition Pakistan under the auspices of the Awqaf Department reflects government-approved interpretations of the historical roles of Sufi saints. And local hagiographies continue to be produced for the benefit of pilgrims and devotees.

Within this context we may consider the more recent hagiographical works devoted to the Sufis of Khuldabad. In the post-Mughul period, two such works, both written in Persian, claim our attention: Āzād Bilgrāmī's *Rawẓat al-awliyā'* (*Garden of the saints*), written in 1152/1740, and Sabzawārī's *Sawāniḥ* (*Incidents*), completed in 1189/1775. Āzād (1116/1704–1200/1786), whose name has already been mentioned, was a well-known scholar and poet in Arabic and Persian.[379] Although he came from a learned family in Awadh, he settled in the Deccan in Dhū al-Qa'da 1152/January 1740, and remained for seven years at a Sufi hospice in Aurangabad. He was also attached to the court of the Nizams, a dynasty whose first three representatives were buried at Khuldabad. *Rawẓat al-awliyā'* is one of his earlier productions, but it shows a careful scholarly approach, based on a thorough knowledge of the manuscripts of *malfūẓāt* texts as well as dynastic histories such as that of Firishta. The book covers the Khuldabad Chishtīs and other saints of that locality whose antecedents are less well known, and it concludes with a section on the kings buried there; royal historiography and hagiography are not separated here.[380] The other eighteenth-century work, Sabzawārī's *Sawāniḥ*, is by an otherwise unknown author.[381] It has thirty-one sections, of which about half are devoted to the Chishtīs of Khuldabad and other ancient saints, while the rest concerns the city of Aurangabad and Sufis of the author's own time. The focus of this work is on Khuldabad and Aurangabad as centers of pilgrimage, with extended rhetorical descriptions of tombs and other buildings, along with brief accounts of the annual *ʿurs* festivals. The historiographical attitude of Sabzawārī, like that of Āzād, mixes royal and hagiographical tendencies in the same way that Mughul-era texts did, with the only addition being the presence of the Nizams as inheritors of Mughul sovereignty in the Deccan.

In the twentieth century, more local hagiographies have emerged in Urdu. Most valuable from the historical point of view is *Rawẓat al-aqṭāb* (*Garden of the world-axes*), published in 1931 to record the antiquarian researches of a learned local schoolteacher named Rawnaq ʿAlī.[382] Like Āzād, he relied on a variety of rare manuscript sources, including the *malfūẓāt*, which he surveyed thoroughly.[383] The book describes mainly the Khuldabad Chishtīs, along with a few other early saints, and it has valuable notes and digressions gleaned by the author from his experience in the Hyderabad civil service. He also periodically addresses memorials to the Nizam, requesting his support for renovation and maintenance of saints' and kings' shrines. There are other small books and pamphlets intended for pilgrims and antiquarians.[384] One of the last gestures of the Nizam's government toward these Sufi saints was a hagiographical booklet in Urdu on the Khuldabad Chishtīs, written by the Hindu prime minister of Hyderabad, Dewan Kishen Pershad.[385] Of these modern hagiographies, the most interesting, and the most recent (1988) was written by a Pakistani novelist and poet, Waḥīda Nasīm, under the title *Shāhān-i be-tāj* (*The uncrowned kings*).[386] The book is prefaced by an Urdu *ghazal*, which she has addressed to the principal Khuldabad saints; this poem (translated in the Conclusion, below) has now become a popular religious song there. Of special benefit to pilgrims are the book's extremely detailed accounts of the saintly and royal tombs. These modern works preserve many of the features of medieval imperial historiography in their exaltation of the kings buried in Khuldabad, and they add to it both the element of hagiographic legend and the modern concern with Sufi saints as missionaries of Islam.

To conclude this historiographical orientation, it may suffice to reiterate the interpretive principles that should govern an attempt to take account of the complex phenomenon of Sufism in history. The initial task has been to indicate the distance that separates modern ideologies (especially nationalism) from the medieval culture that produced the texts under investigation. Only then can one formulate the task of restoring the texts to their original political and religious context. Questions of literary genre need to take priority in this investigation, as the different kinds and classifications of writings are sorted out, with attention to the difference between written and oral sources. Questions of authorship and readership need to be addressed in every case also. All these literary and historiographic differences can best be highlighted when we contrast differing accounts of the same events. Then categories of analysis can be elaborated on the basis of the materials themselves, rather than being deduced from some external framework. These are simple enough strictures, hardly novel in terms of literary and historical criticism. But their application in a systematic fashion to materials from medieval Indo-Muslim culture needs to be carried out far more extensively. The remainder of this study is an attempt to apply these principles to the special case of Khuldabad, in the hope of clarifying some of the wider issues relating to the study of Islam in the south Asian subcontinent.

PART II

Chishtī Sufism at Khuldabad

6

From Delhi to the Deccan

What was the nature of the Chishtī establishment of Burhān al-Dīn Gharīb at Khuldabad? After having situated the historiographical problem of interpreting Sufi texts and documents from the Indo-Muslim courts, we are now in a position to construct a picture of the Sufi circle that surrounded Burhān al-Dīn Gharīb at Khuldabad. The enquiry must begin with a reconsideration of the historiography of Sufism in the Deccan, proposing an alternative to the "Warrior Sufi" hypothesis that Richard Eaton advanced with regard to Bijapur. Next follows a discussion of the Turkish conquest of the Deccan and the role of the Sufis, especially with regard to the transfer of the population of Delhi to the second capital in Daulatabad in 1329. Then, on the basis of the primary *malfūẓāt* texts, it will be possible to make a sketch of the Sufi organization in Khuldabad and the religious teachings and practices of Burhān al-Dīn Gharīb and his followers.[1] The picture is rounded out by a consideration of the interaction between these Sufis and the Indian cultural environment.

The Historiography of Sufism in the Deccan

It is difficult to form any coherent picture of the activities of Sufis in the Deccan before the invasions of the Khaljī sultans of Delhi and the Tughluqs' transplantation of the urban and literate Sufis of Hindustan to Daulatabad. Only the contemporary Persian writings of fourteenth-century Sufis and remarks by a few other chroniclers afford any reliable evidence about Sufis in the Deccan. The legends of Deccani Sufis in the biographical works of the sixteenth and seventeenth centuries are sketchy, while the oral material incorporated in nineteenth-century British gazetteers and modern Urdu hagiographies needs to be reconsidered in terms of their specific agendas, which have been discussed above (Part I, chap. 5).[2] The main problem is that the more recent works tend to distort by interpreting traditional material in terms of contemporary issues and ideological conflicts, which did not even exist when the events under consideration occurred.

The difficulty of establishing a definite picture of Deccani Sufis in the absence of contemporary documentation can be seen from the example of the Junaydī order, which has been recently studied by Muhammad Suleman Siddiqi. Some excerpts from ʿAyn al-Dīn Ganj al-ʿIlm's (d. 795/1393) lost Arabic biographical work on Indian Sufism, *Aṭwār al-abrār*, are preserved in a genealogical scroll in the Junaydī shrine in Gulbarga compiled in the seventeenth century.[3] These excerpts are limited by the narrow purpose of an initiatic genealogy, which is designed to record the legitimacy of the transmission of Sufism to the recorder of the genealogy. Besides this unique fourteenth-century source, we are dependent on fairly recent dynastic chronicles and modern hagiographies for any account of the Junaydīs. What follows is the reconstruction of the Junaydī order that can be gleaned from these recent works.

The first figure in this chain was ʿAlī Jīwarī, a Sufi who grew up and studied in Delhi, went to Daulatabad in the general migration and is said to have died there in 734/1333–34.[4] One of his many students in Daulatabad was Sirāj al-Dīn Junaydī, a descendant of the famous Sufi Junayd Baghdādī, after whom the order was named. He is said to have been born in Peshawar in 680/1281–82, arrived in Daulatabad in 707/1307–8, and moved on to Gulbarga in 770/1368–69, where he was buried in 781/1379–80.[5] The ease with which recent hagiographers record a date like 707/1307 for his arrival in the Deccan is a cause for suspicion, since there was at that time no establishment of religious scholars or Sufis in Daulatabad, prior to the migration from Delhi in 729/1329. He is generously credited with having converted many "idolaters" to Islam during his stay in the village of Kodchian after leaving Daulatabad. Minhāj al-Dīn Tamīmī also studied with ʿAlī Jīwarī in Daulatabad, but is supposed to have left the capital for Gulbarga in 730/1330, much before his fellow students Sirāj al-Dīn and ʿAyn al-Dīn.[6] ʿAyn al-Dīn "Ganj al-ʿIlm" ("treasury of knowledge"), who was born in Delhi in 700/1300–1, studied in Daulatabad with ʿAlī Jīwarī, Shams al-Dīn Damghānī, and others until he went further south to Sagar in 737/1336–37, and to Bijapur in 773/1371–72 where he died in 795/1393. He was a prolific author in subjects such as history and Sufism, and had many disciples.[7]

In the cases of Sirāj al-Dīn Junaydī and ʿAyn al-Dīn Ganj al-ʿIlm there is some documentation from a nonhagiographical source: Firishta in the early seventeenth century made a number of comments about the Junaydīs' relations with the Bahmanī court in Gulbarga, and also cited ʿAyn al-Dīn's historical treatise *Mulḥaqāt-i ṭabaqāt-i Nāṣirī* as one of his sources.[8] On the basis of the above information, one may conclude that there were learned Sufis in Daulatabad who were not Chishtīs, who later migrated from Daulatabad to Gulbarga and Bijapur, although possibly not until after these cities became prominent in the Bahmanī empire. Little else can be said about the Junaydī order. Aside from an unproven assertion about one Sufi's role in converting Hindus to Islam, the modern hagiographer makes no attempt to characterize these Sufis except to extol their learning. They remain vague legends with giant shadows.[9]

The evidence of modern hagiographies and gazetteers about the development of Indian Sufism cannot be accepted at face value. The ideological concerns of these later works fall too easily into extraneous modern patterns that do not fit with the evidence from the earliest sources. Here it is necessary to give detailed consideration to the work of Richard Eaton in his well-researched and original study on *Sufis of Bijapur*. This was the first detailed monograph on the development of Sufism in the Deccan, and despite the particular criticisms that follow, Eaton's study must be considered as an original and ground-breaking study of Indian Sufism. In the absence of contemporary source material for this early period, Eaton was forced to rely on nineteenth-century sources for his analysis of the extension of Sufism to the Deccan frontier in Bijapur. Eaton did not have access to the fourteenth-century sources on the Sufis of Khuldabad, and did not take account of the position of Daulatabad in the development of Deccan Sufism. Using Bernard Cohn's geographical theory of "core zones" forming stable socio-political units and transitional "shatter zones" comprising unstable invasion and migration zones, Eaton described the Bijapur plateau as a "shatter zone" straddling the "cultural fault zone" between the Marathi and Kannada cultural areas.[10] This geographical view of Bijapur as a cultural frontier led Eaton to suggest that "Muslim influence either in the form of political power or the settlement of Sufis could find the most fertile soil in such a shatter zone where Islam represented a third culture system located between the nuclei of two non-Muslim cultures."[11] This intriguing notion does not apply at all to Daulatabad and Khuldabad, which formed a Muslim political center and a Sufi center in the former Yadava capital in the Maratha heartland. The successful transplantation of the Sufi tradition from Delhi to Daulatabad must be explained on other grounds than the geo-cultural frontier theory. Abandoning the frontier theory also requires a critique of its major concomitant, the controversial "Warrior Sufi" theory.[12]

In setting out the grounds for the Warrior Sufi theory, Eaton rightly saw that the British gazetteers had greatly exaggerated the role of Sufis in converting Hindus to Islam. Scholars who had relied on the gazetteers, like Thomas Arnold in his turn-of-the-century *Preaching of Islam*, accepted the picture of Sufis as peaceful missionaries in order to counteract the inaccurate image of Islam being spread by the sword. The problem with this image of Sufis as missionaries is that it was largely based on two late and tendentious historiographies: Mughul imperialism, which recast Sufis into the role of proclaimers of Mughul sovereignty, and the missionary Protestantism of British administrators, an attitude so polemical that it called forth novel missionary and apologetic responses from Hindus, Muslims, and Sikhs.

Modern Muslims have accepted this image, especially since it also fit in with the desire of Indian-born Muslims to link their religious origins to eminent Sufi saints (see Part II, chap. 8, below).[13] Eaton dismissed the portrait of peaceful Sufi missionaries on the grounds that it was a legend based on a pious ideal of pacifism and concocted to serve the cult of saints; any tradition with cultic value, according to this view, is to be viewed with suspicion. Eaton therefore accepted the opposing traditions of Sufi militancy, on the grounds that no cultic value or saintly ideal was involved. Making comparisons with the frontier pickets (*ribāṭs*) that Muslim warriors maintained in other parts of the Islamic world, he suggested that the Sufis were warriors (*ghāzīs*, *bābās*) associated with the armies of the Delhi sultans, and that for a period of perhaps half a century, between the Khaljī invasions and the establishment of the Bahmanī empire (i.e., from 1296 to 1347), militant Sufis played the most important role in establishing a Muslim presence in the southern frontier of the Deccan. "The Warrior Sufi thus appears as the most typical kind of Sufi during [this period]."[14] When examined in the light of the contemporary materials from the Sufis of Daulatabad, however, the examples and comparisons that Eaton used do not sustain the concept of "Warrior Sufis."

To begin from a methodological point of view, the Warrior Sufi theory is questionable at face value in its unconscious projection of the image of fanaticism. The concept of the Muslim fanatic is one that has a long history in European literature, but it reached its apogee in the age of European imperialism. The Sufi and dervish orders did in fact act as agents of opposition to colonial domination in many Islamic countries, primarily because they formed one of the only Islamic social institutions that endured when tottering political regimes fell under the blows of European expansion.[15] The European response was to paint a picture of Muslim fanaticism resisting the civilizing forces of modernity. Thus we find the "Mad Mullah" of Somalia, the fanatical mourids of the Caucasus, the crazed assassins who served the Pir Pagaro in Sind, and the various religious figures in India that the British called "Wahhabis." The phenomenon of self-sacrificing religious activism in the Islamic world is still poorly understood, whether it concerns the Ismaʿīlī "assassins" and Marco Polo's fiction of their hashish use or the modern problem of "terrorism" in the Middle East.[16]

In objecting to the terminology of "fanaticism," I obviously have in mind cases of demonstrated militant religious activism. Eaton's comparison of the Deccani Sufis to the *ghāzī* religious warriors and *bābās* of the Anatolian frontier and the early Ṣafavī state in Iran is inexact on this very point.[17] Contemporary sources show that the mystical philosophy and social role of the Chishtīs of Daulatabad differed markedly from that of the Turkish *bābās* and the Ṣafavīs in Iran, which both combined radical elements of Shīʿism with tribal military affiliations. The early Chishtīs were generally either urban Sufis with close connections to the court or else reclusive teachers who maintained their lodges in remote areas. Though there is no comparable documentation for the teaching activities of the early Bijapuri Sufis, the evidence does not permit us to characterize them as militant, and in fact scarcely permits any characterization at all. In cases where there is no firm evidence of militance, it is best to avoid descriptions of Sufis as people "who granted a quasi-mystical, quasi-militant leader an unquestioning and even fanatical obedience."[18]

Rejecting the legend of Warrior Sufis does not mean that we must rehabilitate the image of Sufis as pacifists who always disapproved of violence. Part of this discussion hinges on the use of the word "Sufi", whether we mean by this the self-conscious participants and interpreters of the Sufi tradition or the social-historical definition, which treats as a Sufi anyone popularly regarded as a saint within an Islamic milieu (Eaton's approach relies on the latter). If we follow the first approach, taking figures like Nizām al-Dīn Awliyā' as Sufis par excellence, then it is safe to say from the available evidence that he was not a warrior, but a literate urban religious figure. It is also true that all of the great Sufis of the Chishtī order had followers who were soldiers. Several of Burhan al-Dīn Gharib's followers fought battles against Hindu opponents as soldiers in the armies of the Tughluqs. These followers were not fully qualified successors (*khalīfa*s) of the shaykh, however, but something analogous to lay followers. The Chishtīs did not disapprove of the soldier's profession on principle, but regarded it as a worldly occupation that, like any other, limited the possibilities of spiritual advancement. Moreover, according to contemporary sources the military activities of Sufi disciples had no missionary or "communalist" flavor at all. My rejection of the image of Warrior Sufis simply means that the principal bearers of the Sufi tradition in India (i.e., the shaykhs) were in general full-time religious leaders, and did not themselves take part in military activities, though some of their followers did.

The evidence for the Warrior Sufi has intrinsic weaknesses, as in the story of Ṣūfī Sarmast of Bijapur, which shows signs of having been composed in recent times on the model of other legends of Deccani Sufis. In one version he was said to have come to the Deccan with seven hundred followers, with whose aid he battled a Hindu raja and converted many Hindus to Islam. Another source maintained that he was an Arab who came to Mathura in northern India, and from there embarked for Sagar in the Deccan with 1,407 disciples riding in palanquins. Doubtless the numbers used here are to some extent based on multiplications of the mystical number seven. The reader familiar with the story of the Chishtīs of Daulatabad will not fail to see a striking resemblance in both versions of Ṣūfī Sarmast's story: the two brothers Muntajib al-Dīn and Burhān al-Dīn Gharīb also are said to have come to

Daulatabad with either seven hundred or fourteen hundred disciples (the sources vary on this point), and their arrival in Daulatabad is commemorated by the "Masjid-i Chahārdih Ṣad Awliyā'," the mosque of fourteen hundred saints. This tradition (discussed in detail below) is very old and occurs in a *malfūẓāt* text written by one of Burhan al-Dīn Gharīb's disciples.[19] The number seven hundred (or its double, fourteen hundred) is probably significant as a round multiple of the sacred number seven, rather than as a statistical count of the migration of Sufis. The similarity in the number of disciples raises the suspicion that Ṣūfī Sarmast's disciples were assigned to him by a modern hagiographer in imitation of the Sufis of Daulatabad. Ṣūfī Sarmast's military exploits also begin to look questionable when compared with a nineteenth-century gazetteer's account of Burhān al-Dīn Gharīb's supposed militancy. According to this version, Burhān al-Dīn Gharīb came to the Deccan with fourteen hundred disciples considerably before ʿAlā' al-Dīn Khaljī's invasion in 1294, and upon the latter's arrival assisted him in his siege of the fortress of Deogir.[20] This is clearly impossible, if we are right in assuming that Burhān al-Dīn Gharīb came to the Deccan over thirty years later, in the general migration imposed by Sultan Muḥammad ibn Tughluq in 1329.[21] If nineteenth-century legends projected an image of militancy onto the retiring and urbane Burhān al-Dīn Gharīb, they may certainly have done the same with Ṣūfī Sarmast. The similarities of these accounts of militancy are so close that they appear to have been coined in the same mint. This evidence suggests an interpretation of Warrior Sufi legends that Eaton considered but rejected: the tales of Sufis battling and converting Hindus may be a garbled interpretation of political history (the invasion from Delhi), in which conquerors were replaced by saints. The Warrior Sufi stories were folk-Muslim legends with complex origins that romanticized and legitimized the conquest of the Deccan.

The sources and motives for the legends of Warrior Sufis can partly be sought in the heroic songs of Indian bards, which provided models for the portrayal of saints as heroes. Eaton has rightly pointed out that some legends seem to confuse putative Sufis like Ṣūfī Sarmast with Turkish military leaders who fought Hindu rajas, so that "this represents a clear confusion of the Muslim hagiographic tradition with political history as remembered by Hindus of the area."[22] The opponent of Ṣūfī Sarmast, Kumāra Rām, was by the sixteenth century the hero of epics and legends still found among the Hindus of Karnataka.[23]

A brief comparison of this finding with other legends of Indian leaders battling against the Turkish invaders suggests that these tales are part of a typical pattern of royal sagas and lays exalting the gestes of local heroes. Bardic composition in the service of royalty is a common literary genre that is well attested in Indian literature. This class of legends includes the heroic lays on the story of Prithviraj, the last Rajput king of Ajmer and Delhi, which

James Tod used in his antiquarian researches on the history of Rajasthan in the 1830s. Another example is Naiñsī's late bardic account of Raja Hammīra, which conflates the exploits of Hammīra with those of his descendants against the Turkish rulers of Malwa, erroneously maintaining that Hammīra captured Sultan Muḥammad ibn Tughluq in single combat, although in reality the two never met.[24] These legendary writings are essentially heroic, the presence of more or less religious language being an incidental accretion from a later age.

Developing a distinction put forward by Bruce Lawrence, we may hypothesize that the legends of Warrior Sufis derive from the saints' Indian followers (of whom only a portion may have formally become Muslims), who participated in the popular cult of pilgrimage to Sufi shrines. Nothing would be more natural for these Indian followers than to perceive the saints in terms of popular Indian heroes like Hammīra or Kumāra Rām, and to make them into warriors capable of fabulous battles with recalcitrant Hindu rajas. In this way legend could remake a shadowy figure like Ṣūfī Sarmast into a hero, and from the likeness of a name portray Pīr Maʿbar K'handā'it as a Hercules wielding an iron sword (from Hindi *k'handa*, "sword, bar").[25] Only from the modern point of view does it appear ironic that the Indian folk imagination has transformed popular Sufi saints into Muslim warriors righteously fighting the infidel. From this point of view, the hostility and violence that rajas are portrayed as offering to the Sufis appear to be elements of the dramatic tension necessary for a good story, not a historical account of the communalistic Hindu-Muslim confrontation of today.[26]

Another possible source for the Warrior Sufi legends was the converse religious process of warriors becoming saints, in which Turkish warriors' tombs became the centers of Muslim martyr cults, sometimes with underlying Hindu elements. The most famous and ancient of the saintly warriors was Sālār Masʿūd of Bahraich in Uttar Pradesh, a soldier from Maḥmūd of Ghazni's (d. 1030) time who is celebrated as Ghāzī Miyāñ ("holy warrior"). Sālār Masʿūd's annual festival is observed according to the Hindu calendar, and contains other Hindu features such as a sacred wedding and elements of sun worship. European observers have found it remarkable that as many Hindus as Muslims attend this festival, in honor of a figure whose main activity, according to the story, was killing Hindu infidels. One explanation for this phenomenon is that in this way both Hindus and Hindu converts to Islam could neutralize the exclusiveness and foreignness of official Islam by integrating it into existing popular religious structures. Thus Hindus have rationalized attending his festival by saying that, despite his violence against Hindus, he must have been on a divinely ordained mission to have succeeded so well.[27]

Many an abandoned Muslim tomb in India has become the focus of a vague sort of worship.[28] The large size of some tombs has often given rise to legends of saints nine feet tall (*naugaza*). It would not be surprising if soldiers in the Deccan assumed after their death a saintly stature quite out of proportion with their earthly lives. Tombs were in any case a novel type of building in India, where cremation is the normal means of disposal of the dead; the only similar structures in Indian architecture were palaces, temples, and hero-stones. Thus it is natural to find the popular imagination attributing both royal heroism and saintliness to the tomb-dweller, regardless of who it may have been. We shall find that the same process of sanctification occured with the kings who were buried at Khuldabad and borrowed holiness from the tombs of saints (Part III, chap. 10, below).

This process of transformation of warriors and even ordinary people into martyrs and saints seems to have begun early, but it was especially common in the late fourteenth century and was often sponsored by royal patrons. A case of popular martyr veneration is the site of the oldest Islamic inscription still in place within India, at the tomb of one Ibrāhīm ibn ʿAbd Allāh at Badreswar in Gujarat. The inscription of 554/1159–60 dates the tomb to the period before Turkish rule, and it clearly gives the name of the otherwise unknown occupant of the tomb. Locally, however, it is considered to be the shrine of Laʿl Shahbāz (also the name of a famous saint of Sind), and legend tells of his death as a martyr fighting against the local Hindu raja.[29] An example from Rajasthan is the epitaph of the six martyrs of Bari Khatu, who are described in a Persian verse inscription attached to a graveyard wall. They are said to have attained martyrdom on the day of the ʿĪd festival in 761/1360, after repelling nine attacks by a force of two hundred horsemen.[30]

In Achalpur, a town in eastern Maharashtra, the legend of Shāh Dola ʿAbd al-Raḥmān hearkens back to the heroic days of Maḥmūd of Ghazni. Shāh Dola ("the bridegroom king") is supposed to have been a nephew of Maḥmūd, and, like Sālār Masʿūd, he was called away from his wedding to avenge a Hindu king's insult to a Muslim saint. In a massive battle in 378/988, he punished the king and dispatched many infidels to hell, at the same time cutting off his own head. His mother built him a tomb, but it eventually fell into neglect. So in 770/1368, he appeared to Sultan ʿAlā' al-Dīn Bahmanī in a dream and ordered him to construct the present tomb.[31] In Malwa, Sultan Maḥmūd Shāh Khaljī rebuilt in 859/1454–55 the tomb of Shaykh ʿAbd Allāh Shāh Changāl, and in an inscription he told how the saint with a large force of soldiers had destroyed the idols in a local Hindu temple and brought about the conversion of Rājā Bhōj to Islam; this is supposed to have taken place either at the time of Maḥmūd of Ghazna or at the beginning of the thirteenth century, at the time of the Khaljī invasion.[32] The same sort of veneration of fallen Muslim warriors took place on the Anatolian frontier as well.[33] The involvement of royal patrons in the erection of shrines to martyrs suggests that the symbolism of holy war against infidels was politically useful to Muslim kings of the fourteenth century. Recent research suggests that the symbolism of holy war in Anatolia was created retrospectively by official Ottoman historians, the religious scholars who worked in the bureaucracy.[34]

There is further reason to suppose that some Muslim rulers in India were quite aware of the tendency to deify kings and warriors, and that they deliberately played upon this religious impulse to advance their own fortunes. Otherwise it is difficult to explain the frequency with which we find reference to kings treated as saints. One of the disciples of the Chishtī leader Naṣīr al-Dīn "Chirāgh-i Dihlī" admitted to having made a pilgrimage to the tomb of Sultan ʿAlā' al-Dīn Khaljī (d. 1296), where he tied a string to the tomb, as people did seeking to have their wishes fulfilled.[35] One of the more curious examples of veneration of kings is the "tomb" of Sultan Muḥammad ibn Tughluq's tooth, built in the village of Ranjani in the Bir district of Maharashtra, evidently during a Deccan campaign in the fourteenth century; one would like to know more about how this structure came to be built.[36] Two fourteenth-century kings of the sultanate of Maʿbar (Madura) in the far south died in battle with the rajas of Vijayanagar, and they are popularly revered as saints and martyrs.[37] Thanks to the writings of royal chroniclers, it is well known that Aḥmad Shāh Bahmanī (d. 1436) assiduously cultivated eminent Muslim mystics such as Gīsū Darāz (d. 1422) in the Deccan and Shāh Niʿmat Allāh Walī (d. 1431) from Iran, so that he himself received the title of "saint" (*walī*) and used it in his coins and inscriptions. He is still widely regarded as a holy man in the Deccan. It is less well known that at his annual festival at Bidar, which is celebrated by the Hindu calendar, the head of the Lingayats (a reform movement of Shiva worshippers) performs the chief rituals.[38] Aḥmad Shāh Walī's son Aḥmad Shāh II (d. 1458) had close relations with Brahmans in spite of protests from Muslim religious scholars, and members of the Dattatreya cult eulogized him as their protector.[39] We may suppose that these kings and perhaps others anticipated Akbar in manipulating both Muslim and Hindu religious symbolism to secure legitimacy with all their subjects.[40]

To summarize, there is reason to question the geo-cultural frontier notion of Islamic expansion in the Deccan, and there are a number of alternate explanations that challenge the theory of Warrior Sufis, whether with respect to Daulatabad or Bijapur. Folk Indian origins combined with royal sponsorship may well be responsible for the martial attributes with which modern hagiographies clothed the Deccani Sufis, as well as for the saintly qualities assumed by otherwise worldly kings and soldiers after death. As a result, the legend of Warrior Sufis may have served cultic purposes far more profound than the later theory of peaceful Sufi missionaries. In order to understand the nature of the Sufi presence in Khuldabad, we shall have to abandon as well the notion, as old as al-Biruni, of the Arab-Islamic and Indic civilizations as static entities opposed at every point.[41] This abstraction covers up the complex interaction of lives, symbols, and societies in medieval India.

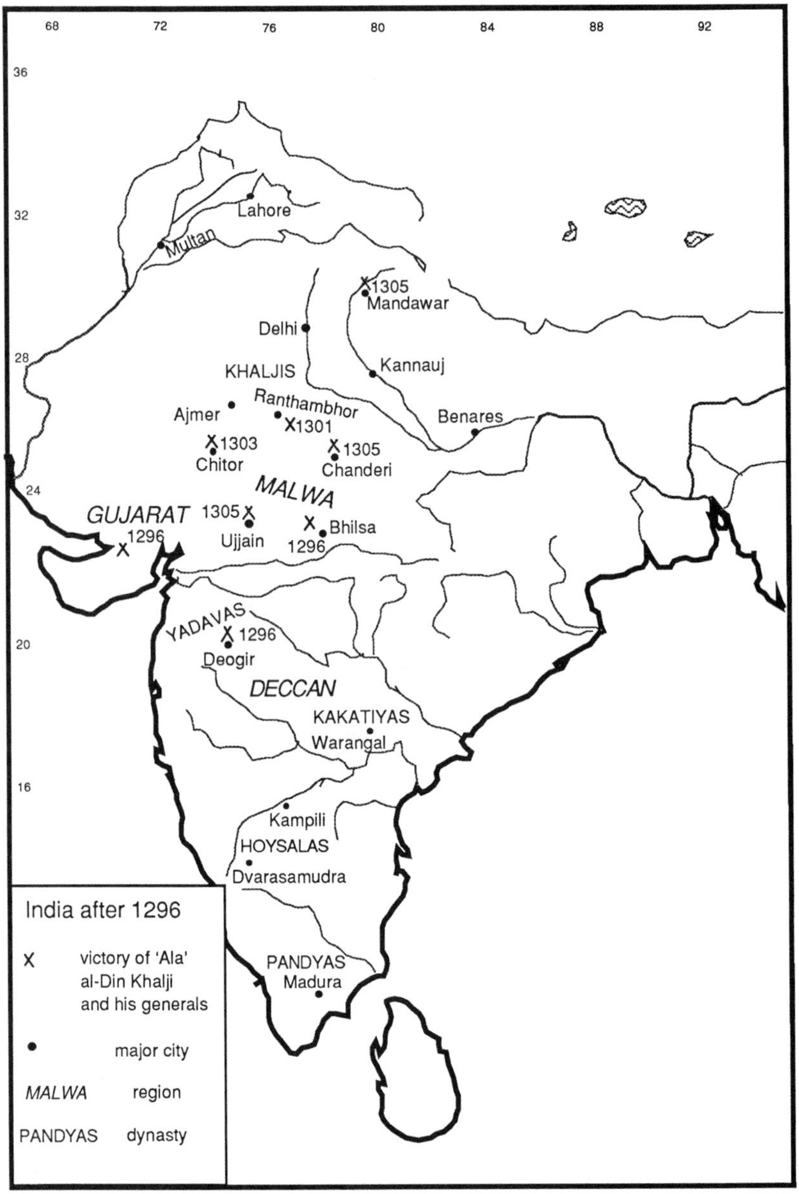

Map 2. India after 1296

Sufism and the Turkish Conquest of the Deccan

It has long been recognized that the Turkish sultans' raids into Indian territories were not motivated by religious fanaticism or iconoclasm, but were quests for booty. Yet the sultans had in mind perennial strategic concerns on the northwestern frontier when they planned the raids on India. The Ghūrid sultans' attack on Hindustan in 602/1205–6 was a raid designed to raise funds to reequip armies depleted by war against the Khwārazm Shāh; the ostensible goal was to raise a force against the pagan Qara Khitai Turks.[42] After the Ghūrids' conquest, the Turkish sultanate of Delhi continued to encroach on Indian territory to the east (the Gangetic plain and Bengal), but the rulers of Delhi had to be constantly on guard against attacks from the ancient northwest invasion route, which they themselves had followed. Mongol troops led by Chingīz Khān reached the Indus River in 1221, and continued to attack India for over a century, threatening Delhi itself in 1303 and 1327. Thus Sultan Balban in 1247 advocated raids on the Indian kingdoms as a means of acquiring the massive funds needed for fielding an army to defend against the Mongol threat.[43] ʿAlāʾ al-Dīn Khaljī's surprise attack on Deogir (Dēvagīrī) in 1296 was certainly a remarkable success for Turkish arms, and it had the extra benefit of solving his personal problems at court with a smashing military victory and a triumphal return to Delhi; the vast wealth of Deogir put ʿAlāʾ al-Dīn into a secure political position and strengthened his chances for succession to the throne. But the invasion of the Deccan was strategically a continuation of the Turkish sultans' policy of using the loot from Indian cities to strengthen defences against central Asian attackers. In this way campaigning against the Indian kingdoms was seen as a necessary part of the Delhi sultanate's battle for survival.

The Turks (then known in Sanskrit inscriptions as Turuṣkas or Turukas) were known for their fighting ability in the Deccan considerably before the Khaljī invasion; the court poet Narendra briefly mentioned the Turkish cavalry in a Marathi composition presented in the Yadava court in 1291. Some skirmishes between Turkish troops and Yadava forces may have taken place as early as 1278, for a Sanskrit royal inscription of that year glorified Ramachandra Yadava as a "Great Boar in succouring the earth from the oppression of the Turukas."[44] ʿAlāʾ al-Dīn Khaljī conceived his invasion of the Yadava kingdom well in advance, after learning of the wealth of Deogir during his highly successful raid on Malwa in 691/1292.[45] The raid was a secret project, which he concealed from his uncle, Sultan Jalāl al-Dīn Fīrūz. ʿAlāʾ al-Dīn Khaljī had made up his mind to seize the throne, and his allies' demands for funds required him to amass an enormous booty. Deogir was too tempting a target to pass up. On the pretext of subduing the recalcitrant ruler of Chanderi in Malwa, ʿAlāʾ al-Dīn departed in 695/1296. In a lightning raid, he surprised the raja in Deogir while the Yadava army was absent and obtained his submission. The vast wealth that Deogir yielded up to plunder gave ʿAlāʾ al-Dīn Khaljī the confidence to return to his estates in Kara and assassinate his uncle at their next meeting, only five months after his departure. He also married a daughter of the raja. Thereafter the Yadavas were technically tributaries of Delhi required to make annual payments, although in their inscriptions they continued to pretend independence, and even falsely claimed to have conquered Qannauj and Varanasi (Benares). An inscription of 1298, interestingly, is a grant for the maintenance of a mosque for Muslims in the Thana district, a sign that the Yadavas, like other Hindu rulers, regarded religion as irrelevant to their relations with the Turks.[46] In any case, the Yadavas administered their kingdom much as before.

The collision of the Turks and the Yadavas produced not only military conflict, but at least one tragic romance, the story of Dewal Rānī and Khiżr Khān. ʿAlāʾ al-Dīn Khaljī had captured and married the queen of Gujarat, Kamala Devī, after her husband fled before the armies of Delhi in 698/1299.[47] The Yadavas then began to neglect their tribute to Delhi, especially after seeing the failure of the sultan's invasion of the Deccan kingdom of Warangal in 1302–3. ʿAlāʾ al-Dīn Khaljī sent his general Malik Kafūr with an army to punish the Yadavas. Malik Kafūr also had instructions to find the fugitive king of Gujarat and demand the princess Dewal, since her mother Kamala Devī was pining away in Delhi and longed to see her daughter, who was still quite young. Singhana the crown prince of Deogir also sought the hand of Dewal, and so her father consented and sent her under escort to Deogir. Malik Kafūr still managed to capture her near Ellora and sent her to Delhi in 706/1307, where she grew up together with the sultan's son Khiżr Khān. Though mere children at the time, the two fell in love, according to Amīr Khusraw's romantic poem *Dewal Rānī Khiżr Khān*, which was written mostly in 1315 at the request of the lovelorn prince and heir apparent. Eventually they were married, despite the initial opposition of Khiżr Khān's mother, and the happy couple lived a life of pleasure and festivity, unaware that the scheming Malik Kafūr was estranging the sultan from his son. During the last illness of ʿAlāʾ al-Dīn, the sultan was persuaded of Khiżr Khān's rebellious intentions and had him imprisoned. Malik Kafūr seized the throne when the sultan died and had Khiżr Khān blinded, but the usurper was himself assassinated, reportedly after forty days, in 717/1316. The blind prince and his princess lived for two comparatively happy years in Gwalior fort, until Quṭb al-Dīn Mubārak had Khiżr Khān and other possible rivals killed after a cousin unsuccessfully attempted revolt.[48]

To return to events in the Deccan, the infamous Malik Kafūr, after sending Dewal Rani to Delhi, had time to compel a new submission from the Yadavas. He brought Raja Ramachandra himself as a captive to Delhi, where Sultan ʿAlāʾ al-Dīn entertained him graciously for six months, so much so that Ramachandra remained loyal to Delhi in subsequent years. When the danger of Mongol attacks on the northwestern frontier lessened, the sultan sent Malik Kafūr on another expedition to Warangal in 709/1309, this time asking Ramachandra to render assistance. The siege was successful, and the fortress yielded in 709/1310, enabling Malik Kafūr to return to Delhi loaded with booty.

By now the fantastic wealth acquired from the Deccan had whetted ʿAlāʾ al-Dīn's appetite for more. Inspired by Malik Kafūr's reports of the kingdoms farther south, the sultan authorized the general to lead a new expedition. The army reached Deogir in 710/1311, where Yadava officers conducted them to the borders of the Hoysala kingdom centered at Dwarasamudra. There was constant warfare between the monarchs of the south, who never seem to have considered an alliance against the Turks. The Hoysala capital was undefended, since Raja Ballala was attacking his neighbors in Madura. Consequently Malik Kafūr easily forced the submission of Ballala and even forced him to lead the Delhi armies on to Madura. Great wealth from the temples of Srirangam and Chidambaram fell into Malik Kafūr's hands, though the Pandyan kings of Madura eventually succeeded in routing the Turkish forces. Muslim troops in the service of the Pandyan king resisted the invading Turks just like the other troops, and only submitted when the king retreated, indicating that here, too, religious factors were irrelevant to the invasion.[49] Still, Sultan ʿAlāʾ al-Dīn was overjoyed at the treasures displayed on Malik Kafūr's return to Delhi in 711/1311.

Up to this point, the Delhi sultans' policy toward the Deccan was simply to raid its treasure-cities, but after the rebellion of Ramachandra's successor Singhana, they were drawn toward annexing the region. The expansion of the Delhi sultanate would ultimately strain its administrative resources to the breaking point, and conquest no longer permitted the ruthless appropriation of wealth that had been possible in formerly enemy territory. Malik Kafūr marched to Deogir to receive the tribute of the Hoysala king, and Singhana's revolt was crushed in 1313. Sultan ʿAlāʾ al-Dīn had coins minted in Deogir, signifying its incorporation into his empire. Malik Kafūr extended a guarantee of peace to the local people and ruled leniently in Deogir until 1315. He then handed over the administration of Deogir to ʿAyn al-Mulk so that he could attend on the sultan on his deathbed, but ambition overpowered him and led him to usurp the throne for a brief time. The confusion in Delhi permitted Harpala Devi, a son-in-law of Ramachandra, to seize Deogir and declare himself king. When the new sultan, Quṭb al-Dīn Mubārak, consolidated his authority late in 1317, he turned to the reconquest of Deogir. The Turkish army's devastation of the countryside cowed Harpala Devi into flight, but the last Yadava king was captured and executed in the presence of the sultan of Delhi. In 717/1317–18 Quṭb al-Dīn renamed Deogir as Quṭbābād and had coins minted there to honor the event. Quṭb al-Dīn's favorite, Khusraw Khān, who had led the Delhi army on this expedition, remained in the Deccan to

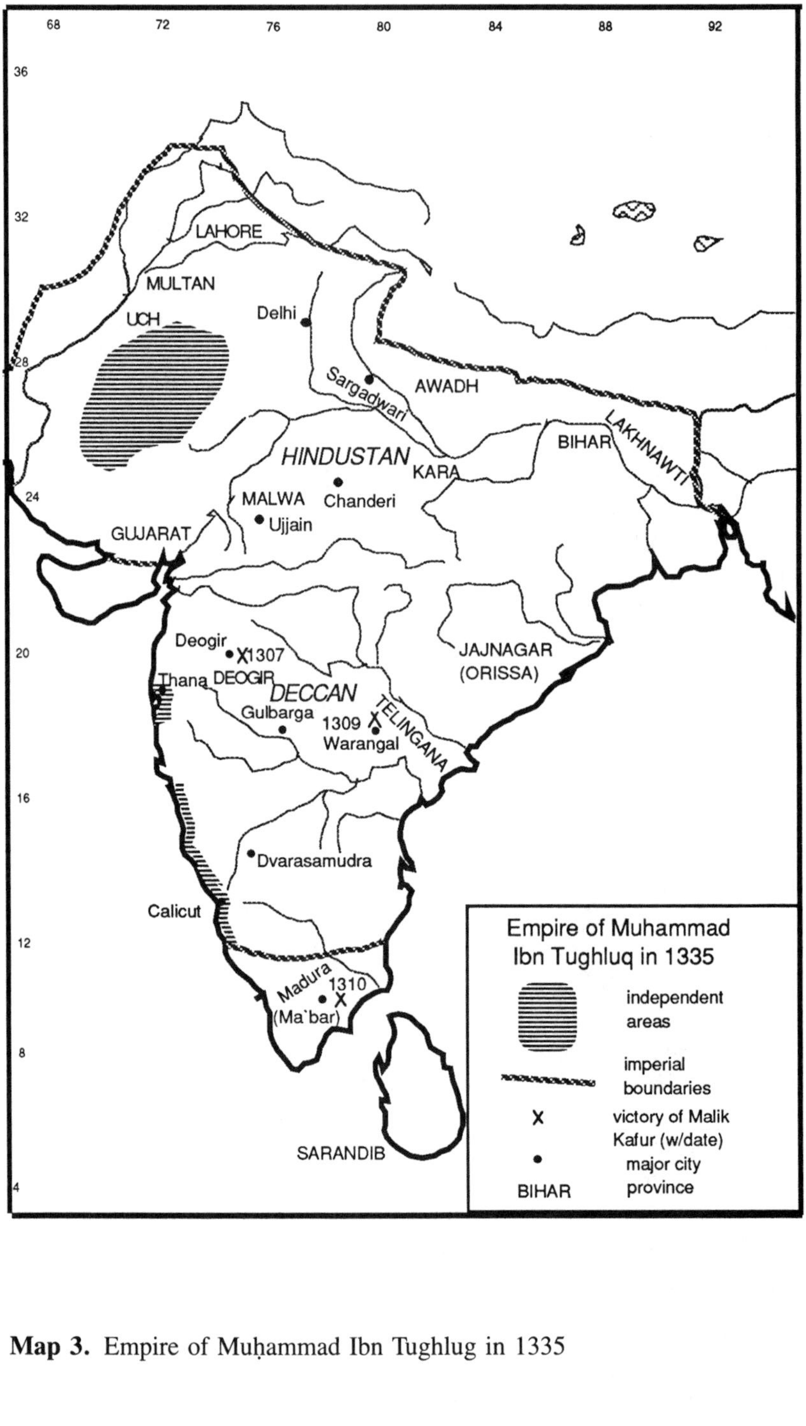

Map 3. Empire of Muḥammad Ibn Tughlug in 1335

quash a revolt by the newly appointed governor of Deogir, Malik Yaklakhī, and unsuccessfully sought to conquer Maʿbar (Madura). New intrigues at court caused the sultan to summon Khusraw Khān to Delhi, where accusations of treason proved all too true, as he assassinated Quṭb al-Dīn in 720/1320 and assumed the title of Sultan Naṣīr al-Dīn for a few short months. Once again, Delhi's tributaries in the Warangal, Deogir, and Dwarasamudra became restive.

The accession of Ghiyās al-Dīn Tughluq took place in a chaotic political situation, but by 721/1321 he was ready to send his son Ulugh Khān, the future Sultan Muḥammad ibn Tughluq, to establish control over all the tributary kingdoms of the Deccan. Another son, Maḥmūd Khān, was placed in charge of Deogir. In 1323 Ulugh Khān succeeded in conquering both Warangal and Maʿbar, and he sent the kings of both countries in chains to Delhi. The new administration was actually unchanged from before, as Ulugh Khān retained the Indian officials of the Deccan kingdoms in their places under the charge of Turkish centurions or commanders of one hundred (*amīrān-i ṣada*). Deogir now served as a useful fortress and staging area for the Tughluqs in subsequent Deccan campaigns. Ulugh Khān turned northeast to invade Orissa in 1324, and then had to return to Delhi to face a new Mongol attack across the Indus.[50] As Sultan Muḥammad ibn Tughluq he ascended the throne in 725/1325, after his father died when a building collapsed on him. The Deccan continued to be turbulent, however, since the governor of Sagar, Bahā' al-Dīn Gurshasp, soon staged an unsuccessful revolt in 727/1326–27, and the sultan pursued him to his refuge in the still independent kingdom of Kampila, and conquered it. It was at this time (728/1328) that Sultan Muḥammad ibn Tughluq decided to make Deogir (now called Daulatabad, "flourishing dominion") a second administrative capital of his empire, to ease the task of government. Administering the vast newly conquered territories proved to be too great a task for the Delhi sultanate, however. Warangal soon regained its independence, the governor of Maʿbar threw off his loyalty to Delhi in 734/1333–34, and in 1336 a former Hoysala officer founded the kingdom of Vijayanagar out of the ruins of Kampila.[51]

The original name of the city was Deogir or Dēvagīrī, and contemporary Persian writers continually use this name. The sultans of Delhi subsequently changed the name of the city, as is known from the coins minted there. Quṭb al-Dīn Mubārak Khaljī (r. 716/1316–720/1320) named it after himself as Quṭbābād, but his successors returned to calling it Deogir until Sultan Muḥammad ibn Tughluq revived the name Quṭbābād in 725–27/1325–27. Briefly Sultan Muḥammad ibn Tughluq turned back to the name Deogir in 727/1327, also calling the city Qubbat al-Islām ("dome of Islam"), before settling on the name of Daulatabad in 728/1328.[52] Arab geographers knew Daulatabad as the second capital along with Delhi.[53]

Soon after establishing Daulatabad as second capital, Sultan Muḥammad ibn Tughluq embarked on one of his most ambitious and controversial projects, to transfer the entire Muslim elite of Delhi to Daulatabad. Medieval authors like Ibn Baṭṭūṭa and Baranī distorted and exaggerated the reasons for this move and its extent, maintaining that the sultan's decision was motivated by petty revenge, and that he completely depopulated the city of Delhi with this irrational decision (they commonly use the phrase "the destruction [*takhrīb*] of Delhi"). Since Delhi still remained a capital, it is not possible to accept Baranī's claim that the capital was shifted to Daulatabad, and that Delhi was destroyed. Modern historians, beginning with Mahdi Husain, have shown both Delhi and Daulatabad were capitals, and that substantial policy reasons dictated the transfer of the Muslim religious classes from one city to the other. Since the move to Daulatabad was the basis for the establishment of a Sufi center in Khuldabad, it will be useful to review here the evidence for the sultan's program, and the various interpretations put upon it.

In preparation for the move, Sultan Muḥammad ibn Tughluq had way stations constructed on the road to Deogir in 727/1326–27. Then in 729/1328–29, the royal household left Delhi for the Deccan, and by royal command they were followed by the religious classes (sayyids, Sufis, *ʿulamāʾ*) and other notables. According to a royal chronicler, the sultan went to great pains to ease the transition by paying compensation for the houses left behind in Delhi, providing travel facilities, and offering free hospitality and gifts for the arrival in Daulatabad.[54] The sultan had carefully planned out the city of Daulatabad, with different quarters for the various classes of society, each with its own markets and other facilities.[55]

Nonetheless, writers from the religious classes unanimously condemned the sultan's motives and cruel methods in transferring the population to Daulatabad. Ibn Baṭṭūṭa maintained that the sultan was annoyed by anonymous poison-pen letters that were left for him in the palace, and so decided to destroy the city.[56] The poet ʿIṣāmī, who championed the Bahmanī revolt, said that the sultan was suspicious of the people and wanted to weaken them.[57] ʿIṣāmī also said that the sultan's police dragged reluctant travelers from their homes by the hair and punished them. The journey apparently took place during the hot season, and inflicted a toll of suffering on the unfortunate people of Delhi.[58] The number of emigrants is difficult to estimate. Mahdi Husain's estimate of twelve hundred is apparently based on ʿIṣāmī's mention of six caravans and the figure of fourteen hundred Sufis given in the hagiographies, but this is not reliable in any statistical sense.[59] ʿIṣāmī, whose grandfather perished en route, claims that only a tenth of the emigrants survived the journey, but that appears to be as exaggerated as his claim that Delhi was emptied of all inhabitants.[60]

Sultan Muḥammad ibn Tughluq's aim in moving the Muslims to Daulatabad was not to depopulate Delhi. Only the Muslim elite were forced to move. ʿIṣāmī did not think it necessary to mention the Hindu population of

Delhi, saying only that this act was God's punishment of the Muslims for their corruption. Ibn Baṭṭūṭa's statements about the complete depopulation of the city were exaggerations based on the universal displeasure of the Sufis and *ʿulamā'* forced to migrate to Daulatabad.[61] Baranī and ʿIṣāmī, when describing the removal of the inhabitants of Delhi, clearly only had the Muslims in mind. Sanskrit inscriptions of 1327 and 1328 indicate that Hindus were living and prospering in Delhi at that time.[62] In 1327 the sultan also embarked on a military construction program in Delhi, building walls to connect old Delhi to Siri, forming the area known as Jahānpanāh.[63] This would scarcely have been done if the sultan planned to leave the city. Daulatabad was not to be a replacement for Delhi. Delhi was still the main administrative capital, and coins continued to be minted there in 727/1326–27, 728/1327–28, and 729/1328–29.[64] When Ibn Baṭṭūṭa saw Delhi in 734/1334, Jahānpanāh was a wonderful city showing no signs of having been destroyed.[65]

The transfer of the Muslim elite of Delhi to Daulatabad also had economic factors behind it. Sultan Muḥammad ibn Tughluq, in order to raise the huge army needed for his project of conquering Khurasan, had to increase the tax yield from the Gangetic farm lands, and the transfer of the Muslim residents had the effect of reducing consumption in the old city of Delhi, theoretically lightening the consumption demand on the farmers.[66] The Muslim residents according to Baranī included the elite and their households.[67] The army remained, and the Hindu peasantry was drafted into the Khurasan army and quartered in the empty sectors of the old city.

Sultan Muḥammad ibn Tughluq in moving the Muslim elite to Daulatabad wished to enroll them in his mission of world conquest. He saw their role as that of propagandists who would adapt Islamic religious symbolism to the rhetoric of empire. He apparently believed, like a number of modern interpreters, that the Sufis could by persuasion bring many of the inhabitants of the Deccan to become Muslims.[68] The goal of converting Hindus was for him primarily a means of advancing his own authority. The sultan's project had a certain plausibility. Hindus of means who cast themselves adrift from the moorings of caste society would have to attach themselves to the court to find a secure anchorage.

The principles and teachings of the early Chishtī Sufis encouraged resistance to the sultan's program. Employment in government service was forbidden to senior disciples, since it almost always involved actions disapproved of in Islamic law, such as accepting salaries derived from non-*sharīʿa* taxes. Moreover, acceptance of the sultan's travel directive was potentially in conflict with the territorial organization of *vilāyat*-dominions, the areas over which Sufi masters exercised authority.[69] To obey the sultan's command would mean giving his order precedence over that of the Sufi shaykh, thus violating the sanctity of the master-disciple relationship. In some individual instances, Niẓām al-Dīn Awliya' permitted disciples to join military expeditions as spiritual advisers or to remain in government service, but in most cases the tendency was to back away from engagement with the sultans.

Niẓām al-Dīn Awliyā' did send some Chishtīs south from Delhi to Malwa and the Deccan before the migration to Daulatabad, not as part of a missionary scheme but to meet the needs of particular people. One such disciple was Shaykh Mūsā Deogīrī, who came to visit and ask his advice.[70] Another was Burhān al-Dīn Gharīb's brother, Muntajib al-Dīn (discussed below). Mīr Khwurd speaks respectfully of two brothers, ʿAzīz al-Dīn and Kamāl al-Dīn, who came to their master Niẓām al-Dīn Awliyā' and expressed the wish to travel somewhere. When they took leave of him, he gave each a *jalālī* coin and said to Kamāl al-Dīn, "You be in Malwa," and he told ʿAzīz al-Dīn, "You be in the domain (*vilāyat*) of Deogir." Though ʿAzīz al-Dīn was dissatisfied with receiving a single coin, Kamāl al-Dīn interpreted it as a sign of their future greatness (*jalāl*, "majesty"). Mīr Khwurd remarks that "the lands of Deogir and Telang were all the followers and servants" of ʿAzīz al-Dīn, whom he had met before the latter's death in Deogir; Kamāl al-Dīn's tomb in Dhar (Malwa) later became the resort of the people of that region.[71] Although these two brothers may have successfully extended the influence of the Chishtī order by their activities, their migration occurred partly due to their own initiative, and cannot be considered evidence for a Chishtī missionary movement.

Niẓām al-Dīn also sent one eminent disciple out from Delhi at the request of a general who was leaving on a mission of conquest. Mīr Khwurd relates that Sultan ʿAlā' al-Dīn Khaljī ordered one of his generals to take a large army to conquer the city of Chanderi in Malwa (Chanderi, a trading center south of Gwaliyar, was on the main route from Delhi to Deogir). The general (probably ʿAyn al-Mulk Māhrū, who led the successful expedition against Chanderi, Dhar, Ujjain, and Mandu in 1305) was an adherent of Niẓām al-Dīn Awliyā'. He approached the shaykh and asked that he send one of his disciples along, so that they should go with the shaykh's protection. Niẓām al-Dīn Awliyā' agreed and appointed Wajīh al-Dīn Yūsuf of Kilokhri, sending him along with the army. In the event, the general's attack was successful, and Yūsuf took up his abode there and became known as Yūsuf Chanderī. In this instance, it was again at the request of another that Niẓām al-Dīn Awliyā' sent this disciple on his mission.[72] A similar case was that of Shams al-Dīn D'hārī, who had worked in the imperial treasury (*dīvān*) before becoming a disciple of Niẓām al-Dīn Awliyā'. Though he expressed a desire to retire as a hermit, Niẓām al-Dīn Awliyā' pointed out that it was no less important to come out from seclusion to benefit others, and he gave Shams al-Dīn an inkpot to signify that he should return to worldly duties. Shams al-Dīn received a land assignment (*iqṭāʿ*) in the Deccan from the government and was buried there.[73] Here too Niẓām al-Dīn Awliyā' allowed a disciple to go to the Deccan in connection with the Tughluqs' imperial expansion.

But the Sufis did not wish to engage in the sultan's program of conversion of Hindus to Islam, since it was basically a program in the service of the empire. This reluctance to participate in Tughluq imperialism was evident in the case of an eminent disciple of Niẓām al-Dīn Awliyā', Shams al-Dīn Yaḥyā, whom the sultan ordered to go to Kashmir and preach (*daʿvat kun*) Islam in the idol-houses. Preaching in support of imperial expansion was not an activity the Sufi could engage in. The shaykh had a dream that Niẓām al-Dīn Awliyā' was summoning him, and grew ill; Sultan Muḥammad ibn Tughluq assumed he was faking to avoid government service, and called him to court. The illness was genuine, however, and the shaykh died instead of following the sultan's order.[74]

As we have seen, the population that Sultan Muḥammad ibn Tughluq transferred to Daulatabad was primarily the religious and intellectual class, and the Chishtī writings tell of a number of Sufis who participated in this migration, often with great reluctance. Mīr Khwurd's youngest uncle, Shams al-Dīn Sayyid Khāmūsh, who was a friend of Burhān al-Dīn Gharīb, died in Deogir in 732/1332.[75] Another of Niẓām al-Dīn Awliyā's disciples who went to the south was Qāżī Sharaf al-Dīn Fīrūzkūhī, who used to read the poems of Ḥasan Sijzī with Mīr Khwurd; he died in Deogir.[76] The difficulty of flouting the sultan's order to live in Daulatabad is illustrated by the story of Niẓām al-Dīn's learned successor Shaykh Fakhr al-Dīn Zarrādī. He had once defied Sultan Muḥammad ibn Tughluq's attempt to force him into government service, but was constrained to join the emigrants to Daulatabad.[77] The story of his attempt to leave on pilgrimage to Mecca, which Mīr Khwurd told as a Chishtī teaching story, has already been discussed (Part I, chap. 5). The language of this account reveals the anxiety that religious officials felt about dealing with the capricious sultan. On hearing of Fakhr al-Dīn's plan to leave Daulatabad, his friend, a judge, told him not to go, since "it is the Sultan's desire that this city should be famed to the ends of the earth because of the presence of scholars, shaykhs, and religious officials. And especially [you should not go] because he will be bound to oppress you." Fakhr al-Dīn was supposedly inspired to sneak away at the instance of a fellow Sufi, Mīr Khwurd's father Sayyid Muḥammad Kirmānī.[78]

Another Sufi forced to go to Daulatabad was Shihāb al-Dīn "the truth-teller" (*ḥaqq-gū*), whom Ibn Baṭṭūṭa described as having tragically fallen afoul of Sultan Muḥammad ibn Tughluq's temper. When the sultan first tried to enroll Shihāb al-Dīn in government, the shaykh refused, and the sultan was so furious that he ordered the jurist Żiyā' al-Dīn Sunamī to pluck out Shihāb al-Dīn's beard. The jurist refused, so both he and the shaykh had their beards plucked out. The sultan then sent Żiyā' al-Dīn to Telengana, where he later became qāżī of Warangal, and he sent Shihāb al-Dīn to Daulatabad for seven years. Shihāb al-Dīn then earned his nickname *ḥaqq-gū* after he returned to Delhi, at a time when the sultan had commanded everyone to call him "Sultan

Muḥammad the Just."[79] Shihāb al-Dīn told the sultan to his face that he was a tyrant and enumerated his injustices, including the ruining of Delhi—the transfer of population to Daulatabad. The sultan's response was to have the shaykh brutally killed, a curious proof of his justice.[80]

Despite the sultan's elaborate plans, the migration to Daulatabad backfired politically to the extent that it generated intense resentment and opposition among those forced to emigrate. The venture was also a failure from an economic point of view. With revolts in Telangana and Maʿbar dissolving the short-lived Tughluq control of the south, and with the devastation caused by bubonic plague in the Deccan and famine in Hindustan, Sultan Muḥammad ibn Tughluq permitted the transplanted Delhiites to leave Daulatabad, probably in 1335.[81] The abandonment of the Daulatabad project was due to the financial reverses that the empire suffered. Incorporation of the Deccan into the empire was more of a financial drain than the old raiding ventures with their low overhead. Consequently, after the sultan's attempts at currency reform failed to remedy the deficit problem, the Khurasan expedition was called off. Instead of bankrolling Tughluq expansionism into central Asia, the Deccan had emptied the Delhi treasury.

Some Sufis and scholars who came to Daulatabad remained and went on to other urban centers in the Deccan, helping to consolidate that Islamic intellectual tradition in the south, which was to some extent what Sultan Muḥammad ibn Tughluq had wished for in ordering the migration. Texts surviving from this period indicate the extent of the dissemination of Islamic culture under the Tughluqs in the Deccan. In the field of belle lettres, Ḥājib-i Khayrāt Dihlawī in 1342 had access to the full range of Persian literature when he compiled a Persian dictionary entitled *Dastūr al-afāżil* (*The canon of the learned*), which he dedicated to a Tughluq official in Gogi (Gulbarga district, Karnataka).[82] In Islamic law, Karīm Khān Nāgawrī wrote an extensive work on Islamic ritual, *Majmūʿ-i Khānī* (*The khān's collection*), along with an equally large sequel, both of which were sponsored by an official of Daulatabad, Bahrām Khān.[83] Zayn al-Dīn Shīrāzī studied the Islamic religious sciences with some eminent scholars in Daulatabad.[84] Others came to Daulatabad after the principal migration of 729/1328–29. One of Mīr Khwurd's uncles, Quṭb al-Dīn Sayyid Ḥusayn Kirmānī (d. 752/1351), accompanied the wazir Aḥmad Ayāz Khwāja-i Jahān to Daulatabad in 732/1331–32. Though he did not wish to go, he could not gainsay the command of Sultan Muḥammad ibn Tughluq; he did, however, manage to persuade the wazir to permit him to retain his Sufi dress and be exempt from government service.[85]

The migration of the Delhi Muslims to Daulatabad had the permanent effect of consolidating the social and cultural traditions of Hindustan in the Deccan. Although some returned to Delhi, those who had put down roots remained to raise their families and tend the graves of those who died.[86] When the sultan gave the order that those who wished to return to Delhi might do so, some did. According to Baranī, two or three caravans of people made the return journey, while those with families settled there remained.[87] Khwāja Tāj al-Dīn Dāwarī, an ardent disciple of Niẓām al-Dīn Awliyā' who was often absorbed in *samā'*, died on the return march to Delhi and was carried on to be buried there.[88] Mawlana Shihāb al-Dīn Imām, who used to lead prayers for Niẓām al-Dīn Awliyā', had gone to Deogir and taken on a number of disciples, but he returned to Delhi and died there.[89] When Burhān al-Dīn Gharīb became seriously ill in 735/1334, his disciples began to pack his belongings, intending to take him back to Delhi. He refused to leave, however, and pointed to the spot where he did his devotions, declaring that he would be buried here.[90] Islam and the Sufi tradition had been transplanted to Khuldabad.

7

Burhān al-Dīn Gharīb's Establishment and Teaching

The *Khalīfa* of Niẓām al-Dīn

What kind of a person was Burhān al-Dīn Gharīb, and what was his position in the Chishtī order as a Sufi teacher? From his own remarks as preserved in the *malfūẓāt* texts, we can construct a picture that is suggestive, with some details. While his family had some religious leanings, they seem not to have encouraged his Sufi vocation very much. He has referred to twin uncles, one of whom taught Islamic law in Daulatabad.[91] He tells a story of his father having preserved a curious document, with the aid of which certain spirits would give one immunity from disturbance.[92] His impulse toward religion was precocious, manifesting long before he reached the age of legal responsibility; he recalls acting as imam at the ʿĪd festival when he was seven years old.[93] At the age of six or seven, he would say the confession of faith and retire into a room to perform *zikr*. At sixteen he decided to remain celibate against his mother's wishes, and fasted continually until she finally gave up her insistence that he marry.[94] Burhān al-Dīn Gharīb at the age of seventeen used to repeat the confession of faith as a spiritual practice, but his father could not distinguish between that and his studies of the standard religious curriculum.[95]

The exact nature of the authority of Burhān al-Dīn Gharīb within the order has been variously interpreted in later hagiographies, and it is best to begin with the evidence found in the *malfūẓāt* texts. Burhān al-Dīn Gharīb himself has described his relation with Niẓām al-Dīn Awliyā' in terms suggesting a very close spiritual relationship, in which he has directly inherited the substance of the authority of the Chishtī masters. Niẓām al-Dīn Awliyā' commented on Burhān al-Dīn Gharīb's jealousy with regard to other visitors.[96] Niẓām al-Dīn observed, "Burhān al-Dīn Gharīb has both eyes on me and does not attend to any other."[97] Burhān al-Dīn Gharīb mentioned how he vigorously defended Niẓām al-Dīn Awliyā' and the practice of *samā'* against hostile criticism.[98] He also instructed a visitor in manners, when the latter had said something offensive to Niẓām al-Dīn Awliyā'.[99] He stated in 733/1333 that he had followed the path of Niẓām al-Dīn Awliyā' for forty years (a number symbolic of perfection), and only on four occasions had he been forced to ask directly for the latter's help.[100] His disciples recorded of him that never in his life did he disrespectfully turn his back toward his master's tomb in Ghiyaspur (a suburb of Delhi).[101] During the last few years of his life, which were marred by constant illness, Burhān al-Dīn Gharīb once confessed that he only remained alive in order to fulfil the instructions of Niẓām al-Dīn Awliyā'.[102]

The nature of Burhān al-Dīn Gharīb's discipleship is partly indicated by other anecdotes from the *malfūẓāt*, which depict Niẓām al-Dīn presenting him with the initiatic regalia of the Chishtīs and confirming his spiritual status. Burhān al-Dīn described himself as having received from Niẓām al-Dīn Awliyā' the "essential" hat of initiation, as opposed to the hat of ordinary discipleship.[103] On the journey from Delhi to Daulatabad, Burhān al-Dīn Gharīb had a cot carried alongside him, in which was the staff of Niẓām al-Dīn.[104] When Burhān al-Dīn Gharīb was on his deathbed, he called for Niẓām al-Dīn's rosary.[105] Other less tangible evidence also attests to the high regard that Niẓām al-Dīn had for his disciple. At their first meeting, Niẓām al-Dīn's attendant announced that Burhān al-Dīn, a poor man (*gharīb*) had arrived; the shaykh remarked that he is indeed poor now, but the whole world will come to know him (thus conferring upon him the epithet *gharīb*).[106] Niẓām al-Dīn Awliyā' is quoted as saying, "Burhān al-Dīn Gharīb is with the *majmū'* ['the group']," apparently meaning the group of those who are saved.[107] Niẓām al-Dīn Awliyā' pronounced the Qur'ānic passage, "Today I have perfected your religion and completed my bounty to you" (Qur'ān 5.3), in reference to Burhān al-Dīn Gharīb's spiritual perfection, when he gave the latter dominion (*vilāyat*) over the Deccan.[108] When a number of disciples one day were discussing the famous Sufi Bāyazīd Bisṭāmī, Niẓām al-Dīn Awliyā' remarked, "We too have a Bāyazīd," indicating Burhān al-Dīn Gharīb.[109] At their last meeting, Burhān al-Dīn Gharīb requested from Niẓām al-Dīn Awliyā' the gift of being under the direct spiritual observation (*naẓar*) of Farīd al-Dīn Ganj-i Shakkar.[110]

A different evaluation occurs in the standard biographical notice of Burhān al-Dīn Gharīb, from the pen of Mīr Khwurd, whose hagiographical writing has been discussed above (Part I, chap. 4 and 5). Mīr Khwurd's initial account of Burhān al-Dīn Gharīb is very laudatory, and described some aspects of the shaykh's ecstatic personality very well:

> He was an example in the matter of belief among the foremost lovers, and he preceded most of the foremost lovers in discipleship. He was a good balm to those disappointed in love and passion, and he was a good remedy for the pain of the lovers and jesters of the day, so that Amīr Khusraw and Mīr Ḥasan [Dihlawī] and other lovers became captivated by his love, because of his graceful nature and passion. . . . In *samāʿ* this saint was completely extreme, experienced much ecstasy, and said the prayers of lovers. He had a distinctive style in dancing, so that the companions of this saint were called "Burhānīs" among the lovers. Whoever was in the presence of this saint for an hour fell in love with the beauty of his saintliness, because of the ecstasy of his passionate words and the purity of his enchanting conversation. There was no better master than he to show the way to servants of God in belief and love. The author many times had the happiness of kissing the feet of that saint, and became captivated by his passionate words.[111]

This early account by one who knew him was widely quoted in later descriptions of Burhan al-Dīn Gharib.[112] In the Chishtī order at large, then, Burhān al-Dīn Gharīb was regarded as an old and dedicated disciple of Niẓām al-Dīn. He was distinguished for his ecstatic temperament and his love of musical sessions.

Yet in the subsequent sections of this biographical notice, Mīr Khwurd focuses on two incidents that show Burhān al-Dīn Gharīb in a less than flattering light. The first occurred when Burhān al-Dīn Gharīb started using a doubled carpet to sit upon, because of his physical weakness. When the news was brought to Niẓām al-Dīn, he became extremely displeased, because he was told that Burhān al-Dīn Gharīb was setting himself up as a master and sitting on the carpet of authority while Niẓām al-Dīn was still alive. Niẓām al-Dīn consequently banished the unfortunate Burhān al-Dīn Gharīb from his presence, and it was only after Amīr Khusraw made a very theatrical intercession that Niẓām al-Dīn consented to forgive his old and distraught disciple.[113] The other incident was the manner in which Burhān al-Dīn Gharīb obtained investiture as a *khalīfa* of Niẓām al-Dīn. In this version, one of Mīr Khwurd's uncles and some other disciples decided to request Niẓām al-Dīn to honor Burhān al-Dīn Gharīb with *khilāfat* as others had been honored (the incident would thus be dated to the last months of Niẓām al-Dīn's life, when he was quite ill). With the aid of Niẓām al-Dīn's personal attendant Iqbāl, they brought Burhān al-Dīn Gharīb to see Niẓām al-Dīn while the latter was resting, presented some articles of Niẓām al-Dīn's clothing, which he then blessed, and in Niẓām al-Dīn's presence announced that Burhān al-Dīn Gharīb was now a fully qualified *khalīfa*. Niẓām al-Dīn's silence was construed as approval.[114]

These two incidents have led some to regard Burhān al-Dīn Gharīb as a nice but doddering old man who offended his master and was only made *khalīfa* because of special pleading.[115] Despite a longtime residence in the Deccan, and an apparent fondness for the shaykh, Mīr Khwurd closed his account of Burhān al-Dīn Gharīb with the barest mention of the latter's sojourn there, adding only that Burhān al-Dīn Gharīb's tomb "today is the pilgrimage center of the people of that region." Although Mīr Khwurd had admired Burhān al-Dīn Gharīb personally, he had fallen away from Sufism when he served in the administration in the Deccan, and so had not kept in touch with Chishtī circles in Daulatabad. Since his reconversion to Sufism had taken place when he returned to Delhi and met Chirāgh-i Dihlī, it was only natural that he regard the latter as the central figure in Chishtī Sufism.

The other follower of Chirāgh-i Dihlī who commented negatively on Burhān al-Dīn Gharīb was Muḥammad al-Ḥusaynī "Gīsū Darāz" (d. 825/1422), so named for his long tresses of hair. According to his oldest biography, Gīsū Darāz had gone with his father to Daulatabad from Delhi in 725/1325, at the age of four, at the time of Muḥammad ibn Tughluq's enforced transfer of the population to the new capital (that event actually took place four years later, in 1329). He remained there for eight more years until he returned to Delhi, and there he became a disciple of Chirāgh-i Dihlī in 733/1333 at the age of twelve.[116] Gīsū Darāz cannot have had much significant contact with Burhān al-Dīn Gharīb during his childhood years in Daulatabad, but many years later, when he passed through the Deccan again, he recalled hearing Burhān al-Dīn Gharīb predict that Gīsū Darāz would obtain spiritual guidance from Chirāgh-i Dihlī. In a conversation recorded in 802/1400, Gīsū Darāz discribed the relationship between Burhān al-Dīn Gharīb and Chirāgh-i Dihlī as that of disciple to master.[117] According to Gīsū Darāz, "Mawlānā Burhān al-Dīn Gharīb had perfect faith in our shaykh, saying just this: 'If I had not been connected to the revered Shaykh al-Islām Niẓām al-Dīn, I would be connected to Mawlānā Maḥmūd [Chirāgh-i Dihlī].'"

Gīsū Darāz illustrated the spiritual superiority of Chirāgh-i Dihlī by several anecdotes. In the first story, Burhān al-Dīn Gharīb's associates criticize Chirāgh-i Dihlī for an apparent lapse of manners, but he is vindicated. In the second, Burhān al-Dīn Gharīb approaches the meditating Chirāgh-i Dihlī, led by Gīsū Darāz himself (who would have been less than four years old at the time), and humbly begs Chirāgh-i Dihlī to pray for him. The third incident was a letter that Burhān al-Dīn Gharīb wrote expressing his admiration and sympathy for Chirāgh-i Dihlī during the sufferings inflicted upon him by the sultan. Gīsū Darāz reflected that it was this suffering that caused Chirāgh-i Dihlī to inherit the saintly authority (*vilāyat*) of Niẓām al-Dīn, which was later transmitted to Gīsū Darāz himself. The trend in these stories is to stress Burhān al-Dīn's recognition of Chirāgh-i Dihlī as the true successor of Niẓām al-Dīn and as his own spiritual superior. Gīsū Darāz complained, however, that some of Burhān al-Dīn Gharīb's associates (in the circle of Yaʿqūb Chanderī) had erroneously supposed that Chirāgh-i Dihlī had learned something about Sufism from Burhān al-Dīn Gharīb; Chirāgh-i Dihlī according to him hotly denied this and said it was quite the reverse: "If some words of dervishes have reached the hearing of Mawlānā Burhān al-Dīn, they have come from this very person [i.e., from me]." Gīsū Darāz was concerned to praise Burhān al-Dīn Gharīb faintly and to preserve the prestige of Chirāgh-i Dihlī (and by extension Gīsū Darāz) as the true successor of Niẓām al-Dīn.

What are we to make of the discrepancies between these accounts of the status of Burhān al-Dīn Gharīb? The negative evaluations of Burhān al-Dīn Gharīb's position come primarily from the followers of Chirāgh-i Dihlī, who viewed him as having succeeded to the authority of Niẓām al-Dīn. In addition to Mīr Khwurd and Gīsū Darāz, Ḥamīd Qalandar also proclaimed the authority of Chirāgh-i Dihlī by elevating him above Burhān al-Dīn Gharīb (above, Part I, chap. 4). Yet the accounts of how Niẓām al-Dīn named his successors do not suggest that any of his followers received a preeminent position. Mīr Khwurd has described the way Niẓām al-Dīn chose the leading disciples from a list of thirty-two candidates, and drew up their diplomas (*khilāfat-nāmas*) according to a strict procedure that Farīd al-Dīn Ganj-i Shakkar had employed. This all took place on 20 Dhū al-Ḥijja 724/20 December 1324, not long before Niẓām al-Dīn's death on 18 Rabīʿ I 725/12 March 1325.[118] Although in that passage Mīr Khwurd did not indicate the exact number of *khalīfas*, his organization of the chapter on Niẓām al-Dīn's *khalīfas* makes it clear that there were ten.[119] As Simon Digby has pointed out, Niẓām al-Dīn did everything he could to discourage competition among his successors; at the time of the investiture of Shams al-Dīn Yaḥyā and Chirāgh-i Dihlī, he minimized the slight precedence given to the former and caused the two to embrace.[120] There is little evidence that any of the *khalīfas* of Niẓām al-Dīn actually vied with one another, but their followers in the next generation could not help playing the game of one-upmanship.

The lesser known Deccan tradition deriving from Burhān al-Dīn Gharīb's followers shows an entirely different picture, however, in which his critics were refuted. Āzād Bilgrāmī minimized the incident of Niẓām al-Dīn's anger with Burhān al-Dīn Gharīb over the carpet, arguing that it was just a case of backbiting.[121] Mīr Khwurd's story of Burhān al-Dīn Gharīb's *khilāfat*, however, posed greater problems; Āzād simply repeated it without comment.[122] Āzād's translator leaped to the defense, though, pointing out that Burhān al-Dīn Gharīb's own references to this event contrasted with Mīr Khwurd's description; instead of using the silence of an ailing saint to approve his own nomination as successor, Burhān al-Dīn Gharīb specified the precise oral instructions that Niẓām al-Dīn gave him when authorizing him to teach.[123] Mīr Khwurd's account of this event seems to belong to the class of rumors regarding Niẓām al-Dīn's feebleness in the month before his death, which some had used to question the credentials of certain *khalīfas*. Mīr Khwurd himself had hastened to dismiss these rumors, arguing that Niẓām al-Dīn was still quite vigorous at the time of the selection of the ten *khalīfas*.[124] Other late hagiographers insisted that Burhān al-Dīn Gharīb had been the first *khalīfa* invested by Niẓām al-Dīn, and they proceeded to enumerate the sacred Chishtī regalia with which he was entrusted.[125]

Burhān al-Dīn Gharīb's followers regarded him as the "world-axis" (*quṭb-i ʿālam*), the supreme figure in the Sufi hierarchy.[126] His reputation became widespread in the Deccan during his lifetime. One of his disciples, Maḥmūd of Lajwara, had been a businessman in Maʿbar, some hundreds of miles to the southeast of Daulatabad, and after becoming a recluse was told by a mysterious saint to seek the perfect master Burhān al-Dīn Gharīb. He has recently arrived in Daulatabad, said the man, and compared to others he is like the sun compared to the moon. When Maḥmūd came to Daulatabad, Burhān al-Dīn Gharīb without being told described the personal appearance of the saint of the south.[127]

Each *khalīfa* of Niẓām al-Dīn was surrounded by disciples who necessarily tended to see their master as the one supreme successor to Niẓām al-Dīn's authority. This quest for paramountcy was reflected in the images of Burhān al-Dīn Gharīb in the writings of his own circle as contrasted with the circle of Chirāgh-i Dihlī. Among Chirāgh-i Dihlī's followers, it was well known that Burhān al-Dīn Gharīb was an older disciple of Niẓām al-Dīn, and that Chirāgh-i Dihlī had often stayed with Burhān al-Dīn Gharīb when he came from Awadh to see Niẓām al-Dīn in Delhi. The relationship between the two men thus became a matter of some concern, and the writings of Ḥamīd Qalandar, Mīr Khwurd, and Gīsū Darāz show a tendency to belittle the spiritual stature of Burhān al-Dīn Gharīb and enhance the status of Chirāgh-i Dihlī. Due to the continued prominence of the Delhi branch of the Chishtīs, and by dint of repetition in later biographical texts, this picture of the relationship between the two has come to dominate the later Chishtī perspective. The discrepancies between the different evaluations of Burhān al-Dīn Gharīb's status, then, derive from competing historiographies within the Chishtī order. For the historian, it is not necessary to decide which is the "correct" version. The most interesting conclusion to be drawn from the variance of the sources is the extent to which the concept of undivided transmission of authority was a driving force in the social implementation of Sufism. Despite Niẓām al-Dīn's clear unwillingness to designate a single successor, later constructions could not resist the temptation to draw a single line of initiatic transmission connecting Sufi disciples to Niẓām al-Dīn and, ultimately, to the Prophet.

The Sufi Master

The authority of the Sufi master elicited a corresponding devotion in the disciple. From anecdotes and remarks in the *malfūẓāt* texts, it is possible to form a picture of the master-disciple relationship that was formulated in the Chishtī order. Burhān al-Dīn Gharīb gave the following description of the ideal Sufi master:

> The perfect master and teacher is that one who is both lover and beloved, both the seeker and the sought, both the impassioned and the impassioning, both the perfect and the perfected, both the enraptured wayfarer and the wayfaring enraptured one, both the astonished and the absorbed. His way is sometimes intoxicated and sometimes sober, at times absorbed and at times effaced. The master is the guide and exemplar.[128]

In theory, the master should be able to comprehend all sides of the complex teaching situation.

The Sufi master-disciple relationship was not conceived of as anything foreign to Islamic tradition. On one occasion Zayn al-Dīn Shīrāzī raised the question of devotion to the master from the perspective of Islamic law. Is it not the case, he asked, that following the master is an additional duty above and beyond that of following the Prophet, and is it not incumbent upon the elect? In that case, contemplating the master is like reciting the *Fātiḥa*, or other practices derived from prophetic example (*sunnat*), like using the saltshaker and praying over food. Burhān al-Dīn Gharīb replied that he wholly concurred with this position.[129]

Frequently Chishtī disciples were depicted demonstrating their reverence for their masters in remarkable ways. Rukn al-Dīn Kāshānī once was summoned to go to Delhi by post-relay, accompanying Sultan Muḥammad ibn Tughluq on horseback. Rukn al-Dīn rode the whole way with his back to Delhi and his face turned to Burhān al-Dīn Gharīb in the direction of Daulatabad. On the trip, every morning after prayer he placed his face on the ground in the direction of his master before proceeding on his way. On hearing of this reverential attitude, Burhān al-Dīn Gharīb said, "his appointment (*gumāshta*) is right (*ḥaqq*), for a person who does thus is appointed by God."[130] In a similar way, Quṭb al-Dīn Dabīr was going to perform pilgrimage to Niẓām al-Dīn, and as soon as he saw the dome (*qubba*) of his tomb, he got off his horse and put his face on the ground, performing the rest of the pilgrimage on foot.[131]

It was also expected that disciples once initiated would no longer make indiscriminate visits to other Sufi masters, if that might detract from their concentration upon their master. Once Rukn al-Dīn Kāshānī had returned from a trip to Delhi, whereupon Burhān al-Dīn Gharīb asked him about the Sufi masters he had seen there. After Rukn al-Dīn mentioned whom he had visited, Burhān al-Dīn Gharīb went on to relate a story about a dervish who had expressly forbidden his son to even look at other Sufis. Rukn al-Dīn became understandably upset upon hearing this account, since he was afraid that his master supposed that he had sought these other Sufis out as teachers.[132]

Likewise the obedience of the disciple to the master's instructions was considered to be essential. Maḥmūd of Lajwara was an ascetic from Maʿbar who had once been initiated and shaven (as was customary) as a disciple of Burhān al-Dīn Gharīb. When it became evident that he was regrowing his hair and only performed supererogatory prayers instead of obligatory rituals, Burhān al-Dīn Gharīb severely reproved him for his bad behavior.[133] Niẓām al-Dīn Awliyā' would sometimes redirect disciples who had decided to go on the *ḥajj* pilgrimage to Mecca. To one disciple, Niẓām al-Dīn observed that from Delhi to Ghiyaspur is nearer than going on *ḥajj*, meaning that it was more important for the disciple to visit Niẓām al-Dīn. Burhān al-Dīn Gharīb's comment on this advice was that when visiting dervishes one should form the intention entirely for God, and then God blesses every step with the reward of the *ḥajj*.[134]

Burhān al-Dīn Gharīb was probably as learned as most of the other successors of Niẓām al-Dīn Awliyā', but he was not a specialist in Islamic law.[135] In this respect he differed considerably from his friend and younger contemporary, Naṣīr al-Dīn Maḥmūd Chirāgh-i Dihlī. The later biographer of the Khuldabad Sufis, Āzād Bilgrāmī, observed that "the path of Shaykh Naṣīr al-Dīn Maḥmūd and most of his successors was the observance of the exemplary practices of the prophetic law and the practice of teaching the religious sciences."[136] The writings of the disciples of Chirāgh-i Dihlī are in fact mostly studies of Islamic law and ritual from the perspective of Sufi piety.[137] And it was not accidental that when Ḥamīd Qalandar tried to flatter Chirāgh-i Dihlī in comparison with Burhān al-Dīn Gharīb, he praised Chirāgh-i Dihlī as a religious scholar equal to the founder of the Ḥanafī legal school, which has always been dominant in India. "Lord! Mawlānā Burhān al-Dīn was a dervish who attained union, but the revered master [Chirāgh-i Dihlī] is an Abū Ḥanīfa in learning, and in asceticism and mastery he is the Shaykh Niẓām al-Dīn of the age."[138] The title that Ḥamīd Qalandar gave to the *malfūẓāt* of Chirāgh-i Dihlī, *Khayr al-majālis* (*The best of assemblies*), is an indirect reference to the religious sciences, recalling the saying that "the best of assemblies is that in which discussion of religious learning (*ʿilm*) takes place."[139]

Once Burhān al-Dīn Gharīb recalled comparing notes with Naṣīr al-Dīn Maḥmūd about what extra petitions they recited during the special prayers (*tarāwīḥ*) performed in Ramaẓān. Typical of the difference in temperament between the two, Burhān al-Dīn Gharīb recited a Persian couplet on seeking union with God, while Chirāgh-i Dihlī uttered an Arabic prayer seeking forgiveness for all humanity.[140] In the *malfūẓāt* of Burhān al-Dīn, works on law are rarely mentioned, but the discourses of Chirāgh-i Dihlī frequently cite legal and theological texts.[141] Burhān al-Dīn Gharīb once mentioned to Niẓām al-Dīn that he had as a child played the part of prayer leader (*imām*) for his playmates, but that he preferred to be a dervish rather than a preacher (*khaṭīb*); Niẓām al-Dīn concurred and told him he would not be a preacher.[142] Burhān al-Dīn Gharīb was impatient with the sterile debates of scholars about the precise manner of washing the hands during ablutions, or the reason for the order of the *sūra*s of the Qur'ān; for him it was more important to exert oneself for the benefit of others.[143] "Our order," he said, "is known for two things: love and compassion."[144]

Islamic learning was nonetheless highly valued in the circle of Burhān al-Dīn. Rukn al-Dīn Kāshānī in his speculative work *Shamā'il al-atqiyā'*, written with the approval of Burhān al-Dīn, made use of many classical works of Qur'ānic commentary, *ḥadīth*, and law, in addition to writings on Sufism.[145] *Ḥadīth* texts were frequently quoted, sometimes interpreted as psychological allegories, as in the saying, "An angel does not enter a house in which there is a dog or a picture on the wall." The dog, in Burhān al-Dīn Gharīb's view, symbolizes the carnal soul (*nafs*), while the pictures stand for the love of things other than God.[146] Some of the stories told by Burhān al-Dīn Gharīb are stock teaching stories that can be found also in classical authors such as al-Ghazālī.[147] Zayn al-Dīn Shīrāzī was also very learned in the religious sciences, though this training took place before he became interested in Sufism.[148] On occasion Zayn al-Dīn Shīrāzī demonstrated his learning in regard to difficult terms from the Qur'ān.[149] Yet law and scholarship were not subjects that Burhān al-Dīn emphasized for their own sake. Rukn al-Dīn Kāshānī's discussion of ritual and legal subjects typically considers them primarily in order to introduce the inner dimension of such practices. Ḥamīd Qalandar may have been correct in calling Burhān al-Dīn Gharib primarily a dervish—a practicing Sufi, rather than a scholar.

Burhān al-Dīn Gharīb's style as a teacher was simple and direct, drawing on a wealth of Sufi narratives and his own vivid metaphors to convey points to listeners. When a fasting visitor declined to partake of a meal, Burhān al-Dīn Gharīb proceeded to tell (with a number of digressions) a series of six stories that emphasized the danger of arrogance for those who fast. In each of the stories, accepting the gift of food from a Sufi saint turns out to be the source of spiritual blessings. We are not told whether the visitor eventually was persuaded to join the meal, but the hint must have been unmistakable.[150] To give an illustration of humility in prayer, Burhān al-Dīn Gharīb gave the example of grass, which is in prostration until it dies. Its mouth faces downward to drink water, and likewise in prayer it is natural to turn the mouth to one's source in prostration.[151] Speaking of renunciation of the world, Burhān al-Dīn Gharīb first likened the world to a shadow, which always sticks to one's body. Since one's shadow can only be faced by turning away from the sun, the world can only be embraced by turning away from God. Continuing with a switch of metaphors, he said that unless one renounces the world, then prayers are like the struggles of a mouse in a bucket. If one first renounces the world, prayers will be really efficacious.[152]

Persian poetry was the basis for the literary culture of Burhān al-Dīn Gharīb's circle, as it was for all Sufis of the subcontinent at this time. Burhān al-Dīn Gharīb related that once when he was sick, he stayed home and read Niẓāmī's great epic poem *Majnūn-Laylī*; Niẓām al-Dīn then visited him and presented him with a hat.[153] On another occasion, he called for Rukn al-Dīn Kāshānī to recite a passage from Khāqānī's *Tuḥfat al-ʿirāqayn* on the vanity of wealth.[154] Burhān al-Dīn Gharīb was often moved to quote or extemporize verses of poetry, which he expected his listeners to be able to memorize on a single hearing.[155] Sometimes a disciple would respond by reciting appropriate verses in the same rhyme and meter.[156] Several examples of poetry composed by Burhān al-Dīn Gharīb's disciples are preserved.[157] One recently discovered poetic testimony is especially valuable as coming from the pen of the poet and *malfūẓāt*-writer Amīr Ḥasan Dihlawī. This is a Persian *masnavī* poem in honor of Burhān al-Dīn Gharīb and his disciples, which Ḥasan must have written not long after arriving in Daulatabad. The opening lines reveal the gratitude that Ḥasan felt for the guidance that Burhān al-Dīn Gharīb offered him:

> Peace like the dawn breeze be upon that head of the circle of the divine secret!
> Peace like the purity of visionaries be upon that candle of creation's palace!
> Peace like the conquest of the seven climes be upon that Burhān al-Dīn, that candle of submission to God!
> By the truth that one may call him "truth" (*ḥaqq*), one can call him the absolute ruler of the world.
> For by the command of [his] allusion, morning and night, I take my path to the rendezvous with his mouth [i.e., his words].
> What good fortune it will be, if some morn or eve he remembers me in this exile (*ghurbat*)!
> I have become "poor" (*gharīb*)—I am his slave! Perhaps I have found the same quality from his name.
> That time of expectation, by way of hope, he sent me, time and again, a prayer messenger.
> The prayer that he sent one morning may be my escort on this path.
> Even now, if God wills, I will find him, and I will lay my head at the feet of that leader.[158]

Teachings and Practices

Among the Sufi practices that receive prominent attention in the *malfūẓāt* of Burhān al-Dīn Gharīb, initiation (*bayʿat*) deserves to be singled out, since it is the beginning of the Sufi path. *Bayʿat* (literally "agreement" or "compact") is regarded as being the formal acknowledgment of religious authority as instituted by the Prophet Muḥammad among his followers. Qur'ānic passages (48.10, 48.18) refer to this agreement as a linkage between humanity and God, with the Prophet as the intermediary. This linkage is considered to be an uninterrupted transmission through the Sufi masters to each generation.[159] The fifth chapter of *Aḥsan al-aqwāl* gives a lengthy description of the main rituals. If someone wishes to be honored with initiation (*bayʿat*), one should fast that day, give alms, and perform ritual prayer. The alms are a thanksgiving offering of food after initiation, while the prayer is the same that is done after being dressed in the *khirqa* cloak. Three conditions must be fulfilled: acceptance (*iqrār*) by the master with a handshake, shaving (*qaṣr yā ḥalq*), and investment with the cloak (a hat or other garment could be substituted for the cloak).[160] On accepting the prospective initiate, the master takes the hand of the disciple in his own hand, and says:

> You have sworn an oath (*ʿahd kardī*) with this broken one, and with the master of this broken one (*khwāja-i īn shikasta*), with the masters of Chisht, and with the followers [of the Prophet, *tābiʿīn*], and with the followers of the followers, and with the Messenger of the Lord of Creation, and with the bearers of the Canopy, and with God Himself. Guard your eye, and guard your tongue. Do not speak evil of anyone nor think evil of anyone. Do not bring harm to anyone, and do not approach forbidden things. Remain on the path of the religious law (*sharʿ*). You have sworn an oath to all of this, so observe these conditions.

The disciple says, "I have sworn an oath to all of this." Then comes the shaving. They take some hair from the right side of the head and from the left, and cut it with scissors. A hat is put on his head, and at this time the master invokes the name of God, and announces (in Arabic) that this is the clothing of piety and the clothing of well-being. The disciple expresses his intention (again, in Arabic) to perform two cycles of supererogatory prayer, with these words: "I intend to pray to God most high two cycles of supererogatory prayer; rejecting all that is other than God, I turn my face to the noble Kaʿba. God is most great." After performing the prayer, he puts his head at the master's feet, and then rises and presents some gift to the master. The disciple joins the ranks of the other companions of the assembly, and the master will then determine his capacity and give him instruction.[161] Special procedures based on the usage of the Prophet Muḥammad governed the initiation of women disciples. Following the directive of a passage in the Qur'ān (60.12), women could undertake initiation with a Sufi shaykh just as women had taken the oath of allegiance to Muḥammad. The procedure, derived from a *ḥadīth* related by ʿUmar, was for the woman to place her hand into a cup of water, after which the shaykh (again following the example of the Prophet) would also put his hand in the water, and then the oath of initiation would be administered.[162]

Initiation, which might be renewed on special occasions, was a frequent occurrence in Burhān al-Dīn Gharīb's circle, and the circumstantial details reveal the importance of this ritual. A typical example is the case of Mawlānā Nūr al-Dīn Ḥāfiẓ Maḥjūb. When he was initiated and shaved, Burhān al-Dīn Gharīb inquired how this action would be received by the man's family. Nūr al-Dīn said that he had permission, but admitted that there had been some criticism of dervishes in his house, on the grounds that some are blind and others had no hair. Burhān al-Dīn Gharīb smiled and then proceeded to relate a number of stories dealing with the theme of seeing through appearances, and cited a *ḥadīth* on the importance of self-examination. With these preliminary pieces of advice completed, the new disciple was given a hat and instructed in the details of supererogatory prayer, with emphasis on the Qur'ānic verses to be recited at different times.[163] When an official named Saʿd al-Dīn Dabīr came to be shaven and initiated, Burhān al-Dīn Gharīb answered his unspoken question about the significance of the hat or cloak. Their absence invalidates the initiation, just as the absence of a master makes it impossible to pursue salvation. In this connection he told the story of Aḥmad Nahāvandī (d. 370/980–81), who fell in love with a Christian princess and ended up becoming a swineherd and converting to Christianity. He was saved from this apostasy only by the intervention of the Prophet as mediated by the chain of Sufi masters.[164] The story of the Sufi who becomes the swineherd of a Christian girl, better known through ʿAṭṭār's tale of Shaykh Ṣanʿān, is told here to indicate the significance of the chain of Sufi masters as the means of salvation; for ʿAṭṭār, the story was told primarily to illustrate the power of love.[165] Some prospective initiates were questioned as to their observance of ritual prayer, and were instructed to be scrupulous about refusing unlawful sources of money.[166] But initiation was not for everyone. Citing the example of Niẓām al-Dīn, Burhān al-Dīn Gharīb pointed out that the master must examine the motivation of would-be dervishes to see if they were inspired by God or by the devil.[167]

In terms of religious practice, prayer in its manifold forms was the central activity in the Chishtī tradition. The five daily ritual prayers required of all Muslims were considered to be basic and obligatory in Sufi circles as well. This comes out in the incident of a disciple named Shams al-Dīn Fażl Allāh, who in a hypersensitive mood declared that he would give up all prayers, since in the Qur'ān (41.46, 45.15) it is said that actions are for the sake of the carnal soul (*nafs*). Burhān al-Dīn Gharīb in turn quoted from the Qur'ān (74.1–6) and from numerous *ḥadīth* to demonstrate that religious actions are for the sake of God. The actions of the heart (including fasting), he pointed out, are not ordinary actions, but are contemplation of God. Shams al-Dīn then expressed his concern that he was committing hypocrisy by not living up to the words of his prayers. Burhān al-Dīn Gharīb then quoted again from the Qur'ān (43.32), "We have apportioned among them their livelihood in the world," to indicate that God decrees everything and that God's will should be recognized in all things. It is worth noting that this advice concludes with a line of Hindi poetry that incorporates part of the Arabic Qur'ān verse.[168]

While it is assumed, then, that the standard ritual prayer (*namāz*) forms part of the Sufi discipline, much attention is focused on supererogatory prayers (*nawāfil*) and chants (*wird*, pl. *awrād*). The longest chapter in *Aḥsan al-aqwāl*, approximately one-fifth of the book, is devoted to a detailed description of many different prayers and chants. We see how Burhān al-Dīn Gharīb instructs the son of Muḥammad Khādim in supererogatory prayers, remarking that both Niẓām al-Dīn and the Prophet Muḥammad used to enjoy the company of children after prayers.[169] These supererogatory prayers, performed at specified times especially during the night, had been a basic feature of Sufi piety for centuries. When a disciple revealed that he had family problems, Burhān al-Dīn Gharīb indicated that prayers using the *sūra*s of the Qur'ān beginning with the word *qul* or "say" (known as the *ṣalawāt al-qalāqil*) were very effective to ward off evil and solve problems. The disciple was told to insert these into his evening ritual prayer and afterward recite seventy-five repetitions of a short Arabic address to God.[170] Chants, however, were more specific and spontaneous, and might consist of special petitions addressed to God.

Once during a discussion of concentration (*himmat*), Burhān al-Dīn Gharīb broke into a short Arabic prayer, "God, give me high concentration so that I do not ask of you anything except for your sake." On hearing this, Zayn al-Dīn Shīrāzī asked if he might not use it as a chant. Burhān al-Dīn Gharīb concurred, saying that a chant is something that one hears and then recites; one ought to use it, for not to do so is like leaving a sharp sword unused.[171] Other special prayers are mentioned, such as the prayer to prevent rain that Qutlugh Khān had given to certain religious scholars.[172] These chants were not to be taught indiscriminately, however. When Burhān al-Dīn Gharīb once described a certain prayer (*du'ā*) that protected a man from attempted murder, a disciple asked to hear it, but the shaykh refused.[173]

The impulse toward interiorization of ritual, so typical of classical Sufism, was the dominant aspect of religious practice among the Khuldabad Chishtīs. Burhān al-Dīn Gharīb explained the levels of interior purification as a transition from practicing Islamic law to undergoing moral transformation, followed by the onset of mystical experience:

> First is external purification (*tazkiya*), which attaches the soul to the religious law. Then comes internal purification (*taṣfiya*), which empties the interior of obscurities, and then the divine lights manifest

within. . . . It is actions, morals, and states. At first men do actions, then they strive beyond that to turn their blameworthy actions to praiseworthy ones—avarice turns to concentration and greed to bravery—and in this way, whatever is blameworthy becomes praiseworthy; this becomes the category of morals. When actions have become morals, then comes emptying (*takhliya*). When obscurities are emptied out, states appear, and divine visitations enter the interior.[174]

This emphasis on interiorization is especially evident in the chapters on rituals in Rukn al-Dīn's *Shamā'il al-atqiyā'*.[175] The Qur'ān's reference to those who are "constantly at prayer" (70.23), for example, is interpreted differently in accord with the diverse classes of people. According to Burhān al-Dīn Gharīb, the vulgar follow this injunction by practicing their five daily prayers and the regular festival prayers during the year; their only concern is that these prayers be performed without sloth or heedlessness, and with precise movement. The elite apply this by performing all supererogatory prayers, with "subjection of the body and presence of the heart," determined to complete all such devotions even in the throes of death. The prophets and the elite of the elite are in a continuous state of obedience and worship throughout their lives and even in death.[176] Similarly, the mystical interpretation of the *ḥajj* pilgrimage is attaining closeness to the divine beloved, and the Sufi fast is not simply abstinence during the days of Ramażān, but a continual deprivation of the soul in order to reach the vision of God in the heart.[177] Alms for the wealthy is to give wealth, and for the *'ulamā'*, it is to teach religious subjects. But the alms of the saints is "to teach the knowledge of wayfaring, to instruct in external and internal practices, and to give up the world and its pomp. The real alms of the most elite of the saints is to give benefits from the purification of the heart and the illumination of the spirit to sincere disciples, and bestow the bounty of passion, love, and the happiness of gnosis and proximity to God to the seekers of the Lord."[178] From the Sufi perspective, the rituals enjoined by Islamic law were most perfectly performed when this inner dimension was added to the external enactment of the ritual.

The Chishtīs also followed distinctive practices based on the master-disciple relationship, such as pilgrimage to tombs of saints and the observation of their death anniversaries.[179] Burhān al-Dīn Gharīb gave explicit directions for the performance of this ritual:

When a dervish wishes to visit the dead, he presents his wish twice to the spirit of the dead, goes out of the house and into the road. He goes reciting what he intended, and when he arrives at the head of the tomb he does not stand at the foot. He stands before the tomb and recites the *Fātiḥa* [Qur. 1] once, the Throne Verse [Qur. 2.255] once, *ilāhukum al-takāthur* [Qur. 102] three times, *Ikhlāṣ* [Qur. 112] ten times, and *durūd* [blessing the Prophet] ten times, and then he returns.[180]

Festivals were held on the death-anniversary (*ʿurs*, literally "wedding") of major saints, and food was blessed and distributed to the faithful. Niẓām al-Dīn used to preserve food from the *ʿurs* of Farīd al-Dīn Ganj-i Shakkar and give it to the sick to heal them.[181] Burhān al-Dīn Gharīb recalled that his own father was in the habit of visiting the tombs of the saints and praying thus: "God, God, by the sanctity of those accepted in your court, make this helpless one accepted in your court!"[182] As this prayer implies, pilgrimage to tombs was not worship of the people buried there, but a worship of God that looked to the saint as a kind of intermediary. Disciples often found guidance from deceased saints in dreams after spending time meditating at their tombs.[183]

The center of activities among the Chishtīs was called the *jamāʿat khāna*, literally "house of gathering." Unlike the *khānqāh* of Iran and central Asia, which might often be a large establishment supported by endowments, the Chishtī *jamāʿat khāna* was essentially the residence of the shaykh. Meals were taken there, people slept there, and the basic teaching activities, interviews, and rituals (including *samāʿ*) also took place in central room of the *jamāʿat khāna*.[184] Early Chishtī masters such as Farīd al-Dīn Ganj-i Shakkar insisted that this was the normal place of association for the order; he reprimanded a disciple who set up a *khānqāh* with an administration big enough to offer opportunities for embezzlement. Farīd al-Dīn Ganj-i Shakkar's concept of *jamāʿat khāna* was that it be hidden from the people, a retreat rather than a showplace. Niẓām al-Dīn Awliyā' also maintained a simple *jamāʿat khāna*, and the same organization was followed by Burhān al-Dīn Gharīb and Zayn al-Dīn Shīrāzī. The desire for privacy was probably the reason for the selection of Khuldabad, several miles away from the Daulatabad fort, as the site for Burhān al-Dīn Gharīb's *jamāʿat khāna*.

Some features of the administration of the *jamāʿat khāna* can be pieced together. Burhān al-Dīn Gharīb's personal attendant Kākā Shād Bakhsh would act as a doorman and general factotum, regulating all access to the shaykh. Some disciples took care of secretarial tasks such as correspondence, writing out letters of authorization, and keeping the accounts for the kitchen. Others undertook menial duties such as carrying water, cooking, and carrying things.[185] Hospitality for visitors was treated as a sacred duty, which Burhān al-Dīn Gharīb emphasized to his disciples.[186] Visiting dervishes would be accommodated for up to three days, after which they were expected either to work, to be absorbed in prayer, or to travel on.[187] Visitors would also be expected to conform to the rules and etiquette of the order. Burhān al-Dīn Gharīb himself was asked to instruct in manners a man who behaved rudely to Niẓām al-Dīn, and he felt that those who persist in rudeness should be refused admittance.[188]

The Disciples

Discipleship (*irādat*, literally "desire"), according to Burhān al-Dīn Gharīb, is an action of the disciple, not the master. It consists of a discipline (*taḥkīm*) imposed on oneself such that one attends to everything said by the master. "The disciple (*murīd*) must become a lover of the master's sainthood, so that he can depart from the power of his own longing, and the desirer (*murīd*) can become the desired (*murād*) of the master."[189] Burhān al-Dīn Gharīb distinguished two kinds of disciple, nominal and real: "The nominal disciple is one whom the master instructs to make the seen unseen and the heard unheard, and to follow the standards of religion. But the real disciple is the one to whom, at the time of instruction, the master speaks of repentance and discipleship, saying, 'Be in our company, and we will be in your company.'"[190] The nominal disciple, a sort of lay follower, is thus taught self-control and the regular practices of religion, but the real disciple is admitted to a relation of intimacy with the master, in which the inner discipline can take place.

Burhān al-Dīn Gharīb had many followers in Daulatabad, and they represented a wide selection of classes and vocations that can be briefly surveyed here. From the casual way in which many individuals are mentioned, it is not always possible to determine their social standing; most are discussed in terms of their closeness to the Sufi master. The outstanding personalities are the principal successors (*khalīfa*s) whom Burhān al-Dīn Gharīb authorized as Sufi teachers; they were, in his terms, "real disciples." Burhān al-Dīn Gharīb had four principal successors in Daulatabad, who exhibited spiritual vocations that differed considerably in their public visibility.

Farīd al-Dīn Adīb,[191] a cultured and pious recluse, was brought by his father to meet Burhān al-Dīn Gharīb at a musical audition (*samāʿ*) at the age of fifteen. A precocious aspirant, he at once formed the resolve to become a disciple of Burhān al-Dīn Gharīb, and with the internal help of his future master, he began reducing his food intake to prepare for asceticism. He became initiated when he was eighteen, though Burhān al-Dīn Gharīb compared him in spiritual maturity to a disciple of thirty years service.[192] The written sources portray him as extremely devout and closely attuned to his master, so that he would come in response to Burhān al-Dīn Gharīb's wish before he was actually called. When overcome by a state of spiritual intoxication, he sought help from Burhān al-Dīn Gharīb, who consoled him by saying that Niẓām al-Dīn had saved them both; Farīd al-Dīn fervently repeated these words.[193] His close relationship with his master was dramatized when he dreamed that Burhān al-Dīn Gharīb pulled him out of a mud hole.[194] Burhān al-Dīn Gharīb said of him, "We have given you every internal and external bounty." He also remarked, "If at the resurrection I am asked what I have brought, I will say that I have brought Farīd."[195] But Farīd was more of a solitary than a guider of souls. When Burhān al-Dīn Gharīb told him that he would become a *khalīfa*, he wept bitterly and prayed to God to take him before his master. Accordingly, he died on 29 Muḥarram 738/17 August 1337, thirteen days before Burhān al-Dīn Gharīb's death.[196]

A *khalīfa* with a particularly inconspicuous lifestyle was Sayyid Naṣīr al-Dīn (now called Naṣīr al-Dīn Pā'oñ Payk, "the footman"), who received his authority along with Zayn al-Dīn Shīrāzī three days after the death of their master.[197] He died sometime before 761/1360, since in that year one of his disciples dreamed that Naṣīr al-Dīn's spirit received the soul of Ḥammād al-Dīn Kāshānī, who died at that time.[198] Only rarely is he mentioned with specific detail in the *malfūẓāt* texts. Once he is the source for a story about someone else, and on another occasion he is quoted as saying that sayyids as descendants of the Prophet Muḥammad are not shaved at initiation, since they wear their hair long by custom (this was the origin of the nickname Gīsū Darāz, meaning "long locks").[199] Otherwise we are only told that he was the source of innumerable miracles, none of which are mentioned.[200]

A much more public role was played by Malik Mubārak, a noble who held the hereditary title Shams al-Mulk. It was at his house that Burhān al-Dīn Gharīb first stayed on his arrival in Daulatabad. His career demonstrates that the line between court life and Sufism could be very hard to define. He and Rukn al-Dīn Kāshānī both attended upon Burhān al-Dīn Gharīb before they became initiated, and after visiting most of the Sufis of Delhi he decided that only Burhān al-Dīn Gharīb could be his master.[201] Mubārak then became initiated as a Sufi, but he remained in service at court at the order of Burhān al-Dīn Gharīb, though he wanted to quit his position and become a dervish. Burhān al-Dīn Gharīb said of him, "he is both a man of affairs (*kāsib*) and a dervish."[202] Mubārak was later promoted in the administration and became a revenue official (*mustawfī-i mamālik*) in Delhi. But on the death of Burhān al-Dīn Gharīb, Mubārak was sent the robe of a *khalīfa* and a diploma of authorization (*ijāzat nāma*) to take on disciples. He accordingly returned to Daulatabad to live as a Sufi, and the displeased sultan therefore seized all his belongings. Despite his position of authority in the Chishtī order, Mubārak avoided receiving visitors, and eventually he went on pilgrimage to Mecca. He died in Khuldabad just two years after the death of Burhān al-Dīn Gharīb, in 740/1340.[203] We shall return to Mubārak in connection with the question of just how close the relationship was between the Sufi center and the court.

Clearly the dominant figure among Burhān al-Dīn Gharīb's successors was Zayn al-Dīn Shīrāzī, who is universally regarded as the chief inheritor of his master's authority. According to Āzād, who has constructed a detailed biography of Zayn al-Dīn Shīrāzī, he was born in Shiraz in 701/1301–2 and came to Delhi with his uncles after performing pilgrimage to Mecca. He accompanied his teacher Kamāl al-Dīn Samāna to Daulatabad in the general move, and he distinguished himself in the Islamic religious sciences. Zayn al-Dīn initially avoided the Sufis, and he disputed the mastery and miracles of

Burhān al-Dīn Gharīb, in particular criticizing the practice of *samāʿ*. He addressed to Burhān al-Dīn Gharīb some thorny questions on the religious sciences, and had them all answered to his satisfaction, so he converted to Sufism. He advanced rapidly, and on 17 Rabīʿ I 737/24 October 1336, on the *ʿurs* festival of Niẓām al-Dīn Awliyā', he obtained the cloak of succession (*khirqa-i khilāfat*).[204]

The master-disciple relationship between Zayn al-Dīn and Burhān al-Dīn Gharīb was very close. Reminiscing some nine years after his master's death, Zayn al-Dīn described him as having succeeded to the position of the representative of the Prophet Muḥammad:

> The Prophet Muḥammad at this time is in the veil. His representatives (*nā'ibān*), such as Imām Jaʿfar Ṣādiq, Ḥasan Baṣrī, Uways Qaranī, Bāyazīd, Junayd, Shiblī, Shaykh al-Islām Niẓām al-Dīn, and Shaykh al-Islām Burhān al-Dīn, have taken care of his position after him. Each of them was in his time the representative of the Prophet. With their protection they bring people to fulfil their religious and worldly goals, so one should entrust oneself to their protection so that by following them all one's affairs should be in order.[205]

By placing Burhān al-Dīn Gharīb in this distinguished lineage, Zayn al-Dīn regarded his master as holding the supreme spiritual position of his time.

In the following description, Zayn al-Dīn uses a Qur'ānic passage (18.18) to describe the remarkable qualities of the perfect master, in a portrait drawn from the likeness of Burhān al-Dīn Gharīb:

> The master is someone for whom perfect mastery is the apportioned state. His spiritual genealogy goes back, one generation after another, to the Prophet. This group has a characteristic, that because of their mildness, benevolence, and character, there is an awe about them—and this is also supported in the Qur'ān, just as God Most High stated to the Prophet in the story of the companions of the cave: "If you observed them, you would have turned away in flight, and you would be filled with dread from them" (Qur. 18.18). . . . This meaning is found in [legal works such as] the *Hidāya*, in Pazdawī, and in all the books of the scholars, although one cannot say it to the masses. But this meaning came true with Shaykh al-Islām Burhān al-Dīn.[206]

In short, Zayn al-Dīn felt that his relationship with his master was of the greatest importance. "Without the protection of Shaykh al-Islām Burhān al-Dīn," he remarked, "how would spiritual wayfaring (*sulūk*) be possible?"[207]

From Burhān al-Dīn Gharīb's *malfūẓāt*, one can get glimpses of the development of Zayn al-Dīn Shīrāzī as a disciple. His initial approach was scholarly and even bookish, and he had to be weaned away from this tendency. We see him asking if he can use an Arabic prayer as a chant, and then asking if he can write down a verse recited by Burhān al-Dīn Gharīb—on this occasion, Burhān al-Dīn refused, saying that he expected one to memorize a verse on the first hearing.[208] It was only slowly that Zayn al-Dīn became accustomed to the position of being a spiritual director and the demands that people made on his time. Zayn al-Dīn complained to Burhān al-Dīn Gharīb that people interrupted his prayers, but Burhān al-Dīn replied in Arabic that "when the brethren come, the supererogatory prayer is finished."[209] But just as Burhān al-Dīn Gharīb had himself acted as a guide during the lifetime of his teacher Niẓām al-Dīn, so did Zayn al-Dīn become adjusted to his new role, receiving the spiritual genealogy from his master as a sign of spiritual perfection.[210]

As a teacher, Zayn al-Dīn Shīrāzī continued to be scholarly in style, and he joined his early training in Islamic law to the Chishtī teachings. He quoted extensively from poets such as Amīr Khusraw, ʿAṭṭār, Niẓāmī, Saʿdī, and Sanāʾī.[211] Works of law and Qurʾān commentary regularly came up for discussion.[212] He used classical Sufi texts and recommended them for the study of his own disciples. When he went to Delhi in 747/1347, he gave to his disciple Ḥasan a copy of al-Ghazālī's *Minhāj al-ʿābidīn* that he himself had written, with instructions that Ḥasan should read and correct the manuscript.[213] Ḥasan, the recorder of Zayn al-Dīn's *malfūẓāt*, also borrowed from his teacher a copy of the *Qūt al-qulūb* of Abū Ṭālib al-Makkī.[214] Zayn al-Dīn referred to other Sufi classics, such as the works of Qushayrī and Hujwīrī.[215] In his use of Sufi writings, Zayn al-Dīn was careful to distinguish between those that were for general use and those with esoteric content. He singled out in particular the controversial works of the Sufi martyr ʿAyn al-Quẓat Hamadānī, the *Tamhīdāt* and *Maktūbāt* (*Letters*), as texts that required special handling. He emphasized that the words of this writer were not to be followed, and that not all can understand them. This was a general principle of esotericism; those who do understand such things should not reveal them or speak of them.[216] Nonetheless, he did quote from ʿAyn al-Quẓāt, and it is clear that the works of this famous Sufi were well known in Khuldabad.[217]

In the experience of Zayn al-Dīn Shīrāzī, Sufism was an interior discipline that has a complex relationship with Islamic law. To abandon Islam and the *sharīʿa*, he noted, is the worst of crimes.[218] Beyond that, he said, "The path of our masters is the path of the heart."[219] The normal requirements of Islamic law (*farāʾiẓ*) and the Prophetic example (*sunna*), in his view, establish regulations of purity as a trial designed to release humanity from the evil results of their free will.[220] The acts of supererogatory worship (*nawāfil*) performed by the Sufis have the further goal of restraining the carnal soul (*nafs*) from forbidden speech and acts.[221] He recommended the following daily schedule:

> One performs the dawn (*bāmdād*) prayer, sits facing the direction of Mecca, and until sunrise is occupied with chants. When the sun rises, one performs morning (*ishrāq*) prayer, and then if one must be involved with some worldly job or relationship, such as trade, work, or negotiations, one is busy with that. Otherwise there is reading and study of spiritual wayfaring, until mid-morning (*chāsht*). Then one performs mid-morning prayer and takes a nap. After arising from the nap, one does ablutions and performs the noon (*zawāl*) prayer. Then one performs the midday (*pīshīn*) prayer, and once again is occupied in a job, necessary relationships, teaching, reading, or studying spiritual wayfaring, until the next prayer. Then one performs the evening (*shām*) prayer, the prayer between evening and nightfall (*bayn al-ʿashā'ayn*), and the bedtime (*khuftan*) prayer, and then one sleeps for a while. Then one does ablutions and performs the vigil (*tahajjud*) prayer. Then the times are finished. Work and affairs are from morning to mid-morning, and from noon to evening.[222]

Spiritual practices had to be flexible, in order to deal with the ever-changing nature of the *nafs*. Thus in discussing fasting, Zayn al-Dīn followed Burhān al-Dīn Gharīb, saying that it is better to break one's fast when others specially offer food, rather than remaining rigidly committed to the fast. But in that case one should only take two or three bites, in order to oppose the *nafs* completely—if fasting is one's idol, one should break it. Likewise one should also oppose the *nafs* by only eating less when it wants more.[223] When asked why Sufi masters sometimes do not permit disciples to go on pilgrimage to Mecca, Zayn al-Dīn replied that this is not an absolute prohibition. Following the master's order becomes an occasion for the disciples to give up their free will, in order to quell the *nafs*.[224]

Zayn al-Dīn Shīrāzī remained in Khuldabad until some months after the outbreak of the rebellion of the centurions led by Ismāʿīl Mukh, who was crowned sultan in Daulatabad in Jumādā I 747/September 1346. But Sultan Muḥammad ibn Tughluq descended upon the rebels, won a decisive victory, and visited severe reprisals upon the population. News of a new rebellion in Gujarat caused him to leave hastily, however, and on 2 Dhū al-Ḥijja 747/16 March 1347, Zayn al-Dīn Shīrāzī along with many of the residents of Daulatabad went north with the army.[225] Evidently the sultan had "invited" the shaykh to accompany him on the road to Gujarat. At some point on this journey, given freedom by the sultan to go where he wished, Zayn al-Dīn decided to stay for an extended period at the major Chishtī shrines in Delhi, meeting all the leading figures of the order, including Naṣīr al-Dīn Maḥmūd Chirāgh-i Dihlī. This was for him a period of intense spiritual exercises. On 30 Rabiʿ I 749/28 June 1348, Zayn al-Dīn said that for two months he had been doing a daily complete recitation of the Qur'ān for the spirit of Niẓām al-

Dīn Awliyā', staying mornings meditating in his tomb. During this time Zayn al-Dīn also took on many disciples. Eventually, after the death of Muḥammad ibn Tughluq, Fīrūz Shāh was crowned, and on 18 Ṣafar 752/16 April 1352, he met with Zayn al-Dīn Shīrāzī and invited him to stay in Delhi. The shaykh declined, saying he wished to return to his master's threshold, so with the sultan's permission he returned at last to Daulatabad, after lengthy sojourns at the tombs of Farīd al-Dīn Ganj-i Shakkar at Ajodhan and Muʿīn al-Dīn Chishtī at Ajmer. The foregoing account is based on the biographical notice by Āzād Bilgrāmī, who had access to three additional *malfūẓāt* texts of Zayn al-Dīn, none of which is now extant.[226]

When he was on his deathbed, Zayn al-Dīn's disciples asked him to name a successor, but he died on 25 Rabīʿ I 771/27 October 1369, without having done so. Zayn al-Dīn's tomb was built opposite that of Burhān al-Dīn Gharīb (see Figures 6 and 7). Since he was the twenty-second in the Chishtī lineage, Zayn al-Dīn is known locally as "the twenty-second master" (*bā'īs khwāja*); there is no twenty-third (see Table 1). Despite this unambiguous statement that there were no successors, later political traditions attempted to fill the gap by suggesting that Zayn al-Dīn bequeathed his authority to Malik Rājā Fārūqī, founder of the kingdom of Khandesh, and a nineteenth-century source even credited him with ten *khalīfa*s.[227] The leadership of the Chishtī order in the Deccan after Zayn al-Dīn seems to have passed after a couple of decades to Muḥammad al-Ḥusaynī Gīsū Darāz. Only in very recent years has a Chishtī lineage emerged claiming descent from Zayn al-Dīn's disciple Shamnā Mīrān (d. 798/1395), whose tomb is in Miraj.[228]

In addition to the *khalīfa*s, the most numerous group of disciples consisted of the ordinary devotees who stayed with Burhān al-Dīn Gharīb or visited him regularly. Nobles, administrators, and the ruling sultan called upon the shaykh, as did religious scholars, soldiers, and other residents of Daulatabad. The Kāshānī family, including both parents and their four sons, were dedicated followers of Burhān al-Dīn Gharīb. The father, ʿImād al-Dīn Kāshānī, never actually became initiated, but expressed the intention of doing so before he died. Their mother, who was a daughter or descendant of Farīd al-Dīn Ganj-i Shakkar, was herself accepted as a disciple.[229] Burhān al-Dīn Gharīb emphasized his closeness to the sons by calling himself their fifth brother, the son of their mother.[230] All four brothers appear to have been officials in the Tughluq administration in Daulatabad, although we have little information about their secular activities. Of the four brothers, Burhān al-Dīn Kāshānī was the only one not to write a *malfūẓāt* collecting Burhān al-Dīn Gharīb's teachings, perhaps because he was less knowledgeable about Sufi customs. When he and his brother Majd al-Dīn were first initiated, he tried to give a gold ring to Burhān al-Dīn Gharīb by way of thanks, but the shaykh gave it back, saying, "By the spirit of Shaykh al-Islām Niẓām al-Dīn! Sell it and spend it. A dervish ought not to receive things of this kind."[231] His concentration on Burhān al-Dīn Gharīb was such that once he received from him in a dream the same chant that his brother Ḥammād al-Dīn had just been taught in waking life.[232] On his wedding day, he became a disciple of Burhān al-Dīn Gharīb, who instructed him to work in the world. He died on the same day as Burhān al-Dīn Gharīb.[233]

Ḥammād al-Dīn Kāshānī was the author of *Aḥsan al-aqwāl*, in which he collected Burhān al-Dīn Gharīb's teachings and arranged them by subject. His scholarship was also expressed in a treatise on Islamic law and two works on Sufism.[234] He was personally very close to his teacher. After searching for a Sufi master for some time, he told Burhān al-Dīn Gharīb he had no desire to meet any more dervishes.[235] We see him on several occasions trading Persian verses with Burhān al-Dīn Gharīb, the latter even reciting a verse that mirrors one Ḥammād al-Dīn is thinking of.[236] In an exchange that may have stimulated Ḥammād al-Dīn to write *Aḥsan al-aqwāl*, Burhān al-Dīn Gharīb told Ḥammād al-Dīn to remember all that he says, so that he too will be in the group (*majmūʿ*) that will be saved.[237] Ḥammād al-Dīn followed the Chishtī meditative regime intently. When preparing for a journey, he received the following Arabic prayer for love from Burhān al-Dīn Gharīb: "God, give me life as your lover, let me die as your lover, and resurrect me beneath the feet of the dogs of your lovers."[238] He helped a fellow disciple, Qāżī Farīd al-Dīn Yūsuf, by suggesting a chant to solve his problems.[239] Twice he made pilgrimage to the tomb of Burhān al-Dīn Gharīb to received posthumous instructions, the last time shortly before his death in 761/1360, in Sagar near Gulbarga, where he is buried in the southwest corner of Ṣūfī Sarmast's tomb. Ḥammād al-Dīn reportedly brought over a thousand people to become disciples of Burhān al-Dīn Gharīb.[240] The confidence that Burhān al-Dīn Gharīb had in Ḥammād al-Dīn is indicated in a scene that took place three days before his death, when the shaykh had Ḥammād al-Dīn renew his initiation, and then instructed him to continue in his prayers and study.[241] Ḥammād al-Dīn informs us that Burhān al-Dīn Gharīb predicted that Ḥammād al-Dīn would become a living saint (*zinda walī*), implying that this did in fact occur.[242]

Majd al-Dīn Kāshānī was perhaps less of a scholar and more of a devotee than his brothers. He was the author of *Gharā'ib al-karāmāt*, a narrative work summarizing the miracles and revelations of Burhān al-Dīn Gharīb, along with a supplement, *Bāqiyat al-karāmāt*, which is no longer extant. Majd al-Dīn has nearly effaced himself in his storytelling, and there are only a few references to him directly. Once when he had a problem, he dreamt that Burhān al-Dīn Gharīb told him that secrets are to be found written in blood; perhaps due to a bookish inclination, he found the solution by reading for days in various books on Sufism.[243] When Burhān al-Dīn Gharīb appeared to be on his deathbed in 737/1337, he asked Majd al-Dīn and Rukn al-Dīn to pray for him with Qur'ānic prayers.[244] Years after, it was Majd al-Dīn who received in a dream certain prayers from Burhān al-Dīn Gharīb that saved the people from the wrath of sultan, after the rebellion of Ismāʿīl Mukh.[245] Majd al-Dīn thus appears primarily as a devotee who stands somewhat in the background among the disciples of Burhān al-Dīn Gharīb.

Rukn al-Dīn Kāshānī was the most prolific writer of the family, having written not only *Nafā'is al-anfās* as a *malfūẓāt* in diary form, but also a Qur'ān commentary entitled *Rumūz al-wālihīn* (*Cyphers of the mad lovers*) and *Shamā'il al-atqiyā'* as an encyclopedia of Sufi teaching. He wrote a good deal of undistinguished Persian poetry, much of it inserted into the topics of *Shamā'il al-atqiyā'*.[246] Burhān al-Dīn Gharīb recognized his literary bent by calling him a "collector of stories" and "the spiritual secretary."[247] Ḥammād al-Dīn also mentions that Rukn al-Dīn wrote a book (unspecified) at the request of a noble, which he took to Burhān al-Dīn Gharīb's tomb for blessing; on his way there a rainstorm began, but the book was miraculously preserved.[248]

Rukn al-Dīn, like his brothers, had a very close relationship with Burhān al-Dīn Gharīb, which deepened as he became more thoroughly imbued with the Chishtī teaching. He records frequent events marking his growing intimacy with Burhān al-Dīn Gharīb. He introduced a number of his friends from court to Burhān al-Dīn Gharīb, and discussed their family problems with him.[249] Burhān al-Dīn Gharīb frequently presented Rukn al-Dīn with the personal effects that formed such an important part of the initiatic process.[250] Once Rukn al-Dīn was about to take his leave, but Burhān al-Dīn Gharīb was in a bad mood, and had him wait. A little while later, Burhān al-Dīn Gharīb felt more cheerful, and so he gave Rukn al-Dīn a robe and sent him on his way.[251] Burhān al-Dīn Gharīb predicted that Rukn al-Dīn's son Ṣāliḥ would also grow up to be worthy and would sit with him as a disciple.[252] Fairly early in their relationship, Rukn al-Dīn asked if he could help share in Burhān al-Dīn Gharīb's illness, but the shaykh warned him that it was too dangerous.[253] When Burhān al-Dīn Gharīb appeared to be on the point of dying in 735/1335, he gave instructions for his burial. Rukn al-Dīn wept and renewed his initiation along with the others. When, the next morning, it appeared that Burhān al-Dīn Gharīb had recovered, a moving exchange took place between the two:

> The revered master (God remember him with good and happiness!) asked me, "Where were you, and what have you done?" I said, "I have been busy praying for my master." He replied (verse): "He said to me, where were you, what did you do? Where was I, what did I do? I sorrowed for you." His eyes filled with tears, and he said, "I know that the devotees have been sad and disturbed on my account." Then he asked, "How are you?" And on that day, I was internally disturbed because of something important. I said, "The master's blessing is for the good." The shaykh began to weep, and extending

> his hand from his sleeping robe, he said, "Put your hand in mine." I put my hand in the hand of the leader of humanity and placed my head at the feet of that rescuer of the people. The shaykh wept and said, "Lord! Lord! Save him!" Several times he said these words. Then he said, "May he grant you one day the happiness of both worlds, and bestow upon you acceptance in both worlds." Then he said, "Go home or to bed." On that day the Real (who is mighty and glorious) bestowed such fortune and happiness [on me].[254]

From this kind of incident it is easy to see how intense the master-disciple relationship was between Rukn al-Dīn Kāshānī and Burhān al-Dīn Gharīb.

As Burhān al-Dīn Gharīb's prayer for Rukn al-Dīn indicates, the Sufi master wished for his disciple success both spiritually and temporally. This follows the pattern already seen in the case of Malik Mubārak, who was instructed to remain in government service until the shaykh's death. Rukn al-Dīn seems to have found the balancing of court life and Sufism difficult to achieve. As early as 733/1332, Rukn al-Dīn requested to be fully initiated, and shaved as a dervish, so that he could give up his government career. Burhān al-Dīn Gharīb divined this wish before it was expressed, and refused, telling him to go back to the palace; he should imitate Aḥmad Maʿshūq and help the people rather than retire into seclusion. This advice was striking enough to have been repeated in three *malfūẓāt* texts.[255] Four years later, in 737/1336, Rukn al-Dīn complained again of the difficulty of working for the administration, when all "the *khān*s, nobles, and princes of this time" ignored his advice. Burhān al-Dīn Gharīb advised him to trust in God.[256]

Among the other prominent disciples was Kākā Shād Bakht (or Shād Bakhsh), the personal attendant of Burhān al-Dīn Gharīb, who was a principal source of many oral accounts incorporated into the *malfūẓāt*. He seems to have been a practical soul who was much concerned about the welfare of his master. When the sultan presented a gift of three thousand tankas, Kākā suggested accepting it, but Burhān al-Dīn Gharīb insisted on distributing it.[257] The shaykh called him "one of the good and pure ones."[258] Burhān al-Dīn Gharīb entrusted him with the responsibility for distributing food and clothing to others.[259] He kept the accounts and later administered the hospice of Burhān al-Dīn Gharīb for nine years after the shaykh's death, and it was he who undertook the project of constructing his master's tomb, as an inscription on the tomb testifies. In order to do this, he went to Delhi to have a workman construct a wooden model of the tomb of Niẓām al-Dīn Awliyā, and brought it down on horseback to serve as a model for the tomb of Burhān al-Dīn Gharīb, which was completed in 744/1343–44; this wooden model was in existence until very recently. Kākā was the first administrator of Burhān al-Dīn Gharīb's shrine, and he died in 747/1346–47.[260]

Another leading disciple was Laṭīf al-Dīn, a nephew of Burhān al-Dīn

Gharīb, who was entrusted with the ceremonial position of holding the toothpick during meals in the hospice.[261] His high status in the group is indicated by his giving counsel to another disciple, Muḥammad Lashkar, when the latter was having difficulties.[262] One account describes his intense concentration on Burhān al-Dīn Gharīb, which caused him miraculously to transform himself into the likeness of a dervish whose appearance was being described by the shaykh.[263] He was singled out to be presented with a woolen garment at the time of Burhān al-Dīn Gharīb's near-fatal illness.[264] While he was extremely pious in matters such as reciting Qur'ān over food, he was also entrusted with the administration of the *dargāh* after the death of Kākā Shād Bakht. According to Āzād, Laṭīf al-Dīn was the administrator of the shrine after the death of Kākā Shād Bakht, and in 761/1359–60 he presented Ḥammād al-Dīn Kāshānī with a special shawl that belonged to the shaykh, and he died soon after.[265] There is some discrepancy about the role of Laṭīf al-Dīn, however, since the revenue memorandum (Appendix B) indicates only that his mother and his descendants received stipends in kind from the shrine's income, but it does not mention him among the administrators of the shrine; this discrepancy may reflect later disagreements over the running of the shrine between the various factions of devotees. We shall return to this revenue document in the context of the later institutionalization of the shrine.

In the second rank of disciples one may count figures such as Shams al-Dīn Fażl Allāh, apparently a brother of Zayn al-Dīn Shīrāzī and a teacher of the Qur'ān.[266] He is referred to in the hagiographical *Gharā'ib al-karāmāt* as being an intoxicated saint of high station, who had been told by a wise dervish that he would meet the Quṭb-i ʿĀlam or "axis of the world." After becoming disciple of Burhān al-Dīn Gharīb, he learned that the latter was indeed the Quṭb al-Aqṭāb or "axis of axes" as defined by Niẓām al-Dīn, and therefore the supreme figure in the spiritual hierarchy.[267] Nonetheless, he was hypersensitive about his own practice, and we see him having qualms about performing any action (including prayer) hypocritically; he is also shown asking whether it is all right to teach children for money (Burhān al-Dīn Gharīb approved).[268]

In the second rank also may be placed Tāj al-Dīn Muḥammad Lashkar, a soldier in the Tughluq garrison at Daulatabad. His relationship with Burhān al-Dīn Gharīb was more worldly than spiritual. His experiences of the miracles of Burhān al-Dīn Gharīb included the latter telling him where to find a lost horse. When he participated with Qutlugh Khān's army in the siege of Kotgir, he was injured by an arrow, but was healed after dreaming of Burhān al-Dīn Gharīb.[269] When Muḥammad Lashkar complained to the shaykh of his family's poverty, Burhān al-Dīn Gharīb predicted that bounty would come to him when the shaykh was no longer there. Muḥammad Lashkar later was named commander of the Badarkot fort and was much better off financially.[270] Around 754/1353, Zayn al-Dīn Shīrāzī named him the third administrator of the shrine of Burhān al-Dīn Gharīb. Muḥammad Lashkar is associated with Mawlānā Rashīd al-Dīn, an old disciple of Niẓām al-Dīn Awliyā'. Little is known of Rashīd al-Dīn's earlier life. One anecdote relates that his brother was reported killed by a highwayman while on the sultan's business; Burhān al-Dīn Gharīb correctly predicted the brother's return.[271] He was the last to speak to Burhān al-Dīn Gharīb, and he became the second administrator of the saint's shrine after Kākā Shād Bakht until his death in 754/1353.[272]

Some members of the Khuldabad circle were brought there forcibly as part of Sultan Muḥammad ibn Tughluq's policy of installing learned men in the government. One such was Qāżī Rafī' al-Dīn Muta'allim, an old disciple of Burhān al-Dīn Gharīb and the author of a *Risāla-i karāmāt* (*Treatise on miracles*). He was chained by the sultan and ordered to serve in the administration Daulatabad. Later, on receiving a summons to the imperial court, he was so disturbed that he fled to Burhān al-Dīn Gharīb for refuge; on the latter's advice, however, he heeded the summons and was fortunately freed from his chains and service.[273]

There were also lay disciples like Ibrāhīm Burhānī, a soldier and poet whose pen name "Burhānī" was taken from his master's name. Evidently he was the poet who composed the verses inscribed on the wall of Burhān al-Dīn Gharīb's tomb.[274] The story is told that he was summoned to army duty by the military commander Malik Ḥājjī Qulghī, but the shaykh correctly predicted his return in three days. On the occasion of that visit, Burhān al-Dīn Gharīb also presciently told him to check his purse; Ibrāhīm in fact caught his own servants rifling it just at that moment.[275]

Burhān al-Dīn Gharīb also had frequent visits from members of the scholarly class. These encounters were not always friendly. 'Azīz al-Dīn Ḥāfiẓ, an expert on Qur'ānic recitation, could not resist showing off his learning in front of Burhān al-Dīn Gharīb. The shaykh took this opportunity to predict the imminent demise of the scholar's teacher.[276] An equally unfortunate situation occurred with Maḥmūd Laṭīf, another visitor who showed off his knowledge to Burhān al-Dīn Gharīb. He died three days later, just as predicted by the shaykh.[277] Another scholar was Fakhr al-Dīn Hānswī, a purely theoretical thinker; it was remarked that he had a relative who was a cheat. His son wanted to become a Sufi with Burhān al-Dīn Gharīb, but the mother was opposed to this.[278] Other religious scholars were more interested in Sufism. Qāżī Farīd al-Dīn Yūsuf was not a disciple, but he requested from Ḥammād al-Dīn Kāshānī one of Burhān al-Dīn Gharīb's chants in order to solve a problem. He stopped using it after a while, but later resumed it successfully after seeing Burhān al-Dīn Gharīb in a dream.[279] Āzād mentions several eminent religious scholars who became disciples of Zayn al-Dīn during his sojourn in Delhi. These included Nūr al-Dīn Imām, an expert on Qur'ānic readings, and Ṣadr al-Dīn Muftī, a descendant of Shihāb al-Dīn Suhrawardī. He claimed that Zayn al-Dīn Shīrāzī's ascetical struggles outweighed those of all other saints.[280]

Women disciples did not have a high profile in the Khuldabad Sufi group. Certain women, such as Burhān al-Dīn Gharīb's mother Bībī Hājira, were highly respected. Bībī Hājira's tomb is next to the shrine of her other son, Muntajib al-Dīn Zar Zarī Zar-bakhsh. The five sisters of Burhān al-Dīn Gharīb, known locally as "The Five Ladies" (*pāñch bībīyāñ*), also had a prominent position.[281] The upkeep of their tombs was one of the tasks assumed by the first administrators of the shrine of Burhān al-Dīn Gharīb (see Appendix B). But only occasionally do we hear of a female disciple, such as Khwān Bībī. Āzād's description of her is therefore worth quoting in full:

> From childhood she was benevolently nurtured in the shade of Mawlānā Zayn al-Dīn. The Mawlānā too had great affection for her, and for that reason she is known as "the adopted daughter" (*mutabannā ṣāḥib-zādī*). She was a great devotee and ascetic. Having mastered the external and internal sciences with the Mawlānā, she attained the rank of unveiling (*mukāshafa*). The story is well known that once the Bībī was in a state of intoxication when it came time to eat. When the table was laid out, she was summoned. Because of this state, she came but could not begin to eat. The Bībī lifted up some bread from the table and stretched out her hand, saying, "Take it!" The master asked, "To whom are you giving the bread?" She replied, "You cannot see that a [illegible] in blessed Mecca is asking for it; I have given it to him." By the truth of the saying, "The seeker of the Lord is masculine," she is known as Mawlānā Bībī Ṣāḥiba.[282]

Here Khwān Bībī is portrayed as a Sufi who excelled both in religious learning and in visionary experience. For that very reason, she was assimilated to the metaphysical model of gender expressed in the saying of the Chishtī poet Jamāl al-Dīn Hānswī (d. 1260): "The seeker of this world is feminine, the seeker of the next world is hermaphrodite, and the seeker of the Lord is masculine."[283] Thus it was that she was given the courtesy title of the learned, Mawlānā. But in general the attitude toward women was the generally tolerant misogyny typical of the time. Once Burhān al-Dīn Gharīb commented on a formula occurring in a Persian prayer that began, "By the sanctity of the good women and the good men." The good women precede the good men, he remarked, because they were so few, while there were many good men. One of these good women was the mother of Rukn al-Dīn Kāshānī, herself a daughter or descendant of Farīd al-Dīn Ganj-i Shakkar. Comparing her to an unnamed woman saint of the previous generation, Burhān al-Dīn noted that Farīd al-Dīn Ganj-i Shakkar had frequently called that saint a man whom God had sent to the world in a woman's form, in order to do the work of the men of God. Finally, Burhān al-Dīn Gharīb concluded that learning from one's mother was a highly important part of spiritual development.[284]

We shall return to the feminine presence in Khuldabad in connection with the later development of local hagiography (Part III, chap. 11).

There are many other names of disciples that occur only once or twice, but even in these instances one can get some of the flavor of what it meant to them to be disciples. Such is the case with ʿAlī Shāh ʿUmar Mihrāpā, who once thought of going to Multan to become a disciple of the Sufis there (the Suhrawardīs), but after meeting Zayn al-Dīn Shīrāzī he changed his mind and stayed in Daulatabad.[285] Once, when troubled by evil thoughts, he went to Burhān al-Dīn Gharīb for advice. Before he could ask his question, the shaykh answered it, speaking of the difficulty of disciplining the carnal soul. "One must drain cups brimful of poison for thirty years, and to overcome the *nafs*, strive and exceed all limits, so that the 'blaming soul' becomes the 'soul at peace.'"[286] We also hear of Muḥammad Rustam, a former drunkard who gave up wine with the help of Burhān al-Dīn Gharīb and subsequently became initiated.[287] Niẓām al-Dīn Yaʿqūb was a visitor who once, seeing Burhān al-Dīn Gharīb look old and tired, wished that the shaykh would glance at him; he did so, observing ironically that the interior is superior to the appearance.[288] Other members of the circle are shown in even briefer vignettes. Majd al-Dīn Khusraw, we are told, used to bring milk to Burhān al-Dīn Gharīb daily. Muḥammad Khādim is shown being ordered to shave an aspirant. His son later got instruction from Burhān al-Dīn Gharīb in *nawāfil* prayers.[289] Khwāja Muḥammad appeared bringing bread and sugar.[290] Ṣūfī Sakhtiyānī used to come once a year, and was warned of his forthcoming death by Burhān al-Dīn Gharīb during the latter's last year of life, so that he had a month to prepare.[291] There were even characters such as a certain Masʿūd, who came and left without even seeing Burhān al-Dīn Gharīb; he was dismissed as one of the mannerless.[292]

Some members of the Khuldabad circle became important as models for later devotees. Writing in the eighteenth century, Āzād Bilgrāmī observed three main hereditary groups that participated in the running of Burhān al-Dīn Gharīb's shrine. One group was the offspring of Burhān al-Dīn Gharīb's sister through her son Laṭīf al-Dīn, and they are called the *mawlā-zādagān* or descendants of the master. This group figures prominently in the shrine's revenue memorandum produced in the late fifteenth century (Appendix B). The second group, the descendants of Muḥammad Lashkar and Rashīd al-Dīn, are called the *murīd*s or disciples, and they also play a significant role in the revenue memorandum. The third group is comprised of the offspring of four brothers named Khayr al-Dīn, Qabūl, Jildak, and ʿAbd al-Rahman, and they are known as the children (*farzandān*) and attendants (*khuddām*) of the shaykh.

The story of their attachment to Burhān al-Dīn Gharīb has become, in the interpretation given by Āzād, a model for all those who in subsequent generations would become disciples. According to this story, a noble once approached Burhān al-Dīn Gharīb and asked his blessing for a son. The shaykh replied that there would be four sons worthy of his service, so the noble promised them to him, and he was warned not to break promises to *faqīrs*. The four sons were born in due course, and all four eventually entered the service of Burhān al-Dīn Gharīb, apparently when they were still quite young. Two parallel accounts reveal tensions between these children and the senior disciples. Khayr al-Dīn and Qabūl were once beaten by Latif al-Dīn for taking grapes from the garden, and they went and complained of this to Burhān al-Dīn Gharīb, who said, "You are my children, and I am your friend." He then pulled up his shirt and showed them that he also bore the bruises of their beating. He told Laṭīf al-Dīn not to bother them any more. In the other incident, Kākā Shād Bakht gave a whipping to ʿAbd al-Raḥmān and Jildak because they disturbed his reading. Again, the two went and complained to the shaykh. On this occasion too he had the marks of the strap on his back. He warned Kākā Shād Bakht and excluded him from the assembly for several days, saying that those who treated his children well also treated him well, and the same held true for ill treatment.[293]

Āzād enlarged further on the importance of Burhān al-Dīn Gharīb's treatment of these children, seeing it as an indication that the shaykh's beneficent influence continued for all future disciples. According to *Bāqiyat al-karāmāt*, Burhān al-Dīn Gharīb said that the children were his disciples without him having to act like a master. The same source records that he said, "I will not let my children slip, if they slip I will not let them fall, and if they fall I will not let them come down." Thus the term "children" is now generalized to mean all disciples, and Āzād gave thanks for the great blessing of the oath Burhān al-Dīn Gharīb had sworn to protect them. Āzād then cited chapter four of *Aḥsan al-aqwāl*, where Burhān al-Dīn Gharīb says that the wise protect the children, meaning that the shaykhs will protect the disciples. In Āzād's view, this means that all disciples in the order will be protected by Burhān al-Dīn. In chapter five of *Aḥsan al-aqwāl*, the shaykh is quoted as saying that someone who is not a disciple of a master but has true devotion to him and follows him is also among the disciples, and will not be excluded from the reward and blessings of his good intention. By this saying, concludes Āzād, all adherents and pilgrims are included in this blessing.[294] The importance of the "children," then, lies not in their character as model Sufis, but in the paradigmatic relationship of grace and sympathy that the Sufi master established with them. The four brothers owed their very existence to the intervention of the shaykh, and he shared intimately in all their experiences, as the twin whipping incidents show. There is no reference to their having any particular spiritual aptitude or practising any form of discipline, indeed, we only know of their getting into mischief. Yet here were people who received the benefit of the shaykh's love and understanding—what better model could there be for the ordinary devotee of later times?

Samāʿ: Listening to Music

One of the most distinctive practices of the Chishtīs was *samāʿ*, or listening to musical recitation of poetry. Although *samāʿ* literally means "listening" or "audition," it is more correct to follow Bruce Lawrence's definition of *samāʿ* as "hearing chanted verse (with or without accompanying instruments) in the company of others also seeking to participate in the dynamic dialogue between a human lover and the Divine Beloved."[295] Since music, particularly instrumental music, has always had an uneasy status in Islamic law, the practice of *samāʿ* has been controversial. In contemporary South Asian Muslim circles, one sometimes hears the argument that the Chishtīs only adopted the questionable practice of *samāʿ* in order to appeal to the music-loving Indian population, as part of a program of conversion.

This position, which seeks to excuse a legally dubious practice by making it serve a higher missionary goal, has no historical justification. *Samāʿ* was a standard topic in the Arabic Sufi manuals of the tenth century, and it was widely practised in Iraq and Iran. There are remarkable similarities between the Chishtī approach to music and that of the great Sufi poet Jalāl al-Dīn Rūmī (d. 1277), whose works were known in northern India. *Samāʿ* was, moreover, restricted in principle to the mystical elite, and according to some was a purely spiritual experience. One early Sufi described it in these words:

> *Samāʿ* is the comprehension of essences by the ear of the heart, the heart's understanding of realities, becoming aware of God's indications and the divine speech and will, the opening up of the tongue of conscience to God, the avoidance of doubt and suspicion, and the conveying of the words of reality by the heart of *samāʿ*."[296]

From the foregoing description, one would take *samāʿ* to be the essential mystical experience, and the direct perception of God by the heart. Yet simply to equate *samāʿ* with some kind of inner experience would be misleading, for *samāʿ* is a form of religious activity involving musical performance that ideally takes place under the strictest of conditions. Demanding psychological and intellectual guidelines, as well as elaborate rules of etiquette, govern the enactment of *samāʿ*. The writings of the Khuldabad Sufis amplify this notion of *samāʿ* as the ecstatic core of the Chishtī tradition, and they emphasize the pursuit of *samāʿ* as a way to union with God that must be combined with severe discipline of the carnal self.

Burhān al-Dīn Gharīb was, probably more than any other senior disciple of Niẓām al-Dīn Awliyā', dedicated to the practice of *samāʿ*. Mīr Khwurd had emphasized this ecstatic attitude, saying that Burhān al-Dīn had "a distinctive style (*ṭarzī alā-ḥida*) in dancing, so that the companions of this saint were called 'Burhānīs' among the lovers."[297] Burhān al-Dīn himself was extremely susceptible to the influence of *samāʿ* as well as spiritual discourses in general.[298] The Khuldabad *malfūẓāt* reveal that *samāʿ* was very popular in the circle of Burhān al-Dīn Gharīb, most notably with Burhān al-Dīn's successor Zayn al-Dīn Shīrāzī, although he had fiercely opposed listening to music before he became a Sufi.[299] *Aḥsan al-aqwāl* is a particularly rich resource on this topic, as chapter twenty-six presents a whole series of rules governing the practice of *samāʿ*. *Shamā'il al-atqiyā'* also contains a comprehensive discussion of the question of *samāʿ* according to both classical Sufi authors and the Delhi Chishtīs. These primary sources furnish an irreplaceable documentation on the Chishtī practice of *samāʿ*.

As a disciple of Niẓām al-Dīn Awliyā', Burhān al-Dīn must have been keenly aware of the controversy that raged in Delhi over the legitimacy of listening to music. This controversy was not new; Sufis in the Islamic heartland had practiced *samāʿ* since the ninth or tenth century, and jurists had not been slow to attack this phenomenon as a suspicious and possibly immoral innovation. Although many of the early Sufi masters joined the musical gatherings to hear mystical verses, they more than anyone were conscious of music's power over the soul for both good and evil; consequently, few approved of it without reservation. A number of Sufi authorities give the impression that *samāʿ* is a kind of stimulant for those whose spiritual nerves have become deadened. Aḥmad al-Ghazālī was one of the minority of early authorities who regarded *samāʿ* as part of the height of Sufi experience. Shaykh ʿAlī Hujwīrī of Lahore, one of the first Sufis to dwell in the Indian subcontinent, showed the ambivalence typical of many shaykhs—he praised *samāʿ* as a source of ecstasy for advanced mystics, but condemned it as a trap of Satan for the unwary novice. The legitimacy of listening to music, in other words, was not a simple question, but depended on the people and circumstances involved.

Under the Delhi sultanate, the Chishtī order was in the middle of the continuing controversy over listening to music, because, in a significant new development, *samāʿ* had now become the central feature of Sufi practice even for novices. As Bruce Lawrence has observed, "in the Indian environment from the period of the Delhi sultanate through the Mughul era (1206–1857) *samāʿ* assumed a unique significance as the integrating modus operandi of the Chishtī order."[300] Thus the Chishtī order stood apart from the Suhrawardī order, which did not emphasize *samāʿ*, and it was even further removed from the conservative jurists. The jurists' opposition took the form of petitions to the sultans of Delhi, seeking a royal decree forbidding the practice of *samāʿ*, while the Chishtīs and their supporters vigorously defended *samāʿ* as permissible under Islamic law. Despite these appeals, both Sultan Iltutmish and Sultan Ghiyās al-Dīn Tughluq refused to outlaw the Chishtīs' observances.[301] Burhān al-Dīn was undoubtedly aware of both the contemporary debate and the reserve of some of the classical Sufi authorities toward *samāʿ*. On one occasion another Sufi, who was not a disciple of Niẓām al-Dīn Awliyā', criticized

Burhān al-Dīn's appearance after *samā*ʿ (it may be that Burhān al-Dīn appeared disheveled or had rent his garments); Burhān al-Dīn responded that this was his master's practice, even if it was not recommended in the great handbook of Sufism, the *ʿAwārif al-maʿārif* of Shaykh Suhrawardī.[302]

With this controversy in mind, it is not surprising to find that Burhān al-Dīn Gharīb and his followers upheld a demanding ethical standard for participants in *samā*ʿ, even as they spiritualized some of the technical rules. Burhān al-Dīn used a framework derived from Islamic law to describe the varying psychological attitudes that lovers of God and lovers of the world bring to the experience of listening to music:

> The master (Burhān al-Dīn) also said, "*Samā*ʿ is of four types. One is lawful, in which the listener is totally longing for God and not at all longing for the created. The second is permitted, in which the listener is mostly longing for God and only a little for the created. The third is disapproved, in which there is much longing for the created and a little for God. The fourth is forbidden, in which there is no longing for God and all is for the created. . . . But the listener should know the difference between doing the lawful, the forbidden, the permitted, and the disapproved. And this is a secret between God and the listener."[303]

Although cast in a legal form, Burhān al-Dīn's analysis of the listener's motivation puts the burden of responsibility on the individual conscience, for the object of one's love is by its nature secret from the law. Similar was the view of Rukn al-Dīn Kāshānī when he was asked if at the judgment *samā*ʿ would weigh in the scale of good or of evil; he replied that *samā*ʿ as the perception of spiritual states did not enter into the scales of actions at all.[304]

The Chishtīs' focus on purified intention as the criterion of genuine *samā*ʿ led them to encourage novices to participate in musical sessions, and to seek genuine ecstasy (*wajd*) even if it meant imitating that ecstasy initially. Many early texts mention the imitation of ecstasy by "empathetic ecstasy" (*tawājud*), which is sometimes characterized by a susceptibility to be inspired by hearing a divine communication even in the voices of animals. The subject of empathetic ecstasy had been an ambiguous one in classical Sufism, because of a general abhorrence of affectation or pretense in any form. The Persian translation of Suhrawardī's *ʿAwārif*, for instance, concentrates much of its discussion of the manners of *samā*ʿ on the horrible nature of empathetic ecstasy, though there is some concession in the case of beginners.[305] Yet with Niẓām al-Dīn Awliyā' there is a new emphasis on linking the grades of ecstasy with the ranks of the participants in *samā*ʿ. Niẓām al-Dīn's disciple, Fakhr al-Dīn Zarrādī, systematized this insight in his treatise on listening to music, *Uṣūl al-Samā*ʿ (*Principles of samā*ʿ). Now empathetic ecstasy (*tawājud*) was seen as a proper response to *samā*ʿ, and one that was intrinsically connected to the ecstasy of divine love. This wholehearted enthusiasm for *samāʿ* became characteristic of later Chishtī writers, such as Masʿūd Bakk (d. 1389) and Ashraf Jahāngīr Simnānī (d. 1422). Burhān al-Dīn Gharīb on occasion did say that empathetic ecstasy was a defect in *samāʿ*, since true ecstasy and spiritual states were the goal; he repeated the advice of Niẓām al-Dīn Awliyā' that if one does not have ecstasy (*wajd*), one should call on the name of God as *al-Wājid*.[306] This insistence on the elite level of experience was unusual, however.

In general, Burhān al-Dīn and his followers approve of empathetic ecstasy, and they prescribe it first of all as a mode of behavior during *samāʿ*. In the ritual, empathetic ecstasy seeks real ecstasy by conforming to the behavior of those who have it. "If someone in *samāʿ* has no ecstasy nor rapture, the rules (*adab*) are that he go stand with the people of ecstasy and conform with them."[307] One can observe this custom in the performance of *samāʿ* even today, when someone goes into a *ḥāl* or spiritual state, and the company rises up to conform to his state. Rukn al-Dīn Kāshānī is explicit on this point: "If a dervish rises from his spiritual state and ecstasy, the companions should conform, and all rise. This is an approved custom, and a fine tradition; to go against it is to abandon sanctity."[308] If, on the other hand, one has not yet attained ecstasy, but only the intermediate experiences of "rapture" (*jazb*) and "taste" (*zawq*), one still must conform with the rest, and sit if they are seated, though movement is permitted. In the receptive mood of the *samāʿ* assembly, one's state can affect others strongly; therefore, if one is overcome by one of the awesome qualities of the divine wrath, one should remain silent to avoid influencing one's companions.[309]

Empathetic ecstasy is also a mode of engagement with the recited verses, so that it becomes an intellectual approach to mystical experience. Rukn al-Dīn Kāshānī gives lengthy explanations of the process of interpretation of poetry and empathetic ecstasy, in a number of passages drawn from his lost work *Rumūz al-wālihīn*.[310] In these comments Rukn al-Dīn truly lives up to his nickname, "the spiritual clerk" (*dabīr-i maʿnawī*). He speaks in this text as an intellectual lay follower of the Sufis. His audience is not only the elite disciples of the Chishtī order, but also the educated Muslims who are interested in Sufism but are not certain how to evaluate it. In his discussion of *samāʿ*, he emphasizes the need for the novice to interpret the verses in terms of the attributes of God. Allegorical interpretation (*taḥmīl*) of the verses of poetry in terms of God or the master is of course a dominant characteristic of Sufi writing, from Sarrāj and Aḥmad Ghazālī to Niẓām al-Dīn Awliyā' and Sharaf al-Dīn Manērī.[311] According to Rukn al-Dīn Kāshānī, this is not to be done except in a theologically correct manner. The negative and positive divine attributes are to be correlated with the symbols of poetry (e.g., the cheek of the beloved as the manifestation of divine beauty). This is a process of deliberate thought (*fikr*) in listening (*istimāʿ*), aided by divine visitations (*wāridāt*). Or more formally, one proceeds through three journeys. "The first is in voice and verse, the second in active attributes, the third in essential attributes. . . . The root of the matter is thought in *samāʿ*."[312] Examples of this kind of interpretation are the qualities of divine beauty and majesty, or grace and wrath, as polar manifestations of the power of God. Doubtless also many verses were then as now referred to the great Sufi masters, whose lives and deaths are still celebrated regularly by such concerts (see Figure 18). As long as one can interpret the poetry in this way, it is a sign of divine guidance, according to Rukn al-Dīn. This is in general a very systematic and intellectualistic approach to *samāʿ*, but one that he feels will lead to transrational ecstasy.

In contrast, a remarkable instance of Burhān al-Dīn's more direct spirituality is his story of the shaykh who heard a lute that was expressing the divine attributes with its strings. "Then he said, 'Lute, if you only knew what you are saying, every one of your strings would break.' No sooner were these words spoken than the strings of the lute broke. The disciples asked what the lute was saying. The master said, 'One string said, "O Merciful," and another string said, "O Compassionate."' "[313] Burhān al-Dīn here alludes to the experience of divine attributes by direct perception. For Rukn al-Dīn, however, the theological interpretation is significant. This intellectualism may be contrasted with a passage that Rukn al-Dīn quotes from al-Ḥallāj, who insisted that *samāʿ* is not limited to words and thought—"that which they hear without notes is not by means of word and voice, but is related to the perception of internal hearing."[314]

On the highest level, however, *samāʿ* derives from spiritual experiences of the most sublime nature. Ever since the time of Junayd of Baghdad (d. 910), it has been common for Sufis to link *samāʿ* with the Qur'ānic theme of the primordial covenant (*mīthāq*) between God and the unborn souls of humanity, when God demanded, "Am I not your Lord (*a-lastu bi-rabbikum*)?" (Qur. 7.172). This moment, for the Sufis, was not only the perfect statement of the divine unity but also the forging of the link of love between God and the soul. Moreover, the music of *samāʿ* is nothing but the reverberation of that primal word of God: "*Samāʿ* is the recollection of the speech of the Covenant, and the burning of the fire of longing."[315] The Sufis describe God as having placed a secret into the human heart that day, which is concealed like a spark in stone, but which blazes forth when struck with the steel of *samāʿ*.[316] Junayd is quoted as saying, "When to the essence of the children of Adam on the day of the covenant there came the words, 'Am I not your Lord,' all the spirits became absorbed by its delight. Thus those who came into this world, whenever they hear a beautiful voice, their spirits tremble and are disturbed by the memory of that speech, because the influence of that speech is in the beautiful voice."[317] In other terms, the source of *samāʿ* is said to be the "rapture" or "attraction" (*jazb*) of God, a kind of energy that irresistibly draws one toward

God. The Egyptian Sufi Dhū al-Nūn (d. 859) said, "*samā*ʿ is God's rapture that agitates (*yazʿaju*) hearts toward God." Alluding to the difference in perspective between lovers of God and lovers of the world, Dhū al-Nūn said further, "*samā*ʿ is the messenger of the Real (*al-ḥaqq*). Whoever listens to God becomes a realizer of truth (*muḥaqqiq*), and whoever listens to the carnal soul becomes a heretic" (*zindīq*).[318] Burhān al-Dīn even traced the spiritual source of one's physical appearance during *samā*ʿ. He said that "*samā*ʿ has two colors, one yellow and the other red. Everyone on whom distance, wrath, and fear descend turns pale, and everyone who has nearness, union, grace, and hope, blushes."[319] In this way, the fundamental modes of separation from God and union with God manifest directly in the color of the human face.

What would most interest an outside observer about *samā*ʿ is to see what are the effects of the ecstasy on the participants, but this is a topic that the sources touch upon only lightly, since the spiritual experience is the goal. One of the most intriguing effects of *samā*ʿ is dancing (*raqṣ*), usually spoken of as a spontaneous expression of ecstasy. It was perhaps only among the Mevlevi dervishes of Turkey that rhythmic dance was regularly practiced as empathetic ecstasy (nowadays the dance of the "whirling dervishes" is performed in concert halls and for tourists).[320] Though the early Sufi masters at best tolerated ecstatic dance, the Chishtīs felt it was a natural effect of the powerful influences of *samā*ʿ. Niẓām al-Dīn Awliyā' is reported as saying, "At the time of *samā*ʿ and recitation, happiness descends on the heart. From the world of emanation to the world of power, then it affects the heart. These are the states which are between kingdom (*mulk*) and angelicity (*malakūt*). When its agitation becomes visible, it is called 'influences' (*āsār*) which have come from the kingdom to the limbs."[321] *Samā*ʿ creates a kind of channel between the heard and the spiritual world, and the surging of its energy overflows into the body and releases itself in dance. An older Sufi source states, "Every limb has a portion and a pleasure in *samā*ʿ. The portion of the eye is weeping, the portion of the tongue is crying out, the portion of the hand is striking the garment, and the portion of the foot is dancing."[322]

There is an enigmatic statement by Qushayrī, frequently quoted in the sources, that runs as follows: "*Samā*ʿ is an invitation, and ecstasy is an intention." By this Qushayrī appears to emphasize the psychological dimension of participation in *samā*ʿ. Curiously enough, the version of this saying cited by Rukn al-Dīn adds an extra phrase, so that it reads, "*samā*ʿ is an invitation, ecstasy is an intention, and dance is union." [323] The additional conclusion, that "dance is union," appears to have been added by some Indian author, perhaps by Rukn al-Dīn himself. It seems to be typical of the Chishtī approach to *samā*ʿ that the ecstatic element has been raised to the dominant position. Other effects of *samā*ʿ include healing and even raising people from the dead.[324] The influence of *samā*ʿ was certainly considered to extend beyond the grave. "Khwāja Jalāl al-Dīn told of being with Burhān al-Dīn Gharīb on an ecstatic occasion, and mentioned Khwāja Ẓuhayr Saqqā' and how tears would fall from his eyes as soon as *samā'* started. Burhān al-Dīn Gharīb suggested that they visit his tomb and perform pilgrimage (*ziyārat*). They did, and Burhān al-Dīn Gharīb told Jalāl that Khwāja Ẓuhayr Saqqā' still had those tears."[325]

This description of *samā'* and the accompanying ecstasy would be incomplete and one-sided without an account of the strict discipline that balanced it. What was the function of these rules? In brief, it was to keep open the avenues of divine influence while attempting to exclude the intrusion of the human ego. These rules were not only derived from the classical manuals of Sufism, but also were ideals that followed the concrete examples of the early Chishtī masters. Most notably, in *Aḥsan al-aqwāl*, Ḥammād al-Dīn Kāshānī records illustrations of these principles from incidents in the circle of Burhān al-Dīn Gharīb, and he also quotes Burhān al-Dīn Gharīb on particular instances of Niẓām al-Dīn Awliyā's behavior during *samā'*. According to Ḥammād, every session began and ended with recitation of the Qur'ān. All the participants were expected to perform ablutions as for ritual prayer, and abstain from chewing betel.[326] It was important not to make *samā'* a mechanical performance. Therefore it should not be held at a fixed time every week, or be made into a profession or a habit.[327] Neither should one be forward or assertive during *samā'*. Since ecstasy was often the result of the listener's interpretation of a verse, the listener would desire to have that verse repeated; it is acceptable for the listener to request repetition, but "if in spite of his desire he submits and does not have them repeat it, God inspires the reciter" to do so.[328]

It is forbidden to question others who are present about the meaning of a verse, since that is usually only a pretext for the questioner to show off his own knowledge, and talk distracts from the real meaning.[329] One should not criticize the singer, for this reduces the performance to an aesthetic occasion; it is better to refer the matter to God.[330] In any case, inspiration is of greater importance in a singer than artistic skill, and is more likely to induce ecstasy.[331] Although the objective is ecstasy, total control of the ego is necessary to achieve this. Therefore it is forbidden to disclose or display the nature of one's spiritual state. Burhān al-Dīn Gharīb has given a whole series of regulations that apply this principle to the physical behavior of participants in *samā'*.[332] For instance, he said, "If a dervish unintentionally raises his hand during audition, audition is no longer proper for him." One should be physically restrained. "A dervish should be sober and never allow his hands or feet to touch another; if this happens anyway, he should pull back."

Another rule states that if one goes to the extent of rolling on the ground, there is a fine to be paid. The example given is Burhān al-Dīn himself, who once had actually been crawling (*lūkīda*, a rare word), and received this penalty. It is doubtful that this lack of control had anything to do with the

"Burhānī" style of dancing that Mīr Khwurd mentioned, since that must have been a measured dance of empathetic ecstasy. One cannot drink anything during a musical session or fan oneself, no matter how hot the weather. Once when someone committed this offense, Niẓām al-Dīn Awliyā' rebuked him in the metaphor of lovers' suffering, "Dervishes consume their blood; what have I to do with sherbeṭ?" One should avoid giving greetings to others during *samā*ʿ, to avoid disturbing anyone's concentration. Zayn al-Dīn Shīrāzī reiterated this emphasis on solitude in the gathering: "If a hundred Sufis are in *samā*ʿ, one walks so that one's skirt does not touch the skirt of another." But since human nature is what it is, mistakes will occur. When mistakes happen, it would be a serious breach of discipline to point this out publicly. If someone is behaving affectedly or without manners, the proper response is to "remain outwardly silent and help inwardly so that the state becomes balanced again. Our master [Burhān al-Dīn] said that one uses this prayer: 'Lord, prevent him from this, and protect me from this!' "[333] There are other rules governing precedence in rituals, the distribution of patched cloaks, gifts to the musicians, and so on, but it is difficult to reconstruct these aspects of the ritual on the basis of the texts alone.

From the writings of the Khuldabad Chishtīs on *samā*ʿ, we can see how Burhān al-Dīn Gharīb stood firmly in the tradition of classical Sufism while at the same time he embodied the particular genius of the Chishtī order. He faced the problem of the ambiguity of *samā*ʿ in Islamic law by putting the burden of ethical responsibility on the individual participant in *samā*ʿ. This emphasis on the contextuality of *samā*ʿ was thoroughly in consonance with the internal orientation of Sufi ethics. Burhān al-Dīn also continued the Chishtī practice of permitting empathetic ecstasy, the imitation of genuine ecstasy, as a way to introduce novices into the higher ranges of spiritual experience.

To avoid the problems of insincerity and affectation in *samā*ʿ, Burhān al-Dīn insisted on the proper spiritual interpretation of the erotic verses recited in *samā*ʿ, and he determined that the psychological basis of *samā*ʿ was to be found in the most profound spiritual experiences of Islamic mysticism. To maintain the purity of this ritual form of meditation, Burhān al-Dīn urged a discipline that was designed to eliminate expression of egotism as well as the habitual attitudes of secular life. We can summarize the Chishtī attitude towards *samā*ʿ—and at the same time stress its importance in Sufism as a whole—by quoting Shaykh ʿUmar al-Suhrawardī:

> The deniers of *samā*ʿ are either ignorant of the example of the Prophet, deluded by their own knowledge, or perverse by nature. Some masters of *samā*ʿ can understand a hundred thousand mysteries filled with treasuries of secrets in the voice of the singer and the verse.[334]

8

The Indian Environment and the Question of Conversion

By the time that the Chishtīs settled in Khuldabad, the Sufi tradition had been established to some extent in northern India for two and a half centuries. Necessarily much of the substance of Sufi teaching and practice derived from models initially elaborated in Iran, Iraq, and central Asia in the previous centuries. Yet our subject here is Sufism in India, and so it may be asked to what extent the Chishtī Sufi center in Khuldabad affected and was affected by the Indian environment. The question of the Indian character of Sufism in south Asia is a complex one, and discussions of it have generally revolved around contentious issues of religion, in particular the issue of conversion to Islam. Particular details of language and custom indicate that a certain amount of Indianization had taken place in the groups upon which the Chishtīs drew for their membership. The primary documents do not, however, suggest that the Chishtīs were involved in any conscious missionary activity designed to convert non-Muslims to Islam; it would be more correct to say that the *malfūẓāt* texts scarcely mention non-Muslims at all. As we have seen, the Chishtīs' emphasis on interiorization was not even oriented to the average Muslim, but to a spiritual elite, and so it can hardly be expected that these Sufis would have devoted themselves to an audience that was totally unfamiliar with the basic points of Islam.

The Sufis' relationship with the Indian environment is most importantly revealed by their use of poetry in Indian regional languages. The Hindawī verses that occur in the Khuldabad texts indicate an Indianization of Sufism, to the extent that Sufis found the local language and imagery appropriate for the expression of their teachings. Although most of these verses occur in contexts of specialized Islamic discourse, it would be wrong to regard them as the vehicles for the dissemination of Islam to non-Muslims; when non-Muslim groups such as the Sikhs appropriated the verses of the Chishtī master Farīd al-Dīn Ganj-i Shakkar (a problem greatly clarified by the Khuldabad texts), they only drew upon those poems that lacked any specifically Islamic character.

Recent methodological essays by scholars of Indian Islam have helped to bring out the issues at stake in the discussion of conversion. Peter Hardy, in particular, has emphasized the vagueness that has surrounded the question of conversion of Islam, and the way in which this question has served as a mode of expression for the authors' own preconceptions or evolving views about their own relationship with Islam.[335] Theories of conversion, in other words, often tell us more about the theorist's views of Islam than anything else. In modern times, the question of conversion to Islam has had many explosive implications ever since it was first raised in a systematic way by British administrators in the nineteenth century. Hardy rightly describes it as being today "a political minefield," especially in the wake of the partition of British India into India and Pakistan.[336] The principal ideological arguments can be classified, loosely, as follows: first, the "religion of the sword" argument, which assumes that conversion to Islam took place primarily by force. Second, the "religion of social liberation" argument, which sees Islam as offering equality to Indians suffering from oppression under the caste system. And third, the "Sufi as missionary" argument, which sees the Sufis as having systematically brought Hindus to Islam by preaching and by indirect means such as force of character.[337] All of these arguments have political implications, and all have the defect of either relying on an excessively literal reading of sources or anachronistically projecting modern concerns onto medieval society.[338]

The "religion of the sword" theory equates Islam with political rule by Muslims, and accepts the triumphalist rhetoric of dynastic chronicles as a statement of the Islamic faith. This theory was first enunciated with respect to India by British administrators such as Sir Henry Elliot, and it plays an important role in modern Hindu nationalism. While evidence suggests that certain Muslim rulers encouraged outward conformity to Islam by repressive means, such actions had a significance that was primarily political. The "religion of social liberation" argument comes, on the other hand, originally from a sixteenth-century Muslim source, and is favored by the liberal wing of south Asian Muslim scholars. This interpretation views Islam as progressive and egalitarian, and thus a boon welcomed by the Indian masses.[339] It has been remarked that whatever value this observation has may be limited to the extreme south of India, where Muslims have generally had a high social status and converts have not been subjected to the limitations of their former caste. This stands in contrast to northern India, where the majority of Muslims in modern times hold relatively low social status.[340] The "Sufi as missionary" theory is more complex, and we shall discuss it further below.

Other, less controversial, factors in the growth of the Islamic population in south Asia include significant immigration by Arabs, Turks, Afghans, and

Iranians, the "political patronage" argument, which points to individuals and groups who received financial rewards and political appointments in exchange for converting to Islam, and intermarriage between Muslim men and non-Muslim women. These processes probably did not involve large numbers of people. Richard Eaton has introduced another thesis, the "ecological" argument, that conversion to Islam was most effective in those areas (western Punjab and Bengal) that were least exposed to Brahmanical culture and shifted from tribal and nomadic lifestyles to agricultural existence under a political system ruled by Muslims. The literate tradition of Islam, through the medium of qāżī judges and Sufi shrines, according to this view, was vastly more effective in stabilizing these local cultures in terms of Islamic values than in areas more firmly linked to the rival literate tradition of the Brahmans.[341] Eaton has also charted a process of gradual conversion to Islam by a process of intergenerational accretion among tribal groups in the Punjab, in connection with the unifying role of one of the great Chishtī shrines, that of Farīd al-Dīn Ganj-i Shakkar.[342] These sociological explanations involve gradual social change over long periods of time, and depart from the Christian model of conversion as a sudden "change of heart" in an individual.

But what of the argument that the Sufi saints were responsible for the conversion of large numbers of Indians to Islam? Again, much depends on what is meant by conversion. It is one thing to show, as Eaton has done, that over many generations the social groups (in this case, tribes of the Punjab) associated with a Sufi shrine show a gradual increase in the proportion of obviously Muslim names, which eventually becomes 100 percent; by that index it can be argued that the Sufi shrine acted as the focus for the Islamization of those groups through a process of accretion over time. It is quite another thing to say that Farīd al-Dīn Ganj-i Shakkar personally engaged in attempting to preach Islam to large numbers of Hindus. For this argument there is practically no evidence in the oldest stratum of Sufi literature. As Bruce B. Lawrence has shown, the *malfūẓāt* texts of the thirteenth and fourteenth centuries refer only to a few isolated cases of individuals who converted to Islam after becoming attracted to the Sufi saints.[343] Niẓām al-Dīn Awliyā' observed that Indians were not drawn to Islam through sermons, and Naṣīr al-Dīn Maḥmūd Chirāgh-i Dihlī never converted anyone to Islam; Gīsū Darāz was unusual in that he engaged with some Indians in disputations, but he complained that they did not follow through with conversion when defeated.[344] While the Chishtīs would doubtless have been pleased to see people attracted to the faith of Muḥammad, the assertion that most Sufis "regarded the conversion of non-Muslims as one of their primary spiritual objectives in India" cannot be supported by contemporary accounts.[345]

The picture of the Sufi as missionary is derived from three later sources: royal historiography, tribal and caste traditions enshrined in late hagiographies and British gazetteers, and nineteenth-century British concepts of Christian missions. Royal historiography contributed to the notion of Sufi missionaries by invoking the aura of Sufi sanctity to legitimize their conquests; this began as early as Muḥammad ibn Tughluq's attempt to force the Chishtīs to preach Islam, a conscription that they resisted (above, Part II, chap. 6). The royal search for religious support widened in the fourteenth century, when rulers saw the foundation of mosques and the encouragement of conversion as a way of broadening their base of support.[346] Hagiographies of the Mughul period begin to discuss Sufis as bringing about the mass conversion of infidels to Islam, generally through the exhibition of miraculous powers. This phenomenon breaks the tension between royal and mystical historiographies, making the Sufis into the agents of imperial expansion (above, Part I, chap. 5). As Simon Digby has pointed out, contests between Sufis and yogis, which were often followed by conversion of the yogi, often had local territorial significance as well, in emphasizing the saint's superiority over other Sufis.[347] Medieval hagiographies often depict famous Sufis as leaving their homes in Iran or central Asia as a result of a dream, in which the Sufi was commanded to go to India to preach to the heathen. Such was the case with Sayyid ʿAlī Hamadānī (d. 786/1385), regarded as the true founder of Islam in Kashmir. Recent scholarly research suggests, however, that such a motive cannot be detected in sources contemporary with the shaykh, who seems rather to have left central Asia as a result of his strained relations with the emperor Tīmūr.[348] Political considerations would also seem to have a role in modern celebrations of the death-anniversaries of Sufi saints, who are sometimes extolled as the missionaries of Islam as if that were their main activity and the sole justification for the reverence in which they are held. This strategy has the effect, in Pakistan, of portraying Sufi saints as the forerunners of the Islamic state, and at the same time it defuses fundamentalist criticism of Sufism by resolutely avoiding any mention of the actual content of Islamic mysticism.

Tribal and caste traditions about conversion, which were often not committed to writing until the nineteenth century, represent a phenomenon difficult to track. These are often only available in nineteenth-century British gazetteers, which emphasized the most bizarre manifestations of popular religion.[349] But the inevitable selection of an eminent early Sufi as the medium for the Islamization of castes and tribes suggests that other motives may be present besides antiquarian research. Lawrence maintains that "those who attached themselves to the Shaykh and to his tomb forged a new lineage of legitimacy for themselves and their descendants."[350] Those who could claim to have been converted to Islam by a Sufi saint could also claim his spiritual and even temporal protection. Conversion stories may have had other important implications at the time when they were told, with respect to asserting one's ancestral position for the British authorities when revenue settlements were being made, or establishing rights to Islamic judicial positions.[351] The role of Christian missionaries served as a model for the Sufi as missionary when nineteenth-century Muslims reconsidered their history under the pressure of colonial rule.[352] The strength of the Christian concept can be judged from the adoption of the word "mission," which has been directly transliterated into Urdu script (as *mishan*), to describe the activities of Chishtī Sufis in the Deccan.[353]

The late hagiographic ideal of the missionary Sufi does not fit, however, with the picture of Sufi discipline and practice as found in the early Sufi manuals. Travel to faraway places, rather than being the result of dreams, is discussed as a difficult task that forms part of the discipline, but never in connection with conversion of non-Muslims. According to the tenth-century authority al-Sarrāj, one travels to get away from other people and to see one's own blameworthy qualities. One travels to meet shaykhs, since that requires manners, humility, desire, forgetting all that one knows, and accepting the shaykh's advice, so it should not be a cause of pride.[354] A more detailed account by Abū Najīb al-Suhrawardī (d. 563/1168) listed the permissible purposes of traveling, in order of priority: *jihād*, *ḥajj*, pilgrimage to the Prophet's tomb, pilgrimage to the mosque of Jerusalem, traveling for learning, to visit shaykhs and brethren, to repair wrongs and ask forgiveness, to learn stories of past Sufis, and finally as self-discipline and to achieve anonymity.[355] While some might argue that *jihād* was the equivalent of conversion, this remained only a theoretical option for most Sufis at this period, and one that was in practice subordinated to royal ambition. Al-Suhrawardī gave detailed rules concerning the behavior of Sufi travelers in the hospices where they generally lodged, but never mentioned public proselytizing. The role of travel as a means of purification and discipline is illustrated by the remark of the other leader of the Suhrawardī order, Shihāb al-Dīn al-Suhrawardī (d. 632/1234): "The influence of travel on taming souls is no less than that of supererogatory prayer, fasting, and ritual prayer."[356]

The only term regularly used in Arabic for missionary activity is *daʿwa* (Persian *daʿvat*), which means "calling, inviting." The only Islamic group that has systematically employed *daʿvat* as a technique to reach outsiders and non-Muslims is the Ismāʿīlī sect, which has for centuries freely adapted local Indian symbolism and integrated it with Islamic themes. The term *daʿvat* occurs in Sufi texts, but with the specific meaning of a master preaching to an elite group of disciples in training. Rukn al-Dīn Kāshānī quotes the Persian translation of Suhrawardī's *ʿAwārif* to define this term as follows:

> *Daʿvat* means to call someone toward something and towards someone, and it is of several types, by wisdom, by preaching, and by disputation, as God Most High said, "Call to the path of your lord with wisdom and fine preaching, and dispute with them by means of that which is best" (Qur. 16.125). That is, "O Muḥammad, by whatever means his carnal soul dominates his heart, call him with a fine

> preaching." This is directed toward the pious ones (*abrār*), by recalling heaven and hell. "And for anyone whose heart dominates his carnal soul, call him with wisdom." This was directed toward the wayfarers and seekers of the Real, who are hopeful of finding internal purity, gnosis, unity, and nearness. This is by hint, and it is a gift. "Say: This is my way; I call toward God with insight, I and whoso follows me" (Qur. 12.108) is the secret of this meaning.[357]

What is especially noticeable about this passage is the exegesis of the three modes of *da'wa* traced to Qur. 16.125. Here "fine preaching" (*maw'iẓa ḥasana*) is equated with reminding the pious of heaven and hell, while "wisdom" (*ḥikma*) is regarded as calling the adept mystics to inner experience by means of hint and allusion. The urge to interiorize religious practice into spiritual experience so preoccupied Rukn al-Dīn that he completely omitted any reference to disputation, the third manner of calling to God. It must be recalled that the principal religious activity of Sufism was the intensive interiorization of Islamic religious practice. Sufis had little patience for dealing with the more literally minded generality of Muslims; most of their teachings were reserved for an elite group. How should they suddenly begin to preach, then, to a mass of non-Muslims who were not even familiar with the basics of Islam? Giving public lectures and admonishment (*tazkīr*) is an activity that the Khuldabad *malfūẓāt* texts associate exclusively with the activities of professional religious scholars.[358] The concept of Sufi missionaries seems almost contradictory when viewed in this light.

The role of the Khuldabad Chishtīs with respect to the spread of Islam in the Deccan has been greatly exaggerated in modern historical literature. Mixing royal and saintly traditions, the British gazetteers and Urdu hagiographies portray the Sufis of Khuldabad as militant warriors in the service of Islam and the state. One typical, rather confused, example is as follows:

> Alāuddin Khaljī and Malik Kāfur led the Muslim military force to conquer Dēvagiri of the Yādavas and Dvārasumadra of the Hōysala and to bring them under the political control of Delhi Sultanate, while the disciples of Nizamuddin Avaliya of Delhi led three consecutive expeditions of their spiritual army for the spread of Islam. Each batch was seven hundred strong. These Sūfi missionaries led a spiritual life and by their spirituality and humanity attracted to themselves not only the Muslims but also low caste Hindus and even a few Brāhmans.[359]

As in the nineteenth-century gazetteer of the Nizam's dominions (above, Part II, chap. 6), here the story of the forced emigration of the fourteen hundred saints to Daulatabad in 1329 has been conflated with the original raid of 'Alā' al-Dīn Khaljī in 1296. The militant image now assigned to the Sufi "army" accords with its supposed missionary activity. Now it may be that the

Khuldabad shrines have acted over the centuries as a focus for the gradual accretion of some of the local population to Islamic practices. In the first available census figures, the district (Circar) of Daulatabad under the Nizam's government in 1849 contained a population of 10.5 percent Muslims, exclusive of the city of Aurangabad. This figure is considerably higher than the average population of Muslims in rural Maharashtra, so there may be reason to suppose that the Chishtī shrines acted as a stimulus toward greater local identification with Islam.[360] But we do not have any contemporary indication that the Khuldabad Sufis ever entertained the idea of missionary activity.

The rare occasions when contemporary non-Muslims are mentioned in the Khuldabad *malfūẓāt* texts scarcely permit one to form any picture of the relations between the Sufis and non-Muslims. The most specific reference to any non-Muslim is the occasional mention of yogis, who are regarded as alchemists (possibly fraudulent ones) with advanced knowledge of medicine and the body.[361] The term "Hindu" only occurs in contexts that describe battles between Turkish forces and Indian soldiers, so that the term appears hardly to have acquired any religious significance as far as the Sufis are concerned.[362] Zayn al-Dīn in many remarks explicitly restricted the role of Sufism to exerting a spiritual influence over Muslims. When Mīr Ḥasan mentioned to Zayn al-Dīn the *malfūẓāt* project that he was writing, he stated that it would be for the benefit of Muslims. This is not surprising, considering that the *malfūẓāt* texts were all written in Persian.[363] Zayn al-Dīn later discussed the problem of the relation between the Sufi and society, saying that a dervish should avoid business affairs, but should care for people and help Muslims.[364] Zayn al-Dīn described the conditions of being a Muslim—principally rituals and distinctive clothing—as being learned from one's parents.[365] Rarely did Zayn al-Dīn allude to practices frowned upon by Islamic law, and it is difficult to tell if these observations are directed to lax Muslims or to non-Muslims.

A story is told of the great influence that Ḥasan Baṣrī held over his contemporaries, so that a Christian converted to Islam. This story occurs in a discussion about whether it is proper to eat with someone who does not pray; Zayn al-Dīn's comment was that one may do so, since it is possible that one may influence that person to the good.[366] In the light of the statements that seem to restrict Sufi activity to the Muslim community, this last remark appears to be directed at nonpracticing Muslims. Zayn al-Dīn only once made an apparent reference to those who are not fully Islamized. When describing those Muslims who learn their duties from their parents, he said that even a little bowing to stone is all right and does not actually destroy their religion; in such a case it is best to wait to correct these people.[367] It may be that this description applies to people who converted to Islam only one or two generations ago, and are not fully weaned away from the practices of idol worship, but it is not possible to be much more specific than that. These "idolatrous" practices might as easily be associated with Mongol religious practices as with

Hindu ones; Mongol troops were certainly present from time to time in Daulatabad.[368]

The Khuldabad Sufis did occasionally refer to conversion to Islam in their discourses, but usually in the context of stock tropes and tales familiar in the Sufi tradition. Much of the interest from these stories touching on conversion centers on the volatile semantic aura surrounding terms such as "idol-worship," "infidelity" (*kufr*), and any account of non-Islamic religions. In Sufi symbolism, these blameworthy terms (along with the vocabulary of wine) were consistently used to indicate transcendental mystical experiences that stood in tension with the external religious law. From al-Ḥallāj to Iranian Sufis such as ʿAyn al-Qużāt Hamadānī and Rūzbihān Baqlī, the theme of mystical infidelity reverberated as a deliberately provocative topos.[369] The Khuldabad Sufis were thoroughly familiar with this complicated symbolism. Rukn al-Dīn Kāshānī, drawing heavily on the writings of ʿAyn al-Qużāt, devoted a section of his compendium of Sufi doctrine to the nuances of mystical infidelity.[370] Stories involving Sufis falling in love with non-Muslim women and then apostatizing from Islam thus involved all the delicious resonances of impassioned love combined with the total abandonment found in mystical infidelity.

Such was the story of Aḥmad Nahāwandī (above, Part II, chap. 7), who fell in love with a Christian princess and became a Christian. Burhān al-Dīn Gharīb used the story to illustrate the ability of the chain of Sufi masters to intervene on behalf of a disciple. Burhān al-Dīn Gharīb followed that tale with the story of a dervish who went to Mongolia and fell in love with a Magian woman (*sic*). When told he had to become a Magian to marry her, he went to the bazaar and bought an idolater's belt (*zunnār*) for himself. A dervish friend of his saw him and asked the reason for him wearing the belt, which the first dervish explained. The second dervish then announced that he too would buy an idolater's belt, in order to be in conformity with his friend. When the woman saw the two idolater's belts, she was deeply impressed to learn that the second dervish had given up his religion also out of friendship for the other. She said, "If your religion is this sort of religion, then tell me the profession of faith," and she became a Muslim.[371] As with Aḥmad Nahāvandī, all turns out well in the end as everyone converts to Islam, but the deliberate flirting with apostasy for the sake of love adds an exciting element of risk to the story. These stories should not be seen as reflections on how best to proselytize among non-Muslims, however. As ʿAyn al-Qużāt had pointed out, non-Muslims are at best counterfeit infidels, since they have not penetrated to the mystical "real infidelity" symbolized by extra-Islamic references.

Other references to conversion can be found in stories intended to demonstrate the nature of the master-disciple relationship. Under the heading of "The Excellence of Obeying the Master," Ḥammād al-Dīn Kāshānī related the following tale from Burhān al-Dīn Gharīb. A disciple once asked a master where to perform his devotions. He was told to go anywhere and meditate, but he persisted in asking for a precise location. The master, possibly feeling irritable, told him to go meditate in an idol temple. Wondering about the wisdom of this course of action, the disciple nonetheless found an idol temple in a nearby village. The idols all fell down before him as soon as he set foot inside the temple. The people of the village revered him as a saint and all became Muslims. When the disciple went to see his master, the whole village followed him, and the master welcomed him and congratulated him, saying, "How wonderful the feet by whose blessing so many people became Muslims." The disciple then blessed the word of the master who sent him to the idol temple.[372] What is especially striking about this story is its close resemblance to the accounts found in the British gazetteers purporting to give historical accounts of the Islamization of certain tribes, due to the miraculous deeds of famous saints.[373] But this story in its context is devoid of any historical reference; the individuals and the places remain nameless, subordinated to a pedagogical purpose.[374] The story of the idol temple is but one in a sequence of many that relate how disciples should carry out the instructions of the master, no matter how strange they may appear. The similar oral traditions found in the gazetteers took stories about discipleship and projected them back to historicize their own relationship with Islam.

One other story from the Khuldabad *malfūẓāt* texts needs to be considered, since it presents a Chishtī master using quasiviolent tactics to cause non-Muslims to convert to Islam. Ḥammād al-Dīn Kāshānī relates the story from Burhān al-Dīn Gharīb that once Farīd al-Dīn Ganj-i Shakkar was visited by a group of black-cloaked dervishes (*siyah-pūsh*). Although they appeared outwardly unremarkable, the shaykh perceived something wrong about them, and he locked their leader into a room for three days, but supplied the others with bread and water. On the third day, the shaykh told the leader that if he became a Muslim, he would be released. The leader agreed, and when he came out it was revealed that beneath his dervish cloak there was an idolater's belt. The leader admitted that for thirty years he had been visiting the hospices of Khurasan and India, but that no one had seen through his disguise before.[375] The purpose of the story, in context, is to demonstrate the ability of the Sufi master to see through appearances and read one's inner thoughts; the heading under which it appears is "The Unveiling of the Saints," in the chapter on "The Miracles of the Saints." It would seem to be unnecessary to seek here a reference to any particular non-Muslim group, such as the black-cloaked pagans (*kāfirān-i siyah-pūsh*) of the Hindu Kush.[376] Burhān al-Dīn Gharīb has elsewhere referred to "black-cloaked dervishes" in a story taking place in Ceylon, so he seems to have had in mind a recognized Sufi garb.[377] It is hard to imagine what non-Muslim group would make a career of masquerading as Sufis and getting free lodging in hospices in Iran and India, simply in order to test the resident Sufis. The term "idolater's belt" (*zunnār*) in

Persian is indifferently applied to a Christian monk's belt, a Zoroastrian belt, or a Brahman's sacred thread.

As in the other conversion stories, this one seems to hold interest for its audience primarily insofar as it uses the extra-Islamic reference to create a tension that is resolved by the insight of the Sufi master. It would be wrong to assume from this story that Farīd al-Dīn Ganj-i Shakkar had a regular program of converting Indians to Islam.

The first references to missionary activities among the Khuldabad Chishtīs come, predictably, in late biographical texts suffused with touches of imperial historiography. In the seventeenth century, Dārā Shikūh maintained that Burhān al-Dīn Gharīb was sent to the Deccan "to spread Islam and guide the residents of those regions. . . . From the blessing of his arrival, most of that group became honored with [conversion to] Islam and became disciples."[378] A century later Sabzawārī, in his account of Burhān al-Dīn Gharīb's brother Muntajib al-Dīn Zar Zarī Zar-bakhsh, said, "He was the eliminator of infidelity and innovative influences, and he was the knower and defender of the faith of *islām*."[379] Without giving any specific information, this statement suggests that the saint somehow opposed paganism and advanced the cause of Islam. Sabzawārī's comment on Burhān al-Dīn Gharīb does not stress opposition to paganism as much as his exemplary religious life: "In Rawża he exhibited the splendor of the practice of the religious laws [and] the inner path (*ṭarīqa*) of *islām* and lived there."[380]

Sabzawārī's tone grows more strident, however, when describing the legendary saints whose arrival in the Deccan is thought to predate the Turkish conquest. He says of Mu'min ʿĀrif that "he revealed transformations and supernatural feats to the mass of infidels, who thereupon became his followers."[381] Regarding the shadowy Jalāl al-Dīn Ganj-i Ravān, Sabzawārī remarks, "by various miracles and numerous supernatural feats he defeated the people of infidelity and sorcery. He confounded the foundation of infidelity and ignorance. He first revealed the sign and the currency of *islām* and made firm the pomp of the religion of Muhammad."[382] Sabzawārī's accounts stand midway between the royal historiography of the Mughul period, with its stress on universal empire, and the miracle-laden drama of popular hagiography. Phrases like "the sign of Islam" (*shiʿār-i islām*) are typical of the vocabulary of political chronicle, and are tied to the concept of imperial expansion.[383] The victory of the saint over the infidels through thaumaturgic battles is a mainstay of the militant hagiography based on epic models (above, Part II, chap. 6). Sabzawārī's accounts of Sufis and their role in conversion to Islam need to be seen as belonging to the late evolution of mixed political and religious hagiographies, rather than as evidence for the self-image of Sufis of the fourteenth century.

The concept of the Sufi shaykh during the Delhi sultanate period was intimately tied to the norms of Islamic scholarship. The assimilation of the *malfūẓāt* texts to the model of *ḥadīth* transmission indicates the centrality of Islamic scholarship to the function of the Sufi teacher (above, Part I, chap. 4). Sufi criticism of the externalist religious scholars (*ʿulamāʾ-i ẓāhir*) has encouraged the assumption that they were indifferent to matters such as Islamic law. Yet in their own understanding, the Sufis were simply religious scholars who had also mastered the internal disciplines; they were the scholars of the internal (*ʿulamāʾ-i bāṭin*). The special documents called *khilāfat-nāma*s, by which the Chishtīs authorized their principal successors, placed the successor into the initiatic line of Chishtī masters that originated with the Prophet Muḥammad. When Niẓām al-Dīn Awliyāʾ authorized Shams al-Dīn Yaḥyā to teach, the document recording this stated that "it is permitted for him to grant the dervish habit to disciples and guide them to the stations of those confirmed in faith, as it was granted to me by . . . Shaykh Farīd . . . [who] received the dervish cloak from . . . Shaykh [Quṭb al-Dīn] Bakhtiyār Awshī . . . [etc.] . . . And ʿAlī received it from . . . Muḥammad the Chosen one."[384] This sequence employed the structure of the initiatic genealogy or "tree" (*shajara*).

The Chishtīs not only regarded their vocation as deriving from the Prophet, but also they made little distinction between their teaching authority and their study of the traditional Islamic sciences. The document by which Farīd al-Dīn Ganj-i Shakkar authorized Niẓām al-Dīn as a successor is simultaneously an authorization to teach a standard Arabic text on theology and law, the *Tamhīdāt* of Abū al-Shakūr al-Sālimī; this *khilāfat-nāma* thus followed the structure of the *ijāzat-nāma*, the typical teaching license of Islamic scholarship.[385] In naming Niẓām al-Dīn as his successor and at the same time authorizing him to teach a text on Islamic theology, Farīd al-Dīn Ganj-i Shakkar showed that the Sufi master could also function as a transmitter of the standard Islamic religious sciences. But none of the *khilāfat-nāma*s contain any instructions regarding the conversion of non-Muslims.

Yet certain Chishtī practices, and the use of Indian vernaculars for poetry, testify to an undeniable Indian element in Sufism. The use of betel leaf with areca nut and lime paste (Hindi *pān-supārī*) as a masticant, which is still universally practised in south Asia, found its way into Chishtī practice as well. In Burhān al-Dīn Gharīb's circle, betel (*tanbūl*) was on special occasions offered to visitors, and instructions for its proper preparation and consumption were included in the descriptions of the manners (*ādāb*) of the hospice.[386] The use of betel was prohibited during the performance of *samāʿ*, although afterward betel and sherbet were provided to the participants.[387] Betel partially chewed by the master was regarded as the cause of miraculous cures, and it was also distributed to disciples after initiation rituals.[388] But it is probably in the Sufi use of the local language, indifferently termed Hindawī (literally, "Indian"), that the strongest indication of Indianization lies.

What, then, was the significance of the use of Indian vernaculars by the Sufis? The Hindawī language that is referred to in the Chishtī *malfūẓāt* texts was close to Old Punjabi, and it was a forerunner of Dakhani Urdu. Some of the oldest samples of this language are found in quotations from Farīd al-Dīn Ganj-i Shakkar, who was a native of the Punjab.[389] The exact role of this language in Indian Sufism is unclear. Indian dialects were undoubtedly the mother tongue for Muslims born in India; Persian and Arabic were the learned languages of the court and the mosque, for which special instruction was necessary. So it can be assumed that, on a practical level, Indian Sufis used these vernaculars in the market and to some extent at home. The more vexed question is that of the use of poetry in the Indian vernaculars, in which Sufi authors played an important role. The Sanskrit-based literary culture of Brahmanic India did not encourage the use of vernaculars for literary purposes. Yet in languages such as Hindi, Punjabi, Sindhi, Bengali, and even the Dravidian languages of the south, a number of important early compositions were written by Sufi poets, who adapted indigenous idioms, genres, and themes for their own purposes.[390] On this subject, too, modern studies have tended to fall into familiar ideological postures, ranging from regionalism to religious chauvinism. Since the Hindi-Urdu controversy of the late nineteenth century, Hindi has become identified with Hinduism and is the preferred official language of India, while Urdu is associated with Islam and holds the equivalent position in Pakistan. The artificiality of this situation is exposed not only by the difficulty of distinguishing between the two tongues on the bazaar level, but also by the impossibility of tracing this political distinction any further back than a century or so.

Since the literary use of Indian languages by Sufis implies some kind of direct contact with Indian culture and religion, the immense weight of received opinion has led many to assume that the Sufis wrote in Indian languages in order to convert Indians to Islam. The historiographical considerations just advanced put this assumption under suspicion. The Khuldabad *malfūẓāt* texts furnish a number of examples of Hindawī poetry that have not been previously considered by scholars. These specimens indicate that the poetry written by the early Chishtīs was in a number of cases aimed at a very restricted audience, consisting of elite Sufis who were familiar with the local language. Incidentally, these verses may help clear up one of the most troublesome problems in Indian literary history, the problem of the authorship of the Farīd verses in the Gurū Granth Ṣāḥib of the Sikhs. Sixteen Hindawī verses plus a few phrases and proverbs can be found in the Khuldabad texts.[391] The manuscripts are all rather late, none predating Aurangzib (d. 1707), and so the poems are predictably somewhat corrupted and difficult to decipher, especially since scribes of the Persian text could not always be expected to recognize the peculiarities of the old dialect. A full study of these verses will need to be undertaken by experts in Punjabi on the basis of a comparison between the Khuldabad manuscript of *Hidāyat al-qulūb* and the Hyderabad copy, to which

I have not had access. Nonetheless, a preliminary examination by Christopher Shackle still permits us to draw some conclusions.[392]

The Hindawī verses in the Khuldabad texts occur in contexts that are heavily laden with Islamic themes, so that their net effect is to add an Indian sensibility that modulates the quality of the Islamic material. In themselves, however, these verses do not convey any distinctively Islamic import, so that it is difficult to imagine them as devices to impart a knowledge of Islam to non-Muslims. The purpose of this kind of poetry seems rather to be that of reinforcing the subject at hand by means of a powerful literary tool that had great appeal to an audience of Indian Sufis. The verses (mostly couplets called *dohras*) address topics such as opposing the self (*nafs*) by serving others, using the image of a mother who is kind to her sons.[393] Burhān al-Dīn Gharīb's disciple Mubārak once was on the point of going to see a dervish who was lodging in the house of a noble, when his master appeared to him in a dream, reciting a riddle verse that dissuaded the disciple from seeking a false master.[394] Here a distinctively Sufi dilemma, whether to approach strange dervishes, is resolved by the earthy language of the poem. Another verse uses the imagery of yogis to make a stern warning against self-deception; it tells the listener not to get covered with ashes like a yogi, simply in order to use the bhang (cannabis liquor) and forehead-mark that are the yogi's trademarks.[395] The main point here, however, is part of the Sufi analysis of the ego, which deludes one into thinking that gnosis has been attained. Frequently the Hindawī quotations are sandwiched between Persian verses and Qur'ānic passages.[396] A picturesque verse on following a difficult road is used to underline the necessity of following the *sharīʿa*, and it is followed by citations from the Qur'ān.[397] The most telling example, however, is a macaronic verse that is only three-fourths Hindawī; the remaining portion is an Arabic quotation from the Qur'ān. Burhān al-Dīn Gharīb recited this verse, perhaps spontaneously, in commenting on the Qur'ānic verse (43.32), "We apportioned among them their livelihood in the life of this world."[398] A verse that is part Hindawī and part Arabic could only be directed at an audience that was firmly ensconced in the Islamic tradition, but at the same time open to having the tradition's nuances explored through Indian imagery.

The subsidiary question of the Farīd material in the Gurū Granth Ṣāḥib concerns some hundred-odd couplets plus a few longer fragments of Hindawī attributed to Farīd al-Dīn Ganj-i Shakkar. This material, which Gurū Arjun collected in his recension of 1604, accompanied the poems of various north Indian saintly figures held to be compatible with the message of the Sikh gurūs. The Farīd verses, the only ones from a Muslim to be included in the Granth, have been the subject of controversy ever since MacAuliffe challenged their authenticity in 1904. In his translation of the Granth, MacAuliffe maintained that it was impossible that these verses attributed to Farīd al-Dīn

Ganj-i Shakkar (d. 664/1265) could have been written by him; instead, he maintained, they must have been written by one Shaykh Ibrāhīm (d. 960/1552), a descendant of Farīd al-Dīn Ganj-i Shakkar known as "Farīd the Second."[399] This hypercritical conclusion was never favorably received within the Sikh community. The authoritativeness of oral tradition was, for the Sikhs, a sufficient guarantee of the authenticity and antiquity of the Farīd verses. Other scholars, while not ruling out the possibility that Farīd al-Dīn Ganj-i Shakkar had composed Hindawī poetry, questioned whether he had, since the known *malfūẓāt* texts made no mention of them, nor was there any literary trace of these verses predating the Granth itself.[400] This is where the Khuldabad texts provide an invaluable documentation, since Zayn al-Dīn Shīrāzī in his discourses quoted seven Hindawī poems by Farīd al-Dīn Ganj-i Shakkar, one of which is found in the Granth.[401] While the undated manuscript containing these quotations from Farīd al-Dīn Ganj-i Shakkar is late, the appropriateness of these verses in their contexts makes interpolation seem unlikely. In that case, at the very least, one can assume that a corpus of poems acknowledged to be Farīd's was in circulation in Chishtī circles within a century after his death (the passage in question was written some time before 766/1364–65, the next date to appear in the text). This evidence favors the strength of the oral tradition of Punjabi poetry, and the continuity of the Sikh Farīd material with the older poems of the Sufi tradition. Thus poems in Indian languages using the full range of Indian idioms could be used by Sufis in thoroughly Islamized contexts while at the same time non-Muslim Indian religious groups could easily appropriate a significant number of the same verses, precisely because they had little distinctively Islamic content. The explanation for the Sufi interest in Indian literature may turn out to be fairly simple, on the aesthetic level. They used Indian poetry because they liked it, and they interpreted it in terms of their own Sufi teachings. If we can take the Sufi adoption of Indian literature as a typical example, then the Indian environment was the world in which these Sufis lived. From it they took attractive materials, whether *pān* leaves or poems, which in this way became ancillary to Sufi teaching and practice.

Figure 1. Chand Minar and Daulatabad Fort

Figure 2. *Naqqār-khāna* Gate, Khuldabad

Figure 3. Outer Entrance to the Shrine Complex of Burhān al-Dīn Gharīb

Figure 4. The Tomb of Burhān al-Dīn Gharīb

Figure 5. The Tomb of Muntajib al-Dīn Zar Zarī Zar Bakhsh

Figure 6. The Shrine Complex of Zayn al-Dīn Shīrāzī

Figure 7. The Tomb of Zayn al-Dīn Shīrāzī

Figure 8. Open tombs of Muḥammad Aʿzam and his wife Awrangī Bībī next to the tomb of Khwān Bībī Sāhiba, in the shrine complex of Zayn al-Dīn Shīrāzī. Women pilgrims who visit Khwān Bībī leave bangles as pledges over the doorway.

Figure 9. The open tomb of the Mughul emperor Awrangzīb in the shrine complex of Zayn al-Dīn Shīrāzī. It is now surrounded by a marble platform and screens erected by the Nizam of Hyderabad.

Figure 10. *Portrait of a Mughal Emperor*, late 18th century. Courtesy Museum of Fine Arts, Boston. © 1991 Museum of Fine Arts, Boston.

Figure 11. *Naqqār-Khāna* (royal drum balcony) overlooking the inner courtyard of the *Dargāh* of Zayn al-Dīn Shīrāzī. Similar ones are found at the shrines of Burhān al-Dīn Gharīb and Muntajib al-Dīn Zar Zarī Zar Bakhsh.

Figure 12. The Tomb of Malik ʿAnbar

Figure 13. The Tomb of Bībī ʿĀ'isha

Figure 14. Mughul Imperialism in the Deccan: Jahāngīr's Fantasy of Destroying Malik ʿAnbar

Figure 15. The Tomb of Sīdī ʿAbd al-Raḥmān

Figure 16. The Tomb of Sayyid Yūsuf al-Ḥusanyī Rājū Qattāl (below, left), the Mosque of Fourteen Hundred Saints (below, right), the Mosque on Hoda Hill (above, left), and the Meditation Chamber of Muntajib al-Dīn Zar Zarī Zar Bakhsh (above, right)

Figure 17. *Qawwals* Performing at the Tomb of Burhān al-Dīn Gharīb

PART III

The Khuldabad Sufis in History

To the Sufism of the textbooks and manuals of discipline it is necessary to add a Sufism of history. The constant interweaving of political and saintly historiographies makes it imperative that the relations between court and shrine be further detailed. The exploration of the historical embodiment of Sufism in society can be undertaken in three stages. The first stage covers the relations between the Chishtīs of Khuldabad and contemporary political figures in the administration of Sultan Muḥammad ibn Tughluq. With the end of active Sufi teaching at Khuldabad after the death of Zayn al-Dīn, the second stage begins, in which the Sufi shrines take on a political role in the legitimation of dynastic authority.

The political role of Khuldabad, which was cemented with regular and increasing endowments, played a part in the development of the nearby Deccan kingdoms (Bahmanīs, Fārūqīs, Niẓāmshāhs) and in the later policies of the Mughuls and the Nizams. The relations between the shrines and the various dynasties are documented by a memorandum written by a shrine trustee in the late fifteenth century and by a series of revenue documents from the seventeenth through nineteenth centuries (these documents are presented as Appendixes B and C). The third stage in the historical distribution of Sufism is through hagiographies that, with the addition of some royal historiography, have been projected onto local cosmologies to form an intricate local sacred geography.

9

Political Relations of the Khuldabad Chishtīs

The teachings of the Khuldabad Chishtīs strictly militated against accepting gifts that could compromise their independence or principles, but there were conditions under which such gifts could be accepted. In the chapter on "The Condition of the Legitimacy of Donations," Ḥammād al-Dīn Kāshānī enumerated a number of specific situations regarding the acceptance of gifts. If someone brings something with the intention of helping someone to be occupied with God, the donation should not be declared unlawful. Burhān al-Dīn Gharīb said, "When the Shaykh al-Islām Niẓām al-Dīn (God sanctify his conscience) gave me authorization (*ijāzat*), he said, 'Take worthy people as disciples, and on the subject of donations, no rejecting, no asking, no saving (*lā radd wa lā kadd wa lā madd*). If anyone brings you something, do not reject it, and do not ask for anything, but if they bring a little of something good, do not reject it to get it increased, and do not accept by specifying everything [one needs].' "[1]

In the same way, Burhān al-Dīn Gharīb observed that one should not sit in the mosque continually looking at the door to see if anyone is bringing something; that nullifies any effort to maintain trust in God.[2] Nor should one ask God for anything; Burhān al-Dīn Gharīb instructed some of his disciples in a prayer that went as follows: "God, give me high concentration so that I ask you for nothing but yourself."[3] Acceptance of gifts was possible, or even necessary, provided that they were unsolicited and not saved up. It was a generally accepted principle that if any gifts were saved, that would prevent any new donations from coming in. Greed and covetousness would act as obstacles to the divine bounty. Farīd al-Dīn Ganj-i Shakkar is quoted as saying, "Nothing comes to the clenched fist. Open up that they may open up; give that you may find."[4] Borrowing was also frowned upon, since that too would interfere with unsolicited donations.[5] From the viewpoint of Islamic law, it is noteworthy that Burhān al-Dīn Gharīb firmly distinguished unsolicited donations (*futūḥ*) from the obligatory alms tax (*zakāt*), and when Zayn al-Dīn was offered something by way of alms tax, Burhān al-Dīn Gharīb advised him to reject it.[6] Also unacceptable was any donation derived from illicit wealth, following the old Sufi teaching regarding the "lawful morsel." Burhān al-Dīn Gharīb related that once a woman had a son who received a horse and cloak from a prince. People congratulated her, but she asked, "What sort of good news is this, that someone gave him something?"[7]

Zayn al-Dīn continued to stress the same principles taught by Burhān al-Dīn Gharīb with respect to gifts. He observed, "dervishes do not think of collecting or spending. [Since they are] sitting next to the treasury of God, whenever they spend, another grace arrives. In the same way, a person sitting next to the edge of a stream does not have any inclination to spend the water. Whenever they do spend, another grace arrives. If dervishes keep treasure, no other expense will ever arrive."[8] Since saving wealth would act as an obstacle to this flowing grace, in principle accepting land grants would be out of the question, since they would provide regular income. Burhān al-Dīn Gharīb, in a testament delivered while he apparently was on the point of death in 735/1335, had quoted the advice of his master Niẓām al-Dīn, that those who follow him should accept no village or stipend (*dih wa idrār*).[9] Thus Zayn al-Dīn said that dervishes have no land-assignment (*iqṭāʾ*) on earth.[10] If renunciation is the Sufi's goal, service to kings will be an impediment. In this connection Zayn al-Dīn told the story of a sick king whom a dervish healed. The dervish refused to accept any reward, since hunger and helplessness were the source of his own power.[11]

A number of government administrators appear in the *malfūẓāt* texts in the role of visitors to the Sufi shaykh. Sometimes these figures are just onlookers, such as Malik Ḥusām al-Dīn Pahlavān-i Jahān, a military leader who was present during a discussion on performing extra prayers.[12] Another such was Niẓām al-Dīn Fīrūz Majmūʿdār ("the auditor"), who came with Rukn al-Dīn Kāshānī during a discussion of preaching.[13] A scribe named Saʿd al-Dīn Dabīr received initiation and heard a discourse about the need for the initiatic hat or cloak.[14] A centurion (*amīr-i ṣada*) named Naṣīr al-Dīn is quoted as the source for an anecdote concerning the disciples of Burhān al-Dīn Gharīb; this soldier may have been among the group of centurions whose revolt later precipitated Delhi's loss of the Deccan.[15] Other notables remain anonymous. Burhān al-Dīn Gharīb gave dates to one unnamed notable (*ʿazīz*). Another notable asking to become a disciple was questioned about his prayer habits and instructed in how to keep good company and use only legal food. An unnamed figure made casual conversation concerning the increase in the price of grain.[16] It is hard to draw any conclusions about the nature of the relationship between Burhān al-Dīn Gharīb and these government figures, except to say that he seems to have had a significant following among administrators.

Other incidents indicate that the influence of Burhān al-Dīn Gharīb at court was considerable, so that some people tried to bribe and influence him to intercede with the authorities on their behalf. A scholar named Mawlānā Muʿizz al-Dīn Khaṭṭāṭ, a friend of Burhān al-Dīn Gharīb, one day brought the shaykh a garment. When presenting it, he admitted he was seeking a favor for a noble called ʿAlā' al-Mulk; Burhān al-Dīn Gharīb rejected this as a bribe. He made it a rule that in such cases, he might listen to the request, but would always refuse the gift, for "dervishes are not bribe-takers."[17] An example of the kind of influence Burhān al-Dīn Gharīb could wield can be seen in the subsequent fate of the same ʿAlā' al-Mulk, as related by Majd al-Dīn Kāshānī in the hagiographical *Gharā'ib al-karāmāt*. Burhān al-Dīn Gharīb's attendant Kākā Shād Bakhsh tells the story that once Sultan Muḥammad ibn Tughluq ordered ʿAlā' al-Mulk to appear at court, and in a fright, the latter went to Burhān al-Dīn Gharīb for help. Courtiers never knew if the unpredictable sultan had summoned them in order to execute them or to reward them. The shaykh, however, prophesied that things would turn out well. ʿAlā' al-Mulk in fact received a robe and court dress (*khilʿat*), and was given the revenue collection (*shughl-i ʿāriḍī*) of Daulatabad and the wazirate. He accordingly headed for the regional capital of Sultanpur and got established there. Afterward he came to Burhān al-Dīn Gharīb, who told him to take care of the needs of some dervishes in Sultanpur. He agreed, but on his return there began to torment and suppress the Sufi devotees and their families in some unspecified way. After Burhān al-Dīn Gharīb heard of this, the sultan's attitude toward ʿAlā' al-Mulk changed, and after hearing reports of the latter's malfeasance the sultan removed him from the post. Once again ʿAlā' al-Mulk spoke to Burhān al-Dīn Gharīb and said that he had been enrolled in the cavalry of Khwāja-i Jahān and was going with him to Delhi. Burhān al-Dīn Gharīb wondered aloud if he would survive the trip, but ʿAlā' al-Mulk optimistically replied that he had no fear because of their close relationship. Burhān al-Dīn Gharīb, ominously, did not reply, and ʿAlā' al-Mulk departed. When ʿAlā' al-Mulk reached Khwāja-i Jahān, he was put to death.[18] This story shows the power of Burhān al-Dīn Gharīb whether as friend or enemy. Government figures who thought they had ingratiated themselves with the shaykh could forfeit their support by alienating the shaykh with anti-Sufi policies.

An especially interesting case of Sufi relations with the government concerns Malik al-Mulūk, a noble who became a disciple of Burhān al-Dīn Gharīb. The unusually full account of their meeting, recounted in three sessions that took place during the space of ten days (16–26 Dhū al-Ḥijja 736/26 July–5 August 1336), can be summarized as follows. This noble's official title was Mukhliṣ al-Mulk Kamrān, and he was a nephew of the central Asian Sufi ʿAlā' al-Dawla Simnānī. His father ʿImād al-Dīn Simnānī was given the title Malik al-Mulūk and governorship of the Deccan principality of Lajwara. The sultan once gave Malik al-Mulūk ʿImād al-Dīn a splendid gift of seventeen lakhs of tankas.[19] The younger Malik al-Mulūk even married a daughter of the sultan. When Rukn al-Dīn Kāshānī first brought Malik al-Mulūk to meet Burhān al-Dīn Gharīb, Malik al-Mulūk expressed his wish to enter the Sufi path; he explained that this was not a sudden decision, but had been on his mind for some time. Kākā Shad Bakhsh confirmed that Malik al-Mulūk had long wished to see Burhān al-Dīn Gharīb. Burhān al-Dīn Gharīb warned him that it is difficult. Malik al-Mulūk said that he had read the Qur'ān sixteen times, and when he demonstrated his ability in recitation of the scripture, Burhān al-Dīn Gharīb was so pleased that he gave Malik al-Mulūk a hat. Observing that Malik al-Mulūk's real name was Maḥmūd, Burhān al-Dīn Gharīb expressed the hope that his life would be "praised" (*maḥmūd*).

A few days later, Burhān al-Dīn Gharīb asked how things were with Malik al-Mulūk. Rukn al-Dīn Kāshānī replied that they had performed Friday prayers at the enclosure of Muntajib al-Dīn, where Rukn al-Dīn taught him special prayers. Malik al-Mulūk told Rukn al-Dīn and his friend Qāẓī ʿĀrif Kāshānī that he was now one of them, and that he was extremely happy to become part of Burhān al-Dīn Gharīb's circle of devotees. Rukn al-Dīn Kāshānī then saw him the next day at Ellora, still wearing the hat presented to him by Burhān al-Dīn Gharīb. Rukn al-Dīn told him to wear it for three days, to preserve it afterward to keep it from getting dirty, but in any case never to wash it. Burhān al-Dīn Gharīb approved of this advice, and added that a robe from the master, when sweaty, should never be washed—thus one should never wear it to the privy, just as in the case of amulets and talismans. Then followed some talk about Malik al-Mulūk's family and political connections. Burhān al-Dīn Gharīb mentioned that he had heard that Malik al-Mulūk was distinguished for his generosity. Rukn al-Dīn Kāshānī replied that his family was liberal to all who were connected to them, uniquely so in their time; they did not stint in giving robes, grain, stipends, or money. Burhān al-Dīn Gharīb then asked whether Malik al-Mulūk was favorably inclined to dervishes. Rukn al-Dīn said that he was a man of good character and very devoted to the Sufis. Burhān al-Dīn Gharīb then reflected that Malik al-Mulūk might be a good influence on some of the disciples who are not yet firm. He further suggested that Malik al-Mulūk be taught the supererogatory dawn prayers.

Again a few days later Burhān al-Dīn Gharīb asked about Malik al-Mulūk, and was told that he wanted to visit the shaykh again, but that the sultan was unhappy with him. Rukn al-Dīn Kāshānī said that the sultan had ordered Malik al-Mulūk to do things that would injure the people, and Malik al-Mulūk was resisting this. Burhān al-Dīn Gharīb approved Malik al-Mulūk's wish to avoid injuring people—one should see God's will in this, he said.[20] It is not clear which of the sultan's policies aroused the opposition of Malik al-Mulūk; it was to be another four years before the centurions of Daulatabad would revolt in 741/1340. Malik al-Mulūk was later deprived of his title (presumably because of his opposition to the sultan), and he was renamed Maḥmūd in fulfillment of Burhān al-Dīn Gharīb's prediction, while his brother ʿAzīz Allāh received the title.[21]

Another important official who was a disciple of Burhān al-Dīn Gharīb was Qutlugh Khān, the tutor to the sultan. Qutlugh Khān was the governor of the Deccan at Daulatabad from 1335 to 1344.[22] Zayn al-Dīn Shīrāzī regarded Qutlugh Khān as a close friend and as a model Sufi. He refers to the manners of Qutlugh Khān during prayer, and quotes him saying that the path has nothing to do with glory.[23] Zayn al-Dīn refers to Qutlugh Khān by three respectful titles: *mawlānā* (lit., "our master"), an epithet for the learned; *ʿālim*, "scholar"; and *dabīr*, "secretary." Reflecting on his early days in Daulatabad, he observed that his meeting with Qutlugh Khān was truly providential; when he was staying alone at the house of Khwāja-i Jahān, God brought the two of them together, and then other friends began to appear.[24] Majd al-Dīn Kāshānī praised Qutlugh Khān as being outwardly a king but inwardly a Sufi, with a style of writing similar to that of ʿAyn al-Qużāt. Majd al-Dīn records that before becoming a Sufi, Qutlugh Khān was summoned by Burhān al-Dīn Gharīb, and came with some trepidation. The shaykh presciently explained to him the significance of the events of his life, so Qutlugh Khān soon became a disciple as ardent as the famous Sumnūn "the Lover."[25]

When Qutlugh Khān was removed from the governorship of the Deccan late in 1344, the sultan replaced him with his brother ʿAlīm al-Mulk and appointed ʿAzīz Khammār to the governorship of Malwa. Qutlugh Khān had been blamed for his laxity toward the centurions (*amīrān-i ṣada*), military officers in charge of a hundred (*ṣad*) soldiers who also collected revenue for the civil administration. ʿAzīz Khammār was given carte blanche by the sultan to undertake reprisals against the centurions, and his harsh measures led directly to the revolt that successfully threw off the authority of Delhi within a few years.[26] Zayn al-Dīn Shīrāzī viewed the governorship of ʿAzīz Khammār as a catastrophe, and he used this story as an example of the results of injustice. According to Zayn al-Dīn, when ʿAzīz Khammār arrived in Malwa, he proceeded to plunder the people ruthlessly, so that they fled to the hills. He seized all their property and turned soldiers loose on the villages and peasants. When the district quickly became ruined, he could no longer provide for his soldiers, who by then were poor, tattered, and afflicted. Qutlugh Khān found out and wrote to the sultan, who replied that anyone who could restore the land assignment could have it. Qutlugh Khān advised summoning ʿAzīz Khammār to court for reprimand and replacement. This was not to be, however, since ʿAzīz Khammār was killed in February or March of 1345, fighting the centurions in Gujarat. Some of the soldiers of Malwa came to Zayn al-Dīn Shīrāzī seeking his prayers, and they were in a wretched condition, confirming the evil deeds of ʿAzīz. Only one soldier appeared to be well-fed and finely dressed. He had refused to plunder the villages or take anything from anyone, but spent what he had lawfully and fed some hungry people. He was accordingly befriended by a saint who loaned the soldier fifty *tanka*s to equip himself, as God's reward for his lawful behavior.[27]

Although he had been removed from the governorship of the Deccan in 745/1344, Qutlugh Khān appears to have returned to Daulatabad when the sultan's armies attempted to put down the revolt there. In September 1346 the successful Deccani rebels had crowned Ismāʿīl Mukh sultan in Daulatabad. Qutlugh Khān's presence some months later in Daulatabad, which is not mentioned in the dynastic chronicles, occurred when Sultan Muḥammad ibn Tughluq came to the Deccan to put down the rebellion. Qutlugh Khān used this opportunity to see Zayn al-Dīn again. In a passage dated 2 Dhū al-Ḥijja 747/16 March 1347, we are told that Qutlugh Khān was present in the assembly of Zayn al-Dīn and asked a question about the meaning of a famous Persian verse.[28] This assembly took place in Ellora, some miles outside Daulatabad, where Zayn al-Dīn was summoned to meet the army of sultan Muḥammad ibn Tughluq after the defeat of Ismāʿīl Mukh's army. He would soon be taken back to Delhi along with all the elite Muslim population of Daulatabad in the company of the future Fīrūz Shāh and other nobles.[29] It appears from his comments to his audience that the shaykh was concerned about the welfare of his followers in the army. He told a story using the metaphor of the army quartermaster looking after horses to illustrate his own position as guide to his disciples. "In this way, the masters do not let disciples depart from their companionship. . . . The master investigates their state in his dominion (*vilāyat*)."[30] Thus in the midst of a rebellion, Zayn al-Dīn and his soldier disciples managed to have a gathering even as the sultan prepared to extract his revenge from the rebels in Daulatabad. According to Āzād, Zayn al-Dīn took advantage of this forced return to northern India to perform pilgrimage at the tombs of the early Chishtī saints in Delhi, Ajodhan, and Ajmer.[31] Zayn al-Dīn would be welcomed back to Daulatabad by the Bahmanī official Muḥammad ʿAyn al-Dīn Khwāja-i Jahān and thirty-four others, on his return sometime after 752/1352.[32]

The Chishtī masters such as Burhān al-Dīn Gharīb tried to stay clear of direct involvement with the court, but they often encouraged disciples to retain government posts, even when the disciples showed signs of wanting to renounce the world. It has already been seen in the case of Malik Mubārak Shams al-Mulk that a senior disciple destined to become one of the master's successors could continue in secular office, at the express command of the master. Rukn al-Dīn Kāshānī on at least two occasions expressed the desire to give up his position for the dervish life, but Burhān al-Dīn Gharīb consistently counseled him to stick to his duty (above, Part II, chap. 7). The same thing occurred in the case of Qutlugh Khān and several others. Zayn al-Dīn reflected on this paradox in an extended series of remarks:

> If someone enters the path of poverty, he should not give up his work and acquisition. Service work and the like does not prevent obedience and trust in God. Whatever they do, they pursue their work. The revered Shaykh al-Islām Burhān al-Dīn had some income (*nān-i amānat*) before his initiation, and after initiation, however much he said to the revered Shaykh al-Islām Niẓām al-Dīn, "I will give it up," permission was not granted until God most high showed his grace and brought him out [of worldly society]. Amīr Khusraw was a courtier, and was distinguished among the poets. Time and again he said to the master [Niẓām al-Dīn], "No one has peace or satisfaction who for a day has spoken eulogies of anyone." He came to the master's presence and cast his turban on the ground, crying out, "How long will I praise these tyrants?" The master said, "Be patient, until God does something." Mawlānā ʿĀlim Dabīr Qutlugh Khān time and again cried out to the shaykh, "I will give up serving the people." The shaykh said, "No, my friend, go to the court and perform your duty, but also pursue your obedience and worship, until God brings something before you." There was a soldier who became attached to the shaykh. After some time, he said, "The decorations of my horse are my impediments. I will give up service and get rid of my horse." The shaykh said, "My friend, God most high gave Ṣāliḥ the Prophet (peace be upon him) a camel, and to the Prophet Jesus (peace be upon him) he gave a donkey. He has given you a horse. Do not get rid of it, endure your sadness, and pursue your work until God does something. A time will come when the divine nature will release you from all impediments. Alone, you cannot extricate yourself from attachments and impediments; God gives release. Until that time, you should be involved with what you have, and obey, worship, give thanks, and be patient."[33]

This list of those who sought renunciation and were advised against it is impressive. Amīr Khusraw, the panegyrist to seven sultans of Delhi, must indeed have sickened over the fantastic hyperbolic poetry he ingeniously churned out for decades. Only in the privacy of the relationship with Niẓām al-Dīn could he give expression to the resentment he felt over this task. It was only someone with a special vocation for the life of renunciation who would be called to it by divine invitation; even Burhān al-Dīn Gharīb had to wait until the proper time. The same thing happened with Mīr Ḥasan, who twice announced to Zayn al-Dīn his intention of renouncing the world; on both occasions he was told to remember God in this world and use his work for God.[34]

One story shows the delicate balance that Burhān al-Dīn Gharīb tried to keep in his relations with the sultan. The hagiographer Majd al-Dīn Kāshānī relates that Sultan Muḥammad ibn Tughluq once came to Daulatabad and asked to see all the *ʿulamā'* and shaykhs. The noble Aḥmad Ayāz Khwāja-i Jahān informed him that he had seen all the religious leaders except Burhān al-Dīn Gharīb. The sultan did not even want to hear the name of this shaykh, as in his youth he had met Burhān al-Dīn Gharīb, but the latter had proved to be so independent (*kamāl-i istighnā'*) that he paid no attention to the future king. But then the sultan decided that he wished to see Burhān al-Dīn Gharīb anyway, and on a Friday after leading prayers he asked to go to the shaykh's house. Amīr Khusraw's son Malik Mubārak ran ahead to tell the shaykh. The noise of the procession reached the house and alarmed Burhān al-Dīn Gharīb, so he prayed that the sultan would not come. As it happened, the sultan suddenly had a change of heart and turned back. At this time, however, the sultan had some problems, and he sent three thousand *tanka*s with Malik Nā'ib Barbak and Fīrūz Shāh as a gift to the shaykh. This sum was conveyed with the express wish that the shaykh give his blessing and help solve the problem. Burhān al-Dīn Gharīb replied that he had no power in his heart to do this, so he returned the gift. The sultan realized that he had infringed upon the customs of the Chishtīs, so he sent the money back with the stipulation that it was only a gift for Burhān al-Dīn Gharīb's attendants. This time it was accepted. Kākā Shād Bakhsh suggested that it be sent to the shaykh's house, where there were already twenty *tanka*s kept. Burhān al-Dīn Gharīb told him instead to bring that money and distribute it, together with the sultan's gift, at once. Majd al-Dīn was present and took part in this distribution. Malik Nā'ib Barbak also witnessed this, and Burhān al-Dīn Gharīb recited to him some admonitory verses about sowing what one reaps. He also sent the sultan a prayer carpet and some dates.[35]

This narrative illustrates the ideal of saintly independence at its height. Burhān al-Dīn Gharīb not only had snubbed the sultan in his youth, but also felt free to refuse his gift, or to accept it under the proper conditions but give it away immediately. Yet the shaykh was also careful to demonstrate his good manners by sending the sultan an appropriate present rather than offend him by overt defiance. There were times, however, when the saints might feel like being a little more blunt, to judge from a passing remark by Zayn al-Dīn. The shaykh was commenting that, just as a sultan can raise the recommended salary of an officer, so the master can forbid a disciple's apparently spiritual plans in order to bring about something better. He then remarked, "the intimates of the All-powerful have no less power and authority than the intimates of the metaphorical emperor (*pādshāh-i majāzī*). But one should not repeat to the people these stories taught at this time."[36] Though the Sufis might regard the sultans as metaphorical rulers in comparison with God, they generally curbed their tongues in public in order to keep from causing friction.

After the death of Burhān al-Dīn Gharīb, when the Deccan became more disturbed due to revolts, the saint's tomb was the people's only refuge in a time of trouble. The situation became especially acute when the sultan crushed the rebel forces in Daulatabad and allowed his soldiers to loot the city indiscriminately.[37] Just prior to the meeting on 2 Dhū al-Ḥijja 747/16 March 1347, at Ellora with the sultan's army, Zayn al-Dīn bitterly blamed the worldliness and indifference to religion that resulted in the sultan's savage reprisals on the population. "Inasmuch as Sultan Muḥammad ibn Tughluq has come to Deogir in the time of Ismāʿīl Mukh, all the people of Daulatabad, Deogir, and the villages have given up hope and washed their hands of life." His disciple Mīr Ḥasan observed that the blood-shedding of the sultan had passed the limit, and the people were greatly disturbed. Zayn al-Dīn then instructed him in five Qur'ānic prayers to prevent misfortune.[38]

A hagiographical account presents a different account of the sultan's reprisals on Daulatabad, which agrees only in locating the salvation of the people in Qur'ānic prayers. Majd al-Dīn Kāshānī depicts the sultan as unleashing in particular his Mongol troops, with the intention of having them slaughter every shaykh and scholar, and enslave all the women and children. The Mongols were to leave no sword in the scabbard for three days after the conquest. When this plan became clear, the people all went to the tomb of Burhān al-Dīn Gharīb, and asked him to help, since this dominion was his. That very night, Majd al-Dīn Kāshānī saw Burhān al-Dīn Gharīb in a dream, who told him to pay attention; the sultan would not be able to carry out his plan to kill everyone. But they must repeat a particular Qur'ānic prayer. When Majd al-Dīn awoke, he at once began repeating this prayer. A few days later the armies of the sultan arrived and defeated Ismāʿīl Mukh and captured Daulatabad, but the plan of the sultan changed. Because of the blessing of the tomb of Burhān al-Dīn Gharīb, God changed the heart of the sultan, who left the people alive with all their possessions and freed the Muslim women and children enslaved by the Mongols. No one was hurt. The nobles and commanders, mostly Mongols, came to the tomb and pressed their faces on the threshold and performed pilgrimage. All the people of the region realized that their salvation was due to the help and protection of Burhān al-Dīn Gharīb. Those who were plundered and dispersed had participated in the rebellion and had themselves plundered the Muslims.

This event goes to show that the shaykh in life and death is the protector of the disciple.[39] This account, which presents an optimistic picture of the sultan's reprisals, also implausibly puts the execution of the nefarious scheme exclusively into the hands of demonic Mongols, who are nonetheless suitably humbled by the saint in the end; their few victims turn out to be guilty rebels, anyway. There may be a faint echo of this story in ʿIṣāmī's description of a stomachache that temporarily persuaded Sultan Muḥammad ibn Tughluq to desist from slaughtering the population of Daulatabad. With his usual malice toward the sultan, ʿIṣāmī maintains, however, that "the Emperor of Delhi continued there for two months during which period he shed much blood of the believers every now and then."[40] Again a historiographical divergence hinges upon the difference between a hagiographical exaltation of the authority of a saint and a royal epic depicting the tyranny of a despised monarch.

The Khuldabad texts portray the Sufis' relations with political power somewhere between independence and interdependence. Sufi principles in theory prevented certain kinds of interactions with kings, especially where gifts of money or land were concerned. The Sufis nonetheless occupied a privileged political position that drew the nobility and government functionaries to their lodges. Some eminent members of the court, like Malik al-Mulūk and Qutlugh Khān, could become close disciples of shaykhs like Burhān al-Dīn Gharīb. What is most surprising is the frequency with which the Chishtī shaykhs refused to entertain the notion that their courtier disciples should renounce the world. The Chishtīs evidently felt that society and religious duty required that the average disciple fulfill the duties of office, while only the rare individual would be of a temperament to give up all worldly connections. The balance between the Sufi establishment and the political power was delicate. Excesses by the court were countered in hagiographical literature by miraculous intervention from the shrine. In history, the Khuldabad Sufis played a role that was certainly religious but undoubtedly political as well.

10

Political History of the Khuldabad Shrines

The Bahmanī Sultans

Although royal chronicles make brief references to Sufis in connection with their main theme of kingship, it is rare to have anything like a detailed administrative account of the relationship between Sufi shrines and the regimes. We are fortunate to have access to a remarkable text (translated as Appendix B), which sheds light on how the once independent shrine gradually became more and more closely associated with the Bahmanī sultans, from the very moment when they rejected Delhi's authority over the Deccan in the mid-fourteenth century. This anonymous document gives new evidence about the shrine's very first encounter with the patronage of kings, and gives a step-by-step chronicle of its increasing dependence on endowments from the Bahmanīs. Moreover, this memorandum demonstrates that the political importance of Khuldabad during the early years of the Bahmanī kingdom was much greater than was previously suspected.[41] Since the last event mentioned in the memorandum occurred in 887/1482, it appears that the text was written by a trustee of the shrine at the end of the fifteenth century, though the manuscript copy dates only from the early eighteenth century.

The document is of considerable importance as evidence for the administration and political role of early Sufi shrines in India. When viewed together with court chronicles and Sufi hagiographies, financial documents such as this reveal the developing role of Sufism in relation to the state, as one of the most significant sources of legitimation for political authority. The document invokes the authority of Burhān al-Dīn Gharīb and Zayn al-Dīn Shīrāzī to sanction the shrine's administration, although this could only be done by drastically revising the views of the Chishtī shaykhs as expressed in the *malfūẓāt* texts. To the extent that this textual revision justified an absorption of the shrines into the sultans' land revenue system, it represents a victory for royal historiography.

The document is also written partly to explain the organization of the shrine's internal administration. As noted above (Part II, chap. 7), by the eighteenth century the shrine attendants were divided into three hereditary groups: (1) the master's descendants (*mawlā-zādagān*), descended from the sister of Burhān al-Dīn Gharīb; (2) the disciples (*murīdān*), descended from Muḥammad Lashkar and Rashīd al-Dīn; (3) the children (*farzandān*), descended from the four brothers Khayr al-Dīn, Qabūl, Jildak, and ʿAbd al-Raḥmān. Only part of this systematic division is reflected in the fifteenth-century document. It uses the compound phrase "devotees and master's descendants" (*bandagān wa mawlā-zādagān*) indiscriminately to refer to all the shrine attendants; at this point *mawlā-zādagān* is a vague term, which might also include descendants of the early Chishtī masters. Yet one of the purposes of the document is to illustrate how Laṭīf al-Dīn, the nephew of Burhān al-Dīn Gharīb, came to be singled out by the shaykh for certain gifts, which entitled his heirs (the *mawlā-zādagān* in the later sense of the term) to a share in the revenues of the shrine.

The memorandum has the appearance of a foundation document, tracing the financial administration of the shrine to the directives of Burhān al-Dīn Gharīb himself. It begins by describing Burhān al-Dīn Gharīb's journey from Delhi to the Deccan at the command of Shaykh Niẓām al-Dīn Awliyā' and his stay at Daulatabad; anachronistically, this is described as taking place in 719/1319–20 instead of 729/1329–30. A visit from his relatives twelve years after his departure from Delhi prompts him to affirm that his disciples and the children of his spiritual masters (*mawlā-zādagān*) are his real relatives. Having thus shown that the Khuldabad center is Burhān al-Dīn Gharīb's real home, the author proceeds to relate, with some significant alterations, the impressive speech made by Burhān al-Dīn Gharīb in 734/1334 when he appeared to be on his deathbed; this speech was recorded in full by Rukn al-Dīn Kāshānī in *Nafā'is al-anfās*. In this speech, Burhān al-Dīn Gharīb, very concerned about observing the imminent death-anniversary (*ʿurs*) of his master Niẓām al-Dīn, entrusted all his possessions to his disciple Kākā Shād Bakhsh and instructed him to distribute gifts and food to all the participants in this important ritual. This speech became the rationale for the later financial organization of the shrine, since in it Burhān al-Dīn Gharīb specifically commanded his follower to incur suitable expenses in the celebration of a saint's death-anniversary. The author has introduced changes into the text, however, to preserve Burhān al-Dīn Gharīb's reputation for absolute poverty, and he leaves out the shaykh's next words, in which he condemned the practice of accepting gifts from kings. By another skilful transition, the author has made Burhān al-Dīn Gharīb's observance of Niẓām al-Dīn's death-anniversary the precedent for the later celebration of Burhān al-Dīn Gharīb's own death-anniversary in Khuldabad. Kākā Shād Bakhsh, we are told, faithfully kept his master's order and also maintained other shrines in the neighborhood.

The main part of the text that follows chronicles the way in which the Bahmanī sultans became involved in supporting the shrine. The document does not mention the story, known to Firishta, that upon his coronation in 748/1347, 'Alā' al-Dīn Ḥasan Bahman Shāh's first action was to order a gift of five *mann* of gold and ten *mann* of silver for the shrine of Burhān al-Dīn Gharīb, in the name of Niẓām al-Dīn (a *mann* is about forty pounds). This princely sum would have been an offering in gratitude for Niẓām al-Dīn's prediction of Ḥasan's future ascent to power.[42] Instead the text begins when Muḥammad ibn Ḥasan, the second Bahmanī sultan (r. 759/1358–776/1375), came on pilgrimage to the tomb of Burhān al-Dīn Gharīb. Ascertaining from his wazir that the shrine had no current endowment from the treasury, he offered to provide it with "a daily prayer-ration" (*waẓīfa-i rūzīna*) of a specified amount of fruit and meat, to be paid out of the taxes normally due from the town. The accounting of the amounts and kinds of fruit and meat is so detailed that it might even satisfy the requirements of a modern internal revenue service. The large amount of food in the prayer ration (fifty pounds of meat, and twice that amount of fruit, daily) incidentally suggests a fairly large and growing population of dervishes in attendance at the shrine. The attendants then had to convey news of this gift to Burhān al-Dīn Gharīb's successor, Zayn al-Dīn Shīrāzī, to ask his approval. Zayn al-Dīn Shīrāzī made a point of determining that the gift had been unsolicited, for it was the rule of the Khuldabad Chishtīs to avoid asking for donations, and only to live on gifts that came unasked. Being satisfied that the sultan's offering fit this requirement, he approved of the gift. From the point of view of the Chishtī tradition, though, this action would be something of a departure. One-time gifts were acceptable, but regular stipends paid out of taxes would appear to come perilously close to institutional dependence. Still, the first steps had apparently been taken, just over twenty years after Burhān al-Dīn Gharīb's death.

Zayn al-Dīn Shīrāzī then is said to have made an even more momentous decision regarding a yearly stipend from an unnamed donor (probably the same sultan), which brought the shrine formally into relationship with the Bahmanī sultan by including him in the Sufis' prayers. Faced with a substantial income, Zayn al-Dīn Shīrāzī appointed Mawlānā Muḥammad Lashkarī trustee over the funds, and instructed him to distribute them among the customary recipients according to the example of Kākā Shād Bakhsh. He further ordered the Sufis always to feed visitors first, and to perform a series of prayers, first for Burhān al-Dīn Gharīb, then for the Chishtī masters, and finally "for the sake of the well-being of the emperor and the Muslims." At this point Zayn al-Dīn Shīrāzī has apparently entered into a closer relationship with royalty than any of the early Chishtī authorities would have tolerated. The author of the memorandum does not comment on this innovation, but concentrates instead on describing the internal administration of the shrine by a series of trustees. The ease with which Zayn al-Dīn here seems to cast off his traditional Chishtī independence for a regular income contrasts strangely with his rigorism in Islamic law. It is likely that the author of the memorandum has reinterpreted Zayn al-Dīn's behavior to suit his purpose of demonstrating the authoritative origins of the shrine administration, as was done in the creative retelling of Burhān al-Dīn Gharīb's testament.

From this point onward, the text reveals a new pattern developing in the shrine's relationship with the sultan, in which some of the leading attendants visited the sultan at his coronation, bringing special gifts, and requested an increase in their stipend. Niẓām al-Dīn Awliyā's order to Burhān al-Dīn, "No refusing, no asking, no saving" (*lā radd wa lā kadd wa lā madd*) seems to have been forgotten, for now they felt no hesitation whatever about asking for support. The shrine's embassy to the sultan took on the appearance of a ritual occasion, since the shrine attendants each time presented food offerings that had been blessed at the tomb (*tabarrukāt*), as well as a turban for the sultan.[43] The shrine attendants in 776/1375 in this way first approached Sultan Mujāhid Shāh, who according to the historian Firishta also visited the shrine of Burhān al-Dīn after his coronation and became a disciple of Zayn al-Dīn Shīrāzī. A slight discrepancy unfortunately attaches to this last report, since Zayn al-Dīn had died five years before the sultan's coronation.[44]

Other kings favored by this embassy were Sultan ʿAlā' al-Dīn Aḥmad II in or after 839/1436 (apparently during his visit to the shrine and not at his coronation), Sultan ʿAlā' al-Dīn Hūmayūn after 862/1458, Sultan Shams al-Dīn Muḥammad III in 867/1463, and Sultan Shihāb al-Dīn Maḥmūd in 887/1482. According to a still legible inscription in the southwest corner of the *dargāh* of Burhān al-Dīn, Sultan ʿAlā' al-Dīn Aḥmad II ordered the construction of the mosque adjacent to the shrine, completed after his death in 862/1458.[45] The trustees probably also visited the coronation of Sultan Niẓām Shāh (r. 865/1460–867/1463), since that event is mentioned in the list of names of shrine functionaries attached to the document.

It appears that whatever king was in control of the fort of Daulatabad needed to become the patron of the Khuldabad shrines, to judge from an incident that took place in 867/1462. When Sultan Maḥmūd Khaljī of Malwa invaded the Deccan, and obtained the surrender of the governor of Daulatabad, one of his first acts during the few months he held the fort was to visit the shrines of Burhān al-Dīn and Zayn al-Dīn, and give donations to the residents.[46]

The Bahmanī sultans regularly confirmed (but did not increase) the special individual pension awarded to the descendants of Laṭīf al-Dīn, the nephew of Burhān al-Dīn Gharīb, to whom the saint gave a woolen cloak in his will. Given the unusual prominence of Laṭīf al-Dīn in this document, it is possible that a member of Laṭīf al-Dīn's family (called *mawlā-zādagān* in

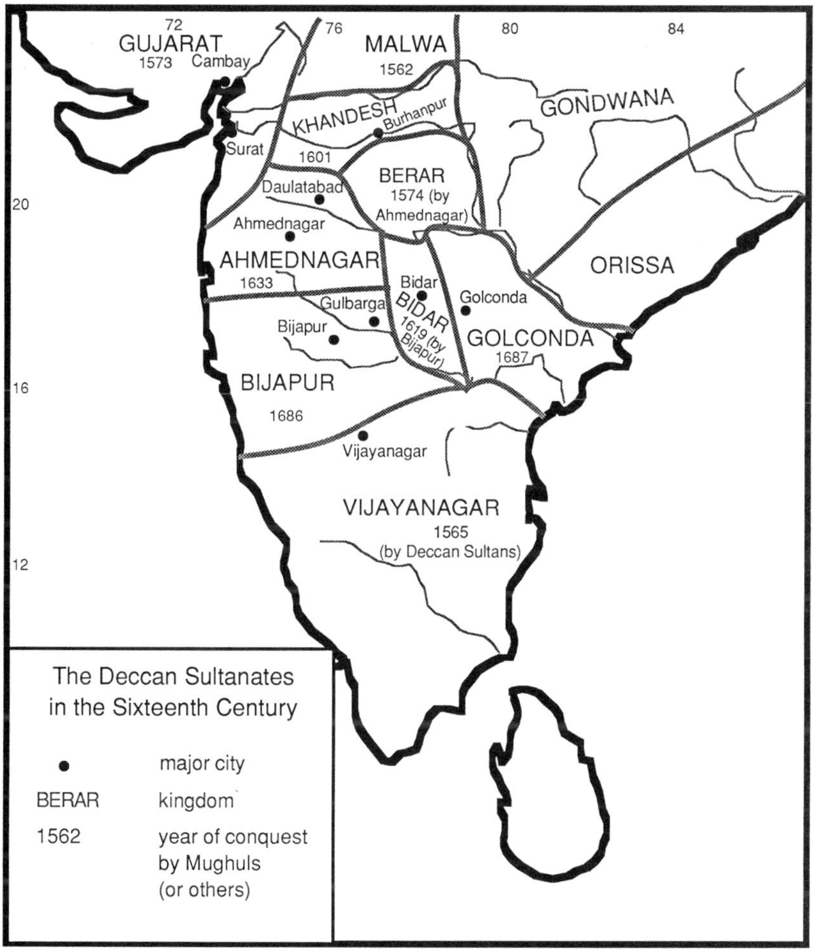

Map 4. The Deccan Sultanates in the Sixteenth Century

later times) was its author. It is evident that this grant went first to Laṭīf al-Dīn's mother, then to his son Fażl, then to Fażl's son Qadan, then to some unnamed relatives, then to Qadan's two sons Jalāl and Bara, and finally to Bara a second time. Tables 4 and 5 indicate the various stipends granted by the Bahmanī sultans to the shrine and to individuals.

The memorandum proper ends abruptly with the mention of the personal stipends presented by Sultan Shihāb al-Dīn Maḥmūd in 887/1482, but does not mention any embassy from the shrine to request an increase nor the amounts awarded to the shrine itself. To the document are attached several lists of names of government and shrine functionaries; the order does not

Table 4. Daily Stipends Given to the Khuldabad Shrines by Bahmanī Sultans

The following terms are used: *mann* (English "maund," about forty pounds), *sīr* ("seer," about two pounds), *k'handī* ("candy," twenty maunds or nearly 500 pounds), *lawāzima* (necessities), a revenue term of uncertain meaning that may indicate cash. The *tanka* was the basic coin of India during this period.

Sultan	*Year*	*Fruit*	*Meat*	*Other*
Muḥammad Ḥasan	1358+	2.5 *mann*	1 *mann*, 10 *sīr*	*lawāzima*
Mujāhid Shāh	1375	7.5 *mann*	3 *mann*, 30 *sīr*	*lawāzima*
ʿAlā' al-Dīn	1436+	15 *mann*	7.5 *mann*	*lawāzima*
Hūmayūn Shāh	1458+	1 *k'handī*, 5 *mann*	? *mann*, 25 *sīr*	*lawāzima*, 19 *tanka*s
Muḥammad Shāh	1463			3 villages, 10 *tanka*s
Maḥmūd Shāh	1482	?	?	?

Table 5. Daily Personal Stipends for Family of Laṭīf al-Dīn

Recipient	*Year*	*Fruit*	*Meat*	*Other*
Laṭīf's mother	1365?	1/2 *mann*	10 *sīr*	no *lawāzima*
Fażl b. Laṭīf	1375	1/2 *mann*	10 *sīr*	
Qadan b. Fażl	1436+	1/2 *mann*	10 *sīr*	no *lawāzima*
Relatives	1458	1/2 *mann*	10 *sīr*	
Jalāl and Bara-i Qadan	1463	1/2 *mann*	10 *sīr*	no *lawāzima*
Bara	1482	1/2 *mann*	10 *sīr*	no *lawāzima*

exactly follow the chronological order established in the main document. The first list contains the names of governors (*t'hānah-dār*s), trustees (*mutawallī*s), and treasury officers (*mushrif*s), grouped in threes in that order, presumably to indicate contemporaries. Then follow separate lists of the Bahmanī kings, the shrine trustees, governors, and judges (qāżīs). So ends the memorandum on the history of the shrine of Burhān al-Dīn Gharīb and the Bahmanīs.

It is doubtful if there were any subsequent Bahmanī endowments of the Khuldabad shrines; as Bahmanī power declined, Daulatabad fell into the hands of Aḥmad Niẓām Shāh in 899/1493, and remained part of the new kingdom of Ahmednagar until the Mughuls captured it in 1042/1633.[47] From the presence in Khuldabad of such tombs as those of Aḥmad Niẓām Shāh Baḥrī (d. 914/1508–9), Burhān Niẓām Shāh (d. 961/1553), and the Niẓām Shāhs' general Malik ʿAnbar (d. 1035/1626), it can be assumed that the Niẓām Shāhs stepped into the role of the Bahmanīs as principal patrons of the Khuldabad shrines. Indeed, though no record comparable to our document survives for the kings of Ahmednagar, we may suppose that Khuldabad was even more important to the Niẓāmshāhs than to the Bahmanīs, for there was no other comparable place of Sufi pilgrimage within the domain of Ahmednagar; the erstwhile Bahmanī empire had other important centers of Sufism in Gulbarga, Bidar, and Bijapur. Firishta records that in 937/1530, after receiving from Bahādur Shāh of Gujarat the royal paraphernalia of the conquered king of Malwa in ceremonies at Burhanpur, Burhān Niẓām Shāh stopped at Daulatabad and "paid his devotions at the shrines of the holy men buried at that place."[48] Probably he was paying tribute to the symbolic authority of Burhān al-Dīn Gharīb over the Deccan. The Niẓāmshāhs even maintained their symbolic connection with Khuldabad after Burhān Niẓām Shāh's adoption of Shīʿism in 944/1537. In accordance with Shīʿi practice, he had his father's bones sent to Kerbala in Iraq, but most of the Niẓāmshāh princes continued to have tombs built in Khuldabad.[49] Inscriptions at the tomb of Muntajib al-Dīn in Khuldabad dated 971/1564 and 1000/1591–92 probably derive from Niẓāmshāh patrons.[50] Murtażā Niẓām Shāh is said to have been "seized with religious enthusiasm" while visiting the tombs of Khuldabad in 984/1576, and he was later temporarily buried there in 996/1587 prior to his reburial in Kerbala.[51] Likewise a king of Bijapur (another Bahmanī successor-state), ʿAlī Ādil Shāh I, was crowned in 1558 in the tomb of a disciple of Zayn al-Dīn Shīrāzī, Shams al-Dīn "Shamnā Mīrān," in Miraj.[52] So the patronage of Sufi shrines continued from one royal dynasty to another.

The Fārūqīs of Khandesh

The Fārūqī kings of Khandesh, a small kingdom straddling the Tapti river valley between Gujarat and the Deccan, maintained that their dynasty too had been nourished and supported by the Sufis of Khuldabad; in this way they gave their rule a religious foundation. Royal historical tradition since Firishta has been unanimous in referring to the long association between the Khuldabad Sufis and the Fārūqī dynasty of Khandesh, though up to now no archival documentation of this connection had come to light.[53] The Fārūqīs named their capital Burhanpur after Burhān al-Dīn Gharīb and the town of Zaynabad across the river Tapti after Zayn al-Dīn Shīrāzī.[54] Sufi traditions record that Burhān al-Dīn stopped at the future site of Burhanpur and prophesied its greatness. It is also said that Malik Rājā (d. 801/1399), first ruler of the Fārūqī dynasty, was a disciple of Zayn al-Dīn; he is said to have founded the two cities in 772/1370.[55] These traditions will be examined more fully below (Part III, chap. 11). In a similar way, royal chronicles maintain that Niẓām al-Dīn Awliyā' prophesied kingship for the founder of the Bahmanī dynasty, and several other examples of this kind of prophecy exist.[56] This kind of saintly legitimation of royal power included dreams through which the sultans received advice from the Sufi, which they would dutifully relay to their troops.[57] It is apparent that royal and saintly historiographies have crisscrossed in these cases; the task of disentangling the opposing viewpoints must now be undertaken.

When first we hear of Malik Rājā (d. 801/1399), founder of the Fārūqī dynasty, he was an ex-wazir fleeing the wrath of Muḥammad Bahman Shāh sometime after 759/1358. According to Firishta, in 772/1370 Malik Rājā received from Sultan Fīrūz Shāh the district of Thalner on the Tapti River, eventually becoming independent around 784/1382 (this account is contradicted by the revenue document, which portrays Malik Rājā as a Bahmanī governor). As he and his descendants used the title *khān*, their realm became known as Khandesh ("country of the *khāns*"). His claim to power derived partly from a genealogical connection with the caliph ʿUmar al-Fārūq, but he also invoked Sufi authority. When Firishta in 1013/1604–5 visited Khandesh, three years after the kingdom's conquest by Akbar, he was told that Malik Rājā had been a disciple of Zayn al-Dīn Shīrāzī, from whom he received an initiatic "robe of discipleship and successorship" (*khirqa-i irādat wa khilāfat*). This Sufi garment was passed down from father to son, to the end of the Fārūqī dynasty over two hundred years later.[58] Strangely enough, the poet ʿIṣāmī in the epic poem *Futūḥ al-salāṭīn* dedicated to the Bahmanīs (751/1350–51) had already described the founder of the Bahmanī kingdom as having received the robe of the Prophet Muḥammad, which had been passed down through twenty-two generations of Sufi shaykhs to Zayn al-Dīn Shīrāzī. Nor was this just any robe that happened to belong to the Arabian Prophet; this was regarded as the very shirt that the Prophet Muḥammad had worn on the night of his ascension to paradise.[59]

Regardless of the difficulty of establishing the authenticity of such relics, their symbolic importance as emblems of spiritual authority is clear.[60] It appears likely that both the Bahmanī and Fārūqī dynasties claimed to have an initiatic robe of the Chishtī Sufis, resembling the ceremonial robe of the caliphs as a relic of the Prophet. At his coronation, the first Bahmanī sultan also adopted the black parasol of the ʿAbbāsī caliphs as part of his court ritual.[61] Later, however, the second Bahmanī sultan, Muḥammad (r. 759/1358–776/1375), sent the queen mother on a state pilgrimage to Mecca, during which she obtained investiture and appropriate symbols from the ʿAbbāsī caliph in Egypt. According to a contemporary source, the explicit purpose of this gesture was to keep future sultans of Delhi from attempting to reconquer the Deccan.[62] The caliph notified Fīrūz Shāh in Delhi that the Deccan had been properly awarded to the Bahmanīs, so Fīrūz Shāh, eager to retain his own caliphal investiture, never troubled the Bahmanīs. For all the pious posturing, though, caliphal symbolism was only useful as a support for kingship. Both royal robes have shaky pedigrees if they are supposed to be the robe of Zayn al-Dīn; the visitor to Zayn al-Dīn's shrine may still see displayed at the annual *ʿurs* festival the robe of the Prophet's ascension, which was handed down in the Chishtī order to Zayn al-Dīn.[63] The story of this initiatic robe has been enlarged by the author of the hagiography *Fatḥ al-awliyā'*, the description of which follows. In this account, the entire Chishtī hierarchy since ʿUsmān Hārwanī (d. 607/1211) had been foretelling the transmission of this robe to Zayn al-Dīn, who thus takes on a great importance as the only legitimate heir of the Chishtīs.[64]

The stories of Sufis foretelling the coronations of founders of dynasties are as curious for their prominence in the works of dynastic historians, as they are suspicious for their absence from the writings of contemporary Sufis. As an example, one of the most important later historical sources for this region is an anonymous author's collection of biographies of Deccan Sufis, *Fatḥ al-awliyā'*. This was written in Burhanpur in 1030/1620 and is now preserved in an apparently unique manuscript at Khuldabad. The testimony of *Fatḥ al-awliyā'* is especially significant for the political and symbolic importance that the Mughuls placed on patronage of Sufism, both in their endowments of shrines and in their patronage of biographical works on saints. The Mughul policy toward Khuldabad (more fully documented below, Part III, chap. 10) was implicitly a continuation of the Fārūqī position, since the Mughuls completely appropriated the Fārūqī historiography after their conquest of Khandesh in 1009/1601. The book begins with a eulogy of Jahāngīr, quotes the old Sāsānian adage that "religion and politics are twins" (*al-dīn wal-mulk tu'amān*), piously expresses thanks to God for the beneficent dynasty ruling Hindustan (i.e., northern India), and concludes with a prayer for the expansion of Jahāngīr's realm to include the entire inhabited world.[65] After another eulogy devoted to the Deccan governor ʿAbd al-Raḥīm Khān-i Khānān, the book then gives the biographies of five Sufis of Khuldabad, followed by the lives of twenty-one Sufis of Burhanpur.[66] The pivotal figure in the book is the first, Burhān al-Dīn Gharīb. *Fatḥ al-awliyā'* describes him as "the master of the entire dominion (*vilāyat*) of the Deccan" according to the order of the supreme Chishtī authority, Niẓām al-Dīn Awliyā' of Delhi. Burhān al-Dīn's position in the Deccan is then unsurpassable, for "one to whom Niẓām al-Dīn gives dominion holds it safely until the Resurrection."[67] The conjunction of Burhān al-Dīn, his Khuldabad successors, and the mystics of the city that bore his name, invokes his authority over the Deccan even as it seeks to advance Mughul claims to sovereignty.

The symbols of legitimacy were doubly important in the first decades of the seventeenth century as the Mughuls planned to expand into the Deccan. In the midst of this political crisis, the author of the *Fatḥ al-awliyā'* tells us that he commenced the book in Burhanpur at the order of ʿAbd al-Raḥīm Khān-i Khānān on 9 Muḥarram 1030/December 1620. The book was compiled with the aid of Jalāl al-Dīn Shāh Nuʿmānī, an aged member of a Burhanpur Sufi family and an expert on local traditions, who had joined the entourage of Khān-i Khānān. The biographical accounts of the Sufis have frequent references to their interaction with the Fārūqī rulers in the fifteenth and sixteenth centuries. Some of the accounts of earlier Sufis are copied directly out of Firishta's appendix on saints. Strangely, the author fails to mention that the Ahmednagar general Malik ʿAnbar had recently defeated the Mughul forces and was actually besieging Burhanpur at the very moment when he commenced writing the book.[68] The author's praise of Mughul power and the eminence of the Deccan governor, Khān-i Khānān, appears to be wishful braggadocio, written while Deccani soldiers were surrounding the city. It is comparable to the fantasy painting commissioned by Jahāngīr, showing him in the act of shooting an arrow at the head of Malik ʿAnbar (Figure 15); unfortunately for Jahāngīr, Malik ʿAnbar and the Deccan were not to be so easily dealt with. *Fatḥ al-awliyāʾ* has a curious political significance. Its ornate rhyming prose and florid expression belie the undertone of urgency that the author must have experienced under these threatening conditions. ʿAbd al-Raḥīm Khān-i Khānān evidently felt that commissioning a hagiography was an important enough task to claim his attention, even in the midst of a siege. By dedicating this work to the saints, he hoped for their assistance in securing the victory hinted at by the book's title. His commission created a work that skilfully weaves the Fārūqī traditions into a new pattern that would support Mughul claims to legitimacy in the context of Jahāngīr's expansion into the Deccan.

The fifteenth-century financial document just described offers an opportunity to measure the Fārūqī imperialist historiography of *Fatḥ al-awliyāʾ* against the rival Bahmanī version. It furnishes evidence that Malik Rājā was associated with the Khuldabad shrines when he was Bahmanī governor of Daulatabad (ca. 772/1370–1 to 784/1382–83); during that period he confirmed the shrine's chief trustee. The traditions about Zayn al-Dīn blessing the Fārūqī foundation of Burhanpur and Zaynabad are evidently anachronistic political reconstructions, but one of the Fārūqī kings (either Malik Rājā or Naṣīr Khān) undoubtedly had some connection with the Khuldabad Sufis and made a substantial land endowment to the Khuldabad shrines; this land endowment continued up to the fall of the dynasty in 1009/1601, when the Mughuls took it over and perpetuated it.

The stories detailing the connection of the Khuldabad Sufis with the founding of the cities of Khandesh have many significant inconsistencies. Though the Fārūqīs were clearly followers of Burhān al-Dīn Gharīb and Zayn al-Dīn Shīrāzī, the Fārūqīs themselves must have worked out at a later date the association of the two saints with the cities named after them. Firishta, followed closely by *Fatḥ al-awliyāʾ*, first told the story that the Fārūqī ruler Naṣīr Khān (d. 1437) became a devoted follower of the Chishtīs through Zayn al-Dīn, an intriguing notion, since Zayn al-Dīn died thirty years before Naṣīr Khān became king. The whole story is suspicious, since it shows Zayn al-Dīn in an uncharacteristically servile role, rushing to congratulate the king on his conquest of the fortress of Asīr (this great victory, incidentally, was achieved by smuggling warriors into the fortress dressed as women). Here is a summary of the story as told by Firishta and *Fatḥ al-awliyā'*:[69] After Naṣīr Khān's conquest of Asir, Zayn al-Dīn came from Daulatabad to congratulate him. All the king's retinue came to meet the saint, and the king invited Zayn al-Dīn to cross the river Tapti, at the future site of Zaynabad, and visit the fort. The shaykh declined, saying his master had not given him permission to cross the river, so the king moved his camp across the river to join Zayn al-Dīn; this site would later become Burhanpur. The king visited Zayn al-Dīn twice a day (or five times, according to Firishta), eventually becoming a fully initiated disciple of Burhān al-Dīn through Zayn al-Dīn Shīrāzī. At this point, Zayn al-Dīn announced, "I have included your offspring, until the Resurrection, in the fruits of allegiance to me, and have accepted them as disciples" (the initiation of the king and the entire Fārūqī dynasty occurs only in *Fatḥ al-Awliyā'*). A couple of weeks later, when Zayn al-Dīn announced his intention of returning to Daulatabad, the king proposed to donate the income from a village district from his kingdom for the upkeep of the shrines of Khuldabad. Nonetheless, Zayn al-Dīn parried the offer in typical Chishtī style, replying, "What do dervishes have to do with villages and districts?" When the king repeated his offer, Zayn al-Dīn again obliquely declined:

> We are in this region of happy name, on that river bank that was the stopping-place of the Sultan and the holy warriors (*ghāzīyan*) of Islam. When you have built a city in the name of Shaykh Burhān al-Dīn, filled with mosques and minbars, make it your capital. And on this river bank where I and the dervishes have come, let them construct a town and a mosque and call it Zaynabad, so that by this means, when the sign of Islam has become current in these two pieces of land, the name of this dervish will become known in this region.[70]

Here ends the account of Firishta. The whole thrust of this account is to demonstrate that the Sufis of Khuldabad not only blessed, but even ordered, the foundation of the capital cities of Khandesh.[71] The historiography behind the story stands in tension with Sufi traditions about Zayn al-Dīn. The part about Zayn al-Dīn being forbidden to cross the Tapti is nonsense, because he went on pilgrimage to the Chishtī shrines of Delhi, Pakpattan, and Ajmer in 747/1346–47.[72] The use of phrases like "the holy warriors of Islam" and "the sign of Islam" belongs to the propagandistic use of Islam in royal chronicles, and is not typical of Sufi texts (above, Part II, chap. 8). This strategy fits in with the Fārūqīs' other main attempt at grounding themselves in an Islamic religious identity, by using the name "Fārūqī" to assert that they were descended from the Caliph ʿUmar.[73]

The Fārūqīs did have an early connection with the Khuldabad shrines, consisting of an endowment of the shrines with land income, and perhaps a relationship of discipleship, but they wanted more than that; they wanted to show that their reign was firmly based on the authority of the most eminent Muslim religious figure in the Deccan. So the Fārūqīs, or their apologists, traced the origin of their historical endowment to the story of the foundation of Burhanpur. *Fatḥ al-awliyā'* added the following postscript to Firishta's story: after Zayn al-Dīn blessed the future cities' sites and departed, the king designated the villages of Bhadgaon and Kandalah for the maintenance of the *faqīrs* residing at the Khuldabad shrines—despite the shaykh's repeated refusal to accept them. It was further maintained that the tax yield from those villages remained an uninterrupted bequest for the shrines from that day forward, a point that the Sufi biographer Muḥammad Ghawsī Manḍawī also made in 1020/1611–12.[74] Since both Ghawsī and *Fatḥ al-awliyā'* base their accounts on traditions current in Burhanpur, we must assume that the Fārūqīs had insisted that their donation was nothing but the proper response to the saintly blessing that ensured their dominion "until the Resurrection." It cannot be doubted that at some point the Fārūqīs settled the revenue from several towns of Khandesh as an income for the Khuldabad shrines; Mughul farmans of Akbar and Jahāngīr perpetuated the Fārūqī endowment, including the Khandesh town of Bhadgaon mentioned in *Fatḥ al-awliyā'*.[75] Naṣīr Khān Fārūqī was known for his generous donations to the religious classes,[76] and both political and Sufi historical sources agree that he founded the cities.[77] But the mention of his bequest in connection with the story of the founding of the two cities is gratuitous, and serves only to create the illusion that his royal authority has a religious foundation; the king's donation, ingeniously, had become proof of the dynasty's sacred origin.

Turning away from the Fārūqīs' apocryphal foundation story, we may now examine one more conflict between royal and saintly historiographies, regarding the quarrel between Zayn al-Dīn Shīrāzī and Muḥammad Shāh Bahmanī. Zayn al-Dīn was apparently willing to defy the Bahmanī Sultan in political matters. The shaykh had aroused Muḥammad Shāh Bahmanī's wrath by receiving and aiding the fleeing Malik Rājā Fārūqī sometime after 759/1358, when the latter had become an ally of the rebel governor of Daulatabad, Bahrām Khān Māzandarānī.[78] The charm of the story makes it worth describing in detail, in order to make clear the differences between the version of Firishta and the account in the discourses of Zayn al-Dīn Shīrāzī himself.

According to Firishta, when Muḥammad Shāh Bahmanī prepared to besiege the rebels in Daulatabad, they fled to Zayn al-Dīn for advice, and he counseled them not to resist, but to flee to Gujarat. Due to the king's indulgence in wine-drinking and other practices contrary to Islamic law, Zayn al-Dīn had been the only Sufi to refuse to swear allegiance to Sultan Muḥammad at his coronation, and now the sultan was enraged at this new evidence of the shaykh's insubordination. He sent for the shaykh and meant to force him to sign a statement of allegiance. In response to the summons, Zayn al-Dīn told the story of a sayyid, a scholar, and a hermaphrodite who were captured by infidels and offered the choice of bowing down to an idol or death. The scholar argued that sins committed under duress are excused, and so he bowed down before the idol. The sayyid did not wish to refute this logic, and was moreover hopeful of the intercession of the Prophet and the imams on judgment day, so he too bowed down. The hermaphrodite alone refused to bow before the idol, saying his life was full of nothing but sin and error, so he could only hope for God's forgiveness if he remained true to the Muslim confession of faith, that there is no god but God. Zayn al-Dīn said he was like that hermaphrodite or worse, and could not come to court or swear his allegiance to the sultan.

The sultan was further incensed at this new impertinence, and sent for the shaykh again, to be brought by force if necessary. This time Zayn al-Dīn crossed the street to the threshold of Burhān al-Dīn Gharīb's tomb, put down his prayer carpet, and said, "Where is the man who will take me away from here?" At this point the king relented, and sought a reconciliation, eventually agreeing to observe the prohibition of liquor, so that the two were on good terms at last. In recognition of the sultan's willingness to implement Islamic law, the saint addressed him by the title *ghāzī* or holy warrior (in an ethical sense), and Sultan Muḥammad was so delighted that he used that title from that time forth.[79] Whether Sultan Muḥammad's donation of a daily prayer ration to the Khuldabad shrines took place or not, in either case Zayn al-Dīn emerges from this account as a man of principle, unmoved by the whims of the sultan.

The version of the story in Zayn al-Dīn's discourses has a very different flavor. Beginning with the statement that "God loves our masters all the time," the shaykh related the following, as recorded by Mīr Ḥasan:

> Inasmuch as Sultan Muḥammad Bahman came to Deogir regarding the affair of Bahrām Khān, he sent his private chamberlain, saying, "Bring Shaykh Zayn al-Dīn to me!" Then he sent the qāżī of the town, but in no way did they bring the shaykh. "But if he does not come, let him confirm my vice-gerency (*khilāfat*) and write his signature to it."[80]

Although the manuscript is badly damaged at this point, it is clear that Zayn al-Dīn then related the story of the wise man, the sayyid, and the hermaphrodite. The story continues, unfortunately in a fragmentary form:

> Then the qāżī sent a decree that the sultan had said, "If the shaykh does not come, he must not stay in my city." The revered master put his prayer carpet on his shoulder and went towards the shrine [of

> Burhān al-Dīn Gharīb]. The sultan again spoke and sent [a message:] "Beware, let him not go to that side." Then the revered master remained in the shrine. . . . Sultan Muḥammad Bahman by means of the sayyid . . . [several lines of fragmentary Persian verses] . . . [The Sulta]n spoke and by means of the sayyid spoke and sent [a message].[81]

That is the end of the story. It is worth noticing what is not mentioned in this version. There is no apparent reference in the Sufi story to the king enforcing prohibition of alcohol in the kingdom, nor to the Sufi addressing the sultan as a *ghāzī*. The royal version ends by having the Sufi legitimize the authority of the king, though the Sufi felt no need to mention this in the *malfūẓāt*; Zayn al-Dīn's own story suggests that the opposition between him and the sultan remained unresolved. The moral of his story was to demonstrate that God loves the saints, not to show that the saints love the kings.

A popular legend of Khuldabad illustrates the poignancy of the transition from traditional Sufi poverty to the more prosaic status of an institution supported by state pension. It is related that "a few hundred years" after the death of Burhān al-Dīn Gharīb, the attendants of his shrine found themselves in great distress, so that they were very near to death from starvation. After they appealed to the influence of the saint, they received consolation in a dream. The following day they found that four or five *tola*s of pure silver had sprouted from the ground right in front of the saint's tomb.[82] They broke up the silver and used it to ward off starvation and to maintain the shrine. The remains of the silver in the pavement are still pointed out to the visitor even today.[83] It might be suggested that this story illustrates the later feeling of nostalgia for the greater purity of the early Chishtī masters. It had been their custom then to live only on the daily unsolicited donations of the pious, and then to distribute to the poor all that remained at the end of the day. The life of poverty, relying on the divine beneficence for sustenance and taking no thought for the morrow, must have appeared truly miraculous to those later attendants, who had come to rely on the benevolence of kings as relayed through a feudalistic administration.

Unfortunately, no documentation is available on the later Fārūqī bequests to Khuldabad, such as the Bahmanī document provides. But since the traditions connecting Burhān al-Dīn and Zayn al-Dīn to Burhanpur were still strong even after the fall of the Fārūqīs, we can assume that this religious connection continued to be expressed through the Fārūqī financial support of the shrines throughout their reign. But this connection between the later Fārūqīs and the Khuldabad Chishtīs would appear to be borne out by the claim of the Nawwābs of Arcot (a principality in the Tamil country) to be connected with the Fārūqīs. The first Nawwāb, Anwār al-Dīn Khān (d. 1162/1749), kept a Fārūqī pretender under his protection and adopted the latter into his family;

by a sort of reciprocal adoption, his official biography seems in this way to regard Anwār al-Dīn Khān as a descendant (via the Fārūqīs) of the caliph ʿUmar al-Fārūq.[84] The Nawwāb also maintained the Fārūqī tradition of patronage of the Chishtī order in the Deccan, so that he was known as "the lover of dervishes."[85]

The political link between Sufis and sultans in the case of Khuldabad was strong indeed. The presence of the attendants of Burhān al-Dīn's shrine at the Bahmanī coronations, and their presentation of a turban to the sultan, suggests that the recognition of the sultan's authority was in some sense dependent on the saint's acknowledgment, and the sultans showed their gratitude for this service over the years by increasing their gifts to the Sufi establishment. A kind of quid pro quo evidently took place in 867/1463 at the Bahmanī capital of Bidar, when the shrine attendants offered to include the sultan in their prayers at the five ritual prayer times; the sultan responded by endowing the shrine with the income from three villages as well as other gifts. In this relationship, the sultans obtained the efficacy of prayers at holy shrines and public recognition as friends of the saints, while the shrine attendants became ever more drawn into financial administration and the problems of landlords.

A similar situation obtained in the kingdom of Khandesh, where the Fārūqī dynasty based its claim to political dominion on the spiritual authority of Burhān al-Dīn Gharīb and his successor Zayn al-Dīn Shīrāzī. Malik Rājā and Naṣīr Khān Fārūqī were also followers of the Khuldabad Sufis, and when the latter built the city of Burhanpur, he created the myth that the Sufis gave his dynasty its origin; at the same time he enrolled his descendants under the saint's protection "until the Resurrection." The Fārūqīs also showed their seriousness by settling the income from two villages on the shrine, making this very donation, which was after all a modest return for a kingdom, the proof of divine favor. Toward the end of the period covered by the document, the sultan of Malwa fleetingly obtained control over Daulatabad and tried to cement his rule with gifts to the shrines, while the Niẓāmshāh dynasty of Ahmednagar eventually took over from the Bahmanīs the role of protectors of Khuldabad, as their numerous mausolea attest. All these dynasties sought from the Khuldabad Sufis an everlasting dominion over the Deccan, which they tried to insure by their donations.

The Mughuls and Nizams

When the Tīmūrī or Mughul (Mongol) dynasty came to power in northern India in the sixteenth century, they as much as their predecessors kept in mind the dependence of political power on religious legitimation. The emperor Jahāngīr called the Sufi pensioners "the army of prayer." The Khuldabad shrines received ample endowments from the Mughuls, which are detailed in a series of revenue documents still preserved at the shrines. When compared with standard histories and Sufi biographical works, these documents reveal once again the political importance of the royal patronage of Sufism as a device by which rulers borrowed legitimacy from religious institutions.

The tombs of the two brothers Burhān al-Dīn and Muntajib al-Dīn Zar Zarī Zar-bakhsh in recent times have formed a single joint institution, known as the "Greater Dargāh Society" (*dargāh-i ḥadd-i kalān*). The other main shrine institution in Khuldabad is the "Lesser Dargāh Society" (*dargāh-i ḥadd-i khurd*), which oversees the tomb of Zayn al-Dīn Shīrāzī, Sayyid Shāh Yūsuf al-Ḥusaynī "Rājū Qattāl" (d. 1331), and some related shrines. The two societies appear to have been formed under the Nizams, since the shrines of Burhān al-Dīn, Muntajibal-Dīn, and Zayn al-Dīn were administered as a single unit during Mughul times. Papers in the collection of Mr. Fariduddin Saleem of Khuldabad, president of the Greater Dargāh Society, document the history of both sets of shrines. The collection of fifteen documents covers a period from 1605 to the early 1800s, and comprises a continuous record of Mughul policy toward these shrines, with documents from every emperor from Akbar to Bahādur Shāh, as well as from the Nizams of Hyderabad. Comparison with other private collections of Mughul revenue documents reveals that the Khuldabad collection is unusually complete and must be regarded as one of the most significant of its kind.

These documents are mostly *farmāns* (royal decrees announcing an official policy) that record the shrine revenues by granting to the client the crown's right to collect taxes on specified lands. It is clear from the two earliest documents in the Khuldabad collection that Mughul patronage of the Khuldabad shrines directly perpetuated the Fārūqī endowment. Akbar had conquered the kingdom of Khandesh in 1601, when he captured the fortress of Asir. His son Dāniyāl was governor of the Deccan at Burhanpur until his demise in 1605. It was shortly after this that Akbar issued his *farmān*, endowing the shrines with the income of villages in the districts of Bhadgaon, Busawal, and Adilabad, all towns in Khandesh. Since Bhadgaon was one of the towns named in Naṣīr Khān Fārūqī's original endowment of 1432 (as reported by *Fatḥ al-awliyā'*), we must assume that Akbar merely approved and continued the same arrangement that obtained under the last of the Fārūqīs, nearly two centuries after its inception. Such is the testimony of Muḥammad Ghawsī Manḍawī and *Fatḥ al-awliyā'*, as noted above. According to Jahāngīr's *farmān* of 1626, Akbar's endowment consisted of an actual yield (*ḥāṣil*) of 1,250,000 *dāms* (equivalent to 31,250 silver rupees). Jahāngīr retained Bhadgaon as the source of the shrine's income, but reduced it in value to an estimated total worth (*jamʿ raqmī*) of 122,400 *dāms*, or 3,060 silver rupees. This is in fact an even greater reduction than it appears, since the actual revenue would always be much less than the estimated total worth.

The Mughuls supported the Khuldabad shrines as an extension of their plan for conquest of the Deccan. Akbar, after his victory over the Fārūqīs, would probably have continued his campaigns against the Deccan kingdoms, but had to return to the north to deal with Prince Salīm's rebellion. During Jahāngīr's reign, Mughul ambitions were frustrated by the tireless Abyssinian general Malik ʿAnbar, who successfully routed the expeditions that Jahāngīr sent against the Niẓāmshāhs of Ahmednagar. Mughul patronage of the Khuldabad shrines was doubtless meant to undermine the authority of the Niẓāmshāhs of Ahmednagar, by claiming to inherit the role of the Fārūqīs as patrons of Khuldabad. An ostentatious display of generosity to the chief spiritual center of the region would thus lend an air of legitimacy to Mughul claims, and would be doubly effective as a provocative intrusion into the heart of the Niẓāmshāhs' territory.

We have already seen the disturbed conditions that led to the commissioning of *Fatḥ al-awliyā'* in 1030/1620. The following year, Prince Shāhjahān managed to bring down a new Mughul army and retaliate by sacking the Niẓāmshāhs' new capital of Khirki (later known as Aurangabad), only a few miles from Khuldabad. During this period, when the issue was still in doubt, Akbar's generous stipend to the Khuldabad Sufis remained in effect (it is interesting to note that the last of the Fārūqīs, Bahādur Shāh, would continue to live in Mughul custody in Agra until his death in 1033/1623–24). After Malik ʿAnbar's submission, the Deccan witnessed Shāhjahān's own rebellion against Jahāngīr, while in the north Maḥābat Khān's coup took place.[86] But the increasing weakness of the Niẓāmshāhs finally permitted Jahāngīr, from his house arrest during Maḥābat Khān's ascendancy, to reduce the Khuldabad endowment to a fraction of its former size in 1626 (A2). Nevertheless, the trustees of the shrine were expected to "pray for the welfare of the conquering dynasty." Both the Mughuls and the Niẓāmshāhs realized that these spiritual centers played an important role in establishing political legitimacy.

The later *farmāns* likewise reflect the varying political and economic conditions of their times. Shāhjahān's bequest of 1635 (A3), for example, recognizes the incorporation of the former Niẓāmshāh possessions into his empire and transfers the source of the shrines' revenue from Khandesh to Daulatabad. He thus abandons the traditional Fārūqī endowment for a local source coming under the new Mughul administration of the Deccan. In addition, the currency used in the next few documents (A3–A5) changes from the copper-based *dām* of Hindustan to the gold-based *hūn* of the Deccan (usually reckoned as the equivalent of 3.5 rupees). The declining amounts of these grants also reflect a more realistic appraisal of the economic conditions of the country. Shāhjahān's initial endowment of 1635, combined with an additional sum suggested by the Deccan governor Khān-i Zamān, totals 10,345.5 *hūns* or 36,209.25 rupees, which reverses Jahāngīr's drastic reduction, and even raises the sum significantly beyond its value under Akbar. By 1638, however, the value of the endowment has again been reduced to 3500 *hūns* or 12,250

Table 6. Summaries of Mughul and Deccan Revenue Documents (from Appendix C)

The following terms are used: the abbreviation Rs. stands for the silver rupee of northern India; the *dām* is a copper coin, one-fortieth of a rupee; the *hūn* (called "pagoda" by Europeans) is a gold coin of the Deccan worth 3.5 rupees; the *bīgha* is a Mughul land measurement of about five-eighths of an acre; the *chāwar* is a Maratha land measurement, equivalent to 120 *bīghas*. "Actual revenue" (*ḥāṣil*) is the amount of income the government expected to realize in taxes on a given portion of land, while "estimated total worth" (*jamʿ-i raqmī*) (abbreviated "est.") was a customary evaluation of total value worth many times the actual revenue. All figures are for annual income.

A. *Dargāhs* of Shaykh Burhān al-Dīn Gharīb, Shaykh Muntajib al-Dīn, and Shaykh Zayn al-Dīn

No.	*Year*	*Reign*	*Endowed Land*	*Value/Action*
A1	1014/1605	Akbar	Bhadgaon + 2 villages	1,250,000 *dāms* (actual) = Rs. 31,250
A2	1035/1626	Jahāngīr	2 villages in Bhadgaon	122,400 *dāms* (est.) = Rs. 3060 (actual)
A3	1046/1636	Shāhjahān	Daulatabad	6845.5 + 3500 *hūns* = Rs. 36,209.25
A4	1047/1637	Shāhjahān	Sara (Daulatabad)	Confirmation of trustees
A5	1047/1638	Shāhjahān	Daulatabad villages	3500 *hūns* (actual) = Rs. 12,250
A6	1080/1669	Awrangzīb	Sara (Daulatabad)	Rs. 741
A7	1101/1690	Awrangzīb	Payan	Confirmation of recipient
A8	1121/1709	Bahādur Shāh	Sara (Daulatabad)	74,106 *dāms* (est.) = Rs. 1175 (actual)
A9	1122/1710	Bahādur Shāh	Bursar Khurd	110,300 *dāms* (est.) = Rs. 1378 (actual)

B. *Dargāh* of Sayyid Yūsuf al-Ḥusaynī Rājū Qattāl

No.	*Year*	*Reign*	*Endowed land*	*Value/Action*
B1	1046/1636	Shāhjahān	Sultanpur	3 (down from 7) *chāwars* = 360 *bīghas*
B2	1238/1823	Sikandar Jāh	Bumiya (Daulatabad)	Rs. 1095 (actual)
B3	1242/1827	[Sikandar Jāh]	———	Confirmation of recipient by Gulbarga shrines

(*continued*)

Table 6. (*Continued*)

C. Other Grants

No.	*Year*	*Reign*	*Endowed Land*	*Value/Action*
C1	1094/1683	Awrangzīb	Sultanpur	30 *bīghas* for a brother and 3 sisters
C2	1122/1710	Bahādur Shāh	Sultanpur villages	282,067 *dāms* = Rs. 3249 (actual) for *dargāhs* of Khwāja Ḥusayn and Khwāja ʿUmar
C3	1256/1840	Trībhavan Dās	———	Rs. 60 for *dargāh of Jalāl Ganj-i Ravān*

rupees (A5). Revenues from the war-torn Deccan eventually dwindled from fifty million to ten million rupees between 1636 and 1652. It was probably Awrangzīb, governor of the Deccan since July 14, 1636, who reduced these benefices as an economy measure during a deficit period. Though the Deccan was returning to normal, Shāhjahān now insisted that Awrangzīb meet administrative expenses with local revenue without benefit of funds from the north.[87] Nonetheless, the Mughuls continued to make substantial gifts to the Khuldabad shrines at various times. Shāhjahān arranged the magnificent sum of one thousand gold *muhrs* (equivalent to 14,000 rupees) for the "truth-seekers" (*ahl-i istiḥqāq*) of Burhanpur and Daulatabad in 1049/1640.[88] An archival source states that Awrangzīb made a personal donation of 500 rupees to the greater *dargāh* in Rajab 1047/November 1637, and he continued to be a frequent visitor to the shrines in the 1650s.[89] Awrangzīb's brother and unsuccessful rival, Dārā Shikūh, also paid a visit to the shrine of Burhān al-Dīn sometime before 1049/1640, as he recorded in his biographical work *Safīnat al-awliyā'*, and it is quite likely he made some donation also.[90] Awrangzīb's *farmān* of 1669 (A6), however, reveals the startling decline in Deccan revenues due to the interminable warfare of the late seventeenth century. Despite the administrative reforms of Murshid Qūlī Khān under Awrangzīb's administration in the 1650s,[91] the campaigns against Golconda and Bijapur, and the war of succession, had been a continuing drain on the Deccan treasury. It is otherwise difficult to explain Awrangzīb's reduction of the endowment to 741 rupees. Awrangzīb continued to remember the shrines in his *farmān* of 1691 (A7), and would be buried in an unmarked tomb outside the shrine of Zayn al-Dīn in 1707 (discussed below). The later bequests of Bahādur Shāh in 1709–10 (A8–9, C2) only confirm the reports of his uncritical generosity. Though the economic situation of India was by now far worse than fifty years previously, he actually raised the amount of revenue for the larger *dargāh* from

1,175 to 1,378 rupees, and settled a revenue property worth 3,249 rupees on the smaller *dargāh*.

After the critical period of Mughul expansion in the Deccan, the Sufi shrines would no longer be counters in such a dramatic political contest, but they continued to play a symbolic role of legitimating temporal power for a considerable time. For example, the small stipend donated by a minor Hindu raja in 1834 (C3) is an interesting tribute to the influence wielded by Sufi shrines across religious lines. More importantly, the nineteenth-century endowments by the Nizams of Hyderabad, several of whom were buried in Khuldabad, further indicate the continuing importance of this sacred center. Sikandar Jāh's *farmān* of 1823 (B2), awarding 3 rupees daily to Shāh Rājū Qattāl's shrine, amounts to 1,095 rupees annually; even allowing for inflation, this sum indicates a commitment comparable to that shown by the Mughul rulers.

In 1849, it was reported that 8.4 percent of the land in the Daulatabad district was untaxed *inʿām* endowment, and that most of the holders of these lands encouraged good farming.[92] The Nizams similarly patronized the greater *dargāh*, though no revenue documents for this connection survive in the Khuldabad collection. Two of the documents (A7, C2) have notations in English, evidently made by some nineteenth-century British officer in the Nizam's administration. Rawnaq ʿAlī, a member of the Nizam's administration, reported that in 1310/1892, the greater *dargāh* were receiving "from some old towns" an unspecified endowment income twice the size of that given to the lesser *dargāh*, while the shrine of Ganj-i Ravān had an income from the towns of Soli Bachan and Nadirabad. The Nizam declared these incomes free of all duty in 1333/1914–15. By 1931, there were over seven hundred attendants (*khuddām*) attached to the greater *dargāh*, over four hundred attached to the lesser *dargāh*, and one hundred fifty attached to the shrine of Ganj-i Ravān; three hundred students were supported by the Nizam's donations, as were charitable kitchens at the tombs of Awrangzīb and the first two Nizams. Growing prosperity in the twentieth century is evident from the annual revenue of Rs. 43,000 from crown land in Sara. According to the Mughul documents, this property was earmarked for the greater dargah from the early 1700s and was continued by the Nizams.[93] After the collapse of the Hyderabad state, the income for the shrines is now negligible, however, but even in the post-1952 period these religious endowments are still theoretically effective.[94] Thus the shadow of the old political patronage of sacred shrines survives.

Though most of these documents record grants of patronage, some of them also mediated disputes over the control of shrine revenues. Disputes between the heirs of the original clients and the boards of trustees appointed to oversee the operations of the shrines have been endemic to the Islamic charitable trusts system, and still require administrative correction.[95] The patron would be in a position to settle these disputes decisively in a manner conducive to his interests. Akbar's *farmān* (A1) sides with the hereditary chief custodian, or "owner of the prayer-carpet" (*ṣāḥib-i sajjāda*), and excludes the trustees (*mutawalliyān*) from the shrine income. This position was reversed twenty years later, when Jahāngīr not only reduced the shrine's revenue drastically but also entrusted it to the attendants (*khādimān*). It is tempting to speculate that this dispute may have had relevance to Mughul imperialism in the Deccan, but it is impossible to know without having further evidence on the participants. Other problems attested in the documents include a rivalry between two factions within the greater dargāh society over income attached to a subsidiary shrine (A7). The case of Ḥāfiẓ ʿAbd al-Shakūr of the lesser dargāh society suggests the decay of political power in the Deccan. In 1823 he received a grant from the Nizam, but had to be confirmed in his position four years later by the hereditary custodians of Sufi shrines in Gulbarga (B2, B3). It is remarkable that this man had to be confirmed by other Sufi shrines; state authority must have been too weak to achieve this resolution.

The juxtaposition of royal tombs alongside Sufi shrines is a phenomenon that parallels the overlay of royal historiography upon hagiography. Royal mausolea in India waver between maintaining splendid isolation and seeking the protection of saintly holiness. Religious and political motives always overlapped, however, in the configuration of a royal tomb. From an architectural perspective, it might be more correct to describe such tombs as mosques with funerary functions, since the tombs invariably have an orientation to the direction of Mecca, and larger mausolea almost always feature a *qibla* niche in the appropriate wall.[96] Some, as in the case of the principal Mughul tombs, were designed as independent structures where perpetual endowments would theoretically ensure that constant prayers were said for the departed monarch's soul. Most of the isolated royal tombs in India are dependent now for their upkeep on the meagre resources of the Archeological Survey, and with the exception of popular tourist attractions like the Taj Mahal, the majority are in a state of complete disrepair. Others, by their location adjacent to or within the precincts of a Sufi shrine, testify to a desire to share in the sanctity of the saints, and perhaps to cement the relationship between the dynasty and the saints. These tombs have fared better for the most part, since they tend to receive care approximating to that lavished on Sufi tombs by devotees. Already by the fourteenth century there had been a tendency for kings to encourage a cult of royal tombs, identifying early members of their lines as saints and martyrs (above, Part II, chap. 6). One suspects that the kings who built their tombs alongside the saints were hedging their bets, anticipating that future generations would generously include them in their devotions.

The process of sanctification of royal tombs, by proximity as it were, is abundantly demonstrated in Khuldabad. Although there are dozens of unidentified tombs scattered throughout the valley, quite a number of tombs within

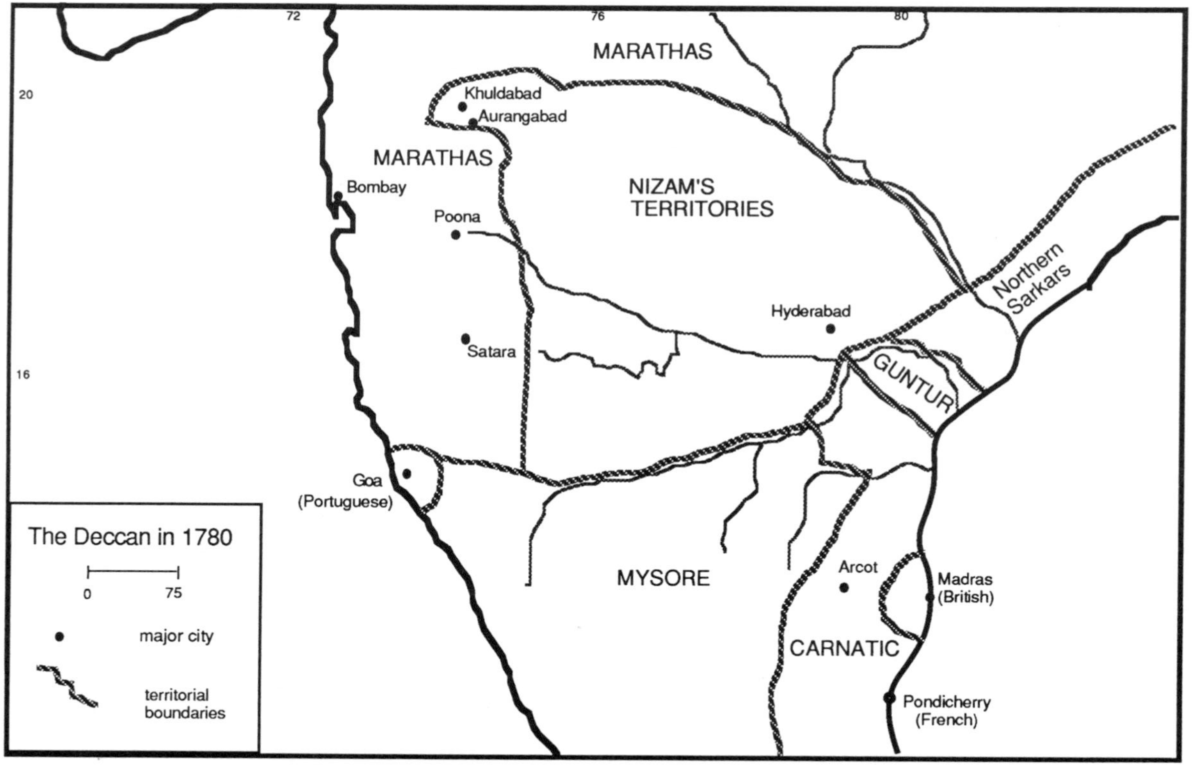

Map 5. The Deccan in 1780

the shrines are identified, of which the following are the most important (see also Table 3 and Map 1). The first Nizam, Niẓām al-Mulk Āṣaf Jāh (d. 1161/1748), was closely attached to the Chishtīs, and even wrote a biography of a contemporary shaykh, Niẓām al-Dīn Awrangābādī (d. 1142/1729).[97] He considered patronage of Sufi saints an important state duty, and stressed this point in his testament to his successor. Both the first Nizam and his successor, Niẓām al-Dawla Nāṣir Jang (d. 1164/1750), were buried along with their wives in separate red sandstone enclosures next to the tomb of Burhān al-Dīn Gharīb (see Figure 6).[98] Niẓām al-Mulk had died near Burhanpur, and after his funeral, his son appropriated revenues from the nearby towns of Bhadgaon and Pipalgaon for his death-anniversary (*ʿurs*) expenses, for sandalwood and roses.[99] The Nizam's choice of Bhadgaon as a source of revenue is striking, since under the Fārūqī and early Mughul endowments, Bhadgaon was the source of revenue for the Sufi shrines of Khuldabad. The third Nizam, Muẓaffar Jang (d. 1751), is buried just south of Burhān al-Dīn's tomb, along with figures such as his uncle Mutawaṣṣil Khān, ʿIważ Khān (d. 1143/1730–31), Jamāl al-Dīn Khān (d. 1159/1746), and others.[100] Other notables are buried in the complex of Yūsuf al-Ḥusaynī Rājū Qattāl: Nawwāb Marḥamat Khān, a governor of Aurangabad; Dā'ūd Khān (d. 1127/1715), a governor of Burhanpur; and Abū al-Ḥasan Tānā Shāh (d. 1111/1699), the last Quṭbshāhī king of Golconda, who was imprisoned in the Daulatabad fort until his death.[101] Most of the archeological maintenance budget expended by the Nizam's government in Khuldabad seems to have been directed at repairing the tombs of just these kings and nobles.[102]

Malik ʿAnbar, the great general of Ahmadnagar who was buried at Khuldabad, was not known for his sanctity during his lifetime. But the process of partial sanctification may be observed in his case as well, since he, his wife Siddī Karīma, and his grandson Siddī ʿAbd al-Raḥmān all have impressive tombs at Khuldabad (see Figures 13, 14, 16). ʿAbd Allāh Ḥabīb al-ʿAydarūs (d. 1631), a Sufi and scholar from southern Arabia, was a friend of Malik ʿAnbar, and also resided at the Bijapur court for a time. His burial next to the tomb of Malik ʿAnbar is probably due to their personal connection, since he was not attached to the Chishtī order.[103] Writing sixty years ago, Rawnaq ʿAlī lamented that Malik ʿAnbar's tomb was not well taken care of, and he urged the Nizam of Hyderabad to see that funds were made available for proper observation of his death-anniversary, just as in the case of a saint (this was not without precedent; in the middle of the nineteenth century, the Niẓāmshāhs' tombs were still maintained by the revenue of several villages).[104] More recently, Waḥīda Nasīm has noted the reverence that local people feel for Malik ʿAnbar, and she has argued that he truly had the character of a saint and dervish.[105]

The most notable case of royal saintliness in Khuldabad is the hue of sanctity attributed to the tomb of Awrangzīb (d. 1119/1707), last of the great

Mughul emperors (see Figure 10). He had often visited Khuldabad as a pilgrim, and the first stipulation in his will had specified that he be buried there: "That they shroud and carry this sinner drenched in sins to the neighborhood of the holy Chishtī tomb of the revered leader, Sayyid and Shaykh, Zayn al-Dīn Dā'ūd Ḥusayn Shīrāzī, since without the protection of that court [of the saints], which is the refuge of forgiveness, there is no refuge for those drowned in the ocean of sin."[106] Aurangzīb felt ambivalent about the tomb veneration, and in keeping with the conservative tone of his later life, he resisted the temptation to build himself a massive imperial mausoleum in the tradition of his forebears. His own simple tomb is technically nothing but an uncovered dirt grave (Figure 9). In the late eighteenth century Sabzawārī described it as follows: "At the foot of the blessed tomb [of Zayn al-Dīn] is the place of the emperor Awrangzīb ʿĀlamgīr, buried no more than a few steps from the shadow of that heaven-displaying threshold. The rainwater of mercy falls on the blessed shrine around the tomb of the late emperor. What good fortune that he has found such a pure place and is resting between two saints who may be called the sun and moon of religion—that is, between the twin tombs that are like the pole stars, of the revered Burhān al-Dīn and Zayn al-Dīn (mercy be upon them)."[107] It presently has a small tree growing on it, and it is surrounded by a marble platform with elegant grillwork, installed by the seventh Nizam in 1341/1922–23. Nearby one also finds the tombs of Awrangzīb's son Muḥammad Aʿẓam and his wife Awrangī Bībī (Figure 8). Awrangzīb's tomb became a place of pilgrimage with a distinctly political tone to it. When the Maratha general Shāhū, grandson of Shivajī, was released from court detention, he collected an army and went to Ahmednagar to visit the place where Awrangzīb died, then on to Khuldabad to visit Awrangzīb's tomb and distribute money to the poor.[108] Though his visit to Khuldabad had the appearance and form of a pilgrimage to a saint's shrine, it was in reality a manifestation of political allegiance.

In the 1930s a herald (*chūbdār*) was always present at the tomb, and at the approach of important visitors, he would bring out gold and silver decorations to adorn the tomb. Due to the Nizam's largesse, there were constant Qur'ān recitations and an open kitchen in the name of Awrangzīb.[109] In the same way, according to oral reports, the Nizam used to make a special visit to Awrangzīb's tomb every year on the death-anniversary, in which he approached it barefoot as the vassal of the Mughul emperor and not as the ruler of an independent kingdom.[110] The Nizam had apportioned a substantial land endowment for the upkeep of the shrine, but after the drastic fiscal reorganization that followed the Indian takeover of Hyderabad, the Nizam Trust now yields only a meagre monthly income of Rs. 6/75 (about fifty cents) for Awrangzīb's tomb.[111] Nowadays Khuldabad has been bypassed by much of the development in Maharashtra, and the Sufi saints are not well known outside the immediate area. But the tourists who come to visit the Ellora caves sometimes stop for tea in Khuldabad, where their guides inform them that the main item of interest in the town is the grave of Awrangzīb.

Just as royal tombs have taken on some of the characteristics of saints' shrines, so too the tombs of saints have felt the impact of royal patrons, who to some extent reconstructed the shrines to suit their own interests. The Sufi tombs of Khuldabad have been retouched and rebuilt many times, and the intermingling of different regional styles in the shrines still needs to be disentangled by architectural historians. The original tomb of Burhān al-Dīn Gharīb was built by his disciples according to a specially constructed model of the tomb of Niẓām al-Dīn Awliyā' in Delhi. A mosque was added by the Bahmanī sultan in 862/1458 (above, Part III, chap. 10), and numerous other reconstructions must have been undertaken at one time or another, since by that time the shrines were totally dependent on royal patronage (see Figures 3–4). One distinctive aspect of the shrine architecture is certainly due to royal patrons, probably the first Nizams: over the main gateway to the city, and in the upper story of the shrines of Burhān al-Dīn Gharīb, Muntajib al-Dīn Zar Zarī Zar-bakhsh, and Zayn al-Dīn, there are located special galleries (*naqqār khānas*) for the performance of court music (Figures 2, 12). Variously known in different Islamic countries as the *ṭabl khāna* ("drum house"), *naqqār* or *naqqāra khāna* ("kettledrum house"), or *nawbat khāna* ("military band house"), this type of building was designed to house the musicians who performed on special large drums associated with Iranian-based court ritual. It was typically performed for royalty at the five daily times for ritual prayer, or three times a day for nobles of lesser rank. The size of the drums and their use were jealously guarded prerogatives.[112] These drums are still used at the shrine of Muʿīn al-Dīn Chishtī at Ajmer, where a five-foot tall drum donated by Akbar may be seen.[113] The *nawbat* drums were still being used in Khuldabad at the annual festival of Muntajib al-Dīn Zar Zarī Zar-bakhsh in the 1960s, but the large drums in the courtyard of Burhān al-Dīn Gharīb's shrine have not been used for some time and now lack covers.[114] Unlike *qawwālī* music deriving from the classical Sufi *samāʿ*, the official court music of the *naqqār khāna* had nothing to do with Sufism, but was an intrusion of royal symbolism into the heart of the Sufi shrines.

The financial documents and architectural monuments of medieval India reveal much when understood in a historical context defined by dynastic history on the one hand and hagiography on the other. The political ambitions of the Muslim rulers of India partly relied on the spiritual authority of Sufi mystics, even when that spiritual authority was reduced to the purely symbolic status of the tomb-shrine. Economic support of these shrines displayed both the strength of the royal authority and its need to secure popular support. In accepting a maintenance from kings, the followers of the Chishtīs of

Khuldabad undoubtedly forfeited their traditional independence along with their poverty, but becoming an explicit part of secular politics was the price of security. Sultans emulated Sufi saints and made their own presence felt in Sufi shrines by building in them structures to celebrate royal authority. The later institutional history of these Sufi shrines shows them to lie at a complicated intersection between the mystical tradition of Islam and royal power.

11

Khuldabad as a Sacred Center in the Local Context

Later hagiographic materials offer a perspective on the Sufis of Khuldabad that is dependent on the royal hagiographies just elaborated, but which also radiate outward to include saints whose connection with history is highly attenuated. Some, such as Bahā' al-Dīn Anṣārī (d. 1515) and Shāh Khāksār (seventeenth cent.) appear to have been drawn to the area by its reputation for holiness and stayed on. Little else is known of them, except that Khāksār was a devotee of Rājū Qattāl. Other local saints have been connected to the early Khuldabad Chishtīs to form a lineage transmitting the dominion of the Deccan region.

These saints sometimes have strong connections to local pre-Islamic culture, and their connections are brought out through colorful legends that reveal saintly power as fundamentally connected with the local landscape. This last phase of history-making can now be explored in terms of the way the Sufis' authority was transmitted and interpreted by later generations, with special emphasis on the Khuldabad-Burhanpur connection and on other local developments in Khuldabad. Hagiographic materials in Persian and Urdu from the Mughul period up to the present day recognize the Sufis of Khuldabad as a potent force for legitimizing both spiritual and political authority, frequently in terms that were intelligible for the local Indian culture. The axis of authoritative symbolism that linked Khuldabad and Burhanpur in this way made possible a local sacred geography for Indian Islam.

The Khuldabad-Burhanpur Axis

The issue of succession to the authority of Burhān al-Dīn Gharīb can be seen most clearly in an obviously political tradition that describes the saint's prediction of the foundation of Burhanpur. *Fatḥ al-awliyā'* gives considerable prominence to this story, which adds the royal Indian symbolism of the elephant and the local symbolism of rivers to a prophecy of dynastic success.[115] In this account, Burhān al-Dīn halted his journey from Delhi to Daulatabad to perform prayers. Standing on a stone in the middle of the river Tapti, he was greatly charmed by the spot, and in his prayers he had a vision of the future city of Burhanpur and prophesied its greatness. The text adds that the stone is known as the *hāt'hī k'harag* (Marathi for "elephant stone"), and that when the Mughul emperor Akbar conquered Burhanpur in 1601, he took a fancy to the stone and had it carved into the likeness of an elephant, as a standing memorial to his conquest. From an oral tradition quoted in a seventeenth-century hagiographic source, we learn a valuable supplementary point, that Burhān al-Dīn Gharīb's prophecy had actually specified that the Fārūqī dynasty would last only until the stone became an elephant.[116] Now the incident has taken on a double significance. Burhān al-Dīn Gharīb's prophecy concerning Burhanpur was undoubtedly of great importance to the Fārūqīs as a foundation myth.[117] But the Mughuls had absorbed Khandesh in 1601, and had taken over the Fārūqī symbols of authority, so that all of the known versions of this story are marked with an addition that in its present form reflects Mughul interests: the story of the elephant stone makes a second prediction of Mughul supremacy implicit in the first one. All that was necessary was for Akbar to recognize the inner aspect of the elephant in the stone and leave it as an imperial monument, as had many an Indian ruler before him. The location of this incident in a river would also convey to a local audience the association of rivers with fertility and power that is typical in Marathi culture. European travelers in the seventeenth century observed that the stone elephant in the Tapti was painted like a temple and worshiped by the "Gentiles."[118] The story thus legitimizes the authority of the Mughuls over Khandesh, deftly combining the spiritual recognition of a Sufi saint with an aura of imperial and cosmic power suggested by the symbolism of the elephant and the river.

Succession to Burhān al-Dīn Gharīb's authority took on a more straightforward guise in the form of shadowy Sufi lineages formed in descent from the saint. It should be emphasized that these lineages belong almost wholly to the realm of hagiography and contain little of the teaching content of the Sufi tradition, unlike the well-documented literary circle that recorded the teachings of Burhān al-Dīn Gharīb in Khuldabad. Especially striking is the case of a lineage of saints who transmitted his authority from Daulatabad to Burhanpur and periodically renewed it by visiting his tomb. The first of these was Sayyid 'Alā' al-Dīn Żiyā' (d. 801/1398–99), whose birth was due to the prognostication of Burhān al-Dīn Gharīb.

Again, the earliest written source is *Fatḥ al-awliyā'*, from which we draw the following summary.[119] It seems that after the move to Daulatabad, one of the duties that Niẓām al-Dīn Awliyā' had laid upon Burhān al-Dīn Gharīb was to look after one of the daughters of the great shaykh Farīd al-Dīn Ganj-i Shakkar. On his weekly Friday visit to the lady, who is usually identified as Bībī ʿĀ'isha, Burhān al-Dīn Gharīb's glance happened to fall upon her beautiful and pious 14-year-old daughter, and he smiled. When the observant mother asked (in Multani dialect) the reason for this smile, he replied that she carried in her womb a saint who had saluted him, so that he was greatly astonished. He knew that she was an unmarried virgin, so he wondered if the saint would be born without a father, like Jesus; that had been the reason for his smile. Bībī ʿĀ'isha was not amused, but pointed out that having made the prediction, he should determine whether the girl is to be properly married or not. Burhān al-Dīn Gharīb then promised that a suitable husband would appear by the following Friday, and so it happened that Sayyid Żiyā' al-Dīn duly appeared, and they were married. Having fulfilled his duty, Sayyid Żiyā' al-Dīn took his leave after three days, and ʿAlā' al-Dīn Żiyā' was born in due time. Everyone brought gifts then, with the exception of Burhān al-Dīn Gharīb, who gave the excuse that he had no possessions. Farīd al-Dīn's daughter observed that he was nonetheless the master of the dominion (*vilāyat*) of the entire Deccan. Thereupon the saint agreed to bestow upon the child the regions of Munki Patan and Khandesh as his future dominion. At any rate, despite Burhān al-Dīn Gharīb's prophecy that the child would become a great teacher of religion, the boy ran away as soon as possible with a singer and lived a dissolute life. Eventually, however, he repented and undertook rigorous asceticism, so that he was finally recognized as the saint predicted by Burhān al-Dīn Gharīb.

Another spiritual linkage enters the story at this point, as ʿAlā' al-Dīn Żiyā' announced that it was necessary for him to get initiation from another Chishtī master in Gujarat, Rukn al-Dīn Chishtī, upon which he himself would initiate all those who are destined to be connected with this Sufi order.[120] Through a complicated series of circumstances, ʿAlā' al-Dīn Żiyā' met and recognized his future disciple Niẓām al-Dīn Idrīs, a strange man who went about with a bow and a stone ball in search of a master who could read his inner soul. Abandoning these implements on the advice of ʿAlā' al-Dīn Żiyā', he went to Gujarat and obtained from Rukn al-Dīn initiatic robes and authorization to teach for ʿAlā' al-Dīn Żiyā'. Niẓām al-Dīn Idrīs became the successor of ʿAlā' al-Dīn Żiyā' and had from him the charge of the dominion of Munki Patan, where he is buried. The tomb of ʿAlā' al-Dīn Żiyā' is in Daulatabad, though presently neglected; the tomb of Bībī ʿĀ'isha and her daughter is to the south of Amīr Ḥasan Dihlavī's tomb just outside Khuldabad (Figure 14). Although the details of this story are romantic, the political impact would be felt through the bestowal of the dominion particularly of Khandesh upon the infant ʿAlāʾ al-Dīn Żiyāʾ. This gift underlined the supreme authority of Burhān al-Dīn Gharīb over the whole Deccan at the same time that it opened up the possibility of expanding the Chishtī order in Khandesh.

The next step took place through a disciple of ʿAlāʾ al-Dīn Żiyāʾ, Shāh Nuʿmān of Asīr (d. 881/1476–77), to whom in turn the dominion of Khandesh would be bequeathed. Once again, the fullest source we have is *Fatḥ al-awliyāʾ*, from which the following details are extracted.[121] Shāh Nuʿmān claimed descent from one of the early Chishtī saints, Mawdūd Chishtī (d. 527/1133), and the travels and circumstances of his ancestors are fully detailed. Shāh Nuʿmān's great-grandfather Muḥammad Ṭāhir is said to have sought a Sufi vocation, with the idea of spreading the Islamic faith, and so he came to India, settling at last in the delightful abode of Daulatabad. In the chronology that follows there is some confusion, probably deriving from the use of different sources. We are now told that Shāh Nuʿmān's religious vocation began at age twelve and at that time he became a disciple of Sayyid ʿAlāʾ al-Dīn Żiyāʾ. After many austerities, he obtained the Chishtī initiatic robe and diploma of authorization together with the dominion of Khandesh.[122] Meditating that night at the resting place of Burhān al-Dīn Gharīb, he perceived in a vision that the city of Burhanpur would soon be founded. Accordingly, in 822/1419 he traveled to Khandesh and visited the future site of Burhanpur, which at that time was still a village called Vaysāna. Pushing on farther, he settled at the base of the mountain fortress of Asīr, where he is buried. His appearance greatly impressed the inhabitants of the place, especially after he caused a spring to come into existence to provide water for ablutions; he named it the Sīwarī, and predicted that it could continue to flow clear for one hundred thirty more years. Some local people became his disciples, and when deer and other animals approached the peaceful hermitage, the men would kill the beasts to prepare the saint's meals. An incidental story relates that the eponymous builder of the fortress of Asīr, Āsā Ahīr, became a disciple of Shāh Nuʿmān as well, and constructed the mighty fort in his honor.[123]

In the meantime, Naṣīr Khān Fārūqī (d. 841/1437), son of Malik Rāja, had declared himself the independent ruler of Khandesh in 801/1398–99, and was living in the town of Thalner. Being greatly drawn to Sufism, he came to visit the shaykh, and had his son do so also (this was ʿĀdil Khān Shahīd, the next ruler of Khandesh). Naṣīr Khān was so eager to spend time with Shāh Nuʿmān that he asked permission to move closer. Shāh Nuʿmān consulted both with God and with the spirit of Burhān al-Dīn Gharīb, and became aware that the "elephant stone" in the Tapti River marked the spot where Burhān al-Dīn Gharīb had prayed, which would become the site of the city of Burhanpur and the capital of the Fārūqīs. Naṣīr Khān gladly received this information, and finally in 835/1431–32, he began to lay the foundations of the city. Shortly afterward he captured the fortress of Asīr by a strategem. On account of the generosity of Naṣīr Khān toward Sufis, his kingdom became a center of the

Chishtī order, to whose members he awarded many stipends and land endowments. The text makes an excursus at this point to relate an additional foundation story, also known to the seventeenth-century historian Firishta, which anachronistically depicts Burhān al-Dīn Gharīb's chief disciple Zayn al-Dīn Shīrāzī (d. 771/1370) coming to congratulate Naṣīr Khān on his conquest of Asīr, at the same time enrolling the Fārūqī dynasty under his protection until the Resurrection.[124] Further stories depict Shāh Nuʿmān's supremacy among spiritual leaders of the region. He is shown humbling a yogi named Shiva Nāth by a demonstration of the ability to transform stones into gold with a glance, so that the yogi converted to Islam, and he also correctly intuited the problems that the Sufi leader Shāh ʿĀlam (d. 880/1475–76) of Gujarat was having with Sultan Maḥmūd Bēgaṛ'ha.

The biography of Shāh Nuʿmān closes on a curious note. Some disciples are puzzled about why Sayyid Niẓām al-Dīn Idrīs is named as Shāh Nuʿmān's master in their spiritual "tree" (*shajara*) documents, rather than Sayyid ʿAlā' al-Dīn Żiyā'. In reply to this question it is said that when Shāh Nuʿmān went to receive his teaching authorization from ʿAlā' al-Dīn Żiyā', the latter took a sip from a cup (*piyāla*) and presented it to the disciple, who then drained it. ʿAlā' al-Dīn Żiyā' then told Shāh Nuʿmān to guard the cup carefully. Shāh Nuʿmān replied, "Your children (*farzandān*) will get it [i.e., discipleship] from me." Thus a reciprocal relationship was worked out, so that Shāh Nuʿmān put the name of Niẓām al-Dīn Idrīs (the spiritual "child" of ʿAlā' al-Dīn Żiyā') in the place of his real master, and ʿAlā' al-Dīn Żiyā's "children" put the name of Shāh Nuʿmān as their master.

At this point it may be noted that the portrayal of the life of Shāh Nuʿmān in *Fatḥ al-awliyā'* repeatedly emphasizes his connection with Burhān al-Dīn Gharīb and the foundation of Burhanpur; this connection takes on the force of revelation both at his initiation by ʿAlā' al-Dīn Żiyā' and later on when questioned by Naṣīr Khān Fārūqī. The importance that the text lays on this relationship is clear also from the final obscure discussion of spiritual genealogy. Although Shāh Nuʿmān was most commonly associated with the local saint Niẓām al-Dīn Idrīs, *Fatḥ al-awliyā'* insists that his real connection was with ʿAlā' al-Dīn Żiyā' (and therefore Burhān al-Dīn Gharīb), from whom the spiritual dominion of the region had been transmitted.

The last figure to receive the authority of Burhān al-Dīn Gharīb was Bahā' al-Dīn Shāh Bājan (d. 912/1507). Born in 790/1388 in Ahmadabad, Shāh Bājan was descended from the caliph ʿUmar ibn al-Khaṭṭāb, and one of his ancestors, Shaykh Aḥmad Madanī, was so eminent a scholar of *ḥadīth* that he resolved questions on the subject by consulting the Prophet at will in his dreams; he also had nightly access to the Prophet's tomb. Shāh Bājan was initiated by his father, with whom he set out on a journey to the Hejaz. When they reached Khurasan, the father had a dream of the Prophet Muḥammad, who informed him that their pilgrimage had already been accepted, and that it was the destiny of the son to go to Burhanpur to teach and lead according to the religious law of Islam. The father then died, and Shāh Bājan returned to India and lived for some years in Delhi with his uncle Shaykh ʿAṭāʾ Allāh, who succeeded to his father's position as Sufi master. Finally prompted inwardly to go to the Deccan, he visited the tomb of Burhān al-Dīn Gharīb in Daulatabad, and then headed for Bidar and became a disciple of Shaykh Manjhlē, a mysterious figure who was himself a disciple of the Chishtī martyr Masʿūd Bakk (d. 1387).[125] After that, he went to Gujarat and spent seven years with dervishes and in retreat, and then finally came to Burhanpur. At some point, Shāh Bājan also became a disciple of Shaykh Raḥmat Allāh ibn Shaykh ʿAzīz Allāh Mutawakkil of Mandu.[126] He was welcomed to Burhanpur by the Fārūqī prince ʿAynā ʿĀdil Shāh (r. 861–909/1457–1503), and lived for many years in Burhanpur. He was extremely popular, and was known for the literary talent in Persian and Gujari poetry displayed in his Sufi treatise *Khizānat-i raḥmat allāh*. So much we learn from *Fatḥ al-awliyā'*, which is for once restrained in describing the authority of a saint.[127]

To fill out the picture of the saint's spiritual connections we are fortunate to have access to *Khizānat-i raḥmat allāh*, in which Shāh Bājan sets out an account of his own destiny that is much more closely linked with Burhān al-Dīn Gharīb.[128] In describing his slow itinerary to Burhanpur, Shāh Bājan revealed that he had thought it best to go first to Khuldabad, since Burhanpur was under Burhān al-Dīn's protection, to seek the blessing and guidance of the saint. Burhān al-Dīn appeared to him three times in dreams with the same message, saying that he was indeed dead, that up to now Burhanpur had been in his own protection, but that he would entrust it to Shāh Bājan. Moreover, Burhān al-Dīn gave Shāh Bājan a written teaching authorization (*ijāzat nāma*) in the dream, and told him to come to Khuldabad to receive a garment (*pīshwāz*) that had been Burhān al-Dīn's, and which was especially reserved as a trust (*amāna*) for Shāh Bājan. Burhān al-Dīn then appeared in a dream to the custodian of his shrine, Shaykh Jīvan, ordering him to give the garment to Shāh Bājan when he arrived as a pilgrim. The custodian did as ordered, and also gave Shāh Bājan an initiatic genealogy (*shajara*). Burhān al-Dīn then appeared in the latter's dream again, twice repeating that "Burhanpur is my station, which I entrust to you," and giving him permission to leave. It was only then that Shāh Bājan was ready to make his way to Burhanpur. Shāh Bājan's connection with Burhān al-Dīn Gharīb reveals how important the latter's authority was in the fifteenth-century Deccan. It shows less political construction than does the lineage of ʿAlāʾ al-Dīn Żiyāʾ and Shāh Nuʿmān. While Shāh Bājan did form an attachment with the Fārūqī dynasty, his relationship with Burhān al-Dīn Gharīb was independent of royal authority. The authority of ʿAlāʾ al-Dīn Żiyāʾ and Shāh Nuʿmān, on the other hand, was (at least in *Fatḥ al-awliyā'*) important only insofar as it led from Burhān al-Dīn Gharīb up to the consolidation of the kingdom of Burhanpur.

The Local Saints of Khuldabad

Aside from overt political connections, the saints of Khuldabad exerted an authority that was widely recognized in the region, in many cases through signs of miraculous power marked with a strong local accent. The earliest among them may have come even prior to the transfer of Delhi's elite to Daulatabad. But since we have no contemporary sources of information about them, nor any historical inscriptions on their tombs, the legendary saints remain misty figures enlarged by the passage of time into giants. The late hagiographical literature praises their greatness but offers little descriptive detail. With only legends of this type available, it is not surprising that even medieval hagiographers have lamented the absence of texts that would shed light on the lives and history of these early saints.[129] Nonetheless, the legends are valuable sources for understanding the way that the power of sainthood was mediated into the local culture.

One of the legendary Sufis was Jalāl al-Dīn, better known by the epithet "Ganj-i Ravān" ("flowing treasure"). He is supposed to have been a disciple, perhaps by one intermediary, of Shaykh Shihāb al-Dīn al-Suhrawardī of Baghdad, and is believed to have come to the area when it was still ruled by a Hindu raja. Some believe that he had been a soldier who fought against Chingīz Khān on the banks of the Indus and was well received by Sultan Iltutmish (d. 634/1236) at Delhi. He is supposed to have come to the Deccan in search of solitude in 634/1236–37.[130] As an example of the vague halo of sanctity that came to surround him we may quote the eighteenth-century author Sabzawārī: "By various miracles and numerous supernatural feats he defeated the people of infidelity and sorcery. He confounded the foundation of infidelity and ignorance. He first revealed the sign and the practice of Islam and made firm the pomp of the faith of Muhammad."[131] Sabzawārī's description gives no details, however, of the feats by which Jalāl al-Dīn may have impressed the local inhabitants. Āzād Bilgrāmī writing some decades earlier only recorded that Jalāl al-Dīn came to Khuldabad before the Chishtīs, and he praised the beauty of the tomb, which overlooks a splendid view of a spring-fed pond, known as the Fairies' Tank (*pariyāñ kā tālāb*); the pastoral beauty of this scene is still impressive today.[132]

It remained for a recent hagiographer, Rawnaq ʿAlī, to record the legends associated with Jalāl al-Dīn. One account states that when he came to Khuldabad he bound and imprisoned a demon or jinn named Āzar beneath a stone on which he had prayed, which is still found to the east of his tomb. This stone is perhaps identical with a large stone *yoni*, which is still in ritual use today by Hindu pilgrims; this once formed the base for a Shiva-*lingam*, and is now found a few feet to the east of the main entrance to the tomb. The presence of this Hindu ritual object suggests that Jalāl al-Dīn's tomb was built at an earlier center for worshipers of Shiva. Also near the tomb is a tree that he caused to bear fruit for his children. Such is the virtue of this tree that barren women may conceive children by eating its fruit. It is said that a hermaphrodite once mocked the saint's powers by eating the tree's fruit; miraculously the hermaphrodite became pregnant and bore a child, though both died soon after. Both parent and child are buried in the courtyard near the tomb, and the site is pointed out with emphasis to the visitor. At the saint's annual festival beginning on 26 Dhū al-Qaʿda, one day (the 29th) is set aside especially for women's participation, and the festival is still quite popular among women. Bathing in water from the Fairies' Tank is recommended to cure illnesses among women. The saint's death-date is recorded as the surprisingly early 644/1247.[133] His reputation as a binder of demons mythologizes him by making him the hero of a cosmic combat. His ability to heal and provide fertility through the tree and the water of the tank provides continuity with the sacred powers of the Maharashtran landscape, and perhaps with earlier Shiva traditions associated with the locality where he is buried.

Another early saint of the region was Mu'min ʿĀrif, whose tomb lies at the foot of the hills due east of the Daulatabad fort. Scarcely anything is known about this figure, nor is it possible to say anything of his connection with Sufism. He is believed to have come to the area before the time of the Khaljī conquest of the Deccan, perhaps around 1200. His name itself, which means "believer" (*mu'min*) and "knower" (*ʿārif*), subsumes him from any particular individuality into the generality of religious virtue. Sabzawārī recorded that Mu'min ʿĀrif was descended from the eighth Shīʿī imam, ʿAlī Rizā', and that his death is observed on 20 Ṣafar, just as in the case of the imam.[134] On this anniversary, songs of lamentation (*marsiyya*) for the sufferings of the Shīʿī imams formed the principal ritual during the eighteenth century. To judge by his descent from an imam and the performance of Shīʿī ritual at his tomb, Mu'min ʿĀrif appears to have been more closely connected to Shīʿī piety than to Sufism. Nowadays these Shīʿī practices are no longer found; the shaykh, now know as Mu'min ʿĀrif Bāqī Billāh, is connected with the Suhrawardī Sufi order, and the customary weekly Thursday visits and annual festival prevail.[135]

According to current oral tradition, Mu'min ʿĀrif came to Deogir when it was still ruled by a Hindu raja. One of his miracles occurred when this raja stole and butchered the cow of a Muslim woman, who then came to appeal to the saint for help. Mu'min ʿĀrif by his supernatural power restored the cow to life, thus demonstrating his divine support; the eventual grave of the cow is still pointed out to visitors.[136] The heterogeneous elements in the story of this saint suggest that different constituencies preserved different traditions about Mu'min ʿĀrif. At one point Shīʿī observances predominated, and for some local devotees the saint acted out the defense of cows against royal repression. The story of the cow in particular sets the usual "Hindu-Muslim" stereotype on its head. As in the case of the veneration of Muslim "holy warriors" by local non-Muslim Indian communities, an Islamic figure has become assimilated to an Indian norm of sanctity, in this case the protection of cows.[137]

Perhaps the most remarkable legendary saint of Khuldabad, however, is Burhān al-Dīn Gharīb's brother Muntajib al-Dīn, better known as Zar Zarī Zar-bakhsh, "the giver of the essence of gold." Although his connection with the Chishtī tradition is beyond doubt, the lack of any contemporary account leaves him in the fog of legend, forever beyond the grasp of our knowledge. Burhān al-Dīn Gharīb only referred twice to his brother in his collected discourses, once in an anecdote concerning the rules of fasting and a second time in a story about Muntajib al-Dīn meeting a madman.[138] While Burhān al-Dīn and his disciples undoubtedly respected Muntajib al-Din, he was not known as a Sufi teacher. Sabzawārī expansively refers to his thousands of disciples and converts, but twentieth-century sources maintain that he had no formal disciples (the case of Sōnā Bā'ī, mentioned below, is obviously exceptional).[139] Literally nothing else is known of the life and teachings of Muntajib al-Dīn. What remains is his impressive tomb (Figure 5), built alongside that of his mother Bībī Hājira, and a small cave to which he used to retreat on the side of Hoda Hill a few furlongs away (overlooking the tomb of Sayyid Yūsuf Ḥusaynī Rājū Qattāl; see Figure 17). Today the fame of Muntajib al-Dīn has outstripped that of any other saint of Khuldabad, and his festival regularly attracts a very large attendance.[140] He is said to have died on 7 Rabīʿ al-Awwal 709/15 August 1309, and I was fortunate to be present as a guest at his seven hundredth death-anniversary festival in Khuldabad in the fall of 1987.

In any case, the reconstruction of the life of Muntajib al-Dīn has focused on his coming to the Deccan to introduce the Chishtī order and spread Islam. The earliest biography of Muntajib al-Dīn is given by Sabzawārī in the eighteenth century, although he draws upon an important tradition that was first articulated in *Fatḥ al-awliyā'* a century earlier. Sabzawārī at first describes Muntajib al-Dīn as a disciple of Niẓām al-Dīn Awliyā', although in a verse immediately following, Muntajib al-Dīn is referred to as a disciple of Farīd al-Dīn Ganj-i Shakkar.[141] In *Fatḥ al-awliyā'*, however, the issue of spiritual dominion (*vilāyat*) comes to the fore immediately. In a lengthy buildup, Niẓām al-Dīn Awliyā' is portrayed in a meditative ecstasy, suddenly interrupted by a divine voice offering the saint any boon he can name. After some hesitation, Niẓām al-Dīn requests that any disciple to whom he gives *vilāyat* will hold it safely until the resurrection without any alteration. Although *vilāyat* also means sainthood (from *valī*, "friend" [of God], saint), the author of *Fatḥ al-awliyā'* has in mind the distribution of saintly authority over the political domain. He describes Niẓām al-Dīn's assignment of the dominion of Delhi to Naṣīr al-Dīn Maḥmūd "Chirāgh-i Dihlī," that of Malwa to Wajīh al-

Dīn Yūsuf, and so on, in this way dividing most of the subcontinent among his chief disciples. In this way Muntajib al-Dīn received the dominion over the entire Deccan.

After Muntajib al-Dīn's departure for Daulatabad, accompanied by seven hundred Sufi saints, some years passed, when suddenly one day Niẓām al-Dīn asked Burhān al-Dīn Gharīb, "Was your brother Muntajib al-Dīn older or younger?" From this Burhān al-Dīn Gharīb guessed that his brother had died, and in a scene drawn out with many dramatic touches, *Fatḥ al-awliyā'* describes how Niẓām al-Dīn then conferred the *vilāyat* of the Deccan upon Burhān al-Dīn Gharīb. When the latter displayed some reluctance to leave his master, Niẓām al-Dīn presented him with his own sandals as a token of their continuing connection, and also ordered seven hundred (or fourteen hundred) of the assembled disciples to accompany Burhān al-Dīn Gharīb in palanquins to the Deccan.[142] In this way the transfer of the Chishtī order to Daulatabad was accomplished, as commemorated by the "Mosque of Fourteen Hundred Saints" in Khuldabad.[143] Thus the transplantation of the Chishtī order takes on a purely spiritual significance, so that it stands in contrast with Sultan Muḥammad ibn Tughluq's forcible removal of the Muslim population of Delhi to Daulatabad in 1329.[144] It will be recalled that one of the main themes of *Fatḥ al-awliyā'* was the subsequent distribution of the dominion of the Deccan from Burhān al-Dīn Gharīb to his successors ʿAlā' al-Dīn Żiyā' and Shāh Nuʿmān, as part of the legitimation of the Fārūqīs' claim to authority. Muntajib al-Dīn's role in this hagiography was to be the prior link in the chain of divinely decreed authority. The tension between *Fatḥ al-awliyā'* and the Tughluq chronicles need not be reduced to a contradiction of sources, in which one is right and the other wrong, but may be considered simply as a tension between different historiographies.[145]

Although Muntajib al-Dīn's epithet Zar Zarī Zar-bakhsh may have been originally symbolic of spiritual riches, it has given rise to a number of legends that explain circumstantially how he was the giver of gold. The epithet does not occur in the early literature, but is found occasionally in Mughul revenue documents of the seventeenth century (sometimes it is also applied to Burhān al-Dīn Gharīb, or even to Niẓām al-Dīn Awliyā'). The first legend, given by the historian Firishta, relates that on the caravan down from Delhi to Daulatabad, by the grace of Niẓām al-Dīn Awliyā', Muntajib al-Dīn miraculously received a gold bar every day to defray the expenses of the fourteen hundred during the journey. A second story, known to the seventeenth-century hagiographer Khwīshagī, maintains that he received a golden robe every morning and evening, which he would sell for money to support his companions. A third version tells how in a time of famine, Muntajib al-Dīn prayed for help for the people, whereupon golden branches grew from the ground (this appears to be related to the story of the silver branches that, according to Rawnaq ʿAlī, appeared by the tomb of Burhān al-Dīn Gharīb). A fourth account states that when the mother of Muntajib al-Dīn was in labor, she had difficulty in giving birth to the child, and the father learned from his master that a saintly personage like Muntajib al-Dīn was not to be born naked. The mother accordingly was given a nugget of gold to eat, and Zar Zarī Zar-bakhsh was born with a golden diaper (*langōṭa*).[146] A fifth story concerns Sōnā Bā'ī, as discussed below.

The feminine role is not prominent in the "classical" hagiographical literature of Chishtī Sufism, but recent writers on the saints of Khuldabad have given a more appreciable account of feminine presence in the spiritual geography of the region. The Five Ladies (*pāñch bībīyāñ*), the sisters of Muntajib al-Dīn and Burhān al-Dīn Gharīb, are buried outside the tomb of Naṣīr al-Dīn Pā'oñ Payk, and they (like Bībī Hājira and Bībī ʿĀ'isha) are recognized as saintly individuals.[147] An anniversary festival also takes place on 21 Shaʿbān at the tomb of Khwān Bībī Ṣāḥiba, the learned and pious adopted daughter of Zayn al-Dīn Shīrāzī, within his tomb complex (see Figure 8).[148] One of the most prominent gardens of Khuldabad, the Banī Bēgam garden (now unfortunately run down), contains the tomb of the wife of the Mughul prince Bīdār Bakht, elder son of Aʿẓam Shāh.[149]

But the most striking woman in the hagiography of Khuldabad is undoubtedly the Hindu princess Sōnā Bā'ī ("gold woman" in Marathi), who became a disciple of Zar Zarī Zar-bakhsh. She is known especially for having constructed the well named after her, the Sōnā Bā'olī (three other less prominent wells are named after her three sisters Bā'olā Bā'ī, Ḍāk Bā'ī, and Kuṭ'hā [or Kūṭ'hā] Bā'ī). The story is told that her father, a Hindu chieftain, was the ruler of the country. When Muntajib al-Dīn arrived in Khuldabad and settled on Hoda Hill, he sent a servant out to fetch water for ablutions. When the servant requested access to the well from an attendant, he was refused, but by good fortune Sōnā Bā'ī happened to be passing by with her companions. Hearing that the already famous Zar Zarī Zar-bakhsh was requesting water, she jestingly replied that he could have water as soon as the well turned to gold. When the servant returned to the saint and relayed the message, he replied, "So be it," and instructed the servant to return, take some water, and then place a handkerchief belonging to Zar Zarī Zar-bakhsh in the well. The servant followed these orders, and Sōnā Bā'ī watched in amazement as the water turned to flowing gold. She then understood the power of the God who could perform such a deed, went to meet the saint, and became his disciple. The gold had led her to the maker of gold. She and her family converted to Islam, and she eventually became an adept mystic.[150] Sōnā Bā'ī's tomb lies under a jasmine tree between the tombs of Zar Zarī Zar-bakhsh and his mother Bībī Hājira.[151] Her well, the Sōnā Bā'olī, still forms part of the itinerary of the festival procession at the *ʿurs* of Zar Zarī Zar-bakhsh. It is suggestive that Zar Zarī Zar-bakhsh is also known locally as Dūlhā Miyāñ, "the noble bridegroom," according to one source because he died young.[152] At least by the seventeenth century, Hindus and Muslims alike participated in all the rituals at the annual festival of Zar Zarī Zar-bakhsh.[153] As with Ghāzī Miyāñ and other heroes who have been assimilated to Indian patterns, Zar Zarī Zar-bakhsh may have taken on the epithet of "bridegroom" for a local population that regarded him as taking part in a *hieros gamos* or sacred marriage with his feminine counterpart.

The multilayered stories about Muntajib al-Dīn Zar Zarī Zar-bakhsh reflect his appeal to different audiences. For the political elite, he is the guarantor of legitimate authority and the possessor of the dominion of the Deccan. Other local groups regard him as a miracle worker in accordance with the promise of his name. Some put his prodigies in the context of feminine spirituality and the wells that form a powerful element in the cosmos of Maharashtra. His sainthood radiates authority in several dimensions at once.

The establishment of Rawza or Khuldabad in the fourteenth century as a center of Sufism in the Deccan created a new spiritual center for Indian Muslims in the region. The Khuldabad-Burhanpur connection was a linkage of spiritual authority through Sufi lineages that ensured saintly protection for the Fārūqī dynasty of Burhanpur. By drawing on the established territorial principle of "dominions" in Sufism, the Fārūqīs were able to use their association with the Chishtīs of Khuldabad to bolster their own authority. Literate Sufis like Shāh Bājan of Burhanpur continued to regard the tomb of Burhān al-Dīn Gharīb in Khuldabad as the center of saintly power in the Deccan. On a more local basis, saints such as Mu'min ʿĀrif and Ganj-i Ravān became famous not through the Persianate literary hagiographies but through legends that represented the symbolic world of Maharashtra. These saints became larger-than-life figures, partaking of the qualities of heroism within the Indian cosmos, by protecting cows, imprisoning demons, and bestowing health and fertility. Muntajib al-Dīn Zar Zarī Zar-bakhsh played a variety of roles for several different audiences, ranging from the political elite to the local cultivators. Khuldabad was a sacred center for Indian Islam in many senses. This was a sacred geography composed of many maps, layered one over the other.

PART IV

Conclusions

What issues does Khuldabad raise for the study of south Asian Islam, Indo-Muslim rule, institutional Sufism, and the Chishtī brotherhood? First, the Khuldabad materials furnish a thorough documentation of multiple historiographies, each with its own narrative interpretation of the authority of the Sufi master. Historical perspectives on the Sufi master have changed drastically over the centuries, and the interpretations of the actions and purposes of the Sufis have changed too. This change in perspective was not apparent as long as the religious history of south Asia was read through the lens of political sources, including both dynastic histories and the late hagiographies in which royalist motives interfered.

The fourteenth-century *malfūẓāt* texts from Khuldabad significantly enlarge our understanding of the formation of this genre of Sufi literature. When placed alongside the well-known *Fawā'id al-fu'ād* of Niẓām al-Dīn and *Khayr al-majālis* of Chirāgh-i Dihlī, the texts on Burhān al-Dīn Gharīb (*Nafā'is al-anfās*, *Aḥsan al-aqwāl*, *Gharā'ib al-karāmāt*, and *Shamā'il al-atqiyā'*) offer a major expansion of the sources on the early Chishtīs. The information conveyed in these narrative accounts of Sufi teaching challenges the received picture of early Indian Sufism. What are we to make of the discrepancies over the status of Burhān al-Dīn Gharīb, who is dismissed as a minor figure by the Delhi-focused branch of Chishtīs (Mīr Khwurd, Ḥamīd Qalandar, Gīsū Darāz, all followers of Chirāgh-i Dihlī), while his disciples in the Deccan depict him as the principal successor to Chishtī authority? Such a question cannot be directly answered by an outsider; one who affirms the authenticity of an initiatic lineage is expressing a personal relationship with the authority of that lineage. For the historian of religion, the diversity that the Khuldabad texts reveal within fourteenth-century Chishtī circles constitutes instead a challenge for historiographic interpretation. An even greater gap is revealed between the Khuldabad *malfūẓāt* and the hagiographies of later centuries, each of which reflects a differing religious and political perspective.

Taking the Khuldabad texts into account therefore makes it more than ever clear that the different types of writing about Sufi saints need to be classified according to their genre and purpose. The "original" *malfūẓāt* texts written by the literate courtier disciples of the Chishtī masters discuss the authority of the Sufi shaykh from a pedagogical perspective, treating it as an oral transmission of Chishtī teachings. The words and actions of the Sufi master, like the *ḥadīth* of the Prophet, are recorded for their blessings and their teaching value, both for the immediate audience and for future generations of would-be disciples. Hagiographies in contrast emphasize initiatic authority as a mediation between God and the saint's followers. These "lives of the saints" stress miraculous power and authority over teaching. The same is true of the "retrospective" *malfūẓāt* texts, which are presented as accounts of the principal Sufi saints as recorded by their chief successors. This historiographic approach has meaning primarily as a guarantee of the salvific power of the lineage from the viewpoint of the ordinary devotee. Sufi biographers and historians with royalist inclinations (e.g., Firishta) treat the authority of Sufi saints as the guarantee of legitimate dominion, which is to be entrusted to the ruling dynasty. Popular tales of the Sufis adapt their names and lives in ways that reflect the local cosmology, often preserving elements of pre-Islamic origin. Late hagiographies from the seventeenth century onward (Dārā Shikūh, Sabzawārī) and oral traditions recorded in nineteenth-century gazetteers depict the Sufis as missionaries of Islam, sent by their masters to convert the heathen. Sometimes the Sufis become warriors and martyrs based on the models of Indian epic heroes.

These multiple perspectives illustrate the ways in which certain groups explain their own relationship with Islam, using the Sufi saint as the medium for that relationship. In recent times the image of the Sufi as missionary has been encouraged by the modern Pakistani state, to support the ideological interpretation of Islam as the basis for government. A competing political image is fostered in India, where Sufis are depicted as tolerant universalists and secularists only tangentially related to Islam. In all these cases the interpretive stance is governed by the aim of the literary genre employed.

The conflict of narratives offers the opportunity for clarifying more precisely the genre to which each text belongs. When the dynastic chroniclers Baranī and ʿIṣāmī described the transfer of the Muslim elite from Delhi to Daulatabad, they called it "the destruction of Delhi," and both regarded it as one of the tyrannical actions that would doom the empire of Muḥammad ibn Tughluq. Their perspective was that of the cultured religious scholar who writes history as a mirror for princes, using the concept of the ideal ruler to measure the behavior of present kings. Muḥammad ibn Tughluq's forcible incorporation of the religious classes into his administrative machinery made him the villain of their chronicles. The ultimate fate of the Sufi mystics who were included in the migration to Daulatabad did not receive any mention in these histories.

In contrast, when later hagiographies (such as *Fatḥ al-awliyā'*) were commissioned by the Fārūqī rulers of Khandesh and by the Mughuls, the coming of the Sufis to Daulatabad was no longer part of the tragic tale of Tughluq misrule; now it was the triumphal arrival of a Sufi saint to claim dominion over the Deccan with his entourage of fourteen hundred saints. Burhān al-Dīn Gharīb's prophecies of the greatness of future kings were matched by the text's unrestrained exaltation of the Chishtī initiatic lineage. Although the elements of this story were taken from hagiography, its purpose was political. Using Khuldabad as the focus of a microstudy makes it possible to bring out the conflicting testimonies, and in this way chart the historiographical landscape with more precision. Narrative conflict need not be reduced to mere contradiction, in which we choose which is right and which is wrong—historiographic interpretation is designed not to bring out a single line of meaning, but multiple refractions of the significance of each event.

Second, the Sufi establishment at Khuldabad, when examined in its historical context, sheds light on the fundamentally nonreligious character of the Indo-Muslim state. The foundations of the Indo-Muslim state were of so varied a nature that it is no longer possible to characterize this era as the "Muslim period" of Indian history. The ideology of religious nationalism is singularly inept when it comes to describing this kind of premodern institution. The powerful traditions of Persian kingship combined with central Asian political ideas derived from Turks and Mongols formed the basis of the Delhi sultanate. Islamic symbolism of the caliphate and administrative structures using *qāżī* judges gave an overlay of religious usage to the sultanate, but the regime itself did not have any formal basis in Islamic law. Patronage of religion was an important function of government, since legitimation of the state in practical terms could only be conferred in this way. Patronage was extended to some non-Muslim religious institutions through the same mechanisms by which Sufi centers and academies for Islamic religious scholars were supported. The use of land endowment as the means of patronage inevitably integrated religious centers, including Sufi shrines, into the government bureaucracy.

Sufism as a spiritual discipline based on master-disciple relationships was potentially in tension with the sultanate over the question of whose authority was to be supreme. *Malfūẓāt* texts from Khuldabad provide extensive details regarding the relations between the Sufis and the Delhi sultanate. While Chishtī principles forbade asking for gifts or receiving regular stipends or land revenue, nonetheless many disciples of Burhān al-Dīn Gharīb were officials in the Tughluq administration in Daulatabad, and it was of interest to the Chishtīs to find out if prospective disciples were generous and well-disposed to dervishes. The Chishtī masters did not directly question the sultanate itself, at least not in public, but they were perpetually on guard to the perversion of authority by brutality and greed. Sometimes individual Sufi disciples would get into conflict with the sultan over particular policies, like the noble Malik al-Mulūk, who believed that the people were suffering unnecessarily (probably from excessive taxation). Several cases are related of disciples in government jobs who felt the contradictions in their positions, and wished to resign and take up a dervish's solitude. Burhān al-Dīn and Niẓām al-Dīn before him consistently counseled their disciples to retain these worldly occupations until their vocation for poverty should become undeniable. Just as the Sufi masters lived in close proximity to the court, but were in principle independent of it, their courtier disciples were expected to perform their duties while trying to remain inwardly focused on their spiritual path.

The conflict of narratives of Sufi-sultan relations gives insight into the different historiographic perspectives underlying the documents. Royalist reworkings of stories about saints tend to annihilate the tension between Sufis and sultans. Custodians of the shrine of Burhān al-Dīn Gharīb in the fifteenth century composed a document (Appendix B) depicting him establishing an administrative structure to run the shrine after his death. In doing so, they made significant alterations to his speech as preserved in *Nafā'is al-anfās*, and they omitted his final advice to avoid accepting gifts from kings. The distance between the fifteenth-century revenue document and the *malfūẓāt* indicates how far the shrine attendants had moved in the direction of the royal establishment. In the absence of an active teaching lineage, the Sufi shrine was totally dependent on kings for support.

Zayn al-Dīn Shīrāzī defied the Bahmanī sultan, and in his *malfūẓāt* he explained the confrontation as evidence of how God loves and preserves the saints. The dynastic chronicler Firishta recorded this event in an entirely different sense, showing the saint becoming reconciled to the sultan and bestowing titles of legitimacy in recognition of the regime's religious policies. Thus even saintly criticism of kings can be transformed into praise by creative revision of hagiography, as Baranī had shown earlier in his version of the story of Fużayl ibn ʿIyāż and Hārūn al-Rashīd. Later documents from the Mughul period reveal the way in which royal donations fluctuated in accordance with the fortunes of Mughul imperial expansion. The royal appropriation of Sufi shrines as devices for legitimation led to the building of many royal mausolea found in or adjacent to Sufi shrines. By the time of the Nizams, special galleries for playing ritual court music were integrated into the architecture of all the major shrines of Khuldabad. The imperial institution, with its implicit quest for world dominion, would leave no corner neglected by its all-pervasive control.

Third, the writings of the Khuldabad Sufis indicate that they framed their spirituality in terms of the Islamic tradition. Chishtī Sufism is a phenomenon thoroughly embedded in an Islamic milieu. Modern fundamentalist rhetoric decries what it sees as "un-Islamic" features in medieval Islamic culture, and Sufism is a convenient scapegoat. Disapproved Sufi activities (such as music and pilgrimage to shrines) are considered to be unfortunate concessions to the "Hindu" environment. Such an ideological interpretation is only possible if one refuses to read Sufi literature. The contents of an extensive Sufi bookshelf (Appendix A) are organized completely in terms of the Islamic religious sciences as studied in India in the fourteenth century. With approximately equal attention to authorities from each Islamic century, Rukn al-Dīn Kāshānī enumerated authorities in the main fields of religious thought, saving the Sufis as the pinnacle of this edifice. It may well be that some modern Muslim thinkers reject some or most of Islamic history as falling short of their ideal, but it is hard to see how the writings of the Khuldabad Sufis could be dismissed in toto as "un-Islamic." The oral teachings of the Chishtīs took on a form explicitly modeled on the transmission of the *ḥadīth* reports of the Prophet. The *malfūẓāt* as a secondary canon had some of the charismatic power that *ḥadīth* has when it still retains the aura of personal oral transmission. Their *sharīʿa*-minded prayer life, personal devotions, psychological discipline, and analysis of the interior life were all oriented toward the Qur'ān and the Prophet Muḥammad.

Yet the Sufi establishment of Khuldabad was not Islamic in a narrow or exclusivist sense. The Chishtīs were clearly Indianized; they used important materials of Indian origin (such as poetry in local languages) to build the edifice of their mystical culture. And as we have seen, despite the abstract symbolism that opposes Arabian Islam to an infidel "Hindu India," old Islamic traditions (preserved by Āzād Bilgrāmī) insisted that India is a holy land for Muslims. Popular legends portray the miracles of the saints of Khuldabad, using reverent terms from the local Indian culture. Zar Zarī Zar Bakhsh won the devotion of the Hindu princess Sōnā Bā'ī at a well, Ganj-i Ravān imprisoned a demon and bestowed fertility, and Mu'min ʿĀrif protected cows. These and similar stories testify to the warm acceptance of these Sufi saints in this part of India; Indian spirituality embraced the memories of these Muslims and gave them a new life. On several levels, then, the Khuldabad Sufis may be called an instance of Indian Islam.

The burden of this book has been analysis, the distinction and separation of literary genres and historiographies. This analysis has been done, as far as possible, in terms of categories that were developed from the materials under consideration. Nonetheless, the categories of theory are always refined and abstracted so that there is inevitably a distance between the theorist's presentation and the phenomenon itself. But once that gap has been created, it is my belief that it is possible to go back to the texts themselves and experience them all the more richly, for they can now be restored with some confidence to their original political and historical context. There is, as Paul Ricoeur pointed out, a "second naivete" that comes after one has demythologized a text. One can no longer accept the narrative with the simple wholeness that it once possessed, but with the aid of the analysis one can see the multiple layering of perspectives, the marvelous overlap of historiographies, that characterizes the density of historical imagination.

Many travelers will continue to pass by Khuldabad, both foreign tourists like Thevenot and indigenous pilgrims like Āzād. Stopping there for a moment, they might consider the enigma posed by this remote valley. Whose are the stately whitewashed tombs? The Sufi saints. Whose are the dark abandoned tombs? Kings unknown. The contrast is vivid and dramatic. To restore these scattered elements to unity, one could perhaps do no better than to quote the ode to Khuldabad by Waḥīda Nasīm:

> This world of light in the mountains' sweet embrace, this is the world's Mount Sinai for those with eyes to see.
> One *Mu'min* settled here a world of knowledge, and here *Ganj-i Ravān* gave a world of blessing.
> The lamp of the Chishtīs here is kindled by strong winds, here *Zar Zarī Zar Bakhsh* scattered gold.
> Till doomsday, seekers of knowledge will come here, so it seems these saints are the proof (*Burhān*) of Sufism.
> *Zayn al-Dīn* adorned the master's court; his essence perfumed the master's garden.
> The humble ones (*Khāksār*) gave it the gift of authority; how many kings have come here and bowed down to them!
> The father of *Gīsū Darāz* came bringing glory and passion; *Bahā' al-Dīn*, the priceless pearl, came all alone.
> The one whom empire ever looked on enviously [Burhān al-Dīn Gharīb] was set there as a precious stone by *Maḥbūb-i Ilāhī* [Niẓām al-Dīn Awliyā'].
> This land sparkles with the light of Chishtī masters; this lawn glitters with sparks from the green dome.
> The puffs of wind become gentle and breeze by; ablutions done, the cloud descends from the mountain.
> *Ḥasan ʿAlā'-i Sanjar* chose to rest here; *Āzād* left his home behind, but this garden suited him.
> In this silent town Sufism's tavern lies; the domes remain a stranger to the changing times.
> This valley is the trustee of the *Tughluq* treasure; the cries of *Khaljī* caravans still echo here.
> Since his nature was not sated by the Amberi Canal, *Malik ʿAnbar*'s thirst brought him to your springs.

ʿĀlamgīr [Awrangzīb] came to this same garden and found rest;
 this is the cradle in which sleep touched *Āṣaf Jāh*.
Simplicity's glory was found in beauty's pride, when *Tānā Shāh*'s
 nature was pacified.
Nasīm comes destitute, bringing a gift of tears; give her, too, a
 full measure with the glance of grace.

Such is the fascination that Khuldabad still exerts. This book is a map of the many different stories that revolve around this center of medieval life. It will serve its purpose best not by championing one story over another, but by being used as a guide for an intellectual pilgrimage of a sort. If the visitor then can contemplate and admire the display, or *tamāshā*, of south Asia's history, in all its rich complexity and contradiction, the journey will have been worthwhile.

PART V

Appendixes

Appendix A. A Sufi Bookshelf: The Bibliography of Rukn al-Dīn Dabīr Kāshānī

The following bibliography was given by Rukn al-Dīn Kāshānī in *Shamā'il al-atqiyā'* to indicate all the sources used in his compilation, whether written or oral. This is probably the most complete listing of the religious and mystical literature in Arabic and Persian that was in general use in the Delhi sultanate. The categories by which the sources are classified are those used by Rukn al-Dīn. Since he like most of his contemporaries used shorthand references, more complete annotation has been supplied from standard biobibliographical reference works, as follows:

GAS, GALS: Carl Brockelmann, *Geschichte der arabischen Litteratur*, 2 vols. plus *Supplementband*, 3 vols. (Leiden: E. J. Brill, 1937–49)

GAS: Fuat Sezgin, *Geschichte des arabischen Schrifttums*, vol. 1 (Leiden: E. J. Brill, 1967)

Lawrence, *Notes*: Bruce B. Lawrence, *Notes from a Distant Flute: The Extant Literature of Pre-Mughal Indian Sufism* (Tehran: Imperial Iranian Academy of Philosophy, 1978)

Munzawī: Aḥmad Munzawī, *Fihrist-i mushtarak-i nuskha-hā-yi khaṭṭī-yi fārsī-yi Pākistān*, vol. 3, *'Irfān* (Islamabad: Markaz-i Taḥqīqāt-i Fārsī-yi Īrān u Pākistān, 1363/1405/1984)

Nizami, *Thirteenth Century:* Khaliq Ahmed Nizami, *Some Aspects of Religion and Politics in India in the Thirteenth Century* (2nd ed.)

Storey: C. A. Storey, *Persian literature: A Bio-Bibliographical Survey* (2 vols.; London: Luzac & Co., 1927–71)

Death dates have been taken from standard hagiographical works in Persian and Arabic. Some variants are noted in parentheses from MS 1197 Persian, Asiatic Society, Calcutta.

I. Qur'ānic Commentaries

1. Sulamī. Abū ʿAbd al-Raḥmān al-Sulamī (d. 412/1021). *Ḥaqā'iq al-tafsīr* (Arabic: GAL I, 201; GALS I, 361). An important early Sufi Qur'ān commentary.
2. Qushayrī. Abū al-Qāsim al-Qushayrī (d. 465/1072). *Laṭā'if al-ishārāt* (Arabic: GAL I, 432; GALS I, 770), another Sufi Qur'ān commentary.
3. *Istighnā*. Muḥammad al-Adfuwī al-Miṣrī (d. 388/988). *al-Istighnā fī ʿulūm al-dīn* (Arabic: GAS I, 46), an early commentary in twenty volumes, of which only one survives.
4. *Kashshāf*. Zamakhsharī (d. 538/1144), the Muʿtazilī scholar. *al-Kashshāf ʿan ḥaqā'iq al-tanzīl* (Arabic: GAL I, 289; GALS I, 507).
5. Zāhidī. Abū Naṣr Aḥmad ibn al-Ḥasan Sulaymanī al-Zāhidī (ca. 519/1125), a scholar from Bukhara. *Laṭā'if al-tafsīr* (Persian: Storey, I, 4; I, 1190).
6. *Baṣā'ir*. Muḥammad ibn Maḥmūd al-Naysābūrī (ca. 529/1134), a scholar at the Ghaznavid court. *Tafsīr-i baṣā'ir-i yamīnī* (Persian: Storey, I, 5).
7. *ʿAzīzī*. Possibly the undated work of Mullā Ḥusayn Kashgarī, *Tafsīr-i ʿazīz* (Persian: Storey, I, 32, no. 40).
8. Mujāhid. Abū al-Ḥajjāj Mujāhid ibn Jabr al-Makkī (d. 104/722), a famous early commentator. *Tafsīr* (Arabic: GAS I, 29).
9. *Tāj al-maʿānī*. Abū Naṣr Maqdisī. *Tāj al-maʿānī* (Persian: known only as a source mentioned in the *tafsīr* of Muḥammad ibn Ḥusayn al-Wā'iẓ Jamāl al-Dīn Astājī, *Zād al-muzakkirīn*, written in 618/1221 in Samarqand [Storey, I, 5, gives his name as Sājī]; cf. Munzawī, I, 55).
10. ʿAyyāshī. Abū Naṣr Muḥammad ibn Masʿūd ibn ʿAyyāsh al-Sulamī al-Samarqandī (ca. 300/923), a Shīʿī commentator. *Tafsīr al-ʿAyyāshī*, or *Tafsīr al-Sulamī* (Arabic: GALS I, 334).
11. Zanjānī. Possibly ʿIzz al-Dīn Ibrahīm ibn ʿAbd al-Wahhāb al-Zanjānī (d. 655/1257), Arabic grammarian (GAL I, 283; GALS I, 497). No commentary is attributed to him.
12. Jurayrī. Possibly Amīr ʿIzz al-Dīn Muḥammad ibn Bahā' al-Din al-Jurīdī (or al-Jūrī), no date. *Kāmil al-tajwīd* (Persian: Storey, I, 45, no. 7; I, 1223), a work on recitation. Alternatively this could be a Qur'ānic commentary by the Sufi Muḥammad al-Jurayrī (d. ca. 311/923).
13. *Ījāz*. Najm al-Dīn al-Nīsābūrī (ca. 553/1158). *Ījāz al-bayān fī maʿānī al-Qur'ān* (Arabic: GALS I, 733).

14. *Tuḥfat al-walad*. Not traced.
15. *Tuḥfat al-islām*. Not traced.
16. *Mustakhlaṣ*. Ḥāfiẓ al-Dīn Bukhārī (d. 693/1294). *Mustakhlaṣ* (Persian: Storey, I, 31, no. 22, n. 1 [hence not the work of Muḥammad Pārsā]; I, 1215), a glossary of the Qur'ān.
17. *Kāshif* [*sic*; cited in the text as *Kashf al-asrār*]. Rashīd al-Dīn al-Maybudī (ca. 520/1126). *Kashf al-asrār wa ʿuddat al-abrār* (Persian: Storey, I, 1190), based on the Sufi commentary of ʿAbd Allāh Anṣārī (no. 184, below).
18. Rafīʿī. Possibly ʿAbd al-Karīm al-Rafīʿī al-Qazwīnī (d. 623/1226), a Shāfiʿī jurist (GAL I, 383; GAS I, 678).
19. *Rumūz*. Rukn al-Dīn Kāshānī, the author of *Shamā'il al-atqiyā'*. *Rumūz al-wālihīn* (Persian); the work only survives in 68 citations in *Shamā'il al-atqiyā'*.
20. *Gharā'ib*. Cited in the text as *Tafsīr-i gharīb*. Not traced.

II. Divine Sayings (*Kalimāt-i Qudsī*), from the following sources and others

21. *Mashāriq al-anwār*. Raḍī al-Dīn al-Ḥusayn al-Ṣaghānī (d. 650/1252). *Mashāriq al-anwār* (Arabic: GAL I, 361; GALS I, 613). A *ḥadīth* collection based on Bukhārī and Muslim.
22. *Āthār-i nayyarayn*. Possibly Abū Muḥammad ibn al-Ḥasan al-Shaybānī (d. 189/805), *Kitāb al-āthār* (Arabic: GAS I, 430), a Ḥanafī collection of *ḥadīth*. Nizami (*Thirteenth Century*, p. 274, no. 15) lists the similarly entitled *Akhbār al-nayyarayn* as a Sufi work.

III. Prophetic Sayings

23. *Mashāriq al-anwār*. See no. 21.
24. *Maṣābīḥ*. Abū Muḥammad al-Ḥusayn Masʿūd al-Farrā al-Baghawī (d. 516/1122). *Maṣābīḥ al-sunna* (Arabic: GAL I, 363–364; GALS I, 620).
25. *Sharḥ-i mashāriq*. Unspecified commentary on no. 21, "introduced for the sake of examples."
26. *Akhbār wa athmār*. Not traced.
27. *Khawāriq*. Not traced.
28. *Riyāḥīn*. Not traced.
29. *Daqā'iq*. Muḥyī al-Dīn al-Nawawī al-Ḥawrānī (d. 676/1278). *Daqā'iq* (Arabic: GAL I, 394; GALS I, 682).
30. *Ṣaḥīḥayn*. The two classical *ḥadīth* collections, both entitled *al-Ṣaḥīḥ* or "correct": Muḥammad Ismaʿīl ibn Ibrāhīm al-Bukhārī (d. 255/869) and Muslim ibn Ḥajjāj al-Qushayrī al-Nīshāpūrī (d. 261/875). (Arabic: GAL I, 160; GALS I, 265).

31. *Jāmiʿ al-wuṣūl*. Majd al-Dīn Abū Saʿādat al-Mubārak (d. 606/1209–10). *Jāmiʿ al-wuṣūl* (Arabic: GAL I, 357; GAL II, 64), a study of *ḥadīth*.
32. Ṣanʿānī. Abū Bakr ʿAbd al-Razzāq ibn Hammām al-Ḥimyārī al-Ṣanʿānī (d. 211/827). *al-Muṣannaf fī al-ḥadīth* (Arabic: GALS II, 333; GAS I, 99).
33. *Tafārīq al-ṣaḥīḥ*. Not traced. Presumably a study of one of the works in no. 30.

IV. Significant Books

34. *Qūt al-qulūb*. Abū Ṭālib al-Makkī (d. 386/996). *Qūt al-qulūb fī muʿāmalat al-maḥbūb* (Arabic: GAS I, 667, 936). A classic source on Sufism.
35. Imām Ghazālī (d. 505/1111). *Sirr Allāh*. This particular title, attributed to the famous scholar, is not extant (GAL I, 419; GALS I, 744).
36. ʿAyn al-Qużāt Hamadānī (d. 525/1131). Writings. See nos. 97ff., below.

V. Sayings of the Companions and Successors of the Prophet

37. Abū Bakr (d. 13/634).
38. ʿUmar (d. 23/644).
39. ʿUthmān (d. 35/656).
40. ʿAlī (d. 40/661).
41. Ḥasan Baṣrī (d. 110/728).
42. Ibn ʿAbbās (d. 68/687–88).
43. Imām Jaʿfar al-Ṣādiq (d. 148/765).
44. Abū Hurayra (d. 57/676).
45. Uways Qaranī (d. 30/651).

VI. Traditions from Books of the Science of Dialectical Theology, which is Called the Divine Science, Containing the Descriptions of the Attributes and Essence of God

46. Abū Ḥanīfa al-Nuʿmān ibn Thābit ("The Greatest Imam," d. 150/767). *Fiqh akbar* (Arabic: GAL I, 168; GALS I, 283). Famous credal statement attributed to the founder of a major school of law.
47. Ḥāfiẓ al-Dīn, *ʿAqīda*. Abū al-Barakāt ʿAbd Allāh Ḥāfiẓ al-Dīn al-Nasafī (d. 710/1310). *al-ʿUmda fī al-ʿaqāʾid* or *al-ʿAqīda al-Ḥāfiẓiyya* (Arabic: GAL II, 196; GALS II, 263). An important Sunnī credal statement.
48. Fakhr al-Dīn Rāzī, *Maʿālim*. Fakhr al-Dīn al-Rāzī (d. 606/1209). *al-Maʿālim fī uṣūl al-dīn* (Arabic: GAL I, 506, no.

5; GALS I, 921, no. 5). A work on principles of jurisprudence by the famous theologian.

49. *Ṣaḥā'if*. Shams al-Dīn Muḥammad ibn Ashraf al-Ḥusaynī al-Samarqandī (ca. 690/1291). *al-Ṣaḥā'if al-ilāhiyya* (Arabic: GAL I, 468; GALS I, 850), a work on dogmatic theology.
50. Nīshāpūrī, *Bidāya*. Not traced.
51. *Uṣūl ṣighār*. Not traced.
52. *Lāmiyya*. Probably the *Lāmiyyat al-ʿajam* of Mu'ayyad al-Dīn al-Ṭughrā'ī (d. 515/1121, GAL I, 247; GALS I, 439).
53. Nasafī. *ʿAqīda*. Same as no. 47 above.
54. *Qawā'id*. Many works with this title.
55. Abū Shakūr Sālimī, *Tamhīdāt*. Abū Shakūr al-Sālimī (5th/11th cent.). *Kitāb al-tamhīd fī bayān al-tawḥīd* (Arabic: GAL I, 419; GALS I, 744), a theological treatise.
56. *Sharḥ-i mantiqī [sic]*. Not traced.
57. Shihāb al-Dīn Suhrawardī (d. 632/1234). *Iʿlām al-hudā* (Arabic: GAL I, 436; GALS I, 789).

VII. Traditions from Significant Books of Jurisprudence, Decisions, and Tales of the Prophets

58. *Manẓūma*. Probably *al-Manẓūma al-Nasafiyya fī al-khilāfiyya* (Arabic: GAL I, 428; GALS I, 761) by Najm al-Dīn al-Nasafī (d. 537/1142).
59. *Muttafaq* (or *Mustaftā*). Not traced.
60. *Kanz*. Ḥāfiẓ al-Dīn al-Nasafī (no. 47 above). *Kanz al-daqā'iq fī al-furū'*, an abridgement of the same author's *al-Wāfī*, a standard textbook on Ḥanafī law (Arabic: GAL II, 196; GALS II, 265).
61. *Dhakhīra*. Possibly the *Kitāb al-dhakhīra al-Burhāniyya* (GAL I, 375; GALS I, 642) of Burhān al-Dīn Maḥmūd al-Bukhārī ibn Māza (d. 573/1177), grandson of al-Ṣadr al-Shahīd (no. 73).
62. *Muḍammarāt*. Not traced.
63. Aḥmad ibn Ḥanbal (d. 241/855). *Musnad* (Arabic: GAL I, 181; GALS I, 309). Fundamental *ḥadīth* collection.
64. Abū al-Layth Samarqandī (d. 373/983). *Bustān al-faqīh* (Arabic: GAL I, 196; GALS I, 347, GAS I, 449), a handbook on law.
65. *Jāmiʿ al-ṣaghīr*. Abū Muḥammad ibn al-Ḥasan al-Shaybānī (no. 22). *al-Jāmiʿ al-ṣaghīr* (Arabic: GAL I, 172; GAS I, 428), a popular work on Ḥanafī law.

66. *Khizānat al-fiqh*. Abū al-Layth al-Samarqandī (no. 64). Another legal work (Arabic: GAL I, 196; GALS I, 347, GAS I, 449).
67. *ʿUmdat al-fiqh*. Not traced.
68. *Sharḥ-i taʿarruf*. A Persian commentary on the Sufi handbook *Kitāb al-taʿarruf li-madhhab ahl al-taṣawwuf* (Arabic: GAS I, 668) of Muḥammad ibn Isḥāq al-Kalabadhi (d. 380/990).
69. *Uṣūl al-Shāshī*. Usually ascribed to Isḥāq ibn Ibrāhīm al-Shāshī (d. 325/937), the *Uṣūl al-Shāshī* (Arabic: GAL I, 174; GALS I, 294) is in fact by Niẓām al-Dīn al-Shāshī (7th/13th cent.; cf. GAS I, 498, n. 1).
70. Ḥusāmī, *Uṣūl*. Muḥammad al-Akhsīkatī Ḥusām al-Dīn (d. 644/1247). *Kitāb al-muntakhab fī uṣūl al-madhhab*, known as *al-Ḥusāmī* (Arabic: GAL I, 381; GALS I, 654), on jurisprudence.
71. Bazdawī, *Uṣūl*. Abū al-Ḥasan ʿAlī ibn Muḥammad al-Pazdawī (d. 482/1089; called al-Bazdawī by Arabic sources). *Kanz al-wuṣūl ilā maʿrifat al-uṣūl* (Arabic: GAL I, 373; GALS I, 637), a widely used text on law.
72. *Mutawaffī* (or *Mustawfī*), the commentary on Bazdawī (no. 71). This title not traced.
73. *Fatāwā kubrā*. Ḥusām al-Dīn ibn Māza al-Ṣadr al-Shahīd al-Bukhārī (d. 536/1141). *al-Fatāwā al-kubrā* (Arabic: GAL I, 374; GALS I, 640), a collection of legal responsa.
74. *Fatāwā Taysīr*. Not traced.
75. *Qiṣaṣ-i Nīkūh* (?—Persian for "good stories," possibly tales of the prophets); cited in the text in Persian (p. 261) as *Qiṣaṣ-i sangūya* or *sangūna* (?).
76. *Kifāya*. Many works with this title.
77. Ṣābūnī, *Bidāya*. Aḥmad ibn Maḥmūd al-Ṣābūnī al-Bukhārī (d. 580/1184). *al-Bidāya min al-kifāya*, an abridgement of his legal work *Kitāb al-kifāya fī al-hidāya* (Arabic: GAL I, 375; GALS I, 643).

VIII. Great Books of the Science of the Path and Reality from the Writings and Works of the Masters Possessing Saintship and the Saints Possessing Saintship

78. *Sirr al-nabī dar ʿālam-i jalāl wa jamāl wa khawāṣṣ wa taʾsīr* (Persian). Not traced.
79. *ʿIṣmat al-anbiyāʾ*. Fakhr al-Dīn Rāzī (above, no. 48); (Arabic: GAL I, 507; GALS I, 922, no. 14).

80. Abū Nuʿaym, *Ḥilyat al-awliyāʾ*. Abū Nuʿaym al-Iṣfahānī (d. 430/1038). *Ḥilyat al-awliyāʾ* (Arabic: GAL I, 362; GALS I, 617). A major biographical work on Sufis.
81. Imām Jaʿfar al-Ṣādiq (d. 148/765), sixth imām of the Shīʿa (GAL I, 220; GALS I, 104; GAS I, 528–531). *Waḥy-i asrār* (or *Asrār al-waḥy*, Arabic: GAS I, 530, no. 7).
82. Abū Ṭālib Makkī. *Qūt al-qulūb*. Same as no. 34 above.
83. *Tarjuma-i qūt al-qulūb*. Persian trans. of no. 34.
84. Muḥammad Tirmidhī (d. ca. 932). *Khatm al-wilāya* (Arabic: GALS I, 356; GAS I, 653). A major early Sufi work.
85. *Tūqān al-ʿārifīn*. Not traced.
86. Shihāb al-Dīn Suhrawardī (no. 57, above). *ʿAwārif al-maʿārif*, an important handbook of Sufi practice (Arabic: GAL I, 440; GALS I, 789).
87. *Tarjuma-i ʿawārif*. One of the numerous Persian translations of no. 86.
88. Najm al-Dīn Rāzī (d. 654/1256). *Mirṣād al-ʿibād* (Persian). A well-known Sufi manual.
89. *ʿUnwān al-mirṣād* (Persian). Probably a summary or commentary on no. 88.
90. ʿAlī Hujwīrī (d. 465/1072). *Kashf al-maḥjūb* (Persian). One of the first Persian Sufi manuals.
91. Imām Ghazālī (no. 35). *Kīmīyā-i saʿādat*. Ghazālī's own Persian reworking of his Arabic classic *Iḥyāʾ ʿulūm al-dīn*, on ethics and mystical religion.
92. *Tarjuma-i Qushayrī*. Persian translation of the Sufi handbook, *al-Risāla al-Qushayriyya*, by Abū al-Qāsim al-Qushayrī (no. 2).
93. *Fikrat al-aṣfiyāʾ*. Not traced.
94. Imām Ghazālī (no. 35). *Maqṣad al-aqṣā* (Arabic: GALS I, 754, no. 53e).
95. Imām Ghazālī (no. 35). *Kunūz al-jawāhir*. This title not traced to Ghazālī.
96. Farīd al-Dīn ʿAṭṭār (d. ca. 617/1220). *Tazkirat al-awliyāʾ*. Well-known Persian hagiography.
97. ʿAyn al-Qużāt Hamadānī (d. 525/1131). *Tamhīdāt*. A classic Persian work on Sufism.
98. ʿAyn al-Qużāt Hamadānī. *Tanzīh al-makān*.
99. ʿAyn al-Qużāt Hamadānī. *Jāvīd nāma*.
100. ʿAyn al-Qużāt Hamadānī. *Rushd nāma*.
101. ʿAyn al-Qużāt Hamadānī. *Zubdat al-ḥaqāʾiq*. An Arabic work on metaphysics (GALS I, 675); often this title is mistakenly used for his Persian *Tamhīdāt*.

102. *Anīs al-arwāḥ*. *Malfūẓāt* of ʿUthmān Hārwanī (d. 607/1211) (Persian).
103. *Dalīl al-ʿārifīn*. *Malfūẓāt* of Muʿīn al-Dīn Sijzī (d. 633/1236) (Persian).
104. *Fawā'id al-sālikīn*. *Malfūẓāt* of Quṭb al-Dīn Bakhtiyār Kākī (d. 633/1235) (Persian).
105. *Rāḥat al-qulūb*. *Malfūẓāt* of Farīd al-Dīn Ajōdhanī (d. 664/1265) (Persian).
106. *Asrār al-mutaḥayyarīn*. *Malfūẓāt* of Farīd al-Dīn Ajōdhanī (no. 105) (Persian).
107. *Fawā'id al-fu'ād*. *Malfūẓāt* of Niẓām al-Dīn Badā'ōnī (d. 725/1325) (Persian).
108. *Nafā'is al-anfās*. *Malfūẓāt* of Burhān al-Dīn Gharīb (d. 738/1337) (Persian).
109. ʿAlī Bihārī. *Zāhidī*. Not traced.
110. *Sawāniḥ*. Aḥmad Ghazālī (d. 517/1123, brother of no. 35). Classic Persian treatise on love.
111. *Sirr allāh* (Persian). Same as no. 35 above.
112. *Rūḥ al-arwāḥ*. Mīr Ḥusaynī Sādat (d. 728/1328). A popular Persian work on Sufism (Lawrence, *Notes*, p. 103, n. 73).
113. Bahā' al-Dīn, successor to Shaykh Kabīr. *Khulāṣat al-ḥaqā'iq* (Arabic). Not traced.
114. Imām Ghazālī (no. 35). *ʿUnwān*. Not traced.
115. Qāżī Ḥamīd al-Dīn Nāgawrī (d. 643/1246). *Ṭawāliʿ al-shumūs* (Lawrence, *Notes*, p. 60). A Persian commentary on the names of God.
116. Qāżī Ḥamīd al-Dīn Nāgawrī. *Sawāniḥ* (Persian). Not extant.
117. Qāżī Ḥamīd al-Dīn Nāgawrī. *Lawāmiʿ* (Persian). Not extant.
118. Qāżī Ḥamīd al-Dīn Nāgawrī. *Maqāṣid* (Persian). Not extant.
119. *ʿUmda-i Junaydī*. Not traced.
120. *Mukhtaṣar-i iḥyā' al-ʿulūm*. An abridgement of the *Iḥyā' ʿulūm al-dīn* of al-Ghazālī (no. 35).
121. *ʿUmdat al-asrār*. Not traced.
122. *Kashf al-asrār*. Same as no. 17, though in the text (p. 359) it is once unaccountably confused with the Arabic work of the same title by Rūzbihān Baqlī (d. 606/1209).
123. Abū Saʿīd Abū al-Khayr (d. 440/1049). *Asrār al-abrār* (?). Possibly a mistake for the *Asrār al-tawḥīd*, a collection of biographical anecdotes about this famous Sufi.
124. *Sukūt al-ʿārifīn*. Not traced.
125. *Asrār al-ʿārifīn*. Not traced.
126. *Tawqīʿ al-ārifīn*. Not traced.
127. *Sirāj al-ʿārifīn*. Not traced.

128. *Ādāb al-murīdīn* (Arabic: GAL I, 436; GALS I, 780). The well-known manual for novices by Abū al-Najīb al-Suhrawardī (d. 563/1168).
129. *Ādāb al-muḥaqqiqīn*. Not traced.
130. *Maʿrifat al-murīdīn*. Not traced.
131. Mawlānā Rūm [a mistake for Jalāl al-Dīn Rūmī's father, Bahā' al-Dīn Walad, d. 628/1231]. *Maʿārif* (Persian), a treatise on Sufism.
132. *Hidāyat al-dhākirīn*. Not traced.
133. *Anīs al-tā'ibīn* (Persian). A treatise by the Sufi Abū Naṣr Aḥmad-i Jām Zhinda-pīl Nāmiqī (d. 536/1141–42).
134. *Asbāb al-maghfirat*. Not traced.
135. *Majmaʿ al-ḥaqā'iq*. Not traced.
136. Shams al-ʿĀrifīn. *Qiwām al-ʿaqā'id*. Not traced.
137. Rukn al-Dīn Kāshānī. *Rumūz al-wālihīn* (Persian). Same as no. 19.
138. Ḥammād al-Dīn Kāshānī. *Ḥuṣūl al-wuṣūl* (Persian). Only extant in six quotations in *Shamā'il al-atqiyā'*.
139. Ḥammād al-Dīn Kāshānī. *Asrār al-ṭarīqat* (Persian). Only extant in five quotations in *Shamā'il al-atqiyā'*.
140. Muhammad Kāshānī. *Ḥujjat al-islām fī jarḥ al-ʿuẓẓām*. Not traced.
141. *Sharf-i faqr*. Not traced.
142. *Guzīda* (Persian). Not traced.
143. *Madārik*. Not traced.
144. *Bawāriq al-ilmāʿ* (Arabic: GAL I, 426; GALS I, 756). Aḥmad al-Ghazālī (no. 100). A defense of listening to music.
145. Sayyid Badr al-Dīn. *Arbaʿīn*. Untraced. A common title for collections of forty (*arbaʿīn*) *ḥadīth*, this title is also cited in the text in Persian (p. 196) with the authorship of Mawlānā Sadīd ʿAwfī (d. 625/1228).
146. *Sirāj al-murīdīn*. Not traced.
147. Imām Ghazālī (no. 35). *Saʿādat nāma* (Persian). Not traced.
148. *Nūr-i nāẓir*. Not traced.
149. Amīr Khusraw. *Rāḥat al-muḥibbīn*. *Malfūẓāt* of Niẓam al-Dīn (no. 107). (Persian).
150. *Rūḥ al-arwāḥ*. Same as no. 112.
151. *Khulāṣat al-ḥaqā'iq*. Same as no. 113. Not traced.

IX. Brief and Abbreviated Treatises of the Ancients and Moderns Specifying the Name of the Book

152. *Munājāṭ-i luṭf-i jalāl wa jamāl*. Not traced.

153. Khwāja Khiżr. *Munājāt-i mihtar Mūsā [Prayers of the Prophet Moses]* (Persian). Not traced.
154. Treatise of Khwāja Bāyazīd Bisṭāmī (d. 261/875) (GAS I, 645).
155. Treatise of Ghawth al-Aʿẓam [i.e., ʿAbd al-Qādir Gīlānī, d. 561/1167] (GAL I, 435, GALS I, 777).
156. Imām Ghazālī. *Sirr Allāh*. Same entry as no. 35.
157. Treatise of Khwāja ʿAbd Allāh ibn Khafīf (d. 371/981; GAS I, 663).
158. Treatise of Sulṭān Ibrāhīm ibn Adham (d. 163/779).
159. Treatise of Khwāja Hubayra Baṣrī, seventh master in the Chishtī lineage.
160. Treatise of Khwāja ʿAlū Dīnawarī, eighth master in the Chishtī lineage.
161. Treatise of Khwāja Junayd (d. 298/910; GAS I, 647).
162. Treatise of Khwāja Shiblī (d. 334/946; GAS I, 660).
163. Treatise of Khwāja Maʿrūf Karkhī (d. 200/815; GAS I, 637).
164. Treatise of Shaykh Baraka, master of ʿAyn al-Qużāt (d. 525/1131).
165. Treatise of Ḥusayn Manṣūr [al-Ḥallāj] (d. 309/922; GAS I, 651).
166. Treatise of Imām Ḥaddādī. Possibly Abū Ḥafṣ Ḥaddād (d. 264/877–88).
167. Treatise of Khwāja Yūsuf Hamadānī (d. 535/1140–41).
168. Treatise of Shaykh Najm al-Dīn Kubrā (d. 618/1221).
169. Treatise of Khwāja Sahl Tustarī (d. 283/896; GAS I, 647).
170. Treatise of Shaykh Sarī Saqaṭī (d. 253/867).
171. Treatise of Khwāja Abū Bakr Wāsiṭi (d. 320/932) (GAS I, 659).
172. Treatise of Shaykh Abū al-Ḥasan [sc. al-Ḥusayn] Nūrī (d. 295/907) (GAS I, 650).
173. Treatise of Shaykh Jamāl al-Dīn Hānswī (d. ca. 664/1265–66).
174. Treatise of Rifāʿī, son of Sīdī Aḥmad. Evidently Aḥmad al-Rifāʿī (d. 578/1182) (GALS I, 780).
175. Treatise of Shaykh ʿAlī Rūdbārī (d. 322/934).
176. Treatise of Khwāja Abū al-Faraj Zanjānī. Not traced.
177. Treatise of Khwāja Muḥammad Ḥarīrī [Jurayrī? Cf. no. 12].
178. Treatise of Khwāja [Abū] Sulaymān Dārānī (d. 215/830–31).
179. Treatise of Khwāja [Ibn] Sīrīn (d. d. 110/729) (GAS I, 665).
180. Treatise of Khwāja Makḥūl. Abū Muṭīʿ Makḥūl ibn al-Faḍl al-Nasafī (d. 318/930) (GAS I, 601).
181. Treatise of Shaykh Abū Mūsā Abū al-Khayr (possibly a mistake for no. 123).

182. Treatise of Shaykh Abū ʿUthmān Maghribī (d. 373/983) (GAS I, 665).
183. *Ḥāshiya-i zubdat al-ḥaqāʾiq* [comm. on no. 101] (Persian).
184. Treatise of Khwāja ʿAbd Allāh Anṣārī (d. 481/1089) (Storey, I, 924).
185. Treatise of Shaykh Muḥyī al-Dīn [ibn] ʿArabī (d. 638/1240) (GAL I, 441).
186. Treatise of Shaykh Jibraʾīl. Not traced.
187. Treatise of Khwāja Shaydā. Not traced.
188. *Dībācha-i kashf*. Not traced.
189. Treatise of Shaykh Sharaf al-Dīn Pānīpatī. Better known as Bū ʿAlī Shāh Qalandar (d. 724/1324).
190. Treatise of Shams al-ḥaqq, Khwāja Shams al-Dīn. Not traced.
191. Treatise of Mawlānā Quṭb al-Dīn. Not traced.
192. *Risāla-i gharīb*. Not traced.
193. *Risāla-i Ḥamīdī*. Not traced.
194. *Risāla-i Saʿīdī*. Not traced.
195. Treatise of Khwāja [Żiyāʾ al-Dīn] Nakhshabī (d. 751/1350), a poet connected to the Chishtī order (Lawrence, *Notes*, pp. 42–44).
196. *Maqṣad al-aqṣā*. ʿAzīz al-Dīn Nasafī (d. 661/1263). A well-known Persian Sufi treatise.
197. *Munkasar al-qulūb*. Not traced.

X. Sayings of the Masters in God, the Elite Saints, and other Realizers of Truth

198. Saying of the Prophet Khiżr.
199. Saying of Khwāja Fużayl ʿIyāż (d. 187/802) (GAS I, 636).
200. Saying of Sulṭān Ibrāhīm Adham (no. 158).
201. Saying of Khwāja Bāyāzīd (no. 154).
202. Saying of Khwāja Junayd (no. 161).
203. Saying of Shaykh Shiblī (no. 162).
204. Saying of Khwāja Dhū al-Nūn Miṣrī (d. 246/861) (GAS I, 643).
205. Saying of Abū Yūsuf Qāżī (d. 182/798) (GAS I, 419).
206. Saying of Bishr Ḥāfī (d. 227/841) (GAS I, 638).
207. Saying of Khwāja Shaqīq Balkhī (d. 194/810).
208. Saying of Imām ʿAbd Allāh Sulamī (no. 1).
209. Saying of Imām Mālik Dīnār (d. 137/748) (GAS I, 634).
210. Saying of Shaykh Abū al-Ḥasan [i.e., al-Ḥusayn] Nūrī (no. 172).
211. Saying of Rābiʿa Baṣrī (d. 185/801).

212. Saying of Khwāja Ḥusayn Manṣūr (no. 165).
213. Saying of Khwāja Sahl Tustarī (no. 169).
214. Saying of Khwāja Yaḥyā Muʿādh (d. 258/872) (GAS I, 644).
215. Saying of Shaykh Abū Saʿīd Abū al-Khayr (no. 123).
216. Saying of Khwāja Sulaymān Dārānī (no. 178).
217. Saying of Khwāja Sarī Saqaṭī (no. 170).
218. Saying of Shaykh ʿUthmān Hārwanī (no. 102).
219. Saying of Shaykh Muʿīn al-Dīn Sijzī (no. 103).
220. Saying of Shaykh Quṭb al-Dīn Bakhtiyār Kākī (no. 104).
221. Saying of Shaykh Farīd al-Dīn Ajōdhanī (no. 105).
222. Saying of Shaykh Niẓām al-Dīn Badā'ōnī (no. 107).
223. Saying of Shaykh Burhān al-Dīn Gharīb (no. 108).
224. Saying of Zayn al-Dīn Dā'ūd Ḥusayn Shīrāzī (d. 771/1369).
225. Saying of Shaykh Ghiyāth al-Dīn. Not traced.
226. Saying of Khwāja ʿAbd Allāh [ibn] Masʿūd (d. 32/653).
227. Saying of Khwāja ʿAbd Allāh Anṣārī (no. 184).
228. Saying of Shaykh Abū Bakr Warrāq (d. 280/893) (GAS I, 646).
229. Saying of Khwāja Abū ʿAlī Daqqāq (d. ca. 406/1015).
230. Saying of Khwāja Nāmiqī (no. 133).
231. Saying of Shaykh Jibra'īl. Not traced.
232. Saying of Khwāja Abū Bakr Ṭamistānī (d. 340/951–52).
233. Saying of Khwāja [Abū] ʿUthmān Ḥīrī (d. 298/910–11).
234. Saying of Khwāja Abū Saʿīd Kharrāz (d. 279/892) (GAS I, 646).
235. Saying of Qays Sāʿida. Possibly the pre-Islamic orator Qays ibn Sāʿida.
236. Saying of Imām Muḥammad Ghazālī (no. 35).
237. Saying of Khwāja ʿAbd Allāh Mubārak (d. 181/797) (GAS I, 95).
238. Saying of Wahb ibn Munabbih (d. 110/728) (GAS I, 305).
239. Saying of Rābiʿa ʿAdawīya (no. 211).
240. Saying of Shaykh Abū ʿAlī Juzjānī (d. ca. 353/964).
241. Saying of Khwāja Aḥmad [Muḥammad] Maʿshūq (5th/11th cent.).
242. Saying of Abū Ṭayyib Sijzī. Not traced.
243. Saying of Shaykh ʿAlī Jurjānī (repetition of no. 240?).
244. Saying of Ibn ʿAṭā' (d. 309/922).
245. Saying of Khwāja ʿAbd Allāh Maṭarī, Treasurer of the Prophet. Not traced.
246. Saying of Khwāja Sumnūn Muḥibb (d. 287/900).
247. Saying of Jalālī. Not traced.
248. Saying of Khwāja Ruwaym (d. 303/915).

249. Saying of Khwāja Muḥammad Sulaymānī. Not traced.
250. Saying of Khwāja Muḥammad Sahl Saʿīd. Not traced.
251. Saying of Makhdūm Sayyid Jalāl Bukhārī (d. 785/1383).
252. Saying of Amīr Yaʿqūb Sūsanī [Sūsī] (d. ca. 300/912).
253. Saying of Mawlānā Sadīd ʿAwfī (no. 145).
254. Saying of Khwāja Qāsim. Not traced.
255. Saying of the old wife of Khwāja Zakī. Not traced.
256. Saying of Khwāja Abū al-Ḥasan Sālim. Not traced.
257. Sayings of other realizers of the truth whose names are not known; since they are realizers of the truth, [the sayings] are written.

Appendix B. A Fifteenth-Century Revenue Memorandum

The text of the following document is appended to MS of *Aḥsan al-Aqwāl* by Ḥammād al-Dīn Kāshānī, collection of Fariduddin Saleem, Khuldabad, pp. 149–57 (MS copied by Fayż Muḥammad son of Ḥāfiẓ Muḥammad Amīn, 27 Rabīʿ II, 6th Regnal Year of Farrukhsiyar [1130/30 March 1718]). For a discussion, see Part III, chap. 10, above, and Tables 4 and 5.

Text

Memoir of the manner of the coming of Shaykh al-Islām wa al-Muslimīn, Quṭb al-Aqṭāb wa al-Muḥaqqiqīn, the revered Sultan Burhān al-Dīn, from the city of Delhi at the command of the revered Shaykh al-Islām Sultan al-Mashāyikh Niẓām al-Ḥaqq wa al-Dīn to the city of Daulatabad. He came down in the year 719 [1319–20] and alighted in the house of Malik Mubārak Shams al-Mulk. Then in 731 [1330–31], his relatives [p. 150] came from Delhi to Daulatabad. Khwānd Kākā told Sultan Burhān al-Dīn that his relatives had come from Delhi. The revered Sultan Burhān al-Dīn said, "Where were my relatives when we were eating *lūbīyā* beans and leftovers (*kunjāra*)?[1] Tell them to go back. Relatives have no connection to my house. Our relatives and children are our devotees and master's descendants (*mawlā-zādagān*)." Because of these words, his relatives chose to attend on him and take up [his] service.

1. Although Burhān al-Dīn Gharīb here is made to complain of *lūbīyā* beans and leftovers, elsewhere it is said that he preferred these humble foods to almonds and sweets (*Shamā'il al-atqiyā'*, p. 154).

After some years Miyān Laṭīf al-Dīn was sitting in his house, relying on God, when the revered Sultan Burhān al-Dīn suffered a very severe illness. He summoned all the lovers to his presence, and said to Kākā Shad Bakhsh, "I have nothing of my own, and it is [a question of] money[2] for the *'urs* of the revered Shaykh al-Islam Niẓām al-Ḥaqq wa al-Dīn. Out of my own [money] I cannot manage, and there will be expenses for the *'urs*. Two people from the group contributed something, but I have nothing to do with that either." Then he turned toward Kākā and said, "Some *tanka*s[3] are here, and a wool cloak, and robes of *bahīram* (?). Give those robes, money, and fruit to the lovers, and give the one wool cloak separately to Mawlānā Laṭīf al-Dīn,[4] and divide up some of the other robes and present them to the devotees. This is a covenant with you, for you do not save anything." [p. 151] This account is written in *Nafā'is al-anfās*.[5]

Later, the revered Burhān al-Dīn passed on in 738 [1337]. After the passing away of the revered Sultan Burhān al-Dīn, Khwānd Kākā for nine

2. Reading *sīm* rather than *siyum*, which would have meant, "It is the third [day] of the *'urs*." But Niẓām al-Dīn's *'urs* is celebrated on the 17th of Rabī' II, and this conversation took place a couple of weeks before the anniversary, on the first of the month; cf. Mīr Khwurd, *Siyar al-awliyā'*, p. 165.

3. The silver *tanka*, during the reign of Sultan Muḥammad ibn Tughluq, was the basic coin of the realm, about fifty of which were equivalent to the gold *tanka*.

4. This nephew and disciple of Burhān al-Dīn Gharīb, whose family figures so prominently in the memorandum and in the shrine's history, was entrusted with overseeing supplies in the khānqāh, and was known for his piety (Āzād, *Rawżat al-awliyā'*, pp. 40–41). The beginning sentence of this account, which places Laṭīf al-Dīn in a prominent position, does not occur in the text of *Nafā'is al-anfās*, but may have been inserted to enhance his role.

5. This episode closely follows the 23rd Majlis (1 Rabī' II, 735) of Rukn al-Dīn Kāshānī's *Nafā'is al-anfās* (p. 92ff.), but with significant changes. Rukn al-Dīn Kāshānī introduces this as Burhān al-Dīn's testament (*waṣīyat*) following upon a long illness from which he did not expect to recover. After arranging for the expenses of the open kitchen, he spoke as follows: " 'Life is not to be depended upon, and it gives me great sorrow that consumes me inside. I have called you so that you may hear that Kākā has received nothing of mine. For the *'urs* of Shaykh al-Islam Niẓām al-Dīn, out of my own [money] I cannot manage, and there will be expenses for the *'urs*. There are not two other people from the group who have contributed anything. But I have nothing to do with that either.' Then he turned toward the revered Kākā, saying, 'I have a few *tanka*s in my possession, and a wool cloak and robes of *bahīram*. Give the robe, the *bahīram* [i.e., the robes of *bahīram*], the fruit, and all the food to the lovers. There is one woolen cloak; give it to Mawlānā Laṭīf al-Dīn. [p. 93] Divide up some of those robes and present them to the devotees. It is a covenant for you, if you [do not] save anything.' " The major difference between the two texts is that the memorandum version eliminates any reference to Burhān al-Dīn personally owning any money or possessions. That omission in Burhān al-Dīn's first sentence contradicts his later order to distribute his possessions. The whole point of the episode in the original *malfūẓāt* version is that he is giving away everything in order to support the *'urs*, and he is encouraging others to do likewise. Even more striking, in view of the main subject of this document, is the omission of Burhān al-Dīn's speech immediately following this episode (*Nafā'is al-anfās*, p. 93), in which he warns his followers that they must avoid gifts from kings if they wish to stay on his path.

years [up to 747/1346–47] kept the work of administration (*tawliyat*) going, whatever currency (*rawish*) [was] included in [the property] of Sultan Burhān al-Dīn or [was] extra: kinds of money of gold and silver, small change (*khwurda*), gold coins, wool cloaks (*ṣūf*), scarlet cloth (*saqallāt*), fine robes (*jāma*), and with the currency of the tombs, such as [those of] Mawlānā Badr al-Dīn Naw-lak'ha, the Five Ladies (*pañch bībīyāñ*), Mawlānā Amīr Ḥasan Dihlawī, Mawlānā Ẓahīr al-Dīn B'hakkarī, Mawlānā Kamāl al-Dīn Ṣāḥib al-Khayrāt, etc.; ritual objects (lit., "the adornment of the presence," *ārāyish-i ḥażrat*): lamp oil, cool water for the fingers (*āb-i angusht-i sard*), sweets, raw and cooked fruit, animal victuals—whatever came as unsolicited gift (*futūḥ*) he divided among the devotees (*bandagān*) [and] *mawlā-zādagān* of the revered Sultan Burhān al-Dīn. In this way he keeps the work going. Kākā told Khwāja Rashīd al-Dīn [to continue], and the Khwāja also kept this same work going faithfully.

After the passing away of the Khwāja,[6] the emperor (*pādshāh*) Sultan Muḥammad Ḥasan[7] came to the city of Daulatabad to make pilgrimage to the shrine (*rawża*) of Sultan Burhān al-Dīn. The devotees and *mawlā-zādagān* were all present. The Sultan glanced at them and asked the wazir, "Do they have something assigned to them from the treasury suitable to their merit, or not?" The wazir said no. Then the Sultan said, "Let them, in lieu of a daily 'prayer ration' (*badal-i waẓīfa-i rūzīna*), be assigned 2 1/2 *mann*[8] of fruit, of meat [p. 152] 1 *mann* and 10 *sīr*[9] with animal fat, and necessities (*lawāzima*),[10] against the taxes of the town (*bar bāj-i qaṣba*)." Then it was assigned and written against the taxes of the town. They came before the revered leader Shaykh Zayn al-Dīn and informed him. The revered leader Shaykh Zayn al-Dīn said, "Did you ask for it? For in our order (*khānwāda*) there is no asking [for gifts]. But if they bring it without being asked, it should not be passed by, as it is said: 'No refusing, no asking, no saving (*lā radd wa lā kadd wa lā madd*).' So take this that you have brought and divide it among you."

Later the devotees and *mawlā-zādagān* brought someone who had sent a sum for annual 'prayer ration' (*mablagh-i waẓīfa-i sālyāna*) before the revered leader Shaykh Zayn al-Dīn and explained it. The revered leader Shaykh Zayn al-Dīn assented, saying to Mawlānā Muḥammad Lashkarī, "We appoint you their trustee and attendant (*mutawallī wa khādim*). Whatever currency there is in unsolicited gifts from the shrine of the revered Sultan Burhān al-Dīn, the

---

6. According to information given below, Rashīd al-Dīn held the office of trustee for seven years, so his death took place ca. 754/1353–34.

7. Muḥammad ibn Ḥasan, the second Bahmanī sultan (r. 759/1358–776/1375).

8. A *mann* (Anglo-Indian "maund") is a weight usually of about forty pounds.

9. The *sīr* ("seer") is about two pounds.

10. The term "necessities" (*lawāzima*) appears to refer to an extra cash benefit of some kind, since some of the rations include it and others do not.

shrine of the revered Shāh Muntajib al-Dīn, and the other tombs, divide it and convey it to the devotees and *mawlā-zādagān*, just as Kākā conveyed it. Now all the devotees and others, consider among yourselves, if a sum or prayer ration of cooked and raw food has been divided and I take some, it is not good. Let us cook it in the kitchen of the revered Sultan [Burhān al-Dīn Gharīb] and, after honoring the visitor and traveler [by feeding them first], let us take what is left over and divide it among ourselves. Then let a *fātiḥa* and a *khatm* [complete Qur'ān recitation] be done to the spirit of the revered Sultan [Burhān al-Dīn] and all the family (*khāndān*) of the Chishtī masters, [p. 153] and let a petition for wants (*istimdād-i khwāsta*) be given with the *fātiḥa*, for the sake of the well-being of the emperor and the Muslims."

After a few years, Khwāja Muḥammad Lashkarī died. He gave the administration of the *khānqāh*, the devotees, and the *mawlā-zādagān* to Khwāja Sharaf al-Dīn, son-in-law of Khwāja ʿAbd al-Rashīd. Khwāja Sharaf al-Dīn also kept the work of administration of the revered shrines going for some years. After his passing away, Khwāja Bara, son-in-law of the former Khwāja [ʿAbd al-Rashīd], was given the administration. During his time, the mother of Miyān Laṭīf al-Dīn[11] performed the *ʿurs* of the revered Sultan [Burhān al-Dīn Gharīb]. She invited the devotees and *mawlā-zādagān*. After paying for the *ʿurs*, the revered lady said, "You are all my brothers. You too, if the revered Sultan Burhān al-Dīn gave us [a place] in his khānqāh, you give us a place among you." Then all the devotees and *mawlā-zādagān* agreed. They had a daily ration of 1/2 *mann* of fruit and 10 *sīr* of raw meat, without necessities, given out [to her] from the customs house (*khāna-i mu'addiyān*).[12]

Several years passed in this way. When Sultan Mujāhid Shāh was crowned,[13] from the devotees and others, Mawlānā Dā'ūd and Mawlānā Musā with a few other lovers took relics (*tabarruk*),[14] food offerings [lit. "bread crumbs," *nān-rīza*, from the shrine], and a turban for Sultan Mujāhid Shāh. After honoring him with the food offerings and turban, they asked the Sultan to increase the prayer ration. Due to their request, he ordered the assignment of a daily prayer ration of 7 1/2 *mann* of fruit, of meat 3 *mann* 30 *sīr* with animal fat, and necessities. [p. 154] At that time Miyān Fażl Allāh ibn Miyān Laṭīf al-Dīn was there. He too was given 1/2 *mann* of fruit and 10 *sīr* of raw

11. This would be the sister of Burhān al-Dīn Gharīb.

12. The phrase "customs house" is a loose equivalent; the *mu'addī-i māliyāt* was an official expected to protect and keep up the roads, in return for which the government granted him the right to accept a yearly salary in cash and kind from imposts; cf. Amīr Jalāl al-Dīn Ghaffārī, *Farhang-i Ghaffārī* (Tehran: Dānishgāh, 1337), VII, 321.

13. ʿAla' al-Dīn Mujāhid, third Bahmanī sultan (r. 776/1375–779/1378).

14. Literally "blessing," this probably means here sacred relics and food offerings distributed at the shrine during the *ʿurs*, some of which is saved for presentation to selected persons like the king.

meat from the customs house. At that time the *t'hāna-dār* [governor] of the region of Daulatabad was Malik Raja Fārūqī.[15] He made Khwāja Bara trustee.

When Sultan ʿAlā' al-Dīn was there,[16] the devotees Mawlānā Ghiyās al-Dīn and Mawlānā Jamāl al-Dīn brought relics, food offerings, and a turban before the Sultan. After honoring him with the food offerings and the rest, they requested an increase in the prayer ration. Due to their request, he ordered an assignment of a daily ration of 15 *mann* of fruit, 7 1/2 *mann* of meat with animal fat, and necessities, against the taxes of government income (*bar bāj-i samt-i dawlat*).

At that time, the relatives of Miyān Qadan ibn Fażl Allāh, the grandson of Miyān Laṭīf al-Dīn, conferred the service of administration on Miyān ʿAbd al-ʿAzīz. In that period the *t'hāna-dār* was Malik Sharaf Parvīz. Just so, he conferred on the relatives a daily ration of 1/2 *mann* of fruit and of raw meat 10 *sīr*, without necessities, from the customs house.

When the coronation of Hūmayūn Shāh took place,[17] the devotees Shaykh Mawlānā Fażl Allāh and Mawlānā Chandan and Mawlānā Mūsā took relics, food offerings, and a turban for the Sultan. After honoring him with the food offerings and the rest, they asked for an increase in the prayer ration. Because of their request, he assigned one *k'handī*[18] five *mann* [p. 155] of fruit and of mutton with fat 25 *sīr*,[19] with necessities. He conferred on the shrine of the revered Shāh Muntajib al-Dīn and the shrine of Amīr Ḥasan Dihlawī a daily ration of 19 *tankas* by way of prayer ration for the devotees and attendants. In that time the *t'hāna-dār* was Malik Muḥammad Parvīz and the trustee was Miyān Chaman Ṣūfī. They gave the relatives 1/2 *mann* of fruit and

15. The founder of the kingdom of Khandesh (r. 772/1370–801/1399). As Mahdī Hussain pointed out, the Fārūqīs were originally governors under the Bahmānīs and not under the Tughluq emperor in Delhi; see his "A Short History of Khandesh," *Quarterly Journal of the Mythic Society* 51 (1960–61), esp. pp. 122–26. The term *t'hānah-dār* corresponds to the term *ṭaraf-dār* used in the Bahmanī kingdom to denote the four governors of the four *aṭrāf* or provinces; cf. H. K. Sherwani, "Bahmānīs," EI^2 I (1960), 923–25, esp. 924.

16. Sultan ʿAlā' al-Dīn Aḥmad II, tenth Bahmanī Sultan (r. 839/1436–862/1458). The encounter described here appears to have taken place at the sultan's visit to the shrine, rather than at his coronation. ʿAlā' al-Dīn had married a princess of the Fārūqī house (Firishta [Nawal Kishōr ed.] II, 280), and must have been keenly aware of the relationship between Burhanpur and Khuldabad; the Bahmanīs' bequests to the shrine may even have been in direct competition with the Fārūqīs' donations.

17. ʿAlā' al-Dīn Hūmayūn, the eleventh Bahmanī sultan (r. 862/1458–865/1461). According to Malkapūrī (*Salāṭīn*, p. 556) no proper coronation took place, due to revolt.

18. The *k'handī*, variously rendered in English as "candy," "candie," or "kandy," was a large weight of twenty *mann*, or nearly 500 pounds. The present increase is thus from 15 to 25 *mann* of fruit.

19. One suspects that a figure has been left out here, perhaps "10 *mann*," that would have represented an increase in the amount of meat over the endowment of ʿAla' al-Dīn, which was 7 1/2 *mann*.

10 *sīr* of raw meat from the customs house, up to the time of Muḥammad Shāh.

When the coronation of Muḥammad Shāh took place,[20] the devotees and *mawlā-zādagān* of the revered Sultan [Burhān al-Dīn], such as Mawlānā Rashīd and others, took relics, food offerings, and a turban. After honoring him with the food offering, they requested an increase in the prayer ration, so that the attendants of the court (*dargāh*) of the revered Shāh should rest easy, and at the five prayer times they would be occupied in praying for the welfare of the emperor. Because of the Mawlānā's request, he conferred several villages (*qaryāt*) on the two shrines; he named three villages (*dih*): the town (*mawżaʿ*) of Sayūr in Kāndāpūr district (*pargāna*), and the towns of Chēklī and Mālīwārī. For the shrine of the revered Shāh Muntajib al-Dīn, for the sake of the prayer ration of the devotees and *mawlā-zādagān*, he gave 10 *tanka*s to the service of that shrine.

At that time the *t'hāna-dār* was Malik Parvīz[21] and the trustee Miyān Muḥammad Chaman, the Qāżī of the shrine was Qāżī Jalāl al-Dīn Ṭūsī; after them, the Qāżī was Shaykh Miyān Jalāl al-Dīn, [and] Miyān Bara-i Qadan,[22] the sons of Miyān [p. 156] Laṭīf al-Dīn. To them too he assigned ½ *mann* of fruit and 10 *sīr* of meat, without necessities. In the same way it was conveyed from the customs house.

When the coronation of Maḥmūd Shāh took place,[23] at that time he made Malik Wajīh *t'hāna-dār*, and Miyān Muḥammad trustee, and Qāżī Shaykhun was qāżī of the shrine. In the same way he assigned to Miyān Bara ½ *mann* of fruit and 10 *sīr* of meat, which they conveyed without necessities from the customs house. Since in the noble age of the late Hūmayūn there were such *t'hāna-dār*s and trustees, so to the offspring of Mawlānā Laṭīf al-Dīn ½ *mann* of fruit and 10 *sīr* of raw meat was conveyed from the customs house.[24]

Names of the Governors (*t'hāna-dar*s), Trustees, and Treasurers (*mushrif*s).

Governor: Quṭb al-Dīn
Trustee: Miyān Manān
Treasurer: Manjhū

20. Shams al-Dīn Muḥammad III, the thirteenth Bahmanī sultan (r. 867/1463–887/1482).

21. Malik Parvīz was the governor of Daulatabad under the previous sultan, and he surrendered the fort in 867/1462 to Sultan Maḥmūd Khaljī of Malwa; cf. U. N. Day, *Medieval Malwa*, p. 157.

22. Miyān Bara (or possibly Bizha) Qadan, who flourished from the 1460s through the 1480s, is to be distinguished from Khwāja Bara, whom Malik Raja Fārūqī confirmed as trustee in the late 1300s.

23. Shahāb al-Dīn Maḥmūd, fourteenth Bahmanī sultan (r. 887/1482-924/1518).

24. It is odd that the main endowment of the shrine is not mentioned here, but only the private endowment of the family of Laṭīf al-Dīn, which is mentioned twice.

At the time of the Niẓām Shāh's coronation:[25]
Governor: Khājī Khān
Trustee: Qāżī Shaykhun[26]

Treasurer: Diyānat Khān
Governor: Kāmil Khān
Trustee: Miyān Bud'hū

Treasurer: Naṣīr al-Dīn
Governor: Mubāriz al-Mulk
Trustee: Miyān Muḥammad

Treasurer: Sakhāwat Khān, Pīr Niʿmat Khān
Governor: Badan Laṭīf
Trustee: Miyān Abu Shakūr

Treasurer: Malik Muḥammad Ghaws ʿurf-i Abū Bakr ibn Abū Shakūr[27]
Governor: Iwānat (?) Khān
Trustee: Miyān Bara

Treasurer: Qāżī Jīwan ibn Ghaws

Governor, Treasurer, and Trustee: Qāżī [p. 157] Ghaws

Treasurer: Qāżī Charchū ibn Ghaws

Emperors[28]

Sultan Mujāhid Shāh
Sultan Muḥammad Ḥasan
Sultan ʿAlā' al-Dīn
Sultan Muḥammad Shāh
Sultan Maḥmūd Shāh
Sultan Hūmayūn Shāh

Trustees[29]

Kākā Shād Bakht (9 years)
Khwāja ʿAbd al-Rashīd (7 years)

---

25. Sultan Niẓām Shāh, the twelfth Bahmanī sultan (r. 865/1461–867/1463).

26. Mentioned in the last paragraph of the text as qāżī under Maḥmūd Shāh's reign (887/1482-924/1518), more than twenty years after Niẓām Shāh's coronation.

27. The recurrence of the name "Ghaws" in the next few lines indicates a family succession to the office of *mushrif* at this time.

28. This list of six Bahmanī sultans is not in chronological order.

29. This list is also out of order; Muḥammad Lashkarī should come third, after ʿAbd al-Rashīd.

Khwāja Sharaf al-Dīn, son-in-law of ʿAbd al-Rashīd (5 years)
Khwāja Bara, son-in-law of ʿAbd al-Rashīd
Khwāja Muḥammad Lashkarī
Khwāja ʿAbd al-ʿAzīz[30]
Khwāja ʿAbd al-Karīm
Miyān Ṣūfī
Miyān Aḥmad Maḥmūd
Miyān Bara[31]
Miyān Mīrān Maḥmūd
Miyān Chaman[32]
Qāżī Shaykhun[33]
Miyān Manan
Agha Miyān

Governors

Malik Rājā Fārūqī
Malik Parvīz[34]
Malik Muḥammad Parvīz[35]
Malik Wajīh ʿAlī Muḥammad[36]
Malik Quṭb al-Dīn
Kamāl Khān
Mubāriz al-Mulk
Mukhtaṣṣ Khān
Farḥat Khān
Iwānat (?) Khān
Maʿrūf Khān

Qażīs

ʿAlī Ṭūsī
Qāżī Niẓām Dā'ūd Ṭūsī
Qāżī Dā'ūd Niẓām Ṭūsī

30. Trustee at coronation of Mujāhid Shāh (776/1375).

31. Mentioned in connection with the reign of Muḥammad Shāh (867/1463–887/1482), he was a descendant of Laṭīf al-Dīn.

32. Mentioned as trustee at the coronations of Hūmayūn (862/1458) and Muḥammad (867/1463).

33. After appearing as qāżī under Maḥmūd Shāh's reign (887/1482-924/1518), the same figure is now listed as a trustee.

34. Coronation of Sultan Muḥammad (867/1463).

35. Coronation of Hūmayūn (862/1458).

36. Probably the Malik Wajīh at the time of Maḥmūd's coronation (887/1482).

Qāżī Jalāl al-Dīn Ṭūsī
Qāżī Muḥammad Jalāl Ṭūsī[37]
Shaykh Miyān Qāżī ibn Shaykh Miyān

Writer and owner Muḥammad Fayż, son of Ḥāfiẓ Muḥammad Amīn, attendant of the luminous shrine ———.

37. Coronation of Muḥammad Shāh (867/1463).

Appendix C. Mughul and Deccan *Farmāns* from Khuldabad

The following summaries are based on microfilm printout copies of the original Persian documents from the collection of Fariduddin Saleem of Khuldabad. Lack of space as well as the condition of the manuscripts precludes a complete transcription and translation here. These summaries are not exhaustive, but include the principal data while omitting administrative formulas and the more technical financial notations. Dates of documents are given in the Mughuls' solar *ilāhī* calendar, the lunar Islamic *hijrī* calendar, and the Gregorian calendar, separated by slashes, with calculated equivalents in brackets. Conversions are based on V. S. Bendrey's *Tārīkh-i-ilāhī* (Aligarh: Centre of Advanced Study, Department of History, Aligarh Muslim University, 1972), with the difference that Bendrey's Old Style (Julian) dates are corrected into New Style (Gregorian). For a discussion of the documents, see above, Part III, chap. 10, and the summary in Chart 6.

A. *Dargāhs* of Shaykh Burhān al-Dīn Gharīb, Shaykh Muntajib al-Dīn, and Shaykh Zayn al-Dīn

A1. Date: 27 Tīr, 50 *ilāhī*/[2 Rabī' I 1014]/[18 July 1605].[1]

Reign: Akbar

1. This is evidently identical with a *farmān* preserved in the Andhra Pradesh State Archives in Hyderabad, identified as Museum 7993, and briefly described in the *Proceedings of the Indian Historical Records Commission* 46 (1979), p. 289. None of the other *farmāns* in this collection seems to survive in an administrative copy.

Endowment: Bhadgaon village in Burhanpur district, and two villages in the districts of Bhusawal and Adilabad.[2]

Recipient: Shaykh Zayn al-Dīn Muḥammad, son of Shaykh Khān Muḥammad, heir of Sultan Burhān al-Dīn and Shāh Muntajib.

Stipulations: Half the income is designated for living expenses of the custodians, and half for the annual festival (*ʿurs*), the open kitchen, shawls, and lamps. Exemption from various taxes is guaranteed. The chief custodian of the shrine (*ṣāḥib-i sajjāda*) has exclusive control over these revenues, from which the trustees (*mutawalliyān*) are excluded.

Endorsements: Mīrān Ṣadr-i Jahān, *ṣadr*; Muḥammad Ṭāhir, reporter (*wāqiʿa-niwīs*); Rām Dās.[3]

A2. Date: 28 Tīr, 21 *ilāhī* regnal/24 Shawwāl 1035/[19 July 1626].[4]

Reign: Jahāngīr.

Endowment: Longaon and Karab villages in Bhadgaon district, with an estimated total revenue (*jamʿ-i raqmī*) of 122,400 *dāms*, from the beginning of the autumn (*kharīf*) crop of Pars-īl (third year of the Turkish duodecenary cycle).[5]

Recipient: Shrine of Sultan Burhān al-Dīn and Shāh Zayn al-Dīn and the attendants thereof.

---

2. Bhadgaon is a town on the Girna River, fifty miles north of Khuldabad, Bhusawal is a junction town on the Tapti River, and Adilabad is a major town on the Purna River.

3. Mīrān Ṣadr-i Jahān Pihānī (d. 1020/1611) was the officer in charge of religious endowments (*ṣadr*) under Akbar from 997/1599 (according to H. Blochmann, trans., *The A'in-i Akbari* by Abu 'l-Fazl ʿAllami, I, 282), and subsequently served in the same capacity under Jahāngīr. Shāhnawāz Khān reported of him, that "during his tenure of office as the *Ṣadr* of Jahāngīr he gave away so many maintenance lands that Āṣaf Khān Jaʿfar reported to the king that Mīrān had given away in five years what Akbar had granted in fifty years" (Ṣamṣām-ud-Daula Shāhnawāz Khān and his son ʿAbdul Ḥayy, *The Maāthir-ul-Umarā*, trans. H. Beveridge, revised by Baini Prashad [Patna: Janaki Prakashan, 1979], II, 79–80).

4. This grant was made when Jahāngīr was in Kabul, where Maḥābat Khān had put him under virtual house arrest in an attempt to take over the administration. During this time Jahāngīr visited many local saints while plotting his eventual return to power, and so granting this endowment presumably fit in with his conspicuously religious behavior during this time. See further Beni Prasad, *History of Jahāngīr* (Allahabad: The Indian Press [Publications] Private Ltd., 1962), p. 384.

5. Estimated total revenue (*jamʿ-i raqmī*) was a customary evaluation not necessarily identical with actual revenue (*ḥāṣil*); cf. H. H. Wilson, *A Glossary of Judicial and Revenue Terms* (London: Wm. H. Allen & Co., 1855; reprint ed., Delhi: Munshiram Manoharlal, 1968), pp. 229b, 202a. The *dām* is a copper coin equivalent to one fortieth of a silver Hindustani rupee (Wilson, p. 121b).

Stipulations: Revenue to be used for expenses. Recipients are to pray for the welfare of the ruling dynasty.

Endorsements: Khān-i Jahān,[6] Fāżil Khān.[7] Records the actual revenue (*ḥāṣil*) of the old endowment as 1,250,000 *dams*, which has been reduced on the advice of Āṣaf Khān.[8]

A3. Date: 20 Āzar [9 *ḥijrī* regnal]/[14 Rajab 1046]/[12 December 1636].[9]

Reign: Shāhjahān.

Endowment: 6,845 ½ *hūns* from villages in Daulatabad district, plus twenty-one shawls; also, on the recommendation of Khān-i Zamān, 3,500 *hūns* from the town of Rawża (i.e., Khuldabad).[10]

Recipient: Sultan Burhān al-Dīn, etc.

Stipulations: Local revenues are to be used for expenses. Recipients are to pray for the welfare of the ruling dynasty.

A4. Date: 6 Muḥarram, 11 regnal/1047/[31 May 1637].[11]

Reign: Shāhjahān.

Endowment: Sara village in Daulatabad district, from beginning of autumn crop of Pars-īl.[12]

---

6. Khān-i Jahān Lōdī (d. 1040/1631) was a courtier and great favorite of Jahāngīr; from the year of this *farmān*, he had been given charge of the entire Deccan (*The Maāthir-ul-Umarā*, I, 798). His sympathy for Sufism is evident also in his later attraction to the eminent Shaykh Fażl Allāh of Burhanpur (ibid., I, 804).

7. Āqā Afżal Fāżil Khān (d. 1058/1648) was a close associate of Khān-i Jahān and served under him in the Deccan at this time (*The Maāthir-ul-Umarā*, I, 549).

8. This Āṣaf Khān is better known as Āṣaf Jāhī (d. 1051/1641), brother of Nūr Jahān and close counselor of Jahāngīr. His advice to reduce the grant must have come after his own release from the custody of Maḥābat Khān, during the time Jahāngīr was under house arrest (*The Maāthir-ul-Umarā*, I, 289).

9. The year is obliterated on the front, but is supplied on the endorsement.

10. Khān-i Zamān was the governor of the northern Deccan (or Balaghat) from 1627 to 1637; see *The Maāthir-ul-Umarā*, I, 217. It is notable that the endowment has now been regularized into the Mughul administrative system in the Deccan. Not only has the old Fārūqī endowment from Khandesh been replaced with a local grant from the Daulatabad area, but also the currency valuation has been made in terms of the gold-based Deccan *hūn* (usually translated "pagoda") in place of the silver-based *dām* (cf. Wilson, p. 211b).

11. This document was issued in Agra, just three weeks after Awrangzīb's marriage to Dilrās Bānū; cf. Saksena, *History of Shāhjahān*, p. 315.

12. This is evidently the village today called Sarai, two miles from Khuldabad (*Aurangabad District, Maharashtra State Gazetteers* p. 1176).

Recipient: Shaykh Burhān al-Dīn, Shaykh Muntajib al-Dīn, Shaykh Zayn al-Dīn, and in particular the prior trustees of the shrines.[13]

Stipulations: Revenues to be used for the annual festival, open kitchen, etc. Exemptions from various taxes are guaranteed.

Endorsements: Mīr Muḥammad Hāshim, *ṣadr*; ʿAbd al-Raḥīm, reporter.

A5. Date: 9 Ramażān, 11 regnal/1047/[25 January 1638].

Reign: Shāhjahān.

Endowment: Villages in the Daulatabad district, with a yield (*mablagh*) of 3500 *hūns*.[14]

Recipient: Sultan Burhān al-Dīn, etc. (obliterated on front, but supplied in endorsement).

Endorsement: Cites previous decree of 9th regnal year (cf. A3 above) conferring four villages from Daulatabad district, with a yield of 3,500 *hūns*.

A6. Date: 4 Rajab, 12 regnal/1080/[28 November 1669].

Reign: Awrangzīb.

Endowment: Sara village in Daulatabad district.

Recipient: Shaykh Burhān al-Dīn, Muntajib al-Dīn, Zayn al-Dīn.

Stipulations: Revenues to be used for annual festival, open kitchen, etc. As hoped by the trustees and residents, the previous endowment is renewed. Exemptions from various taxes are guaranteed.

Endorsement: Cites memorandum (*yād dāsht*) of Friday, 24 Rabīʿ I, 12 regnal/1080/[22 August 1669], and a decree of Muḥarram, 11 regnal, stating the actual revenue (*ḥāṣil*) of the village to be 741 rupees in 1077/1666. Ḥājji Yāsīn, *ṣadr*.

A7. Date: 24 Shaʿbān, 34 regnal/[1101]/[2 June 1690] (a copy, with some errors corrected).[15]

---

13. This represents a change in the fortunes of the shrines, since in Akbar's farmān the trustees (*mutawalliyān*) were excluded from the shrine's revenues in favor of the hereditary custodian.

14. Again the income of the shrine has been reduced, by the loss of the 6845 1/2 *hūns* of document A3, above.

15. At this time Awrangzīb was probably at Bijapur; see Saqi Mustʿād Khān, *Maasir-i ʿAlamgiri* (sic), trans. Sir Jadu-nath Sarkar (Calcutta: Royal Asiatic Society of Bengal, 1947), p. 204.

Reign: Awrangzīb.

Recipient: Shaykh Niʿmat Allāh and the attendants of the shrines of Shāh Burhān al-Dīn and Shāh Muntajib al-Dīn.

Stipulations: Confirms recipients' rights against the claims of Shaykh Darvīsh Muḥammad and attendants of the shrine of Shaykh Zayn al-Dīn, concerning the village of Payan (?) endowed to the shrine of Khwāja Ḥusayn (father of Zayn al-Dīn), which was normally under the control of Zayn al-Dīn's shrine.[16] Endorsement in English, "Compared and found correct," with illegible date and signature.

A8. Date: 4 Jumādā II, 3 regnal/1121/[11 August 1709].

Reign: Bahādur Shāh.[17]

Endowment: Sara, in Daulatabad district, with a total revenue of 74,106 *dams*, and an actual revenue of 1,175 rupees.

Recipient: Shaykh Burhān al-Dīn, Zayn al-Dīn, Muntajib al-Dīn.

Stipulations: From second third of the spring (*rabīʿ*) crop of Ūd-īl (second year in cycle), for the annual festival, open kitchen, etc.

Endorsement: Amjad Khān, *ṣadr*; Ghulām ʿĪsā, reporter. Murshid Qūlī Khān's seal confirms that according to a decree of Awrangzīb, and a memorandum of the Amīr al-Umarā', this grant was confirmed from crown lands (*khāliṣa*) for the shrines' expenses in the name of one Mubārak Khān. Contains lengthy eulogies of the Niẓām al-Mulk Āṣaf al-Dawla.[18] Cites two of Awrangzīb's decrees (including no. A6 above, of the twelfth regnal year).

A9. Date: 7 Rajab, 4 regnal/[1122]/[1 September 1710].

Reign: Bahādur Shāh.

Endowment: Bursar Khurd, in Kanhar district, Daulatabad region, with total revenue of 110,300 *dāms*, and actual revenue of 1,378 rupees, from the spring crop of Pars-īl, instead of the villages formerly held (cf. A8, above).[19]

16. This document evidently reflects a split within the organization that jointly administered the three shrines of Burhān al-Dīn, Muntajib al-Dīn, and Zayn al-Dīn. On the shrine of Khwāja Ḥusayn, see no. C2, below.

17. For this monarch's reverence for saints, and his reckless generosity, see William Irvine, *Later Mughals*, ed. Jadunath Sarkar (New Delhi: Oriental Books Reprint Corporation, 1971), pp. 136–38.

18. It is likely that this noble, who became the first Niẓām of Hyderabad, assisted in securing this endowment; his devotion to the saint is evident from the fact that he was buried in the precincts of Burhān al-Dīn's shrine.

19. For Bursar Khurd, see *Gazetteer*, p. 1070.

Recipient: Attendants of the shrines of Shaykh Burhān al-Dīn, Muntajib al-Dīn, and Zayn al-Dīn.

Stipulations: To be used only for living expenses. Recipients are to pray for the welfare of the ruling dynasty.

Endorsement: Cites memorandum of 28 Āzar, 3 regnal/17 Shawwāl, 1121/[20 December 1709]. Sayyid Amjad Khān, *ṣadr*; Ghulām ʿĪsā, reporter. Specifies actual revenue of endowment as 1378 rupees and 10 *ānās*. Signatures of Niẓām al-Mulk Āṣaf al-Dawla, Muʿaẓẓam Khān, Ikhlāṣ Khān, and Mīrzā Shāhnawāz Khān (as deputy to Āṣaf al-Dawla) are recorded. Specifies revocation of the previous endowment of Sara village by Awrangzīb in regnal years 11 and 12 (cf. A6, above). Refers to gift of the villages of Sankuli (?) and Tajnapur, with total revenue of 1,000 rupees, for the upkeep of the attendants of the shrines; the latter, however, preferred the present grant of 1378 rupees 10 *ānās*.

B. *Dargāh* of Sayyid Yūsuf Rājū Qattāl

B1. Date: 25 Tīr, 81 *ilāhī*/9 regnal/[11 Ṣafar 1046]/[15 July 1636] ("copy in agreement with the original").

Reign: Shāhjahān.

Endowment: 3 *chāwar*s by *sharʿī* gaz, equivalent to 360 *bīgha*s by *ilāhī* gaz, from previously held land, to replace 7 *chāwar*s from Sultanpur village.[20]

Recipient: Shrine of Sayyid Rājū, for sandalwood, roses, and lamps, and for the sustenance of Mullā Wāḥid ibn Aḥmad, the attendant.

Stipulations: Recipient is to use the products of the land for his sustenance, and to pray for the welfare of the ruling dynasty. Exemptions from various taxes are guaranteed.

Endorsement: Cites memorandum of 31 Urdibihisht, 9 *ilāhī* regnal/14 Dhū al-Ḥijja 1045/[20 May 1636]. Mawlawī Khān, *ṣadr*. Cites memoranda of ʿAbd al-Raḥmān, of 16 Tīr, 9 *ilāhī* regnal/[2 Ṣafar 1046]/[6 July 1636], and of Afżal Khān.

B2. Date: 15 Jumādā I 1238/[28 January 1823].

---

20. The *chāwar* is a Maratha land measure, usually the equivalent of 120 square *bīgha*s. The *bīgha* is about five eighths of an acre. Measurement is made by a yardstick measure, here the *ilāhī* gaz instituted by Akbar (33 inches), or the *sharʿi gaz*. For these terms, see Wilson, pp. 85b, 107b, 171b.

Reign: Sikandar Jāh, Nizam of Hyderabad.

Endowment: Bumiya (?) village in Daulatabad region, with an actual revenue of 3 rupees (i.e., per day), half of which is to be paid monthly from the beginning of 1237.

Recipient: Ḥāfiẓ ʿAbd al-Shakūr, son of Ḥāfiẓ Muḥammad ʿAlī, attendant of the shrine of Sayyid Rājū Qattāl and Sayyid Zayn al-Ḥaqq.

Endorsement: Seal of Farrukhsiyar. Cites previous grant of village (name illegible) yielding 8 *ānā*s per day, and a memorandum of 17 Rabīʿ I, 4 regnal/[1222]/[25 May 1807], in the names of Fayż Allāh, Raḥmat Allāh, and Muḥammad (illegible), for sandalwood, roses, and lamps for the shrine, from 1 Shaʿbān, 4 regnal. Endorsement in Marathi.[21]

B3. Date: 5 Dhū al-Qaʿda 1242/[31 May 1827] ("copy in agreement with the original").

Reign: (Sikandar Jāh).

Recipient: Muḥammad ʿAbd al-Shakūr, son of Ḥāfiẓ Muḥammad ʿAlī, of the sons of Mullā Wāḥid al-Dīn Aḥmad, attendant of the shrine of Shāh Rājū Qattāl.

Stipulations: Recipient is confirmed as sole legitimate attendant of the shrine.

Endorsement: Rather than being a government document, this has been issued under the seals of Sayyid Shāh Asad Allāh Muḥammad Akbar al-Ḥusaynī, chief custodian of the Greater Shrine (*rawża-i kalān*) in Gulbarga, and Sayyid Shāh Ḥabīb Allāh Muḥammad Aṣghar al-Ḥusaynī, chief custodian of the shrine of Gīsū Darāz (*rawża-i khwāja*) at Gulbarga.

C. Other Grants

C1. Date: 14 Ramażān, 27 regnal/1094/[6 September 1683].

Reign: Awrangzīb.

Endowment: Thirty *bīgha*s as measured by *ilāhī* gaz, from Sultanpur district in the region of Daulatabad.

Recipient: Unspecified on front, but see endorsement.

Stipulations: Revenues to be used for necessities. Recipients are to pray

21. One *ānā* equals one-sixteenth of a rupee (Wilson, p. 24a), so this document raises the income from one-half rupee to three rupees per day.

for the welfare of the ruling dynasty. Exemptions from various taxes are guaranteed.

Endorsement: Muḥammad Saʿīd, reporter, on the basis of a memorandum from the late treasurer Sharīf Khān, dated 29 Jumādā II, 27 regnal/1094/[25 June 1683], signed also by Fażā'il Khān and Bahrmand Khān, citing the date of 21 Jumādā II, 25 regnal/[1092]/[16 July 1681]. The grant is to be divided among four people, with half going to a son (name illegible) of Ḥājjī Shaykh Ṣaghīr, and the other half to be shared by three sisters, Bībī Rābiʿa, Bībī ʿĀ'isha, and Bībī Bānū Begum.[22]

C2. Date: Rabīʿ II, 4 regnal/[1122]/[June 1710].

Reign: Bahādur Shāh.

Endowment: Bhandegaon village and Jaʿfarabad village in Sultanpur district of Daulatabad region, with total revenue of 282,067 *dāms*, and actual revenue of 3,249 rupees.[23]

Recipient: Shrine of Khwāja Ḥusayn, father of the Shaykh al-Islam (Zayn al-Dīn), and shrine of Khwāja ʿUmar, uncle of the Shaykh al-Islam, in the care of Shaykh Abū al-Khayr.[24]

Stipulations: From the spring crop of Qawī-īl, for annual festival, adornments for the shrine, sustenance of attendants.

Endorsement: Cites memorandum of 14 Ramażān, 5 regnal/1122/5 Ābān *ilāhī*/[6 November 1710]. Amjad Khān, *ṣadr*. Endorsement in English, partially obscured by repairs, reading, " . . . and compared", with illegible date and signature, apparently identical to the English notation on A7 above.

C3. Date: 21 Rajab 1256/[18 September 1840].

Reign: Rājā Trībhavan Dās.

Endowment: 5 rupees monthly for sandalwood, roses, etc., from Shaʿbān 1256/[October 1840].

Recipient: Attendants of the shrine of Shāh Jalāl Ganj-i Ravān.[25]

---

22. This document is a stipend for the support of living individuals rather than a shrine grant.

23. For these villages, see *Gazetteer*, pp. 1064, 1110.

24. For Khwāja Ḥusayn (d. 27 Shaʿban, 752/1349) and his brother Khwāja ʿUmar, see Rawnaq ʿAlī, *Rawżat al-aqṭāb*, pp. 141–43; ʿĀzād, *Rawżat al-awliyā'*, p. 90.

25. This saint, whose original name was Jalāl al-Dīn Kharaqānī, is said to have been the disciple of a student of Shaykh Shihāb al-Dīn Suhrawardī of Baghdad (d. 1234). See ʿĀzād, *Rawżat al-awliyā'*, p. 130.

NOTES

Preface

1. Jean de Thevenot, *The Travels of Monsieur de Thevenot into the Levant* (London, 1687), reprinted in *Indian Travels of Thevenot and Careri*, ed. Surendranath Sen, Indian Records Series (New Delhi: National Archives of India, 1949), p. 105.

2. Ghulām ʿAlī Āzād Bilgrāmī, *Rawżat al-awliyāʾ al-maʿrūf bi-nafaḥāt al-aṣfiyāʾ*, Urdu translation by Muḥammad ʿAbd al-Majīd (Hyderabad: Maṭbaʿ-i Karīmī, n.d. [1345/1926–27]), pp. 1–2. The phrase *rawża-i bā-ṣafāʾ* ("pure garden") is Āzād's chronogram for the year of the book's composition, 1152/1739.

3. Syed Hossain Bilgrami and C. Willmott, *Historical and Descriptive Sketch of His Highness the Nizam's Dominions* (2 vols., Bombay: The Times of India Steam Press, 1883–84), II, 715. "Kerbella" (Karbalāʾ in Iraq) is the site of the martyrdom of the Imam Ḥusayn in 680, and is considered as a most sacred pilgrimage center among Shīʿī Muslims.

4. Thus the approach of this study differs considerably from that of P. M. Currie, *The Shrine and Cult of Muʿīn al-Dīn Chishtī of Ajmer*, Oxford University South Asian Studies Series (Delhi: Oxford University Press, 1989).

5. The name Khuldabad was given to the town after the burial there of the emperor Awrangzīb (d. 1707), from his postmortem epithet *khuld-makān*, "stationed in eternity."

6. Shams al-Dīn Muḥammad Ḥāfiẓ Shīrāzī, *Dīvān* [ed. Qāsim Ghanī] (Tehran: Amīr-i Kabīr, 1352/1973), p. 50, no. 49.

Part One

1. Abú Naṣr ʿAbdallah B. ʿAlí al-Sarráj al-Ṭúsí, *The Kitáb al-Lumaʿ fi ʾl-Taṣawwuf*, ed. Reynold Alleyne Nicholson, "E. J. W. Gibb Memorial" Series, vol. XXII (London, 1914; reprint ed., London: Luzac & Company Ltd., 1963), pp. 20–22, where he also quotes Ibn Isḥāq's history of Mecca on the pre-Islamic use of the term Sufi to describe one who circumambulated the Kaʿba.

2. Sarrāj, p. 22.

3. There are still some who defend a return to "traditional scholarship" consisting of the abstract study of influences, as in the recent work of Julian Baldick, *Mystical Islam: An Introduction to Sufism* (London: I. B. Tauris & Co. Ltd., 1989).

4. This crosscultural process is the subject of my *The Pool of Nectar: Islamic Interpretations of Yoga* (forthcoming from the State University of New York Press).

5. See Annemarie Schimmel, *Mystical Dimensions of Islam* (Chapel Hill: University of North Carolina Press, 1975), pp. 8–11, for an overview of early studies of Sufism.

6. Sarrāj, pp. 3–4.

7. Jacqueline Chabbi, "Remarques sur le développement historique des mouvements ascétiques et mystiques au Khurasan, IIIe/IXe siècle–IVe/Xe siècle," *Studia Islamica* 46 (1977), pp. 5–72.

8. Abdurrahman Habil, "Traditional Esoteric Commentaries on the Quran," in *Islamic Spirituality: Foundations*, ed. Seyyed Hossein Nasr, World Spirituality: An Encyclopedic History of the Religious Quest, vol. 19 (New York: Crossroad, 1987), pp. 24–47.

9. For a brief survey of Sufi biographical literature, see my "From Hagiography to Martyrology: Conflicting Testimonies to a Sufi Martyr of the Delhi Sultanate," *History of Religions* XXIV/4 (May 1985), pp. 308–27.

10. For a discussion of the early Sufi trials, see my *Words of Ecstasy in Sufism*, SUNY Series in Islam (Albany: State University of New York Press, 1984), esp. part III.

11. See my *Words of Ecstasy in Sufism*, part I, for a discussion of ecstatic expressions.

12. See my "Mystical Language and the Teaching Context in the Early Sufi Lexicons," in *Mysticism and Language*, ed. Steven T. Katz (Oxford University Press, forthcoming).

13. Schimmel, pp. 98–99.

14. Sarrāj, p. 150.

15. Sarrāj, p. 167.

16. Sarrāj refers to this intensification as "emphasis (*tashdīd*) on his [God's] saying, 'Fear God as much as you are able' (Qur. 64.16)" (*Lumaʿ*, p. 87).

17. Junayd, in Sarrāj, p. 42.

18. Rūzbihān Baqlī, *Sharḥ-i shaṭḥiyyāt*, ed. Henry Corbin, Bibliothèque Iranienne, no. 12 (Tehran: Département d'Iranologie de l'Institut Franco-Iranien, 1966), pp. 546–47.

19. Sarrāj, p. 41.

20. See Schimmel, pp. 109–130, for extended comments on the states and stages.

21. See my "Mystical Language and the Teaching Context in the Early Lexicons of Sufism."

22. Schimmel, pp. 155–67.

23. Sarrāj, pp. 257–63, where the invocations are listed as a type of Sufi literature, along with letters, poetry, and testaments; an example is Khwāja ʿAbdullah Ansari, *Intimate Conversations*, trans. Wheeler M. Thackston, Jr. (New York: Paulist Press, 1978).

24. Schimmel, pp. 167–78.

25. Schimmel, pp. 178–86.

26. James Robson, trans., *Tracts on Listening to Music* (London, 1938); D. S. Margoliouth, trans., "Devil's Delusion of Abū'l Faraj ibn al-Jawzi," *Islamic Culture* 19 (1945), pp. 180–88, 272–89, 376–83.

27. See, for example, the discussion of Hujwīrī, pp. 331–67, trans., pp. 393–420.

28. Hujwīrī, pp. 188–217, trans., pp. 210–41; Schimmel, pp. 199–213

29. Abū Nuʿaym Aḥmad ibn ʿAbd Allāh al-Iṣfahānī, *Ḥilyat al-awliyā' wa ṭabaqāt al-aṣfiyā'* (10 vols., Egypt: Maktabat al-Khānjī, n.d.), X, 252–53.

30. R. A. Nicholson, *Studies in Islamic Mysticism* (Cambridge, 1921; reprint ed., Cambridge: Cambridge University Press, 1967), p. 46. Cf. also Fritz Meier, *Abū Saʿīd-i Abū l-Ḫayr (357–440/967–1049), Wirklichkeit und Legende*, Acta Iranica 11 (Leiden: E. J. Brill, 1976), pp. 310–11, who suggests that this type of behavior predates Abū Saʿīd.

31. Abū al-Najīb al-Suhrawardī, *A Sufi Rule for Novices, Kitāb Ādāb al-Murīdīn*, trans. Menahem Milson (Cambridge: Harvard University Press, 1975).

32. Marshall G.S. Hodgson, *The Venture of Islam: Conscience and History in a World Civilization*, vol. II, *The Expansion of Islam in the Middle Periods* (Chicago: University of Chicago Press, 1974), pp. 214–17.

33. Fritz Meier, "Ḫurāsān und das Ende der klassischen Ṣūfik," *La Persia nel medioevo* (Rome: Accademia Nazionale dei Lincei, 1971), pp. 545–70.

34. Ibn Battutah, *Travels in Asia and Africa 1325–1354*, trans. H. A. R. Gibb, ed. E. Denison Ross and Eileen Power (London, 1926; reprint ed., Karachi: Indus Publications, 1986), p. 316.

35. Muḥammad ibn Munawwar, *Asrār al-tawḥīd*, cited by A. Bausani, "Religion in the Saljuq Period," in J. A. Boyle, ed., *The Cambridge History of Iran*, vol. 5, *The Saljuq and Mongol Periods* (Cambridge: At the University Press, 1968), p. 300.

36. Khaliq Ahmad Nizami, *Some Aspects of Religion and Politics in India During the Thirteenth Century* (Bombay: Asia Publishing House, 1961), p. 249.

37. A. K. S. Lambton, "Quis Custodiet Custodes: Some Reflections on the Persian Theory of Government, I, " *Theory and Practice in Medieval Persian Government* (London: Variorum Reprints, 1980, pp. 138–39.

38. Nizami, pp. 248–53.

39. Abū Ḥāmid al-Ghazālī, *Iḥyā' ʿulūm al-dīn* (Cairo: Dār al-Shuʿab, n.d.), part 7, pp. 1273–74; Ira M. Lapidus, *Muslim Cities in the Later Middle Ages* (Cambridge: Harvard University Press, 1967; Student edition, Cambridge: Cambridge University Press, 1984) p. 106.

40. Ghazālī, *Iḥyā' ʿulūm al-dīn,* Kitāb al-halāl wa al-ḥarām, *bāb*s 4–6, pp. 886–914.

41. Nizami, p. 241, quoting *Maktūbāt-i Ghazālī*, p. 7.

42. Nizami, p. 243, quoting (without translation) the *Dīvān-i Jamāl al-Dīn Hānsvī*, II, 45.

43. James Dickie, "Allah and Eternity: Mosques, Madrasas and Tombs," in George Michell, ed., *Architecture of the Islamic World: Its History and Social Meaning* (London: Thames and Hudson, 1978), pp. 15–48, esp. pp. 43–44.

44. Hodgson, pp. 95–98, 220–22.

45. For the Mughul administration of *suyurghal*s, see Abū 'l-Fażl 'Allāmī, *The Ā'īn-i Akbarī*, trans. H. Blochmann, 2nd ed. rev. by D.C. Phillott (New Delhi: Oriental Books Reprint Corporation, 1977 [1927]), I, 278–85.

46. Lapidus, pp. 73–74.

47. Ibn al-Jawzī, *Talbīs Iblīs* (Beirut: Dār al-Kutub al-ʿIlmiyya, n.d.), p. 175.

48. See my "An Indo-Persian Guide to Sufi Shrine Pilgrimage," in *Manifestations of Sainthood in Islam*, ed. Grace Martin Smith and Carl W. Ernst (forthcoming).

49. For juristic opposition to Sufi practices, see Muhammad Umar Memon, *Ibn Taymiya's Struggle Against Popular Religion* (The Hague: Mouton, 1982).

50. Hujwīrī, pp. 50–56; trans., pp. 62–69.

51. Hodgson, II, 218.

52. P. Hardy, *Historians of Medieval India: Studies in Indo-Muslim Historical Writing* (London: Luzac & Company Ltd., 1960), pp. 1–20.

53. Sir H. M. Elliot, *The History of India as told by its own Historians, The Muhammadan Period*, ed. John Dowson (8 vols., London, 1867–77; reprint ed., Allahabad: Kitab Mahal, n.d.).

54. See the critical studies, corrections, and additions in Shāpūrshāh Hormasji Hodīvālā, *Studies in Indo-Muslim History, A Critical Commentary on Elliot and*

Dowson's History of India as told by its Own Historians (2 vols., Bombay: S. H. Hodivala, 1939, 1954); Mohammad Habib, "Introduction to Elliot and Dowson's *History of India*, vol. II, " in *Politics and Society during the Early Medieval Period, Collected Essays of Professor Mohammad Habib*, ed. K. A. Nizami (New Delhi: People's Publishing House, 1974), pp. 33–110; Khaliq Ahmad Nizami, *Supplement to Elliot & Dowson's History of India* (2 vols., Delhi: Idarah-i Adabiyat-i Delli, 1981).

55. Elliot, "Original Preface," I, xix.

56. Ibid., I, xxii.

57. Hardy, ibid., discusses the reasons for the political focus of British historians of India, which continues to follow the "sources" method in such works as the *Cambridge History of India*, vol. 3, *Turks and Afghans*, ed. Sir Wolseley Haig (Cambridge: Cambridge University Press, 1928).

58. For the development of nationalist trends in Indian historiography, see R. C. Majumdar, "Nationalist Historians," in C. H. Philips, *Historians of India, Pakistan and Ceylon* (London: Oxford University Press, 1961), pp. 416–28; J. S. Grewal, "Concepts and Interpretations of Medieval Indian History," in *Medieval India: History and Historians* (Amritsar: Guru Nanak University, 1975), pp. 135, 138–39; Bruce T. McCully, "The Origins of Indian Nationalism According to Native Writers," *The Journal of Modern History* 7 (1935), pp. 295–314.

59. John E. E. D. Acton, "Nationality," in *The History of Freedom* [1862], ed. John Neville Figgis and Reginald Vere Laurence (London: Macmillan and Co., Limited, 1922), pp. 270–300; Carlton J. H. Hayes, *Nationalism: A Religion* (New York: The Macmillan Company, 1960), pp. 164–82; Hans Kohn, "Nationalism," *International Encyclopedia of the Social Sciences* (1968), XI, 63–70.

60. Mohammad Habib, "Introduction," in Khaliq Ahmad Nizami, *Some Aspects of Religion and Politics in India in the Thirteenth Century*, IAD Religio-Philosophical Series, 2 (2nd ed., Delhi: Idarah-i Adabiyat-i Delli, 1978), pp. xi-xxii.

61. The term "historiomachy" was coined by Eric Voegelin to describe the rivalry of ecumenic symbolisms in the Hellenistic age; cf. his *Order and History*, vol. 4, *The Ecumenic Age* (Baton Rouge: Louisiana State University Press, 1974), pp. 111–13.

62. K. M. Munshi, "Foreward," in R. C. Majumdar, ed., *The History and Culture of the Indian People*, vol. V, *The Struggle for Empire* (Bombay: Bharatiya Vidya Bhavan, 1957), pp. vii, xi-xii.

63. Peter Hardy estimates that 20 out of 416 pages of al-ʿUtbī's *Ta'rīkh-i yamīnī* (Tehran, 1345 solar) deal with India, and just four and a half pages of Gardīzī's *Zayn al-akhbār* (Tehran, 1347 solar) record expeditions to India; see "The Growth of Authority over a Conquered Political Elite: The Early Delhi Sultanate as a Possible Case Study," in *Kingship and Authority in South Asia*, ed. J. F. Richards (Madison: University of Wisconsin, 1978), p. 205.

64. C. E. Bosworth, "The imperial policy of the early Ghaznawids," in *The Medieval History of Iran, Afghanistan and Central Asia* (London: Variorum Reprints, 1977), essay XI, pp. 54–55.

65. See Paramatma Saran, "The Turkish Conquest of Northern India," in *The Struggle for Empire*, pp. 125–29; Ashirbadi Lal Srivastava, "A Survey of India's Resistance to Mediaeval Invaders from the North-West: Causes of Eventual Hindu Defeat," *Journal of Indian History* 43 (1965), pp. 349–68; and the review article of J. F. Richards, "The Islamic Frontier in the East: Expansion into South Asia," *South Asia* 4 (1974), pp. 90–109.

66. The idealized portrait of Maḥmūd is fully realized by the time of the Seljuks, and is a major theme in Delhi sultanate authors such as Baranī and ʿIṣāmī; cf. Aziz Ahmad, *Studies in Islamic Culture in the Indian Environment* (Oxford: Oxford University Press, 1964; reprint ed., Lahore, 1970), p. 79. Modern eulogistic comments on Maḥmūd can be found in Muḥammad Ikrām, *Āb-i Kawsar*, pp. 59–62, partially translated as S. M. Ikram, *Muslim Civilization in India*, ed. Ainslie T. Embree (New York: Columbia University Press, 1964), pp. 24–26.

67. The telling phrase is used by R. C. Majumdar, "Indian Historiography: Some Recent Trends," in *Historians and Historiography in Modern India*, ed. S. P. Sen (Calcutta: Institute of Historical Studies, 1973), p. xxiii. But feelings of religious communalism still simmer in this work. The editor criticizes (p. xii) what he sees as the condescending attitude of the C. H. Philips volume (above, n. 58) and attacks (p. xiii) the unnamed Aligarh school for its "officially inspired" political interpretation of medieval Hindu-Muslim relations. The problem of positivism and nationalism also occurs in modern Arab historiography; cf. Abdallah Laroui, *The Crisis of the Arab Intellectual: Traditionalism or Historicism?*, trans. Diarmid Cammell (Berkeley: University of California Press, 1976), p. 25.

68. Voegelin, p. 58.

69. See Bruce B. Lawrence, *Shahrastānī on the Indian Religions*, Religion and Society 4 (The Hague: Mouton, 1976), pp. 17–29.

70. Yohanan Friedmann, "The Origins and Significance of the Chāch Nāma," in *Islam in Asia*, vol. I, ed. Yohanan Friedman (Boulder: Westview Press, 1984), pp. 23–37. Friedman argues (pp. 33–34) that the portions concerning the local dynasty and class structure derive from later Indian Muslim sources.

71. John Block Friedman, *The Monstrous Races in Medieval Art and Thought* (Cambridge: Harvard University Press, 1981), pp. 6ff.

72. C. E. Dubler, "ʿA<u>dj</u>ā'ib," EI² I, 103–4; Buzurg ibn Shahriyar (ca. 342/953), *The Book of the Marvels of India* [French trans.] from the Arabic by L. Marcel Devic, English trans. Peter Quennell (New York: Lincoln MacVeagh, Dial Press, 1929); cf. GALS I, 404.

73. S. Maqbul Ahmad, ed., *India and the Neighbouring Territories as described by the Sharif al-Idrisi*, Part One (Arabic Text) (Aligarh: Muslim University, 1954), pp. 24, 28.

74. As an example, see *The Fihrist of al-Nadīm*, ed. and trans. Bayard Dodge (2 vols., New York: Columbia University Press, 1970), pp. 826–36.

75. On the term *hindu*, see Wilfrid Cantwell Smith, *The Meaning and End of Religion: A New Approach to the Religious Traditions of Mankind* (New York: New

American Library, 1964), pp. 59–63, 249–52; Henry Yule and A.C. Burnell, *Hobson-Jobson, A Glossary of Colloquial Anglo-Indian Words and Phrases*, ed. William Crooke (London, 1903; reprint ed., New Delhi: Munshiram Manoharlal, 1979), s.vv. "Hindoo," "India." Europeans also used the term Gentoo (from Portuguese *gentio*), to describe the "Gentiles" or native inhabitants of India.

76. See Annemarie Schimmel, "Turk and Hindu: A Poetical Image and its Application to Historical Fact," in *Islam and Cultural Change in the Middle Ages*, ed. Speros Vryonis, Jr. (Wiesbaden: Otto Harrassowitz, 1975), pp. 107–26.

77. Abū al-Qāsim Firdawsī, *Shāh nāma*, ed. Muḥammad ʿAlī Furūghī (Tehran: Intishārāt-i Jāwīdān, n.d.), p. 329, column 1, line 9. The Brahman sages whom Alexander later meets (ibid., pp. 340–41) are not described as Hindu, but are rather compared to Greek philosophers in their disdain for the world. On images of India in the *Shāh nāma*, see Peter Hardy, "The Growth of Authority," p. 206.

78. Schimmel, "Turk and Hindu," p. 112.

79. "*Táríkh Yamíní* of ʿUtbí," trans. H. M. Elliot, in Elliot and Dowson, II, 14–52.

80. Bosworth, "The Development of Persian Culture under the Early Ghaznavids," p. 42.

81. Eduard Sachau, trans., *Alberuni's India* (London, 1888; reprint ed., Delhi: S. Chand & Co., 1964).

82. Ibid., p. 5.

83. Ibid., p. 17.

84. Ibid., p. 5.

85. On the terms *dīn* and *islām*, see W. C. Smith, ch. 4, pp. 75–108.

86. Minhāj-e-Sirāj-e-Juzjānī, *Ṭabaqāt-e Nāṣirī* (*sic*), vol. II, ed. ʿAbd-ul-Ḥaiy Ḥabībī Afghānī, Panjab University Oriental Publications, 30 (Lahore: University of the Panjab, 1954), p. 604; Minhāj-ud-Dīn Abū-ʿUmar-i-ʿUsmān, *Ṭabaḳāt-i-Nāṣirī*, trans. H. G. Raverty (2 vols., Calcutta, 1881; reprint ed., Oriental Books Reprint Corporation, 1970), II, 766. Post-Mongol Persian chronicles in central Asia still referred to the Hindu primarily as a slave or bandit: see ʿAláʾu ʾd-Dín ʿAṭá Malik-i-Juwayní, *The Taʾríkh-i-Jahán-Gushá*, ed. Mírzá Muḥammad ibn ʿAbduʾl-Wahháb-i-Qazwíní, "E. J. W. Gibb Memorial" Series, XVI, 1–3 (3 vols., London: Luzac & Co., 1912, 1916, 1937), I, 27, 109, 143; II, 59, 143.

87. Minhāj-i Sirāj, II, 643–45 (Muḥammad), 712–717 (Arabic poem by ʿAlī's friend Yaḥyā Aʿqab predicting the Mongols' downfall); trans. Raverty, II, 869 ff., 1281–82 (Raverty did not think these prophecies worth translating, and omitted them derisively). Cf. also II, 691–94, trans. Raverty, II, 1157–64, for the miraculous foiling of the Mongol plot to exterminate all Muslims.

88. On the death of the last caliph, see Minhāj-i Sirāj, II, 708–9; trans. Raverty, II, 1252–61. To end on an upbeat note, Minhāj-i Sirāj looks hopefully to the conver-

sion of the Mongol leader Barkā Khān, grandson of Chingīz Khān (II, 717–21; trans. Raverty, II, 1283–93).

89. Minhāj-i Sirāj, II, 642, trans. Raverty, II, 869–79 (with minor changes; emphasis mine).

90. Minhāj-i Sirāj introduces to history the adulatory portrait of Maḥmūd of Ghazna as the champion of Islam, modelled on the belles lettristic anecdotes of Niẓāmī ʿArūżī (ca. 1160); now it seems that Maḥmūd was born under the same heavenly sign that attended the beginning of Islam, and his birth was heralded by the sudden shattering of an Indian idol temple (trans. Raverty, I, 76–80).

91. Muḥammad Ikrām, *Āb-i Kawsar* (5th ed., Lahore: Idāra-i Siqāfat-i Islāmiyya, 1984), pp. 128–29.

92. Minhāj-i Sirāj, II, 705; trans. Raverty, II, 1234, note 8.

93. Peter Hardy, *Historians of Medieval India*, p. 114.

94. Amīr Khusraw, *Khazā'in al-futūḥ*, trans. M. Habib (Madras, 1931), p. 49, as cited in Aziz Ahmad, "Epic and Counter-Epic in Medieval India," *Journal of the American Oriental Society* 83 (1963), p. 470.

95. Hardy, *Historians*, p. 115; see ibid., pp. 68–93 for an analysis of Amīr Khusraw's rhetorical approach to history.

96. Ahmad, p. 741; Hardy, *Historians*, pp. 94–110. For ʿIṣāmī, too, Maḥmūd of Ghazna is the "standard-bearer of Islam" and arch-enemy of idolatry (ibid., p. 108).

97. Żiyā' al-Dīn Baranī, *Fatāwā-i jahāndārī*, ed. Afsar Saleem Khan, Publication of the Research Society of Pakistan, no. 25 (Lahore: University of the Punjab, 1972), p. 18.

98. Hardy, p. 128.

99. "*Mir-át-i Masʿúdí*," trans. R. B. Chapman, in Elliot and Dowson, II, 513–49.

100. Ibid., II, 522.

101. Ibid., II, 525; this is attributed to the mythical *Tārīkh-i Maḥmūdī* from which ʿAbd al-Raḥmān Chishtī claimed to have gotten the story of Sālār Masʿūd.

102. Ibid., II, 541.

103. Kerrin Graefin v. Schwerin, "Saint Worship in Indian Islam: The Legend of the Martyr Salar Masud Ghazi," in *Ritual & Religion among Muslims of the Subcontinent*, ed. Imtiaz Ahmad (Lahore: Vanguard, 1985), pp. 143–61.

104. Ernst, "From Hagiography to Martyrology."

105. For condemnation of the Zoroastrian worship of Ahūrā in an Indian Muslim legal text, see Maḥmūd ibn Aḥmad ibn Abū al-Qāsim ibn Aḥmad Ṭā'ifī, *Khulāṣat al-aḥkām fī dīn al-islām* (written 755/1354), MS 1 Fārsiyya Fiqh, University Żamīma,

Maulana Azad Library, Aligarh Muslim University, p. 62; another copy is MS 2562 Persian, India Office Library, London.

106. Anonymous, *Manāfiʿ al-qulūb* (dedicated to the Sufi master Naṣīr al-Dīn Maḥmūd "Chirāgh-i Dihlī" [d. 1356]), MS 66 Fiqh Fārsī, Salar Jung Museum Library, Hyderabad, fol. 51b (another copy is in the Buhar Collection, National Library, Calcutta); Abū Bakr ibn Muḥammad al-Qurayshī al-ʿAlawī al-Sindī al-Pātarī (15th cent.), *al-Fatāwā al-ʿAlawīya*, MS 490 Arabic, Asiatic Society, Calcutta, fol. 218b.

107. Ṭā'ifī, p. 63, where the Indian festivals of Holī and Dīwālī are expressly forbidden to Muslims. For further examples of legal responsa from the sultanate period, see David H. Partington's edition and translation of the text by Ḍiyā' al-Dīn al-Sūnamī, "The *Niṣāb al-Iḥtisāb*, an Arabic Religio-Legal Text," Ph. D. dissertation, Princeton University, 1961, esp. p. 49, no. 35 (prohibiting *dhimmī* fairs).

108. Y. Friedmann, "A Contribution to the Early History of Islam in India," *Studies in Memory of Gaston Wiet*, ed. Myriam Rosen-Ayalon (Jerusalem: Hebrew University of Jerusalem, 1977), pp. 318–19, with references.

109. Ibid., p. 324.

110. Annemarie Schimmel, *Islam in the Indian Subcontinent*, Handbuch der Orientalistik IV.3 (Leiden: E. J. Brill, 1980), p. 4.

111. Qāżī Aṭhar Mubārakpūrī, *Khilāfat-i rāshida awr Hindūstān* (Delhi, 1972; reprint ed., Sukkur: Fikr o Naẓar Publications, 1986), p. 18; this book, together with its continuations *Khilāfat-i Umawiyya awr Hindūstān* and *Khilāfat-i ʿAbbāsiyya awr Hindūstān*, constitutes the Urdu translation of his compendious Arabic work, *al-ʿIqd al-thamīn fī futūḥ al-Hind wa man warada fīhā min al-ṣaḥāba wa al-tābiʿīn* (Delhi: Nadwat al-Muṣannifīn, 1969).

112. Amīr Khusraw, *Masnavī-i nuh sipihr* (Calcutta, 1949), pp. 151–57, as quoted by Waris Kirmani, *Dreams Forgotten, An Anthology of Indo-Persian Poetry* (Aligarh: Department of Persian, Aligarh Muslim University, 1984), pp. 83–85.

113. Ghulām ʿAlī Āzād al-Bilgrāmī, *Subḥat al-marjān fī āthār Hindūstān*, ed. Muḥammad Faḍl al-Raḥmān al-Nadwī al-Sīwānī (2 vols., Aligarh: Jāmiʿat ʿAlīgarh al-Islāmiyya, 1976–80), I, 9–10.

114. See Schimmel, *Dimensions*, Index, s.v. "Light, of Muḥammad"; Āzād, I, 21–22.

115. Ibid., I, 24–28.

116. Ibid., Introduction, p. 18.

117. Ibid., Introduction, p. 6; John Voll, "Muḥammad Ḥayāt al-Sindī and Muḥammad ibn ʿAbd al-Wahhāb, an Analysis of an Intellectual Group in Eighteenth-century Madīna," *Bulletin of the School of Oriental and African Studies* 38 (1975), pp. 32–39.

118. Āzād, p. 8.

119. Ibid., I, 63. Rabīʿ ibn Ṣabīḥ was a *ghāzī* warrior and *ḥadīth* scholar from Iraq who died in Sind (ibid., I, 64–65). The importance attached to this scholar as far as India is concerned is overrated, since his scholarly work was all done in Basra, and he died within a year of his arrival in Sind; see Yohanan Friedmann, "The Beginnings of Islamic Learning in Sind—A Reconsideration," *Bulletin of the School of Oriental and African Studies* 37 (1974), esp. pp. 660–61.

120. Agehananda Bharati, *Hindu Views and Ways and the Hindu-Muslim Interface* (Delhi, 1981).

121. R. C. Majumdar, "Ideas of History in Sanskrit Literature," in C. H. Philips, p. 13; A. L. Basham, "The Kashmir Chronicle," in ibid., pp. 57–65.

122. Wilfred Cantwell Smith, *The Meaning and End of Religion*, p. 62.

123. Rama Shankar Avasthy and Amalananda Ghosh, "References to Muhammadans in Sanskrit Inscriptions in Northern India—A.D. 730 to 1320," *Journal of Indian History* 16 (1936), pp. 24–26, 161–84, esp. nos. 1–5, 49.

124. J. F. Fleet, "Sanskrit and old Canarese Inscriptions, relating to the Yâdava Kings of Dêvagíri," *Journal of the Bombay Branch of the Royal Asiatic Society* 12, no. 33 (1876), p. 19.

125. George Roerich, trans., *Biography of Dharmasvāmin* (Patna: K. P. Jayaswal Research Institute, 1959), pp. 61–61f., 98. Despite the use of the term Turuṣka in the text, the translator's introduction (pp. v, xiv, xviii-xxi) invariably refers to "Muslim soldiers."

126. Krishna Chaitanya, *A New History of Sanskrit Literature* (New York: Asia Publishing House, 1962), pp. 282–83.

127. Aziz Ahmad, "Epic and Counter-Epic in Medieval India," p. 473.

128. Ibid.

129. Chaitanya, p. 350.

130. Aziz Ahmad, "Epic and Counter-Epic in Medieval India," p. 473.

131. The one reference to Islam in the *Prithvī Rāj Rāsō* depicts Tātār Khān reading a verse from the Qur'ān and having his troops touch the book before battle. The presence of Arabic words (*mashwara*, *muṣḥaf*) in these verses suggests a late date of composition; see Chand Bardāī, *The Prithirāj Rāsau*, trans. A. F. Rudolf Hoernle (Calcutta: Baptist Mission Press, 1886), part II, vol. I, p. 10, verses 16–17. Although the term Hindu is used (pp. 18, 22, 60, 62, 63), it is opposed to *mleccha*.

132. Ahmad, p. 474.

133. Ibid., p. 475.

134. M. C. Joshi, "Some Nagari Inscriptions on the Qutb Minar," *Proceedings of Seminar on Medieval Inscriptions (6–8th Feb. 1970)* (Aligarh: Aligarh Muslim University, 1974), p. 25.

135. Ibid. Joshi renders *prasāda* as "by the grace of" instead of treating it as the noun for "temple," which would be normal in an inscription (I am grateful to Dr. Ariel Glucklich for his comments on this inscription).

136. D. C. Sircar, "Veraval Inscription of Chaulukya-Vaghela Arjuna, 1264 A.D.," *Epigraphia Indica* (1961), pp. 141–43.

137. Ibid., p. 144. The Arabic inscription that records this same endowment (pp. 149–50) naturally omits the Sanskrit terms.

138. R. Nath, *History of Mughal Architecture*, vol. I (Atlantic Highlands, N.J.: Humanities Press Inc., 1982), p. 7; cf. pp. 6–10, 68–69 (Sanskrit text).

139. Z. A. Desai, "A Persian-Sanskrit Inscription of Karna Deva Vaghela of Gujarat," *Epigraphia Indica, Arabic and Persian Supplement* (1975), pp. 13–20.

140. D. C. Sircar, p. 145.

141. Norman P. Ziegler, "Some Notes on Rajpūt Loyalties During the Mughal Period," in *Kingship and Authority in South Asia*, ed. J. F. Richards, p. 235.

142. Shankar Gopal Tulpule, *Classical Marāṭhī Literature*, History of Indian Literature IX/4 (Wiesbaden: Otto Harrassowitz, 1979), pp. 334–35.

143. Eleanor Zelliot, "A Medieval Encounter between Hindu and Muslim: Eknath's Drama-Poem *Hiṇdu-Turk Saṃvād,"* in *Images of Man: Religion and Historical Process in South Asia*, ed. Fred W. Clothey (Madras: New Era Publications, 1982), p. 171.

144. Ch. Vaudeville, *Kabīr*, vol. I (Oxford: At the Clarendon Press, 1974), pp. 92–95.

145. The last quotation is from *Stories of Indian Saints, Translation of Mahipati's Marathi "Bhaktavijaya,"* trans. Justin E. Abbott and Narhar R. Godbole (2 vols.; Poona, 1933; reprint ed., Delhi: Motilal Banarsidass, 1982), II, 146–52 (ch. 44), which gives a complete but slightly misleading version. The preceding quotations are from the superior translation of excerpts of the story by Hugh van Skyhawk, "Vaiṣṇava Perceptions of Muslims in 18th Century Mahārāṣṭra" (paper presented at conference on regional varieties of Islam in premodern India, University of Heidelberg, July 1989), pp. 9–10.

146. Mircea Eliade, *Yoga: Immortality and Freedom*, trans. Willard R. Trask, Bollingen Series LVI (2nd ed.; Princeton: Princeton University Press, 1969), pp. 5–6, 100.

147. Gokhale, p. 157, citing G. B. Nirantar, *Marathi Vangmayacha Paramarsha* (Poona, 1971), pp. 181–82.

148. Ibid., p. 157, citing D. K. Kelkar, *Marathi Sahityache Simhavalokana* (Poona, 1963), p. 89.

149. V. D. Rao, "The Maratha Bardic Poetry," *The Modern Review* 124 (1969), pp. 749–52.

150. Gokhale, pp. 162–71, gives a detailed survey of modern Maratha views of Islam.

151. P. N. Oak, *The Taj Mahal is a Hindu Temple* (3rd ed., New Delhi: P. N. Oak, 1974).

152. Wilfred Cantwell Smith, "The Crystallization of Religious Communities in Mughul India," in his *On Understanding Islam: Selected Studies*, Religion and Reason 19 (The Hague: Mouton, 1981), pp. 177–96.

153. Ibid., p. 195.

154. Eric Voegelin, *The Ecumenic Age*, pp. 114ff.

155. H. A. R. Gibb, "An Interpretation of Islamic History," "Evolution of Government in Early Islam," and "Arab-Byzantine Relations under the Umayyad Caliphate," in *Studies on the Civilization of Islam*, ed. Stanford J. Shaw and William R. Polk (Boston: Beacon Press, 1962), pp. 3–61.

156. S. D. Goitein, "A Turning-Point in the History of the Muslim State," in *Studies in Islamic Institutions* (Leiden: E. J. Brill, 1966), pp. 149–67; H. A. R. Gibb, "The Social Significance of the Shuubiya," in *Studies on the Civilization of Islam*, pp. 62–73.

157. Hubert Darke, trans., *The Book of Government or Rules for Kings* (New Haven: Yale University Press, 1960).

158. E. G. Browne, *A Literary History of Persia*, II, 129–47.

159. Clifford Bosworth, "The Development of Persian Culture under the Early Ghaznavids," *Iran VI* (1968), pp. 33–44, reprinted in his *The Medieval History of Iran, Afghanistan and Central Asia* (London: Variorum Reprints, 1977), essay no. 18.

160. Oleg Grabar and Sheila Blair, *Epic Images and Contemporary History: The Illustrations of the Great Mongol Shahnama* (Chicago: University of Chicago Press, 1980); Martin Bernard Dickson and Stuart Cary Welch, *The Houghton Shahnameh* (2 vols., Cambridge: Harvard University Press, 1981).

161. Zabīḥ Allāh Ṣafā, "Ḥamāsa-hā-yi tārīkhī wa dīnī dar ʿahd-i Ṣafavī," *Īrān nāma I* (1361/1982), pp. 5–21.

162. Schimmel, "Turk and Hindu."

163. K. A. Nizami, "The Early Turkish Sultans of Delhi," in Habib and Nizami, pp. 280–85.

164. K. A. Nizami, "Muhammad Bin Tughluq," in Habib and Nizami, pp. 563–65. Afsar Saleem Khan calls the new composite state an "Indo-Muslim polity" rather than a purely Turkish one; cf. Introduction to Żiyā' al-Din Baranī, *Fatāwā-i Jahāndārī*, p. 71.

165. For the theory of universal empire in Hindu tradition, see André Wink, *Land and Sovereignty in India, Agrarian Society and Politics under the Eighteenth-*

century Maratha Svarājya (Cambridge: Cambridge University Press, 1986), pp. 12–19.

166. A recent example of the romantic wish to see modern Hindu nationalism in medieval India is V. S. Naipaul's *India: A Wounded Civilization* (New York: Vintage Books, 1978).

167. Afsar Saleem Khan, Introduction to Baranī, pp. 25, 31, 40–46.

168. Gāyumars, the primal human in Iranian myth, is also the first king according to the traditions recorded in Firdawsī's *Shāh nāma*. Gāyumars naturally has no place in the family of the biblical or Qur'ānic Adam, except in an artificial political construction such as Baranī's.

169. Baranī, *Fatāwā*, pp. 334ff.

170. Afsar Saleem Khan, Introduction to Baranī, pp. 68–70.

171. Ibid., p. 102.

172. Baranī, *Fatāwā*, pp. 200, 222.

173. Afsar Saleem Khan, Introduction to Baranī, p. 89.

174. Baranī, *Fatāwā*, pp. 140–41.

175. Ibid., p. 232.

176. Afsar Saleem Khan, Introduction to Baranī, p. 72.

177. Ibid., pp. 102, 273.

178. Baranī, *Fatāwā*, pp. 272–73.

179. Ibid., pp. 233–34.

180. Ibid., pp. 95, 140.

181. Ibid., pp. 114, 336ff. (Alexander).

182. Afsar Saleem Khan, Introduction to Baranī, pp. 118–19.

183. Baranī, *Fatāwā*, p. 233.

184. Ibid., p. 237.

185. Ibid., p. 108.

186. Oleg Grabar, *The Formation of Islamic Art* (New Haven: Yale University Press, 1973), pp. 45–48.

187. Ibn Battutah, *Travels in Asia and Africa 1325–1354*, trans. H. A. R. Gibb, ed. E. Denison Ross and Eileen Power (London, 1926; reprint ed., Karachi: Indus Publications, 1986), pp. 148, 308, where Ibn Baṭṭūṭa proclaims Abu ʿInan of Morocco as supreme over the seven others.

188. Baranī, *Fatāwā*, p. 252.

189. Żiyā' al-Dīn Baranī, *Tārīkh-i Fīrūz Shāhī*, ed. Sayyid Aḥmad Khān under the supervision of W. Nassau Lees and Kabīr al-Dīn (Calcutta: Asiatic Society of Bengal, 1860–62), pp. 262–64, Urdu trans., Sayyid Mu'īn al-Ḥaqq (Lahore: Urdu Science Board, 1983), pp. 389–91.

190. The idea of the Mongol conquest as a religious one was not peculiar to Baranī. According to the Persian historian Vaṣṣāf, the Jewish wazīr Sa'd al-Dawla (executed in 1291) unsuccessfully tried to convince the Īl-Khān ruler Arghūn that Chingīz Khān had been a prophet, and that Arghūn as a descendant of Chingīz Khān had inherited this office; adopting this policy would then amount to founding a new religious community (*umma*) that would replace Islam. Cf. Alessandro Bausani, "Religion under the Mongols," *The Cambridge History of Iran*, vol. V, ed. J. A. Boyle (Cambridge: Cambridge University Press, 1968), p. 541.

191. Baranī, *Tārīkh*, pp. 264–66, Urdu trans., pp. 391–93.

192. Banarsi Prasad Saksena rejects the account on historical grounds in "Alauddin Khaljī," in Habib and Nizami, pp. 336–37.

193. Although 'Alā' al-Din was supposed to have prohibited alcohol in Delhi, it was for the reason that it contributed to rebellion and conspiracy; Banarsi Prasad Saksena, "Alauddin Khaljī," in Habib and Nizami, pp. 349–50.

194. Although 'Alā' al-Mulk only specified the consolidation of Khaljī rule over Hindustan, i.e., northern India, his inclusion of Chanderi, Dhar, and Ujjain in central India as areas to be conquered implicitly suggests the possibility of military action against rajas of the Deccan.

195. Baranī, *Fatāwā*, p. 18. Baranī completely misrepresents Shafi'ī's position; cf. Banarsi Prasad Saksena, "Alauddin Khaljī," in Habib and Nizami, p. 363.

196. Baranī, *Tārīkh*, pp. 291–92, Urdu trans., pp. 427–28; Banarsi Prasad Saxena, "Alauddin Khaljī," in Habib and Nizami, pp. 352–66.

197. Saxena, pp. 361–62.

198. Afsar Saleem Khan, Introduction to Baranī, pp. 40–41.

199. Ibid., p. 19.

200. Muḥammad Ikrām, *Āb-i Kawsar*, pp. 128–29, citing Baranī's *Ṣaḥīfa-i na't-i Muḥammadī*, as published in *Darbār-i millī*, pp. 78–80; there this debate is said to have occurred in the realm of Iltutmish, with the minister Niẓām al-Mulk Junaydī furnishing the practical argument against extermination of Hindus.

201. Baranī, *Fatāwā*, pp. 167–68, apparently describes the wealth and freedom enjoyed by Hindus in his own time; cf. translation of the passage by Banarsi Prasad Saxena, "Alauddin Khaljī," in Habib and Nizami, pp. 355–56.

202. Afsar Saleem Khan, Introduction to Baranī, p. 122, also attributing the Seljuk wazir Niẓām al-Mulk's wrath against Ismā'īlī heretics to a similar political expediency.

203. Banarsi Prasad Saxena, "Fīrūz Shāh Tughluq," in Habib and Nizami, pp. 609–10.

204. K. A. Nizami, "The Futuhat-i-Fīrūz Shāhī As A Medieval Inscription," *Proceedings of the Seminar on Medieval Inscriptions*, pp. 28–35.

205. B. N. Goswamy and J. S. Grewal, *The Mughals and the Jogis of Jakhbar, Some Madad-i-Maʿāsh and Other Documents* (Simla: Indian Institute of Advanced Study, 1967); id., *The Mughul and Sikh Rulers and the Vaishnavas of Pindori, A Historical Interpretation of 52 Persian Documents* (Simla: Indian Institute of Advanced Study, 1969).

206. Grewal and Goswamy, *Jogis*, pp. 20–21; J. J. Modi, "The Parsees at the Court of Akbar, and Dastur Meherji Ráná," *Journal of the Bombay Branch of the Royal Asiatic Society*, vol. 21, no. 58 (1901), reprinted in *Contributions on Akbar and the Parsees*, ed. B. P. Ambashthya (Patna: Janaki Prakashan, 1976), with facsimiles, transcriptions, and translations of the relevant revenue documents.

207. Yūsuf Husain Khān, ed., *Farmans and Sanads of the Deccan Sultans* (Hyderabad: State Archives, Government of Andhra Pradesh, 1963), no. 14, pp. 40–41; for samples of *agrahāram* grants, see M. G. Dikshit, *Selected Inscriptions from Maharashtra (5th to 12th Century A.D.)*, Swiya Grantha Mala, no. 67 (Poona: Bharat Itihas Samshodhaka Mandal, 1962), pp. 106–9.

208. Iqtidar Husain Siddiqi, "Wajh-i-Maʿash Grants under the Afghan Kings (1451–1555)," *Medieval India, A Miscellany II* (1972), pp. 19–45; W. H. Siddiqi, "Religious Tolerance As Gleaned From Medieval Inscriptions," *Proceedings of the Seminar on Medieval Inscriptions*, pp. 53–58; Upendra Nath Day, *Medieval Malwa, A Political and Cultural History, 1401–1562* (Delhi: Munshī Ram Manohar Lal, 1965), Appendix D, "The Jains in Malwa," pp. 422–28, 437–39; K. D. Swaminathan, "Two Nawabs of the Carnatic and the Sri Rangam Temple," *Medieval India: A Miscellany* III (1975), pp. 184–87; M. A. Ansari, *Administrative Documents of Mughul India* (Delhi: B. R. Publishing Corporation, 1984), giving a series of twenty documents from the Jangams of Benares, dated from 1563 to the 1720s.

209. David Morgan, *The Mongols* (Cambridge, Mass.: Basil Blackwell, 1990), p. 44.

210. Grewal and Goswami, p. 22; other terms used include *madad-i maʿāsh* ("means of living") and *inʿām* ("benefice").

211. G. A. Deleury, *The Cult of Viṭhoba* (Poona: Deccan College, 1960), p. 39.

212. W. H. Siddiqi, "Religious Tolerance As Gleaned From Medieval Inscriptions," p. 53, citing the Sanskrit inscription published by P. B. Desai, *Epigraphia Indica*, vol. 32 (1957–58), p. 168.

213. Athar Alī, "The Religious Issue in the War of Succession," *Medieval India Quarterly* V (1963), pp. 80–87.

214. Jnan Chandra has discussed Awrangzīb's patronage of Hindus in a series of articles in the *Journal of the Pakistan Historical Society*: "Awrangzīb and Hindu

Temples," V (1957), pp. 254ff.; "'Ālamgīr's Grants to Hindu Pujaris," VI (1958), pp. 55–65; "'Ālamgīr's Patronage of Hindu Temples," VI (1958), pp. 208–13; "'Ālamgīr's Tolerance in the Light [of] Contemporary Jain Literature," VI (1958), pp. 269–72; "'Ālamgīr's Grant to a Brahmin," VII (1959), pp. 99–100. See also S. M. Jaffar, "Religious Views of Akbar and Aurangzeb as Disclosed by Contemporary Archives," *The Proceedings of the All Pakistan History Conference, First Session, Karachi, 1951* (Karachi: Pakistan Historical Society, 1952), pp. 271–75.

215. For examples, see Hardy, "The Growth of Authority," pp. 202, 205, 208; N. Venkataramanayya, *Early Muslim Expansion in South India* (Madras: University of Madras, 1942), pp. 121–22.

216. W. Doderet, "A Fourteenth Century Marathi Inscription," *Bulletin of the School of Oriental and African Studies* 5 (1930), pp. 37–42, recording the trust established by the minister of a local ruler of the Koṇkaṇ for offerings to be used in temple worship; the inscription is dated 769 according to the Islamic *hijrī* calendar (1367 C.E.), and therefore assumes some kind of Muslim overlord.

217. Speros Vryonis, *The Decline of Medieval Hellenism in Asia Minor and the Process of Islamization from the Eleventh through the Fifteenth Century* (Berkeley: University of California Press, 1971), p. 402.

218. Ibid., p. 356.

219. Hardy, "The Growth of Authority," p. 194.

220. Avasthy and Ghosh, "References to Muhammadans in Sanskrit Inscriptions," p. 181, no. 46.

221. For South Asia as "the realm of the universal Emperor," see Wink, *Land and Sovereignty in India*, p. 16.

222. D. C. Sircar, *Studies in Indian Coins* (Delhi: Motilal Banarsidass, 1968), p. 19.

223. Dines Chandra Sircar, *Select Inscriptions bearing on Indian History and Civilization*, vol. II (Delhi: Motilal Banarsidass, 1983), pp. 650–51; idem, *Studies in Indian Coins*, p. 19. This Sanskrit version of the Muslim profession of faith forms an interesting counterpart to the first Muslim coins struck in North Africa in the seventh century, which contained a similar formula in Latin: *non est deus nisi solus deus cui non socius alius*, "there is no god but the one God who has no partner"; cf. K. A. C. Creswell, *Early Muslim Architecture*, 2 vols. (2nd ed., New York: Hacker Art Books, 1979), I, 131.

224. Sircar, *Select Inscriptions*, pp. 653–65, 673. More complete listings can be found in Edward Thomas, *The Chronicles of the Pathan Kings of Dehli* (Delhi: Munshiram Manoharlal, 1967), and in H. Nelson Wright, *The Coinage and Metrology of the Sulṭāns of Dehlī* (Delhi: Manager of Publications, Government of India, 1936).

225. S. K. Bhuyan, *Annals of the Delhi Badshahate, Being a translation of the old Assamese chronicle Pādshāh-Buranji* (Gauhati: Government of Assam, Department of Historical and Antiquarian Studies, 1947), pp. 55–56, 58.

226. The name of the priest, Sarbabhaum, has overtones of the Indian concept of world dominion, Sanskrit *sārvabhauma* meaning "possessing the entire earth"; see Wink, *Land and Sovereignty*, p. 16, n. 31.

227. Ibid., pp. 74, 76.

228. A curious later example is the genealogy that the Ranas of Udaipur constructed on the basis of the Persian *Shāh nāma*, tracing their descent from Persian shah Nūshīrvān's son Noshizad and the daughter of the Roman emperor. The Sisodia Rajputs likewise at one time claimed to be descended from Mahā Bānū, daughter of Yazdigard, the last Sāsānian king of Iran. These adoptions of Iranian royal genealogy by Rajputs show how compelling the authority of Persian kingship could be. Cf. James Tod, *Annals and Antiquities of Rajast'han, or The Central and Western Rajpoots of India*, 2 vols. (London: George Routledge & Sons Limited, 1914 [reprint of 1829–32 ed.]), I, 192.

229. Vasundhara Filliozat, *Épigraphie de Vijayanagar du début à 1377* (Paris: École Française d'Extrême Orient, 1973), p. 23, no. 35; p. 24, no. 36; p. 41, no. 50; p. 90, no. 101; p. 130, no. 138. In Sanskrit, *suratrāṇa* is the attested rendering of the Arabic title *sulṭān*; see Avasthy and Ghosh, "References to Muhammadans in Sanskrit Inscriptions," p. 180, no. 44.

230. Hermann Kulke, "Ein hinduistischer Tempel unter muslimischer Herrschaft," *Saeculum* 27 (1976), pp. 366–75.

231. Prof. Srinivasachari, "Gingee," in Habib and Nizami, pp. 1106–08; George W. Spencer, "Crisis of Authority in a Hindu Temple under the Impact of Islam: Srirangam in the Fourteenth Century," in *Religion and the Legitimation of Power in South Asia*, ed. Bardwell Smith (Leiden: E. J. Brill, 1978). A related literary work is the Sanskrit *Madhurā Vijaya* by Gangādevi, queen of Vijayanagar, which describes in the most colorful epic terms the overthrow of the sultanate of Madura (Maʿbar) in the late fourteenth century. See Chaitanya, p. 282; S. Selvin Kumar, "A Case Study of Madura Vijayam," in *Bias in Indian Historiography*, ed. Devahuti (Delhi: D. K. Publications, 1980), pp. 236–39; and K. A. Nilakanta Sastri, *Sources of Indian History with Special Reference to South India* (New York: Asia Publishing House, n.d.), p. 83.

232. Wink, *Land and Sovereignty in India*, p. 218.

233. K. A. Nizami, "The Early Turkish Sultans of Delhi," in Habib and Nizami, p. 219, citing ʿAbd al-Razzāq's *al-Ḥawādith al-jāmiʿa* (Baghdad), p. 263, and Baranī, pp. 103–5, who tells of Qāżī Jalāl ʿArūs bringing from the caliph in Baghdad a book written by the caliph al-Ma'mūn, detailing the pious behavior of the caliph Hārūn al-Rashīd. The latter account sounds suspiciously like the other fictitious ancient books that Baranī concocted in his *Fatāwā-i jahāndārī*.

234. Abdul Karim, *Social History of the Muslims in Bengal (Down to A.D. 1538)* (Dacca: Asiatic Society of Pakistan, 1959), p. 47.

235. Thomas W. Arnold, *The Caliphate* (Oxford: Clarendon Press, 1924; reissued with an additional chapter by Sylvia G. Haim, Lahore: Oxford University Press, 1965), p. 87.

236. Arnold, p. 105.

237. K. A. Nizami, "Muhammad Bin Tughluq," in Habib and Nizami, pp. 537–83.

238. Fīrūz Shāh, *Futūḥāt-i Fīrūz Shāhī*, ed. Shaikh Abdur Rashid (Aligarh: Department of History, Muslim University, 1954), pp. 18–19; Arnold, p. 105.

239. Mahdi Husain, *Tughluq Dynasty* (Calcutta: Thacker Spinck & Co. [1933] Pvt. Ltd., 1963), p. 277; Nizami, "Muhammad Bin Tughluq," in Habib and Nizami, p. 537.

240. Arnold J. Toynbee, *A Study of History* (London: Oxford University Press, 1954), VII, 7–16.

241. R. P. Tripathi, *Some Aspects of Muslim Administration in India*, pp. 36–37, cited in Habib and Nizami, p. 284. Claims of caliphal support by minor kings in India were in the same way challenges to Tughluq supremacy; cf. the claim of the sultan of Maʿbar, Nāṣir al-Dīn Maḥmūd Damghān Shāh, in a coin of 745/1344–45, claiming to be "helper of the Commander of the Faithful," cited by S. A. Q. Husaini, "The Sultanate of Maʿbar," in *History of Medieval Deccan (1295–1724)*, ed. H. K. Sherwani and P. M. Joshi (2 vols., Hyderabad: Government of Andhra Pradesh, 1973–74), I, 65.

242. Minhāj-i Sirāj, *Ṭabaqāt-i Nāṣirī*, pp. 639–40; not translated by Raverty, II, 858, on the grounds that it was "scarcely worth insertion here."

243. Arnold, pp. 106, 109–11.

244. Badr-i Chāch, *Qaṣā'id*, with *Farhang* by Muḥammad Hādī ʿAlī (Cawnpore: Nawal Kishor, 1884), pp. 14 (lines 1–4, 7, 9, 10), 15 (lines 3, 6).

245. Some other odes of Badr-i Chāch are translated by Sir Henry Elliot in Elliot and Dowson, II, 567–73.

246. Āzād Bilgrāmī, *Khizāna-i ʿĀmira*, cited by Shiblī Nuʿmānī, *Shiʿr al-ʿajam* (Islamabad: National Book Foundation, 1972 [1341]), IV, 125.

247. Amīr Khusraw, *Dīwān-i nihāyat al-kamāl*, ed. Sayyid Yāsīn ʿAlī Niẓāmī Dihlawī (Delhi: Maṭbaʿ-i Qayṣariyya, 1332), pp. 42, 43.

248. Mohammad Wahid Mirza, *The Life and Works of Amir Khusrau* (Delhi: Idarah-i Adabiyat-i Delli, 1974), p. 126, n. 4.

249. S. A. Q. Husaini, "The Sultanate of Maʿbar," in Sherwani and Joshi, I, 65.

250. ʿIṣāmī, *Futūḥ al-salāṭīn*, ed. Mahdī Ḥusayn (Agra, 1938), p. 573. Jalāl al-Dīn Muḥammad Shāh, sultan of Bengal, claimed the title of caliph in coins minted in 824/1430, although he had previously received investiture from the caliph in Egypt and acknowledged it in earlier coinage (Abdul Karim, *Social History of the Muslims in Bengal*, p. 47).

251. Muḥammad ʿAbd al-Jabbār Mulkapūrī, *Tazkira-i salāṭīn-i Dakan*, vol. I, *Dar bayān-i salāṭīn-i Bahmaniyya* (Hyderabad: Maṭbaʿ-i Fakhr-i Niẓāmī, n.d.), p. 70.

252. ʿAyn al-Dīn Bījāpūrī, *Mulḥaqāt-i ṭabaqāt-i Nāṣirī*, quoted by ʿAbd al-Jabbār Mulkapūrī, *Tazkira-i salāṭīn-i Dakan*, p. 239 (ʿAyn al-Dīn's work is no longer available, since ʿAbd al-Jabbār's unique copy was destroyed).

253. Meier, *Abū Saʿīd*, pp. 327–29, surveys examples of this "hagiographic motif."

254. See my "From Hagiography to Martyrology," pp. 325–26.

255. A. K. S. Lambton, "The Theory of Kingship in the *Nasihat ul-Muluk* of Ghazali," in *Theory and Practice in Medieval Persian Government* (London: Variorum Reprints, 1980), p. 51.

256. A. K. S. Lambton, "Quis Custodiet Custodes: Some Reflections on the Persian Theory of Government, I," in *Theory and Practice in Medieval Persian Government*, pp. 137–38, citing Rāzī's *Mirṣād al-ʿibād*; cf. the translation by Hamid Algar, *The Path of God's Bondsmen from Origin to Return*, Persian Heritage Series, no. 35 (Delmar, N.Y.: Caravan Books, 1982).

257. Lambton, "Quis Custodiet Custodes," p. 147.

258. Lambton, "The Theory of Kingship," p. 148; Afsar Saleem Khan, Introduction to Baranī, p. 120.

259. Sayyid Muḥammad Mubārak al-ʿAlawī al-Kirmāni Mīr Khwurd, *Siyar al-awliyā'*, (Delhi: Maṭbaʿ-i Muḥibb-i Hind, 1302/1884–85; reprint ed., Islamabad: Markaz-i Taḥqīqat-i Fārsī-i Īrān u Pākistān, 1398/1978), pp. 322–23.

260. Afsar Saleem Khan, Introduction to Baranī, pp. 24–25.

261. Baranī, *Fatāwā*, pp. 21–23; Baranī as usual provides a spurious ancient source for the story, in this case a *Tārīkh-i khulafā-i ʿAbbāsī* ascribed to the philologian al-Aṣmāʿī.

262. Afsar Saleem Khan, Introduction to Baranī, pp. 49–53.

263. Khaliq Ahmad Nizami, "Introduction," in Ḥamīd Qalandar, comp., *Khayr al-Majālis*, ed. Khaliq Ahmad Nizami (Aligarh: Department of History, Muslim University, 1959), pp. 49–58.

264. ʿAbd al-Raḥmān ibn Aḥmad Jāmī, *Nafaḥāt al-uns min ḥażarāt al-quds*, ed. Mahdī Tawḥīdīpūr (Tehran: Kitābfurūshī Maḥmūdī, 1337/1959), pp. 323–31.

265. Bruce B. Lawrence, "The *Lawā'iḥ* of Qāḍī Ḥamīd ad-dīn Nāgaurī," *Indo-Iranica* 20 (1975), pp. 34–53; id., *Notes from a Distant Flute, The Extant Literature of pre-Mughal Indian Sufism* (Tehran: Imperial Iranian Academy of Philosophy, 1978), pp. 60–62.

266. See my "From Hagiography to Martyrology," pp. 317ff.

267. The collection of Abū Yazīd's sayings by al-Sahlajī, *Kitāb al-nūr min kalimāt Abī Ṭayfūr*, was edited by ʿAbd al-Raḥmān Badawī as *Shaṭaḥāt al-Ṣūfiyya*,

part 1, *Abū Yazīd al-Bisṭāmī*, Darasāt Islāmiyya 9 (Cairo, 1949). Louis Massignon reconstructed the traditional body of Ḥallāj's sayings in *Akhbār al-Ḥallāj, Recueil d'oraisons et d'exhortations du martyr mystique de l'Islam*, ed. and trans. Louis Massignon and Paul Kraus, Études Musulmanes IV (3rd ed., Paris: Librairie Philosophique J. Vrin, 1957).

268. Fritz Meier, *Abū Saʿīd*, pp. 19–21.

269. Ibid., p. 22, n. 9.

270. Jalāl al-Dīn Rūmī, *Fīhi mā fīhi*, ed. Badīʿ al-Zamān Furūzānfar (Tehran: Shirkat-i Sihāmī-i Nāshirīn-i Kutub-i Īrān, 1338/1959); A. J. Arberry, trans., *Discourses of Rūmī* (London: John Murray, 1961).

271. Muḥammad Taqī Bahār, *Sabk-shināsī yā tārīkh-i taṭawwur-i nasr-i Fārsī* (2nd ed., 3 vols.; Tehran: Mu'assasa-i Chāp wa Intishārāt-i Amīr-i Kabīr, 1337/1959), II, 198.

272. Meier, p. 21.

273. Ziya-ul-Hasan Faruqi, trans., "Fawa'id-ul-Fu'ad of Khwajah Hasan Dehlawi," *Islam and the Modern Age* 13 (1982), 33–44, 126–41, 169–80, 210–28; 14 (1983), 195–213; 15 (1984), 25–36, 167–92; 16 (1985), 231–42, etc. Bruce B. Lawrence's complete translation of *Fawā'id al-fu'ād* is forthcoming. For a description of several other *malfūẓāt*, see Khaliq Ahmad Nizami, "Historical Significance of the Malfuz Literature of Medieval India," in his *On History and Historians of Medieval India* (New Delhi: Munshiram Manoharlal Publishers Pvt. Ltd., 1982), pp. 163–97.

274. Amīr Ḥasan ʿAlā' Sijzī, *Fawā'id al-Fu'ād*, ed. Muḥammad Laṭīf Malik (Lahore: Malik Sirāj al-Dīn and Sons, Publishers, 1386/1966). The text is divided into five "books" recording the sessions of Niẓām al-Dīn in chronological order, from Shaʿbān 707/January 1308 to Shaʿbān 722/August 1322.

275. On the works of Ḥasan, see M. I. Borah, "The Life and Works of Amir Hasan Dihlavi," *Journal of the Royal Asiatic Society of Bengal, Letters* VII (1941), 1–59; Ḥasan Dihlawī, *Dīwān*, ed. Masʿūd ʿAlī Maḥwī (Hyderabad: Ibrahimiyah Steam Press, 1352/1933). The name "Sanjarī" sometimes attached to Ḥasan derives from a mistaken reading of "Sijzī" (i.e., from Seistan in eastern Iran).

276. Mīr Khwurd, *Siyar al-awliyā'*, p. 318. See also Borah, p. 52.

277. Ḥasan Sijzī, *Fawā'id al-fu'ād*, p. 49.

278. Ibid., pp. 50–51.

279. Ibid., p. 39.

280. Ibid., p. 199.

281. Mīr Khwurd (pp. 362–63) quotes an Arabic document in the handwriting of Niẓām al-Dīn, praising Abū Hurayra and his mantle, and equating it as a repository of knowledge with the cloak (*khirqa*) of ʿAlī, the very same cloak with which Muḥammad wrapped ʿAlī, Ḥasan, Ḥusayn, and Fāṭima as the "people of the house" (*ahl al-bayt*).

282. Barani, *Tārīkh-i Firūz Shāhī*, p. 347, as quoted by Nizami, *Thirteenth Century*, p. 198.

283. Lawrence, *Notes*, p. 45, referring to *Durar-i Niẓāmiyya* (MS 183 Persian, Buhar Collection, National Library, Calcutta). Cf. Nizami, "Introduction," in Ḥamīd Qalandar, comp., *Khayr al-majālis*, p. 1.

284. Muḥammad Shakīl Aḥmad Ṣiddīqī, *Amīr Ḥasan Sijzī Dihlawī, ḥayāt awr adabī khidmāt* (Lucknow: Muḥammad Shakīl Aḥmad Ṣiddīqī, 1979), pp. 218–71.

285. Nizami, *Thirteenth Century*, p. 374.

286. Lawrence, *Notes*, pp. 28–30, translating *Khayr al-majālis*, *majlis* 18, pp. 69–70.

287. Ḥamīd Qalandar, *Khayr al-majālis*, p. 31.

288. Ibid., p. 218.

289. Muḥammad Gīsū Darāz, *Jawāmiʿ al-kalim*, p. 134, cited by Nizami, Introduction to *Khayr al-majālis*, p. 5, n. 2.

290. Ibid., p. 47.

291. Paul Jackson, "Khair Al-Majalis: An Examination," in *Islam in India: Studies and Commentaries*, vol. 2, *Religion and Religious Education*, ed. Christian W. Troll (Delhi: Vikas Publishing House Pvt Ltd., 1985), pp. 34–57.

292. K. A. Nizami, Introduction to *Khayr al-majālis*, p. 6 (citing *Jawāmiʿ al-kalim*, p. 135).

293. Ḥamīd Qalandar, *Khayr al-majālis*, p. 279.

294. Ibid., pp. 123–24. Jackson ("Khair Al-Majalis," p. 35) too hastily dismissed this type of anecdote in his analysis of the text.

295. Kendall A. Folkert, "The 'Canons' of 'Scripture,'" in *Rethinking Scripture: Essays from a Comparatives Perspective*, ed. Miriam Levering (Albany: State University of New York Press, 1989), pp. 170–79.

296. Ḥamīd Qalandar, *Khayr al-majālis*, pp. 8–9. This book is not extant. According to the seventeenth-century biographer Khwīshagī, the book was entitled *Nafā'is al-anfās* (*Maʿārij al-wilāya* I, 347, cited by Nizami, *Khayr al-majālis*, p. 4, n. 1); this is quite unlikely, however, in view of Burhān al-Dīn Gharīb's *malfūẓāt* of the same name compiled by Rukn al-Dīn Kāshānī, which was well-known in the Deccan, according to Rukn al-Dīn's brother Ḥammād al-Dīn (*Gharā'ib*, p. 3).

297. *Khayr al-majālis*, pp. 9–10.

298. Ibid., pp. 284–85.

299. Ibid., p. 10.

300. Ibid., p. 12.

301. Ibid., p. 279.

302. Majd al-Dīn Kāshānī, *Gharā'ib al-karāmāt*, MS Fariduddin Saleem, Khuldabad. In the introduction the author states that it was written after Rukn al-Dīn's *Nafā'is al-anfās* and Ḥammād al-Dīn's *Aḥsan al-aqwāl*, and the formulas used in benediction of Burhān al-Dīn Gharīb (*ṭayyaba allāhu marqadahu*) indicate that it was written after the latter's death, possibly with additions as late as 766/1364–65.

303. *Gharā'ib al-karāmāt*, p. 14. This incident, which occurs as the first *mukāshafat* or revelation in the book, has a certain prominence, mirroring that given to the contrary story, which Ḥamīd Qalandar likewise put at the beginning of his book.

304. Ibid., p. 31.

305. Rukn al-Dīn Dabīr Kāshānī, *Nafā'is al-anfās*, MS Fariduddin Saleem, Khuldabad, containing 135 pages. Another copy exists at the library of Nadwat al-ʿUlama' academy in Lucknow.

306. *Nafā'is al-anfās*, p. 3.

307. Ibid.

308. Ibid., p. 4.

309. Ibid., p. 10.

310. Ḥammād al-Dīn Kāshānī, *Aḥsan al-aqwāl*, MS in collection of Mr. Fariduddin Saleem, Khuldabad, containing 149 pages, copied by Fayż Muḥammad son of Ḥāfiẓ Āmīn in 1130/1718. Another MS is in the collection of K. A. Nizami, Aligarh; cf. Khaliq Ahmad Nizami, "A Note on *Ahsan-al-Aqwal*," *Journal of the Pakistan Historical Society* 3 (1955), pp. 40–44. Additional copies are found at Aligarh (no. FM 318) and Osmania University (nos. 478 and 1479).

311. E.g., the use of the word *khayr* (good) instead of *na* (not) as a negative (cf. modern Persian *nakhayr*, "no"), to ward off ill omen, as in the phrase *khayr dānam*, "I do not know" (a few examples are seen in *Aḥsan al-aqwāl*, pp. 14, 44, 68). This habit of speech can still be observed in Punjabi and in Turkish today.

312. Ḥammād al-Dīn Kāshānī Chishtī, *Aḥsan al-aqwāl Urdū al-maʿrūf bi-afżal al-maqāl*, trans. Muḥammad ʿAbd al-Majīd (Hyderabad, 1342; reprint ed., Miraj: Ganj Bakhsh Publications, 1987). There are notable discrepancies between the Khuldabad MS and the Urdu translation, with a significant number of practices appearing in one text but not the other.

313. Ḥammād al-Dīn, *Aḥsan al-aqwāl*, p. 147.

314. Ibid., p. 141.

315. Ibid., p. 4.

316. Majd al-Dīn Kāshānī, *Gharā'ib al-karāmāt wa ʿajā'ib al-mukāshafāt*, MS in collection of Mr. Fariduddin Saleem, Khuldabad, containing 83 pages. The copy was begun 1 Muḥarram 1315 (June 2, 1897) and completed 15 Dhū al-Qaʿda 1317 (April

16, 1900), copied in a ragged hand by Muḥammad Walī Allāh wuld-i Ḥājī Walī Muḥammad. Another copy is in the Salar Jung Museum Library, Hyderabad, MS 876 Tarājim Fārsiyya. A copy is supposed to exist in the Andhra Pradesh State Oriental Manuscript Library, Hyderabad (formerly the Āṣafiyya Library), but I was unable to get access to it. A MS was reported to be in the library of the Panchakki Khānqāh in Awrangabad (now in custody of the Awqaf Department of Maharashtra), but a search in 1981 proved fruitless; cf. "Literary Treasures of Aurangabad," *Islamic Culture* XVI (1942), p. 451, note.

317. Ibid., p. 3.

318. Ibid., pp. 6–12.

319. *Nafā'is al-anfās*, pp. 100, 123.

320. *Gharā'ib al-karāmāt*, pp. 17–18, 22, 39, 43, 45, 46, 49, 74, 75.

321. Ibid., pp. 13–16, 18, 23, 25, 26, 28, 30, 33–35, 37, 39, 42, 44, 47.

322. I am not aware of the existence of any copies of this text, but some quotations are given in the standard modern Urdu hagiography of Khuldabad by Rawnaq ʿAlī, *Rawżat al-aqṭāb al-maʿrūf bi-maẓhar-i āṣafiyya* (Lucknow: Dilgudāz Press, 1931), and in the translator's notes to the 1739 hagiography by Ghulām ʿAlī Āzād Bilgrāmī, *Rawżat al-awliyā'* pp. 13, 19, 25, 31–32, 41, 45, 86, 135.

323. Majd al-Dīn, *Gharā'ib al-karāmāt*, p. 12.

324. Rukn al-Dīn ibn ʿImād al-Dīn Dabīr Kāshānī Khuldābādī, *Shamā'il al-atqiyā'*, ed. Sayyid ʿAṭā' Ḥusayn, Silsila-i Ishāʿat al-ʿUlūm, 85 (Hyderabad: Maṭbūʿa Ashraf Press, 1347). A few fascicles of an earlier and somewhat defective edition were published by Shāh Khayrat Ḥusayn Firdawsī (Hyderabad: Abū al-Maʿālī, 1326/1908), but it was never completed, due to a flood that destroyed the press (Sayyid ʿAṭā' Ḥusayn, introduction to *Shamā'il al-atqiyā'*, p. 4). The editor of the Ashraf Press lithograph used as the basis for the edition a MS dated Shaʿbān 1151 (November 1738), and compared it with MSS dated Ṣafar 998 (December 1589), Rabīʿ I 1245 (September 1829, in the Āṣafiyya collection), and Rabīʿ I 1334 (January 1916, a Khuldabad MS). Other examples are MS 1836 Persian (Ethé), India Office Library, London, and MS 29767/14, Subḥān Allāh Collection, Aligarh Muslim University, Aligarh.

325. An annotated translation of this "Sufi bookshelf" forms Appendix A.

326. These works include Rukn al-Dīn's *Rumūz al-wālihīn* (68 citations), his *Tafsīr-i rumūz* (perhaps the same work, 10 citations), and two writings by Ḥammād al-Dīn: *Ḥuṣūl al-wuṣūl* (6 citations) and *Asrār al-ṭarīqat* (5 citations). It is tempting to speculate that the frequently mentioned *Risāla-i gharīb* (49 citations) was written by a member of this circle, but its authorship is nowhere indicated.

327. Jonathan Z. Smith, "Sacred Persistence: Toward a Redescription of Canon," in his *Imagining Religion: From Babylon to Jonestown* (Chicago: University of Chicago Press, 1978), p. 45.

328. Rukn al-Dīn, *Shamā'il al-atqiyā'*, p. 3.

329. Shams Allāh Qādirī, *Urdū-i qadīm* (Lucknow: Tej Kumār, 1967), pp. 118–19, citing the Urdu translation of *Shamā'il al-atqiyā'* by the Quṭbshāhī-era writer Mīrān Yaʿqūb in 1078/1667–68, MS 663 Taṣawwuf Urdu, Āṣafiyya collection; ibid., appendix, pp. 56–57, giving an excerpt. A more extensive sample of the Urdu translation is found in Sayyida Jaʿfar, *Dakanī nasr kā intikhāb* (New Delhi: Taraqqī Urdu Bureau, 1983), pp. 104–20. A scholar at Marathwada University in Aurangabad is preparing a modern Hindi translation of *Shamā'il al-atqiyā'* for publication, on the basis of the Urdu version.

330. Burhān al-Dīn Gharīb is quoted in *Shamā'il al-atqiyā'* by name sixteen times (pp. 21, 47, 53, 68, 69, 98, 137, 151, 201, 232–33, 238, 316, 382, 383, 384, 381), and as "the revered master" (*khidmat-i khwāja*) another sixteen times (pp. 52, 53, 68, 137, 149, 168, 207, 210, 213, 217, 222, 252, 261, 276, 281, 418).

331. Rukn al-Dīn, *Shamā'il al-atqiyā'*, p. 4.

332. Baranī, in Nizami, *Thirteenth Century*, p. 197.

333. Lawrence, *Notes*, pp. 21, 97; K. A. Nizami, "The *Sarur-u's-Sudur*," *Proceedings of the Indian History Congress, Nagpur Session* (1950), pp. 167–69.

334. Ḥasan Sijzī, *Fawā'id al-fu'ād*, p. 76.

335. Mohammad Habib, "Chishti Mystics Records of the Sultanate Period," *Medieval India Quarterly* 1 (1950), pp. 1–42; reprinted in *Politics and Society During the Early Medieval Period, Collected Works of Professor Mohammad Habib*, vol. I, ed. K. A. Nizami (New Delhi: People's Publishing House, 1974), pp. 385–433, esp. pp. 401–25.

336. See also Khaliq Ahmad Nizami, *The Life and Times of Shaikh Farid-u'd-Din Ganj-i-Shakar*, IAD Religio-Philosophy Series no. 1 (Delhi: Idarah-i Adabiyat-i Delli, 1955; reprint ed., 1973), pp. 118–20; Bruce B. Lawrence, "*Afzal-ul-fawa'id*—a reassessment," in *Life, Times & Works of Amīr Khusrau Dehlavi, Seventh Centenary*, ed. Z. Ansari (New Delhi: National Amīr Khusrau Society, 1976), pp. 119–31.

337. Ibid., p. 124.

338. Habib, "Chishti Mystics Records," I, 430.

339. E.g., Ṣabāḥ al-Dīn ʿAbd al-Raḥmān, *Bazm-i Ṣūfiyya* (Aʿẓamgaṛh: Dār al-Muṣannifīn, 1949).

340. Nizami, Introduction to *Khayr al-majālis*, p. 7.

341. *Anīs al-arwāḥ*, *Dalīl al-ʿārifīn*, *Fawā'id al-sālikīn*, *Rāḥat al-qulūb*, and *Asrār al-mutaḥayyarīn* (a previously unmentioned compilation of Farīd al-Dīn Ganj-i Shakkar's sayings) occupy nos. 102 to 106 in the bibliography, and Amīr Khusraw's *Rāḥat al-muḥibbīn* is no. 149. *Fawā'id al-fu'ād* is no. 107 and *Nafā'is al-anfās* is no. 108. See Appendix A.

342. *Fawā'id al-sālikīn*, cited in *Shamā'il al-atqiyā'*, pp. 31, 46; *Rāḥat al-muḥibbīn*, on pp. 58, 65, 67, 93; *Asrār al-mutaḥayyarīn*, on p. 403.

343. Mīr Ḥasan, *Hidāyat al-qulūb wa ʿināyat ʿullām al-ghuyūb*, MS in collection of Mr. Fariduddin Saleem, Khuldabad, containing 392 pages, but lacking colophon (the last 32 pages are almost completely destroyed). One other copy exists, MS 353 Taṣawwuf Fārsī, Ahdhra Pradesh Oriental Manuscript Research Library [Āṣafiyya], Hyderabad, but I could not get access to it.

344. Ibid., pp. 1–2, recalling by the phrase "pearl-bearing words" both *Fawā'id al-fu'ād*, p. 49, and *Shamā'il al-atqiyā'*, p. 4.

345. On pp. 2, 3, and 4 are given the dates of 7, 8, and 9 Rajab 745/14–16 November 1344; on p. 158, 2 Dhū al-Ḥijja 747/16 March 1347; on p. 245, simply the year 766/1364–65; on p. 262 (apparently out of order), *shab-i barāt* (14 Shaʿbān) 755/3 September 1354; on p. 332, 7 Dhū al-Ḥijja 768/4 August 1367; and on p. 336, 10 Rabīʿ I 769/4 November 1367.

346. *Hidāyat al-qulūb*, pp. 44, 213.

347. Ibid., pp. 102, 124.

348. These texts by Bahā' al-Dīn Zakariyyā include *al-Awrād*, ed. Muḥammad Miyān Ṣiddīqī (Islamabad: Markaz-i Taḥqīqāt-i Fārsī-i Īrān u Pākistān, 1398/1978), a collection of prayers in Arabic for different times and days, aimed at a popular audience; *Shurūṭ al-arbaʿīn fī julūs al-muʿtakifīn*, an Arabic manual on retreat, which has been published with an Urdu translation (Muḥammad Laṭīf Farīdī, *Anwār-i ghawsiyya* [Lahore: Shuʿāʿ-i Adab, 1955]) although the sole MS is now lost; and a short *Risāla* or epistle on Sufi practice, written at the request of a disciple, published by Shamīm Maḥmūd Zaydī, *Aḥwāl u āsār-i Shaykh Bahā' al-Dīn Zakariyyā wa khulāṣat al-ʿārifīn* (Islamabad: Markaz-i Taḥqīqāt-i Fārsī-i Īrān u Pākistān, 1353/1974), pp. 103–9.

349. K. A. Nizami, "Bahā' al-Dīn Zakariyyā," EI², I (1960), p. 912, referring to the fifteenth-century hagiographer Jamālī. The anonymous hagiography entitled *Khulāṣat al-ʿārifīn*, edited by Zaydī, *Aḥwāl u āsār*, pp. 123–71, consists of anecdotes of Bahā' al-Dīn as narrated by the later Suhrawardī master Jalāl al-Dīn Bukhārī (d. 785/1384) and by the Chishtī masters Farīd al-Dīn Ganj-i Shakkar and Niẓām al-Dīn Awliyā'.

350. Lawrence, *Notes*, p. 64, citing the *Kanz al-fawā'id* (sayings of Ṣadr al-Dīn ʿĀrif), the *Majmaʿ al-akhbār* (sayings of Rukn al-Dīn Abū al-Fatḥ), and the *Fatāwā-i Ṣūfiyya* (on both of the latter).

351. Carl Brockelmann, *Geschichte der arabischen Litteratur, Supplementband* (Leiden: E. J. Brill, 1938), II, 310, citing MSS in Leiden, Oxford, Paris, and Istanbul, as well as an abridgement by ʿAlā' al-Dīn Muḥammad al-Ḥiṣnī al-Dimashqī. A brief excerpt is given by Gustavus Fluegel, *Lexicon Bibliographicum et Encyclopædicum a Mustafa ben Abdallah Katib Jelebi Dicto et Nomine Haji Khalfa Celebrato Compositum* (London: Oriental Translation Fund, MDCCCXLV), IV, 360–61.

352. A. S. Bazmee Ansari, "Djalāl al-Dīn Ḥusayn al-Bukhārī," EI² I (1965), 392; Lawrence, *Notes*, p. 69; Riazul Islam, "Collections of the Malfuzat of Makhdum-i-Jahanian (1307–1388) of Uchh," in *The Proceedings of the All Pakistan History*

Conference, First Session, 1951 (Karachi: Pakistan Historical Society, 1952), pp. 211–16.

353. Lawrence, *Notes*, pp. 76–78. See now Paul Jackson's translation of one of Sharaf al-Dīn's *malfūẓāt*, *Khwān-i Pur Niʿmat (A table laden with good things)* (Delhi: Idara-i Adabiyyat-i Delli, 1986).

354. Bruce B. Lawrence, "*Afzal-ul-fawa'id*—a reassessment," pp. 120, 122.

355. Marilyn R. Waldman, "Primitive Mind/Modern Mind: New Approaches to an Old Problem Applied to Islam," in *Approaches to Islam in Religious Studies*, ed. Richard C. Martin (Tucson: The University of Arizona Press, 1985), pp. 91–105.

356. G. H. A. Juynboll, *The Authenticity of the Tradition Literature: Discussions in Modern Egypt* (Leiden: E. J. Brill, 1969), pp. 71, 87.

357. Wilfred Cantwell Smith, "Scripture as Form and Concept," in *Rethinking Scripture: Essays from a Comparatives Perspective*, ed. Miriam Levering (Albany: State University of New York Press, 1989), p. 45.

358. Mīr Khwurd, pp. 372–74.

359. Currie, pp. 39, 49, 55–56.

360. Mohammad Habib, "Chishti Mystics Records," pp. 392–93.

361. Mīr Khwurd, pp. 262–83.

362. Kamāl al-Dīn held the title Ṣadr-i Jahān, or minister in charge of charitable trusts, under both Ghiyās al-Dīn Tughluq and Muḥammad ibn Tughluq; cf. Baranī, *Tārīkh-i Fīrūz Shāhī*, pp. 428, 454, Urdu trans., pp. 613, 649.

363. Mīr Khwurd, pp. 283–85.

364. *Fawā'id al-fu'ād*, pp. 415–16.

365. *Nafā'is al-anfās*, p. 66.

366. Ibn Battutah, trans. Gibb, pp. 95, 256; *Nafā'is al-anfās*, p. 130. The same story of the dervishes and the mother elephant is told without names by Rūmī in his *Masnavī* (III, 69–171); cf. Reynold A. Nicholson, ed. and trans., *The Mathnawí of Jalálud'dín Rúmí*, "E. J. W. Gibb Memorial" Series IV (8 vols., London, 1925–40; reprint ed., London: Luzac & Co. Ltd., 1977), translation vol. II, 8–13, lines 69–171.

367. Bahā' al-Dīn Maḥmūd Nāgawrī Chishtī, *Urdū tarjuma-i kitāb-i sirr al-ʿārifīn yaʿnī ḥālāt-i mashāyikh-i Chishtiyya* (Lahore: Allāh Wālē kī Qawmī Dukān, 1974). A Persian MS copy is in the collection of K. A. Nizami in Aligarh; cf. *Tārīkh-i mashāyikh-i Chisht* (2nd ed., Delhi: Idāra-i Adabiyyat-i Dellī, 1980–85), I, 192, n. 2. This text appears to be the same as the one by Bahā' al-Dīn entitled *Asrār al-mashāyikh* found in the Āṣafiyya catalogue (III, 362, no. 192).

368. This branch of the Chishtiyya derives from Quṭb al-Dīn Bakhtiyār Kākī through Badr al-Dīn Ghaznavī and Shihāb al-Dīn ʿĀshiq to ʿImād al-Dīn. For references, see Niẓāmī, *Tārīkh*, I, 211–12.

369. Bahā' al-Dīn Nāgawrī, *Ḥālāt*, p. 130.

370. The section on saints in Firishta's *Gulshan-i Ibrāhīmī* (Lucknow: Nawal Kishor, 1281/1864–65) occupies pp. 374–418.

371. The historical works of Badā'ūnī and Abū al-Fażl contain more or less extensive biographical sections on Sufis, as do many of the chronicles of regions such as Gujarat.

372. Examples of authors who wrote both religious and political histories are Muḥammad Ṣādiq, author of a hagiography (*Kalimāt al-ṣādiqīn*), a court history (*Ṣubḥ-i ṣādiq*), and an important mixed biographical work (*Ṭabaqāt-i Shāhjahānī*); and ʿĀqil Khān Rāzī (d. 1108/1696), who wrote both a history of Awrangzīb and a *malfūẓāt* of his Sufi master Burhān al-Dīn Rāz-i Ilāhī.

373. Examples that come to mind include the account of Muḥammad Chishtī assisting Maḥmūd of Ghazna's raid on Somnath, cited by Jāmī and quoted in the *Mir'āt-i Masʿūdī*, in Elliot and Dowson, II, 525. The traditional accounts of Muʿīn al-Dīn Chishtī's role in assisting the Ghūrid conquest of Ajmer call for reconsideration in this light.

374. The vast Persian hagiographical literature, much of it produced in India, is described in C. A. Storey's *Persian Literature: A Bio-bibliographical Survey,* 2 vols. (London: Luzac & Co. Ltd., 1927–71), I, 923–1067. A useful survey in Urdu, focusing on the Mughul period, is found in Ẓuhūr al-Dīn Aḥmad, "Awliyā'-i kirām kē tazkirē," in *Tārīkh-i adabiyyāt-i Musulmānān-i Pākistān u Hind*, ed. Maqbūl Beg Badakhshī, vol. 4, part 2, *Fārṣī adab (1526–1707)* (Lahore: Punjab University, 1971), pp. 620–57. See also Marcia K. Hermansen, "Interdisciplinary Approaches to Islamic Biographical Materials," *Religion* 18 (1988), pp. 163–82.

375. Muḥammad Ghaws Gwāliyārī, *Awrād-i ghawsiyya* (MS 446 Persian Curzon, Asiatic Society, Calcutta), fols. 97b-107b.

376. See my *Words of Ecstasy*, pp. 124–25.

377. Eric Voegelin, *The Ecumenic Age*, pp. 2–6, 64–67.

378. Bruce B. Lawrence, "Biography and the 17th-Century Qadiriyya of North India," paper presented at the conference on Regional Varieties of Islam in Premodern India, University of Heidelberg, July 1989.

379. Cf. Storey, *Persian Literature*, I, 855–66.

380. This work is best accessible in the Urdu translation by ʿAbd al-Majīd, which contains many footnotes and six appendices, providing useful information taken from sources that are now lost.

381. Sabzawārī, *Sawāniḥ*, MS 285 Persian, Asiatic Society, Calcutta. Another copy is supposed to be at Osmania University, Hyderabad, under the title *Tazkira-i awliyā'-i Dawlatābād*.

382. Rawnaq ʿAlī, *Rawẓat al-aqṭāb al-maʿrūf ba-maẓhar-i Āṣafī* (Lucknow: Dil-gudāz Press, 1349/1931).

383. Rawnaq ʿAlī, pp. 11–16. Some of these texts, such as *Bāqiyat al-karāmāt* and *Dalīl al-sālikīn* (an abridgement of *Hidāyat al-qulūb*), are no longer available.

384. Muḥammad ʿAlī Khān's *Tazkira-i awliyā'-i Khuldābād Sharīf* (Hyderabad: Commercial Book Depot, n.d.) is part of a series of local hagiographies of Deccan towns; Nūr al-Dīn wuld Muḥammad ʿUmar's *Taʿāruf chand awliyā'-i ikrām Khuldābād sharīf* (Aurangabad: Āzād Printers, n.d.) contains notes on various saints' and kings' tombs.

385. This booklet, entitled *Rawża-i sharīf*, was published in the 1930s, according to local scholars in Khuldabad, but I have not seen any copy. Kishen Pershad's interest in Sufism is hinted at by Harriet Ronken Lynton and Mohini Rajan, *The Days of the Beloved* (New Delhi: Orient Longman Limited, 1974; reprint ed., 1988), p. 124.

386. Waḥīda Nasīm, *Shāhān-i bē-tāj* (Karachi: Maktaba Āṣafiyya, 1988). The author has enthusiastically published here (pp. 9–10) some correspondence from me about her poem, as well as (pp. 155–63) my preliminary summaries of the Khuldabad Mughul revenue documents (above, Appendix C). Thus even the foreign researcher enters into hagiography.

Part Two

1. In what follows, no reference will be made to the didactic Persian poem *Tuḥfat al-naṣā'iḥ*, often attributed to the saint of Khuldabad Yūsuf al-Ḥusaynī Rājū Qattāl, since the researches of Simon Digby have decisively ruled out that attribution; cf. his "The *Tuḥfa i naṣā'iḥ* of Yūsuf Gadā: An Ethical Treatise in Verse from the Late Fourteenth-Century Dehlī Sultanate," in *Moral Conduct and Authority: the Place of Adab in South Asian Islam*, ed. Barbara Metcalf (Berkeley: University of California Press, 1983), pp. 91–123.

2. The strictures on the Urdu sources also apply to the massive Arabic biographical dictionary of Indian Muslims by the learned ʿAbd al-Ḥayy ibn Fakhr al-Dīn al-Ḥasanī (d. 1341/1923), *Nuzhat al-khawāṭir wa bahjat al-masāmiʿ wa al-nawāẓir* (9 vols., 2nd ed., Hyderabad: Dā'irat al-maʿārif al-ʿUthmāniyya, 1386/1966–). It draws upon Arabic, Persian, and Urdu sources of all periods, and is by far the most comprehensive reference book of its kind, but its use of sources is completely uncritical.

3. Muhammad Suleman Siddiqi, *The Bahmani Ṣūfīs*, IAD Religio-Philosophy (Original) Series no. 19 (Delhi: Idarah-i Adabiyat-i Delli, 1989), pp. 95–107.

4. ʿAbd al-Ḥayy, II, 88–89, citing an otherwise unknown fourteenth-century *malfūẓāt* text called *Jāmiʿ al-ʿulūm*, also says he had gone to Baghdad and become a disciple of Shaykh Shihāb al-Dīn ʿUmar Suhrawardī himself, the founder of the Suhrawardī order; he quotes a modern Urdu work called *Tārikh al-awliyā'* for the saint's date of death.

5. ʿAbd al-Ḥayy, II, 143, where he is called Rukn al-Dīn ibn Sirāj al-Dīn; cf. Mulkāpūrī, *Tazkira-i awliyā'-i Dakan* I, 391–93, where the only date given is that of his death.

6. ʿAbd al-Ḥayy, II, 167.

7. Ibid., 95–96. Shams al-Dīn Damghānī was a well-known scholar of Delhi who had studied the religious sciences alongside of Niẓām al-Dīn Awliyāʾ; ibid., II, 146. Mulkāpūrī (I, 538–41), which is evidently ʿAbd al-Ḥayy's source, cites the *Rawża-i awliyāʾ-i Bījāpūr* as giving ʿAyn al-Dīn's birth date as 706/1306–7.

8. Firishta, tr. Briggs, II, 310, 319, 350, 398 (Sirāj al-Dīn). On ʿAyn al-Dīn's history, see also ʿAbd al-Ḥayy Ḥabībī's note in al-Juzjānī, *Ṭabaqāt-i Nāṣirī* (Lahore: Dānishgāh-i Panjāb, 1954), II, 829–30.

9. The same is true of most of the figures whose biographies appear in works like Mulkāpūrī's *Tazkira-i awliyaʾ-i Dakan*. Historians like Muḥammad Ikrām have attempted to use these biographies, but the results are not satisfactory; cf. *Āb-i Kawsar*, pp. 357–62, on Sufis in the Deccan before the migration, and p. 364, where he lists several Sufis who may or may not have come to Daulatabad at the time of the migration or by order of Niẓām al-Dīn Awliyāʾ.

10. Eaton, pp. 4–5.

11. Ibid., p. 13.

12. Most reviewers of Eaton's book who criticized this theory have been content merely to deny the existence of Warrior Sufis without offering any sustained objections.

13. Bruce B. Lawrence, "Early Indo-Muslim Saints and Conversion," *Islam in Asia*, vol. I, *South Asia*, ed. Yohanon Friedman (Boulder: Westview Press, 1984), p. 121.

14. Eaton, p. 33.

15. The remarks of John Voll on "neo-Sufism," though presented as an abstract typology, provide a suggestive beginning to understanding the role of Sufism in relation to colonialism; cf. his *Islam: Continuity and Change in the Modern World* (Boulder: Westview Press, 1982), index, s.v. "neo-Sufism."

16. The problem of understanding the "self-sacrificer" (*fidāʾī*) in Islamic history is obviously too large to discuss here, but it may be observed that almost all descriptions of fanaticism, from Marco Polo's story of the assassins down to current journalistic books on terrorism, rest primarily on the evidence of opponents, and do not attempt to consider the self-interpretation of the groups in question.

17. Eaton, pp. 34–38.

18. Ibid., p. 27.

19. *Gharāʾib al-karāmāt*, p. 9, where it is said that Nizām al-Dīn Awliyāʾ ordered 700 or 800 saints to be in the company of Burhān al-Dīn Gharīb.

20. Bilgrami and Willmott, *Historical and Descriptive Sketch of His Highness the Nizām's Dominions* II, 721.

21. Amīr Ḥasan Dihlawī records the presence of Burhān al-Dīn Gharīb in Delhi in sessions occurring in 708/1308–9 and 716/1316 (*Fawā'id al-fu'ād*, pp. 24, 55, 73, 143), and Burhān al-Dīn Gharīb also seems to have been present at the death of Niẓām al-Dīn in 725/1325, if we can rely on the accounts of his obtaining *khilāfat* during the last year of the shaykh's life.

22. Eaton, p. 25.

23. A. Krishnaswami, *The Tamil Country under Vijayanagar* (Annamalainagar: Annamalai University, 1964), p. 22ff.

24. Mahdi Husain, *Tughluq Dynasty*, p. 110. A list of these Sanskrit and Rajasthani sources is given in Habib and Nizami, pp. 1183–85.

25. The presence of names or epithets such as Tīgh-i Barahna (Persian for "naked sword") should not be mistaken for evidence of concrete military activities (Eaton, p. 33). This is simply a rough Persian translation of his Muslim name Ḥusām al-Dīn (Arabic for "sword of the faith"), and the name has given rise to the legend of his always carrying a naked sword, an example of the "onomastic" process familiar to folklorists; cf. *Tazkira-i awliyā'-i Dakan*, I, 394, where the sword emerges from his tomb like excalibur to confirm the authority of Gīsū Darāz over the Deccan. K'handā'it may be the Hindi translation of the same name. A number of Sufis also carried the alarming epithet Qattāl ("killer"), but in the biographical literature this name only applies to those who performed extensive asceticism and meditation, and have "killed" the carnal soul; cf. the eccentric ʿAyn al-Dīn Qattāl, in *Mir'āt al-asrār* (Urdu trans.), II, 455, and the recluse Ṣadr al-Dīn Rājū Qattāl, in *Akhbār al-akhyār*, p. 145.

26. Muḥammad Ikrām accepts these accounts from Mulkāpūrī's *Tazkira-i awliyā'-i Dakan* as factual (*Āb-i Kawsar*, p. 362).

27. Kerrin Graefin V. Schwerin, "Saint Worship in Indian Islam,"pp. 153–54, 157–58.

28. In 1981 I observed villagers performing rituals at the impressive twelfth-century tomb of "Sultan Ghārī," one of the Turkish Ghurid princes buried near Palam west of New Delhi. The participants, when questioned about the identity of the "saint" (*buzurg*) buried there, variously maintained that it was someone who had died quite recently or else hundreds of years ago.

29. W. E. Begley, *Monumental Islamic Calligraphy from India* (Villa Park, Ill.: Islamic Foundation, 1985), p. 25.

30. N. M. Ganam, "Epitaph of Six Martyrs from Bari Khatu in Rajasthan," *Epigraphia Indica, Arabic and Persian Supplement* (1973), pp. 10–14.

31. *Census of India 1961*, vol. X, *Maharashtra*, pt. VII-B, *Fairs and Festivals in Maharashtra* (Delhi: Manager of Publications, Government Central Press, 1969), pp. 207–9.

32. Upendra Nath Day, *Medieval Malwa, A Political and Cultural History, 1401–1562* (Delhi: Munshi Ram Manohar Lal, 1965), p. 436; J. Burton-Page, "Dhār. 2.—Monuments," *Encyclopedia of Islam*, II, 219.

33. Irène Beldiceanu-Steinherr, "La Vita de Seyyid 'Alî Sultan et la conquête de la Thrace par les Turcs," in *Proceedings of the Twenty-Seventh International Congress of Orientalists*, Ann Arbor, Michigan, 13–19 August 1967 (Wiesbaden, 1971), pp. 275–76.

34. Rudi Paul Lindner, *Nomads and Ottomans in Medieval Anatolia*, Indiana University Uralic and Altaic Series, vol. 144 (Bloomington: Research Institute for Inner Asian Studies, Indiana University, 1983), pp. 1–9, 34–36. I owe this reference to Richard Eaton.

35. Ḥamīd Qalandar, *Khayr al-majālis*, pp. 241–42.

36. *Antiquarian Remains in Hyderabad State* (Hyderabad: Archeological Department, 1953), p. 9, no. 11.

37. These were Shams al-Dīn ʿĀdil Shāh (r. 757–61/1356–59) and ʿAlāʾ al-Dīn Sikandar Shāh (r. 774–79/1372–78); cf. S. A. Q. Husaini, "The Sultanate of Maʿbar," in Sherwani and Joshi, I, 68–69.

38. P. M. Joshi, "Economic and Social Conditions under the Bahmanīs," in Sherwani and Joshi, I, 166, 170.

39. Ibid., in Sherwani and Joshi, I, 209 (cf. II, 590).

40. To notice but one example, the traveler Ioannes Oranus observed that some Hindus held Akbar to be the tenth incarnation of Vishnu; cf. J. Talboys, ed., *Early Travels in India (16th & 17th Centuries)* [Calcutta, 1864; reprint ed., Delhi: Deep Publications, 1974], p. 78. Although Abū al-Fażl does not mention this particular gambit, it has the signs of a carefully planted political use of religious symbols. For Akbar, see now Khaliq Ahmad Nizami, *Akbar & Religion* (Delhi: Idarah-i-Adabiyat-i-Delli, 1989).

41. Eaton, p. 38; cf. E. Sachau, trans., *Alberuni's India* (Delhi: S. Chand & Co., 1964 [1888]) I, 17–26.

42. K. A. Nizami, "Foundation of the Delhi Sultanate," in Habib and Nizami, p. 183, quoting Juwaynī's *Tārīkh-i jahān-gushā* (Tehran, 1311), II, 37. Juwaynī says Shihāb al-Dīn Ghūrī was raising an army "under pretext of *ghazwa*" (or holy war) against the Qara Khitai.

43. Peter Jackson, "Delhi: A Vast Military Encampment," in *Delhi Through the Ages*, pp. 21–22, citing Juzjānī's *Ṭabaqāt-i Nāṣirī* (II, 57) on Balban.

44. P. M. Joshi and Mahdi Husain, "Khaljis and Tughluqs in the Deccan," in Sherwani and Joshi, I, 35. The authors suggest that the inscription, and similar claims in later inscriptions, refers to military action against Muslim officials on the coast between Goa and Chaul, but there were no Turkish authorities there at the time. Baranī (*Tārīkh-i Fīrūz-Shāhī*, pp. 222–23, Urdu trans. p. 339) says that the people of Deogir had "never heard of Islam," explaining that "no emperor, khan, or king had reached those regions."

45. Barani, pp. 220–21.

46. P. M. Joshi and Mahdi Husain, "Khaljis and Tughluqs in the Deccan," I, 35, 40.

47. Ibid., I, 41.

48. Mohammad Habib, *Hazrat Amir Khusrau of Delhi* (Lahore: Islamic Book Service, 1979 [reprint of 1927 ed.]), pp. 53–66.

49. Amīr Khusraw, *Khazā'in al-Futūḥ*, trans. Mohammad Habib, p. 90, cited in K. A. Nizami, "Foundation of the Delhi Sultanate," in Habib and Nizami, p. 189.

50. Banarsi Prasad Saksena, "Ghiyasuddin Tughluq," in Habib and Nizami, pp. 469–73.

51. P. B. Desai, "The Foundation of Vijayanagar," in Sherwani and Joshi, I, 138–39.

52. P. L. Gupta, "Coinage," in Sherwani and Joshi, II, 430.

53. Mahdi Husain, *Tughluq Dynasty*, p. 173.

54. K. A. Nizami, "Muhammad Bin Tughluq," in Habib and Nizami, p. 510, citing Yaḥyā Sirhindī, *Tārīkh-i Mubārak Shāhī*, p. 102.

55. K. A. Nizami, "Muhammad Bin Tughluq," in Habib and Nizami, p. 511, quoting Shihāb al-Dīn ʿUmarī's *Maṣālik al-Abṣār*, trans. Otto Spies, pp. 18–19.

56. Ibn Baṭṭūṭa, p. 204.

57. K. A. Nizami, "Muhammad Bin Tughluq," in Habib and Nizami, p. 507.

58. Ibid., in Habib and Nizami, p. 513.

59. *Tughluq Dynasty*, p. 158, estimating that each caravan conveyed two hundred people, for a total of twelve hundred. Husain constructed this figure to agree with a sign on the Daulatabad road that read, "Here came twelve hundred saints," evidently a mistake on his part for the traditional figure of fourteen hundred, still preserved in the name of the Mosque of Fourteen Hundred Saints (Masjid Chahārdih Awliyā') in Khuldabad.

60. K. A. Nizami, "Muhammad Bin Tughluq," in Habib and Nizami, p. 514. For the text of ʿIṣāmī's remarks, see Mahdi Husain, trans., *Futūḥu's Salāṭīn or Shāh Nāmah-i Hind of ʿIṣāmī* (New York: Asia Publishing House, 1977), III, 675–89, lines 8460–64.

61. *Tughluq Dynasty*, p. 173.

62. Ibid., p. 146.

63. Jackson, p. 25, citing *Tughluq Dynasty*, pp. 166–68.

64. *Tughluq Dynasty*, p. 163. Mahdi Husain maintained that the poet Badr-i Chāch also testified to the vitality of Delhi in 727, by writing the city's chronogram in the phrase *fa-dkhulūhā*, "enter it" (ibid., p. 166), but this appears to be a mistake. In

the *Qaṣā'id* of Badr-i Chāch (Kanpur: Nawal Kishore, 1884), p. 90, the phrase is *wa-dkhulū fīhā*, which yields 744, referring to the construction of Khurramabad fort by Ẓahīr al-Juyūsh. The latter noble participated in Sultan Muḥammad ibn Tughluq's struggle against Taghī's rebellion in Gujarat and Ḥasan Bahmanī's revolt in 748/1347; Baranī, *Tārīkh-i Fīrūz Shāhī*, pp. 516, 520, Urdu trans., pp. 729, 735.

65. *Tughluq Dynasty*, p. 173, citing *Maṣālik al-Abṣār*.

66. Jackson, pp. 23–27.

67. Baranī, p. 473 (*khawāṣṣ-i khalq; mardum-i guzīda wa chīda*), cited in Jackson, p. 25, n. 78; cf. *Tughluq Dynasty*, pp. 146ff.

68. *Tughluq Dynasty*, p. 144; Mohammad Habib, in Habib and Nizami, p. 509.

69. K. A. Nizami, "Muḥammad Bin Tughluq," in Habib and Nizami, p. 512.

70. *Nafā'is al-anfās*, p. 125.

71. Mīr Khwurd, pp. 207–8.

72. Mīr Khwurd, p. 296. It was only after ʿAyn al-Mulk's expedition that these cities came under the Delhi administration; cf. Banarsi Prasad Saksena, "Alauddin Khalji," in Habib and Nizami, p. 395.

73. Mīr Khwurd, p. 328; *Akhbār al-akhyār*, p. 110. ʿAbd al-Ḥayy (II, 53–54) points out that Shams al-Dīn's grave is in D'hāraseoñ in the Deccan, so presumably his surname "D'hārī" signifies that place rather than Dhar in Malwa. Mīr Khwurd and ʿAbd al-Ḥaqq say his land assignment was in Zafarabad, which in the Tughluq empire was a town near Jawnpur in Awadh, but it is possible that the Deccan town also received this name ("flourishing dominion") during the Tughluq campaigns there.

74. *Tughluq Dynasty*, p. 150; Mīr Khwurd, p. 238.

75. Mīr Khwurd, p. 230.

76. Ibid., p. 319; cf. p. 137, where he interprets a verse for Niẓām al-Dīn Awliyā'.

77. Ibid., pp. 262–83.

78. Ibid., pp. 283–85.

79. Sultan Muḥammad ibn Tughluq had coins struck with this epithet (*ʿādil*), and also named the fort of ʿAdilabad in Delhi in the same way; Mahdi Husain, *Tughluq Dynasty*, p. 56.

80. Ibn Baṭṭūṭa, in ʿAbd al-Ḥayy, II, 54–56, where he is called Shihāb al-Dīn ibn Shaykh al-Jām al-Khurāsānī, and was executed by beheading after torture; ʿAbd al-Ḥayy believes this took place in 741/1340–1. ʿAbd al-Ḥayy lists separately Shihāb al-Dīn ibn Fakhr al-Dīn al-Mīrat'hī "Ḥaqq Gū" (II, 58), following the version in *Gulzār-i abrār* in which the shaykh beat the sultan with his shoes for declaring that the prophethood of Muḥammad was not final; his punishment was to be thrown off the

palace roof three times until he was killed. The story in *Gulzār-i abrār* has a legendary appearance, in that the shaykh's death is explained as the punishment for his disobedience to his father years before (Muḥammad Ghawsī Manḍawī, *Azkār-i abrār, Urdū tarjuma-i gulzār-i abrār*, trans. Fażl Aḥmad Jēwarī [Agra: Maṭbaʿ-i Mufīd-i ʿĀmm, 1326/1908; reprinted., Lahore: Islamic Book Foundation, 1395/1975], pp. 46–47). A briefer version of this story is found in ʿAbd al-Ḥaqq, who only describes the shaykh as refuting the sultan and calling him a tyrant, and then being thrown off the fort (*Akhbār al-akhyār*, p. 131). All these stories have the appearance of being variants of the same tale.

81. Baranī, p. 481.

82. Mahdi Husain, in *Futūḥu's Salātīn*, Appendix A, pp. 923–27; Iqtidar Husain Siddiqui, "Farhang Literature of the 14th Century as a Source of Information for the Socio-political History of the Delhi Sultanate," in *Papers on Medieval Indian History* (Hyderabad: Indian History Congress, 1978), typescript.

83. Karīm Khān Nāgawrī, *Majmūʿ-i Khānī*, MSS 1782 and 2376 Persian, Bodleian Library, Oxford; MSS 2572, 2573, and 2574 (*Tatimma-i Majmūʿ-i Khānī*) Persian (Ethé), India Office Library. Mahdi Husain (*Tughluq Dynasty*, p. 575) identifies this Bahrām Khān with Qutlugh Khān, the governor of Daulatabad and admirer of Burhān al-Dīn Gharīb.

84. These include Kamāl al-Dīn Samānawī (ʿAbd al-Ḥayy, II, 113).

85. Mīr Khwurd, p. 228. ʿAbd al-Ḥayy (II, 33), citing Mīr Khwurd, says Sayyid Ḥusayn returned to Delhi and died there, though this return is not mentioned in the printed text of *Siyar al-awliyā'*.

86. Baranī, p. 474.

87. Ibid., p. 481; Urdu trans., p. 686 (three caravans); cf. K. A. Nizami, "Muḥammad Bin Tughluq," in Habib and Nizami, pp. 490, 527.

88. Mīr Khwurd, p. 321.

89. Ibid., pp. 300–301.

90. *Gharā'ib al-karāmāt*, p. 51. Āzād (*Rawżat al-awliyā'*, p. 28) interprets this as part of the general migration back to Delhi.

91. *Nafā'is al-anfās*, no. 3, p. 18.

92. Ibid., no. 4, p. 22.

93. Ibid., no. 38, p. 121.

94. *Gharā'ib al-karāmāt*, pp. 6–7.

95. *Nafā'is al-anfās*, no. 31, p. 109.

96. Ibid., no. 7, p. 38.

97. *Hidāyat al-qulūb*, p. 146.

98. *Nafā'is al-anfās*, no. 10, p. 49.

99. Ibid., no. 17, p. 80.

100. Ibid., no. 12, p. 56.

101. *Aḥsan al-aqwāl*, chapter 3, p. 42.

102. *Gharā'ib al-karāmāt*, p. 51.

103. *Nafā'is al-anfās*, no. 10, p. 50. Although the word "essential" does not appear in the manuscript, in the passage where Burhān al-Dīn Gharīb describes which kind of hat he was given, another version preserved by Muḥammad ʿAbd al-Majīd emphasizes that Niẓām al-Dīn gave Burhān al-Dīn Gharīb the "essential" hat; cf. Āzād, *Rawẓat al-awliyā'*, p. 14, n. 1.

104. *Aḥsan al-aqwāl*, chapter 7, p. 55; *Gharā'ib al-karāmāt*, p. 27, also mentions this staff, which is called the staff of Farīd al-Dīn Ganj-i Shakkar.

105. *Nafā'is al-anfās*, no. 23, p. 93.

106. Āzād Bilgrāmi, *Rawẓat al-awliyā'*, p. 12, quoting the lost *malfūẓāt* of Zayn al-Dīn Shīrāzī, *Ḥubbat al-maḥabba*.

107. *Nafā'is al-anfās*, no. 36, p. 119. The term *majmūʿ* in this context has also been interpreted to mean "character, bounty, and divine knowledge" (Āzād, p. 11, n. 1).

108. *Gharā'ib al-karāmāt*, p. 11.

109. Ibid., p. 52.

110. *Nafā'is al-anfās*, no. 1, p. 9.

111. Mīr Khwurd, *Siyar al-awliyā'*, pp. 288–89.

112. E.g., *Akhbār al-akhyār*, pp. 93–94.

113. Mīr Khwurd, *Siyar al-awliyā'*, pp. 289–91.

114. Ibid., pp. 291–92.

115. Muhammad Habib did not even include Burhān al-Dīn Gharīb among the ten successors of Niẓām al-Dīn Awliya', but only listed nine out of Mīr Khwurd's list of ten; cf. Muhammad Habib, *Ḥażrat Niẓām al-Dīn Awliyā'* (Lahore: Progressive Books, 1974), pp. 134–35.

116. Shah Muḥammad ʿAlī Sāmānī, *Siyar-i Muḥammadī*, ed. and Urdu trans. Nazīr Aḥmad Qādirī Sikandarpūrī, Silsila-i Maṭbūʿāt-i Sayyid Muḥammad Gīsū Darāz Academy, Gulbarga, no. 3 (Gulbarga: Sayyid Muḥammad Gīsū Darāz Academy, 1399/1979), pp. 9, 13.

117. *Jawāmiʿ al-kalim*, pp. 239–40. Gīsū Darāz's biographer mentions his visit in 801/1399 to the grave of his father, Sayyid Shāh Yūsuf al-Ḥusaynī Rājū Qattāl,

which is in Khuldabad, but he does not record any visit to the tomb of Burhān al-Dīn Gharīb at that time.

118. Mīr Khwurd, *Siyar al-awliyā'*, pp. 230–33.

119. The ten successors were Shams al-Dīn Yaḥyā, Naṣīr al-Dīn Maḥmūd Chirāgh-i Dihlī,Quṭb al-Dīn Munawwar, Ḥusām al-Dīn Multānī, Fakhr al-Dīn Zarrādī, ʿAlā' al-Dīn Nīlī, Burhān al-Dīn Gharīb, Wajīh al-Dīn Yūsuf, Sirāj al-Dīn ʿUsmān, and Shihāb al-Dīn Imām; cf. Mīr Khwurd, *Siyar al-awliyā'*, chapter 4, pp. 233–302.

120. Simon Digby, "*Tabarrukāt* and Succession among the Great Chishtī Shaykhs," in *Delhi Through the Ages: Essays in Urban History, Culture and Society*, ed. R. E. Frykenberg (Delhi: Oxford University Press, 1986), pp. 63–103, esp. pp. 78–79.

121. Āzād, *Rawẓat al-awliyā'*, p. 12.

122. Ibid., pp. 14–15.

123. Muḥammad ʿAbd al-Majīd, in *Rawẓat al-awliyā'*, pp. 13–14, n., quoting *Aḥsan al-aqwāl*, chapter 16, pp. 82–83.

124. Muḥammad ʿAbd al-Majīd, ibid.; Digby, "*Tabarrukāt*," p. 79.

125. Jamālī, *Siyar al-ārifīn'*, Urdu trans., p. 94 (Burhān al-Dīn Gharīb as first *khalīfa*); *Fatḥ al-awliyā'*, MS in collection of Fariduddin Saleem, Khuldabad, p. 23 (Chishtī cloak); Sabzawarī, *Sawāniḥ*, fol. 4b (turban, cloak, and prayer carpet; this author avoids referring to Mīr Khwurd's critical stories altogether). Dārā Shikūh regarded the four chief disciples of Niẓām al-Dīn as being Amīr Khusraw, Chirāgh-i Dihlī, Burhān al-Dīn Gharīb, and Amīr Ḥasan Dihlawī; cf. *Safīnat al-awliyā'*, ed. Mr. Beale (Agra: Madrasa-i Āgrah, 1853), p. 167.

126. *Gharā'ib al-karāmāt*, pp. 37–38.

127. Ibid., p. 16, where the man is described as a member of the invisible hierarchy, one of the *awtād* and *abdāl*. Burhān al-Dīn Gharīb later reproved the same Maḥmūd of Lajwara for excessive asceticism and bad behavior, *Nafā'is al-anfās*, no. 30, p. 106.

128. Burhān al-Dīn Gharīb, in *Shamā'il al-atqiyā'*, p. 29.

129. Burhān al-Dīn Gharīb, in *Nafā'is al-anfās*, p. 59.

130. *Aḥsan al-aqwāl*, p. 41.

131. Ibid., p. 42. Cf. also *Nafā'is al-anfās*, p. 128, where Bahā' al-Dīn Zakariyyā once sat with his rear to Mecca and his face to his master Shihāb al-Dīn Suhrawardī, upon which the latter remarked that a disciple's prayer-direction (*qibla*) is his master. This kind of story is frequently met with in hagiographical literature, as a metaphor for complete devotion to the master.

132. *Nafā'is al-anfās*, pp. 65–66 (unfortunately the microfilm copy of the MS is defective here and does not reveal the outcome of this conversation).

133. Ibid., p. 106.

134. *Aḥsan al-aqwāl*, p. 45.

135. His references to legal texts are comparatively rare; cf. *Nafā'is al-anfās*, 109 (the *Hidāya* of Marghinānī), 22 (the *Manẓūma*).

136. Ghulām ʿAlī Āzād Bilgrāmī, *Subḥat al-marjān*, p. 76.

137. Some examples of the writings of Chirāgh-i Dihlī's disciples are the following: Muḥammad Mujīr ibn Wajīh al-Dīn, *Miftāḥ al-jinān*, MS 2565 Persian, India Office Library (cf. also Rieu, I, 40–41; Munzawī, IV, 2459, no. 4298), on religious duties; Ṣadr al-Dīn Ḥakīm, *Ṣaḥā'if dar ʿilm al-akhlāq*, MS 2175 Persian, India Office Library, on ethics; anon., *Fawā'id-i Maḥmūd Khānī*, MS 55 Fiqh Fārsī, Salar Jung Library, Hyderabad, on Islamic law (also entitled *Manāfiʿ al-qulūb*, MS 66 Fiqh Fārsī, Salar Jung Library); Rukn al-Dīn, *Ṭurfat al-fuqahā'*, MS 50 Fiqh Fārsī, Salar Jung Library, Hyderabad, a large rhymed treatise in 15,486 couplets composed in 775/1374 on Ḥanafī law.

138. *Khayr al-majalis*, p. 12.

139. Mīr Khwurd, *Siyar al-awliyā'*, p. 148.

140. *Nafā'is al-anfās*, p. 52.

141. Legal and theological works mentioned by Chirāgh-i Dihlī include Pazdawī, *Uṣūl al-Shāshī*, *Shirʿat al-islām*, Quddūrī, the *Kashshāf* of Zamakhsharī, the *Mashāriq al-anwār*, the *Hidāyat*, etc.; cf. *Khayr al-majālis*, index, p. 304, for references.

142. *Nafā'is al-anfās*, p. 121.

143. Ibid., p. 116.

144. *Aḥsan al-aqwāl*, p. 80.

145. See Appendix C.

146. *Nafā'is al-anfās*, p. 129.

147. E.g., the story of the bride with smallpox and her husband's pretense of blindness for twenty years (*Nafā'is al-anfās*, p. 11) can be found in al-Ghazālī's *Iḥyā' ulūm al-dīn*, III.3.7 (Cairo: Dār al-Shuʿab, n.d.), pp. 1525–26.

148. Āzād, *Rawżat al-awliyā'*, p. 96.

149. *Nafā'is al-anfās*, p. 60, on Qur. 12.33 and the term *iṣrāf*.

150. Ibid., pp. 24–32.

151. Ibid., p. 114.

152. Ibid., pp. 118–119.

153. Ibid., p. 50. Niẓāmī is also quoted in *Gharā'ib al-karāmāt*, p. 66.

154. *Nafā'is al-anfās*, p. 55.

155. Ibid., p. 58. A verse of Burhān al-Dīn Gharīb is quoted in *Shamā'il al-atqiyā'*, p. 191, along with a similar verse by Naṣīr al-Dīn Maḥmūd Chirāgh-i Dihlī.

156. *Nafā'is al-anfās*, p. 127.

157. Ibid., pp. 90–91 (Rukn al-Dīn's poem celebrating Burhān al-Dīn Gharīb's recovery from illness), 132 (Rukn al-Dīn's poem on the ʿĪd festival); *Gharā'ib al-karāmāt*, pp. 79–83 (Majd al-Dīn's elegy on Burhān al-Dīn Gharīb).

158. Amīr Ḥasan Dihlawī, in Ṣiddīqī, *Amīr Ḥasan Sijzī*, pp. 409–10. This poem also contains praises of several of Burhān al-Dīn Gharīb's disciples, including Muḥammad Lashkar and Rukn al-Dīn Kāshānī.

159. Rukn al-Dīn Kāshānī, *Shamā'il al-atqiyā'*, pp. 45–46.

160. Elsewhere (*Nafā'is al-anfās*, p. 81), Burhān al-Dīn Gharīb observed that in former times the novices also used to carry wood, cook, and wash clothes as part of their beginning service, but that these customs were no longer observed in India.

161. *Aḥsan al-aqwāl*, chapter 5, pp. 46–47.

162. *Shamā'il al-atqiyā'*, pp. 48–49.

163. *Nafā'is al-anfās*, p. 11.

164. Ibid., pp. 43–45.

165. An English version of the story of Shaykh Ṣanʿān can be found in Farid ud-Din Attar, *The Conference of the Birds*, trans. Afkham Darbandi and Dick Davis (Hammondsworth, Middlesex: Penguin Books, 1984), pp. 57–75. The sources for the story are discussed by Muḥammad Javād Mashkūr, ed., in his introduction to Farīd al-Dīn ʿAṭṭār Nīshāpūrī, *Manṭiq al-ṭayr* (3rd ed., Tehran: Nāṣir-i Khusraw, 1968), pp. xxiii–xxx. Burhān al-Dīn Gharīb may have recalled the name of Aḥmad Nahāvandī as a mistake for Shaykh Ṣanʿān, since Aḥmad Nahāvandī is known for an incident in which a disguised Christian became his disciple and then converted to Islam; cf. Jāmī, *Nafaḥāt al-uns*, pp. 147–48. The confusion between Nahāvandī and Ṣanʿān becomes obvious when the same story is cited again in *Shamā'il al-atqiyā'*, p. 55, and Farīd al-Dīn ʿAṭṭār is mentioned there as a supporter of Nahāvandī against the criticism of religious scholars.

166. *Nafā'is al-anfās*, pp. 95–96.

167. Ibid., p. 87.

168. Ibid., pp. 111–13.

169. Ibid., p. 85.

170. Ibid., pp. 16–17.

171. Ibid., p. 57, reading (in the prayer) *as'ala* instead of *yas'ala*.

172. Ibid., p. 83.

173. Ibid., p. 29.

174. *Aḥsan al-aqwāl*, pp. 77–78.

175. *Shamā'il al-atqiyā'*, chapters 15–22, pp. 72–94.

176. Ibid., p. 75.

177. Ibid., pp. 87–88, 91.

178. Ibid., p. 94.

179. For a discussion of Chishtī pilgrimage practices as understood in the twelfth/eighteenth century, see my "An Indo-Persian Guide to Sufi Shrine Pilgrimage."

180. *Aḥsan al-aqwāl*, p. 16.

181. Ibid., p. 67.

182. Ibid., pp. 76–77.

183. Ibid., pp. 144–45.

184. Mohammad Salim, "Jamaʿat-Khana of Shaikh Nizamuddin Auliya of Delhi," *Proceedings of the Pakistan Historical Conference* III (1953), pp. 183–89; K. A. Nizami, "Some Aspects of *Khānqāh* Life in Medieval India," *Studia Islamica* 8 (1957), pp. 51–70; S. Babs Mala, "The Sufi Convent and its Social Significance in the Medieval Period of Islam," *Islamic Culture* LI/1 (1977), pp. 31–52.

185. Āzād, *Rawżat al-awliyā'*, p. 39.

186. *Nafā'is al-anfās*, p. 75.

187. *Aḥsan al-aqwāl*, p. 10.

188. *Nafā'is al-anfās*, pp. 80, 96.

189. *Shamā'il al-atqiyā'*, p. 53.

190. Ibid., p. 52.

191. Āzād, *Rawżat al-awliyā'*, pp. 60–65, quoting from *Bāqiyat al-karāmāt*, distinguishes between this Farīd al-Dīn Adīb, nicknamed "Tuḥfa-i Ilāhī" (the divine gift), and another Farīd al-Dīn Adīb called Khaṭṭāṭ or calligrapher, both of whom are buried in a group of four tombs to the west of the tomb of Muntajib al-Dīn Zar Zarī Zar-bakhsh. The latter is supposed to have acted as prayer leader for the former. These may have been one and the same person, since Burhān al-Dīn Gharīb praised the calligraphy of Farīd al-Dīn Adīb, his *khalīfa*, as being superior to that of his teacher (*Gharā'ib al-karāmāt*, p. 56). See also Rawnaq ʿAli, pp. 62–65, and Waḥīda Nasīm, pp. 73–76.

192. *Gharā'ib al-karāmāt*, p. 57.

193. *Aḥsan al-aqwāl*, p. 41.

194. Ibid., p. 142.

195. Ibid., p. 146, with slightly different wording in *Gharā'ib al-karāmāt*, p. 56.

196. *Gharā'ib al-karāmāt*, p. 59.

197. *Shamā'il al-atqiyā'*, pp. 34–35.

198. Āzād, *Rawżat al-awliyā'*, pp. 8, 86.

199. *Aḥsan al-aqwāl*, pp. 48, 139.

200. *Gharā'ib al-karāmāt*, p. 64.

201. *Aḥsan al-aqwāl*, pp. 33, 42.

202. Ibid., p. 146.

203. *Gharā'ib al-karāmāt*, pp. 65–70. According to Āzād (p. 138), Mubārak's death anniversary is 5 Shawwal, which makes his death date 12 April 1340. Mubārak, whose personal name was Fakhr al-Dīn, is known now as Pīr Mubārak Kārwān Chishtī (Āzād, p. 133; Rawnaq ʿAlī, pp. 280–81).

204. Āzād, *Rawżat al-awliyā'*, pp. 95–99. Rukn al-Dīn Kāshānī, however, states (*Shamā'il al-atqiyā'*, 34–35) that Zayn al-Dīn Shīrāzī and Sayyid Naṣīr al-Dīn received their *khilāfat-nāmas* and were named *khalīfas* three days after the death of Burhān al-Dīn Gharīb.

205. *Hidāyat al-qulūb*, pp. 52–53.

206. Ibid., p. 113 (this passage dates to sometime between 745/1344 and 747/1347). The *Hidāya* of al-Marghinānī (d. 593/1197) is one of the most popular handbooks of Ḥanafī law, and Pazdawī (see Appendix A, no. 71) is the author of another legal text.

207. *Hidāyat al-qulūb*, p. 153.

208. *Nafā'is al-anfās*, pp. 57–58.

209. *Aḥsan al-aqwāl*, p. 21.

210. *Hidāyat al-qulūb*, p. 146; *Aḥsan al-aqwāl*, p. 146.

211. In *Hidāyat al-qulūb*, he quotes from Amīr Khusraw (p. 237), ʿAṭṭār (pp. 191, 202, 240, 264, 270, 271, 340), Awḥad-i Kirmānī (p. 63), Khāqānī (p. 302), Niẓāmī (pp. 226, 237), Saʿdī (pp. 26, 44, 106, 106, 156, 236, 265, 288, 299, 366), and Sanā'ī (pp. 90, 98).

212. E.g., the Qur'ān commentary of Imām Zāhid (Appendix A, no. 5), quoted in *Hidāyat al-qulūb*, pp. 238–39, 317.

213. *Hidāyat al-qulūb*, p. 159, and p. 255 for another reference to this work (cf. GAL I, 423; GALS I, 751/38, II, 566).

214. *Hidāyat al-qulūb*, p. 224; cf. Appendix A, no. 34.

215. *Hidāyat al-qulūb*, p. 30 (Qushayrī, cf. Appendix A, no. 92), 379 (Hujwīrī's *Kashf al-Maḥjūb*).

216. *Hidāyat al-qulūb*, p. 332.

217. Ibid., p. 377; Appendix A, nos. 36, 97–101.

218. *Hidāyat al-qulūb*, p. 277.

219. Ibid., p. 314.

220. Ibid., p. 230.

221. Ibid., p. 237.

222. Ibid., p. 293.

223. Ibid., pp. 259–60.

224. Ibid., p. 181.

225. Ibid., p. 158. Cf. ʿIṣāmī, trans. Mahdi Husain, lines 10039–191, pp. 784–94; Haroon Khan Sherwani, "The Bahmani Kingdom," in Habib and Nizami, pp. 965–69.

226. Āzād, *Rawżat al-awliyā'*, pp. 99–116. The three lost *malfūẓāt* are *Dalīl al-sālikīn* by ʿAzīzī, *Ḥubbat al-qulūb min maqāl al-maḥbūb*, and *Ḥubbat al-maḥabba*. The last takes place after his return from Delhi, beginning Rajab 755/August 1354 and going to the end of his life.

227. Āzād, *Rawżat al-awliyā'*, pp. 121 (citing *'Ishq-i rabbānī*), 129–30. Zayn al-Dīn's failure to appoint a successor is reflected in initiatic genealogies. One shows him surrounded by six disciples (Sayyid al-Sādāt, Amīr Ḥasan, Mawlānā Yaʿqūb, Shāh Kūchak, Sayyid Shamnā Mīrān, and Sayyid Zayn Yūsuf) but no *khalīfa* (copy of *shajara* document in collection of Nuruddin Khuldabadi, Aurangabad). Another names five disciples: Shams al-Dīn, Yaʿqūb Qandhārī, Yaʿqūb, Shah Kūchak, and Qāżī Ḥamīd al-Dīn ibn Qiwām Bābī (*shajara* document of Khwāja Aḥmad ibn Khwāja Abdāl, in *dargāh* of Zayn al-Dīn Shīrāzī).

228. The current leader of the Miraj center is Sayyid Ḥusayn ibn Sayyid ʿAbd al-Raḥmān, known as Belgaum Wale Sahib, who commissioned a new edition of the Urdu translation of *Aḥsan al-aqwāl* in 1987.

229. *Aḥsan al-aqwāl*, p. 147; *Nafā'is al-anfās*, no. 7, pp. 34–35. The term "offspring of the master" (*mawlā-zāda*) must refer to a descendant of Farīd al-Dīn, since Niẓām al-Dīn Awliyā' was celibate.

230. *Nafā'is al-anfās*, no. 35, p. 118.

231. *Aḥsan al-aqwāl*, p. 11.

232. Ibid., p. 143.

233. *Gharā'ib al-karāmāt*, p. 47.

234. Āzād, *Rawżat al-awliyā'*, p. 8, n. 2, citing *Manāfiʿ al-muslimīn* on law and *Risāla-i ḥuṣūl al-wuṣūl* and *Asrār al-ṭarīqa* on Sufism; the latter two are cited several times in *Shamā'il al-atqiyā'*.

235. *Aḥsan al-aqwāl*, p. 42.

236. *Gharā'ib al-karāmāt*, p. 22; *Nafā'is al-anfās*, p. 127.

237. *Nafā'is al-anfās*, p. 119.

238. *Aḥsan al-aqwāl*, p. 80.

239. Ibid., p. 144.

240. Āzād, *Rawżat al-awliyā'*, pp. 8, 13, 31–32, 86, citing *Bāqiyat al-karāmāt*.

241. *Gharā'ib al-karāmāt*, p. 71.

242. *Aḥsan al-aqwāl*, p. 147.

243. Ibid., p. 144.

244. *Nafā'is al-anfās*, p. 118.

245. *Gharā'ib al-karāmāt*, p. 76.

246. The poetry of Rukn al-Dīn is also cited in *Aḥsan al-aqwāl*, pp. 58, 80, 82.

247. *Aḥsan al-aqwāl*, p. 147; *Shamā'il al-atqiyā'*, p. 3.

248. *Gharā'ib al-karāmāt*, pp. 73–74.

249. *Nafā'is al-anfās*, pp. 15, 17, 47.

250. Ibid., pp. 77 (carpet, *tāqiya*, toothbrush, and hat), 123 (cloak), 133 (hat).

251. *Aḥsan al-aqwāl*, p. 18.

252. Ibid., p. 147.

253. *Nafā'is al-anfās*, p. 10.

254. Ibid., pp. 92–95.

255. *Aḥsan al-aqwāl*, p. 138, *Gharā'ib al-karāmāt*, pp. 29–30, and *Nafā'is al-anfās*, p. 52. Other accounts of Aḥmad Muḥammad Maʿshūq do not shed light on his role in politics; Niẓām al-Dīn only mentioned him as an intoxicated soul who was excused from prayer (*Fawā'id al-fu'ād*, pp. 436–37, 439; cf. Jāmī, *Nafaḥāt*, pp. 309–10, who describes an encounter between Muḥammad Maʿshūq and Abū Saʿīd ibn Abū al-Khayr in Tus).

256. *Nafā'is al-anfās*, pp. 107–8.

257. Āzād, *Rawżat al-awliyā'*, p. 27.

258. *Aḥsan al-aqwāl*, p. 146.

259. *Nafā'is al-anfās*, p. 92.

260. *'Abd al-Majīd,* in Āzād, *Rawżat al-awliyā'*, pp. 34 (with text of the inscription), 42. The wooden model was still in existence when this book was published in 1933, according to ʿAbd al-Majīd, and it was treated as a sacred relic, but according to the shrine attendants it is now destroyed. That loss is unfortunate, since it would have shown how the tombs of Niẓām al-Dīn and Burhān al-Dīn originally looked, prior to the centuries of repairs and alterations by later patrons.

261. *Aḥsan al-aqwāl*, p. 35.

262. Ibid., p. 136.

263. *Gharā'ib al-karāmāt*, p. 15.

264. *Nafā'is al-anfās*, p. 92.

265. Āzād, *Rawżat al-awliyā'*, pp. 40–44.

266. Ibid., pp. 123–24, citing *Nafā'is al-anfās* (p. 47).

267. *Gharā'ib al-karāmāt*, p. 37.

268. *Nafā'is al-anfās*, pp. 111–14, 130.

269. *Gharā'ib al-karāmāt*, pp. 15, 75.

270. *Aḥsan al-aqwāl*, p. 136.

271. *Gharā'ib al-karāmāt*, pp. 23–25.

272. Ibid., p. 78. Although the revenue memorandum (Appendix B) speaks of the second administrator of the shrine as ʿAbd al-Rashīd, no such person is named in any of the *malfūẓāt* texts, so I assume that it is the same person as Rashīd al-Dīn, especially because of the association of the latter with Muḥammad Lashkar (called "Lashkarī" in the memorandum) as founder of the shrine faction called *murīd*s. Since the revenue memorandum stipulates that the fourth and fifth administrators of the shrine were both sons-in-law of "ʿAbd al-Rashīd" (i.e., Rashīd al-Dīn), then on the basis of this assumption, the control of the shrine would have rested primarily with the *murīd* group at least until 801/1399.

273. *Gharā'ib al-karāmāt*, p. 39.

274. Āzād, *Rawżat al-awliyā'*, p. 34.

275. *Gharā'ib al-karāmāt*, pp. 43–44. Baranī lists a Malik Ḥājjī as one of the officials under Ghiyās al-Dīn Tughluq (Persian text, p. 424; Urdu trans., p. 607).

276. *Aḥsan al-aqwāl*, p. 141.

277. *Gharā'ib al-karāmāt*, p. 22.

278. *Nafā'is al-anfās*, p. 110.

279. *Aḥsan al-aqwāl*, p. 144.

280. Āzād, *Rawżat al-awliyā'*, pp. 99, 120.

281. Ibid., pp. 86, 89, names these five women as Bībī ʿĀ'isha, Bībī Amīna, Bībī Khadīja, Bībī Maryam, and Bībī Sāra, and describes them as sisters of Zar Zarī Zarbakhsh. Other sources only name the first four as sisters of Burhān al-Dīn Gharīb (*ʿIshq-i rabbānī*, p. 91; *shajara* in collection of Nuruddin Khuldabadi).

282. Āzād, *Rawżat al-awliyā'*, p. 127.

283. Cf. Annemarie Schimmel, *As Through a Veil: Mystical Poetry in Islam* (New York: Columbia University Press, 1982), p. 155 with n. 79.

284. *Nafā'is al-anfās*, p. 35.

285. *Aḥsan al-aqwāl*, p. 140.

286. *Gharā'ib al-karāmāt*, p. 42.

287. Ibid., p. 45.

288. *Aḥsan al-aqwāl*, p. 140.

289. *Nafā'is al-anfās*, pp. 14, 86.

290. Ibid., p. 74.

291. *Gharā'ib al-karāmāt*, p. 70.

292. *Nafā'is al-anfās*, p. 97.

293. *Aḥsan al-aqwāl*, pp. 138–39, relating both stories; Āzād, pp. 44–45, adds the detail of Kākā's punishment.

294. Āzād, *Rawżat al-awliyā'*, pp. 45–46.

295. Bruce B. Lawrence, "The Early Chishtī Approach to Samāʿ," in *Islamic Society and Culture: Essays in Honour of Professor Aziz Ahmad*, ed. Milton Israel and N. K. Wagle (New Delhi: Manohar, 1983), p. 72.

296. *Tarjuma-i Qushayrī*, cited in *Shamā'il al-atqiyā*, p. 356.

297. Mīr Khwurd, *Siyar al-awliyā'*, p. 289.

298. *Nafā'is al-anfās*, p. 8.

299. Āzād Bilgrāmī, *Rawżat al-awliyā'*, pp. 96 (Zayn al-Dīn), 124 (Shams al-Dīn Fażl Allāh); Majd al-Din Kāshānī, *Gharā'ib al-karāmāt*, p. 56 (Farīd al-Dīn Adīb).

300. Lawrence, p. 73; this article is an excellent summary of the development of *samāʿ* from the classical Sufis to the Chishtīs.

301. For details of the controversy, see Khusro Hussaini, *Sayyid Muḥammad al-Ḥusaynī Gīsū Darāz: On Sufism* (Delhi: Idarah-i Adabiyat-i Delli, 1985), pp. 121–25.

302. *Nafā'is*, p. 49.

303. *Shamā'il*, pp. 347–48. This distinction is reproduced by Gīsū Darāz; Hussaini, p. 128.

304. *Shamā'il*, pp. 356–57.

305. Mu'izz al-Dīn Kāshānī, trans., *Miṣbāḥ al-hidāya, tarjuma-i 'awārif* (Lucknow: Nawal Kishore, n.d.), pp. 148–54; cf. also Lawrence, p. 82. Lt.-Col. Wilberforce Clarke translated some of the relevant passages from this text in *The 'Awarifu 'l-Ma'arif*.

306. *Aḥsan al-aqwāl*, ch. 28, p. 132.

307. *Shamā'il*, p. 360.

308. Gīsū Darāz argues that the company, by joining in with the ecstatic, creates solidarity with him and avoids distracting him by their different behavior (Hussaini, p. 134).

309. Ibid.

310. *Shamā'il*, pp. 343–44, 354–55, 358, 359.

311. For the latter's views on *samā'*, see Sharaf al-Dīn Manērī, *The Hundred Letters*, trans. Paul Jackson, The Classics of Western Spirituality (New York: Paulist Press, 1980), pp. 382–93.

312. *Shamā'il*, pp. 354–55.

313. Ibid., p. 370; the same story is told in *Nafā'is al-anfās*, p. 47, but there the conclusion is that not all Qur'ān readers understand it.

314. *Shamā'il*, p. 357.

315. Ibid., p. 356.

316. Ghazālī, quoted in *Shamā'il*, p. 357.

317. *Shamā'il*, pp. 357–58.

318. Ibid., p. 356.

319. Ibid., p. 358, with a fuller version in *Aḥsan al-aqwāl*, p. 134.

320. Hussaini, p. 120.

321. *Risāla-i shamsiyya*, in *Shamā'il*, p. 360, apparently quoting from Niẓām al-Dīn; cf. Hussaini, p. 161, n. 131.

322. *Shamā'il*, p. 360; this appears to be from Qushayrī, cf. Hussaini, p. 121.

323. From Qushayrī (Beirut ed., p. 154, cit. Lawrence, p. 79), without the last phrase about dance.

324. *Nafā'is*, pp. 83 (Badr al-Dīn Samarqandī healed by *samā'*), 68–70 (problem of *samā'* at funerals causing deceased dervishes to rise up before the Resurrection).

325. *Gharā'ib*, p. 32. Ẓuhayr was known for his participation in *samā'* in Delhi; cf. *Nafā'is*, p. 62.

326. *Aḥsan al-aqwāl*, p. 129.

327. Ibid., pp. 134–35; *Shamā'il*, p. 359.

328. *Shamā'il*, p. 360.

329. Ibid.

330. Ibid., p. 361.

331. Ibid.

332. The following examples are taken from *Aḥsan al-aqwāl*, ch. 26, pp. 128–35.

333. *Shamā'il*, p. 360, also *Aḥsan al-aqwāl*, p. 135.

334. 'Umar al-Suhrawardī, cited (as "Shaykh al-Shuyukh") in *Shamā'il*, p. 352.

335. P. Hardy, "Modern European and Muslim Explanations of Conversion to Islam in South Asia: A Preliminary Survey of the Literature," in *Conversion to Islam*, ed. Nehemia Levtzion (New York: Holmes & Meier Publishers, 1979), pp. 68–99.

336. Hardy, "Conversion," p. 70.

337. The terms are those used by Richard Eaton, "Approaches to the Study of Conversion to Islam in India," in *Approaches to Islam in Religious Studies*, ed. Richard C. Martin (Tucson: University of Arizona Press, 1985), pp. 106–23.

338. The prevalence of anti-Islamic bias characterizes the only attempt at a statistical study of the subject, K. S. Lal's *Growth of Muslim Population in Medieval India (A.D. 1000–1800)* (Delhi: Research, 1973). John Richards suggests, however ("The Islamic Frontier," p. 105), that despite the general bias of Lal's book, his theory of the enslavement of Indian captives as a source of converts may have merit. Nonetheless, the book remains highly speculative; the population figures for Indian Muslims in 1200 are calculated backward from the British censuses of India between 1881 and 1941. Lal's thesis of forced conversions likewise projects backward from nineteenth-century attitudes.

339. The original source of this theory was the *Tuḥfat al-mujāhidīn* of Zayn al-Dīn, written in Malabar around 987/1579–80, who referred to conversion to Islam as a means of abandoning low status in the caste system (Hardy, "Conversion," pp. 82–83).

340. Abdul Malik Mujahid, *Conversion to Islam: Untouchables' Strategy for Protest in India* (Chambersburg, Pa.: Anima Books, 1989).

341. Eaton, "Approaches to Conversion," pp. 118–19.

342. Richard M. Eaton, "The Political and Religious Authority of the Shrine of Baba Farid in Pakpattan, Punjab," in *Moral Conduct and Authority: the Place of Adab in South Asian Islam*, ed. Barbara Metcalf (Berkeley: University of California Press, 1983), pp. 333–56.

343. Bruce B. Lawrence, "Early Indo-Muslim Saints and Conversion," pp. 110ff.

344. Lawrence, "Conversion," pp. 111–14, quoting *Fawā'id al-fu'ād* (Cawnpore: Nawal Kishore, 1885), pp. 182–83 (Lahore ed., pp. 305–9); Mohammad Habib, "Shaikh Nasiruddin Mahmud Chiragh-i-Dehli as a Great Historical Personality," in his *Politics and Society*, I, 368.

345. Aziz Ahmad, *Studies in Islamic Culture in the Indian Environment* (Oxford, 1964; reprint ed., Lahore: Oxford University Press, 1970), p. 84.

346. According to Mullā Dā'ūd Bīdarī (d. 817/1414–15), it was the kings who wished to spread Islam and build mosques; cf. Mulkapūrī, *Tazkira-i salāṭīn-i Dakan*, p. 92, quoting his unique copy (now lost) of Bīdarī's *Tuḥfat al-salāṭīn*.

347. Simon Digby, "Encounters with Jogis in Indian Sufi Hagiography," unpublished paper delivered at the School of Oriental and African Studies, January 1970, pp. 12ff., as cited by Lawrence, "Early Indo-Muslim Saints," p. 117.

348. Muḥammad Riyāż, *Mīr Sayyid ʿAlī Hamadānī*, pp. 38–43.

349. The legends about Farīd al-Dīn Ganj-i Shakkar converting large numbers of Hindus to Islam derive from the Mughul-era *Jawāhir-i Farīdī* and British gazetteers; cf. Nizami, *Life and Times*, p. 107, n. 3.

350. Lawrence, "Early Indo-Muslim Saints," p. 119.

351. Hardy, "Conversion," pp. 98–99.

352. Arnold, *The Preaching of Islam*, pp. 285–87.

353. "Amīr Ḥasan and Burhān al-Dīn Gharīb and a great assembly of revered Sufis also went to Daulatabad. Lord Burhān al-Dīn Gharīb was counted as the master of the dominion of the Deccan. He was the most illustrious *khalīfa* of Sulṭān al-Mashāyikh (Niẓām al-Dīn). To the end of his life he worked to fulfill Sulṭān al-Mashāyikh Niẓām al-Dīn Awliyā's mission (*mishan*) of propagating religion (*tablīgh-i dīn*)" (Ṣiddīqī, *Amīr Ḥasan Sijzī Dihlawī*, p. 163).

354. Al-Sarrāj, Lumaʿ, p. 416.

355. Al-Suhrawardī, *Ādāb al-Murīdīn*, ed. Milson, no. 106, p. 52. This text is no. 128 in Rukn al-Dīn's bibliography (Appendix A).

356. Shihāb al-Dīn Suhrawardī, *Miṣbāḥ al-hidāyat*, Persian trans. of the *ʿAwārif al-maʿārif* by ʿIzz al-Dīn Kāshānī (Lucknow: Nawal Kishōr), pp. 204–7. A Persian translation of the *ʿAwarif* is no. 87 in Rukn al-Dīn's bibliography (Appendix A).

357. Rukn al-Dīn Kāshānī, *Shamā'il al-atqiyā'*, p. 27.

358. *Nafā'is al-anfās*, pp. 15–16, 99, 110.

359. M. G. Panse, "Religion and Politics in the early Mediaeval Deccan (A.D. 1000–1350)," *Journal of Indian History* 45 (1967), pp. 683–84, where the author also

accepts as fact the legend of Shāh Dola Raḥmān Shāh, the Ghaznavid-era militant Sufi (above, Part II, chap. 6).

360. W. H. Bradley, "Statistics of the Circar of Dowlutabad," *Madras Journal of Literature and Science* 36 (1849), p. 531, citing figures of 154,767 total rural district population, of which 138,376 were Hindus and 16,391 Muslims. More recent census figures show relative growth by the Muslim population for the modern district as a whole (12.67% in 1901, 13.85% in 1961, and 17.74% in 1971). In 1971, outside of Aurangabad, the total population was 1,805,753, of which 1,571,885 were non-Muslims and 233,868 Muslims, making a rural Muslim population of 12.95%. See *Aurangabad District, Maharashtra State Gazetteers* (2nd ed., Bombay: Gazetteers Department, Government of Maharashtra, 1977), pp. 277–78.

361. Burhān al-Dīn Gharīb and Rukn al-Dīn Kāshānī discussed a certain yogi from Navsari and his fraudulent alchemical techniques, which only had intermittent success due to their reliance on drugs and spirits (*Nafā'is al-anfās*, pp. 72–73). Zayn al-Dīn Shīrāzī mentioned a yogi of 70 years who could eat anything, and he mentioned remedies "used by skilled physicians and experienced yogis" (*Hidāyat al-qulūb*, pp. 149, 346).

362. *Gharā'ib al-karāmāt*, pp. 61–62, 75.

363. *Hidāyat al-qulūb*, p. 95.

364. Ibid., p. 154.

365. Ibid., p. 111.

366. Ibid., p. 92.

367. Ibid., p. 111.

368. *Gharā'ib al-karāmāt*, pp. 75–77.

369. see Ernst, *Words of Ecstasy in Sufism*, part II, esp. p. 75.

370. Rukn al-Dīn, *Shamā'il al-atqiyā'*, pp. 228–35.

371. *Nafā'is al-anfās*, p. 45

372. *Aḥsan al-aqwāl*, pp. 52–53.

373. Farīd al-Dīn Ganj-i Shakkar in this way is supposed to have brought about the conversion of tribes such as the Sials in the Punjab; cf. Nizami, *Life and Times*, pp. 107–8.

374. Such is also the case in a story told of the famous early Sufi ʿAbd Allāh Anṣārī of Herat. At his funeral, which was attended by Christians and Jews as well as Muslims, seventy men were unable to lift up his bier. When two Sufis appeared and easily lifted it up, all the Jews and Christians became Muslims due to the saint's blessings. This story is told in a chapter concerning the acceptance of the Sufi master's authority; cf. *Aḥsan al-aqwāl*, p. 75.

375. *Aḥsan al-aqwāl*, pp. 66–67; cf. also Nizami, *Life and Times*, pp. 106–7, and Lawrence, "Early Indo-Muslim Saints and Conversion," p. 115.

376. Nizami, *Life and Times*, p. 106, n. 5.

377. *Nafā'is al-anfās*, pp. 6–8.

378. Dārā Shikūh, *Safīnat al-awliyā'*, p. 172.

379. Sabzawārī, *Sawāniḥ*, fol. 6b.

380. Ibid., fol. 8a.

381. Ibid., fol. 25a.

382. Ibid., fol. 23b.

383. For the use of the phrase "the sign of Islam" (*shiʿār-i islām*) in an imperialistic context, see Żiyā' al-Dīn Baranī, *Fatāwā-i Jahāndārī*, pp. 12, 14, 141, 217.

384. Mīr Khwurd, *Siyar al-awliyā'*, pp. 239–41, reproduced by Nizami, *Thirteenth Century*, pp. 351–52; trans. John Alden Williams, *Themes of Islamic Civilization* (Berkeley: University of California Press, 1971), pp. 355–57.

385. Mīr Khwurd, *Siyar al-awliyā'*, pp. 127–29, reproduced in Nizami, *Thirteenth Century*, pp. 349–50. The *Tamhīdāt* of al-Sālimī (fifth/eleventh cent.) is no. 55 in the bibliography of Rukn al-Dīn Kāshānī (Appendix A).

386. *Aḥsan al-aqwāl*, pp. 15, 37.

387. Ibid., pp. 129, 134.

388. Ibid., pp. 141, 147.

389. Nizami, *Life and Times*, p. 106.

390. See Schimmel, *As Through a Veil*, pp. 135–70; Ali S. Asani, "Amīr Khusraw and Poetry in Indic Languages," *Islamic Culture* LXII/2 (1988), pp. 50–62.

391. The Hindawī verses and sayings are found in *Nafā'is al-anfās*, p. 113; *Aḥsan al-aqwāl*, pp. 79, 95, 103 (inferior versions in the Urdu trans., pp. 67, 81, 118); *Hidāyat al-qulūb*, pp. 22, 99, 187, 190, 191, 193, 196, 226, 238, 264, 269, 278, 288, 335; *Shamā'il al-atqiyā'*, p. 146.

392. I would like to express my thanks to Professor Shackle for his kindness in undertaking a preliminary analysis of these poems. Shackle has explored the problem of early Sufi poetry (including the Farīd material) in "Early Muslim vernacular poetry in the Indus valley: its contexts and its character," paper presented at the conference on Regional Varieties of Islam in Premodern India (prior to 1750), University of Heidelberg, July 1989.

393. *Aḥsan al-aqwāl*, p. 95.

394. Ibid., p. 143. On the basis of Shackle's translation, I conjecturally interpret this verse as follows: "How many black and yellow [cows] graze in the jungle, Will the water be sweet, when there is salt in the drink?" The implication is that just as cows do not graze in the jungle, one cannot find sweetness (i.e., spiritual knowledge) in a salty drink (a false master).

395. *Hidāyat al-qulūb*, p. 187.

396. One verse (*Hidāyat al-qulūb*, p. 193) follows on a Persian couplet from Niẓāmī, both in illustration of the Prophet Muḥammad's purpose of turning away from the world; another couplet (*Hidāyat al-qulūb*, p. 226), on enduring the criticism of the world, occurs between a Persian verse of Niẓāmī and an Arabic verse.

397. *Hidāyat al-qulūb*, p. 278.

398. *Nafā'is al-anfās*, p. 113.

399. Max Arthur MacAuliffe, *The Sikh Religion: Its Gurus, Sacred Writings and Authors* (6 vols., Oxford: Oxford University Press, 1904; reprint ed., New Delhi: S. Chand & Co., 1978), VI, 357.

400. Nizami, *Life and Times*, p. 121. See also Attar Singh, "Sheikh Farid and the Punjabi Poetic Tradition," in Gurbachan Singh Talib, ed., *Perspectives on Sheikh Farid* (Patiala: Baba Farid Memorial Society, 1975), pp. 225–33.

401. *Hidāyat al-qulūb*, p. 226, gives a verse nearly identical with śloka 7 of Farīd (trans. MacAuliffe, VI, 394; also trans. Talib, p. 240). The other Farīd verses are in ibid., pp. 187, 190, 191, 238 (Persian *rubā'ī*), 264, 269, 278; another saying of his is given in *Shamā'il al-atqiyā'*, p. 146.

Part Three

1. *Aḥsan al-aqwāl*, pp. 82–83.

2. Ibid., p. 86.

3. Ibid., p. 98.

4. Ibid.

5. Ibid., p. 25.

6. Ibid., p. 84

7. Ibid., p. 97.

8. *Hidāyat al-qulūb*, pp. 3–4.

9. *Nafā'is al-anfās*, p. 93.

10. *Hidāyat al-qulūb*, p. 126.

11. Ibid., p. 31.

12. *Nafā'is al-anfās*, p. 135.

13. Ibid., p. 15.

14. Ibid., pp. 43, 47.

15. *Aḥsan al-aqwāl*, p. 138.

16. *Nafā'is al-anfās*, pp. 50, 95, 127.

17. *Aḥsan al-aqwāl*, p. 12.

18. *Gharā'ib al-karāmāt*, pp. 19–21.

19. Baranī, *Tārīkh-i Fīrūz Shāhī*, Urdu trans., p. 657. Baranī also (p. 711) mentions Malik Mukhliṣ al-Mulk as the administrator of one of the four divisions of the Maratha province.

20. *Nafā'is al-anfās*, pp. 98–107.

21. *Gharā'ib al-karāmāt*, p. 21.

22. K. A. Nizami, "Muhammad bin Tughluq," in Habib and Nizami, p. 562; Haroon Khan Sherwani, "The Bahmani Kingdom," in ibid., p. 965. Mīr Ḥasan (*Hidāyat al-qulūb*, p. 16), who was a government functionary, refers to the possibility that he may go to Delhi with Qutlugh Khān, in a passage dated 9 Rajab 745/16 November 1344, only a few weeks before Qutlugh Khān's departure on 28 Rajab 745/5 December 1344.

23. *Hidāyat al-qulūb*, pp. 75, 140.

24. Ibid., p. 301.

25. *Gharā'ib al-karāmāt*, pp. 33–34. For other anecdotes concerning Qutlugh Khān, see Āzād, *Rawżat al-awliyā'*, pp. 19–20, note.

26. Nizami, "Muhammad bin Tughluq," in Habib and Nizami, pp. 541–45.

27. *Hidāyat al-qulūb*, pp. 342–44.

28. Ibid., p. 167. This was the verse that Quṭb al-Dīn Bakhtiyār Kākī was listening to when he died during *samā'*; see Lawrence, *Notes from a Distant Flute*, p. 22.

29. Baranī, *Tārīkh*, p. 516; Urdu trans., p. 728.

30. *Hidāyat al-qulūb*, pp. 162–63.

31. Āzād, *Rawżat al-awliyā'*, p. 98, although Āzād mistakenly states that the sultan successfully suppressed the revolt and returned to Delhi with Zayn al-Dīn in his entourage. The sultan's route took him instead to Gujarat and Sind, where he died vainly endeavoring to suppress another rebellion.

32. *Hidāyat al-qulūb*, p. 186.

33. Ibid., pp. 141–142.

34. Ibid., pp. 25, 51.

35. Āzād, *Rawżat al-awliyā'*, pp. 26–27, quoting Ḥammād al-Dīn Kāshānī (apparently an error for Majd al-Dīn Kāshānī), *Bāqiyat al-karāmāt*.

36. *Hidāyat al-qulūb*, p. 183.

37. Baranī, *Tārīkh*, p. 516; Urdu trans., p. 728.

38. *Hidāyat al-qulūb*, p. 158. In a later passage (p. 315), Mīr Ḥasan's brother Malik Nat'hū complains desperately of the actions of the army of Delhi, but it is difficult to date this portion of the manuscript.

39. *Gharā'ib al-karāmāt*, pp. 75–77.

40. 'Iṣāmī, trans. Mahdi Husain, pp. 790–1, lines 10142–151; p. 793, line 10176. Haroon Khan Sherwani, "The Bahmani Kingdom," in Habib and Nizami, p. 968, states that the sultan did not remain long in Daulatabad before starting off to suppress the revolt of Taghī in Gujarat.

41. Firishta gives only a couple of references (Mahomed Kasim Ferishta, *History of the Rise of the Mahomedan Power in India, Till the Year A.D. 1612*, trans. J. Briggs [4 vols. Reprint ed., Lahore: Sang-e Meel Publications, 1977] II, 323–25, 329) to the Bahmanī attachment to the shrine of Burhān al-Dīn Gharīb, and stresses more the Bahmanī patronage of Sufis such as Sayyid Muḥammad al-Ḥusaynī "Gīsū Darāz" (II, 388–89, 392, 397–98), Shaykh Sirāj al-Dīn Junaydī (II, 310, 319, 350, 398), and Shāh Ni'mat Allāh Walī (II, 418–19).

42. Firishta, trans. Briggs, II, 277; cf. Niẓāmī, *Tārīkh-i mashāyikh-i Chisht*, p. 260, and Mulkapūrī, *Tazkira-i salāṭīn-i Dakan*, p. 70.

43. The historians Firishta and Ṭabāṭabā have noticed the custom for both religious scholars and Sufis to be present and assist at the coronations of the Bahmanī kings, though they do not mention the representatives of the Khuldabad shrines; cf. M. A. Muttalib, "Laws: The Deccan Sultanates and Muslim Law," in Sherwani and Joshi, II, 476, 478.

44. Firishta (trans. Briggs), II, 329.

45. A. A. Kadiri, "Inscriptions of the Bahmānīs of Deccan," *Epigraphia Indica, Arabic and Persian Supplement* (1964), pp. 38–41. During the reign of the same sultan, the governor Malik Parwīz ibn Qaranfal constructed in 861/1457 another mosque next to the Zaynsar tank (named after Zayn al-Dīn Shīrāzī) in Kaghzipura (ibid., p. 37). The same Malik Parwīz had also been responsible for the construction of the Chand Minār and mosque in the Daulatabad fort in 849/1445; cf. M. F. Khan, "Some Important Inscriptions from Daulatabad," *Journal of the Epigraphical Society of India* 11 (1984), pp. 101–5.

46. U. N. Day, "Malwa," in Habib and Nizami, p. 922, citing the *Ma'āsir-i Maḥmūd Shāhī*.

47. Radhey Shyam, "The Niẓām Shāhīs," in Sherwani and Joshi, I, 232, 274.

48. Firishta, trans. Briggs, III, 138.

49. There is some confusion about the identification of the numerous Niẓām Shāh tombs in Khuldabad, almost all of which lack any inscription. Āzād Bilgrāmī in

the late eighteenth century only mentioned the tomb of Niẓām al-Mulk Burhān Shāh Baḥrī, d. 961/1553; cf. *Rawżat al-awliyā*, p. 89; cf. also p. 149, where the editor's note cites Firishta on the numerous Niẓāmshāhī princes' tombs near Daulatabad. Half a century ago Rawnaq ʿAlī described the great dome near Sayyid Rājū Qattāl's tomb as containing two kings' tombs; cf. *Rawżat al-aqṭāb*, p. 89, n. 1 (the disposal of Aḥmad Shāh's bones), p. 89, n. 2, identifying the great tomb as Aḥmad Niẓām Shāh's and the tomb on the west terrace outside as Burhān Niẓām Shāh's. Curiously, tombs of Aḥmad Niẓām Shāh and Burhān Niẓām Shāh also exist at Ahmednagar; cf. Radhey Shyam, "The Niẓām Shāhīs," in Sherwani and Joshi, I, 242, n. 92, and Z. A. Desai, "Architecture—Bahmanī Succession States," in Sherwani and Joshi, II, 264, 267 (where the tomb commonly assigned to Burhān Niẓām Shāh is simply called "the largest of the Khuldabad tombs"). Firishta records that Burhān Niẓām Shāh was reburied in Kerbala (trans. Briggs, III, 144). Malik ʿAnbar is, however, also said to be buried in the town (named after him) of Amrapur, thirty-two miles north-east of Ahmednagar; cf. Jogindra Nath Chowdhuri, *Malik Ambar, A Biography Based on Original Sources* (Calcutta: M. C. Sarkar & Sons Ltd., 193), pp. 129–31. He built but clearly did not occupy another tomb in Gulbarga in 1008/1599–1600; cf. *Antiquarian Remains in Hyderabad State*, p. 12, no. 6.

50. Rawnaq ʿAlī, p. 54.

51. Firishta, trans. Briggs, III, 159, 164.

52. B. D. Verma, "ʿĀdil Shāhī Epigraphy in the Deccan (Miraj and Kolhapur)," *Journal of the University of Bombay* 8 (1939), p. 14.

53. P. Hardy, "Fārūḳids," *Encyclopaedia of Islam*, new ed., II, 814–16 (1965).

54. Mohammad Shafī, "Burhān al-Dīn Gharīb," *Encyclopaedia of Islam*, new ed., I, 1328–29 (1960).

55. ʿĀzād Bilgrāmī, *Rawżat al-awliyā'*, pp. 107–8. Mahdi Hussain remarks that the long endurance of the Fārūqī dynasty was "the fruit of the prayers and supplications of the sponsor saint Shaikh Zain-ud-din of Daulatabad . . . the accepted guru and spiritual guide of all the members of the house" ("Arberry's Legacy of Persia and New Lights on Khandesh," Part I, *Indo-Iranica* 8 [1955], p. 19).

56. Ḥājji Dabīr Ūlughkhānī, *Ẓafar al-wālih bi-Muẓaffar wa ālih, An Arabic History of Gujarat*, ed. E. Denison Ross, Indian Texts Series (3 vols., London: John Murray, for the Government of India, 1910–28), I, 52; Mahdī Ḥusayn, "A Short History of Khandesh," *Quarterly Journal of the Mythic Society* 51 (1960–61), 122. On Niẓām al-Dīn Awliyā' and the Bahmānīs, see Sayyid ʿAlī Ṭabāṭabā, *Burhān-i ma'āsir*, Silsila-i Makhṭūṭāt-i Fārsiyya, 2 (Delhi: Maṭbaʿ-i Jāmīʿa, 1355/1936), p. 12. Other traditions link the prophecy of ʿAla' al-Dīn Aḥmad Bahmān Shāh's kingship to the Sufi shaykh Sirāj al-Dīn Junaydī; cf. H. K. Sherwani, "The Bahmānīs," in Sherwani and Joshi, I, 149. The later Chishtī Sufi Gīsū Darāz similarly is said to have predicted the coronation of the future Aḥmad Bahman Shāh; cf. Ṭabāṭabā, p. 48.

57. J. S. King, trans., *The History of the Bahmanî Dynasty, Founded on the Burhân-i Ma,âsir* (London: Luzac and Co., 1900), p. 12, cites ʿAlā' al-Dīn Ḥasan

Bahman Shāh's dreams of Uways Qaranī, a contemporary of the Prophet. Yūsuf ʿĀdil Shāh (d. 916/1510), the first sultan of Bijapur, is recorded as having dreams of Khiżr predicting his rise to empire; cf. P. M. Joshi and M. A. Nayeem, "Fuzuni Astarabadi's *Futuhāt-i ʿAdil Shahi*—An Unpublished Persian MS. in the British Museum—*Some Extracts*," *Islamic Culture* LIII/3 (1979), pp. 169–70.

58. Firishta, II, 277; Āzād Bilgrāmī, p. 108; Rawnaq ʿAlī, p. 209; Mahdī Husain unaccountably translates the phrase as "robe of desire and assent" ("Khandesh," p. 127), though it has a very specific twofold meaning, implying status both as an ordinary disciple (*murīd*) and as a fully qualified successor or representative (*khalīfa*).

59. ʿIṣāmī, *Futūḥ al-salāṭīn yaʿnī shāhnāma-i Hind*, ed. Āghā Mahdī Ḥusayn (Agra: Educational Press, 1938), pp. 7–9; trans. Agha Mahdi Husain, *Futūḥ'us Salāṭīn or Shāhnāmah-i Hind of ʿIṣāmī*, 3 vols. (New York: Asia Publishing House, 1967–77), I, 9–13. See also ʿIṣāmī's eulogies of Burhān al-Dīn Gharīb (text, pp. 439–41; trans., III, 691–92) and Zayn al-Dīn (text, pp. 442–44; trans., III, 695–97).

60. Cf. Digby, "*Tabarrukāt*." Modern Chishtīs of the Punjab, counting the angel Gabriel as the first of the twenty-two links, hold that Niẓām al-Dīn Awliyā' gave this shirt to Chirāgh-i Dihlī rather than Burhān al-Dīn Gharīb, and that it was buried with Chirāgh-i Dihlī; cf. Khwāja Ghulām Farīd (d. 1329/1911), *Maqābīs al-Majālis*, Urdu trans. Wāḥid Bakhsh Siyāl (Lahore: Islamic Book Foundation, 1399/1979), pp. 354–55.

61. ʿAbd al-Jabbār Mulkapūrī, *Tazkira-i Salāṭīn-i Dakan*, p. 70.

62. ʿAyn al-Dīn Bījāpūrī, *Mulḥaqāt-i Ṭabaqāt-i Nāṣirī*, quoted by ʿAbd al-Jabbār Mulkapūrī, *Tazkira-i Salāṭīn-i Dakan*, p. 239 (ʿAyn al-Dīn's work is no longer available, since ʿAbd al-Jabbār's unique copy was destroyed).

63. Āzād Bilgrāmī, pp. 127–128. This robe is believed to be the one worn by the Prophet during his ascension (*miʿrāj*), described by Niẓām al-Dīn Awliyā' as having been handed down to his day; cf. *Shamā'il al-atqiyā'*, pp. 56–57, quoting *Qiwām al-ʿaqā'id*.

64. *Fatḥ al-awliyā'*, pp. 26–34.

65. Ibid., pp. 4–7.

66. The MS of *Fatḥ al-awliyā'* in the unique Khuldabad copy is undated and breaks off abruptly in the middle of page 146; the handwriting is tolerably clear except pp. 21–28, which are in a vile shikasta. The table of contents on page 16 lists biographies of the following: (1) Burhān al-Dīn Gharīb, p. 18; (2) Zayn al-Dīn Shīrāzī, p. 26; (3) ʿAlā' al-Dīn Żiyā', p. 37; (4) Niẓām al-Dīn Idrīs, p. 46; (5) Shāh Nuʿmān Asīrī, p. 50; (6) Bahā' al-Dīn Shāh Bājan, p. 65; (7) Niẓām al-Dīn Shāh B'hakārī, p. 69; (8) Sharaf al-Dīn Shāh Shahbāz, p. 83; (9) Shāh Manṣūr Majzūb, p. 94; (10) Aḥmad Ḥājī, p. 115; (11) Niẓām al-Dīn ibn Shāh Nuʿmān, p. 119; (12) ʿAbd al-Ḥakīm ibn Shāh Bājan, p. 132; (13) Jalāl al-Dīn ibn Niẓām al-Dīn, p. 121 [reversed in the text with the preceding entry]; (14) Ibrāhīm Kalhūrā Sindhī, p. 135; (15) Jalāl Qādirī, p. 135; (16) Jalāl Mattū, p. 138; (17) Lashkar Muḥammad ʿĀrif [omitted]; (18) Sayyid Muḥammad Qādirī, p. 138; (19) Sayyid Ibrāhīm B'hakarī [omitted]; (20) Abū Jīv ibn

Khiżr Tamīmī, p. 141; (21) ʿAbd al-Raḥīm Kabīr [omitted]; (22) Sayyid Bahlūl [omitted]; (23) Shāh Panāh [omitted]; (24) Ibrāḥīm Ṣiyān [omitted]; (25) ʿĪsā [Jund Allāh] [omitted]; (26) Muḥammad Afżal [omitted]. Since eight biographies are omitted, only eighteen are given in the text.

67. Ibid., pp. 19–20.

68. Banarsi Prasad Saksena, *History of Shāhjahān of Dihlī* (Allahabad: Central Book Depot, 1958), pp. 19–55.

69. Firishta, II, 279, repeated in a shortened form, ibid., II, 401; *Fatḥ al-awliyā'*, pp. 55, 57–58.

70. The version of this speech in *Fatḥ al-awliyā'* is shorter, and eliminates the references to Zaynabad altogether: "We are in this region [Burhanpur], of happy name, for it was the stopping-place of the Sultan [i.e., Burhān al-Dīn Gharīb]. This is enough, that a city will flourish in his name, for the sign of Islam will become current in this piece of land."

71. Muḥammad Ghawsī relates this story of Burhān al-Dīn himself, while he describes the unnamed donor (presumably Malik Rājā, in another anachronism) as the prefect (*shiḥna*) of the ancient town of Vāysān (or Vīsānah, the traditional name for the site that became Burhanpur); cf. Ghawsī, *Azkār-i abrār*, p. 90.

72. Rawnaq ʿAlī, pp. 199–202.

73. Cf. Firishta (Newal Kishore ed.), II, 277, describing the genealogical tree at one time preserved in the Fārūqī library, tracing the generations in Malik Raja's descent from ʿUmar; ibid., II, 280, where the soldiers of Berar held it an honor to die as martyrs fighting for the heir of ʿUmar.

74. Anonymous, *Fatḥ al-awliyā'*, pp. 57–58; Ghawsī, p. 90. Ghawsī notes that he had visited Rawża (Khuldabad) toward the end of the Fārūqī period in 1001/1592–93 for the *ʿurs* of Burhān al-Dīn Gharīb, which was attended by people "of all countries" (ibid.).

75. See documents A1 and A2 in Appendix C.

76. Firishta (Nawal Kishōr ed.), II, 277.

77. Firishta ([Nawal Kishōr ed.], II, 278, 280) says that he founded Burhanpur at the beginning of his reign, and that the Bahmanī armies sacked it in 841/1437; *Fatḥ al-awliyā'*, p. 55, says the cities were founded in 835/1431–32; cf. Āzād, pp. 107–8. The early Fārūqī kings were all buried in their first capital at Thalner, and the first to be buried in Burhanpur was Naṣīr Khān's great grandson, ʿĀdil Khān Fārūqī, in 866/1461–62; cf. Ḥājji Dabīr Ūlughkhānī, I, 52–54.

78. Mahdī Ḥusayn, p. 124.

79. Firishta (trans. Briggs), II, 383 ff., where Zayn al-Dīn is always misspelled "Ein-ood-Deen"; Āzād, p. 103; Siddiqi, *The Bahmani Ṣūfis*, pp. 129–31.

80. *Hidāyat al-qulūb*, p. 373.

81. Ibid., pp. 374–75. I was unable to compare this passage with the Hyderabad copy (MS 353 Taṣawwuf Farsī, Andhra Pradesh Oriental Manuscript Research Library [Āṣafiyya], Hyderabad), where this episode occurs on p. 348.

82. Ghulām ʿAlī Āzād, *Rawżat al-awliyā'*, p. 33. This story is related from the *Tārīkh-i Khurshīd Jāhī*.

83. L. F. Rushbrook Williams, *A Handbook for Travellers in India, Pakistan, Nepal, Bangladesh and Sri Lanka (Ceylon)* (22nd ed., New York: Barnes & Noble Books, Harper and Row Publishers, 1975), pp. 145–46.

84. Burhān ibn Ḥasan, *Ṭūzak-i-Wālājāhī*, trans. S. Muḥammad Ḥusayn Nainar, Part I (Madras: University of Madras, 1934), pp. 3–5.

85. See my "An Indo-Persian Guide to Sufi Shrine Pilgrimage," n. 22.

86. Banarsi Prasad Saksena, *History of Shāhjahān of Dihlī* (Allahabad: Central Book Depot, 1958), pp. 19–55.

87. Jadunath Sarkar, *History of Aurangzib* (Bombay: Orient Longman Ltd., 1973 [1912]) I-II, 22–23, 99–100.

88. ʿAbd al-Ḥamīd Lahawrī, *Pādshāh nāma*, ed. Kabīr al-Dīn Aḥmad and ʿAbd al-Raḥīm, Bibliotheca Indica (Calcutta, 1872), II, 180.

89. Yūsuf Husain Khān, *Selected Documents of Shāh Jahan's Reign* (Hyderabad: Daftar-i Mulk wa Dīwānī, 1950), no. 11; Sarkar, *Aurangzib* I-II, 95.

90. Muḥammad Shafīʿ, "*Safīnat al-awliyā'* kē ēk nā-yāb nuskha kā ḥāl," *Maqālāt muntakhaba-i majalla-i dānishkāda-i khāvar-shināsī*, ed. Wazīr al-Ḥasan ʿĀbidī (Lahore: Dānishgāh-i Panjāb, 1387 h./1346 sh./1968), p. 131.

91. Sarkar, *Aurangzib*, I-II, 105–10.

92. Bradley, "Statistics of the Circar of Dowlutabad," pp. 487, 514.

93. Rawnaq ʿAlī, *Rawżat al-aqṭāb al-maʿrūf bi-maẓhar-i Āṣafiyya* (Lucknow: Dilgudāz Press, 1931), pp. 23–39. The lesser *dargāh*'s revenues were probably still supplied (as in B1) from Sultanpur and six other villages, as mentioned by Bradley, "Statistics of the Circar of Dowlutabad," p. 526. For reasons that are not clear, the population of Khuldabad declined slightly from 3,085 in 1849 (Bradley, p. 525) to 2,843 in 1318/1900–1 (Rawnaq ʿAlī, p. 22), though the number of houses increased from 416 to 645.

94. *Aurangabad District, Maharashtra State Gazetteers*, p. 665; Fariduddin Saleem, oral communication, Khuldabad, September 1981.

95. S. Khalid Rashīd, *Wakf Administration in India: A Socio-Legal Study* (New Delhi: Vikas Publishing House Pvt. Ltd., 1978).

96. James Dickie, "Allah and Eternity: Mosques, Madrasas and Tombs," in *Architecture of the Islamic World: Its History and Social Meaning*, ed. George Michell (London: Thames and Hudson, 1978), pp. 43–44.

97. Niẓāmi, *Tārīkh*, V, 173, 175–76, notes that this book is no longer extant.

98. P. Setu Madhava Rao, *Eighteenth Century Deccan* (Bombay: Popular Prakashan, 1963), pp. 61–62, 66–67).

99. Rawnaq ʿAlī, p. 183, n.

100. For these notables, see Shāhnawāz Khān, *The Maāthir-ul-Umara*, I, 310 ('Iważ Khān and Jamāl al-Dīn Khān); II, 647 (Mutawaṣṣil Khān); II, 648–50 (Muẓaffar Jang).

101. Rawnaq ʿAlī, p. 51.

102. Archeological Department of His Highness the Nizam's Dominions, *Annual Report 1323–24 Fasli (1914–15)* (Calcutta: Baptist Mission Press, 1916), p. 6; *Annual Report 1345 Fasli (1935–36)* (Calcutta: Baptist Mission Press, 1938), p. 12.

103. Eaton, *Sufis of Bijapur*, pp. 127–29.

104. Bradley, "Statistics," p. 525.

105. Waḥīda Nasīm, pp. 87–90.

106. Awrangzīb's testament of twelve articles, Persian text published in Municipal Gazette, Lahore, 1908, quoted by ʿAbd al-Majīd in Āzād, p. 148.

107. Sabzawārī, fol. 14b.

108. Bilgrami and Willmott, II, 719.

109. Rawnaq ʿAlī, pp. 231–32.

110. Interview, Mr. Hussaini, Lahore, 1986.

111. Nisār Aḥmad, son of Ḥājj Burhān Bakhsh, Khādim of Awrangzīb's tomb, in an interview at Khuldabad, July 1986.

112. H. G. Farmer, "Ṭabl Khāna," *Encyclopedia of Islam*, 1st ed., *Supplement*, pp. 217–22; Affan Seljuq, "Some Notes on the Origin and Development of Naubat," *Journal of the Malay Branch of the Royal Asiatic Society* 49 (1976), pp. 141ff.

113. Samples of this music may be heard on *Music from the Shrines of Ajmer and Mundra*, recorded by John Levy, Lyrichord Discs, LLST 7236, recorded in 1962.

114. *Fairs and Festivals of Maharashtra*, p. 175.

115. For the cosmic and royal symbolism of elephants in India, see Heinrich Zimmer, *Myths and Symbols in Indian Art and Civilization*, ed. Joseph Campbell, Bollingen Series VI (Princeton: Princeton University Press, 1946; reprint ed., 1974), pp. 102–9.

116. Niẓām al-Dīn Aḥmad ibn Muḥammad Ṣāliḥ (17th cent.), *Karāmāt al-awliyā'*, MS 6273 Sherani, University of the Punjab, Lahore, fol. 271a, quoting an anonymous contemporary Sufi. Anachronistically, Burhān al-Dīn Gharīb is made to

deliver this prophecy to one of the rulers of this dynasty, which only began several decades after his death.

117. Muʿīn al-Dīn Nadwī, *Burhānpūr, gahwāra-i ʿilm, dār al-surūr, markaz-i rūḥāniyyat* (Burhanpur: Jāmiʿa Ashrafiyya, 1978), pp. 66–71 (the stone is referred to here in Hindi as *hat'hiyā chaṭān*).

118. *Gazetteer of the Bombay Presidency*, vol. XII, *Khandesh* (Bombay: Government Central Press, 1881), p. 590, citing Ogilby's *Atlas* (1670), V, 237, and Thevenot, *Voyages* (1666), V, 214 (where the carving of the elephant, from a reddish stone, is attributed to Shāhjahān, in commemoration of a favorite fighting elephant). It was reported to be so lifelike as to deceive elephants coming to the river to drink; cf. Joannes De Laet, *The Empire of the Great Mogol*, trans. J. S. Hoyland, annotated by S. N. Banerjee (1928; reprint ed., New Delhi: Oriental Books Reprint Corporation, 1974), p. 30. By the nineteenth century the stone elephant was reported to have disappeared; cf. Thomas Bacon, *The Oriental Annual* (London: Charles Tilt, 1840), p. 130. But Nadwī, *Burhānpūr,* p. 69, says that the elephant stone now lies some distance from the edge of the river, due to changes in its course over the years.

119. *Fatḥ al-awliyā'*, pp. 37–50. This is the source of all the accounts in Urdu hagiographies: Muḥammad ʿAbd al-Jabbār Mulkapūrī (which is the only source to give the death date), *Maḥbūb al-waṭan, tazkira-i awliyā'-i Dakan* (Hyderabad: Maṭbaʿ-i Raḥmānī, n.d.), I, 530–538, citing an otherwise unknown work, *Tārīkh-i mashāhīr-i Burhānpūr*; Rawnaq ʿAlī, *Rawżat al-aqṭāb al-maʿrūf bi-maẓhar-i Āṣafiyya* (Lucknow: Dilgudāz Press, 1931), pp. 257–65; Muḥammad ʿAlī Khān Mujaddidī Naqshbandī al-Qādirī, *Tazkira-i awliyā'-i Khuldābād sharīf* (Hyderabad: Commercial Book Depot, n.d.), pp. 130–40; Abū Muḥammad Muṣliḥ, *Awliyā'-i Dakan awr Qur'ān* (Hyderabad: ʿĀlamgīr Taḥrīk-i Qur'ān, n.d. [1352/1934]), pp. 22–24.

120. This is evidently Rukn al-Dīn Mawdūd Kān-i Shakkar-i Nahrawālah (b. 705/1305–6, d. 811/1409), who was the son of ʿAlam al-Dīn Muḥammad, and began to study Sufism at the age of 25; he later exchanged views with Gīsū Darāz. Cf. Ghawsī, *Gulzār-i abrār*, Urdu trans., pp. 138–39.

121. *Fatḥ al-awliyā'*, pp. 50–65. The only other contemporary account (Ghawsī, *Gulzār-i abrār*, Urdu trans., pp. 196–97) is very brief despite the author's having visited Shāh Nuʿmān's popular annual *ʿurs* festival on two different occasions. Ghawsī writes that Shāh Nuʿmān's master was Sayyid Niẓām al-Dīn, whose tomb in Munki Patan is very near a large Hindu temple called Mūrtīpūr near the Bān Gāngā River.

122. The text distinctly says that the initiatic regalia came "from his great-grandfather Khwāja Muḥammad Zāhid [sc. Ṭāhir?] to Khwāja Rukn al-Dīn" (*Fatḥ al-awliyā'*, pp. 52–53). Since Sayyid ʿAlā' al-Dīn Żiyā' had died in 801/1398–99, it is not clear when Shāh Nuʿmān might have met him or obtained his authorization, or what he did for the next twenty-one years. Possibly this Rukn al-Dīn is the same as the one in Gujarat by whom ʿAlā' al-Dīn Żiyā' was initiated through correspondence, and who died in 811/1409.

123. Historians such as Firishta always refer to Āsā Ahīr as the builder of the fortress, but they fail to mention Shāh Nuʿmān in this regard.

124. Firishta, II, 279, repeated in a shortened form, ibid., II, 401. Virtually all dynastic chronicles repeat this story; e.g., Muḥammad Hādī Kamwar Khān, *Haft gulshan-i Muḥammad Shāhī* (ca. 1132/1719–20), MS Or 1795, British Library, fol. 248b.

125. On Masʿūd Bakk, see my "From Hagiography to Martyrology," pp. 317ff. Masʿūd Bakk was also, according to Mohammad Shafī, an ardent admirer of Burhān al-Dīn Gharīb, whom he praised in his poem *Yūsuf u Zulaykhā*; cf. "Burhān al-Dīn Gharīb," EI², I, 1328–29. Evidently Shafī had access to this poem, otherwise thought lost, but his manuscript library in Lahore is now inaccessible due to legal problems.

126. In an otherwise almost identical account, Ghawsī relates that Shāh Bājan's father died when he was four, and then at age fourteen he became a disciple of Raḥmat Allāh; Shāh Bājan then took the road for Arabia alone and at that point had the dream of the Prophet telling him to go to Burhanpur (*Gulzār-i abrār*, p. 213).

127. *Fatḥ al-awliyā'*, pp. 65–69. The same account is given by Mulkapūrī, *Tazkira-i awliyā'-i Dakan*, I, 188–93, who cites the otherwise unknown *Tuḥfa-i jalālī* as his source; he also relates from *Mishkāt al-nubuwwa* two stories about Shāh Bājan's love of music.

128. Nadwī, *Burhānpūr*, pp. 74–76, quoting the Persian text of *Khizānat-i raḥmat allāh*.

129. Āzād Bilgrāmī, *Rawżat al-awliyā'*, p. 130.

130. Muḥammad Nūr al-Dīn wuld Muḥammad ʿUmar, *Taʿāruf chand awliyā'-i ikrām-i Khuldābād sharīf* (Aurangabad: Āzād Printers, n.d.), pp. 2–3.

131. Sabzawārī, *Sawāniḥ*, fol. 23b.

132. Āzād Bilgrāmī, *Rawżat al-awliyā'*, p. 130.

133. Muḥammad ʿAbd al-Majīd, trans., *Rawżat al-awliyā'*, p. 130, n., citing the nineteenth-century universal history *ʿIshq-i rabbānī*.

134. It seems that 20 Ṣafar appears to be a mistake for 29 Ṣafar, the generally accepted date for the death of ʿAlī Rizā' in 203/818; cf. *Mir'āt al-asrār*, I, 211.

135. Waḥīda Nasīm, pp. 35–38.

136. Oral report, Yahya Maghrebi, Panchakki Khanqah, Aurangabad, September 1981. In October 1987, I was told the same story in Khuldabad, with the variation that the raja was a Jain.

137. Kerrin Graefin V. Schwerin, "Saint Worship in Indian Islam." The participation of both Muslims and non-Muslims in such festivals suggests that widely differing interpretations of this ceremony coexist at the same time.

138. Ḥammād al-Dīn Kāshānī, *Aḥsan al-aqwāl*, pp. 71–72 (also cited by Sabzawārī, *Sawāniḥ*, fol. 7b); Rukn al-Dīn Kāshānī, *Nafā'is al-anfās*, p. 85.

139. Sabzawārī, fol. 7a; Rawnaq ʿAlī, p. 54, n. 2.

140. *Census of India 1961*, vol. X, *Maharashtra*, Part VII-B, *Fairs and Festivals in Maharashtra* (Delhi: Manager of Publications, Government Central Press, 1969), pp. 175–76; *Awrangabad District, Maharashtra State Gazetteers*, p. 1031.

141. Sabzawārī, *Sawāniḥ*, fols. 6b–11a. An anonymous universal history, *ʿIshq-i rabbānī* (apparently written in the nineteenth century), records that Muntajib al-Dīn was born in 675/1276–77, and Burhān al-Dīn Gharīb in 654/1256–57, making the latter 21 years older (MS in collection of M. ʿAbd al-Haiy, Khuldabad), p. 91; cited also in Āzād, *Rawża*, p. 49, n., and Rawnaq ʿAlī, p. 46).

142. *Fatḥ al-awliyāʾ*, pp. 21–23.

143. On this mosque, see Āzād, *Rawża*, p. 86. The number of seven hundred disciples accompanying a peregrinating saint is commonly found in Indian Sufi sources. One tradition portrays Niẓām al-Dīn Awliyāʾ as having initiated seven hundred perfected disciples (Mandavī, *Gulzār-i abrār*, pp. 84–85). Sayyid ʿAlī Hamadānī (d. 786/1385), the famous Sufi of Kashmir, is said to have gone there from Iran accompanied by seven hundred sayyids; cf. Muḥammad Riyāż, *Aḥwāl u āsār u ashʿār-i Mīr Sayyid ʿAlī Hamadānī*, p. 48. The number seven hundred is probably to be taken metaphorically, as suggested by K. A. Nizami, *Tārīkh-i mashāyikh-i Chisht*, I, 230. Rawnaq ʿAlī lists thirteen of Muntajib al-Dīn's companions (pp. 46–47) and seventy-five disciples of Burhān al-Dīn Gharīb (pp. 156–60); Waḥida Nasīm lists one hundred twenty-three disciples of Burhān al-Dīn Gharīb (p. 164–75).

144. Some suggest that Muḥammad ibn Tughluq sent the Delhi Sufis to Daulatabad at the command of Niẓām al-Dīn Awliyāʾ (Waḥida Nasīm, p. 25).

145. Cf. Āzād, *Rawżat al-awliyāʾ*, p. 16.

146. Muḥammad ʿAlī Khān, *Tazkira*, pp. 25–27.

147. Āzād, *Rawżat al-awliyāʾ*, p. 86; Muḥammad ʿAlī Khān, *Tazkira*, p. 110 (their annual festival is held on 10 Shaʿbān).

148. Rawnaq ʿAlī, p. 224; Āzād, *Rawżat al-awliyāʾ*, pp. 126–27.

149. Rawnaq ʿAlī, p. 26.

150. Āzād, *Rawżat al-awliyāʾ*, pp. 54–55, n.; Waḥīda Nasīm, pp. 69–71.

151. Rawnaq ʿAlī, p. 51.

152. Muḥammad ʿAlī Khān, *Tazkira*, p. 27.

153. Sabzawārī, *Sawāniḥ*, fols. 9a-b.

BIBLIOGRAPHY

The bibliography does not include every title mentioned in the book, but includes all sources providing evidence relating to the interpretations presented in the book. Dates are provided for the compilation of manuscripts, and where known, the date of copying. It is arranged by subject, and alphabetized by author, according to the following outline:

1. Primary Sources on Sufism and Islam
   A. Discourses (*malfūẓāt*)
   B. Biographies (*tazkirāt*)
   C. Speculative and Mystical Treatises
   D. Other Islamic Religious Sciences
2. Dynastic Chronicles and Court Poetry
3. Revenue Documents
4. Epigraphy and Numismatics
5. Travel Literature and Gazetteers
6. Modern Secondary Studies
7. Reference Works

Abbreviations

BSOAS	*Bulletin of the School of Oriental and African Studies*
EI[1]	*The Encyclopaedia of Islam*. Edited by T. Houtsma et al. 4 vols. plus Supplement. 1st ed., Leiden: E. J. Brill, 1913–38.
EI[2]	*The Encyclopaedia of Islam*. Edited by H. A. R. Gibb et al. 2nd ed., Leiden: E. J. Brill, 1960-.
EIAPS	*Epigraphia Indica, Arabic and Persian Supplement*
IC	*Islamic Culture*
JIH	*Journal of Indian History*
JPHS	*Journal of the Pakistan Historical Society*
MIM	*Medieval India: A Miscellany*
PAPHC	*The Proceedings of the All Pakistan History Conference, First Session, Karachi, 1951*. Karachi: Pakistan Historical Society, 1952.

PSMI *Proceedings of the Seminar on Medieval Inscriptions (6–8th Feb. 1970).* Aligarh: Aligarh Muslim University, 1974.

SI *Studia Islamica*

1. Primary Sources on Sufism and Islam

*A. Discourses (*malfūẓāt*)*

Farīd, Khwāja Ghulām. *Maqābīs al-majālis*. (Persian.) Urdu translation by Wāḥid Bakhsh Siyāl. Lahore: Islamic Book Foundation, 1399/1979. Compiled 1893–1901.

Ḥasan ʿAlā' Sijzī, Amīr. *Fawā'id al-fu'ād*. (Persian lithograph.) Edited by Muḥammad Laṭīf Malik. Lahore: Malik Sirāj al-Dīn and Sons, Publishers, 1386/1966. Partial English edition: Ziya-ul-Hasan Faruqi. "Fawa'id-ul-Fu'ad of Khwajah Hasan Dehlawi." *Islam and the Modern Age* 13 (1982), pp. 33–44, 126–41, 169–80, 210–28; 14 (1983), pp. 195–213; 15 (1984), pp. 25–36, 167–92; 16 (1985), pp. 231–42, etc. Compiled 1307–22.

Ḥasan, Mīr. *Hidāyat al-qulūb wa ʿināyat ʿullām al-ghuyūb*. (Persian MS.) Khuldabad: Fariduddin Saleem. Compiled 1344–67.

Ḥusaynī, Muḥammad Akbar. *Jawāmiʿ al-kalim*. (Persian lithograph.) Edited by Ḥāfiẓ Muḥammad Ḥāmid Ṣiddīqī. Osman Ganj [Hyderabad]: Intiẓāmī Press, 1356/1937–38. Compiled 1400–1401.

Kāshānī, Ḥammād al-Dīn. *Aḥsan al-aqwāl*. (Persian MS.) Khuldabad: Fariduddin Saleem. Compiled ca. 1338; copied 1718. Urdu translation by Muḥammad ʿAbd al-Majīd. Hyderabad, 1342/1923–24; reprint ed., Miraj: Ganj Bakhsh Publications, 1987.

Kāshānī, Majd al-Dīn. *Gharā'ib al-karāmāt wa ʿajā'ib al-mukāshafāt*. (Persian MS.) Khuldabad: Fariduddin Saleem. Compiled ca. 1340; copied 1897–99.

Kāshānī, Rukn al-Dīn Dabīr. *Nafā'is al-anfās*. (Persian MS.) Khuldabad: Fariduddin Saleem. Compiled 1331–37.

Qalandar, Ḥamīd. *Khayr al-majālis*. (Persian.) Edited by Khaliq Ahmad Nizami. Aligarh: Department of History, Muslim University, 1959. Compiled 1354–55.

*B. Biographies (*tazkirāt*)*

ʿAbd al-Ḥaqq Muḥaddis Dihlawī al-Bukhārī. *Akhbār al-akhyār fī asrār al-abrār*. (Persian lithograph.) Edited by Muḥammad ʿAbd al-Aḥad. Delhi: Maṭbaʿ-i Mujtabā'ī, 1332/1913–14.

ʿAbd al-Ḥayy ibn Fakhr al-Dīn al-Ḥasanī. *Nuzhat al-khawāṭir wa bahjat al-masāmiʿ wa al-nawāẓir*. (Arabic.) 9 vols., 2nd ed., Hyderabad: Dā'irat al-maʿārif al-ʿUthmāniyya, 1386/1966–1392/1972.

ʿAbd al-Raḥmān Chishtī. *Mirʾāt al-asrār*. (Persian.) Urdu translation by Wāḥid Bakhsh Siyāl. 2 vols., Lahore: Sufi Foundation, 1402/1982.

Aḥmad ibn Khwāja Abdāl, Khwāja. *Shajara* scroll (initiatic genealogy). (Persian MS.) Khuldabad: *Dargāh* of Zayn al-Dīn Shīrāzī. n.d.

ʿAlī, Rawnaq. *Rawẓat al-aqṭāb al-maʿrūf ba-maẓhar-i Āṣafī*. (Urdu lithograph.) Lucknow: Dilgudāz Press, 1349/1931.

Āzād al-Bilgrāmī, Ghulām ʿAlī. *Subḥat al-marjān fī āthār Hindūstān*. (Arabic.) Edited by Muḥammad Faḍl al-Raḥmān al-Nadwī al-Sīwānī. 2 vols., Aligarh: Jāmiʿat ʿAlīgarh al-Islāmiyya, 1976–80.

———. *Rawżat al-awliyāʾ al-maʿrūf bi-nafaḥāt al-aṣfiyāʾ*. (Persian.) Urdu translation by Muḥammad ʿAbd al-Majīd. Hyderabad: Maṭbaʿ-i Karīmī, n.d. [1345/1926–27].

Bahāʾ al-Dīn Maḥmūd Nāgawrī Chishtī. *Urdū tarjuma-i kitāb-i sirr al-ʿārifīn yaʿnī ḥālāt-i mashāyikh-i Chishtiyya*. (Urdu lithograph.) Lahore: Allāh Wālē kī Qawmī Dukān, 1974.

Dārā Shikūh. *Safīnat al-awliyāʾ*. (Persian lithograph.) Edited by Mr. Beale. Agra: Madrasa-i Āgrah, 1853.

Fatḥ al-awliyāʾ. (Persian MS.) Khuldabad: Fariduddin Saleem. Compiled 1620.

Ghawsī Manḍawī, Muḥammad. *Azkār-i abrār, Urdu tarjuma-i gulzār-i abrār*. Trans. Fażl Aḥmad Jēwarī. (Urdu lithograph.) Agra: Maṭbaʿ-i Mufīd-i ʿĀmm, 1326/1908; reprint ed., Lahore: Islamic Book Foundation, 1395/1975.

Iṣfahānī, Abū Nuʿaym Aḥmad ibn ʿAbd Allāh, al-. *Ḥilyat al-awliyāʾ wa ṭabaqāt al-aṣfiyāʾ*. (Arabic.) 10 vols., Egypt: Maktabat al-Khānjī, n.d.

ʿIshq-i rabbānī. (Persian MS.) Khuldabad: Mohd. Abdul Hai. n.d. [19th cent.].

Jamālī, Ḥāmid ibn Fażl Allāh. *Siyar al-ʿārifīn*. (Persian.) Urdu translation by Muḥammad Ayyūb Qādirī. Lahore: Markazī Urdu Board, 1976.

Jāmī, ʿAbd al-Raḥmān ibn Aḥmad. *Nafaḥāt al-uns min ḥażarāt al-quds*. (Persian.) Edited by Mahdī Tawḥīdīpūr. Tehran: Kitābfurūshī Maḥmūdī, 1337/1959.

"Mīr Khwurd," Sayyid Muḥammad Mubārak al-ʿAlawī al-Kirmānī. *Siyar al-awliyāʾ*. (Persian lithograph.) Delhi: Maṭbaʿ-i Muḥibb-i Hind, 1302/1884–85; reprint ed., Islamabad: Markaz-i Taḥqīqāt-i Fārsī-i Īrān u Pākistān, 1398/1978.

Muḥammad ʿAlī Khān. *Tazkira-i awliyāʾ*-i Khuldābād sharīf. (Urdu lithograph.) Hyderabad: Commercial Book Depot, n.d. [ca. 1985].

Mulkapūrī, Muḥammad ʿAbd al-Jabbār. *Maḥbūb al-waṭan, tazkira-i awliyāʾ-i Dakan*. (Urdu lithograph.) 2 vols., Hyderabad: Maṭbaʿ-i Raḥmānī, n.d.

Nasīm, Waḥīda. *Shāhān-i bē-tāj*. (Urdu lithograph.) Karachi: Maktaba Āṣafiyya, 1988.

Sabzawārī. *Sawāniḥ*. (Persian MS.) Calcutta: Asiatic Society, no. 285. Compiled 1780.

Ṣāliḥ, Niẓām al-Dīn Aḥmad ibn Muḥammad. *Karāmāt al-awliyā'*. (Persian MS.) Lahore: University of the Punjab, no. 6273 Sherani. n.d. [17th cent.].

Sāmānī, Shah Muḥammad ʿAlī. *Siyar-i Muḥammadī*. (Persian lithograph.) Edited with Urdu translation by Nazīr Aḥmad Qādirī Sikandarpūrī. Gulbarga: Sayyid Muḥammad Gīsū Darāz Academy, 1399/1979.

Shajara scroll (initiatic genealogy). (Persian MS.) Aurangabad: Nuruddin Khuldabadi (photostat copy). n.d.

C. Speculative and Mystical Treatises

ʿAṭṭār Nīshāpūrī, Farīd al-Dīn. *Manṭiq al-ṭayr*. (Persian.) Edited by Muḥammad Javād Mashkūr. 3rd ed., Tehran: Nāṣir-i Khusraw, 1968. English edition: *The Conference of the Birds*. Translated by Afkham Darbandi and Dick Davis. Hammondsworth, Middlesex: Penguin Books, 1984.

Baqlī, Rūzbihān. *Sharḥ-i shaṭḥiyyāt*. (Persian.) Edited by Henry Corbin. Bibliothèque Iranienne, no. 12. Tehran: Département d'Iranologie de l'Institut Franco-Iranien, 1966.

Ghazālī, Abū Ḥāmid al-. *Iḥyā' ʿulūm al-dīn*. (Arabic.) Cairo: Dār al-Shuʿab, n.d.

Gwāliyārī, Muḥammad Ghaws. *Awrād-i ghawsiyya*. (Persian MS.) Calcutta: Asiatic Society, no. 446 Curzon. n.d. [16th cent.].

Kāshānī Khuldābādī, Rukn al-Dīn ibn ʿImād al-Dīn Dabīr. *Shamā'il al-atqiyā'*. (Persian lithograph.) Edited by Sayyid ʿAṭā' Ḥusayn. Silsila-i Ishāʿat al-ʿUlūm, no. 85. Hyderabad: Maṭbūʿa Ashraf Press, 1347/1928–29.

Kāshānī, Muʿizz al-Dīn. *Miṣbāḥ al-hidāya, tarjuma-i ʿawārif* [Persian translation of the Arabic *ʿAwārif al-maʿārif* of Shihāb al-Dīn ʿUmar al-Suhrawardī]. (Persian lithograph.) Lucknow: Nawal Kishōr, n.d. Partial English edition: Sahrwardī [sc. Suhrawardī], Shahābu-d-Dīn ʿUmar bin Muḥammad-i. *The ʿAwarifu'l-Maʿarif*. Persian translation by Maḥmūd bin ʿAlī al Kāshānī. Translated by Wilberforce Clarke. London, 1892; reprint ed., New York: Samuel Weiser, 1970.

Manērī, Sharaf al-Dīn. *The Hundred Letters*. Translated by Paul Jackson. The Classics of Western Spirituality. New York: Paulist Press, 1980.

Robson, James, trans. *Tracts on Listening to Music*. London: Oriental Translation Fund, 1938.

Sarráj al-Ṭúsí, Abú Naṣr ʿAbdallah B. ʿAlí al-. *The Kitáb al-Lumaʿ fi 'l-Taṣawwuf*. (Arabic.) Edited by Reynold Alleyne Nicholson. "E. J. W. Gibb Memorial" Series, vol. XXII. London, 1914; reprint ed., London: Luzac & Company Ltd., 1963.

Suhrawardī, Abū Najīb, al-. *A Sufi Rule for Novices, Kitāb Ādāb al-Murīdīn*. Translated by Menahem Milson. Cambridge: Harvard University Press, 1975.

D. Other Islamic Religious Sciences

Ibn al-Jawzī, Abū al-Faraj. *Talbīs Iblīs*. Beirut: Dār al-Kutub al-ʿIlmiyya, n.d. Partial English edition: Margoliouth, D. S., trans., "Devil's Delusion of Abū'l Faraj ibn al-Jawzi." *IC* 19 (1945), pp. 180–88, 272–89, 376–83, etc.

Manāfiʿ al-qulūb. (Persian MS.) Hyderabad: Salar Jung Museum Library, no. 66 Fiqh Fārsī. n.d. [14th cent.].

Partington, David H., ed. and trans. "The *Niṣāb al-Iḥtisāb* [of Ḍiyā' al-Dīn al-Sunamī], an Arabic Religio-Legal Text." Ph. D. dissertation, Princeton University, 1961. n.d. [14th cent.].

Pātarī, Abū Bakr ibn Muḥammad al-Qurayshī al-ʿAlawī al-Sindī, al-. *al-Fatāwā al-ʿalawiyya*. (Arabic MS.) Calcutta: Asiatic Society, no. 490. n.d. [15th cent.].

Ṭā'ifī, Maḥmūd ibn Aḥmad ibn Abū al-Qāsim ibn Aḥmad. *Khulāṣat al-aḥkām fī dīn al-islām*. (Persian MS.) Aligarh: Maulana Azad Library, University Żamīma, no. 1 Fārsiyya Fiqh. n.d. [14th cent.].

2. Dynastic Chronicles and Court Poetry

Abū 'l-Faẓl ʿAllāmī. *The Ā'īn-i Akbarī*. (Persian.) Translated by H. Blochmann and H. S. Jarrett. 2nd ed. revised and edited by D. C. Phillott and Jadu-Nath Sarkar. 3 vols., Calcutta, 1927–39; reprint ed., New Delhi: Oriental Books Reprint Corporation, 1977.

Badr-i Chāch. *Qaṣā'id*. Edited by Muḥammad Hādī ʿAlī. (Persian lithograph.) Cawnpore: Nawal Kishōr, 1884.

Baranī, Żiyā' al-Dīn. *Fatāwā-i jahāndārī*. (Persian.) Edited by Afsar Saleem Khan. Publication of the Research Society of Pakistan, no. 25. Lahore: University of the Punjab, 1972.

———. *Tārīkh-i Fīrūz Shāhī*. (Persian.) Urdu translation by Sayyid Muʿīn al-Ḥaqq. 2nd ed., Lahore: Urdu Science Board, 1983.

Bhuyan, S. K., trans. *Annals of the Delhi Badshahate, Being a translation of the old Assamese chronicle Pādshāh-Buranji*. Gauhati: Government of Assam, Department of Historical and Antiquarian Studies, 1947.

Chand Bardāī. *The Prithirāj Rāsau*. (Hindi.) Translated by A. F. Rudolf Hoernle. Calcutta: Baptist Mission Press, 1886.

Elliot, Sir H. M. *The History of India as told by its own Historians, The Muhammadan Period*. Edited by John Dowson. 8 vols., London, 1867–77; reprint ed., Allahabad: Kitab Mahal, n.d.

Firdawsī, Abū al-Qāsim. *Shāh nāma*. (Persian.) Edited by Muḥammad ʿAlī Furūghī. Tehran: Intishārāt-i Jāwīdān, n.d.

Firishta, Abū al-Qāsim. *Gulshan-i Ibrāhīmī*. (Persian lithograph.) Lucknow: Nawal Kishōr, 1281/1864–65. English edition: Ferishta, Mahomed Kasim. *History of the Rise of the Mahomedan Power in India, Till the Year A.D. 1612*. Translated by J. Briggs. 4 vols., London, 1829; reprint ed., Lahore: Sang-e Meel Publications, 1977.

Ḥasan, Burhān ibn. *Ṭūzak-i-Wālājāhī*. (Persian.) Translated by S. Muḥammad Ḥusayn Nainar. Part I. Madras: University of Madras, 1934.

ʿIṣāmī. *Futūḥ al-salāṭīn yā shāhnāma-i Hind*. (Persian.) Edited by Mahdī Ḥusayn. Agra: The Educational Press, 1938. English edition: *Futūḥu's Salāṭīn or Shāh Nāmah-i Hind of ʿIṣāmī*. Translated by Mahdi Husain. 3 vols., New York: Asia Publishing House, 1977.

Juwayní, ʿAláʾu 'd-Dín ʿAṭá Malik. *The Taʾríkh-i-Jahán-Gushá*. (Persian.) Edited by Mírzá Muḥammad ibn ʿAbdu'l-Wahháb-i-Qazwíní. "E. J. W. Gibb Memorial" Series, XVI, 1–3. 3 vols., London: Luzac & Co., 1912, 1916, 1937.

Khān, Muḥammad Hādī Kamwar. *Haft gulshan-i Muḥammad Shāhī*. (Persian MS.) London: British Library, no. Or 1795. Compiled 1719–20.

Khusraw, Amīr. *Dīwān-i nihāyat al-kamāl*. (Persian lithograph.) Edited by Sayyid Yāsīn ʿAlī Niẓāmī Dihlawī. Delhi: Maṭbaʿ-i Qayṣariyya, 1332/1913–14.

Kirmani, Waris. *Dreams Forgotten, An Anthology of Indo-Persian Poetry*. (Persian.) Aligarh: Department of Persian, Aligarh Muslim University, 1984.

Lahawrī, ʿAbd al-Ḥamīd. *Pādshāh nāma*. (Persian.) Edited by Kabīr al-Dīn Aḥmad and ʿAbd al-Raḥīm. Bibliotheca Indica. 3 vols., Calcutta: Asiatic Society of Bengal, 1872.

Mulkapūrī, Muḥammad ʿAbd al-Jabbār. *Maḥbūb al-waṭan, tazkira-i salāṭīn-i Dakan*. Vol. 1, *Dar bayān-i salāṭīn-i Bahmaniyya*. (Urdu lithograph.) Hyderabad: Maṭbaʿ-i Fakhr-i Niẓāmī, n.d.

Minhāj-i Sirāj-i Juzjānī. *Ṭabaqāt-i Nāṣirī*. (Persian lithograph.) Vol. 2. Panjab University Oriental Publications, 30. Edited by ʿAbd-ul-Ḥaiy Ḥabībī Afghānī. Lahore: University of the Panjab, 1954. English edition: *Ṭabaḳāt-i-Nāṣirī*, translated by H. G. Raverty. 2 vols., Calcutta, 1881; reprint ed., Oriental Books Reprint Corporation, 1970.

Niẓām al-Mulk. *The Book of Government or Rules for Kings*. (Persian.) Translated by Hubert Darke. New Haven: Yale University Press, 1960.

Saqi Mustʿād Khān. *Maasir-i ʿAlamgiri*. (Persian.) Translated by Sir Jadu-nath Sarkar. Calcutta: Royal Asiatic Society of Bengal, 1947.

Shāhnawāz Khān, Ṣamṣām-ud-Daula, and his son ʿAbdul Ḥayy. *The Maāthir-ul-Umarā*. (Persian.) Translated by H. Beveridge. Revised by Baini Prashad. 2 vols., Calcutta, 1941–52; reprint ed., Patna: Janaki Prakashan, 1979.

Ṭabāṭabā, Sayyid ʿAlī. *Burhān-i maʾāsir*. (Persian lithograph.) Silsila-i Makhṭūṭāt-i Fārsiyya, 2. Delhi: Maṭbaʿ-i Jāmiʿa, 1355/1936. Partial English edition: *The His-*

tory of the Bahmanî Dynasty, Founded on the Burhân-i Ma,âsir. Translated by J. S. King. London: Luzac and Co., 1900.

Ūlughkhānī, ʿAbd Allāh Muḥammad ibn ʿUmar al-Makkī al-Āṣafī, "Ḥājjī Dabīr". *Ẓafar al-wālih bi-Muẓaffar wa ālih, An Arabic History of Gujarat*. (Arabic.) Edited by E. Denison Ross. Indian Texts Series. 3 vols., London: John Murray, for the Government of India, 1910–28.

3. Revenue Documents

Ambashthya, B. P., ed. *Contributions on Akbar and the Parsees*. Patna: Janaki Prakashan, 1976.

Ansari, M. A. *Administrative Documents of Mughul India*. Delhi: B. R. Publishing Corporation, 1984.

Khān, Yūsuf Husain, ed. *Farmans and Sanads of the Deccan Sultans*. Hyderabad: The State Archives, Government of Andhra Pradesh, 1963.

———. *Selected Documents of Shāh Jahan's Reign*. Hyderabad: Daftar-i Mulk wa Dīwānī, 1950.

Chandra, Jnan. "ʿĀlamgīr's Grants to Hindu Pujaris." *JPHS* VI (1958), pp. 55–65.

———. "ʿĀlamgīr's Grant to a Brahmin." *JPHS* VII (1959), pp. 99–100.

———. "ʿĀlamgīr's Patronage of Hindu Temples." *JPHS* VI (1958), pp. 208–13.

———. "ʿĀlamgīr's Tolerance in the Light [of] Contemporary Jain Literature." *JPHS* VI (1958), pp. 269–72.

———. "Awrangzīb and Hindu Temples." *JPHS* V (1957), pp. 254–57.

Farmāns. Khuldabad: Fariduddin Saleem. See Appendix C.

Goswamy, B. N., and J. S. Grewal. *The Mughal and Sikh Rulers and the Vaishnavas of Pindori, A Historical Interpretation of 52 Persian Documents*. Simla: Indian Institute of Advanced Study, 1969.

———. *The Mughals and the Jogis of Jakhbar. Some Madad-i-Maʿāsh and Other Documents*. Simla: Indian Institute of Advanced Study, 1967.

Jaffar, S. M. "Religious Views of Akbar and Aurangzeb as Disclosed by Contemporary Archives." *PAPHC*, pp. 271–75.

Revenue Document. Khuldabad: Fariduddin Saleem. See Appendix B.

Siddiqi, Iqtidar Husain. "Wajh-i-Maʿash Grants under the Afghan Kings (1451–1555)." *MIM* II (1972), pp. 19–45.

4. Epigraphy and Numismatics

Avasthy, Rama Shankar, and Amalananda Ghosh. "References to Muhammadans in Sanskrit Inscriptions in Northern India—A.D. 730 to 1320." *JIH* 16 (1936), pp. 24–26, 161–84.

Begley, W. E. *Monumental Islamic Calligraphy from India*. Villa Park, Ill.: Islamic Foundation, 1985.

Desai, Z. A. "A Persian-Sanskrit Inscription of Karna Deva Vaghela of Gujarat." *EIAPS* (1975), pp. 13–20.

Dikshit, M. G. *Selected Inscriptions from Maharashtra (5th to 12th Century A.D.)*. Swiya Grantha Mala, no. 67. Poona: Bharat Itihas Samshodhaka Mandal, 1962.

Doderet, W. "A Fourteenth Century Marathi Inscription." *BSOAS* 5 (1930), pp. 37–42.

Filliozat, Vasundhara. *Épigraphie de Vijayanagar du début à 1377*. Paris: École Française d'Extrême Orient, 1973.

Fīrūz Shāh. *Futūḥāt-i Fīrūz Shāhī*. Edited by Shaikh Abdur Rashid. Aligarh: Department of History, Muslim University, 1954.

Fleet, J. F. "Sanskrit and old Canarese Inscriptions, relating to the Yâdava Kings of Dêvagíri." *Journal of the Bombay Branch of the Royal Asiatic Society* 12, no. 33 (1876), pp. 1–50.

Ganam, N. M. "Epitaph of Six Martyrs from Bari Khatu in Rajasthan." *EIAPS* (1973), pp. 10–14.

Joshi, M. C. "Some Nagari Inscriptions on the Qutb Minar." *PSMI*.

Kadiri, A. A. "Inscriptions of the Bahmānīs of Deccan." *EIAPS* (1964), pp. 38–41.

Khan, M. F. "Some Important Inscriptions from Daulatabad." *Journal of the Epigraphical Society of India* 11 (1984), pp. 101–5.

Siddiqi, W. H. "Religious Tolerance As Gleaned From Medieval Inscriptions." *PSMI*, pp. 53–58.

Sircar, Dines Chandra. *Select Inscriptions bearing on Indian History and Civilization*. Vol. 2. Delhi: Motilal Banarsidass, 1983.

———. *Studies in Indian Coins*. Delhi: Motilal Banarsidass, 1968.

———. "Veraval Inscription of Chaulukya-Vaghela Arjuna, 1264 A.D." *Epigraphia Indica* (1961).

Verma, B. D. "ʿĀdil Shāhī Epigraphy in the Deccan (Miraj and Kolhapur)." *Journal of the University of Bombay* 8 (1939), p. 12–51.

5. Travel Literature and Gazetteers

Aurangabad District, Maharashtra State Gazetteers. 2nd ed., Bombay: Gazetteers Department, Government of Maharashtra, 1977.

Bacon, Thomas. *The Oriental Annual*. London: Charles Tilt, 1840.

Bilgrami, Syed Hossain, and C. Willmott. *Historical and Descriptive Sketch of His Highness the Nizam's Dominions*. 2 vols., Bombay: The Times of India Steam Press, 1883–84.

Bīrūnī, Abū Rayhān al-. *Alberuni's India*. Translated by Eduard Sachau. London, 1888; reprint ed., Delhi: S. Chand & Co., 1964.

Bradley, W. H. "Statistics of the Circar of Dowlutabad." *Madras Journal of Literature and Science* 36 (1849), p. 481–551.

Buzurg ibn Shahriyar. *The Book of the Marvels of India*. Translated from Arabic to French by L. Marcel Devic. English translation by Peter Quennell. New York: Lincoln MacVeagh, Dial Press, 1929.

Census of India 1961. Vol. 10, *Maharashtra*. Pt. 7-B, *Fairs and Festivals in Maharashtra*. Delhi: Manager of Publications, Government Central Press, 1969.

Gazetteer of the Bombay Presidency. Vol. 12. *Khandesh*. Bombay: Government Central Press, 1881.

Ibn Battutah. *Travels in Asia and Africa 1325–1354*. Translated by H. A. R. Gibb. Edited by E. Denison Ross and Eileen Power. London, 1926; reprint ed., Karachi: Indus Publications, 1986.

Idrīsī, Sharīf al-. *India and the Neighbouring Territories as described by the Sharif al-Idrisi*. Part One (Arabic Text). Edited by S. Maqbul Ahmad. Aligarh: Muslim University, 1954.

Laet, Joannes De. *The Empire of the Great Mogol*. Translated by J. S. Hoyland, annotated by S. N. Banerjee. 1928; reprint ed., New Delhi: Oriental Books Reprint Corporation, 1974.

Thevenot, Jean de. *The Travels of Monsieur de Thevenot into the Levant*. London, 1687; reprint ed., *Indian Travels of Thevenot and Careri*. Edited by Surendranath Sen. Indian Records Series. New Delhi: National Archives of India, 1949.

6. Modern Secondary Studies

Acton, John E. E. D. "Nationality." In *The History of Freedom* [1862], edited by John Neville Figgis and Reginald Vere Laurence, pp. 270–300. London: Macmillan and Co., Limited, 1922.

Ahmad, Aziz. "Epic and Counter-Epic in Medieval India." *Journal of the American Oriental Society* 83 (1963), pp. 470–76.

———. *Studies in Islamic Culture in the Indian Environment.* Oxford: Oxford University Press, 1964; reprint ed., Lahore, 1970.

Aḥmad, Ẓuhūr al-Dīn. "Awliyā'-i kirām kē tazkirē." (Urdu.) In *Tārīkh-i adabiyyāt-i Musulmānān-i Pākistān u Hind,* edited by Maqbūl Beg Badakhshī, Vol. 4, Part 2, *Fārṣi adab (1526–1707),* pp. 620–57. Lahore: Punjab University, 1971.

Alī, Athar. "The Religious Issue in the War of Succession." *Medieval India Quarterly* V (1963), pp. 80–87.

Ansari, A. S. Bazmee. "Djalāl al-Dīn Ḥusayn al-Bukhārī." EI², I, 392.

Antiquarian Remains in Hyderabad State. Hyderabad: Archeological Department, 1953.

Archeological Department of His Highness the Nizam's Dominions. *Annual Report 1323–24 Fasli (1914–15).* Calcutta: Baptist Mission Press, 1916.

———. *Annual Report 1345 Fasli (1935–36).* Calcutta: Baptist Mission Press, 1938.

Arnold, Thomas W. *The Caliphate.* Oxford: Clarendon Press, 1924; reissued with an additional chapter by Sylvia G. Haim, Lahore: Oxford University Press, 1965.

———. *The Preaching of Islam: A History of the Propagation of the Muslim Faith.* 2nd. ed., London, 1913; reprint ed., Lahore: Shirkat-i-Qualam, 1956.

Asani, Ali S. "Amīr Khusraw and Poetry in Indic Languages." *IC* LXII/2 (1988), pp. 50–62.

Bahār, Muḥammad Taqī. *Sabk-shināsī yā tārīkh-i taṭawwur-i nasr-i Fārsī.* (Persian.) 2nd ed., 3 vols., Tehran: Mu'assasa-i Chāp wa Intishārāt-i Amīr-i Kabīr, 1337/1959.

Bharati, Agehananda. *Hindu Views and Ways and the Hindu-Muslim Interface.* Delhi, 1981.

Borah, M. I. "The Life and Works of Amir Hasan Dihlavi." *Journal of the Royal Asiatic Society of Bengal, Letters* VII (1941), pp. 1–59.

Bosworth, C. E. *The Medieval History of Iran, Afghanistan and Central Asia.* London: Variorum Reprints, 1977.

Boyle, J. A., ed. *The Cambridge History of Iran.* Vol. 5, *The Saljuq and Mongol Periods.* Cambridge: At the University Press, 1968.

Browne, E. G. *A Literary History of Persia.* 4 vols., Cambridge, 1902–21; reprint ed., Cambridge: Cambridge University Press, 1957.

Burton-Page, J. "Dhār. 2.—Monuments." EI², II, 219.

Chabbi, Jacqueline. "Remarques sur le développement historique des mouvements ascétiques et mystiques au Khurasan, IIIe/IXe siècle-IVe/Xe siècle." *SI* 46 (1977), pp. 5–72.

Chaitanya, Krishna. *A New History of Sanskrit Literature.* New York: Asia Publishing House, 1962.

Chowdhuri, Jogindra Nath. *Malik Ambar. A Biography Based on Original Sources.* Calcutta: M. C. Sarkar & Sons Ltd., 1934.

Creswell, K. A. C. *Early Muslim Architecture.* 2 vols., 2nd ed., New York: Hacker Art Books, 1979.

Currie, P. M. *The Shrine and Cult of Muʿīn al-Dīn Chishtī of Ajmer.* Oxford University South Asian Studies Series. Delhi: Oxford University Press, 1989.

Day, Upendra Nath. *Medieval Malwa, A Political and Cultural History, 1401–1562.* Delhi: Munshī Ram Manohar Lal, 1965.

Deleury, G. A. *The Cult of Viṭhoba.* Poona: Deccan College, 1960.

Dharmasvāmin. *Biography of Dharmasvāmin.* Translated by George Roerich. Patna: K. P. Jayaswal Research Institute, 1959.

Dickie, James. "Allah and Eternity: Mosques, Madrasas and Tombs." In *Architecture of the Islamic World: Its History and Social Meaning*, edited by George Michell, pp. 15–48. London: Thames and Hudson, 1978.

Digby, Simon. "*Tabarrukāt* and Succession among the Great Chishtī Shaykhs." In *Delhi Through the Ages: Essays in Urban History, Culture and Society*, edited by R. E. Frykenberg, pp. 63–103. Delhi: Oxford University Press, 1986.

Dubler, C. E. "ʿAdjā'ib." EI², I, 203–04.

Eaton, Richard M. "Approaches to the Study of Conversion to Islam in India." In *Approaches to Islam in Religious Studies*, edited by Richard C. Martin, pp. 106–23. Tucson: University of Arizona Press, 1985.

———. "The Political and Religious Authority of the Shrine of Baba Farid in Pakpattan, Punjab." In *Moral Conduct and Authority: the Place of Adab in South Asian Islam*, edited by Barbara Metcalf, pp. 333–56. Berkeley: University of California Press, 1984.

———. *Sufis of Bijapur 1300–1700: Social Roles of Sufis in Medieval India.* Princeton: Princeton University Press, 1978.

Eliade, Mircea. *Yoga: Immortality and Freedom.* Translated by Willard R. Trask, Bollingen Series LVI. 2nd ed.; Princeton: Princeton University Press, 1969.

Ernst, Carl W. "An Indo-Persian Guide to Sufi Shrine Pilgrimage." In *Manifestations of Sainthood in Islam*, edited by Grace Martin Smith and Carl W. Ernst. Forthcoming.

———. "From Hagiography to Martyrology: Conflicting Testimonies to a Sufi Martyr of the Delhi Sultanate." *History of Religions* XXIV (1985), pp. 308–27.

———. "Mystical Language and the Teaching Context in the Early Sufi Lexicons." In *Mysticism and Language*, edited by Steven T. Katz. Oxford: Oxford University Press, forthcoming.

———. *Words of Ecstasy in Sufism*, SUNY Series in Islam. Albany: State University of New York Press, 1984.

Farmer, H. G. "Ṭabl Khāna." EI[1], *Supplement*, pp. 217–22.

Folkert, Kendall A. "The 'Canons' of 'Scripture.'" In *Rethinking Scripture: Essays from a Comparatives Perspective*, edited by Miriam Levering, pp. 170–79. Albany: State University of New York Press, 1989.

Friedman, John Block. *The Monstrous Races in Medieval Art and Thought*. Cambridge: Harvard University Press, 1981.

Friedman, Yohanan. "The Beginnings of Islamic Learning in Sind—A Reconsideration." *BSOAS* 37 (1974), pp. 659–64.

———. "A Contribution to the Early History of Islam in India." In *Studies in Memory of Gaston Wiet*, edited by Myriam Rosen-Ayalon, pp. 309–33. Jerusalem: Hebrew University of Jerusalem, 1977.

———. "The Origins and Significance of the Chāch Nāma." In *Islam in Asia*, vol. 1, *South Asia*, edited by Yohanan Friedmann, pp. 23–37. Boulder: Westview Press, 1984.

Gibb, H. A. R. *Studies on the Civilization of Islam*. Edited by Stanford J. Shaw and William R. Polk. Boston: Beacon Press, 1962.

Goitein, S. D. "A Turning-Point in the History of the Muslim State." In *Studies in Islamic Institutions*, pp. 149–67. Leiden: E. J. Brill, 1966.

Grabar, Oleg. *The Formation of Islamic Art*. New Haven: Yale University Press, 1973.

Grabar, Oleg, and Sheila Blair. *Epic Images and Contemporary History: The Illustrations of the Great Mongol Shahnama*. Chicago: University of Chicago Press, 1980.

Grewal, J. S. "Concepts and Interpretations of Medieval Indian History." In *Medieval India: History and Historians*, pp. 133–40. Amritsar: Guru Nanak University, 1975.

Habib, Mohammad. "Chishti Mystics Records of the Sultanate Period." *Medieval India Quarterly* 1 (1950), pp. 1–42; reprinted in *Politics and Society During the Early Medieval Period, Collected Works of Professor Mohammad Habib*, edited by K. A. Nizami, I, 385–433. 2 vols., New Delhi: People's Publishing House, 1974.

———. *Hazrat Amir Khusrau of Delhi*. Lahore: Islamic Book Service, 1979 [reprint of 1927 ed.].

———. *Hażrat Niẓām al-Dīn Awliyā'*. (Urdu.) Lahore: Progressive Books, 1974.

Habib, Mohammad, and Khaliq Ahmad Nizami. *A Comprehensive History of India*. Vol. 5, *The Delhi Sultanat (A.D. 1206–1526)*. New Delhi: People's Publishing House, 1970; reprint ed., 1982.

Habil, Abdurrahman. "Traditional Esoteric Commentaries on the Quran." In *Islamic Spirituality: Foundations*, edited by Seyyed Hossein Nasr, pp. 24–47. World

Spirituality: An Encyclopedic History of the Religious Quest, vol. 19. New York: Crossroad, 1987.

Hardy, Peter. "Fārūḳids." EI², II, 814–16.

———. "The Growth of Authority over a Conquered Political Elite: The Early Delhi Sultanate as a Possible Case Study." In *Kingship and Authority in South Asia*, edited by J. F. Richards, pp. 192–214. Madison: University of Wisconsin, 1978.

———. *Historians of Medieval India: Studies in Indo-Muslim Historical Writing*. London: Luzac & Company Ltd., 1960.

———. "Modern European and Muslim Explanations of Conversion to Islam in South Asia: A Preliminary Survey of the Literature." In *Conversion to Islam*, edited by Nehemia Levtzion, pp. 68–99. New York: Holmes & Meier Publishers, 1979.

Hayes, Carlton J. H. *Nationalism: A Religion*. New York: Macmillan Company, 1960.

Hodgson, Marshall G.S. *The Venture of Islam: Conscience and History in a World Civilization*. Vol. 2, *The Expansion of Islam in the Middle Periods*. Chicago: University of Chicago Press, 1974.

Husain, Mahdi. "A Short History of Khandesh." *Quarterly Journal of the Mythic Society* 51 (1960–61), pp. 120–28, 180–86; 52 (1961–62), pp. 6–20; 53 (1962–63), pp. 30–40.

———. *Tughluq Dynasty*. Calcutta: Thacker Spinck & Co. (1933) Pvt. Ltd., 1963.

Hussaini, Khusro. *Sayyid Muḥammad al-Ḥusaynī Gīsū Darāz: On Sufism*. Delhi: Idarah-i Adabiyat-i Delli, 1985.

Ikrām, Muḥammad. *Āb-i Kawsar*. (Urdu.) 5th ed., Lahore: Idāra-i Siqāfat-i Islāmiyya, 1984.

———. *Muslim Civilization in India*. Edited by Ainslie T. Embree. New York: Columbia University Press, 1964.

Irvine, William. *Later Mughals*. Edited by Jadunath Sarkar. New Delhi: Oriental Books Reprint Corporation, 1971.

Islam, Riazul. "Collections of the Malfuzat of Makhdum-i-Jahanian (1307–1388) of Uchh." *PAPHC*, pp. 211–16.

Jackson, Paul. "Khair Al-Majalis: An Examination." In *Islam in India: Studies and Commentaries*. Vol. 2, *Religion and Religious Education*, edited by Christian W. Troll, pp. 34–57. Delhi: Vikas Publishing House Pvt. Ltd., 1985.

Jackson, Peter. "Delhi: A Vast Military Encampment." In *Delhi Through the Ages: Essays in Urban History, Culture and Society*, edited by R. E. Frykenberg, pp. 18–33. Delhi: Oxford University Press, 1986.

Jaʿfar, Sayyida. *Dakanī nasr kā intikhāb*. (Urdu.) New Delhi: Taraqqī Urdu Bureau, 1983.

Joshi, P. M., and M. A. Nayeem. "Fuzuni Astarabadi's *Futuhāt-i ʿAdil Shahi*—An Unpublished Persian MS. in the British Museum—Some Extracts." *IC* LIII (1979), pp. 163–77.

Juynboll, G. H. A. *The Authenticity of the Tradition Literature: Discussions in Modern Egypt*. Leiden: E. J. Brill, 1969.

Karim, Abdul. *Social History of the Muslims in Bengal (Down to A.D. 1538)*. Dacca: Asiatic Society of Pakistan, 1959.

Krishnaswami, A. *The Tamil Country under Vijayanagar*. Annamalainagar: Annamalai University, 1964.

Kulke, Hermann. "Ein hinduistischer Tempel unter muslimischer Herrschaft." *Saeculum* 27 (1976), pp. 366–75.

Kumar, S. Selvin. "A Case Study of Madura Vijayam." In *Bias in Indian Historiography*, edited by Devahuti, pp. 236–39. Delhi: D. K. Publications, 1980.

Lal, K. S. *Growth of Muslim Population in Medieval India (A.D. 1000–1800)*. Delhi: Research, 1973.

Lambton, A. K. S. "Quis Custodiet Custodes: Some Reflections on the Persian Theory of Government, I." *SI* V (1956), pp. 125–48, reprinted in *Theory and Practice in Medieval Persian Government*, essay 2. London: Variorum Reprints, 1980.

Lapidus, Ira M. *Muslim Cities in the Later Middle Ages*. Cambridge: Harvard University Press, 1967; Student edition, Cambridge: Cambridge University Press, 1984.

Lawrence, Bruce B. "*Afzal-ul-fawa'id*—a reassessment." In *Life, Times and Works of Amīr Khusrau Dehlavi, Seventh Centenary*, edited by Z. Ansari, pp. 119–31. New Delhi: National Amīr Khusrau Society, 1976.

———. "Biography and the 17th-Century Qadiriyya of North India." Paper presented at the Conference on Regional Varieties of Islam in Pre-modern India, University of Heidelberg, July 1989.

———. "The Early Chishtī Approach to Samāʿ." In *Islamic Society and Culture: Essays in Honour of Professor Aziz Ahmad*, edited by Milton Israel and N. K. Wagle, pp. 69–93. New Delhi: Manohar, 1983.

———. "Early Indo-Muslim Saints and Conversion." In *Islam in Asia*. Vol. 1, *South Asia*, edited by Yohanan Friedmann, pp. 109–45. Boulder: Westview Press, 1984.

———. "The *Lawā'iḥ* of Qāḍī Ḥamīd ad-dīn Nāgaurī." *Indo-Iranica* 20 (1975), pp. 34–53.

———. *Notes from a Distant Flute, The Extant Literature of pre-Mughal Indian Sufism*. Tehran: Imperial Iranian Academy of Philosophy, 1978.

———. *Shahrastānī on the Indian Religions*. Religion and Society 4. The Hague: Mouton, 1976.

Lindner, Rudi Paul. *Nomads and Ottomans in Medieval Anatolia*. Indiana University Uralic and Altaic Series, vol. 144. Bloomington: Research Institute for Inner Asian Studies, Indiana University, 1983.

MacAuliffe, Max Arthur. *The Sikh Religion: Its Gurus, Sacred Writings and Authors*. 6 vols., Oxford: Oxford University Press, 1904; reprint ed., New Delhi: S. Chand & Co., 1978.

Mahipati. *Stories of Indian Saints. Translation of Marathi "Bhaktavijaya."* Translated by Justin E. Abbott and Narhar R. Godbole. 2 vols.; Poona, 1933; reprint ed., Delhi: Motilal Banarsidass, 1982.

Majumdar, R. C., ed. *The History and Culture of the Indian People*. Vol. 5, *The Struggle for Empire*. Bombay: Bharatiya Vidya Bhavan, 1957.

———. "Indian Historiography: Some Recent Trends." In *Historians and Historiography in Modern India*, edited by S. P. Sen, pp. xvii-xxiii. Calcutta: Institute of Historical Studies, 1973.

———. "Nationalist Historians." In *Historians of India, Pakistan and Ceylon*, edited by C. H. Philips, pp. 416–428. London: Oxford University Press, 1961.

Mala, S. Babs. "The Sufi Convent and its Social Significance in the Medieval Period of Islam." *IC* LI (1977), pp. 31–52.

McCully, Bruce T. "The Origins of Indian Nationalism According to Native Writers." *The Journal of Modern History* 7 (1935), pp. 295–314.

Meier, Fritz. *Abū Saʿīd-i Abū l-Ḫayr (357–440/967–1049), Wirklichkeit und Legende*. Acta Iranica 11. Leiden: E. J. Brill, 1976.

———. "Ḫurāsān und das Ende der klassischen Ṣūfik." In *La Persia nel medioevo*, pp. 545–70. Rome: Accademia Nazionale dei Lincei, 1971.

Memon, Muhammad Umar. *Ibn Taymiya's Struggle Against Popular Religion*. The Hague: Mouton, 1982.

Morgan, David. *The Mongols*. Cambridge, Mass.: Basil Blackwell, 1990.

Mubārakpūrī, Qāẓī Aṭhar. *Khilāfat-i rāshida awr Hindūstān*. (Urdu.) Delhi, 1972; reprint ed., Sukkur: Fikr u Naẓar Publications, 1986.

Mujahid, Abdul Malik. *Conversion to Islam: Untouchables' Strategy for Protest in India*. Chambersburg, Pa:. Anima Books, 1989.

Nadīm, al-. *The Fihrist of al-Nadīm*. Edited and translated by Bayard Dodge. 2 vols., New York: Columbia University Press, 1970.

Nadwī, Muʿīn al-Dīn. *Burhānpūr, gahwāra-i ʿilm, dār al-surūr, markaz-i rūḥāniyyat*. (Urdu.) Burhanpur: Jāmiʿa Ashrafiyya, 1978.

Nath, R. *History of Mughal Architecture*. Atlantic Highlands, N.J.: Humanities Press, 1982.

Nicholson, R. A. *Studies in Islamic Mysticism*. Cambridge, 1921; reprint ed., Cambridge: Cambridge University Press, 1967.

Nizami, Khaliq Ahmad. "Bahā' al-Dīn Zakariyyā." EI², I, p. 912.

———. "The Futuhat-i-Fīrūz Shāhī As A Medieval Inscription." *PSMI*, pp. 28–35.

———. "Historical Significance of the Malfuz Literature of Medieval India." In *On History and Historians of Medieval India*, pp. 163–97. New Delhi: Munshiram Manoharlal Publishers Pvt. Ltd., 1982.

———. *The Life and Times of Shaikh Farid-u'd-Din Ganj-i-Shakar*. IAD Religio-Philosophy Series no. 1. Delhi: Idarah-i Adabiyat-i Delli, 1955; reprint ed., 1973.

———. "A Note on *Ahsan-al-Aqwal*." *JPHS* 3 (1955), pp. 40–44.

———. "The *Sarur-u's-Sudur*." *Proceedings of the Indian History Congress, Nagpur Session* (1950), pp. 167–69.

———. "Some Aspects of *Khānqāh* Life in Medieval India." *SI* 8 (1957), pp. 51–70.

———. *Some Aspects of Religion and Politics in India in the Thirteenth Century*, IAD Religio-Philosophical Series, 2. 2nd ed., Delhi: Idarah-i Adabiyat-i Delli, 1978.

———. *Tārīkh-i mashāyikh-i Chisht*. (Urdu.) Vols. 1 and 5, 2nd ed.; Delhi: Idāra-i Adabiyyat-i Dellī, 1980–85.

Nūr al-Dīn wuld Muḥammad ʿUmar. *Taʿāruf chand awliyā'-i ikrām Khuldābād sharīf*. (Urdu.) Aurangabad: Āzād Printers, n.d.

Panse, M. G. "Religion and Politics in the early Mediaeval Deccan (A.D. 1000–1350)." *JIH* 45 (1967), pp. 673–87.

Prasad, Beni. *History of Jahāngīr*. Allahabad: Indian Press (Publications) Private Ltd., 1962.

Qādirī, Shams Allāh. *Urdū-i qadīm*. (Urdu.) Lucknow: Tej Kumār, 1967.

Rao, P. Setu Madhava. *Eighteenth Century Deccan*. Bombay: Popular Prakashan, 1963.

Rao, V. D. "The Maratha Bardic Poetry." *The Modern Review* 124 (1969), pp. 749–52.

Richards, J. F. "The Islamic Frontier in the East: Expansion into South Asia." *South Asia* 4 (1974), pp. 90–109.

Riyāż, Muḥammad. *Aḥwāl u āsār u ashʿār-i Mīr Sayyid ʿAlī Hamadānī*. (Persian.) Islamabad: Markaz-i Taḥqīqāt-i Fārsī-i Īrān u Pākistān, 1405/1364/1985.

Ṣabāḥ al-Dīn ʿAbd al-Raḥmān. *Bazm-i Ṣūfiyya*. (Urdu.) Aʿẓamgaṛh: Dār al-Muṣannifīn, 1949.

Ṣafā, Zabīḥ Allāh. "Ḥamāsa-hā-yi tārīkhī wa dīnī dar ʿahd-i Ṣafavī." (Persian.) *Īrān nāma* I (1361/1982), pp. 5–21.

Saksena, Banarsi Prasad. *History of Shāhjahān of Dihlī*. Allahabad: Central Book Depot, 1958.

Salim, Mohammad. "Jamaʿat-Khana of Shaikh Nizamuddin Auliya of Delhi." *Proceedings of the Pakistan Historical Conference* III (1953), pp. 183–89.

Sarkar, Jadunath. *History of Aurangzib*. 5 vols., 2nd ed., 1952; reprint ed., Bombay: Orient Longman Ltd., 1973.

Sastri, K. A. Nilakanta. *Sources of Indian History with Special Reference to South India*. New York: Asia Publishing House, n.d.

Schimmel, Annemarie. *As Through a Veil: Mystical Poetry in Islam*. New York: Columbia University Press, 1982.

———. *Islam in the Indian Subcontinent*. Handbuch der Orientalistik IV.3. Leiden: E. J. Brill, 1980.

———. *Mystical Dimensions of Islam*. Chapel Hill: University of North Carolina Press, 1975.

———. "Turk and Hindu: A Poetical Image and its Application to Historical Fact." In *Islam and Cultural Change in the Middle Ages*, edited by Speros Vryonis, Jr., pp. 107–26. Wiesbaden: Otto Harrassowitz, 1975.

Schwerin, Kerrin Graefin v. "Saint Worship in Indian Islam: The Legend of the Martyr Salar Masud Ghazi." In *Ritual & Religion among Muslims of the Sub-continent*, edited by Imtiaz Ahmad, pp. 143–61. Lahore: Vanguard, 1985.

Seljuq, Affan. "Some Notes on the Origin and Development of Naubat." *Journal of the Malay Branch of the Royal Asiatic Society* 49 (1976), pp. 141–44.

Shackle, Christopher. "Early Muslim Vernacular Poetry in the Indus Valley: Its Contexts and its Character." Paper presented at Conference on "Regional Varieties of Islam in Premodern India (prior to 1750)." University of Heidelberg, July 1989.

Shafī, Mohammad. "Burhān al-Dīn Gharīb." EI^2, I, 1328–29.

Sherwani, H. K. "Bahmānīs," EI^2, I, 923–25.

Sherwani, H. K., and P. M. Joshi, eds. *History of Medieval Deccan (1295–1724)*. 2 vols., Hyderabad: The Government of Andhra Pradesh, 1973–74.

Shiblī Nuʿmānī. *Shiʿr al-ʿajam*. (Urdu.) Islamabad: National Book Foundation, 1972.

Ṣiddīqī, Muḥammad Shakīl Aḥmad. (Urdu.) *Amīr Ḥasan Sijzī Dihlawī, ḥayāt awr adabī khidmāt*. Lucknow: Muḥammad Shakīl Aḥmad Ṣiddīqī, 1979.

Siddiqi, Muhammad Suleman. *The Bahmani Ṣūfis*. IAD Religio-Philosophy (Original) Series no. 19. Delhi: Idarah-i Adabiyat-i Delli, 1989.

Siddiqui, Iqtidar Husain. "Farhang Literature of the 14th Century as a Source of Information for the Socio-political History of the Delhi Sultanate." *Papers on Medieval Indian History*. Hyderabad: Indian History Congress, 1978, typescript.

Singh, Attar. "Sheikh Farid and the Punjabi Poetic Tradition." In *Perspectives on Sheikh Farid*, edited by Gurbachan Singh Talib, pp. 225–33. Patiala: Baba Farid Memorial Society, 1975.

Skyhawk, Hugh van. "Vaiṣṇava Perceptions of Muslims in 18th Century Mahārāṣṭra." Paper presented at Conference on "Regional Varieties of Islam in Premodern India (prior to 1750)." University of Heidelberg, July 1989.

Smith, Jonathan Z. "Sacred Persistence: Toward a Redescription of Canon." *Imagining Religion: From Babylon to Jonestown*. Chicago: University of Chicago Press, 1978.

Smith, Wilfred Cantwell. *The Meaning and End of Religion: A New Approach to the Religious Traditions of Mankind*. New York: New American Library, 1964.

———. "The Crystallization of Religious Communities in Mughul India." In *On Understanding Islam: Selected Studies*, pp. 177–96. Religion and Reason 19. The Hague: Mouton, 1981.

———. "Scripture as Form and Concept." In *Rethinking Scripture: Essays from a Comparatives Perspective*, edited by Miriam Levering. Albany: State University of New York Press, 1989.

Spencer, George W. "Crisis of Authority in a Hindu Temple under the Impact of Islam: Srirangam in the Fourteenth Century." In *Religion and the Legitimation of Power in South Asia*, edited by Bardwell Smith. Leiden: E. J. Brill, 1978.

Srivastava, Ashirbadi Lal. "A Survey of India's Resistance to Mediaeval Invaders from the North-West: Causes of Eventual Hindu Defeat." *JIH* 43 (1965), pp. 349–68.

Swaminathan, K. D. "Two Nawabs of the Carnatic and the Sri Rangam Temple." *MIM* III (1975), pp. 184–87.

Tod, James. *Annals and Antiquities of Rajast'han, or The Central and Western Rajpoots of India*. 2 vols., London, 1829–32; reprint ed., London: George Routledge & Sons Limited, 1914.

Tulpule, Shankar Gopal. *Classical Marāṭhī Literature*. History of Indian Literature IX/4. Wiesbaden: Otto Harrassowitz, 1979.

Vaudeville, Ch. *Kabīr*. Vol. 1. Oxford: At the Clarendon Press, 1974.

Venkataramanayya, N. *Early Muslim Expansion in South India*. Madras: University of Madras, 1942.

Voegelin, Eric. *Order and History*. Vol. 4, *The Ecumenic Age*. Baton Rouge: Louisiana State University Press, 1974.

Voll, John. *Islam: Continuity and Change in the Modern World*. Boulder: Westview Press, 1982.

———. "Muḥammad Ḥayāt al-Sindī and Muḥammad ibn ʿAbd al-Wahhāb, an Analysis of an Intellectual Group in Eighteenth-century Madīna." *BSOAS* 38 (1975), pp. 32–39.

Vryonis, Speros. *The Decline of Medieval Hellenism in Asia Minor and the Process of Islamization from the Eleventh through the Fifteenth Century*. Berkeley: University of California Press, 1971.

Waldman, Marilyn R. "Primitive Mind/Modern Mind: New Approaches to an Old Problem Applied to Islam." In *Approaches to Islam in Religious Studies*, edited by Richard C. Martin, pp. 91–105. Tucson: University of Arizona Press, 1985.

Williams, John Alden. *Themes of Islamic Civilization*. Berkeley: University of California Press, 1971.

Wink, André. *Land and Sovereignty in India. Agrarian Society and Politics under the Eighteenth-century Maratha Svarājya*. Cambridge: Cambridge University Press, 1986.

Zaydī, Shamīm Maḥmūd. *Aḥwāl u āsār-i Shaykh Bahā' al-Dīn Zakariyyā wa khulāṣat al-ʿārifīn*. (Persian.) Islamabad: Markaz-i Taḥqīqāt-i Fārsī-i Īrān u Pākistān, 1353/1974.

Zelliot, Eleanor. "A Medieval Encounter between Hindu and Muslim: Eknath's Drama-Poem *Hiṇdu-Turk Saṃvād.*" In *Images of Man: Religion and Historical Process in South Asia*, edited by Fred W. Clothey, pp. 171–95. Madras: New Era Publications, 1982.

Ziegler, Norman P. "Some Notes on Rajpūt Loyalties During the Mughal Period." In *Kingship and Authority in South Asia*, edited by J. F. Richards. Madison: University of Wisconsin Press, 1978.

Zimmer, Heinrich. *Myths and Symbols in Indian Art and Civilization*. Edited by Joseph Campbell. Bollingen Series VI. Princeton: Princeton University Press, 1946; reprint ed., 1974.

7. Reference Works

Bendrey, V. S. *Tārīkh-i-ilāhī*. Aligarh: Centre of Advanced Study, Department of History, Aligarh Muslim University, 1972.

Brockelmann, Carl. *Geschichte der arabischen Litteratur*. 2 vols. plus 3 suppl. vols., Leiden: E. J. Brill, 1938–42.

Fluegel, Gustavus. *Lexicon Bibliographicum et Encyclopædicum a Mustafa ben Abdallah Katib Jelebi Dicto et Nomine Haji Khalfa Celebrato Compositum*. 8 vols., London: Oriental Translation Fund, 1845.

Ghaffārī, Amīr Jalāl al-Dīn. *Farhang-i Ghaffārī*. 8 vols., Tehran: Dānishgāh, 1337/1958.

Munzawī, Aḥmad. *Fihrist-i mushtarak-i nuskha-hā-yi khaṭṭī-yi fārsī-yi Pākistān*. Vol. 3, *ʿIrfān*. Islamabad: Markaz-i Taḥqīqāt-i Fārsī-yi Īrān u Pākistān, 1363/1405/1984.

Sezgin, Fuat. *Geschichte des arabischen Schrifttums*. Vol. 1. Leiden: E. J. Brill, 1967.

Storey, C. A. *Persian Literature: A Bio-bibliographical Survey*. 2 vols., London: Luzac & Co., Ltd., 1927–71.

Wilson, H. H. *A Glossary of Judicial and Revenue Terms*. London: Wm. H. Allen & Co., 1855; reprint ed., Delhi: Munshiram Manoharlal, 1968.

Yule, Henry, and A.C. Burnell, *Hobson-Jobson, A Glossary of Colloquial Anglo-Indian Words and Phrases*. Edited by William Crooke. London, 1903; reprint ed., New Delhi: Munshiram Manoharlal, 1979.

INDEX OF NAMES

A

B

Farīd al-Dīn Ganj-i Shakkar (d. 664/1265), 63, 66, 78, 119, 122, 132; and story of black-cloaked dervishes, 163; descendants of, 321 n. 229; on not saving gifts, 191; Punjabi poetry of, 155, 167–68, 329 n. 394, 330 n. 396; portrayed as missionary, 164, 327 n. 349, 328 n. 373; retrospective **malfūẓāt** of, 77, 79; teaching authorization of, 165
Farīd al-Dīn Yūsuf, Qāżī (fourteenth cent.), 139, 143
Fārūqīs, 207–9; patronage of Khuldabad shrines, 210, 217; patronage of Sufism, 210, 212, 214–16, 333 n. 55
Fatāwā-i jahāndārī. *See* Baranī, Żiyā' al-Dīn
Fatḥ al-awliyā', 91, 209–12, 228, 230, 235; contents of, 334 n. 66; political character of, 243
Fawā'id al-fu'ād. *See* Ḥasan Dihlawī, Amīr
Fażl Allāh al-Mājawī (fourteenth cent.), 81
Firdawsī, Abū al-Qāsim (d. 416/1025–26), **Shāh nāma**, 23, 39–40
Firdawsīs, 81
Firishta, Abū al-Qāsim (d. after 1033/1623–24), 54, 91, 98, 203, 210, 231; as source for **Fatḥ al-awliyā'**, 210; on Fārūqīs, 207–8, 211
Fīrūz Shāh (d. 790/1388), 41, 48; seeks caliphal investiture, 56, 59, 208; patronage of Sufism by, 60, 138, 196, 198
Five Ladies (**pānch bībīyān**) (fourteenth cent.), 144, 324 n. 281; tomb of, 237
Fużayl ibn ʿIyāż (d. 187/803), 11, 61, 244

G

Gāyumars, 39, 42, 293 n. 168
Gentoo, 287 n. 75
Gharā'ib al-karāmāt. *See* Majd al-Dīn Kāshānī
Ghazālī, Abū Ḥāmid al- (d. 505/1111), 15, 16, 61, 136
Ghazālī, Aḥmad al- (d. 517/1123), 148
Ghazna, 40
Ghiyās al-Dīn Tughluq (d. 725/1325), 58, 111, 148
Ghiyaspur, 119, 125
Ghulām Farīd (d. 1329/1921), 334 n. 60
Ghur, 40
Ghūrids, 107
Gīsū Darāz, Muḥammad al-Ḥusaynī (d. 825/1422), 105, 138, 315 n. 117, 325 n. 308, 332 n. 41, 333 n. 56; on Burhān al-Dīn Gharīb, 121, 123
God, 43
Golconda, 223
Greater Dargāh Society, 216, 219, 220
Gujarat, 137, 195, 229, 231
Gulbarga, 98, 116, 139, 207, 221
Gurū Granth Ṣāḥib, authenticity of Farīd verses in, 166–68
Gwaliyar, 114

H

Habib, Mohammad (1894–1971), 77
Ḥāfiẓ ʿAbd al-Shakūr (ca. 1238/1823), 221
Ḥāfiẓ Shīrāzī (d. 791/1389), xxix, xxx
Ḥājib-i Khayrāt Dihlawī (fourteenth cent.), 116
Ḥākim II, al- (caliph, d. 753/1352), 56
Ḥallāj, Ḥusayn ibn Manṣūr al- (d. 309/922), 8, 63
Ḥamīd al-Dīn Nāgawrī, Qāżī (d. 641/1244), 63
Ḥamīd al-Dīn Suwāli Nāgawrī (d. 675/1276), 77
Ḥamīd al-Dīn Żarīr, 69
Ḥamīd Qalandar (fourteenth cent.), 69, 125; attitude to Burhān al-Dīn Gharīb, 70, 122, 123; **Khayr al-majālis**, 68–71, 78, 125

I

J

K

L

M

N

INDEX OF TERMS AND SUBJECTS

Abbreviations:

Ar.:	Arabic
H.:	Hindi
Per.:	Persian
Skt:	Sanskrit
Tur.:	Turkish

T